# Media Anthropology

# Media Anthropology

Editors

## Eric W. Rothenbuhler
Texas A&M University

## Mihai Coman
University of Bucharest, Romania

SAGE Publications
Thousand Oaks ■ London ■ New Delhi

*For information:*

Sage Publications, Inc.
2455 Teller Road
Thousand Oaks, California 91320
E-mail: order@sagepub.com

Sage Publications Ltd.
1 Oliver's Yard
55 City Road
London EC1Y 1SP
United Kingdom

Sage Publications India Pvt. Ltd.
B-42, Panchsheel Enclave
Post Box 4109
New Delhi 110 017  India

Printed in the United States of America.

*Library of Congress Cataloging-in-Publication Data*

Media anthropology / edited by Eric W. Rothenbuhler, Mihai Coman.
    p. cm.
Includes bibliographical references and index.
ISBN 1-4129-0670-9 (pbk.)
    1. Mass media and anthropology. 2. Visual anthropology.
3. Anthropology—Computer network resources. 4. Anthropology in
popular culture. I. Rothenbuhler, Eric W. II. Coman, Mihai.
P96.A56M43 2005
301—dc22

                                2004026098

This book is printed on acid-free paper.

05   06   07   08   09   10   9   8   7   6   5   4   3   2   1

| | |
|---|---|
| *Acquiring Editor:* | Margaret H. Seawell |
| *Editorial Assistant:* | Jill Meyers |
| *Project Editor:* | Claudia A. Hoffman |
| *Copy Editor:* | Catherine M. Chilton |
| *Typesetter:* | C&M Digitals (P) Ltd. |
| *Indexer:* | Kathy Paparchontis |

# CONTENTS

# PREFACE

This is an interdisciplinary reader in media anthropology. It should be of interest to scholars and students in communication, journalism, anthropology, sociology, and allied disciplines. It is dedicated to the idea that the media are cultural phenomena, worthy of study using the concepts and methods anthropologists have developed for the study of indigenous cultures—adapted, of course, to global media markets, technologies, and industrial systems.

This book represents a convergence of issues and interests in anthropological approaches to the study of media. In various disciplines and under a variety of labels, work relevant to media anthropology has been accumulating for years. This growth has not been well organized, though, and this name for a field of study, although used, has not yet been widely recognized. The purpose of the book, then, is to promote the identity of the field of study; identify its major concepts, methods, and bibliography; comment on the state of the art; and provide examples of current research. In original articles and a couple of selected reprints, leading scholars from several countries and academic disciplines introduce the issues, review the field, forge new conceptual syntheses, and apply the ideas in ongoing research.

The book is designed to provide useful source materials for a large number and diversity of scholars, to be useful in teaching, and to represent the diversity of thinking in media anthropology across the various fields and disciplines in which it is found. First and foremost, we bring together both anthropologists and media scholars, discussing and applying each other's work. This begins with the editors, one of whom was trained in anthropology while practicing journalism and who later became a journalism teacher and the other of whom was trained as a media scholar and learned anthropology in the course of his research and teaching. The book is not slanted toward one or the other audience but is designed to be useful in both anthropology and media studies and wherever else anthropological approaches to media studies are of interest.

Second, the book includes accessibly written introductions, overview articles from varying points of view, and research examples. Some chapters are guides to the literature, some show the concepts being applied in research, others are essays promoting alternative views of media phenomena—news as stories, for example, or celebrity as religion. Students can read the whole book through; more advanced scholars can choose the parts most useful to their own work. Teachers can choose among the sections to fit their courses.

Throughout the book, we combine contrasting views and intellectual orientations, presenting the whole as more of a moderated discussion than an argument for any one intellectual position. In addition to representing both media scholars and anthropologists, each with their own professional dispositions, each major topic is addressed by at least two scholars, often with sharply contrasting approaches. Ritual, myth, religion, news, the Internet, media events, ethnography, and integration of theory and practice each receive multiple chapters covering contrasting views. The opening sections of the book offer four distinct takes on the very nature of media anthropology. The important debate about whether the adaptation of the spirit of ethnography in media and cultural studies is legitimately anthropological is addressed in multiple chapters. This intellectual diversity serves at least four purposes: It represents the field, it provokes the reader, it aids students especially, and it increases the number of people who can find useful material in the book.

A unique and valuable aspect of the book is the section called "Theory Into Practice." Here we reflect on how the anthropological approach to media studies can inform media practice. This section of the book engages value debates, arguing that anthropological concepts and methods could improve the teaching and practice of journalism in particular and media in general. Again we bring scholars of varying perspectives and experience to the discussion, representing idealistic hopes, some disillusionment, and realistic appraisals.

# ACKNOWLEDGMENTS

The idea for this book arose in conversations with Gerd Kopper, Director of the Erich Brost Center for European Journalism at the University of Dortmund (Germany), at the close of the Media Anthropology doctoral workshop held under the auspices of the Erich Brost Center in January 2001. Mihai Coman was the Erich Brost Visiting Professor that year and had organized the workshop; Eric Rothenbuhler was a visiting faculty participant. We thank the Brost Center for its generous support of the workshop and its visiting professorship, Katharina Hadamik and Rolland Schroeder; members of the staff; and, most especially, the student participants who made that week such a rich experience.

Dr. Kopper's support for the project has been consistent and generous. We spent a week in February 2003 in residence at the Brost Haus, and the Brost Center supported travel for Dr. Coman to New York in May 2004. The book could not have been completed without those weeks of working together. The U.S. Department of State, through the U.S. Embassy in Bucharest, supported Dr. Coman's participation in the 2004 International Communication Association convention in New Orleans.

The Media Studies Program at New School University, where Dr. Rothenbuhler was Director of Graduate Studies from 2001 to 2004, contributed to the project by providing research and editorial assistants, funds for the translation of two chapters, and equipment and office support—including the loan of a laptop so he could continue with final editing tasks while making the move to Texas A&M University. Dr. Rothenbuhler joined the Department of Communication there in August 2004, and the department has been equally supportive, supplying research assistants, a generous office staff, and more. Thanks also to faculty colleagues at both universities for their interest and encouragement.

Katharina Hadamik at the Brost Center coordinated our visits to Dortmund, was a wonderful host, participated in hours of valuable conversation, and has given our project her enthusiastic vote of confidence from the beginning. Dan Cherubin and Eric Logan assisted Dr. Rothenbuhler with various editorial tasks. Paul Grant translated the chapters by Drs. Dayan and Lardellier. Alexandru Ulmanu worked with Mihai Coman in translating and editing some chapters. Thanks to Elizabeth Bird, Nick Couldry, Roger Delbarre, Antonio La Pastina, Jack Lule, Carolyn Marvin, Bernard Miege, Pierre Moeglin, John Pauly, Marsha Siefert, Carol Wilder, and many other friends, colleagues, and correspondents for thoughtful remarks and encouragement. David Morley was an early supporter of the project. Elihu Katz recommended some of the chapter authors. We thank several reviewers, including Ien Ang, David Black, Richard Chalfen, Larry Gross, Larry Grossberg, Nicholas Packwood, Wesley Shumar, Christina Wasson, and Barbie Zelizer; some anonymous reviewers also provided useful suggestions. Margaret Seawell has been a valuable advocate and a thoughtful and flexible editor; she, Claudia Hoffman, Kate Chilton, and everyone else at Sage have been wonderfully helpful. Most of all we thank our chapter authors, who have been quick and patient, terse and voluble, and whose contributions have made this book a success.

Dr. Coman expresses his gratitude to the Fulbright Commission for a research grant in 1999, and he thanks his wife, Cristina, and children Ioana and Ion, for supporting his work and accepting him as physically present and mentally absent during the frantic periods during which we were looking for contributors, writing chapters, and editing the book. Dr. Rothenbuhler thanks Jane Martin, his wife and friend. She has consistently recommended that this project be a priority and tolerated the laptop, manuscripts, and distraction on vacations and during our move from New York to Texas. Without that support in the summer of 2004, the book would have come out 6 months later. We both thank our students for many years of thoughtful discussions, provocative questions, and daily challenges at the Universities of Bucharest, Iowa, and Dortmund and the New School.

# 1

# THE PROMISE OF MEDIA ANTHROPOLOGY

MIHAI COMAN AND ERIC W. ROTHENBUHLER

Media anthropology grows out of the anthropology of modern societies, on one hand, and the cultural turn in media studies, on the other. It turns its attention from "exotic" to mundane and from "indigenous" to manufactured culture but preserves the methodological and conceptual assets of earlier anthropological tradition. It prepares media studies for more complete engagement with the symbolic construction of reality and the fundamental importance of symbolic structures, myth, and ritual in everyday life.

Even though it does not have to invent new theories and methods, media anthropology is not a mere exercise of mechanically applying anthropologists' concepts and techniques to media phenomena. The identity of anthropology among the disciplines is based on the development of a distinct conceptual sphere with its own debates, on the more frequent use of those ideas and methods, and hence on the capacity to explain their objects of study according to that specific conceptual lexicon. In taking concepts and methods developed in the specific intellectual community of cultural anthropology (applied and fashioned on specific fields and on specific cultural forms and thus tuned to their traditional objects of study and their traditional debates) into media studies, we face a dilemma

common to all interdisciplinary fields of study, as well as to the growth and change of any of the human sciences in this globalizing world: how "universal" or "local" are those concepts and methods—and in how many different modalities, geographically, culturally, logically, empirically, historically? How should they be adapted to their new objects of study and intellectual fields? How much loyalty or fundamentalism to their original forms and fields is appropriate?

In this chapter, we will address these questions in regard to ethnography as method and idea, ritual, myth, and religion as widely used concepts of media anthropology and in terms of levels of generality. The chapter closes with a brief discussion of the promise of media anthropology and of our perspective on the potential contributions of this field of inquiry to its home disciplines of communication and anthropology and to larger currents of intellectual life.

## METHOD

One important debate is about whether classical ethnography is necessary to everything called anthropological, or is the adaptation of the spirit of ethnography in media and cultural studies legitimately anthropological? Applying ethnographic methods to modern societies had already produced a dispute regarding methodological purity within anthropology, even before ethnographic ideas were widely adopted in neighboring fields. Where is the dividing line between doing an ethnography in the classic sense and doing research that is ethnographic in some aspects? How important is that line? The questions become more intransigent in regard to the specific study of media audiences, as illustrated by these two contrasting quotations from the debate.

> Most of this work is based on interviewing audiences in their homes, and critics have argued that the label "ethnography" is misleading, because detailed participant observation is minimal and actual immersion in the daily practices and social worlds of the people studied is almost inexistent. (Spitulnik, 1993, p. 298)

> My own feeling is that despite these clear differences, reception studies can still properly be called ethnographic. It is true that they are not based on extensive fieldwork in distant lands, but they do share some of the same general intentions as anthropological research. . . . If the means of investigation are not always identical, then the aims of inquiry can be. (Moores, 1993, p. 4)

La Pastina (chapter 14, this volume) argues for anchoring media studies research in the traditions of cultural anthropology:

> Audience ethnography needs to be repositioned as a fieldwork-based, long-term practice of data collection and analysis. This practice allows researchers to attain a greater level of understanding of the community studied and maintain self-reflexivity and respect toward those they are attempting to understand within the everyday life of the community.

Placing his reflections in the context of discussions of intertextuality, Peterson (chapter 13, this volume) maintains that ethnographic investigation is two headed, like Janus: It tries to understand and re-present the phenomena of society and culture, as well as its own discourse, in a permanent effort of reflexivity and self-reflexivity. Thus media anthropology has, in some sense, to expand ethnography.

To the study of media, ethnography brings an attention to cultural difference, a commitment to close observation and recording, the provision of "thick" descriptive detail designed to reveal the contexts that give actions meanings to a community, reflexive engagement with the voices of one's hosts, and attention to the contiguity of what is being described to broader aspects of social process. Media ethnography attempts to tease out layers of meaning through observation of and engagement with the everyday situations in which media are consumed, the practices by which media are interpreted, and the uses to which media are put (see Peterson, chapter 13; La Pastina, chapter 14; and Murdock and Pink, chapter 15).

*Participant observation, qualitative methods,* and *open-ended interviewing* appeared as methods and terms of debate in communication and media studies before *ethnography* and *ethnographic* became common. There has been a tendency to lump them all together, blurring the distinctiveness of the anthropological method. Debates about phenomenology and hermeneutics were prevalent at the time (early 1980s). Although those philosophical debates have faded to the background, there still tends to be something vaguely, even romantically, phenomenological and hermeneutic about *ethnography* and *ethnographic* as those terms are used in the communication literature. The investigator's intention to achieve a deeper understanding of other people's life experiences thus counts for as much as the actual details of research procedures. If, in a given cultural context, these goals can be achieved without extended residential immersion in a foreign culture, then by the standards of most media scholars the process can still be called ethnography.

Our three Internet chapters present a useful contrast and illustrate some of these tendencies. None is a classic ethnography; each has some claim to the ethnographic tradition. Danet's participant observation and interviewing could be called an online ethnography, focused on a symbol world that exists in the flow of image, text, and interactive turns on an Internet server. Hoover and Parks' work depends on qualitative analysis of transcripts from extensive open-ended interviews. It can be labeled ethnographic in its efforts to understand participants' own experiences in their own terms, contextualized by the researcher's analysis of the situation. Hammer stretches the spirit of ethnography the farthest, although still falling within the grand tradition of the human sciences that it represents. She makes reference to her time as a participant in the online groups she is discussing, but reporting of the observed details of a social world plays a relatively minor role; use of the analytic concepts built up in a century of such work is relatively larger. However, it is still at least philosophically ethnographic to the extent that those concepts and her orientation to her materials address lived experience.

The two of us, Coman and Rothenbuhler, have a pragmatic attitude toward method in research and a disdain for territorial debates between disciplines. Whatever well-applied method produces useful answers to interesting questions is fine. That is why ethnography came to be classic in anthropology, because it produced useful answers to interesting questions. Most certainly, the value of the classic method to classic research should continue to be taught in anthropology. Scholars from other fields, too, can learn much from that work; neither of us could have done any of our own work without a deep appreciation of that tradition and much reading of its literature. Due respect should be paid, and there is no better place to look for guidance than to the classic exponents. Yet the tradition will change, and good ideas will be imitated and adapted to new uses in new circumstances.

A key difference with the classic anthropological ethnographies is that media ethnography does not, usually, take place fully outside the researcher's culture. When researchers turn their attention to their own cultures, even some of the more distinct corners of them, some of the—shall we say—*sacred* characteristics of the classical ethnographic experience are missing. One does not travel far to be there, the journey and the life is not strenuous, one does not need to learn a new language or wholly unfamiliar customs, values, and modes of behavior; the researcher is not fully isolated from home, in all

its senses. These characteristics, very real, have generated a mystique for ethnography, but there is no need to transform a mystique into a dogma. Even short periods spent in field, allied with previous knowledge that the researcher brings to the field, can produce partial, yet focused, knowledge of aspects of group life. Valuable interpretive accounts can be based on relatively small periods of observation, focusing on media texts as much as people and activities. If the ethnographic goals are achieved, the research activity is itself legitimately ethnographic—whether or not it fulfills all the requirements of the classical ethnographic field experience. Finally, in purely pragmatic terms, media ethnography has been worth the risk. These studies have yielded a lot of new and exciting information on the media, putting the "classical" assumptions of media studies, as well as ethnography, into new light.

## CONCEPTS

In the anthropological approach to mass media, several established concepts are finding relatively new uses: culture (and acculturation, cultural change, cultural diffusion, assimilation, globalization), religion (cult, sacred and profane, transcendence, belief, cosmology, liturgical order, themes and motifs), ritual (ceremony, magic, commemoration, celebration, liminality), myth, narrative, performance, representation, and symbol can all be found in this book and the larger literature. Here in the introduction, we single out ritual, religion, and myth for more discussion.

### Ritual

The concept that has received the most numerous applications and the most interesting developments in media anthropology has been *ritual*. Many of these references to the ceremonial universe can be surprising to scholars more familiar with the anthropological definitions and uses. At one end, we find a reductive interpretation of the concept: the ritual is a sum of formalized, repetitive, stereotypical acts. In this line,

Tuchman (1978) launched the phrase "strategic rituals" to name the standardized working procedures of journalists. In the same line, other scholars have considered the regular consumption of television programs or the periodic reading of newspapers or romance novels as ritual behaviors (Goethals, 1981; Lull, 1988; Morley, 1992). At the other end stands the expansive, metaphoric interpretation of the concept as the ritual perspective of communication proposed by Carey (1988); ritual appears as a form of realization and expression of social communication, as a "model for" communication processes centered not on the transfer of information, but on the sharing of a common culture. In consensus with this perspective, even though inspired from another paradigm (associated with Victor Turner), Dov Shinar (chapter 25) builds a complex interpretative system centering on sociocultural change and the functions of communication in these processes. In his conception, ritual is the instrument through which society manages change; the anthropological theories and concepts offer a scientific lexicon to name and interpret the actors' behavior, the institutional destructuring and restructuring processes, and the dialectic of values and symbols that support these transformations.

From another perspective, at one end, we find the creation of new concepts of ritual to account for new phenomena in the mass communication universe and, at the other end, the often mechanical, blind application of established terminology from cultural anthropology. The latter situation is evident in the use of the notion of liminality as a universal key that explains at the same time the consuming behavior of the public, the journalists' reactions in the newsroom, the global functioning of television, and the experiences lived by participants in a media event. All this without taking into consideration the "liminoid" concept through which Turner (1982) was adapting the initial concept from the explanation of phenomena in nonmodern societies to the explanation of phenomena of the modern world. In the same way, the term *magic* is sometimes evoked metaphorically to explain television's power of attraction, without any connection with the rich conceptualizations of magic in the anthropological literature (cf., later, the same point in regard to myth).

As an example of work that borrowed from anthropology to create a new approach to explain ritual phenomena in the mass communication universe, the best known approach is the one built by Dayan and Katz (1992) around the concept of media event. The theoretical vision of their book has inspired numerous studies, which have broadened the sphere of phenomena that could be integrated in this new ritual category: highly mediated marriages and funerals of representative personalities, political or religious visits, sporting events, festivals, pilgrimages, music concerts, and political celebrations and confrontations. In all these cases, the mediation, even to the point of remaking, of already accepted prestigious ceremonies leads to amplification of the ritual in regard to the number of participants, the area of geographic distribution, the magnitude of experiences, as well as to the modification of ceremonial elements—the ritual script, the form of public speeches, the role of the masters of ceremony, the interpretations, and the attributed significations (see Coman, chapter 5, this volume).

Starting from this model, other scholars have launched different conceptual constructs: media rituals (Couldry), "ceremonial television" (Dayan), disaster marathon (Liebes). In these cases, we are not talking of identifying social manifestations that could be labeled as media events but of new concepts of media anthropology. "Media rituals (in the sense in which I am using the term) are actions that are capable of standing in for wider values and frameworks of understanding connected with the media" (Couldry, chapter 6, this volume). The disaster marathon contradicts the classic scheme of media events because "whereas the success of media events is due to the union of establishment and broadcasters, disaster marathons, brought about by an outside power (natural or human), surprise establishment and media alike, sometimes paralyzing the establishment, leaving media in charge of lost and horrified viewers" (Liebes & Blondheim, chapter 18, this volume). Dayan's work has shown a trajectory within and yet independent of his collaboration with Katz. Dayan and Katz used the term *media events* to describe their work across the 1980s and to title their book in 1992. The French translation in 1996 was actually a reworking in important ways, and its title in English would be "ceremonial television." This is not exactly "media events," and in interesting ways. It narrows the focus to television, shifts the emphasis from event to process, and draws attention to the markers that distinguish this kind of television, the ceremonial, from ordinary television.

All these new categories, far from being simple scholastic exercises, show that at the interface between the ritual universe and mass communication, syncretic manifestations of a great variety appear, based in both media and ceremony. Their identification, analysis, and conceptualization represent a possibility for a more subtle understanding of the complex transformations of modernity affecting mass media, public spheres, and *imaginaire social.*

The ritualistic approaches to mass communication stem from the conceptions of Durkheim and Turner. The differences between the two schools of thought are not as great as they may look at a superficial glance—see Dayan and Couldry (chapters 16 and 6, respectively, this volume) and Rothenbuhler (1988, 1998). In the first perspective, the ritual produces and maintains social integration; in the second, it contributes to the management of social change (generated by social conflicts, power relations, personal affliction, social dramas, natural disasters) and, implicitly, to the restoration of social order and integration. Because media anthropologists do not mechanically take over these theoretical models, it would be more adequate to talk of neo-Durkheimian and neo-Turnerian approaches. Thus, Couldry (chapter 6) argues for rethinking media ritual to make room for new connections: between the power of contemporary media institutions and modern forms of government and between an understanding of ritual and the disciplinary practices of surveillance. The same critical approach to Durkheim's legacy

is also found in this volume in the studies of Dayan, Lardellier, Rothenbuhler, Thomas, and Zelizer. The Turnerian model is implied in the very concept of media event, as is especially clear in the typologies proposed by Dayan and Katz for various forms of media events. Defining *contest* as "transformative ceremonies," Dayan and Katz (1995) wrote: "The ceremony itself represents a 'liminal' moment, a break in the routinized social time. . . . It offers society opportunity to discover that there are alternatives to its choices and, in doing so, it partially reveals the anxieties, the chaos, the effervescence of genesis" (p. 166).

Victor Turner's legacy is evident in this volume in the studies devoted to the creation of new rituals to surpass a critical event: Rothenbuhler analyzes the emergence of ceremonial forms around Ground Zero that allowed processing and recovery from the significance of the attacks on 9-11. Liebes and Blondheim study the fabrication of ritual behaviors among the actors in a "disruptive event," the journalists who create a "disaster marathon," and the public of such a "media disaster." Zelizer reveals the appearance of ritualistic reactions in the production, distribution, and use of photographs of reactions to traumatic events, to control the social and individual traumas produced by it. On the other hand, the Turnerian model lies at the root of processual approaches that bring about the emergence of new rites not only through various combinations of cultural symbols (be they verbal, body, or object) but also through the ritualization of behaviors until then not included in the sphere of the ceremonial actions. In chapter 6, Couldry unveils the passing from an "interlocking mass of practices" to an ensemble of media rituals, and Coman stresses the mechanism of ritualization of journalists' discourses, which allows them to exercise a "ritual mastery" over the fabrication and legitimation of socially acceptable versions of the events.

The application of ritual in media studies has produced not only numerous case studies but also numerous theoretical debates, reflected in the chapters here as well as in the larger literature. Several major themes structure this debate.

*The Relation Between Consensus and Conflict.* Media rituals and media ritualization can be considered mechanisms through which individuals are connected to the global social world, see it as a concrete and powerful entity, and become aware of being part of a more than imaginary community (see Dayan, Lardellier, Rothenbuhler, Thomas), but, just as well, rituals and ritualization can be forms of expression and public acceptance of a rupture in the social texture, of conflicts between groups, of the exercise and naturalization of power (see Couldry, Coman, Liebes & Blondheim, Shinar).

*The Relation Between Public Participation and Passive Consumption.* Whether they have an integrative function or serve to contest the existing order, media events should generate active manifestations of the public. The mobilization of the public should be visible either at the level of the established forms of public spheres or at the level of public "sphericules," such as homes or pubs (see Dahlgren, chapter 30, this volume). Some authors maintain that media events generate, to use Dayan's felicitous formula, "a spiral of affirmation" that produces and expresses the public's mobilization (see Dayan, Rothenbuhler, Zelizer), but there is also the possibility that these manifestations do not generate a response, or not the expected response (see Couldry).

*The Localized or Delocalized (Diasporic) Character of Mediated Rites or of Media-Constructed Rites.* The ritual, as it has been identified and defined in classic anthropology, may have a center and a periphery, but it cannot extend its effects beyond a certain area (determined by the coexistence of the participants). The intervention of the mass media allows the dissemination of the ritual to enormous geographical areas and, thanks to television, in full simultaneity with the "original" performance. These "diasporic ceremonies" (Dayan & Katz, 1992) present a double paradox: They cancel both the distance between center and periphery (thus creating a ubiquitous center) and that between in situ participants and those participants in front of TV sets (creating a unity of experiences); at the same time, they subscribe media events within a new localization, through the creation of privileged places for the collective consumption of televised broadcasts (the home, the pub, the street).

## Myth

Another concept that has enjoyed much use in the study of media is myth. The way in which myth appears in media studies unveils the contrast between the anthropological approach and the media studies applications: The disciplines involved in studying myth (the history of religions, comparative mythology, the anthropology of symbolic forms, literary theory, the history of the imaginary, and psychoanalysis) do not have a unitary definition, tending, rather, to a variety of concepts. Cultural anthropology's view of myth generates a vague and ever-contested field. By contrast, in media studies, the tendency has been toward a relatively simple use of the term.

The mythological dimensions of mass culture have been investigated at two levels and from two different perspectives. A large part of the literature has focused on narrative patterns and figures considered to represent modern "mythologies" in movies, TV programs, advertising, music, sports, and other entertainments. This research has centered on the cultural industries, focusing on those products meant for entertainment, which have aesthetic status and nonreferential content. These creations have been studied with conceptual tools from art and literature, the history of the imaginary, hermeneutics, and psychoanalysis. The relation to concepts and interpretations derived from the history of religions and comparative mythology is secondary.

There are fewer studies of *news stories* that have the discursive characteristics of myth or that function for specific social groups as myth. In the case of news, we have media texts that are obligated to be verifiable reports of events in real time and space. These media products are thus endowed with instrumental status and referential content; news stories, under that paradigm, then, would not be expected to involve mythological representations. In spite of all this, many recent studies show that some news media texts build a new level of meaning, deeply anchored in the codes and symbolic vocabulary of the targeted community, starting from and going beyond the referential dimension. The discourse of news media challenges the anthropology of mass media to illustrate how and why there appear, in the field of information and denotation, symbolic constructs and uses whose origins, functions, or means of representation have a mythic significance. "In characterizing television and other media as mythic they are identified as instances of the central symbol system of the society at hand and therefore worthy of the careful treatment anthropologists accord to myth" (Rothenbuhler, 1998, p. 90).

The studies in this volume unveil two major approaches to the relation between myth and media. One consists in placing narration as the common element and identifying mythical attributes in journalistic discourse. The second approach focuses on cognitive processes as the intersection between news stories and myth.

The first perspective is illustrated by Lule in chapter 10. He follows the ways in which various news accounts are constructed through the actualization of cultural archtypes—the "eternal stories":

> Many news stories have no relation to myth. Many news stories are derived from rudimentary story forms and professional conventions of the trade, such as inverted pyramid leads or easy formulas for writing speeches, sports results, or fire stories. . . . Sometimes, however, in describing some experience, in reporting some event, reporters and editors draw upon a fundamental story of earthly existence, a universal and shared story of humankind, and they use that story to instruct, inform, celebrate, or forewarn. Like myth tellers from every age, journalists can draw from the rich treasure trove of archetypal stories and make sense of the world.

For Lule, as well as for others inspired by this paradigm, the mythic status of journalistic accounts derives from the actualization of a pre-existing archetype from the distant past in the representation of a current event. This archetype works simultaneously as a cultural framework,

an epic pattern, and a reserve of meanings. It is applicable to the specific situation the journalists are referring to and offers a surplus of meaning that makes the event easier to understand and accept. The archetype becomes established in time and is available for several uses, without being influenced by social context, cultural system, or the specific genres into which it is placed and adapted.

Lule's position is echoed by the analyses of Schudson, Berkowitz, and Bird, who, putting the story at the basis of journalistic discourse, come to identify structures and mechanisms generating significations commonly across the particularities of different stories and situations. Thus, Schudson, after underlining the predictable, formulaic structure of news stories, after showing how narrative conventions can determine the organization of information, comes to the conclusion that news stories can be conceived of as "part of a process of producing collective meaning rather than transmitting information." What Berkowitz maintains for the specific case of "what-a-story" could be generalized to the ensemble of studies referring to journalistic norms and procedures: "That is, if what-a-story news pertains to big stories—those stories with large social meaning and significance—then what lurks within is the same cultural stuffing from which myth is made." Narrative structures control the process of fixing the unexpected event into a communicable product, and mythical themes offer a series of acceptable significations: "Not only does the mythical framework provide shape for a what-a-story, it also comes equipped with an ending to both the story and the work process."

Bird takes an intermediary position in this configuration, her chapter evoking elements from both strategies: both the way in which epic schemes transmitted by a certain cultural tradition model the fabrication process of journalistic versions of the facts ("reporters learn to find familiar stories in disparate events") and the relation between psychological or knowledge processes that make such a combination possible. In the CJ case analyzed by Bird, the collective, confused fear of AIDS allowed the transformation of the journalistic account into an epic legendary theme, and then into a mythological construction. In this situation, the journalistic mythical narrative functions in the same way as the disaster marathons described by Liebes and Blondheim, the ritualization of photo and photo consumption analyzed by Zelizer, or the fabrication of ad hoc rituals and of heroic narratives analyzed by Rothenbuhler—they all allow fears, traumas, and uncertainties to be surpassed through the game of symbolic constructions.

The second approach to myth is also illustrated by Coman's analyses. He considers that myth and news stories have elaboration processes in common, based in similar cultural and cognitive logics:

> Journalistic crisis stories, like myths, are meaningful due to their very unlikelihood and absurdity. The system of interpretation they suggest does not confer meaning on the story, but on everything else ("a tout le reste," in Lévi-Strauss's words); that is, on the social order affected by the crisis spectrum. Their discourse is not argumentative, but symbolical. In other words, it does not reproduce existent and acknowledged patterns; instead, it produces and mentally experiments on potential patterns of reality. (Coman, chapter 5, this volume)

## Religion

Another concept found in most examples of media anthropology is religion—and, implicitly, sacred, profane, cult, belief, saint, and so on. One might say that the core idea of media anthropology is that the disenchantment of the world cannot happen and that, even though religion is no longer a dominant institution, multiple and complex forms of religiosity are reborn in modern societies. On a first level, religions can manifest themselves using various modern resources, such as the media, yet stay within circumscribed social spheres. Thus Hoover and Park (chapter 23) analyze religious-seeking processes on the Internet, processes that bring about the subjective character of the religious act within an elasticity of practices. The study shows that religious activity on

the Internet is not determined by the digital medium but follows other motivations, habits, and activities. Hoover and Park document a series of interactions: between the Internet and other media, between the Internet and traditional religious commitments and beliefs, between religious needs and more vaguely spiritual impulses.

Rothenbuhler's proposal that the media serve as the church of the cult of the individual may appear diametrically opposed to the topic of Hoover and Parks' study, as it makes no reference to the institutionalized religions and focuses on advertising and celebrity instead. Yet there is continuity with the individualistic seeking of some of Hoover and Parks' respondents and with a vision of social life in which religious orientations and behaviors are ubiquitous and inevitable. If individualism is the religion of modernity, media anthropology shows how it is celebrated and proselytized.

In his turn, Dayan (chapter 16) underlines the force with which the Vatican creates a religious public sphere (which he defines as a "credoscape"), using not only the Pope's traditional visits (and the correlated believers' pilgrimages) but also television's capacity to transmit and recreate rituals, to federate audiences, transforming them into communities of believers, and to offer a "prefiguration" of an imaginary community, "confirming its existence and aiming to maintain it."

On a second level, one can notice the interpretation of mass media as a macrosubstitute for religion—what Thomas (chapter 8) defines as "more or less syncretized arrangements of an emerging media religiosity with a cultural dynamism of its own." From this perspective, television institutes both "an endless, eternal liturgy, aimed in principle at infinity—indeed, as a liturgical order" and a cosmology, based on media products that "thematicize the archaic-anthropological conflicts." The liturgical and cosmological dimensions of television combine "the permanent 'now' of topicality and the 'history-less-ness' of the ever topical"; by that, it functionally substitutes for religion because, comprising the temporary and the eternal, the plane of daily routine and the fundamental truths, it offers order and sense to the world we live in.

## LEVELS OF GENERALITY

Levels of generality are an issue of important differences among investigators, although they are seldom a matter of explicit debate. The dominant tendency in anthropology today is a commitment to particularism, to local knowledge, bounded arguments, deeper understandings of more particular circumstances. This is, of course, not the only possibility, and the drive to larger, more general knowledge claims is present in the current literature as well as in the history of anthropology. Indeed, macrotheoretical perspectives, such as political economy, cultural materialism, or even the presumption that all knowledge is local, necessarily entail general knowledge claims. So do presumptions about the general usefulness and proper conduct of research methods. Harris (1968), Geertz (1983, 1988), and others have discussed these issues thoroughly and well (see Ginsburg, chapter 2; Hobart, chapter 3; and Osorio, chapter 4, this volume).

In media studies, interest in anthropology rose in the search for alternatives to social-psychological effects research, with its dependence on surveys, experiments, and content analysis. The focus on culture, the emphasis on symbols and meanings, and the alternative methods were strongly attractive. The focus on particulars came along, but it was not the primary attraction. Indeed, for many media and communication scholars, the older version of anthropology, with its emphasis on cross-cultural commonalities, is more attractive than the more current emphasis on particularism and reflective, contextual knowledge. Many communication scholars are prepared to see what is common to Greek myth; the religions and rituals of the Aborigine, Tikopia, Neur, and Ndembu; the ceremonial life and artwork of the Tlingit and Kwakiutl; the myths of various South American Indians; the televised Olympic games; and newspaper articles. Please, this is too much for the practicing anthropologist of today—and few, if any, media scholars

would make explicit claims to commonalities across such a wide range. It is a tendency, though, that is often implied in writing that jumps in the space of two sentences from discussing Victor Turner's studies of Ndembu ritual to our own studies of television audiences. Is it a mistake, a misunderstanding of what anthropology is and how to use its ideas? Or is this a useful freedom in the movement of ideas, with important insights generated by startling new comparisons?

Another perspective on these questions focuses on "vertical" shifts between surface and deeper structures rather than on "horizontal" shifts between local and global, or specific and general. Media contents and products are neighborhoods, of a sort, in which information and symbol, rationality and imagination, cohabit. The anthropological view is more attentive to the symbolic content and signifying structures of cultural products. For the anthropologist, information and rationality are special cases of symbolic structures, processes, and expressions. Bringing this frame from cultural anthropology to media studies, we do not generalize by comparing cultural forms but by comparing processes of thinking.

The media create and impose symbolic systems of thought and enunciation of reality, operating like the cultural forms traditionally studied by anthropologists using such concepts as ritual, ceremony, myth, the sacred, magic, and liminality. In other words, media are cultural systems of the social construction of reality. This construction is made under distinct circumstances, with the tools of symbolic reasoning rather than argumentative reasoning. The anthropological approach asserts that these images are accepted precisely because they have the status of symbolic constructions and, having that status, they function and signify the same way that mythical and ritual systems belonging to nonmodern societies do.

Such a vision, which proposes interpretation of media phenomena in terms of the theories and concepts of cultural anthropology, shows that symbolism, far from being a residual element of journalistic communication, for example, is one of its fundamental factors. This perspective forces us to reconsider theories regarding the role of the media in the construction of the public space and in the creation of the modern social imagination; it requires us to rethink the rapport between the rational and the nonrational in the construction of mediated public space (Coman, 2003).

## WHAT IS THE PROMISE OF MEDIA ANTHROPOLOGY?

*More Adequate Understanding of a World That Cannot Be Disenchanted.* The great historical process of secularization that has produced modern economies, governments and political systems, educational systems, and formal religions constrained to their specific institutional spheres cannot, nevertheless, produce a fully disenchanted world. The relation of the human mind and its environments—though secular institutional structures many of those environments may be—will always contain elements of mystery, magic, and ritual. Mythical structures and narrative logics will continue to have influence alongside cause-effect analyses. Choices will be based on values and faith as often as on instrumental reasoning. No field of the social sciences can come to terms with the objects of its study without concepts and methods appropriate to that reality.

Media studies in particular addresses a world founded on texts and discourse. There would be no media audiences or organizations, media technologies would be of no concern, without the texts and discourses around which they are organized. The social relations and political realities of the media system, and hence the consequences of their operation, are founded in communication processes. Paradoxical though it may seem, then, in a culture that values rationality above all things, understanding how the shaman uses text and performance to effect cures is at least as important to media studies as the rational actor model that has dominated Western philosophy and the social sciences (see Allen, chapter 26; Bruns, chapter 27; and Kopper, chapter 29, this volume).

*New Uses in New Social Worlds for Concepts and Methods That Have Already Given a Century of* *Good Service.* It may be a scholastic pleasure, but we are, after all, people of the academy. One of the promises of media anthropology is the discovery of new uses for good, old ideas. Due to their aptness, their elasticity, and the importance of their referents, the core ideas of cultural anthropology have already proven useful, with appropriate adaptations, for 100 years or more, in the study of social groups all over the globe. This is an invitation to media scholars to join that grand tradition and to anthropologists to turn their light on a challenging new subject matter. This will test the elasticity of the anthropological concepts and the cognitive flexibility of the scholars who do the work. We are already convinced of its usefulness for understanding the media and for understanding the social worlds touched by them.

*An Approach to Media That Is Tuned to the Particular in the General, the Local in the Global, the Transient and Circumstantial in the Enduring and Universal.* For decades, the study of the media has been bedeviled by a set of problems that have recently come into prominent discussion under the heading of local and global. Media studies is not unique in this regard, but it may be one of the stronger cases among the human sciences.

The media have been introduced as new technologies, and they constitute a separate institutional sphere; what they do is recognizably a different version of previously existing activities. This has helped produce the strong tendency toward asking very general questions: What are the effects of the media? What do they do? What difference does television make to politics, sports, music, education? What the media do is communication, and each bit of it is unique, each historical moment of it is different, each participant is a willful, interpreting, individual actor. The generalizations have been enormously difficult to come by.

Cultural anthropology has dealt with a structurally similar problem, although in different ways with different results. Classical anthropology also had very general ambitions: What is the nature of the primitive mind? What is the origin of religion? Of course, these ambitions have been tempered over the decades, just as media scholars are always working to shape and temper the public's interest in "the effects" of "the media" into more precise and answerable questions. But under the influence of those classical ambitions, anthropology has developed concepts and methods tuned to the conflict between empirical work in very particular, very unique settings and the drive for more generalizable knowledge claims in the published literature. Anthropological theory tends to operate at a much higher level of analysis than anthropological investigations. The relation between the two can only be managed with concepts that are relatively formalistic, if not content free, with the specifics provided by the empirical materials under investigation. Durkheim's famous definition of the sacred, for example, does not say what it is; he defines it as that which any given people take as beyond question. Therefore, the category of the sacred may be found in any given society, even as the contents of that category vary so widely that one culture's sacred is another's profane.

The literature of cultural anthropology is filled with concepts that define cultural structures and processes and leave their empirical contents as matters for ethnographic investigation. These concepts, as well as this strategy in regard to the relation of the empirical and the theoretical, can be turned now to media studies.

# REFERENCES

Carey, J. (1988). *Communication as culture*. Boston: Unwin Hyman Press.

Coman, M. (2003). *Pour une anthropologie des medias* [Toward an anthropology of the media]. Grenoble, France: Presses Universitaires de Grenoble.

Dayan, D., & Katz, E. (1992). *Media events: The live broadcasting of history*. Cambridge, MA: Harvard University Press.

Dayan, D., & Katz, E. (1995). Télévision d'intervention et spectacle politique [Televisual intervention and political spectacle]. *Hermes, 17-18*, 163-186.

Geertz, C. (1983). *Local knowledge: Further essays in interpretive anthropology*. New York: Basic Books.

Geertz, C. (1988). *Works and lives: The anthropologist as author*. Stanford, CA: Stanford University Press.

Goethals, G. (1981). *The TV ritual*. Boston: Beacon Press.

Harris, M. (1968). *The rise of anthropological theory*. New York: Columbia University Press.

Lull, J. (1988). Constructing rituals of extension through family television viewing. In J. Lull (Ed.), *World families watch television*. London: Sage.

Moores, S. (1993). *Interpreting audiences: The ethnography of media consumption*. London: Sage.

Morley, D. (1992). *Television audiences and cultural studies*. London: Routledge.

Rothenbuhler, E. W. (1988). The liminal fight: Mass strikes as ritual and interpretation. In J. C. Alexander (Ed.), *Durkheimian sociology: Cultural studies* (pp. 66-89). Cambridge, England: Cambridge University Press.

Rothenbuhler, E. W. (1998). *Ritual communication: From everyday conversation to mediated ceremony*. Thousand Oaks, CA: Sage.

Spitulnik, D. (1993). Anthropology and mass media. *Annual Review of Anthropology, 22*, 293-315.

Tuchman, G. (1978). *Making news: A study in the construction of reality*. New York: MacMillan.

Turner, V. (1982). Liminal to liminoid, in play, flow, ritual: An essay in comparative symbology. In V. Turner (Ed.), *From ritual to theatre: The human seriousness of play* (pp. 20-60). New York: Performing Arts Journal Publications.

# Part I

## HISTORIES AND DEBATES

"For many years, mass media were seen as almost a taboo topic for anthropology, too redolent of Western modernity and cultural imperialism for a field identified with tradition, the non-Western, and the vitality of the local" (Ginsburg, chapter 2). Instead, this type of research has attracted scholars from other academic fields and backgrounds. Approaches to media anthropology have been developed by selecting concepts and methods from cultural anthropology, combining them into new configurations, and applying them to the various fields of mass communication—often in direct contrast with anthropological delineations.

This disciplinary crossover has had two results: (a) the absence of a significant corpus of works on mass media done by "legitimate" anthropologists and (b) the existence of numerous studies on media production, circulation, and consumption based on methods labeled *ethnographic* and on concepts one would consider as "specifically" anthropological, carried out by scholars from other disciplines and fields of study.

These results have led to two opposed reactions. Some deny the legitimacy of mass media anthropology as a field and discipline of cultural anthropology, for fear that this combination of domains, methods, and theories cannot be coherent. On the other hand is a tendency to enthusiastic claims for the novelty and the revelations offered by such an approach; these were founded on the sometimes naïve use or abuse of concepts and methods attributed to cultural anthropology. For many scholars, the metaphoric extrapolation of concepts to label mass communication phenomena as myth, ritual, liminal, or magical seemed to be productive, giving the sensation that it offered new keys of interpretation.

The "betwixt and between" position of such works has also had another consequence: the lack of a commonly accepted name and definition for the new field. Several phrases are used to define it: media anthropology, anthropology of mass media, mass communication anthropology, anthropology of culture and media. Several definitions were suggested by Allen (1994); Askew (2002); Ginsburg, Abu-Lughod, and Larkin, (2002); Spitulnik (1993); and others. Osorio (chapter 4) proposes an integrative perspective: "Anthropology is the social science that studies culture. Therefore, mass media anthropology is the field within anthropology that studies the way in which culture shapes society through the mass media." Ultimately, debates over labels and definitions are merely scholastic. It is more important to ask ourselves if there is a field for media anthropology and, if so, what challenges it poses.

The field of media anthropology comprises "the production, circulation, and consumption of mass mediated forms" (Ginsburg, chapter 2), in both modern and nonmodern societies. The phrase "mass mediated forms" implies an extraordinary variety, from movies to print media, from radio and television to the Internet, from recorded music to advertising and, potentially, fashion and design. An equal variety and greater number of cultural processes and products is implied, from broadcasting the Olympics worldwide to the broadcasts of a small ethnic community's radio station, from the national unity affirmed through popularizing traditional ceremonies to consuming a favorite soap opera in the solitude of one's home, from religious manifestations on the Internet to the production routines of journalists, from debates in numerous "public sphericules" (Gitlin, 1998) to video games, from the global circulation of news, entertainment, and ads to producing a corporate newsletter, and more. What could be the common denominator in all these cultural phenomena? What could be the research agenda and the fields of media anthropology?

The studies so far reveal a great variety of preoccupations, fields, investigation methods, and theoretical horizons. One refers to the use of media techniques and media systems by anthropologists to (a) better record, "save," and disseminate the social practices of the insiders; (b) promote anthropology; or (c) improve journalistic practices. Another refers to the investigation of the ways in which different indigenous groups use media to disseminate their culture and to affirm a specific identity. Another perspective looks to mass media as a specific field, employing cultural anthropological methods and concepts to interpret "media culture." Within this field, we would include (i) the study of the influence of channels (oral, textual, audiovisual, or Internet) on media content or media consumption; (ii) the studies of the processes through which these cultural products are institutionally created and distributed by specialists in mass media industries; (iii) the investigation of processes by which these products are consumed and invested with meanings by different audiences; and (iv) the analysis of media contents. All these phenomena could be adressed at local, national, transnational, or global levels and in relationship with various social agencies.

The heterogeneity of such approaches could suggest that the meeting between cultural anthropology as a discipline and mass communication phenomena as a field of research is an accidental and nondurable one. As Hobart underlines in his chapter, media studies researchers could have resorted to cultural anthropology for a belief that anthropology is invoked "at precisely the point at which scientific approaches to society prove manifestly inadequate." Anthropologists could also have turned to mass media because, confronted with the disappearance of their object of study materially, much effort has gone into anthropologists recouping it conceptually. By contrast, emphasizing "[the] several intertwined legacies of thought within anthropology and media studies," Ginsburg (chapter 2) considers that the interest in mass media production and consumption goes back even to the beginnings of anthropology as a science. As they developed, these concerns have come to define an independent field, whose ground is given by the correlation between cultural creation and its mediation, or, later, popularization in various civilizations and ages: "One might think of these linked processes of the cultural production of media, its circulation as a social technology, and the relationship of mediated worlds to self-fabrication as existing on a continuum." This implies that media studies and cultural anthropology are not opposed disciplines but complementary approaches.

In the same line of thought, Osorio (chapter 4) maintains that we do not have to develop new methods for this area of knowledge, as we do not study the mass media in itself but as "the vehicle of the transmission of culture." Media anthropology thus appears as a continuation of classic anthropology, following the same great themes—assimilation, acculturation, diffusion, cross-cultural circulation of symbols, narratives, myths, and rituals—although via more complex and powerful communication systems than those anthropology had been studying in the past. In consensus with this perspective, Coman states in chapter 5 that it is not only the object of study (the production, distribution, and re-production of culture) that brings anthropology close to mass communication but also the fundamental symbolic processes implied: "The anthropological perspective further claims that these images are accepted and assumed precisely because they have the status of *symbolic constructs,* and that, having that status, they function and signify in the same way as mythical systems and rituals of nonmodern societies." In other words, media anthropology continues cultural anthropology's preoccupation from the very beginning to identify those processes that lay at the basis of cultural production in any society, from anywhere on the planet, at any time; media anthropology is about revealing the common logic, the thinking structures that, beyond the fractures of history and geography, unveil the profound unity of the human mind.

## REFERENCES

Allen, S. (1994). What is media anthropology? A personal view and a suggested structure. In S. Allen (Ed.), *Media anthropology: Informing global citizens* (pp. 15-32). Westport, CT: Bergin-Garvey.

Askew, K. (2002). Introduction. In K. Askew & R. Wilk (Eds.), *The anthropology of media,* (pp. 1-13). London: Blackwell.

Ginsburg, F. D., Abu-Lughod, L., & Larkin, B. (Eds.). (2002). *Media worlds: Anthropology on new terrain.* Berkeley: University of California Press.

Gitlin, T. (1998). Public spheres or public sphericules? In T. Liebes & J. Curran (Eds.), *Media, ritual and identity* (pp. 169-174). London: Routledge.

Spitulnik, D. (1993). Anthropology and mass media. *Annual Review of Anthropology, 22,* 293-315.

# 2

# MEDIA ANTHROPOLOGY

## An Introduction

FAYE GINSBURG

In 1993, in a comprehensive review essay, Debra Spitulnik invoked the insights of Stuart Hall[1] and other sociologically grounded media scholars to call for more engagement by anthropologists with "mass media as vehicles of culture, as modes of imagining and imaging communities" (Spitulnik, 1993, p. 295). Years later, a fertile domain of study—the anthropology of media—has emerged, along with a general reconceptualization of anthropology that addresses our changing relationship with informants as our cultural worlds grow ever closer (Marcus, 1996). The social domains we need to track to understand contemporary lives increasingly are shaped by processes of late capitalism, requiring multisited research strategies (Gupta & Ferguson, 1997; Hannerz, 1996). Anthropologists studying media—from their political economy to their presence in everyday lives—are developing research that will help us understand the way these forms are affecting people around the globe, part of a larger effort to create an "anthropology of the present" (Fox, 1991).

For many years, mass media were seen as almost a taboo topic for anthropology, too redolent of Western modernity and cultural imperialism for a field identified with tradition, the non-Western, and the vitality of the local. As media are becoming more ubiquitous even in remote locales, an increasing number of anthropologists have recognized not only the necessity of attending to their presence but also their significance. As anthropologists attempt to account for the growing importance of the presence of film, television, video, and radio as part of the everyday life of people throughout the world, we have taken up with new interest the study of the production, circulation, and consumption of mass mediated forms (Abu-Lughod, 1993, 1997; Appadurai, 1996; Dickey, 1993; Dornfeld, 1998; Mankekar, 1999; Marcus, 1996; Michaels, 1994; Pedelty, 1995; Rofel, 1994; Spitulnick, 2002), as well as visual culture, broadly conceived (Edwards, 2001; MacDougall, 1998; Marcus & Myers, 1995; Pinney, 1998; Ruby, 2000). People who are studying these forms as vehicles for the mediation and expression of social processes and cultural meanings are working in field sites as diverse as BBC boardrooms (Born, 1998), villages in upper Egypt (Abu-Lughod, 2002), fan clubs in south India (Dickey, 1993), radio stations in

**Author's Note:** A revised version of Fieldwork at the Movies in *Exotic No More* (MacClancy, Ed.) Copyright © 2002, University of Chicago Press.

Zambia (Spitulnick, 2002), and popular talk shows in Bolivia (Himpele, 2002).

The anthropology of mass media is informed by several intertwined legacies of thought within anthropology and media studies. Studies of feature films and propaganda were carried out during and following World War II, for example (Bateson, 1948; Mead & Metraux, 1953; Powdermaker, 1950), within the American culture and personality paradigm, and later as part of a developing field of studies in visual communication.[2] Following that lineage, a number of scholars link their work on media to the field of visual anthropology (Banks & Morphy, 1997; Ginsburg, 1998; Pinney, 1998; Ruby, 2000), often bringing a critical revision of that field through the lens of postcolonial scholarship, especially on ethnographic, documentary, and popular film practices, past and present (Rony, 1996; Shohat & Stam, 1994). Others focus on its empirical counterpart in the production of a variety of alternative (Downmunt, 1993; Juhasz, 1995; Riggins, 1992), diasporic (Gillespie, 1995; McLagan, 2002; Naficy, 1993) and small media practices (Haynes, 1997; Manuel, 1993; Sreberny-Mohammadi & Mohammadi, 1994) by people who until recently were only objects of and never producers in the enterprise of cross-cultural representation.

Another related strand of thought, closely identified with the journal *Public Culture,* emerges from those interested in how processes of modernity, postmodernity, and globalization actually work on the ground, tracking the cultural effects of transnational flows of people, ideas, and objects—in some cases mediated by film, video, and television—that are instrumental in creating a sense of a social world that is rapidly "respatializing" culture and power in ways that characterize fin de siecle cultural life (Marcus, 1997). This scholarship builds, in particular, on the work of two key scholars whose work addresses the mediation of the structures and processes of nationalism and consciousness: Benedict Anderson's (1991) groundbreaking insights into the role of print—and now other—media in the creation of the "imagined communities" of nation states, and the extension of Anderson's Durkheimian frame

to a broader notion of the social imaginary[3] and Jurgen Habermas's (1989) articulation of the historical emergence of the public sphere (and the ensuing debates and critiques of that model articulated by Robbins, 1993; Fraser, 1993; Calhoun, 1992; and others). The work of Arjun Appadurai (1996) has been particularly influenced by these thinkers and in turn has been influential in synthesizing their frameworks with anthropological concerns and methods. In his model, media is a central part of public culture, particularly important to the articulation of the national and transnational through local processes. His influential essay on "global ethnoscapes" points to the significance of the spread of film, television, video, and photography throughout the world. Attending to the ways in which satellite and video technologies transcend nation-state boundaries that were sustained more easily through print and terrestrial television, he argues for the increasing significance of "the imagination" in the production of culture and identity in the contemporary world.

> More persons in more parts of the world consider a wider set of "possible" lives than they ever did before. One important source of this change is the mass media, which present a rich, ever-changing store of possible lives, some of which enter the lived imaginations of ordinary people more successfully than others. Important also are contact with, news of, and rumors about others in one's social neighborhood who have become inhabitants of these faraway worlds. The importance of media is not so much as direct sources of new images and scenarios for life possibilities but as semiotic diacritics of great power, which also inflect social contact with the metropolitan world facilitated by other channels. (Appadurai, 1991, p. 198)

In his 1996 edited volume *Connected: Engagements with Media,* George Marcus also focuses on electronic and visual media of various kinds and how they operate increasingly as "a direct and intimate complement to the self and self-capacity" (p. 10).

The significance of media as a hermeneutic for entering and comprehending the contemporary social world is especially clear in a number of recent groundbreaking projects that provide models for how programmatic claims about media can actually guide research. Lila Abu-Lughod's work on the production, circulation, and impact of Egyptian television melodrama serials is exemplary: She tracks how these are intended to operate (although they do not always succeed) as social technologies, through which modern citizens are produced and subjectivities are partially constituted. In one of her recent articles on the social life of these narrative forms as they move from producers to audiences, she demonstrates how, by staging interiorities through heightened emotional display, these serials encourage the embrace of individuality over kinship, a key transformation in the making of modern subjects (Abu-Lughod, 1998).

Finally, Pierre Bourdieu's (1993) framing of the field of cultural production—the system of relations (and struggles for power) among agents or institutions engaged in generating the value of works of art and creating cultural capital for themselves—has been especially influential for those whose emphasis is on the institutional sites of the production of media work. For example, in his innovative ethnography, Barry Dornfeld (1998) draws on Bourdieu's model to understand the production of a public television series as a "cultural field" in which producers are always prefiguring audiences in their work. This position, he argues, calls more generally for "rethinking and bridging the theoretical dichotomy between production and consumption, between producers' intentional meanings and audience members' interpreted meanings and between production studies and reception studies" (Dornfeld, 1998, 12-13).

One might think of these linked processes of the cultural production of media, its circulation as a social technology, and the relationship of mediated worlds to self-fabrication as existing on a continuum. On one end is the more self-conscious cultural activism in which cultural material is used and strategically deployed as part of a broader project of political empowerment, providing a "third space" (Bhabha, 1989) for indigenous and minoritized groups, as well as what some have called Third Cinema (Pines &

Willemen, 1989), often created in circumstances under which choices are heavily constrained and political mobilization is incipient (Downmunt, 1993; Juhasz, 1995; McLagan, 1996; Riggins, 1992). In the middle range are reflexive but less strategic processes in which the imaginative encounter with cinematic or televisual images and narratives may be expressive or constitutive of a variety of social worlds, such as the transnational links that video, television shows, films, and computer networks provide for diasporic communities (Gillespie, 1995; McLagan, 1996; Schein, 2002). On the other end of the continuum are the more classic formations of mass media, which require institutional framings and imply some dimension of social segregation between producers and audiences. Anthropological research on these mediations focuses on the complex and divergent ways in which national cinemas (Bikales, 1997; Faraday, 2000; Ganti, 2002) and television in Third World settings operate, tracking the often unstable relation between intention and effect as these media are put to the service of constituting modern citizens, through a variety of forms, notably in popular soap operas, telenovelas, melodramatic serials (Abu-Lughod, 2002; Mankekar, 1999; Miller, 1992; Rofel, 1994; Salamandra, 1998; Yang, 2002), cultural programming (Hobart, 2002), and talk shows (Gordon, 1998; Himpele, 2002) and how these are intended and understood in relation to larger conjunctures and in a variety of settings, from production to distribution to consumption.

Because anthropologists so frequently locate themselves in non-Western and "out of the way" places, the research offers not only a thick, vertically integrated, and multisited sense of the social life of media but also engages with how this occurs outside the circuits of First World settings, which have provided an ethnocentric frame for much academic discussion of media, until quite recently. Ironically, even those arguing about and against cultural imperialism (Schiller, 1991) or researching the exporting of American culture through the circulation of popular film and television programs (Ang, 1985; Liebes & Katz, 1990; Silj, 1988) nonetheless presume the centrality of

American media. In an effort to correct that, ethnographers and scholars in media studies are attending increasingly to the circulation of media in settings not dependent on Western hegemonic practices, such as the export of Hindi cinema (Pendakur & Subramanyam, 1996) and Mexican telenovelas (Sinclair, 1996).

At the same time, anthropological research on mass media reiterates the insufficiency of bounded concepts of culture as a way of understanding contemporary lives in our own or other societies. As Lila Abu-Lughod (1997) argued in considering the impact of Egyptian serials in the life of Zaynab, an older peasant woman living in a peasant village in Upper Egypt,

> Television is an extraordinary technology for breaching boundaries and intensifying and multiplying encounters among life worlds, sensibilities, and ideas. . . . It brings into Zaynab's home, her conversations and her imagination a range of visions and experiences that originated outside her community . . . hardly unusual produced elsewhere and consumed in a variety of localities. Even if it ultimately helps create something of a "national habitus" or hints of a transnational habitus, television is most interesting because of the way it provides material which is then inserted into, interpreted with, and mixed up with local but themselves socially differentiated knowledges, discourses and meaning systems. . . . Television, in short, renders more and more problematic a concept of cultures as localized communities of people suspended in shared webs of meaning. (p. 122)

Scholars developing ethnographies of media usually begin with an interest in understanding questions generated by the phenomenon itself, often motivated by a desire to comprehend the popularity, power, and passion attached to certain kinds of media production and viewing (e.g., why is Indian cinema so popular among Hausa men in northern Nigeria?). It quickly becomes apparent in almost every case that answering these questions leads to an appreciation of the complexity of how people interact with media in a variety of social spaces and the resulting shifts in the sense of the local as its relation to broader social worlds becomes almost a routine part of everyday life.

Understanding the social relations of media production, circulation, and reception in this way entails a grounded focus on the everyday practices and consciousness of social actors as producers and consumers of different forms of media. Their interests and responses shape and are shaped by a variety of possible subject positions: cultural, generational, gendered, local, national, regional, and transnational communities of identity requiring an increasingly complex and plural notion of audience. Indeed, these multiple identities may be part of a single social subject's repertoire of cultural resources:

> An Egyptian immigrant in Britian, for example, might think of herself as a Glaswegian when she watches her local Scottish channel, a British resident when she switches over to the BBC, an Islamic Arab expatriate in Europe when she tunes in to the satellite service from the Middle East and a world citizen when she channel surfs on CNN. (Sinclair, Jacka, & Cunningham, 1996, p. 25)

Our work is distinguished by an effort to track, qualitatively and with the kind of cultural knowledge that enables what Geertz (1973) calls "thick description,"[4] the practices, consciousness, and distinctions that emerge for people out of their quotidian encounters with media; however, these are also always situated within the context of a broader social universe. To comprehend that reality, studies are increasingly multisited, tracking the various social players engaged when one follows the object—a television serial or film as it moves from elite directors to consumers (Dickey, 1993; Mankekar, 1999), or the object itself, such as a cassette recorder (Manuel, 1993), radio (Spitulnik, 2002), or even radio sound (Taachi, 1998) as it circulates through a variety of milieux. Whether in our own societies (Dornfeld, 2002; McLagan, 2002) or elsewhere, ethnographers look at media as cultural artifacts enmeshed in daily lives, to see how they are imperfectly articulated with (and sometimes created as a counter to) larger hegemonic processes of modernity, assimilation, nation building, commercialization, and globalization, but in terms that draw attention to how those processes are being localized.

Perhaps because of the intensity and self-consciousness of the concern with media's possible deleterious effects, as well its utopian possibilities, most of us carrying out research on media with indigenous or other subaltern groups also have an activist engagement with this work (Philipsen & Markussen, 1995), as supporters and even catalyzers of activity, bringing cameras to communities and assisting in the logistics of projects (Asch, 1991; Carelli, 1988; Ginsburg, 2002; Michaels, 1994; Prins, 2002; Turner, 2002) or helping to develop visibility, funding, and circulation systems for the work (Berger, 1995; Fleming, 1991; Ginsburg, 2003; Meadows & Molnar, 2001; Wortham, 2000). In a less direct but equally engaged concern, Abu-Lughod (1997) points out that studying popular television "is particularly useful for writing against the grain [of global inequalities] because it forces us to represent people in distant villages as part of the same cultural worlds we inhabit—worlds of mass media, consumption, and dispersed communities of the imagination" (p. 128). Some have argued that these projects go beyond advocacy, as authorial relations are reversed and "the anthropologist's voice supplements that of indigenous people" (Marcus, quoted in Palattella, 1998, p. 50), underscoring the ways in which we are increasingly "complicit" with our subjects when engaged with such material (Marcus, 1997), as we find ourselves jointly engaged in the project of objectifying and representing culture. This relationship grows even more complex, as anthropologists (and fellow travelers) are beginning to study cyberspace (e.g., McLagan, 1996; Miller & Slater, 2000), a site of sociality in which the research takes place (in part) through the medium of study itself.

One can see a trajectory in the theorizing of the relationship between culture and media over the last half century, as the objectification of the category of culture becomes ever more widespread, and the observer becomes increasingly implicated as a participant. In the early work on mass media, culture operated as a kind of unconscious Durkheimian indicator of the national, which was interpreted in metaphors of personality types in the work of Mead, Bateson, Weakland, Wolfenstein, and others in the 1950s. When, in the 1990s, anthropologists began to turn their attention to film and television once again, they looked at media not so much as a reductive mirror but as a social force in which culture was a resource in struggles for political and economic hegemony over the representation of society in mass media, from efforts to shore up state control over television to the development of the Third Cinema movement, which was part of a global anticolonial project. Most recently, scholars are developing research that will help us rethink abstract notions such as globalization, to see how new technologies and economies of late modernity are being framed both by "the new international division of cultural labor" (Miller, 1998, p. 371), as well as practices on the ground (or rooftops, as satellite dishes proliferate!), as people at every end of the social spectrum—from Rupert Murdoch's STAR TV to the videographers in Hmong communities dispersed across the globe—are engaging with mediascapes that increasingly escape the control of national political structures and economies, rearranging, in the process, the ways in which cultural formations are spatialized and imagined. For many social theorists interested in media as a site for either social possibilities or cultural decay, the question is still open as to whether even alternative media practices inevitably "eat their young" because of the impossibility of escaping the discursive and institutional structures that even small media require. Although the lack of resolution is undoubtedly healthy for intellectual debate, an unanticipated dimension of continued research during an era of ever widening penetration and availability of media is the way in which we are increasingly implicated in the representational practices of those we study, a social fact that brings absolute and welcome closure to the allochronic tendencies of the field that Fabian (1983) warned against.

Anthropologists at last are coming to terms with the inescapable presence of media as a contemporary cultural force engaged with the mediation of hegemonic forms and resistance to them; the growth and transnational circulation of public culture; the creation of national and activist social imaginaries, with the development of media as new arenas for political expression and the production of identity. Such research offers a salutary effect on anthropology, as well as media studies, opening up new questions regarding the production and circulation of film and electronic media throughout the world, in non-Western as well as Western societies, potentially resituating the "looking relations" (Gaines, 1988) that take place between and among cultures and across boundaries of inequality.

## NOTES

1. Hall (1997) argues that as the mass media "have progressively *colonized* the cultural and ideological sphere" (p. 207) they have increasingly provided "a basis on which groups construct an image of the lives, and accomplishment meanings, practices, and values of *other* groups and classes" as well as "the images, representations and ideas around which the social totality can be coherently grasped as a *whole*" (p. 207).

2. Sol Worth's approach, developed in the 1970s, reflected the theoretical preoccupations of that time with structural semiotics and ethnoscience. Although he also developed a interest in the political economy and global reach of media, Worth's focus on the anthropology of visual communication looked primarily at how films made by any group of people could provide visual maps of worldviews and cognitive categories, serving as a kind of window onto the native's point of view. Later, influenced by Worth's ideas and efforts, Jay Ruby, along with Worth's student Richard Chalfen, initiated the first Masters in Visual Anthropology in the United States at Temple University, with a focus on culture and communication, which included the social uses and cultural meanings of film, television, video, and photography.

3. See a useful discussion of the concept of the imaginary in Lilley (1993).

4. For an excellent discussion of how the notion of "thick description" enters into ethnographies of mass media, see Abu-Lughod (1997).

## REFERENCES

Abu-Lughod, L. (1993). Finding a place for Islam: Egyptian television serials and the national interest. *Public Culture*, 5(3), 493-514.

Abu-Lughod, L. (1997). The interpretation of culture(s) after television. *Representations, 59*, 109-133.

Abu-Lughod, L. (1998). Television and the virtues of education. In N. Hopkins & K. Westergaard (Eds.), *Directions of change in rural Egypt* (pp. 147-165). Cairo: American University in Cairo Press.

Abu-Lughod, L. (2002). Egyptian melodrama: Technology of the modern subject? In F. Ginsburg, L. Abu-Lughod, & B. Larkin (Eds.), *Media worlds: Anthropology on new terrain* (pp. 115-133). Berkeley: University of California Press.

Anderson, B. (1991). *Imagined communities: Reflections on the origins and spread of nationalism*. London: Verso.

Ang, I. (1985). *Watching* Dallas: *Soap opera and the melodramatic imagination*. New York: Methuen.

Appadurai, A. (1991). Global ethnoscapes: Notes and queries for a transnational anthropology. In R. Fox (Ed.), *Recapturing anthropology* (pp. 191-210). Santa Fe, NM: School of American Research Press.

Appadurai, A. (1996). *Modernity at large: Cultural dimensions of globalization*. Minneapolis: University of Minnesota Press.

Asch, T. (1991). The story we now want to hear is not ours to tell—relinquishing control over representation: Toward sharing visual communication skills with the Yanomamo. *Visual Anthropology Review, 7*(2), 102-106.

Banks, M., & Morphy, H. (Eds.). (1997). *Rethinking visual anthropology*. New Haven, CT: Yale University Press.

Bateson, G. (1948). Cultural and thematic analysis of fictional films. In D. G. Haring (Ed.), *Personal character and cultural milieu* (pp. 117-123). Syracuse, NY: Syracuse University Press.

Berger, S. (1995). Move over Nanook. *Wide Angle, 17*(1-4, Special issue), 177-192.

Bhabha, H. (1989). The commitment to theory. In J. Pines & P. Willemen (Eds.), *Questions of Third Cinema* (pp. 111-132). London: British Film Institute.

Bikales, T. (1997). *From "culture" to "commercialization": The production and packaging of an African cinema in Ougadougou, Burkina Faso*. Unpublished doctoral dissertation, New York University, New York.

Born, G. (1998, April). *Between aesthetics, ethics and audit: Reflexivities and disciplines in the BBC*. Talk presented at the Department of Anthropology, New York University, New York.

Bourdieu, P. (1993). *The field of cultural production*. New York: Columbia University Press.

Calhoun, C. (Ed.). (1992). *Habermas and the public sphere*. Cambridge, MA.: MIT Press.

Carelli, V. (1988, May). Video in the villages. *Commission on Visual Anthropology Bulletin*, pp. 10-15.

Dickey, S. (1993). *Cinema and the urban poor in South India.* Cambridge, England: Cambridge University Press.

Dornfeld, B. (1998). *Producing public television.* Princeton, NJ: Princeton University Press.

Dornfeld, B. (2002). Putting American public television documentary in its places. In F. Ginsburg, L. Abu-Lughod, & B. Larkin (Eds.), *Media worlds: Anthropology on new terrain* (pp. 247-263). Berkeley: University of California Press.

Downmunt, T. (Ed.). (1993). *Channels of resistance: Global television and local empowerment.* London: British Film Institute.

Edwards, E. (2001). *Raw histories: Photographs, anthropology, and museums.* New York: Berg.

Fabian, J. (1983). *Time and the other.* New York: Columbia University Press.

Faraday, G. (2000). *Revolt of the filmmakers: The struggle for artistic autonomy and the fall of the soviet film industry.* University Park: Pennsylvania State University Press.

Fleming, K. (1991, Summer). Zacharias Kunuk: Videomaker and Inuit historian. *Inuit Art Quarterly, 24*, 2-8.

Fox, R. (Ed.). (1991). *Recapturing anthropology: Working in the present.* Santa Fe, NM: School of American Research Press.

Fraser, N. (1993). Rethinking the public sphere: A contribution to the critique of actually existing democracy. In B. Robbins (Ed.), *The phantom public sphere* (pp. 1-32). Minneapolis: University of Minnesota Press.

Gaines, J. (1988). White privilege and looking relations: Race and gender in feminist film theory. *Screen, 29*(4), 12-27.

Ganti, T. (2002). The (H)Indianization of Hollywood by the Bombay film industry. In F. Ginsburg, L. Abu-Lughod, & B. Larkin (Eds.), *Media worlds: Anthropology on new terrain* (pp. 281-300). Berkeley: University of California Press.

Geertz, C. (1973). *The interpretation of cultures.* New York: Basic Books.

Gillespie, M. (1995). *Television, ethnicity, and cultural change.* London: Routledge.

Ginsburg, F. (1998). Institutionalizing the unruly: Charting a future for visual anthroplogy. *Ethnos, 63*(2), 173-201.

Ginsburg, F. (2002). Screen memories: Resignifying the traditional in indigenous media. In F. Ginsburg, L. Abu-Lughod, & B. Larkin (Eds.), *Media worlds:*

*Anthropology on new terrain* (pp. 77-104). Berkeley: University of California Press.

Ginsburg, F. (2003). *Atanarjuat* off-screen: From "media reservations" to the world stage. *American Anthropologist, 105*, 827-832.

Gordon, J. (1998). Becoming the image: Words of gold, talk television, and Ramadan nights on the little screen. *Visual Anthropology, 10*(2-4, Special issue), 247-264.

Gupta, A., & Ferguson, J. (1997). Discipline and practice: "The field" as site, method, and location in anthropology. In A. Gupta & J. Ferguson (Eds.), *Anthropological locations* (pp. 1-46). Berkeley: University of California Press.

Habermas, J. (1989). *The structural transformation of the public sphere* (T. Burger with F. Lawrence, trans.). Cambridge, MA: MIT Press.

Hall, S. (1997). *Representation: Cultural representations and signifying practices.* London: Sage.

Hannerz, U. (1996). *Transnational connections.* New York: Routledge.

Haynes, J. (Ed.). (1997). *Nigerian video film* (Rev. ed.). Athens: Ohio University Press.

Himpele, J. (2002). Arrival scenes: Complicity and media ethnography in the Bolivian public sphere. In F. Ginsburg, L. Abu-Lughod, & B. Larkin (Eds.), *Media worlds: Anthropology on new terrain* (pp. 476-500). Berkeley: University of California Press.

Hobart, M. (2002). Live or dead? Transforming Balinese theater into television. In F. Ginsburg, L. Abu-Lughod, & B. Larkin (Eds.), *Media worlds: Anthropology on new terrain* (pp. 548-603). Berkeley: University of California Press.

Juhasz, A. (1995). *AIDS TV: Identity, community, and alternative video.* Durham, NC: Duke University Press.

Liebes, T., & Katz, E. (1990). *The export of meaning: Cross-cultural readings of "Dallas."* New York: Oxford University Press.

Lilley, R. (1993). Claiming identity: Film and television in Hong Kong. *History and Anthropology, 6*(2-3), 261-292.

MacDougall, D. (1998). *Transcultural cinema.* Princeton, NJ: Princeton University Press.

Mankekar, P. (1999). *Screening culture, viewing politics: An ethnography of television, womanhood, and nation in postcolonial India.* Durham, NC: Duke University Press.

Manuel, P. (1993). *Cassette culture: Popular music and technology in North India.* Chicago: University of Chicago Press.

Marcus, G. (1996). Introduction. In G. Marcus (Ed.), *Connected: Engagements with media* (pp. 1-18). Chicago: University of Chicago Press.

Marcus, G. (Ed.). (1997). *Cultural producers in perilous states*. Chicago: University of Chicago Press.

Marcus, G., & Myers, F. (1995). Introduction. In G. Marcus & F. Myers (Eds.), *The traffic in culture: Refiguring anthropology and art* (pp. 1-51). Berkeley: University of California Press.

McLagan, M. (1996). Computing for Tibet: Virtual politics in the post-Cold War era. In G. Marcus (Ed.), *Connected: Engagements with media* (pp. 159-194). Chicago: University of Chicago Press.

McLagan, M. (2002). Spectacles of difference: Cultural activism and the mass mediation of Tibet. In F. Ginsburg, L. Abu-Lughod, & B. Larkin (Eds.), *Media worlds: Anthropology on new terrain* (pp. 90-112). Berkeley: University of California Press.

Mead, M., & Metraux, R. (1953). *The study of culture at a distance*. Chicago: University of Chicago Press.

Meadows, M., & Molnar, H. (2001). *Songlines to satellites: Indigenous communications in Australia, the South Pacific, and Canada*. Leichardt: Pluto Press.

Michaels, E. (1994). *Bad aboriginal art: Tradition, media, and technological horizons*. Minneapolis: University of Minnesota Press.

Miller, D. (1992). The young and the restless in Trinidad: A case of the local and the global in mass consumption. In R. Silverstone & E. Hirsch (Eds.), *Consuming technology*. London: Routledge.

Miller, D., & Slater, D. (2000). *The Internet: An ethnographic approach*. London: Berg.

Miller, T. (1998). Hollywood and the world. In J. Hill & P. C. Gibson (Eds.), *The Oxford guide to film studies* (pp. 371-382). New York: Oxford University Press.

Naficy, H. (1993). *The making of exile cultures: Iranian television in Los Angeles*. Minneapolis: University of Minnesota Press.

Palatella, J. (1998). Pictures of us. *Lingua Franca, 8*(5), 50-57.

Pedelty, M. (1995). *War stories: The culture of foreign correspondents*. New York: Routledge.

Pendakur, M., & Subramanyam, R. (1996). Indian cinema beyond national borders. In J. Sinclair, E. Jacka, & S. Cunningham (Eds.), *New patterns in global television: Peripheral vision* (pp. 69-82). London: Oxford University Press.

Philipsen, H. H., & Markussen, B. (Eds.). (1995). *Advocacy and indigenous film-making*. Aarhaus, Denmark: Intervention Press.

Pines, J., & Willemen, P. (Eds.). (1989). *Questions of Third Cinema*. London: BFI.

Pinney, C. (1998). *The social life of photographs*. London: Blackwell.

Powdermaker, H. (1950). *Hollywood, the dream factory*. Boston: Grosset & Dunlap.

Prins, H. (2002). Visual media and the primitivist perplex: Colonial fantasies and indigenous imagination in the decolonization of the Fourth World. In F. Ginsburg, L. Abu-Lughod, & B. Larkin (Eds.), *Media worlds: Anthropology on new terrain* (pp. 105-130). Berkeley: University of California Press.

Riggins, S. H. (1992). *Ethnic minority media: An international perspective*. London: Sage.

Robbins, B. (Ed.). (1993). *The phantom public sphere*. Minneapolis: University of Minnesota Press.

Rofel, L. (1994). Yearnings: Televisual love and melodramatic politics in contemporary China. *American Ethnologist, 21*(4), 700-722.

Rony, F. (1996). *The third eye: Race, cinema, and ethnographic spectacle*. Durham, NC: Duke University Press.

Ruby, J. (2000). *Picturing culture: Explorations of film and anthropology*. Chicago: University of Chicago Press.

Salamandra, C. (1998). Moustache hairs lost: Ramadan television serials and the construction of identity in Damascus, Syria. *Visual Anthropology, 10*(2-4, Special issue), 227-246.

Schein, L. (2002). Mapping Hmong media in diasporic space. In F. Ginsburg, L. Abu-Lughod, & B. Larkin (Eds.), *Media worlds: Anthropology on new terrain* (pp. 229-245). Berkeley: University of California Press.

Schiller, H. (1991). Not yet the post-imperialist era. *Critical Studies in Mass Communication, 8*, 13-28.

Shohat, E., & Stam, R. (1994). *Unthinking Eurocentrism: Multiculturalism and the media*. New York: Routledge.

Silj, A. (1988). *East of Dallas: The European challenge to American television*. London: British Film Institute.

Sinclair, J. (1996). Mexico, Brazil, and the Latin world. In J. Sinclair, E. Jacka, & S. Cunningham (Eds.), *New patterns in global television: Peripheral vision* (pp. 33-66). London: Oxford University Press.

Sinclair, J., Jacka, E., & Cunningham, S. (Eds.). (1996). *New patterns in global television: Peripheral vision*. London: Oxford University.

Spitulnik, D. (1993). Anthropology and the mass media. *Annual Review of Anthropology, 22*, 293-315.

Spitulnik, D. (2002). Mobile machines and fluid audiences: Rethinking reception through Zambian radio culture. In F. Ginsburg, L. Abu-Lughod, & B. Larkin

(Eds.), *Media worlds: Anthropology on new terrain* (pp. 532-560). Berkeley: University of California Press.

Sreberny-Mohammadi, A., & Mohammadi, A. (1994). *Small media, big revolution: Communication, culture, and the Iranian revolution.* Minneapolis: University of Minneapolis Press.

Taachi, J. (1998). Radio texture: Between self and others. In D. Miller (Ed.), *Material cultures: Why some things matter.* Chicago: University of Chicago Press.

Turner, T. (2002). Representation, politics and cultural imagination in indigenous video: General points and Kayapo examples. In F. Ginsburg, L. Abu-Lughod, & B. Larkin (Eds.), *Media worlds: Anthropology on new terrain* (pp. 131-153). Berkeley: University of California Press.

Wortham, E. C. (2000). News from the mountains: Redefining the televisual borders of Oaxaca. *World Studio Sphere 2000, 5,* 32-33.

Yang, M. M.-h. (2002). Mass media and transnational subjectivity in Shanghai: Notes on (re)cosmopolitanism in a Chinese metropolis. In F. Ginsburg, L. Abu-Lughod, & B. Larkin (Eds.), *Media worlds: Anthropology on new terrain* (pp. 302-338). Berkeley: University of California Press.

# 3

---

# THE PROFANITY OF THE MEDIA

MARK HOBART

---

How should we best imagine the relationship of anthropology and media studies? Will this be a fruitful union? Arguably, anthropology and media studies are at their best when they are *critical*, in the double sense not only of interrogating and seeking to understand the conditions of possibility of their subjects' thinking, but also of their own criteria and practices of inquiry. Thus I will consider how critical reflection on revered anthropological tenets has surprising implications for the presuppositions of media studies. I will start with a critical analysis of an anthropological venture into media studies, then show how it invites a radical (i.e., critical presuppositional) rethinking of a "hegemonic text" of media studies, Stuart Hall's (1980) "Encoding/Decoding."

## SHIPS PASSING IN THE NIGHT?

Speaking as an anthropologist, I would say that a brief critical reading suggests there is a curious sense of something lacking in media studies itself, which has inspired hope among some critical media scholars of finding the missing bits in anthropology. For example, discontent with the inadequacies of the quantitative and macro studies of media has led to interest in qualitative, or ethnographic, approaches. David Morley (1992), noting the problems inherent in ethnographic description, and Ien Ang (1996), commenting on its potentially infinite contextualism, both deferred to the work of the totemic figure of Clifford Geertz.

Significantly, media scholars invoke anthropology at precisely the point at which scientific approaches to society prove manifestly inadequate. The appeal to intensive participatory ethnography complicates naturalism and scientism beautifully because it highlights the dialogic relationship between the ethnographer's and the subjects' practices of knowing, explaining, justifying, and so on. Johannes Fabian (1990) has argued that ethnography is best thought of as a performance interpolated into the other performances that constitute social life. However, recourse to practice dismantles totalizing accounts of cultures, which, despite their protestations to the contrary, leaves most anthropologists and cultural studies specialists without an object of study.

---

**Author's Note:** My thanks to Ron Inden and Richard Fox, who gave invaluable comments on the first and final drafts of this chapter, respectively.

Choosing Geertz as the representative anthropologist is not fortuitous, as he is widely imagined as a proponent of strong culturalism, an antidote to naturalist or economistic reductivism. Close study of Geertz's work shows his culturalism to be supplementary. Culture is strapped onto "hard . . . political, economic, stratificatory realities" and "biological and physical necessities" (Geertz, 1973, p. 30). Culture is the gunk that plugs the holes in existing theories, the while proclaiming itself new and different. Geertz's model of culture is, in fact, a conventional account of articulation that allows interpretive freedom without challenging the ontological status of the elements it articulates. This account of culture has a long pedigree in German Idealism (Hobart, 2000), however, which leaves media studies awkwardly embracing a murky transcendentalism.

Anthropology's obvious critical contribution to media studies is recognizing the problems of ethnocentrism, which pervades cultural, communication, and media studies. Anthropologists' denunciations of others' ethnocentrism, however, verge on the disingenuous, as it is questionable how satisfactorily anthropologists have addressed the issue.

On a stronger reading of culture, it becomes clear that the anthropologists' task is not just to inquire into different ways of thought and action. It is to understand the presuppositions that motivate such thinking and acting and so to appreciate how other people explain, represent, and mediate events and actions. Anthropologists here are poised between noncommensurate discourses, the disjunctures between which give rise to many of our critical dilemmas. Taken seriously, this deprives anthropologists of a critical turn of mind in regard to the possibility of closure, of epistemological grounding or certainty (Fabian, 1991). The anthropologist as a unitary knowing subject emerges as an impossible fiction, as we are obliged to participate in an open, unfinalizable dialogue. Such a radical account of critical understanding invites anthropology and media studies to interrogate one another in a dialogic engagement that problematizes the discursive unity of inquiry, the subjects and objects of study, and the nature of representation and mediation.

## ANTHROPOLOGY MEETS THE MODERN WORLD

Quite apart from their long-standing interest in visual anthropology and ethnographic film, anthropologists, who often resemble the predatory acephalous lineages they study, have engaged in their favourite pastime of ragbag colonizing or liberating of other disciplines through direct nounal assault—frequently by declaring a new subfield, "the anthropology of . . . x," "x" in this instance being media (e.g., Askew & Wilk, 2002; Ginsburg, Abu-Lughod, & Larkin, 2002). Although many such works have the modest and useful aim of ethnographic inquiry, others are more intellectually expansionist and determined to claim the contemporary relevance of anthropology in new fields. One such piece appeared recently in *Anthropology Today,* a magazine aimed at popularizing anthropology. I wish to consider it carefully for several reasons. Its author is a seasoned anthropologist, writing in a publication of the Royal Anthropological Institute, which represents the august and authoritative voice of British anthropology.[1] In its enthusiasm to show just what anthropology can do for—and to—cultural and media studies, revealingly it displays its intellectual underwear.

In "Born a Lady, Became a Princess, Died a Saint," Bill Watson (1997) asked, pertinently, what exactly was going on in the aftermath of the death of Princess Diana. Goaded by the absence of anthropological enunciation on these events, his aim was to demonstrate anthropology's contemporary relevance to the study of mass media and popular culture. To do so, he had to come up with a distinctive explanation. It turned upon two trusty (indeed, rusty) anthropological standbys: the essentially sacred nature of royalty and the significance of sacrifice. Both are captured in a single truth: "Diana is for British society the royal sacrificial victim" (p. 6). Quite apart from the rather quaint notion that there is such a unitary thing as British society, to which anthropologists mysteriously have privileged access, the whole gamut of events surrounding Princess Diana's death, and apparently their refraction in distant parts of the globe, can be reduced to the formula "*royal = sacred = died for our (the nation's) sins*" (p. 6; unless indicated otherwise, all italics are in the original). It was this cultural formula that articulated the "collective emotion" (p. 4). As with most grand anthropological pronouncements, it enshrines a certain magnificent universality and timelessness, of which history tends to make a mockery. Subsequent media coverage of Diana's death raised questions not only about the grimy politics of Diana's apotheosis but why all the dissenting voices felt they had to keep quiet.

What concerns me is not so much Watson's explanation of events after Diana's death as what his argument presupposes. Like the dog that did not bark in the Sherlock Holmes story, the piece is significant for what it does not say—especially about the importance of the media in anthropological analyses.

## The Death of an Argument

Watson's article is important because, almost in the strict Derridean sense, it deconstructs itself to reveal familiar presuppositions about agency, media, ontology, and the nature of anthropological argument itself.

Royalty, it transpired, was not just sacred in 1990s Britain; its sacredness rises above history, place, and culture. Commenting on Diana's brother's remarks at her funeral, Watson (1997) argued:

> Anthropologists can surely not fail to see here an instance of the much documented phenomenon of a challenge being made to the legitimacy and sacred status of the monarch by a principle which would, formulaically at least, carry equal weight to the principle of divine kingship, namely the claim that *vox populi, vox dei*. This republican cry in terms of British history may be of relatively recent date, but it reflects an institution well documented in anthropological and historical scholarship. When the Chinese emperor

loses the mandate of heaven or when the Shilluk king loses his strength, then the people and the people's spokesman must intervene for the sake of the nation to ensure a proper succession. (p. 6)

Although the image of Shilluk kings and Chinese emperors rubbing shoulders with the Windsors and their affines is charmingly ecumenical, invoking scholarly authority to impose contemporary, contested, and arguably vacuous European categories (the nation, the people, republicanism) on the whole history and diversity of the world is problematic: as if power and social divisions everywhere lined up conveniently.

Anthropologists dwell much upon authority. However, to accept uncritically that royalty everywhere is always sacred rather begs the question: We know how to identify sacredness and royalty unambiguously, uncontrovertibly, and universally by applying the categories that were handed down to us! In place of critical dialogue, Watson has imposed a stultifying monologue in the name of anthropological authority.

Of Princess Diana's death, Watson (1997) states: "There can be little doubt that what we witnessed at the time, pace the cynical interpretations of Common Room philosophers, was the articulation of collective emotion" (p. 4).

Leaving aside how you would determine that the same emotion was shared by millions of people, Watson used "articulation" as a synonym for "expression," as if there were some abstract collective mind that seeks instantiation in the world. It is surprising that he ignored, or was ignorant of, an alternative to this dualistic ontology. In cultural studies, *articulation* has come to have the double sense of *to utter* and *to link*. Thus structures, far from being unitary, noncontradictory, stable, transcendent entities, as in Watson's fixed conjunctions, are treated as moments of arbitrary closure, the partial, incomplete products of acts of articulatory practices. According to Hall (1996c), articulation emerges as

> the form of the connection that *can* make a unity of two different elements, under certain conditions. It is a linkage which is not necessary, determined, absolute and essential for all time. You have to ask under what

circumstances *can* a connection be forged or made? The so-called "unity" of a discourse is really the articulation of different, distinct elements which can be rearticulated in different ways because they have no necessary "belongingness." (p. 141).

There are at least two readings. Structure is not necessarily engraved in stone but is open to a degree of rearticulation, under circumstances that remain unspecified. When it is given a strong reading, however, articulation replaces structure with an account of action as situated, underdetermined, and so partly contingent. Subjects are thus those moments of lack of structural determination (Laclau, 1990). The difference is significant.

The problem of analyses such as "Born a Lady" is that the entities being articulated (e.g., "collective emotion") are blissfully unclear. So is the question of who decides what constitutes a collectivity and under what circumstances. (Now, done well, such carefully situated analyses are precisely what anthropology can bring to media studies.) The appeal of such arguments lies partly in the way they sweep a whole pile of awkward questions under the carpet, thus saving our sense of mastery over explanation, if not over events, from seeming in tatters. What counts as evidence and what constitutes an explanation, when you have the actions, contradictory utterances, and commentaries of many different people and groups with different interests? There is the classical hermeneutic question of how to avoid the "selfconfirmability" and assess the relative validity of different interpretations. Then there are the far less often considered issues of how you arrive at—let alone rethink, if need be—the criteria for assessing validity itself in the first place.

## Ultimate Interpretations

What sorts of activity are contemporary commentators such as Watson engaged in when they interpret? At one stage, Watson appears to be establishing global resemblances, but later, he appears to try to divine a deeper meaning, some previously hidden truth beneath appearances. The first begs the question of how you establish the resemblances to begin with. In the second, interpretation involves revealing the depth that emerges—such as the revelation that royalty is sacred and Diana a sacrifice—"as an absolutely superficial secret" (Foucault, 1990, p. 62). If, however, the modern world is distinguished by the endlessness of interpretation, "it is simply because there is nothing to interpret. There is nothing absolutely primary to interpret, because at bottom everything is already interpretation" (p. 64).

Watson (1997) regarded superficiality and the failure to ground representations in an absolute truth as properties of the media. However, not only are media representations inextricable from the conditions of contemporary interpretation, but there is no unitary essence that one can label *the media*, as media practitioners endlessly complain of in media studies' generalizations.

Behind this interpretive morass is a problem of representation. To represent (in whatever sense) something or someone presupposes that they are in some way absent. The possibility of "absolute representation, the total transparency between the representative and the represented, means the extinction of the relationship of representation" (Laclau, 1990, p. 38). Effective representation therefore depends on the imperfection of the relationship in practice. Put another way, as Nelson Goodman (1968) pointed out, you can never represent something as itself. You can only represent it as something else. Representing is an act that transforms what it addresses but appears to underwrite its originality and authenticity. Summing up the life and death in 1997 of Princess Diana as "ritual, collective behaviour, the force of symbols, death and mortuary rituals" (Watson, 1997, p. 3) conjures up a reverse Philosopher's Stone. The complexities of contemporary lifestyles are transmuted with a nostalgic flourish into tribalized trivia.

## The Unmediated Truth

This brings us to a crucial point in Watson's article that raises important issues for media studies more generally. Diana's death had to be different from other famous media-celebrated deaths, whether Marilyn Monroe's or James Dean's. The solution was neat.

> The celebrity of pop-idols is artificial. Like Presidents they are man-made, created by their fans. They are in this respect false idols, creations of cults and sects, powerful images, but *in the last resort unsupported by any transcendental ideology or theology and hence unreal and inauthentic.* Diana however belongs to a very different category: she is very much real and authentic precisely because she is perceived as not being created by the media or the public. (Watson, 1997, p. 5, italics added)

I assure you, I did not make this up. Let me single out two themes: (a) media celebrity is artificial, "man-made," and thus "inauthentic"; (b) reality and authenticity are functions of some transcendental template.

Watson touched with unerring aim on two widespread presuppositions about the media. They involve artifice, dissemblance, lack of groundable truth—features, as I noted, of interpretation itself. They are the noise, distortion, and pollution that obscure, suppress, or poison authentic communication. The media are, in short, profane: the locus, medium, or even the source of profanity. Only what is not made, what is not touched by this profanity but is set apart (sacred) under transcendental guarantee is real and authentic. To rescue what is of lasting value from the transient, the essential from the accidental, reality from appearance, the "influence" of the media must be exorcized.

The profane world is not simply dirt, turpitude, and sin, or even everyday life in all its ordinariness and banality. It is a competitive, rootless, alienated world. On the one hand stands unity, in the form of community, communion, and genuine human communication; on the other, a world as imagined by Hobbes and Durkheim in harness. Less obviously, but more important, the profane is imagined as a world of difference and diversity, set against a world in which difference is finally transcended and unity prevails.

At this point, the reason for the pervasive use of dichotomy in such accounts becomes apparent.

It is necessary to sustain the incoherences of the constitutive idealism. Try imagining a world without difference. It would, on almost any account, be a world without language, signification, or culture. At best, sacred beings would be reduced to indifferent mumblings—a point nicely appreciated by mediums in many parts of the world. What bearing, though, does this divagation have on media studies? Quite simply, historically, the idea of communication in European thinking has been linked to ideas of community and communion—in other words, as Victor Turner (1969) pointed out, of *communitas,* of an ideal and unsustainable sharing and unity—not a good theoretical basis for a theory of everyday human interaction. In the world of the "pure," unmediated object, would you have to avoid books, newspapers, television, Internet, speech? Indeed, you would not learn of the death of Princess Diana at all. This is less longing for a cloistered world *au recherche du temps perdu* than for a world that never existed.

## Getting Down to Business

Anthropology, rubicund with age, might be excused its excesses. So can we turn to lean, mean media studies born in the cauldron of post-Gramscian Marxist sociology and political economy for a thoroughly modern analysis of the issues? Central to the emergence of media studies as a discipline are several works by Stuart Hall, including notably "Encoding/Decoding" (1980) and *The Rediscovery of Ideology* (1982), in which Hall distinguished and distanced critical media studies from "mainstream" American mass communication research. Arguing against these behavioural models and drawing on television as the example, Hall tried to temper communication as the transmission of referential messages by framing it through

> a structure produced and sustained through the articulation of linked but distinctive moments—production, circulation, distribution/consumption, reproduction . . . a "complex structure in dominance" sustained through the articulation of connected practices . . . The "object"

of these practices is meanings and messages in the form of sign-vehicles of a specific kind organized, like any form of communication through the operation of codes within the syntagmatic chain of a discourse. (Hall, 1980, p. 128)

The presupposition that communication rests on transmission of messages containing meaning remains intact. The social circumstances of its working are simply added. Two interesting words, *discourse* and *practice*, make their appearance, suggesting a possibly serious revision of otherwise conventional concepts. *Discourse*, however, is used in a weak linguistic sense, not a stronger sociologically constitutive manner, which is surprising in a work that sets out to socialize communication. The role of *practice* in this account will emerge shortly.

How does meaning, and so ideology, get into the messages and get extracted? According to Hall (1980), "The discursive form of the message has a privileged position in the communicative exchange . . . [and] the moments of 'encoding' and 'decoding,' though 'relatively autonomous' in relation to the communicative process as a whole, are *determinate* moments" (p. 129).

The model not only links structure to practice and explains how discursive closure works on the messages; it can also account for degrees of understanding or misunderstanding, which

> depend on the degrees of identity/non-identity between the codes which perfectly or imperfectly transmit, interrupt or systematically distort what has been transmitted. . . . What are called "distortions" or "misunderstandings" arise precisely from the *lack of equivalence* between the two sides of the communicative exchange. (Hall, 1980, p. 131)

This lack of equivalence enables different subject positions, from which viewers may notionally decode programmes. That is, they may accept the meaning that the producers desire (the *dominant-hegemonic* position), adapt such meanings according to their own position (using a *negotiated* code), or engage in systematic critical reading (using an *oppositional* code; Hall, 1980, pp. 136-138).

The importance of Hall's work has been justly recognized as offering a critical alternative to positivistic and normative sociology. But is Hall's argument quite as radical as is often assumed? And what are its theoretical assumptions?

"Encoding/Decoding" highlights how communication is structured, but what is the status of transmission models and their messages? They still provide the transcendental guarantee of communicability, but with new, added imperfection. Including structure compensates for the shortcomings of the old models in several ways.[2] Noise—the dreaded distortion that plagues dreams of near-perfect communication—now ceases to be a technical problem and is attributable to society, class, or capital working themselves out through media practices. Practice, it turns out, has the task of specifying how structure instantiates itself in process.

The entire apparatus of basic transmission models remains in place, however. Codes still transmit messages "perfectly or imperfectly." Communication still works through "symbolic vehicles constituted within the rules of 'language'" (Hall, 1980, p. 128). Rather more interesting is that Hall clings to "the conduit metaphor of language" (Reddy, 1979), according to which speech and images are containers of meanings, an account that presupposes the classical idealist dichotomy between message (form, appearance) and meaning (essence). Strapped onto bog standard 1970s semiology, we have schoolboy "commonsense" semantics, the "good sense" behind which dropped off some time after Classical Greece. Hall has carefully to tiptoe around the critical thinking coming out of France at the time. His account of practice is simply how structure manages to affect action. At no point does he consider the radical alternative sense of the pragmatic; namely, that humans engage in all sorts of practices of asserting, denying, questioning, deceiving, and so forth in which communication and understanding are at once partial and underdetermined judgments on moments in the histories of such practices and contestable claims within such histories.

To distinguish a critical media from a communications studies approach, Hall needs to frame the referential function of televisual language and images, which bring to the foreground issues of accuracy and bias in representation. To show deep structure at work through underlying ideological closure, Hall (1980) seizes on another dichotomy:

> It is at the connotative *level* of the sign that situational ideologies alter and transform signification . . . The level of connotation of the visual sign, of its contextual reference and positioning in different discursive fields of meaning and association, is the point where *already coded* signs intersect with the deep semantic codes of a culture. (p. 133)

Oddly, Hall insists on trying to analyze complex discursive practices using the notion of signs. It is like trying to build a space rocket out of matchsticks. As Ricoeur (1976) noted, signs are so primitive as to be unable even to deal with the relation of predication on which sentences are based, let alone more complex utterances, such as texts. Both these, being of different, logically more complex, orders, require quite different kinds of analysis.[3] Textuality, famously, introduces context, through the hermeneutic circle (Ricoeur, 1981). And we have not yet even broached the question of intertextuality, of the preunderstandings and learned practices of reading and interpretation required to understand a text in the first place, not to mention the question of why the literary notion of "text" should be applied to the social analysis of television programmes. We start to see why Hall fights shy of theory. It would make life distinctly more complicated. Perhaps he was wise to stick to signs with easily decipherable meanings that enable him to emasculate context and keep the show on the road.

A notion crucial to Hall's argument, as his title suggests, is "code." It has to fulfil several tasks at once. It must mobilize structure and bring it to bear on media production and reception, as well as "concealing the practices of coding that are present" (Hall, 1980, p. 132). It must recreate reality, now naturalized, so that ideology is made invisible and so easily insertable into messages, which are therefore easily swallowable. To do so, code must simplify the vast diversity of human textuality and visuality into apprehensible and easily analyzable form. It must encompass a bewildering range of possible contexts of reference and situations of use. What is more, code must have a classical hermeneutic structure (in other words, a surface appearance) that deceives ordinary mortals and must yield at the hands of the initiated expert to reveal hidden depths that motivate the whole. Fortunately, initiates—in the guise of media studies specialists—are at hand, summoned into life by "Encoding/Decoding."

So what is the remarkable intellectual apparatus through which this is all achieved? It turns out to be none other than a highly conventional and rigid notion worked out by structuralist semiologists for signs, which has precious little to do with textual or discursive analyses that you might have expected for such complex textual and discursive processes. At this point, Hall's interesting attempt to introduce practice into the study of media collides with, and is defeated by, his structuralist inclinations. Bakhtin (1986), developing Volosinov's trenchant critique of structural theories of speech and language, located a significant part of the problem in how the inevitably open, contestable, and partly contingent nature of context is reified and fixed: "A context is potentially unfinalized; a code must be finalized. A code is only a technical means of transmitting information; it does not have cognitive, creative significance. A code is a deliberately established, killed context" (p. 147).

A code is not a fact of nature, culture, or language but an act of power by an analyst. Earlier, in claiming to know the meaning of Diana's death, Watson was less deciphering a code than reifying and overinterpreting a situationally labile context in the name of reality.

The issue is not trivial. In eliminating the gamut of possible contexts and situations of use, Hall adopts a distinctive epistemological position of imagining society as

> a *founding totality* which presents itself as an intelligible object of "knowledge" (*cognitio*) conceived as a process or re-cognition . . . Against this essentialist vision we tend nowadays to accept the *infinitude of the social,* that is, the fact that any structural system is limited, that it is always surrounded by an excess of meaning which it is unable to master. (Laclau, 1990, p. 90)

Hall reiterates the essentialist proposition that the object of knowledge is not just conveniently finite: It is, in principle, fully accessible to the expert knowing subject. Thus, far from being radical, Hall has to fly in the face of his own main intellectual sources, which argue that the knower does not transcend the known, to reassert the epistemological hierarchy of the knower over the known. He also quietly presupposes the idea of a founding totality—the return of the repressed sacred, which the initiated mind can recognize behind appearances and circumstances.

Hall needs codes to get to his central object of study—ideology. The kind of codes he is interested in

> clearly contract relations for the sign with the wider universe of ideologies in a society. These codes are means by which power and ideology are made to signify in particular discourses. . . . They are, if you like, the fragments of ideology. (Hall, 1980, p. 134)

Ideology is the means through which Hall (1980) claims to be able to determine which are the "preferred readings" of the "dominant cultural order" (p. 134) and to identify the pollutant afflicting the masses that intellectuals have to scrub off. Writing specifically about this use of ideology in Marxist writings, Laclau (1990) notes that such "order—or structure— no longer takes the form of an underlying essence of the social; rather it is an attempt—by definition unstable and precarious— to act over that "social," to *hegemonize* it" (p. 91).

In contrast to Hall's massive structures of power and meaning encoded in dominant-hegemonic positions, the social always threatens to elude such structuration—to "seduce" it, in Baudrillard's (1990) terms. It is slightly tricky for someone who positioned himself (or has been positioned) as the key theoretical figure in two related disciplines, cultural and media studies, to turn a blind eye to what does not suit him, calling them "excesses of theory." It would seem to require something close to hubris airily to dismiss the sustained and carefully argued critique of your position by the philosopher whose ideas you admit were constitutive of those disciplines (e.g., Hall, 1996c, pp. 142-146).

Hall's (1980) account of the working of ideology in the media presupposes false consciousness. Viewers are imagined as liable to lapse into false consciousness or wallow benightedly in it as their default state. Nor are producers immune, as there are "professional codes" to keep them "within the hegemony of the dominant code" (p. 136). Laclau's (1990) second argument against such accounts of ideology is that "the notion of false consciousness only makes sense if the identity of the social agent can be fixed. It is only on the basis of recognizing its true identity that we can assert that the consciousness of the subject is 'false'" (p. 91).

Hall's argument leaves him in the arrogant—and untenable—position of being able to determine accurately the status of everyone else's consciousness because, standing outside and above the slough of codes, ideology, and the entire apparatus of the profane, he can judge clearly and dispassionately.

The alternative to such epistemological omniscience is to address the difficult implications of acknowledging that

> the identity and homogeneity of social agents was an illusion, that any social subject is essentially decentred, that his/her identity is nothing but the articulation of constantly changing positionalities. But, if any social agent is a decentred subject . . . in what sense can we say that subjects misrecognize themselves? The theoretical ground that made sense of the concept of "false consciousness" has evidently dissolved. (Laclau, 1990, p. 92)

Nor is Hall in a position to dismiss this as so much highfalutin poststructuralist theory (see Chen, 1996), of little relevance to the stern realities of contemporary politics, because he himself recognized the impossibility of treating subjects as unitary and centered (Hall, 1996b).

Finally, ideology is a double-edged sword. For, it follows that

> the ideological would be the will to "totality" of any totalizing discourse. And insofar as the social is impossible without some fixation of meaning, without the discourse of closure, the ideological must be seen as

constitutive of the social. The social only exists as the vain attempt to institute that impossible object: society. Utopia is the essence of any communication and social practice. (Laclau, 1990, p. 92)

Laclau unerringly puts his finger on the transcendentalism latent in both the concepts of communication and Marxist accounts of social practice. More prosaically, Hall's revelation of ideology and hegemony at work in the media itself turns out to be ideological and hegemonic! His analysis of the mass media also involves a totalizing discourse, which, thanks to Watson, we can now appreciate as presupposing a transcendental sacred space occupied by the superior knowing subject of the university academic. Viewed from anthropology, Hall's argument emerges as a sustained fugue about the profanity of the media, enshrined in the contrapunct of ideology. Even so spankingly modern a discipline as media studies, for all "its sometimes dazzling internal theoretical development" (Hall, 1996a, p. 272) has not managed to exorcise the profane—it just changed its name.

## FUTURE ENGAGEMENT?

So what is the theoretical ground of cultural studies on Hall's account? It turns out to be a thing of sheds and patches. But what is the price of this theoretical incoherence—indeed, incontinence? Hall's disdain for the excesses of theory is well known, if slightly surprising for someone widely considered the theoretical godfather of cultural and media studies. But what are the implications of this disdain? Hall is hoist on his own ideological petard: He turns out to be as much part of the problem as the solution. Hall may lay claim to political radicality, but when "Encoding/Decoding" is analyzed, any claim to intellectual radicality is vacuous. Especially considering the theoretically revolutionary times he was writing in, Hall occupies not just a conservative, but even a fairly reactionary, epistemological position. It requires an act of will not to wonder whether it is precisely these drawbacks that have

made him such a luminary in the Anglo-Saxon intellectual world.

My point is not that there is something peculiarly wrong with either anthropology or media studies. By contemporary standards, they are rather more coherent than most academic disciplines.[4] My aim is to show that a critical analysis of scholarly presuppositions can yield surprising results that fly in the face of, and undermine, disciplinary orthodoxies. What excites me is the possible unpredictability in the outcome of any engagement of media studies and anthropology. In the meantime, the lesson for ambitious young scholars to draw would seem to be: Theoretical incoherence and incontinence pay. Just please do not bother to project any resulting profanity onto the media.

## NOTES

1. I trust Bill Watson, who is an old colleague and a cherished sparring partner, will forgive my use of his work as a good example of contemporary British anthropological thinking.

2. The "object" remains meanings and messages (as noted earlier). "A 'raw' historical event cannot, *in that form*, be transmitted by, say, a television newscast. Events can only be signified within the aural-visual forms of the televisual discourse" (Hall, 1980, p. 129).

3. Matters are more complicated still, both because of the issues surrounding how images are analyzed and the relationship between images and text. Using connotation and denotation to address relations of predication, textuality, and imagery is slightly like using a tin opener and strawberry jam as tools to engineer the space rocket.

## REFERENCES

Ang, I. (1996). Ethnography and radical contextualism in audience studies. In *Living room wars: Rethinking media audiences in a postmodern world*. London: Routledge.

Askew, K., & Wilk, R. (Eds.). (2002). *The anthropology of media: A reader*. Oxford, England: Blackwell.

Bakhtin, M. M. (1986). From notes made in 1970-71. In V. W. McGee, C. Emerson, & M. Holquist (Eds.), *Speech genres and other late essays* (V. W. McGee, Trans.) Austin: University of Texas Press.

Baudrillard, J. (1990). *Seduction* (B. Singer, Trans.). New York: St. Martin's Press.

Chen, K.-H. (1996). Post-marxism: Between/beyond critical postmodernism and cultural studies. In D. Morley & K.-H. Chen (Eds.), *Stuart Hall: Critical dialogues in cultural studies*. London: Routledge.

Fabian, J. (1990). *Power and performance: Ethnographic explorations through proverbial wisdom and theater in Shaba, Zaire*. Madison: University of Wisconsin.

Fabian, J. (1991). Dilemmas of critical anthropology. In L. Nencel & P. Pels (Eds.), *Constructing knowledge: Authority and critique in social science*. London: Sage.

Foucault, M. (1990). Nietzsche, Freud, Marx. In G. L. Ormiston & A. D. Schrift (Eds.), *Transforming the hermeneutic context: from Nietzsche to Nancy*. Albany: New York State University Press.

Geertz, C. (1973). *The interpretation of cultures*. New York: Basic Books.

Ginsburg, F., Abu-Lughod, L., & Larkin, B. (Eds.). (2002). *Media worlds: Anthropology on new terrain*. Berkeley: University of California Press.

Goodman, N. (1968). *Languages of art*. Indianapolis, IN: Bobbs-Merrill.

Hall, S. (1980). Encoding/decoding. In S. Hall, D. Hobson, A. Lowe, & P. Willis (Eds.), *Culture, media, language: Working papers in cultural studies, 1972-79*. London: Unwin Hyman.

Hall, S. (1982). The rediscovery of ideology. In M. Gurevitch, T. Bennett, J. Curran, & J. Woollacott (Eds.), *Culture, society and the media*. London: Methuen.

Hall, S. (1996a).Cultural studies and its theoretical legacies. In D. Morley & K.-H. Chen (Eds.), *Stuart Hall: Critical dialogues in cultural studies*. London: Routledge.

Hall, S. (1996b). Introduction: Who needs "identity"? In S. Hall & P. Du Gay (Eds.), *Questions of cultural identity*. London: Sage.

Hall, S. (1996c). On postmodernism and articulation: An interview with Stuart Hall. In D. Morley & K.- H. Chen (Eds.), *Stuart Hall: critical dialogues in cultural studies*. London: Routledge.

Hobart, M. (2000). *After culture. Anthropology as radical metaphysical critique*. Yogyakarta, Indonesia: Duta Wacana Press. Retrieved November 22, 2004, from http://www.criticalia.org.

Laclau, E. (1990). *New reflections on the revolution of our time*. London: Verso.

Morley, D. (1992). *Television, audiences and cultural studies*. London: Routledge.

Reddy, M. (1979). The conduit metaphor: A case of frame conflict in our language about language. In A. Ortony (Ed.), *Metaphor and thought*. Cambridge, England: Cambridge University Press.

Ricoeur, P. (1976). *Interpretation theory: Discourse and the surplus of meaning*. Fort Worth: Texas Christian University Press.

Ricoeur, P. (1981). The model of the text: Meaningful action considered as a text. In J. B. Thompson (Ed. & Trans.), *Hermeneutics and the human sciences*. Cambridge, England: Cambridge University Press.

Turner, V. (1969). *The ritual process*. London: Routledge & Kegan Paul.

Volosinov, V. N. (1973). *Marxism and the philosophy of language* (L. Matejka & I. R. Titunik, Trans.). Cambridge, MA: Harvard University Press.

Watson, C. W. (1997). "Born a lady, became a princess, died a saint": The reaction to the death of Diana, Princess of Wales. *Anthropology Today, 13*(6), 3-7.

# 4

## Proposal for Mass Media Anthropology

Francisco Osorio

The purpose of this chapter is to answer the question: What would an anthropology of mass communication look like? On one hand, we already have the answer. What we have to do is look for it in the research that has been conducted from the 1970s up until today. In reviewing that material, we will find that the area is open for a proposal due to the large number of open-ended questions that exist. For example: What should be studied? What theory should be used? Are standard anthropological methods effective? Is there a distinct anthropological approach to the study of mass media? How does anthropology's contribution compare to that of the other social sciences studying the subject?

## The Subject Matter

The object of study of mass media anthropology is the system of cultural transmission through mass media. When someone asks what anthropologists study in regard to the mass media, a quick answer might be television or radio. Looking at the media anthropologists have studied, however, we can also add the press, the Internet, cassettes, and videotapes. Anthropologists even consider talking drums to be a form of mass media. Nevertheless, we do not study objects solely because they could have some value in and of themselves. We study culture. Again, the question is: What do anthropologists look for in the mass media? If we take the content into account, a plethora of directions come to our eyes. Some researchers study politics and rituals, others household space use. The list continues on: consumerism, gender, genre, identity, imperialism, globalization, health, perception, indigenous media, and so on. Of course, they are all culture, in one sense. The point is that we cannot understand, from these individual foci, what our subject of study is.

Anthropology is the social science that studies culture. Therefore, mass media anthropology is the field within anthropology that studies the way in which culture shapes society through the mass media. Mass media has been approached in many ways. Mass media anthropology's perspective says we are interested in how a way of being (woman, ethnic, nationhood, etc.) is transmitted to people by a process of mass communication.

Mass media is the current mechanism through which culture diffuses. People know their particular way of being through exposure to television and other principal mass media. This contemporary phenomenon should be the primary subject matter of mass media anthropology. I will fully develop this argument as we continue.

An anthropology of mass communication must follow cross-cultural research in nation-states, minority groups, indigenous societies, and any other form of social organization that could develop throughout the 21st century. In societies in which mass media is not yet the vehicle of the transmission of culture (i.e., hunter-gatherer), there is no place for mass media anthropology.

## METHODOLOGY

The discipline already has methods with which to study the mass media developed by the "culture at a distance" school in the 1950s. So far, all the anthropological knowledge on mass media that we have gained has been through the application of our standard methods. Communication scholars have widely used these anthropological methods. It is fair to say, then, that, methodologically speaking, anthropology is well equipped to study the mass media.

Why is this so? It is interesting that a mass phenomenon does not require a mass method such as surveys. Anthropologists rely on personal experience to study a global fact. This is not surprising, considering that anthropologists study culture, which is both public and personal. We access human society by talking with individuals of a given place. In that sense, there is no need to justify the mass media as an object of study because, in the study of mass media as in the study of any other cultural matter, anthropology is an observational science of society in particular settings (e.g., family viewing).

## CALL FOR ANTHROPOLOGICAL CONCEPTS

The reader should not to be surprised if I return to the 1970s to look for anthropological concepts, because this was the decade in which the direct relationship between anthropology and mass communication began. James W. Carey (1989) helped in this process by writing *Communication as Culture*. As a communication scholar, he was able to relate a classical concept, such as ritual, to a new theory, such as symbolic anthropology, and apply them to the definition of communication. From that time on, we can distinguish two distinct views of communication, the transmission view and the ritual view.

However, this was just the first step, because Carey proposed an *approach*. What we have been waiting for ever since is a *theory*. Carey's essay was an invitation to anthropology to contribute to the study of mass communication. He took the first step by basing his distinctions on anthropological concepts. Direct attempts have been made by Spitulnik (1998) and Michaels (1991) and later ones by further research in the 1990s on national identity and television. It is interesting that Pamela Landers (1974) made a similar call within anthropology, using the concept of myth to understand American television. Hers is also an exploratory work, laying out what time has proven to be a useful resource of ideas (Abeles, 1988; Auge, 1986; Katz, 1989; Marvin, 1999; McLeod, 1999; Rothenbuhler, 1998). She approached the subject saying that the role of mythology could be the same as the role of prime-time television in American life. Her essay invites us to think about a theory that could justify this relationship.

The communication scholar Carolyn Marvin (1999) takes the ritual view a step further in communication research. She argues that the mass media is a myth-and-ritual mechanism of American nationalism. Marvin was able to think out the logical consequences of relating myth, ritual, and the mass media. In doing so, she has proven that we are justified in exploring the relationship between anthropology and mass communication using classical concepts from the study of magic and religion.

Yet another communication scholar, Michael Schudson (1989), takes the main anthropological concept (culture) and applies it to the study of television. Schudson is interested in examining the direct influence of cultural objects; that is, he questions whether exposure to certain symbols or messages in various media actually lead people to change how they think about the world or act in it. He argues that certain conditions of cultural objects may produce a change in a person's behavior. In his words, sometimes culture works and sometimes it does not. The term *work* is understood here as "produces a change in behavior." In my view, the most important condition to be explored by anthropology is what Shudson calls *resonance*. The first papers in mass media anthropology highlight this idea, which can be described as the cultural preconditions that allow the mass media to find a place in a given culture to the degree that said culture already had a place for them. In other words, the mass media have to be relevant to the host culture if they are to make sense or have meaning. The mass media do not have intrinsic meanings but resonate in a given culture; that is, it is the host culture that accepts or rejects the mass media. Certain conditions therein make possible the relationship. Therefore, mass media is culturally dependent on resonance conditions. The important question to ask here is: On which resonance conditions are mass media culturally dependent? In my view, time is the shared cultural mechanism of mass media. I argue that cultures use television precisely as they use time. This is possible because time is the common structure between mass media and culture. If this is correct, then we can understand why television is so easily used by world cultures: People use television as they have always used time. There is nothing new to learn. Television already had a structural place in human society. Barbara Adam (1994) distinguishes four dimensions in the perception of time: clock time, timing, temporality, and tempo. Consider timing. Anthropological studies show that television viewing punctuates time. In other words, cultures use television as "when-time": the moment in which certain activities have to occur (eat, sleep, gather, etc.). Television is thus perceived as timing (a mode in which time is perceived around the world). The argument is as follows: If time is timing, and television is time, then television is timing. The

explanation: Cross-culturally, television is timing because timing is one of the cultural structures of time, and television shares this common structure with time.

## Anthropological Concepts That Might Be Useful

In reviewing both communication and ethnographical research, we find that scholars have been using anthropological concepts but not a theory for mass media developed within anthropology. The concepts appearing with more frequency are assimilation, acculturation, diffusion, and ritual (including myth and rite of passage). Anthropologists use mainly the first two concepts, communication scholars the third, and both use the fourth. Related anthropology from the 1980s and 1990s has been using hermeneutics terminology, European thought, and (obviously) classical concepts.

### Ritual

Anthropologists such as Auge and Turner and communication scholars such as Carey, Marvin, Dayan, and Katz have been applying the theory of magic and religion to mass communication for some time. This well-established research area finds some synthesis in Eric Rothenbuhler's (1998) *Ritual Communication: From Everyday Conversation to Mediated Ceremony*. The ritual view of communication has been developed as a contribution for mass communication, mainly from a functional point of view. The anthropology of magic and religion includes concepts such as ritual, myth, liminality, and rite of passage. Communication scholars see in these concepts analytical tools to stress the integrative functions of the mass media. Anthropologists use them to highlight the central aspects of political and media events. The theory of magic and religion is a well-established research area in anthropology, applied to traditional societies. Communication scholars discovered in the 1970s that this knowledge could also be used to understand mass media in industrial society. Anthropologists confirmed this perspective in the 1980s and 1990s. Together, they all agreed with the assumption that there is no necessity to modify the concepts because they are taken from indigenous societies. There is always a need for a mechanism to keep society going.

## Assimilation and Acculturation

Richard Thompson (1996) says that assimilation is the process by which individuals of a foreign or minority culture enter the social positions of the standard or dominant culture. Although assimilation is a process experienced by individuals, it has often been studied in its sociological aspects with an emphasis on the assimilation rates of immigrant and minority groups.

According to Thomas Glick (1997), acculturation is the process of culture change set in motion by the meeting of two autonomous cultural systems, resulting in an increase of similarity of one to the other. In 1936, a special committee of the Social Science Research Council wrote a memorandum for the study of acculturation. The document was published in *American Anthropologist* by Robert Redfield, Ralph Linton, and Melville Herskovits. It said:

> Acculturation comprehends those phenomena which result when groups of individuals having different cultures come into continuous first-hand contact, with subsequent changes in the original cultural patterns of either or both groups. Under this definition, acculturation is to be distinguished from *culture-change*, of which it is but one aspect, and *assimilation*, which is at times a phase of acculturation. It is also to be differentiated from *diffusion*, which, while occurring in all instances of acculturation, is not only a phenomenon which frequently takes place without the occurrence of the type of contact between peoples specified in the definition given above, but it constitutes only one aspect of the process of acculturation. (p. 150)

Acculturation, assimilation, and diffusion have a strong relationship with persuasion research within mass communication research. I think the persuasion school would be interested in the concept, as it relates to whether and how the mass media have a direct influence on individuals, but communication scholars will be disappointed with the anthropological answer. Within anthropology, there is currently no theory explaining what to do to successfully introduce an element from one culture to another.

## Diffusion

Thomas Glick (1997) says that diffusion is the transmission of elements from one culture to another. Such elements, he says, are transmitted by agents using identifiable media and are subject to different barrier or filter effects. It is one of the processes of acculturation but may lack the close contact between people that acculturation presupposes. Within this concept, Glick differentiates two other terms: (a) *Stimulus diffusion,* which is a concept elaborated by Kroeber (1948)to describe the reinvention of an element transmitted across a social or cultural barrier to bring it into congruence with the values of the recipient culture, and (b) *diffusionism,* which posits an exogenous origin for most elements of a specific culture or cultural subject. Diffusionism, as an anthropological school, dates from the late 19th century, when it emerged from the debate over whether social institutions are independent in origin of or arise out of borrowing knowledge through contact. The focus of this debate was to explain why the family, as a unit, for example, was found in every society anthropologists came to study.

Among communication scholars, the two most important contributors to this area of research are Katz, Levin, and Hamilton (1963) and Rogers (1971). With M. Levin and H. Hamilton, Elihu Katz wrote "Traditions of Research on the Diffusion of Innovation." In it, they define the process of diffusion as (a) the acceptance, (b) over time, of (c) some specific item (e.g., an idea or practice) (d) by individuals, groups, or other adopting units that are linked to (e) specific channels of communication, (f) a social structure, and (g) a given system of values or a culture. Among the authors' purposes in this article was the unification of an area of research that had been developed independently by anthropology, rural sociology, education, public health, marketing researchers, and folklorists.

In 1971, Everett Rogers published *Communication of Innovations: A Cross-Cultural Approach*. This book summarizes the research of 1500 publications on diffusion. It is important because it understands diffusion as a special type of communication, concerned with the spread of messages carrying new ideas. Rogers says that the main elements in the diffusion of new ideas are the (a) innovation (b) communicated through certain channels (c) over time (d) among the members of a social system. Rogers argues, among the generalizations supported by the 1500 publications, that the mass media channels are more effective at spreading knowledge of innovations, whereas interpersonal channels are more effective at forming and changing attitudes toward these new ideas.

What about anthropology? Perhaps the closest relationship found between diffusion and the mass media within anthropology has been the study of the talking drum. If we agree with the thesis that mass media are to be found in all kinds of societies, then we can study some of their manifestations. To do that, I looked into the Human Relations Area Files Database, a nonprofit institution founded in 1949 at Yale University. In the communication section, this database codes (a) gestures and signs, (b) transmission of messages, (c) dissemination of news and information, (d) press, (e) mail, (f) telephone and telegraph, (g) radio and television, (h) public opinion, (i) proxemics, and (j) Internet communications. The description of *transmission of messages* says that this category is used to index information about technologically simple transmission of messages. It includes information on signaling devices (e.g., fire, smoke, blinker, semaphore), signal codes (e.g., drum language, flag codes, Morse code), cryptography, use of carrier birds and animals, messenger and human courier systems, and so on. Among this wide variety of media and cultures, perhaps the best known example is the talking drum. The anthropologist Helen Marie Hogan (1967), studying extensively the

components of communicative acts among the Ashanti, describes different media used by the Ashanti for announcing public summonses: gong, hoe, speaking horn, signal drum, talking drum, and even guns. In this example, the goals vary, from assembling all the people, to assembling women or elders, to informing people of a chief's approach, to inviting people to the palace for a meal, to informing people of an important person's funeral. The communication scholar Yael Warshel (1999) argues that the talking drum is a medium often neglected in light of the telegraph. Nevertheless, she says, talking drums should be recognized for their early achievements in time and space conquest, their ability to overcome the burden of language, and, most important, for their strategic ability to convey coded public communication. For example, she says, without the aid of the drum to communicate across far reaches of space, the Ashanti Empire would not have been able to sustain control for as long as it did. This is an excellent example of the role of the mass media in an ethnographic context.

## THEORY

Anthropologists have primarily tested communication knowledge using concepts developed in communication research and classical anthropology, but the real question remains open: Can an anthropology of mass communication bring us a new and fresh perspective to understanding mass media?

All of anthropology's mass media research can be grouped into three main schools: cultural imperialism, hermeneutics, and functionalism. Each of these schools has generated a distinct theory about the relationship between people, television, and culture (see Figure 4.1).

The cultural imperialism school argues that people are greatly influenced by television. It views culture as determining behavior. The role of people is passive reception. Simply put, this school categorizes the experience of watching television as one of *absorption*. Accordingly,

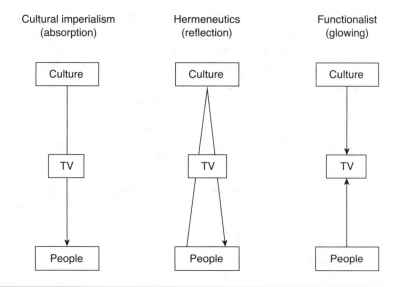

| Cultural imperialism (absorption) | Hermeneutics (reflection) | Functionalist (glowing) |

**Figure 4.1**      Anthropological Schools in Mass Communication

proponents of this school hold American television to be the cause of consumerism and the reason women are changing their roles in traditional societies. They further believe that nation-states can use television to create and reinforce a given order.

Cultural imperialism comes out of the critical school in social sciences known as the Frankfurt School. As a Marxist-based theory, it argues that the ownership of the mass media has a direct influence on media content and dictates, therefore, what is being learned by the audience. The main focus of observation, by scholars of cultural imperialism, is not the audience, whom they perceive to be merely passive receivers, but those who control the content of the media, their motives and purposes.

For example, Miller (1998), studying the Yucatec Maya, argues that audience studies have overlooked the wider social, political, and economic contexts of the relationship between media and audiences. They have to consider that media messages transmitted for consumption are institutional expressions of the dominant social structures and therefore have to be recognized as politically charged. Miller says that the culture of the Yucatec Maya is "contested," because mass media provoke community members into a conflict

between embracing the global sphere or reaffirming ties to local identity and established patterns of behavior.

Unfortunately for this theory, there is no empirical support for its thesis. Some anthropologists use this school while writing their analysis but do not provide evidence to support it. Others use its assumptions to highlight the "resistance" of local cultures to foreign content. Regardless, terms such as *resistance, imperialism,* and *contested* have proved to be empty of empirical content.

The hermeneutic school argues that television reflects culture to people. There is a double hermeneutics in this process. On one hand, people produce culture; on the other, culture defines people's behavior. According to this school, the human process of understanding deposits into cultural elements modes of being that define us. In other words, we learn how to behave by observing preexisting cultural elements. Hermeneutics says that television facilitates this observation. People go to television to watch a prime-time soap opera, for example, but in doing so, they are observing how to be a member of society and are learning the symbols of their national identity. From a hermeneutical point of view, television reflects. That is to say, we recognize ourselves not by watching our face in a mirror but by interpreting ourselves indirectly through local talk shows or American sitcoms (even if we belong to a different culture). In this sense, television is like any other work of art: a novel, theater performance or painting, each summing for us who we are as members of a specific time and place.

The hermeneutical viewpoint is widely accepted by social scientists and the anthropological school led by Clifford Geertz. Based on quite different assumptions (namely hermeneutics and semiotics) than the other two schools, it argues that people do not learn their culture through a process of deep self-observation. People do not ask themselves what their culture is or how to live in their society; quite the contrary—they learn by observing the outside world. Where do they look for this world? In cultural objects such as books, soap operas, or role playing in school. The process of human understanding consists mainly in this: to put oneself out in the world to return fulfilled. It is only in the world that we make ourselves humans, because culture is public.

For example, Davila (1998), studying a Puerto Rican television comedy show, says that although sponsored by an American company (the show is called *El Kiosko Budweiser* and was originally developed as an advertising campaign), the show is better understood as a multilayered text, displaying contemporary Puerto Rican society to itself in some of its contradictory multiplicity. The show provides a venue for a Puerto Rican creation, full of everyday language, mannerisms, and humor.

Unfortunately, this theory lacks an empirical mechanism with which to explain how these processes actually happen. Unlike the cultural imperialism school, hermeneutics has a major role for both the individual and mass media. Nevertheless, hermeneutical research, although appealing in theory, cannot tell us, for example, the mechanism for interpreting local values while watching foreign programming. It is difficult for practitioners to agree in the actual use of hermeneutics. Although literary studies have helped the process, the diversity of methods and techniques dilute the ability of the program to differentiate one interpretation from the other.

The functionalist school argues that television is an integral element of society. According to this school, if we want to understand people or culture, we have to look for television and its role in society. This is the classical school in anthropology, and it is therefore not surprising that the discipline followed the media effects tradition in mass communication studies. This is the school that combined myth, ritual, and television. According to it, the function of television is to integrate society by building national identity. Functionalism was more or less abandoned by anthropologists during the 1980s and 1990s.

## CULTURE AS TRANSMISSION: THE STRONG SENSE

In this section, I propose an anthropological explanation of the relationship between culture and the mass media (especially television). I base this proposition on the anthropological research results from the 1970s through the 1990s and on my previous argument for television and time, discussed earlier in this chapter.

As far as we know, culture is not transmitted genetically, yet what makes us a human being is culture. The question then, is how culture is transmitted. During the 20th century, we faced a new phenomenon as anthropologists: culture transmitted through mass media, especially television. Anthropological studies support the fact that mass media are the primary vehicle for the transmission of culture. This is the main effect of a medium such as television: the transmission of culture and the shaping of human society. For anthropology, the mass media is now in the center of the discipline.

This knowledge is supported by anthropological research on the world's nations, minorities, and indigenous societies. In the few cultures in which mass media do not exist, the vehicle for the transmission of culture is language as personal communication. Classical anthropology argues that language is the vehicle of the transmission of culture. What mass media anthropological studies add is that language must not be understood only as face-to-face contact but also as mass communication.

For example, anthropologists have always known that kinship is a core structure of society. What is new for us is the way in which the Batak of Indonesia transmit kinship: by cassettes (Rodgers, 1986). Tape-cassette dramas are the new vehicle through which the Batak transmit kinship, as they move away from marriage alliance and patrilineal clan descent to a system of family relationships. In India, people are using newspaper advertisements to find potential spouses, replacing the traditional way of arranged marriages (Das, 1980). From a theoretical point of view, communication scholars have shown that American and British soap operas can be explained through the anthropological study of kinship (Liebes & Livingstone, 1994), and they have used ethnography to understand family viewing (Lull, 1990).

Anthropologists have also studied myths and rituals. What is new for us is the relationship between them and television: We learn our myths and rituals by watching television, and its societal functions (integration) are now carried out by the mass media (Abeles, 1988; Auge, 1986; Handelman, 1990; Landers, 1974; McLeod, 1999; Turner, 1985). Communication scholars support the same relationship (Carey, 1989; Dayan & Katz, 1992; Marvin, 1999; Rothenbuhler, 1998). Anthropologists such as Abeles, Handelman, and McLeod also relate ritual, television, and politics. The same goes for communication scholars such as Dayan, Katz, and Marvin.

Anthropologists have also studied the political organization of cultures. What is new for us is that television has the cross-cultural effect of being a medium for shaping national identity, whether through state-owned, commercial, or indigenous television. In other words, culture as politics is transmitted through television.

These examples can be read in either a weak or a strong sense. The weak sense argues that either (a) mass media is merely one of the mechanisms for the transmission of culture or (b) some cultural elements are currently transmitted through the mass media. The strong sense argues that mass media are the vehicle of the transmission of culture. In what follows, I will support the strong sense. My argument is not valid in hunter-gatherer societies that do not use the mass media, but it is valid in indigenous societies and any other societies that do use it.

The strong sense argues that in the process of the evolution of societies, mass media (especially television) became the primary vehicle of the transmission of culture. Societies that use mass media would be quite different if they had not used it. In our present society, this is the way in which culture is transmitted. As anthropologists, we know that historically this was not always so. Be that as it may, anthropology now needs an updated theory of its subject matter to understand what is happening within contemporary culture. The strong thesis lets us understand why television viewing is pervasive, why cultures all over the world adopt television, and why societies continue watching television after their initial cultural contact—briefly, because it is the primary medium by which culture is transmitted.

If I am right, I can explain the cross-cultural characteristics and effects of television that anthropologists have found through their mass media research.

One important and well-documented feature of the television set is that its use is not culturally specific. This means that in every culture in which television is present, people most often use the television set to watch television. This may seem obvious, but it is not. No society worships the television set. No society builds a ceremonial place for the television set inside or outside of the house. There is empirical research showing that television viewing does not alter basic family patterns of spatial use, either in indigenous societies or in nation-states (Kent, 1985). Some societies watch television privately, but others do it collectively (Adra, 1996; Liechty, 1994; Pace, 1993). In the latter, relatives and close friends are invited into the living room. Some neighbors watch the small television set through street windows. Nevertheless, the house (space) remains the same, and the television set is only there to be used as a television set and for nothing more (I include here its use as a video monitor).

I am not saying that particular individuals, in many societies, always follow this pattern (artists have used the television set for great works of art, indeed, and some people build great houses with home theaters in mind), but so far, anthropologists have found no culture that systematically uses the television set to built fences, for example. Societies universally use the cultural artifact for the same and only purpose of watching television programming. Individual use is quite diverse, of course.

Also, there are not culture-specific designs for the television set. The television set is not made to be accepted for a given culture. This is not the case with radio. In Zambia (Spitulnik, 1998), the radio set "Saucepan Special" was designed by the Ever Ready Company of London to popularize African radio listening during the 1950s. It was constructed over a saucepan and painted blue because that color does not have negative associations in African society (according to the Rhodesian colonial officials of that time).

Television viewing is pervasive (everybody watches television). The cost of the television set is irrelevant. In rural Yemen, its value is 3 months' work (Adra, 1996), and similar prices do not stop sales in other societies around the world. Australian Aborigines own their television station (Michaels, 1991). In places with no electricity, car batteries are used. Nation-states such as India, China, and Brazil reach almost every part of their territories through their broadcasting. Television is not only available but accepted.

Cross-culturally, no society excludes, by definition, some of their members from watching television. In fact, anthropological studies say that families spend large amounts of time watching television, that children are heavier viewers than adults are, and that women in traditional societies tend to watch more television than men. We also know that television viewing is the dominant evening and night activity of people.

This is not to say that, for example, families do not sometimes forbid their children to watch television, especially if the children's homework is not finished, but anthropologists so far have not found any culture that *by definition* excludes a particular age group or gender from watching television. As anthropologists, we know that some indigenous societies *hide* some cultural elements from certain members, but this is not the case with television.

Anthropologists, relying mainly on participant observation, have documented that the television drama is people's favorite genre. This antecedent is related to other findings, such as that female characters represent moral forces in society, that viewers have stereotypical perceptions of the sex roles of TV characters, and that viewers perceive sitcom characters as "fantastic" and dramatic characters as "real." The latter means that no culture is naïve. Even if the program is from another culture, every society puts the content in perspective. Some situations can be misunderstood, others can be meaningless, but no culture is a naïve receiver. Not one.

Every society has been in contact with programs from another culture. We now know that local culture can be transmitted through a program produced elsewhere. Even if the program is produced locally, it can take elements from a foreign culture to transmit local culture (Davila, 1998). Unlikely as it may seem, programs produced by one culture can be fully understood by another culture (therefore, there is no place here for cultural relativism). Nevertheless, no culture can impose their meanings on others.

Some readers might be thinking that anthropologists have merely confirmed the old beliefs of communication studies. This is the point: We did not know if there were reasons to believe in mass media generalizations until anthropologists conducted cross-cultural research. Anthropologists have accomplished one of the missions: ethnography.

## References

Abeles, M. (1988). Modern political ritual: Ethnography of an inauguration and a pilgrimage by President Mitterrand. *Current Anthropology, 29*(3), 391-404.

Adam, B. (1994). Perceptions of time. In T. Ingold (Ed.), *Companion encyclopedia of anthropology* (pp. 503-526). London: Routledge.

Adra, A. (1996). The "other" as viewer: Reception of Western and Arab televised representations in rural Yemen. In P. Crawford (Ed.), *The construction of the viewer: Media anthropology and the anthropology of audiences.* Hojbjerg, Denmark: Intervention Press.

Auge, M. (1986). Teleculture heroes; or, a Night at the Embassy. *Current Anthropology, 27*(2), 184-188.

Carey, J. (1989). *Communication as culture: Essays on media and society.* Boston: Unwin Hyman.

Das, M. (1980). Matrimonial advertisements: An examination of its social significance in mate selection in modern India. *Man in India, 60*(3/4), 187-203.

Davila, A. (1998). *El Kiosko Budweiser:* The making of a "national" television show in Puerto Rico. *American Ethnologist, 25*(3), 452-470.

Dayan, D., & Katz, E. (1992). *Media events: The live broadcasting of history.* Cambridge, MA: Harvard University Press.

Glick, T. (1997). Acculturation. In T. Barfield (Ed.), *The dictionary of anthropology.* New York: Blackwell.

Handelman, D. (1990). *Models and mirrors: Towards an anthropology of public events.* Cambridge, England: Cambridge University Press.

Hogan, H. (1967). *Ethnography of communication among the Ashanti.* Unpublished doctoral dissertation, Anthropology Department, University of Pennsylvania, Philadelphia.

Katz, E. (1989). Mass media effects. In E. Barnouw, G. Gerbner, W. Schramm, et al. (Eds.), *International Encyclopedia of Communications* (Vol. 2, 492-497). Oxford, England: Oxford University Press.

Katz, E., Levin, M., & Hamilton, H. (1963). Traditions of research on the diffusion of innovation. *American Sociological Review, 28*(2), 237-252.

Kent, S. (1985). The effects of television viewing: A cross-cultural perspective. *Current Anthropology, 26*(1), 121-126.

Kroeber, A. L. (1948). *Anthropology* (2nd ed.). New York: Harcourt, Brace.

Landers, P. (1974). Prime time television: Mythology of a complex society. *Studies in Visual Communication, 5*(3), 1-5.

Liebes, T., & Livingstone, S. (1994). The structure of family and romantic ties in the soap opera: An ethnographic approach. *Communication Research, 21*(6), 717-741.

Liechty, M. (1994). *Fashioning modernity in Kathmandu: Mass media, consumer culture, and the middle class in Nepal.* Unpublished doctoral dissertation, Department of Anthropology, University of Pennsylvania, Philadelphia.

Lull, J. (1990). *Inside family viewing: Ethnographic research on television's audiences.* London: Routledge.

Marvin, C. (1999). *Blood sacrifice and the nation: Myth, ritual, and the American flag.* Cambridge, England: Cambridge University Press.

McLeod, J. (1999). The sociodrama of presidential politics: Rhetoric, ritual, and power in the era of teledemocracy. *American Anthropologist, 101*(2), 359-373.

Michaels, E. (1991). A model of teleported texts (with reference to Aboriginal Television). *Visual Anthropology, 4*(3/4), 301-323.

Miller, C. (1998). The social impacts of televised media among the Yucatec Maya. *Human Organization, 57*(3), 307-314.

Pace, R. (1993). First-time televiewing in Amazonia: Television acculturation in Gurupa, Brazil. *Ethnology, 32*(2), 187-206.

Redfield, R., Linton, R., & Herskovits, M. (1936). Acculturation. *American Anthropologist, 38*, 149-152.

Rodgers, S. (1986). Batak tape cassette kinship: Constructing kinship through the Indonesian national mass media. *American Ethnologist, 13*, 23-42.

Rogers, E. (1971). *Communication of innovations: A cross-cultural approach.* New York: Free Press.

Rothenbuhler, E. (1998). *Ritual communication: From everyday conversation to mediated ceremony.* London: Sage.

Schudson, M. (1989). How culture works: Perspectives from media studies on the efficacy of symbols. *Theory and Society, 18*, 153-180.

Spitulnik, D. (1998). Mediated modernities: Encounters with the electronic in Zambia. *Visual Anthropology Review, 14*(2), 63-84.

Thompson, R. (1996). Assimilation. In D. Levinson (Ed.), *Encyclopedia of cultural anthropology.* New York: Henry Holt.

Turner, V. (1985). Liminality, Kabbalah, and the media. *Religion, 15*, 205-217.

Warshel, Y. (1999). *Communication and the talking-drum.* Unpublished manuscript, Annenberg School for Communication, University of Pennsylvania, Philadelphia.

# 5

# CULTURAL ANTHROPOLOGY AND MASS MEDIA

## A Processual Approach

MIHAI COMAN

## MASS MEDIA, MYTH, AND RITUAL

As vast and numerous as the anthropological approaches on mass media may be, in the following paragraphs I will focus on the relationship (rarely approached by classical anthropologists) between media content and the concepts of myth and ritual. My anthropological approach stems from the hypothesis that mass media, like non-modern manifestations studied with the aid of concepts such as myth, rite, sacred, liminality, magic, and so on, create and impose symbolic systems of thinking surrounding reality and of articulating it in cultural constructs that are accessible and satisfying to their audience. In other words, the anthropological view starts with the premise that mass media are a cultural system for the social construction of reality and the claim that this construction is made, under certain circumstances, with instruments that are not part of argumentative rationality but of symbolic rationality. It follows that mass media cannot be conceived of as a go-between, mediating or covering certain cultural constructs—a situation in which

their role is only to carry and remodel messages designed and made by other social instances. On the contrary, the anthropological approach imposes a perspective that places mass media at the center of the process of social construction of reality, as an institution that generates specific discourses and logics. The products incorporating such values are distributed to the public and are assumed by the public as edifying images about the world, understandable in themselves, in agreement with its expectations, norms, hopes, and fears. A further claim for the anthropological perspective is that these images are accepted and assumed precisely because they have the status of *symbolic constructs* and that, having that status, they function and signify in the same way as the mythical systems and rituals of nonmodern societies. What follows is not a reduction of the media to mere relics of rite and myth and the avoidance of any specific differences or notes. On the contrary, I propose that with such a view, certain mass media phenomena may be read or interpreted into the framework of anthropological concepts, which can explain the processes of mythologizing or ritualization of reality through media discourse.

Most analyses resorting to basic anthropological concepts come down to two great perspectives: ritualistic interpretation and mythological interpretation.

From the point of view of a ritual universe, the press is viewed in two ways:

1. As a *component* of ritual manifestation, a component conveying a specific symbolic force

2. As a *ritual agent,* a constitutive factor, producing special rites

The fundamental book written by D. Dayan and E. Katz (1992) ventured a successful name for this reality ("media events") and, what is more important, a number of persuasive analyses, a conceptual vocabulary, a proposal for a typology, and an angle of approach that have become referential. According to this approach, mass media have the same role and effect in relation to sociocultural phenomena that they have in relation to ceremonies: They *amplify* an element of the ceremony—the audience (physical or affective) participation, the prestige of officiating agents or other actors, the structure of the ceremonial script, or the public significance of the event (for critical perspective, see Becker, 1995; Coman, 2003; Couldry, 2003; Rothenbuhler, 1998).

The many research studies conducted in this area, most inspired by Dayan and Katz's study, show that when the mass media cover a public ceremony or an event involving ritual behavior schemata, they alter it as follows:

1. They impose a new delineation and a new configuration on the components of the ceremony being covered, emphasizing the officiating agents and the actors, who have now become stars. Under the circumstances, one could even talk about a *new ceremonial scripting* that appears under mass media influence (Carey, 1998; Coman, 1994, 1996; Couldry, 2003; Dayan & Katz, 1995; De Repetigny, 1985; Peri, 1997; Pink, 1997).

2. The media bring a change of emphasis: They place the center of interest of the ritual performance at the emotional level (of actors and officiating agents), leaving the ritual structure in the shadow (Couldry, 2000; Dayan, 1999, 2000; Pink, 1998; Tsaliki, 1995).

3. They disseminate a festive language and mood, assumed as a festive way of life by the receptors (Alexander & Jacobs, 1998; Crivello, 1999; Davis, 1998; De Repetigny, 1985; Rothenbuhler, 1989).

4. They create an "enclave" within the ritual, in which journalists become "apostolic" narrators and privileged actors (Coman, 1994, 1996; Hallin & Mancini, 1991; Liebes, 1998; Lundby, 1997).

From a second perspective, some scholars suggest that mass media are also generators of a specific, modern, ritual type. The press's power to be a *ritualizing* factor was explored in two types of social configuration: small groups in their daily life and collectives in their moments of social mobilization.

The first level of analysis targeted mainly the processes of reception of mass media content. These studies conferred upon television viewing (and newspaper reading) the capacity to set the rhythms of home life and to install a sort of "daily rituality." Starting sometimes from careful ethnographic descriptions, other times only from theoretical considerations, many scholars claim that these fixed encounters with the same shows (and stars) regulate the interactions between receptors and mass media, receptors and the outside world, and receptors and the universe of private existence. Moreover, the rites of mass media consumption dramatize the consumption of cultural products, introduce patterns of behavior, generate collective solidarity forms, and even offer existential security (Barrios, 1988; Goethals, 1981; Real, 1996; Riggs, 1996; Silverstone, 1994). In observing these studies, the anthropologist cannot but notice that the notion of ritual is used to name and add meaning to (a) identical and regulated behavior, (b) certain acts of simultaneous reception of certain messages (therefore *communitary*), and (c) certain dramatically charged content with the power to interpret the world. We notice that, out of the broad pallette of features that single out rituals, those selected derive from the regularity of performance, which brings to the foreground, for this type of behavior, the value of "communication without information" (Rothenbuhler, 1998). That is not enough for labeling a social behavior a ritual.

Much more fascinating, although less researched, is the other level of analysis, according to which the mass media are seen as *ritual agents* capable of ritualizing social activities, on a large scale. Dayan and Katz (1992) emphasized a tendency of political actors to cause events (that had nothing ceremonial through content, context, or meaning) to be "ritualized" for the purpose of offering a solution to complex, difficult political situations. For Dayan and Katz, these ritualizations of politics (played out specifically for the press) have a transformative purpose, ensuring a passage from a tense situation to a balanced one. The ritualized act makes possible, acceptable, and significant an event previously considered unimaginable. When the accent shifts from the ritual pattern to the ritualization process, it is possible to study the processes by which the media have ritualized manifestations that, although they had some formal elements, had neither the cyclic character nor the form or purposes of a ritual. This perspective opens interesting possibilities of renewing theories on the social role of the press, on the public space, and on the ceremonial universe.

From the perspective of myth and theories of myth, mass media may be seen

1. As a storage bin in which mythical constructs may be preserved and reactivated

2. As a *maker* of myths and mythical units in the modern world

In all these studies, the relationship between media contents and myths is justified by the premise (often assumed implicitly) that the mass media system is, on the whole, a form of "modern" actualization of *premodern cultural models*. Articulated by the opposition between high and popular culture, this argument consigns to the former values such as rationality, a reflective character, seriousness, moral responsibility, and so on and places at the other pole the irrational dimension, spontaneity, entertainment (pleasure),

absence of sophisticated ethical standards, and so on (see chapter 11).

I believe an anthropological view of mass media should focus on the forms and processes media employ to build a symbolic representation of reality by means of myth and ritual. In other words, we should turn from the study of the forms of coverage of myth and ritual to exploring the *ritualization* and *mythologization* of reality by the media. This approach would include studies that assert that "this mythical archetype is present in this news story" or "this ceremony influences media coverage and formats" and bring a further processual approach to earlier, vague analogies such as "media messages and myths have identical functions" and "media consumption and rituals have identical functions." Research from this new angle should concentrate on the processes through which media introduce a ritualized or mythological perspective to the image of the world they offer, as well as to their particular manner of structuring the image of reality.

## THE RITUALIZATION

In their well-known study, Dayan and Katz (1992) posited that the creation of a media event could result not only in special coverage of ceremonies but in generating certain media ceremonial manifestations; that is, in generalizing the ceremonial pattern in areas within or without mass media, areas that are essentially nonritual. These particular types of media events, "the transformative events (ceremonies)," as they were further researched by the two authors in a subsequent study (Dayan & Katz, 1995), referred to political and journalistic acts being ritualized so that they would overcome an institutional barrier:

> A transformative ceremony represents a turning point. The proclamation of a new future retrospectively reorganizes the history that led to the ceremonial moment. The ceremony itself represents a "liminal" moment, a break in the routinized social time. It blocks history in its development. It offers society the opportunity to discover that there are alternatives to its choices and, in doing so, it partially

revives the anxieties, the chaos and the effervescence of geneses. New projects are initiated and, from their perspective, the past is reinvented and collective memory is reorganized. (Dayan & Katz, 1995, p. 166)

Transformative events (ceremonies) are based not on a ritualization of nonritual manifestations but on a change of ritual pattern. They are built by extrapolating the symbolic resources of a ritual pattern available in a given culture and applying them to formalized or ceremonialized events. The protocol of official visits whose ceremonialization is not rich in symbols can be restructured and covered as a rite of passage, itself able to generate a symbolic frame, a radically changed public attitude, and an original view of the future political development and historical evolution. For instance, political planners and the media presented the Pope's visit to Poland or Saadat's to Israel not as a sum of regular protocols but as a means of experiencing, at a symbolic level, potential, although still unaccepted, political realities. In other words, these events generated "subjunctive rituals" (Turner, 1969) in which what is not yet, but could be, acquired for a short time a concrete form.

As explained earlier, transformative events are instances in which ceremonies are restructured or situations formalized to replicate the matrix and code of other, symbolically richer, ceremonies. Mass media contribute to the interpretation, legitimization, and development of the new ritual pattern. We might ask ourselves whether media might gain a more complex role and operate also as instruments of *ritualization;* that is, of radical displacement of an event from its usual frame into a ceremonial frame.

The concept of ritualization relates, first, to ethological theories. Ideas originating in research on animal behavior overlapped with developments in cultural anthropology, bringing the performative facet of ceremonies to the foreground and leaving their structural dimension in the background. The concept of *performance* became the framework for interpreting ritual activities.

In other words, ritual comes to be seen as performance in the sense of symbolic acts specifically meant to have impact on an audience and entrust their interpretative appropriation. Second, the notion of performance as a theoretical tool for approaching certain activities comes to be used as descriptive of the fundamental nature of those activities; in other words, a model of ritual activities provides the criteria for what is or is not ritual. Third, although performance may become a criterion for what is or is not ritual, insofar as performance is broadly used for a vast spectrum of activities, there is no basis to differentiate among ways of performing. (Bell, 1992, p. 42)

The numerous definitions of ritualization are seldom intricately elaborated and seem strictly operational in character. For R. Grimes (1995), "ritualization is enactment in the face of imagined, socially experienced or mythologically constructed receptivity" (p. 69). In his elaborated study of the ritual system, R. Rappaport (1999) claims that "the formalization of acts and utterances, themselves meaningful, and the organization of those formalized acts into more or less invariant sequences impose ritual form on the substance of those acts and utterances, that is on their significata" (p. 29). Catherine Bell (1992) moves away from these previous studies because they "identify ritual with communicative functions and thus qualify all or almost all activities as rituals" (p. 73). Bell employs the term *ritualization* to "draw attention to the ways in which certain social acts strategically contrast with other activities" (p. 74). She considers ritualization as part of a more complex class of behaviors, which she calls "practices," following Bourdieu. Thus,

viewed as a practice, ritualization involves the very drawing, in and through the activity itself, of a privileged distinction between ways of acting, specifically between those acts being performed and those being contrasted, mimed or implicated somehow. That is, intrinsic to ritualization are strategies for differentiating itself—to various degrees and in various ways—from other ways of acting within any particular culture. At a basic level, ritualization is the production of these differentiations. At a more complex level, ritualization is a way of acting that specifically establishes a privileged contrast, differentiating itself as more important or powerful. (Bell, 1992, p. 90)

Consequently, "since practice is situational and strategic, people engage in ritualization as a practical way of dealing with some specific circumstances" (Bell, 1992, p. 92). By means of these behavior strategies, people generate and legitimize differences from other practices, and "the degree of difference is itself strategic and a part of the logic and efficiency of the act" (p. 93). Ritualization appears under specific circumstances and uses several "basic operations" that the rituals of the shared culture have already established: formalization of behavior; establishment of basic oppositions; repetition; space and time restructuring; and introduction of symbolic, noninstrumental meanings for the respective practices. Ritualization is marked by a special form of social control:

> Ritual mastery is the ability—not equally shared, desired or recognized—to: (1) take and remake schemes from the shared culture that can strategically nuance, privilege or transform, (2) deploy them in the formulation of a privileged ritual experience, which in turn, (3) impresses them in a new form upon agents able to deploy them in a variety of circumstances beyond the circumference of the rite itself. (Bell, 1992, p. 116)

From this point of view, ritualization is a mechanism that not only produces specific differences (such as those between current practices and symbolic ones) but that can be employed in the struggle for power, as it generates hierarchies and defines hegemonic order (Bell, 1992, p. 216).

It is obvious that journalists exert "ritual mastery," because they have a privileged position in relation to the events and the audience, they have the power to offer and impose variants for the respective events (variants that the shared culture of the audience could acknowledge), and they can attribute meanings that mold the social imaginary. In other words, they can reorganize reality through their discourse according to some "strategic differences." Dramatizing certain aspects of the events and, especially, their efforts to gain access to them, journalists succeed in shifting the focus from the re-presentation of the events to the re-presentation of the media class and

system as leading actor of the respective events. I believe ritualization is a mechanism that allows journalists to establish their position and social role through their discourses, presenting themselves as representatives of Culture in situations that mark and legitimize social differences and endow the journalists (for a short time) with ritual mastery of the processes of debating and interpreting events of great importance for the group.

Journalists resort to ritualization, or rather, to the ritualized construction of meanings, when routine procedures can no longer be applied mechanically—that is, when they can no longer build meaning within the usual reference frameworks. In such instances, stereotypical methods of professional behavior are canceled and replaced by schemata of communicative behavior specific to ritual agency. On the other hand, I think it would be absurd to claim that, by covering events, journalists create and impose rituals the audience ought to perform. Journalists do not manufacture rituals but a *ritualized image* of certain events, which favors "differences" by focusing on specific acts, specific actors, or specific spatial and temporal circumstances. There are two types of journalistic activities that use the methods and codes of the ceremonial system to promote a ritualized image that imposes strategic differences by:

1. Selecting certain acts of the actors of the event and presenting them as elements that define and attribute meaning to a situation. This meaning is built by reference to a ritual-like pattern familiar to both journalists and their audience. The ritual pattern offers ready-made meanings that can be applied to critical events to make them meaningful. Through this procedure, journalists set strategic differences and build a ritually encoded variant of the event by using the actors' declarations and acts.

2. Employing a culturally defined narrative and labels to interpret the event as out of the ordinary, as something that retains and transmits symbolic values that surpass the proper event values. Thus, journalists ritualize the image of reality they are building and, through this mechanism, they legitimize a privileged difference between this event and others presented by the press.

The ritualized variant of events is generated when journalists feel the need to fill in a gap of meaning or, on the contrary, when they want to attribute a surplus of meaning to some situations—especially to those implying an element of formalization and possessing a certain symbolic potential. Facts are reordered and interpreted as part of a ritual pattern—in other words, as if not belonging to the usual schemata of routine events and the common frameworks of interpretation. Thus it is the ritual pattern, not necessarily the structure of a specific type of ritual, that is applied to reality. This leads to the transference of a particular cultural system's interpretation to events belonging to a different system of cultural reference altogether. For instance, all summits imply acts of protocol, but the summit analyzed by Hallin and Mancini (1991) had a specific political connotation and possessed a superior meaning potential: The USSR's political openness involved numerous ambiguities, contradicted the frame of thought introduced by the Cold War, and gave rise to a strange mixture of fear and hope. In this context, journalists ceremonialized the event, placing it in the domain of historical turning points. This ritualized interpretation of facts allowed the summit to be presented as if it were the representation of an already-made (symbolic) pattern, as if history had already been encoded in a preexistent schema, as if journalists were in the position of sacred "officials"—those who know the truth beyond conjectures, who pass sentences and know beforehand how the respective events are going to be considered. We might use the same concept to interpret the "stances" journalists maintain during crisis situations. Zelizer's study (1992) identifies four ostentatiously assumed roles through which journalists ritualized their positions and built strategically marked variants of John F. Kennedy's assassination:

In this capacity, journalists secured their central position in the story and reinforced their authority by adopting four journalistic stances: eyewitness, representative, investigator and interpreter. These roles allowed journalists a repertoire of ways to situate themselves in association with Dallas, providing different foundations for the claim to be legitimate tellers of its story. By highlighting different dimensions of practice that were central to the professional codes of journalism, each role linked journalists with ongoing discourse about journalistic practice, professionalism, and the legitimization of television news. (Zelizer, 1992, p. 131)

By ritualizing their role, journalists promoted, legitimized, and secured their authority to control the process of reporting and retelling of events; that is, to dominate the process of constructing variants of reality according to the audience's expectations.

Ritualization is one of the most powerful instruments for promoting journalistic *authority*. In fact, it gives journalists the opportunity to exert total control over the process of variant reality construction and, through it, to acquire the legitimacy inherent to this position. When they present an event under normal circumstances, "the journalists' interpretative hypotheses and instruments of analysis derive from their own experience, their own reasoning, their own culture—all of these combined with the methods specific to the journalist's profession" (Charaudeau, 1997, p. 173). This means that their authority derives from the authority of the media system, of the press institution they represent, and of the profession (which grants them resources different from those of normal witnesses or investigators from other professions). As presented here, ritualization is accomplished by (a) presenting events as if they had preestablished and immutable order and meaning and (b) by setting this order and meaning within the reference system specific to ritual. Within this framework, meanings appear as preexisting (preceding the event), and those who report the sequence of facts and their meaning appear as agents of generally acknowledged truths. In cases of ritualization, journalists surpass the authority limits imposed by the social standing of their profession and present themselves as the "voice" of the entire society, as ritual agents celebrating a great event: They no longer speak for their profession but for the entire social body. This explains why they give up normal working procedures and the usual journalistic language and tone. Far from being perceived as violations of their professional code, these transgressions are promoted as indicators of the new standing of the media. Thus ritualization appears as a method of exerting control over the processes of construction and negotiation of views of reality. Employing this method, journalists draw attention, by means of a strategic difference, to a "privileged" variant of events and consecrate the ritual mastery of their group, which promotes and validates their own version.

## THE MECHANISMS OF MYTHOLOGIZATION

Anthropologists have historically had little concern for the acts or mechanisms that construct myths out of certain cultural prefabs, under specific circumstances and through specific processes. Obviously, such a process would be difficult to explore in "exotic" fields, where scholars searched for products of tradition and expected to find a confirmation of the exotic and the archaic in the very mythical texts. The ideology of tradition concealed the dynamics of archaic mythologies and generated the feeling of stable, self-reproducing systems. Under the circumstances, there were few studies of the processes that build myths or of which texts with a different cultural status are changed into myths. On the other hand, when anthropologists focused on modern mythologies, the respective studies identified mythologization with the mere representation of (hagiographic) narrative schemata or the representation of characters (the hero, the martyr, the saint, the miracle) pertaining to the archaic cultural background.

Following Lévi-Strauss, I am inclined to believe that, to understand myths, we must consider them systems of logical operations. Moreover, to understand how myths signify, we must understand the operations by which they are built; that is, the processes of mythologization.

> Unlike a linguistic construction that orders, questions or informs and which all members of a culture or subculture can understand if provided with a suitable

context, a myth never offers those listening to it a pre-established meaning. A myth proposes an interpretation defined only in terms of its construction rules. For those who belong to the culture in which the respective myth developed, this interpretation confers meaning not to the myth itself, but to the other elements of the respective culture (that is, to the representations of the world, history, society, more or less internalized by the members of that culture, and to the questions posed by the reality surrounding them). Generally speaking, these disparate elements do not form a coherent ensemble and more often than not they contradict each other. The intelligibility offered by myth allows their articulation into a coherent ensemble. (Lévi-Strauss, 1983, p. 199)

From this perspective, the myth is not the constructed text, but rather the process of constructing a text (which is unstable and changeable anyway). In other words, the myth is an instance of collage, *bricolage*, created out of basic cultural units for the purpose of constructing narratives to operate as systems of interpretation for events. These processes are based on an ensemble of logical operations, through which various possibilities of interpreting the surrounding world are explored. For this reason, myth (mythical thinking) appears as "a giant combinatorial machine" (Lévi-Strauss, 1971, p. 501), which builds

> a table of possibilities for the social groups . . . to find specific formulae to solve issues of internal organization or to promote an image of prestige against their opponents. The formulae developed by myth are thus able to acquire practical use and in this respect, we might say that mythical speculation overtakes action. Mythical speculation never seems content with offering a unique solution to an issue; as soon as it has been formulated, the answer enters a game of transformations in which all the other possible answers are generated simultaneously or sequentially. (Lévi-Strauss, 1983, p. 232)

In a situation of crisis, journalists have to confer meaning on events (that are often threatening, absurd, and meaningless) with the help of stories built on available cultural units. As already pointed out, the crisis affects society and questions its values and norms. Coming through this crisis means not only solving a situation but also rebuilding (sometimes for real, other times only symbolically) the social edifice. Therefore, the discourse on crisis must simultaneously deal with two realities: that of the ongoing events and that of the society on trial. Mythologization is an instrument perfectly adapted to the double challenge and double discourse. It uses a story (actually, the relevant facts) to raise questions about the values, institutions, expectations, and fears of a society by symbolically reconstructing these facts. The story thus built offers a frame of interpretation for the respective crisis (a meaning that can be accepted within the code system specific to a collective). Usually, this story is unlikely, exaggerated, dramatic, and contradictory. When analyzed later, both journalists and observers will label it a media bias, and the professional group will employ a complex ideological machinery to restore the journalists' reputation and to place the causes of the errors outside the profession. They will invoke the difficult access to the events, the scarcity of sources, the impossibility of verifying them, the risk factors, the manipulative intentions of the spin doctors, and so on. And then, when they are confronted with the next crisis, the same exaggerated, incomplete, dramatic stories will reappear in spite of the warnings and the acquired "experience." This phenomenon is not an accident caused by the journalists' lack of ability or the great prowess of some evil spin doctors. On the contrary, this phenomenon represents a structural constant deriving from the double function of journalistic discourse during crisis (it describes events, and it preserves social order).

Journalistic crisis stories, like myths, are meaningful due to their very unlikelihood and absurdity. The system of interpretation they suggest does not confer meaning on the story but on everything else ("*a tout le reste*" in Lévi-Strauss's words); that is, on the social order affected by the crisis spectrum. Their discourse is not argumentative but symbolic. In other words, it does not reproduce existent and acknowledged patterns; instead, it produces and mentally experiments on potential patterns of reality. Following Lévi-Strauss (1971), it means that these stories "represent

rather momentary and context-dependent answers to issues raised by potential adaptations and contradictions otherwise impossible to solve" (p. 562). According to the Lévi-Straussian framework, the elements of the text do not have an intrinsic meaning but a structural one. They are defined by metonymical relations (oppositions, symmetries, permutations, inversions, etc.) with other elements in other (opposed or complementary) variants and by metaphorical relations (of substitution) with respect to the subjacent logical structures and cultural codes. Within this permanently unstable system, in which new variants replace old ones at a fast pace, each element can be both signifying and signified (Lévi-Strauss, 1971, p. 362) or both relation and term (p. 568). This fact explains the apparent lack of consistency of the stories. In their successive changes, they attempt to propose various patterns of intelligibility. For this purpose, they, like myth, regularly construct various stories referring to the same events. In these stories, various "characters" pertaining to the existent cultural heritage mediate through their actions and features between opposite and apparently irreconcilable categories— categories that are appropriated or assimilated by the existing crisis. Thus, within the ensemble of texts focusing on a crisis, journalistic discourse provides a system of interpretation that one can accept, understand, and use to discuss unexpected situations that would otherwise be unacceptable and definitely incomprehensible. Or, as Silverstone (1983) puts it:

> As Lévi-Strauss himself consistently points out the myth and sacred are themselves fully locked both to the empirical realities of their host society and to the persistent patterns of social and cultural life for which that society must find some kind of solution. What they do above all is provide an ultimately rational explanation of the non-rational, coherent and entirely acceptable narrative of what is often incoherent and terrifyingly unacceptable. As in the myth of preliterate society so too on television, those transformations are accomplished by and in their narratives. (p. 141)

The mythologization process is specifically related to situations of crisis. On such occasions, journalists have to resist the pressure of both the confusing, chaotic, meaningless, and often threatening facts and the audience's expectations and anxieties. All these elements that can lead to potential bias are emphasized by the newsroom editor's activity (through pressures referring to the acceleration, simplification, and dramatization of the events). Mythologization, like Janus, looks both ways and satisfies two types of requirements. It structures facts into epic constructions that, though permanently unstable, provide accessible systems of interpretation and, simultaneously, it restructures the society's system of representations to provide convenient and negotiable symbolic configurations.

Under the circumstances, I do not define mythologization as the mere translation of events into topoi inspired from or transmitted by ancient mythologies—even if such processes can take place. Mythologization is more than a simple mechanical copying of epic-symbolic schemata. It is a neverending process of collage, using all the units of the cultural heritage. This collage generates successive sets of stories open to interpretations, negotiations, and modifications within the frame of social dialogue. Under normal circumstances, journalistic stories are more "transparent"; that is, they refer more "openly" to contingent realities to which the representatives of the audience have direct or indirect access through legitimate sources. At the same time, because of this dazzling referential dimension, they do not reveal the systems of representations on which journalistic discourse and the social imagination, thus built and legitimized, are based. Let us not forget that for the last few decades, the unveiling of these hidden ideologies has represented a priority for all critical studies focusing on mass media.

In situations of crisis, stories follow one after the other at great speed; they contradict or melt into each other, turn opaque and self-referential. They reveal less and are less meaningful with respect to their own coherence or that of their referent (the facts in question). They send to and signify more values and systems. In a way, mythologization is a mechanism of dereferentialization (despite the fact that journalists maintain the external indexes of referentiality: invoking or quoting sources, gathering backup figures and data, assuming balance and neutrality, etc.). The stories thus built lean more on characters, epic schemata, values, and symbols pertaining to the audience's cultural heritage and less on the facts, characters, causes, and social mechanisms of the respective crisis. This happens because the main priority (even if not obvious to the creators of journalistic stories) is not the factual description and the scientific interpretation of the event but the return to the symbolic balance threatened by the crisis. Mythologization allows journalists to preserve an authoritative, socially acknowledged standing in the intricate process of outlining the perspectives of a crisis and of meeting social expectations. It offers the professional group and society in general the opportunity to avail themselves of and work with polysemous symbolic constructs adaptable to various types of discourse and capable of contributing to the redefinition of the social order and its systems of constitutive values.

# References

Alexander, J., & Jacobs, R. (1998). Mass communication, ritual and civil society. In T. Liebes & J. Curran (Eds.), *Media, ritual and identity* (pp. 23-41). London: Routledge.

Barrios, L. (1988). Television, telenovelas and family life in Venezuela. In J. Lull (Ed.), *World families watch television*. London: Sage.

Becker, K. (1995). Media and the ritual process. *Media, Culture and Society, 17*(4), 629-646.

Bell, C. (1992). *Ritual theory, ritual practice.* New York: Oxford University Press.

Carey, J. (1998). Political ritual on television: Episodes in the history of shame, degradation and excommunication. In T. Liebes & J. Curran (Eds.), *Media, ritual and identity* (pp. 42-69). London: Routledge.

Charaudeau, P. (1997). *Le discours d'information médiatique* [Of mediated informations]. Paris: Nathan.

Coman, M. (1994). La victime et le vainqueur: La construction mythologique de la visite du roi Mihai en Roumanie par le discours de la presse roumaine [The victim and the victor: The mythological construction of the visit of King Mihai of Romania through the discourse of the Romanian press]. *Reseaux, 12*(66), 179-191.

Coman, M. (1996). L'événement rituel: Médias et cérémonies politiques (La Place de l'Université à Bucarest en 1990) [The ritual event: Media and political ceremonies (the Plaza of the University of Bucharest in 1990)]. *Reseaux, 14*(76), 11-29.

Coman, M. (2003). *Pour une anthropologie des medias* [Toward an anthropology of the media]. Grenoble, France: Presses Universitaires de Grenoble.

Couldry, N. (2000). *The place of media power: Pilgrims and witnesses of the media age.* London: Routledge.

Couldry, N. (2003). *Media rituals: A critical approach.* London: Routledge.

Crivello, M. (1999). La télévision mémorielle? Jubilés historiques et récits médiatiques à la télévision française (1950-1999) [Memorial television? Historic jubilees and mediated stories from French television (1950-1999)]. *Médiatiques, 17,* 8-11.

Davis, C. A. (1998). A oes heddwech: Contesting meanings and identities in the Welsh national Eisteddfod. In F. Hughes-Freeland (Ed.), *Ritual, performance, media* (pp. 141-159). London: Routledge.

Dayan, D. (1999). Madame se meurt. Des publics se construisent. Le jeu des médias et du public aux funerailles de Lady Diana [The Lady is dead. New publics arise. The media and the public play with Lady Diana's funerals]. *Quaderni, 38,* 49-68.

Dayan, D. (2000). Les grands événements médiatiques au miroir du rituel [Great media events through the mirror of ritual]. In P. Brechon & J.-P. Willaime (Ed.), *Médias et religions en miroir* [Media and religion face to face] (pp. 245-264). Paris: Presses Universitaires de France.

Dayan, D., & Katz, E. (1992). *Media events: The live broadcasting of history.* Cambridge, MA: Harvard University Press.

Dayan, D., & Katz, E. (1995). Télévision d'intervention et spectacle politique [Televisual intervention and political spectacle]. *Hermes, 17-18,* 163-186.

De Repetigny, M. (1985). La visite du pape à Québec (spectacle et spiritualité) [The visit of the Pope to Québec (spectacle and spirituality)]. *Communication: Informations, Medias, Theories, Pratiques, 7*(2), 33-43.

Goethals, G. (1981). *The TV ritual.* Boston: Beacon Press.

Grimes, R. (1995). *Beginnings in ritual studies.* Columbia: University of South Carolina Press.

Hallin, D., & Mancini, P. (1991). Summits and the constitution of the public sphere: The Reagan-Gorbaciov meetings as televisual media events. *European Journal of Communication, 6*(12), 349-365.

Lévi-Strauss, C. (1971). *Mythologiques. Vol. IV. L'homme nu* [Mythologies. Vol. 4. The new man]. Paris: Plon.

Lévi-Strauss, C. (1983). *Le regard éloigné* [The distant glance]. Paris: Plon.

Liebes, T. (1998). Television's disaster marathons: A danger for democratic processes. In T. Liebes & J. Curran (Eds.), *Media, ritual and identity* (pp. 71-85). London: Routledge.

Lundby, K. (1997). The web of collective representations. In S. Hoover & K. Lundby (Eds.), *Rethinking media, religion and culture* (pp. 146-164). London: Sage.

Peri, Y. (1997). The Rabin myth and the press: Reconstruction of the Israeli collective identity. *The European Journal of Communication, 12*(4), 435-458.

Pink, S. (1997). *Women and bullfighting: Gender, sex and the consumption of tradition.* Oxford: Berg.

Pink, S. (1998). From ritual sacrifice to media commodity. In F. Hughes-Freeland (Ed.), *Ritual, performance, media* (pp. 121-140). London: Routledge.

Rappaport, R. A. (1999). *Ritual and religion in the making of humanity.* Cambridge, England: Cambridge University Press.

Real, M. (1996). *Exploring media culture.* London: Sage.

Riggs, K. (1996). The case of the mysterious ritual: Murder dramas and older women viewers. *Critical Studies in Mass Communication, 13*(4), 309-323.

Rothenbuhler, E. (1989). Values and symbols in orientation to Olympics. *Critical Studies in Mass Communication, 6*(2), 138-157.

Rothenbuhler, E. (1998). Ritual communication: From everyday conversation to mediated ceremony. London: Sage.

Silverstone, R. (1983). The right to speak: On a poetic for television documentary. *Media, Culture and Society, 5.*

Silverstone, R. (1994). *Television and everyday life.* London: Routledge.

Tsaliki, L. (1995). The media and the construction of an "imagined community: The role of the media events on Greek television. *European Journal of Communication, 10*(3), 345-370.

Turner V. (1969). *The ritual process.* New York: Aldine.

Zelizer, B. (1992). *Covering the body: The Kennedy assassination, the media and the shaping of collective memory.* Chicago: University of Chicago Press.

# Part II

## CONCEPTS AND METHODS

The application of established concepts from cultural anthropology in media studies has produced not only numerous case studies but numerous theoretical debates, as well. Echoing these debates, the contributors to this section of the book address the legitimacy and conceptual implications of applying anthropological theories and methods in this domain and the necessary adaptations of these concepts and methods to their new uses.

Couldry and Lardellier, each from his own perspective, reflect on the relation between mass media and ritual, building on both classic Durkheimian theories and conflict theories. Couldry develops a new approach to the media rituals concept, proposing its integration into a neo-Durkheimian evaluation of the role of mass media in the functioning of society, an evaluation that is not blinded by the illusion of representation, through ritual, of a real social cohesion. He argues that in media we construct not only events, places, or worlds but (especially) differences and hierarchies of events, places, and worlds; in this way, media rituals consecrate and naturalize media-related categories and boundaries and structure our representations of the world in terms of power and conflict. Lardellier places himself at the other end of the discussion, stressing the consensual and reconciliatory functions of media events. He reveals the role of cultural memory in the construction and acceptance of a media event and, later, its transformation into a vector of other forms of collective memory. From this perspective, Lardellier proposes a rethinking of the relation between media and history in which media are not making history banal but *are* history, in the making.

Thomas and Rothenbuhler address the question of religion in its various manifestations. Thomas shows that the relation between religion and television can be addressed in several ways: the self-presentation of religions on TV; the intrusion of religious symbols, motifs, roles, and stories in fictional and nonfictional programs; and the absorption of religious rituals and practices by the television system, which creates the experience of transcendence through television. Anchoring himself in the latter perspective, Thomas stresses the capacity of television to offer "distinctive, cultural communication forms of religion" through its capacity to build a liturgical order and cosmological worldview. Rothenbuhler proposes to consider the media as the church of the cult of the individual. His system is constructed on the bases of the Durkheimian vision of the legitimacy of the cult of the individual as religious practice and interactionist theories of communication and ritual. Rothenbuhler develops the distinction between celebrity and reputation, which allows him to follow the media production of hagiography and ghost stories and to underline the idea that the cult of the individual may be the dominant religious force in modern Western societies.

Lule, Coman, and Schudson approach the mythical and narrative dimension of news stories. For Lule, the mythic status of journalism derives from the actualization of pre-existing archetypes from the distant past in news stories of present events. The archetype perpetuates in time, and is available for, several uses, without being influenced by social context, cultural system, or the specific genres into which it is placed and adapted. Schudson starts from the structural ambiguity of news stories, which are "responsible not only to literary convention but to a faithful rendering and even a verifiably faithful rendering of what really happened." His analysis unveils the role of a culture's epic vocabulary and of narrative structures in configuring journalistic coverage of events: The narrative dimension functions as a catalyst of the symbolic construction processes of reality, based on symbolic representations, possibly anchored in myth. Coman maps the field of debate on the presence of myth in the journalistic discourse. He identifies, in the bibliography on this topic, three major approaches—archetypal, functionalist, and cognitive—and evaluates the theoretical frame and the weaknesses specific to each paradigm. Coman reveals the conceptual difficulties of twinning two cultural systems considered so radically different (myth as fiction and news stories as factual accounts) and underlines the limits of approaches that do not take into account the processual dimension specific to mechanisms of the mythologization of journalistic accounts.

LaPastina and Murdoch and Pink reopen the already thick file of debates and confrontations on the application of ethnographic research methods to media phenomena. It is not at all an easy topic because of differences of opinion and fieldwork that separate, at one end, the partisans of applying ethnographic methods without restrictions and sometimes not in a rigorous manner and, at the other end, the supporters of strict methodology, based on applying point by point the precepts of the ethnography of nonmodern societies. Murdoch and Pink propose the reinterpretation of ethnographic practice through frames of intertextuality; LaPastina suggests refreshing audience ethnography through a dynamic approach to the complexity of phenomena, which he calls "media engagement."

Each of the studies in this section echoes analyses, ideas, polemics, and interrogations from all of the other chapters of the book. The efforts to reflect on the exchanges of research methods, concepts, theories, and visions between cultural anthropology and media studies have generated a rainbow of challenging ideas, interpretations, and theoretical reflections. Regardless of the positions expressed by each author, it is evident that all contributors are aware of the fact that only an ensemble of well-elaborated conceptual tools, referring to both the objects and the methods of analysis, can give media anthropology identity and legitimacy.

# 6

# Media Rituals

## Beyond Functionalism

### Nick Couldry

In the past decade, a consensus has begun to emerge on a new approach to media research that escapes the confines of earlier media studies.[1] This new approach seeks to work not just on the level of media texts and institutions but on the broader and more subtle ways in which the very *existence* of media in our societies transforms those societies, for good or ill. If Joshua Meyrowitz's (1994) term *medium theory* smacks too much of technological determinism, a better label for this shift might be *mediation*:[2] What do we mean when we say our societies are "mediated," and what are the long-term implications of this for their distribution of power? The question, if in different language, can be traced back to Lazarsfeld and Merton's (1969) classic essay "Mass Communication, Popular Taste and Organized Social Action"; it consolidates James Carey's (1989) later and better known call for more attention to the "ritual mode of communication." The radical nature of this shift, however, has largely been obscured by a particular reading of such questions, including the "ritual" dimensions of media processes, within an all-too-comfortable functionalist understanding of how contemporary societies hold together, *if* they do. In this chapter, I want to show what it means to think about mediation *beyond* a functionalist framework.

The term *ritual* inevitably brings with it the contested legacy of anthropology and the sociology of religion. In particular, it summons the highly ambiguous figure of Emile Durkheim: ambiguous because his ideas spanned the most urgent questions of contemporary sociology and an "armchair anthropology" (Pickering, 1984) that seems rather quaint to us now; ambiguous also because the implications of Durkheim's analysis of the social bond (and its grounding in ritual forms) for our understanding of *power* are quite uncertain. Carey was right to be uneasy about the Durkheimian legacy, but wrong (as Eric Rothenbuhler, 1993, pointed out) to suggest that he could or did work outside it. The way forward, rather, must lie through *more* (and more rigorous) examination of anthropological theory in media

**Author's Note:** This chapter draws on the argument of my recent book, *Media Rituals: A Critical Approach* (2003), especially pages 5-6 and 51-52. Thanks to Routledge for granting permission to reproduce this material.

research, not less. The blindness of most media researchers to anthropology has been noted before (Dayan & Katz, 1992; Elliott, 1982), but the vision of anthropological theory that has so far been offered to media research is partial, to say the least. It has brought to the foreground the functionalist aspects of Durkheim and the related work of Victor Turner, ignoring many other promising paths: for example, Maurice Bloch's (1989) work on ritual and power and Pierre Bourdieu's (1991) reinterpretation of Durkheim and the study of media making as a social process in contemporary cultural anthropology (see Ginsburg, 1994). Even less attention has been given to exciting recent work on ritual by anthropologists of religion (Bell, 1992, 1997; Smith, 1987; see also Handelman, 1998). Once these new connections are opened up, other connections with social theory become possible— for example, to the work of Foucault (1981) on "rituals of confession" and governmentality (although I will not have space to pursue these here). The result, I believe, is to enrich media theory considerably and, perhaps, to contribute something to anthropological theory as well.

Before I go any further, let me get one definitional point out of the way. By *media*, I will mean not any media, or process of mediation, but particularly those *central* media (primarily television, radio, and the press, but sometimes film and music, and increasingly also computer-mediated communication via the Internet) through which we imagine ourselves to be connected to the social world. This is the commonsense notion of "*the* media," although in the age of media digitalisation its precise reference point is changing to some degree. *The* media (in this sense) are involved in what I will call "the myth of the mediated centre": the belief, or assumption, that there is a centre to the social world and that, in some sense, the media speak "for" that centre. This myth underlies our orientation to television, radio, and the press (and, increasingly, the Internet), and our tendency to regard the massive concentration of symbolic power in those media institutions as legitimate. Symbolic power (if concentrated in this way) is a socially sanctioned "power of constructing reality" (Bourdieu, 1991,

p. 166), and the practices I will call *media rituals* draw on and, in turn, reinforce the assumed legitimacy of the media's own concentration of symbolic power.

I will be working here both with and against our instinctive sense of what the term *ritual* means. I want to rethink commonsense notions of *ritual* to address the complexity of contemporary media's impacts on social space. Understanding media rituals is not simply a matter of isolating particular performances (rituals) and interpreting them; it is a matter of grasping the whole social space within which anything like ritual in relation to media becomes possible. The result is to enrich, but certainly not simplify, our account of ritual; this chapter presents merely some extracts from a longer, more detailed argument (see Couldry, 2003).

## WHY WE STILL NEED THE TERM *RITUAL*

To introduce the term *ritual* to the study of media requires some defence (Corner, 1999). It is as well to note at the outset how the term has been used by anthropologists.

There have been three broad approaches to ritual in anthropology. These have understood ritual respectively as (a) habitual action, (b) formalised action, and (c) action involving transcendent values. The first definition is uninteresting, as it is unclear what ritual here adds to the idea of regular action or habit; I will not pursue this further. The second and third approaches are more interesting. Formalised action is more than habit, as it insists that ritual involves a pattern, form, or shape that gives meaning to that action. To see ritual from the third perspective—as action involving or embodying broad, even transcendent, values—is compatible with the second approach but shifts the emphasis away from questions of pure form and toward the particular values that ritual action embodies. It is the second and third senses of the term *ritual* in which I am interested in this chapter.

Immediately, however, there is an objection to retaining a term such as *ritual* in contemporary cultural analysis. Doesn't it fly in the face of many claims that we live in an age of "de-traditionalisation" (Heelas, Lash, & Morris, 1994), without anything so formalised as ritual, except as a relic of the past? Doesn't it ignore, specifically, the progressive multiplication and diversification of media outputs and media technologies in an age of media "plenty" (Ellis, 2000)?

Behind this objection is a rather unhistorical assumption, that ritual, including ritual in the media field, is simply a matter of preserving past forms, such as in religious ritual. Why ignore the possibility, however, that new forms of ritual may be being generated right now, perhaps especially through the media's operations? Ritual, I want to argue, remains an important term for grasping what media do and how social institutions work. Just as ritualised action turns our attention to "something else," a wider, transcendent pattern "over and above" the details of actions,[3] raising questions of form, so too it is the media's influence on the forms of contemporary social life—the transcendent patterns within which the details of social life make sense—that is puzzling, and which I intend to capture by the term *media rituals*. Media rituals, in broad terms, refers to the whole range of situations in which media themselves "stand in" for something wider, something to do with the fundamental organisational level on which we are, or imagine ourselves to be, connected as members of a society. This can cover a range of situations: media events; pilgrimages to media sites; the media's claims to represent "reality," as in "reality TV"; and media sites at which individuals may make public disclosures of private aspects of their lives (talk shows): see Couldry (2003).

There is a greater flexibility to the term *ritual* than is often realised. Ritual has often been associated with claims that it produces, or maintains, social integration. This is a reading associated particularly with the tradition of social thought derived from the great French sociologist Emile Durkheim, or at least one reading of Durkheim. But there are other interpretations of ritual. Anthropological theorists, such as Maurice Bloch and Pierre Bourdieu, have connected ritual not with the affirmation of what we share in common (the affirmation of real "community") but with the management of conflict and the masking of social inequality. Unfortunately, in media analysis, whenever ritual has been introduced, it is the first, "integrationist," understanding of "ritual that has dominated"—and it is precisely this association of ritual with social integration and with the standard integrationist reading of Durkheim that we need to challenge.

We need to rethink ritual, and particularly media ritual, to make room for new connections: between the power of contemporary media institutions and modern forms of government (Giddens, 1985). For too long, media theorists have analysed the most dramatic examples of media power (the great media events of televised coronations and state funerals) in isolation from questions of government. As Armand Mattelart (1994) argues, the result is an impoverished account of the media's role in modernity and, therefore, a misreading of media's ambiguous contribution to the ritual dimension of modernity, including late modernity.

Implied in my approach, unavoidably, is a wider perspective on how media contribute to contemporary societies' holding together, if in fact they do. The approach I take to media rituals will be post-Durkheimian and antifunctionalist. These terms require some explanation. To be "post-Durkheimian" is not to abandon Durkheim's social theory as a reference point but to rethink our relation to Durkheim in a radical fashion, by dropping any assumptions that underlying and motivating ritual is always the achievement of social order. To be "antifunctionalist" generalises the first point: It means opposing any form of essentialist thinking about society, not only functionalist accounts of society's workings (and media's role in them) but also the idea that society is essentially disordered and chaotic (indeed, it is a rejection of any notion of social order that prevents some postmodern social theorists from seeing how much Durkheim still has to offer in explaining contemporary media rhetorics, once we work outside functionalist assumptions). The point therefore (and here there is a clear difference with postmodern social theory: for example,

Lash, 2002, p. 215) is not that Durkheim is fundamentally wrong or outmoded in his prioritisation of ritual, sacred and profane, and other related ideas but that, to grasp the continuing power of Durkheim's ideas, we must discard the functionalist framework that shaped his work and consider the question of social order (and its construction) from a new perspective.

## THE DURKHEIMIAN LEGACY

Durkheim's sociology of religion (especially in *The Elementary Forms of Religious Life*, 1912/1995) is the unavoidable reference point for any account of ritual that is interested in wider questions of social order. It was Durkheim who insisted on the need to grasp the dimension of social life that transcends the everyday. He called this "the serious life," *la vie sérieuse* (Rothenbuhler, 1998, pp. 12-13, 25), and saw religion as its main, although not its only, manifestation. Durkheim, however, understood religion in a rather special sense. For him, religion "is first and foremost a system of ideas by means of which individuals imagine the society of which they are members and the obscure yet intimate relations they have with it" (1912/1995, p. 227).

Religion, then, for Durkheim, is not about cosmic order (its usual reference point), but about the way social beings imagine the social bond that they share as members of a group. Durkheim argued that our experiences of being connected as members of a social world are at the root of our most important categorisations of that world; they are at the root in particular of the sacred-profane distinction, which, Durkheim argues, underlies all religion in the usual sense of the term.

This argument can be broken down into three stages:[4]

1. At certain key times, we experience ourselves explicitly as social beings, as members of a shared social whole.

2. What we do in those moments, at least in Durkheim's imagined Aboriginal case, is focussed on certain shared objects of attention, such as totems, and certain rituals that confirm the meaning of these "sacred" objects or protect them from the "profane."

3. The distinctions around which those moments of shared experience are organised—above all, the distinction between sacred and profane—generate the most important categorisations through which social life is organised. This, in Durkheim's view, explains the social origin of religion and religious behaviour and the centrality of the sacred-profane distinction in social life.

Needless to say, in seeking to draw insights from Durkheim's argument, I am not making claims here about the sociology of religion. If this seems cavalier on the face of it, it is justified by the breadth of implication built into Durkheim's original argument (Lukes, 1973, p. 484). Paradoxically, Durkheim's insights, although projected back into the past, were in fact directed at an urgent question for contemporary sociology: How, if at all, do societies cohere? More specifically: Are there certain central categories through which we perceive the social world, and what is their origin? These questions are as relevant to contemporary media as they are to contemporary religion.

I am, of course, not the first to seek to apply Durkheim's argument about religion in this way. Since the late 1970s, there have been a number of approaches that elsewhere I call "neo-Durkheimian" (Couldry, 2003, p. 61), notably Dayan and Katz's (1992) famous thesis on media events. There is not the space here to explore these arguments in detail. Instead I want to emphasise that neo-Durkheimian arguments have a great asset: Unlike many other approaches to the media, they take seriously our sense that much more is at stake in our relationship to the media than just distracted forms of image consumption. They share a concern to address the "excessive" dimension of the media's social impacts, but they also diverge from my argument in a crucial way. What is distinctive about the post-Durkheimian use of Durkheim that I propose is its emphasis not on any *real* social basis for media's integrative social role but instead on the process of social *construction* that underlies the apparent fit of ritual analysis to modern societies of Durkheimian (or neo-Durkheimian) analyses, particularly their media aspects.

We are *not*, in fact, gathered together by contemporary media in the way neo-Durkheimian arguments suggest. Even in the most dramatic cases of media events, this is only an approximation; in most others, it is purely a "conventional expectation" (Saenz, 1994, p. 576). On the contrary, I want to argue, we can only explain the ritual dimensions of media if we operate without mystifying functionalist assumptions. This means reading Durkheim against the grain, or at least against the grain of his most influential interpreters.

From this perspective, Durkheim's concerns with social order are important, but as tools to prise open (rather than take at face value) contemporary claims, especially media claims, to represent social cohesion. Helpful here is Pierre Bourdieu's (1991, p. 166) reinterpretation of Durkheim as a thinker whose interest in social categories was based not on the assumption that they embody something "universal" about the human mind or social fabric but on the belief that the claims to universality inherent in such categories are a fundamental, and highly political, dimension of our contested social "orders." Far from assuming that contemporary mediated societies do hold together (with the help of media or otherwise)—a dangerous assumption (Lukes, 1975)—we should see the very idea of "social order," mobilised in claims that rituals "integrate" societies, as the result of a constant production (Hall, 1977, p. 340).

This might sound, at first blush, like another version of the very functionalism I am claiming to move beyond, but in fact it is quite different. There is nothing functionalist about taking the media's claims to have a function very seriously, not for their truth, but for their rhetorical and, indeed, social effects. Far from believing in a stable, self-reproducing, social macrostructure underlying these claims, we are simply recognising (as the anthropologist Don Handelman suggests) that social networks have "media through which members communicate to themselves in concert about the characters of their collectivities, as if

these do constitute entities that are temporarily coherent" (Handelman, 1998, p. 15).

In contemporary societies dominated by media forms, the rhetorical pressures to believe in such "convergences" are particularly great; to the extent that "everything works as if"[5] there were a functioning social whole, media, and media rituals, are central to that construction. This is why media rituals need to be studied.

## WHAT AND WHERE ARE MEDIA RITUALS?

The nonfunctionalist approach to rituals (including media rituals) is less interested in them for themselves—as expressions of this or that idea—than it is in the wider social processes of "ritualization," through which something like (media) ritual comes into being at all. The term *ritualization* connects with a recent shift in thinking about ritual in the anthropology of religion, especially the work of Catherine Bell (1992, 1997), who draws not only on Durkheim but on Bourdieu and Foucault. Ritualization encourages us to look at the links between ritual actions and wider social space and, in particular, at the practices, beliefs, and categories,[6] found right across social life, that make specific ritual actions possible. In this section, I want to develop this idea both in terms of ritual in general and in terms of media rituals in particular.

The emphasis in ritual analysis needs to shift away from questions of meaning and toward questions of power.[7] Power is intertwined with the very possibility of contemporary ritual; similarly, media power (by which I mean the particular concentration of symbolic power in media institutions)[8] is intertwined with the very possibility of media rituals. But how exactly can we understand this link, and where is it made? Power (following Foucault and many others) is not just in one place, but dispersed across social space, so the link cannot occur just through the workings of those exceptional moments we call ritual. The link between ritual and power must be more regular, more embedded in everyday practice than that. We need a concept (absent from Durkheim) of the wider social space where ritual is generated. It is there that key categories are generated so that they can be drawn on in the formalised distinctions of ritual performance. I call this space the *space of ritualisation* (Bell, 1992).

What space might this be? I use the word *space* here metaphorically, as a convenient term to refer to the whole interlocking mass of practices that must be "in place" for there to be ritual action oriented to the media. In complex societies, the tightly defined contexts of formal ritual (religious ritual and, equally, media ritual) are relatively rare: This is why theories of detraditionalisation appear to make the persistence of ritual implausible. It is better, however, to think of the ritual process as stretched across multiple sites—indeed, across social space as a whole (Silverstone, 1981, pp. 66-67). We can expect that wider landscape of ritualisation to be highly uneven in terms of its power relations. In the case of the media, that space is formed around one central inequality— the historic concentration of symbolic power in media institutions—an equality which is naturalised through many detailed patterns, particularly the categories (such as those of "media" and "ordinary" person, of "liveness," and so on: See Couldry, 2000, pp. 42-52) through which we understand our actions and orientations in relation to the media. Without this wider landscape, the patterned actions I call media rituals (to be clarified shortly!) would not make sense.

Studying media rituals in this nonfunctionalist way is the opposite of isolating particular moments and elevating them to special, even "magical," significance. On the contrary, it means tracing the antecedents of media rituals in the patterns, categories, and boundaries at work everywhere, from press and magazine comment, to television newscasts, to our everyday talk about celebrities, to the way we act when we go on television. Behind the patterns, however, lies the construction of an assumed value: the transcendental "value" associated with "the media" that is based on their presumed ability to represent the social whole. My emphasis on categories, which is Durkheimian in spirit, might seem strange. In complex social worlds, with so many contradictory belief systems, can there really be any central categories that have a privileged relationship to social order (or what passes for it)? Paradoxically, there can, and a striking feature of contemporary media and media rituals is precisely the way in which they make natural (against all the odds) the idea that society is centred and the related idea that some media-related categories ("reality," "liveness," "media person," and so on) are of overriding importance. This is the paradox of the media's social role in late modernity, an age when the real basis of myth (in a unified social community) is less plausible than ever before, yet the apparent basis of myth is more actively worked on and constructed than ever before.

To retain the term *ritual* in this way, however, means resisting some powerful sceptics who have attacked the vagueness of the term in anthropology (Goody, 1977) and in media studies (Becker, 1998; Corner, 1999). All the more of a problem, you might think, when we qualify the notion of ritual as extensively as I have here. Let me be more specific about how I am using the term *ritual* in relation to media.

Media rituals (in the sense in which I am using the term) are actions that are capable of standing in for wider values and frameworks of understanding connected with the media. This connection works as follows:

1. The formalised actions comprising media rituals are structured around certain media-related *categories*.

2. Those categories (themselves, as already mentioned, reproduced much more widely across the whole ritual space of the media) encode, or stand in for, an underlying *value* associated with the media.

3. This value is the sense that media themselves *represent* the social itself (they are our "natural" access point to social space).

An example would be the organisation of ritualised meetings with celebrities that revolves around the distinction between the "media person" (or celebrity) and the "ordinary person."

The wider resonance, or framing, of such acts derives from the way that the media person–ordinary person distinction replicates a broader hierarchy between people, things, and places "in" the media over people, things, and places not "in" the media; this naturalised hierarchy, in turn, helps reinforce the special status of media themselves. This is what underlies, for example, the common reading of celebrities and their stories as if they stood for something more, something central about contemporary social life.

Media rituals, then, like all rituals, do not so much express order as naturalise it. They formalise categories, and the differences or *boundaries* between categories, in performances that help them seem natural, even legitimate; in this case, the boundaries and category differences on which the apparently "natural" social legitimacy of media institutions is based (Couldry, 2000). This way of thinking about the relations between ritual and power is, of course, very much at odds with the implications of traditional Durkheimian readings of ritual. I am drawing instead on Pierre Bourdieu's (1991) radical revision of Durkheimian notions of ritual in his chapter "Rites of Institution." The ritual dimension, for Bourdieu, of the classic rite of passage (from boy to man) lies not in affirming community via the expression of certain transcendental values but in naturalising the arbitrary boundaries on which the very *possibility* of the rite of passage depends: that is, the assumption that the male-female distinction (which divides in advance those who can undergo the rite of passage and those who cannot) is socially central (Bourdieu, 1991, pp. 117-118). For Bourdieu, rituals are "rites of institution," which institute as natural, and seemingly legitimate, certain key category differences and boundaries (for a fuller discussion, see Couldry, 2003, pp. 27-28).

In developing this post-Durkheimian account of ritual and of media rituals, I would like to note that there are other links to areas of anthropological theory not usually associated at all with the Durkheimian tradition. Ritual appears to be both necessary and open to individual appropriation and reflection, as every ritual performance is always only a rough approximation of some imagined form. This potentially puzzling aspect of ritual is at the root of Maurice Bloch's analysis. Maurice Bloch (turning usual approaches to ritual on their head in a way that recalls Barthes's [1972] notion of myth as a "turnstile" that alternates continually between "reality" and "myth") argues that this very *ambiguity* of ritual is central to its effectiveness (Bloch, 1989, p. 130). It is rituals' oscillation between timeless history and contingent adaptation that allows us to believe in their overriding "truth." It is precisely this type of ambiguity that we need to grasp in understanding some well-known contemporary ritual forms; for example, reality game shows, such as *Big Brother* (Couldry, 2002).

This argument is not, however, an attempt to reinstall ideology in media analysis through the back door. The relationship between rituals and belief is a complex one, far from any simple notion that ritual action expresses ideological contents that are explicitly believed. Clearly, in the case of the media, there is no such explicit media credo (even if someone claimed there was one, it would be quickly disavowed as such), but this does not contradict the idea that the media's authority depends on the incessant work through which the categories underlying media rituals are reproduced.

## THE MEDIA'S RITUAL CATEGORIES

In this section I want to explain more fully the categories of thought at play in media rituals and so complete my account of what we mean by the term *media rituals* in a nonfunctionalist framework. For convenience, let's call these categories "the media's ritual categories." What are they? First, and most important, these basic categories differentiate between anything *in* or *on* or associated *with* "the media" and anything that is not. There is no type of thing in principle to which this difference can not apply; that is what it means to say that it is a *categorical* difference. Like Durkheim's distinction between sacred and profane, the media's ritual categories cut across everything in the social world—anything can be "in" the media. The difference between what is in and not in the media is therefore not natural but a difference that, through continual usage, is constructed as natural (Couldry, 2000, p. 41).

We can observe ourselves and others constructing, as different, things, events, people, places, or worlds in the media. We see this in the construction of particular events as "media events" or in the construction of specific media places as places of "pilgrimage" and in the category differences that get drawn between media people and nonmedia people, such as in the construction of celebrities, stars, and "personalities."

So far, we have looked at the category difference, and hierarchy, between what is in the media and what is not. This is the primary distinction through which the myth of the mediated centre is naturalised. There are important secondary differences as well, however; these derive from the assumption that what is in the media must have higher status than what is not, but they are distinct in their reference point. For example, the term *liveness* derives from the status of what is presented in the media but suggests a little more explicitly that the reason media things matter more is that they are part of society's current "reality." That reality is changing from moment to moment, as media coverage changes, which means that whatever is being shown *now* must, relatively, have a higher status than what is no longer being shown: hence the status of live transmission. Even more explicit, but still naturalised, are the distinctions drawn between the "reality" of the different things media present: for example, the debates about "reality TV" and the pursuit of the "really real" moment of "true" emotion in a televised talk show (Couldry, 2003, chapters 6 and 7).

The media's ritual categories, like all important organising categories, are reproduced in countless different circumstances. It is these categories that in media rituals are worked upon and further naturalised through bodily performance. Once again, it is Bourdieu's work on ritual that is particularly helpful in understanding this link (particularly that part of Bourdieu's work that draws on Durkheim's close collaborator, Marcel Mauss). Ritual, Bourdieu argues, is not an abstract expression of an idea but, instead, a pattern of thought realised through embodied performance; ritual enactment is inseparable from the "practical mastery" of the ritual agent who has internalised the key distinctions and categories on which the ritual is based (Bourdieu, 1977, pp. 87-95, discussed by Bell, 1992, pp. 107-108).

The anthropologist of religion Catherine Bell has usefully developed these ideas to argue that it is such practical mastery that is the endpoint of religious ritualisation, "the body invested with a 'sense' of ritual" (Bell, 1992, p. 98). Our sense of ritual—of certain forms of action as having heightened significance—is one way in which broad hierarchies are reinforced through the details of local performance. In this way, ritual performance suggests a "higher" order of things:

> Fundamental to all strategies of ritualization . . . is the appeal to a more embracing authoritative order that lies beyond the immediate situation. Ritualization is generally a way of engaging some wide consensus that those acting [in ritual] are doing so as a type of natural response to a world conceived and interpreted as affected by forces that transcend it. (Bell, 1997, p. 169)

This notion of ritualisation is perfectly adapted, as already suggested, to help us understand media rituals and their deep hinterland in everyday media-oriented practice.

Now, at last, we are in a position to explain more specifically what types of action might count as media rituals. Let me first approach this through the types of places where we might look for media rituals (there are a number of possibilities, still little researched or studied):

- ▣ Sites where people cross from the nonmedia world into the media world, such as studios, or any place where filming or media production goes on
- ▣ Sites where nonmedia people expect to encounter people (or things) in the media (for example, celebrities)
- ▣ Moments in which nonmedia people perform for the media; for example, posing for a camera, even if this takes place in the course of action that is otherwise not formalised

In all these situations, people act out category differences that reproduce in condensed form the idea, or derivatives of the idea, that media are our "natural" access point to society's "centre." What types of action might these be? Here are some examples:

- People calling out as their presence "on air" is acknowledged (the studio chat show host turns to them and asks them to clap, "show what they feel")[9]
- People either holding back, or rushing forward, at the sight of a celebrity
- People holding back before they enter a place connected with the media, so as to emphasise the boundary they cross by entering it
- Performances by media people that acknowledge their own specialness before a crowd of nonmedia people
- Performances by nonmedia people when they are in certain types of formalised media context, such as a talk show

How far, in any particular situation, mere ritual*isation* flips over into the formality of a full-blown media ritual is a matter of empirical detail. The key point to understand, however, is that the antifunctionalist notion of media rituals developed here spans both media rituals as such and the wider space of ritualisation that lies behind them and that sustains them. The concept of media ritual and ritualisation therefore links, in a single explanatory arc, intense moments of personal media performance (someone revealing private truths before unknown millions on a talk show) and the everyday banality of a whole room turning round because a celebrity is thought to have entered the room. Both these examples—and all the different kinds of situations that lie between them—are part of how we live out as truth the "myth of the mediated centre."[10]

## CONCLUSION

The approach offered here aims to confound the conventional association of "ritual" with the preservation of some assumed traditional social

"order." On the contrary, the complexities of this account—and particularly its resolute antifunctionalism—are designed to address a paradox that is profoundly and even distinctively modern. This is a paradox of ambiguity. It was Henri Lefebvre who fixed on the ambiguity of everyday life in his writings in the early days of electronic media (Lefebvre, 1958/1991, p. 18): The ambiguity that comes from the way the private space of everyday life is already crossed by countless trajectories of power (the economy, political order, media narratives). So, too, in assessing the media's wider social consequences, we cannot separate out our hopes, our myths, our moments of togetherness and personal expression, on the one hand, or conflict, on the other hand, from the mediated social forms they now almost always take and the uneven power relations on which those forms are based. To understand this, we need, certainly, a model of the media's ritual dimensions, but it must be one that has moved beyond any vestiges of functionalism.

The result is to return to James Carey, but without either the functionalism or the neglect for questions of power that, because Carey attributed them to Durkheim, led him to deny the theoretical legacy he shared in common with Durkheim (Rothenbuhler, 1993). It was Carey who put the paradox and challenge of the media's social impacts better than anyone else: "reality is a scarce resource . . . the fundamental form of power is the power to define, allocate, and display that resource" (1989, p. 87).

How can we doubt that the fundamental question about mediation is a question of power, the uneven distribution of the power to influence representations of social "reality"? A post-Durkheimian view, however, holds onto Philip Elliott's (1982) insight in one of the first, but still one of the best, essays on media and ritual: "ritual . . . is a structured performance in which not all participants are equal" (p. 145). So, too, inevitably, are even the most apparently unifying moments of our media experience. That is the point of applying Durkheim's insights to a world in which all possibilities of "acting in common"[11] are already mediated through social forms (media forms) that are inseparable from highly uneven effects of power.

## NOTES

1. See, most recently, Gitlin (2002).

2. See Martin-Barbero (1993), Couldry (2000), Silverstone (in press).

3. For example, Myerhoff (1977, p. 199), Lewis (1980, p. 25), Douglas (1984, pp. 63-64), Smith (1987, pp. 109-110), Humphrey and Laidlaw (1994, pp. 88-89), Rappaport (1999, p. 24). See also Carey (1989, p. 21) and Rothenbuhler (1998, p. 57) in media theory.

4. For more detail, see Couldry (2000, chapters 1 and 3), drawing on Durkheim (1912/1995).

5. See Bourdieu (1977, p. 203, note 49).

6. See Bell (1992, 1997); Asad (1993, pp. 87-79); Handelman (1998, p. x), and, above all, Bourdieu (1977, 1991). See, in media studies, Saenz (1994, p. 584).

7. See Bourdieu (1991), Asad (1993, p. 53), Bell (1997, pp. 81-82), Elliott (1982, p. 145), and Bloch (1989).

8. See Couldry (2000, chapter 1).

9. This is the aspect of Karin Becker's (1995) excellent article that perhaps comes closest to the approach developed here.

10. See Couldry (2003, chapter 3) for more discussion.

11. I am referring here to Durkheim's (1995) fundamental claim that "society can *only* feel its influence in action, and [society] is not in action unless the individuals who compose it are assembled and *act in common*" (p. 421, italics added; discussed in Stedman Jones, 2001, p. 214).

## REFERENCES

Asad, T. (1993). *Genealogies of religion.* Baltimore, MD: Johns Hopkins Press.

Barthes, R. (1972). *Mythologies.* London: Paladin.

Becker, K. (1995). Media and the ritual process. *Media Culture and Society, 17,* 629-646.

Becker, K. (1998). The Diana debate. *Screen, 39*(3), 289-293.

Bell, C. (1992). *Ritualt theory, ritual practice.* New York: Oxford University Press.

Bell, C. (1997). *Ritual: Perspectives and dimensions.* New York: Oxford University Press.

Bloch, M. (1989). *Ritual history and power.* London: Athlone Press.

Bourdieu, P. (1977). *Outline of a theory of practice.* Cambridge, England: Cambridge University Press.

Bourdieu, P. (1991). *Language and symbolic power.* Cambridge, England: Polity.

Carey, J. (1989). *Communication as culture.* Boston: Unwin Hyman.

Corner, J. (1999). *Media ritual and identity* [review]. *European Journal of Cultural Studies, 2*(3), 416-419.

Couldry, N. (2000). *The place of media power.* London: Routledge.

Couldry, N. (2002). Playing for celebrity: *Big Brother* as ritual event. *Television and New Media, 3*(3), 283-294.

Couldry, N. (2003). *Media rituals: A critical approach.* London: Routledge.

Dayan, D., & Katz, E. (1992). *Media events: The live broadcasting of history.* Cambridge, MA: Harvard University Press.

Douglas, M. (1984). *Purity and danger.* London: Routledge.

Durkheim, E. (1995). *The elementary forms of religious life* (K. Fields, Trans.). Glencoe, IL: Free Press. (Original work published 1912)

Elliott, P. (1982). Press performance as political ritual. In H. Christian (Ed.), *The sociology of journalism and the press.* Keele, England: University of Keele.

Ellis, J. (2000). *Seeing things.* London: IB Tauris.

Foucault, M. (1981). *The history of sexuality* (Vol. 1). Harmondsworth, England: Penguin.

Giddens, A. (1985). *The nation-state and violence.* Cambridge, England: Polity.

Giddens, A. (1991). *Modernity and self-identity.* Cambridge, England: Polity.

Ginsburg, F. (1994). Culture/media: A mild polemic. *Anthropology Today, 10*(2), 5-15.

Gitlin, T. (2002). *Media unlimited.* New York: Henry Holt.

Goody, J. (1977). Against ritual. In S. Moore & B. Myerhoff (Eds.), *Secular ritual.* Amsterdam: Van Gorcum.

Hall, S. (1977). Culture, media and "the ideological effect." In J. Curran, M. Gurevitch, & J. Woollacott (Eds.), *Mass communications and society.* London: Edward Arnold.

Handelman, D. (1998). *Models and mirrors: Towards an anthropology of public events* (2nd ed.). Oxford, England: Berg.

Heelas, P., Lash, S., & Morris, P. (Eds.). (1994). *De-traditionalization.* Oxford, England: Blackwell.

Humphrey, C., & Laidlaw, J. (1994). *The archetypal actions of ritual.* Oxford, England: Clarendon Press.

Lash, S. (2002) *Critique of information.* London: Sage.

Lazarsfeld, P., & Merton, R. (1969). Mass communication, popular taste and organized social action. In W. Schramm (Ed.), *Mass communications research.* Urbana-Champaign: Illinois University Press.

Lefebvre, H. (1991). *Critique of everyday life* (Vol. 1, J. Moore, Trans.). London: Verso. (Original work published 1958)

Lewis, G. (1980). *Day of shining red: An essay on understanding ritual.* Cambridge, England: Cambridge University Press.

Lukes, S. (1973). *Emile Durkheim: His life and work.* Harmondsworth, England: Penguin.

Lukes, S. (1975). Political ritual and social integration. *Sociology, 29,* 289-305.

Martin-Barbero, J. (1993). *Communication culture and hegemony.* London: Sage.

Mattelart, A. (1994). *The invention of communication.* Minneapolis: University of Minnesota Press.

Meyrowitz, J. (1994). Medium theory. In D. Crowley & D. Mitchell (Eds.), *Communication theory today.* Cambridge, England: Polity.

Myerhoff, B. (1977). We don't wrap herring in a printed page: Fusion, fictions and contingency in secular ritual. In S. Moore & B. Myerhoff (Eds.), *Secular ritual.* Amsterdam: Van Gorcum.

Pickering, W. (1984). *Durkheim's sociology of religion.* London: Routledge & Kegan Paul.

Rappaport, R. (1999). *Ritual and religion in the making of humanity.* Cambridge, England: Cambridge University Press.

Rothenbuhler, E. (1993). Argument for a Durkheimian theory of the communicative. *Journal of Communication, 43*(3), 148-153.

Rothenbuhler, E. (1998). *Ritual communication.* Thousand Oaks: Sage.

Saenz, M. (1994). Television viewing as a cultural practice. In H. Newcomb (Ed.), *Television: The critical view.* New York: Oxford University Press.

Silverstone, R. (in press). Mediation and communication. In C. Calhoun, C. Rojek, & B. Turner (Eds.), *The international handbook of sociology.* London: Sage.

Smith, J. Z. (1987). *To take place: Toward theory in ritual.* Chicago: Chicago University Press.

Stedman Jones, S. (2001). *Durkheim revisited.* Cambridge, England: Polity.

# 7

# RITUAL MEDIA

## Historical Perspectives and Social Functions

PASCAL LARDELLIER

TRANSLATED BY PAUL GRANT

T his chapter attempts to demonstrate how many rites and media maintain a pragmatic relationship (in the primary Austinian sense of the term), linking their symbolic, political, and institutional effects. To this extent, we can rightly evoke the "ritual media"[1] forms of expression and concept, which maintain a dialectical relationship, to mix their effects in a *performative* manner.[2]

Opening a dialogue from afar with Daniel Dayan and Elihu Katz's work *La Télévision Cérémonielle* [Ceremonial Television],[3] we will examine the eloquent durability of ritual media, as well as the surprising ability of information techniques and social communication to ritualize their discourse and the modes of collective participation that are induced as a result.

It is not only audiovisual media that are concerned with this problematic. Giving historical resonance to our point, we will demonstrate that more than four centuries ago in the France and Europe of the *Ancien Règime* (that of the 16th and 17th centuries), political rites maintained a very tight relationship with the ceremonial publications that perpetuated them by granting them a form of textual and iconographic eternity.

We will also establish the fundamental role allocated to the gaze as an instance of legitimation and a vector of belonging during these ritual programs. For ceremonial media "produce the communities to whom they address themselves" (Dayan); they produce these communities by way of a common gaze and shared emotions, by this intuition of history, which takes hold of their "spect-actors,"[4] transporting them into another space-time barely softened by the technical rectory: It is the veritable fact of *seeing*, and of *seeing with*, that creates the conditions for political change. Starting out singular, the ritual gaze subsumes itself in a collective gaze and there reconstitutes itself to find the symbolic means of *performing* the ceremonial spectacle, to the point of transforming political and institutional realities.

Always needing witnesses to establish their legitimacy, the ritual media put their "diasporic communities" (Katz & Dayan) in contact with

---

**Author's Note:** This chapter owes much to Daniel Dayan and Elihu Katz's *Ceremonial Television.*

history and contribute to the reinforcement of social bonds that are placed at a level where the audience is recast and reunited with regard to the retransmission, rich with symbolic effectiveness, thanks to its active participation in the spectacle.

Media and rites are thus complementary, having as their common goal collective participation and sometimes even universal communion, thanks to the power of "seeing with." The lens of the televisual camera constitutes from now on, and at the same time, a panoptic eye and a universal mirror or screen. How fortunate for "those in charge."

## RITES AND MEDIA : CROSSED INTERESTS, LINKED EFFECTS

To begin with, some evidence: The big institutional rites are *naturally* established in the media, the ritual retransmissions that perpetuate them being, if not obligatory,[5] at least obliged—in journalistic jargon, "impossible to circumvent." In fact, the quasitotality of important political events (visits from heads of state, nominations, royal weddings, funerals) is retransmitted with television and even radio. These events are reported at greater length by the newspapers, via special supplements. It would seem that something of capital importance for the various political regimes and institutions is played out in this way.

The primary virtue of these media retransmissions, in comparison with former rites, resides in the fact that they increase the audience of the big rites, conferring upon them a true universality. This is crucial when we again become conscious of the functions of adhesion and belonging fulfilled by the rites, as well as the power of aggregation— linked to the potential for emotivity and dramatization that conceal audiovisual media. Thus, to the seemingly candid question posed by Daniel Dayan, "Can one become a pilgrim without ever leaving his room?" the answer is undoubtedly *yes*.

More than inert partners of the event, the media today in fact constitute "necessary passages," guarantors of the existence of the rite, payees of the social and historical construction of the event. For, as Dayan says,

It is clear that television doesn't play the part of an indifferent "tube," of a simple transmission system of the event, but that its technical nature doubles through a rhetoric aimed at shaping the spectators' answers, imposing upon them if not the exact contents, at least a certain register of experience, and proposing roles to them which, even if they negotiate them, form part of the construction or the definition of the situation presented.[6]

Residing in the insight that the media today are necessary to the historical construction of public events is the innovation and force of this media anthropology approach, represented by E. Katz, D. Dayan, B. Myerhoff, M. Coman, and J. McAloon. The media anthropology approach sets media studies free from those approaches that grant too little importance to the cultural context of reception and the modes of collective appropriation of the ritual contents. It revalues the socioeconomic analyses, which neglect to take into account the anthropological base of the programming of certain types of broadcasts. Erring on this point, these quantitative approaches appear forgetful of the deep aspirations of the communities and institutions (even of the media) *coming to the rite* to live a "dramatized social dramaturgy" (according to V. Turner[7]), whose sublime character far exceeds the usual audiometric and social questions specific to media interrogations.

In this sense, anthropology, applied to the media simultaneously and in a double circular motion, renews anthropology by opening up to contemporary objects (specifically the audiovisual) but also the study of the media, by revealing the adhesive force of certain types of programs that situate their influence well beyond that of the programs of "everyday television." The ritual media thus cultivate a specificity that is linked as much to their contents as to their social effects.

The institutions organizing the big ritual ceremonies attach great importance to their mediatizations, often assuming sufficient importance to allow themselves to disorganize the schedules of the usual programs (as Daniel Dayan says), but there is also a certain finality assigned to these retransmissions: Nothing less than an inscription in history and, above all, the community sharing of this collective conscience, which will always result in social regeneration.

Thus the mediated rite is not a "subrite" or ersatz ritual, an avatar that technical acquisition would soften: On the contrary, it is a rite demultiplied, vectorized, made potentially universal and "eternal,"[8] and which finds in the modes of participation and "consumption" that it generates the conditions of a symbolic action suitable to the in situ rite in general. Between the two there exists a difference in degree but not a difference in kind.

In fact, certain functions and quasisimilar finalities are granted to the great political and religious ceremonies, as well as to their media retransmissions and preservation: legitimacy, allegiance, membership, via the effects of "seeing with."[9] We must also not forget the primarily normative character of the rite, which "works for order"[10] and in favor of the institutions, always contributing to legitimize them.

## THE SYMBOLIC POWER OF MEDIA RITES

Media rites liberate themselves from the political and religious spheres to find new places, new actors, and new typically postmodern practices. Here the worlds of sports and "cultural industries" form new territories of preference, the only obligation of the media ritualization residing in the media's ability to script and dramatize these events. It is also important that the principal actors of these rites (movie stars, famous athletes, various celebrities) hold some degree of charisma, in the absence of which the ceremony will be not attractive, credible, or legitimate. Movies, sports, and even television now produce dedication and awards ceremonies ad nauseam. They ostensibly plagiarize the established ritual codes, awkwardly seeking, through an inappropriate austerity, to summon symbolic efficacy, with the risks and dangers of the ritual's becoming soft, banalized in these "profane liturgies,"[11] which are no longer such.

When their subjects are not dishonoured, the ritual media play the part of symbolic operators invading the legitimation process of the actors and the institutions summoning it. The authors of

*ceremonial television* are formal: The importance seems to be for a community or an institution to have access to an antenna, to have the right to retransmission. Seeing a historical event in the pacified context of its ritualization means that its "spect-actors" are able to assure themselves that a specific change is inescapable and, more important, that it has occurred. This change, "played" by the institutional actors, indeed occurs in the eyes of its witnesses. That is how many contemporary revolutions, violent or " velvet," were played, and won, with the antenna, and were in fact already accomplished by the time their retransmission was authorized, just like the convocation of the States-General, when the drafting of grievance reports allowed the French revolutionary elan to express itself and find its intrinsic dynamics. These ritual programs shape the conditions of change through the media at the same time that they socially authorize them.

## THE LONG GENEALOGY OF THE MEDIA RITUAL

The work of Daniel Dayan and Elihu Katz had the great merit, in the mid-1990s, of clarifying the deeply anthropological dimension of televisual programs when they retransmit rites of a political or religious nature. These media rites have increased in power since the end of World War II, acquiring (thanks to the audiovisual element) a visibility and social power that multiplies by ten the effects of the traditional ceremonies. However, the emergence of ritual media does not date from the appearance of television in the middle of the 20th century, far from it: Their history is hundreds of years old. Well before the emergence of the audiovisual, methods of adopting other forms and supports were known, all with the same goals in mind: to praise the great, to legitimize institutions already in place, and to create the emotional conditions of popular adhesion to celebration. All of this works together to "manufacture" the official story in a very pragmatic way.

Even before the 15th century, chronicles and other "official reports," published as soon as was possible, accompanied all the great political and religious events, marriages, crownings, nominations, solemn entrances, the taking up of duties, visits, burials, and oaths. The media of the time fulfilled this function of "setting in memory," and therefore of perpetuation, as much as of commemoration and homage. The ritual media intend to leave a trace in history that testifies to the inevitably historical dimension of the event in which they take part at the same time that they give an account of it, and this is true of every epoch.

## Gaze, Voice, and Memory: Vectors of a Ritual Media Pragmatic

The ritual media do not therefore create a genre sui generis, smooth and compact: Differences of technical order, among others, separate them. It would not be very appropriate to put in the same category as the televised retransmissions of crownings and burials the anthologies that, in the 16th century, recounted royal triumphs, even though these were quite as ritual in their form, content, and modes of "editorial consumption."

Although the subject covered is the same and the canons of the genre have, ultimately, evolved very little over the centuries, distinctions must be made between the ritual media of immediacy, such as direct audiovisual media, and others, such as these ceremonial works, which gained in longevity what they lost in the moment. Still, if the techniques are different, it seems that it is the mode of gazing at these ritual media and their political essence that make it possible to consider them as fundamentally analogous, belonging to the same family.

In fact, one could consider that it is above all by this relation of the gaze that the ritual media create their communities, the televiewers being transformed into eyewitnesses of history, which is played and written before their eyes. To look at is to recognize and to take part; witnessing the event's broadcast is to belong to the community, which celebrates itself through this retransmission. In this sense, the gaze of the audience on these mediated ritual spectacles is always active:

It also contains political recognition, establishing the citizenship and the religious or political membership of those who voluntarily exercise it.

Let us reaffirm how much the body, the mobilization and the exercise of all the senses (in particular the sight, and therefore hearing) are crucial elements of the accomplishment of the rite as "total spectacle," complete guarantors of its symbolic effectiveness. Dayan and Katz say,

> This gestural dimension reaffirms itself. But this time it is transposed no longer on to a discursive act, but to the exercise of the gaze . . . by the intermediary of these roles, the simple presence of the televiewers is shaped in a kind of act.[12]

It is not only the gaze that produces belonging and legitimacy in this way. For the rite always arises from the establishing of a context of dramatization, in which other physical factors occur on both sides.

The same applies to the ritual voice, which could not be light, lively, or cheerful unless it seriously failed in its mission of austerity. When great political ceremonies are broadcast on television, the journalists are no longer simply commentators or analysts: They become panegyrists for the duration of the rite and its retransmission. The tone they choose to employ will prove crucial, reentering "the production of history" in a straight line.[13]

Because the rites are mediated, one might think that there is no direct contact or true interaction between the ceremonial actors and the televiewers. In fact, the former inevitably take into account the camera and, therefore, the televiewers as well; as for the latter, they respond to the spectacle with emotional demonstrations, destroying the distance imposed by technique by overinvesting their emotional reactions and, above all, by the sharing of a gaze. We must not forget that all rites are, by nature, spectacle—but, within the framework of its televised retransmission, the media ritual is also scripted and redirected.

What televiewer has not been moved, sometimes even to tears, while watching a ritual television program: marriage, nomination, or, *a fortiori*, the burial of a celebrity? A form of communication and, even, an indirect but no less powerful communion is thus instituted.[14] Further, this mode of participation is often produced in an abyss by the media, which, at the time of the broadcast of great political or religious ceremonies, place cameras in public places, such as cafes that are retransmitting the ceremony, and even in the homes of volunteer families. The "meta-reports" are then able to tell how "the event was lived by the man in the street," by "Mr. Everyone."

It goes without saying that these extremely consensual reports systematically accord a large part to the emotional demonstrations, collective happiness, and ecstasy before the beauty of the lived rite "as if one were there."[15] This constitutes the counterpoint as well as the complement of the ritual construction of these historical images, fitting to retain as an event because it is a double relationship with the memory of the event, as much the social and the historical, that establishes the ritual media.

Let us return to the ceremonial works that related the triumphs and royal entrances in the France of the *Ancien Règime*. A remarkable logic of correspondence and preservation was put in place, from the event to the book and from text to images. These anthologies, with the means available to them (inevitably more limited than those of the contemporary audiovisual techniques), were often "synesthesic," making visible the architectures and the processions, audible the orations of municipal officials, and comprehensible the Greek and Latin mottoes. Above all we should contemplate the great copper engraving placed at the end of the volume, which reproduced the procession through the city by including all its protagonists in synoptic and panoptic movement, assembling the exhaustivity of ritual space-time. Offering a linearity to the event, these ceremonial books endeavored to typographically reproduce that which was the political rite in situ. The official, ephemeral procession was perpetuated by means of a book, chapter by chapter. In turn, the reader became both the spectator and the privileged actor, who, strolling through the collection, sauntered in the same way by proxy in a civic procession and a monarchical ideal, from one point to the next, by reviving each one of these ritual moments, finally understanding, thanks to the erudition of the authors, the secret intelligence of the rite and its thousand symbolic and scenographic subtleties.

In this patient inveiglement, these anthologies and their engravings establish one of their profound raisons d'etre. The two-dimensional surface of the book, aided by these synesthetic artifices, maintained the ritual, festive, and event-like nature of the triumph. A new iconographic and rhetorical perspective was thus established, perennializing the ephemeral character of the rite. What the work lost in density and in life, it regained in longevity. The collection celebrated memory, protesting against the transitory and ephemeral character of the rite. Without a written account of a royal entrance, nothing would have reached us; the event would have definitively disappeared, evaporated in the transience of its unfolding.

The Renaissance engravings that decorate the anthologies reporting triumphs and royal entrances, like the official photographs taken today at great political and religious rites, nevertheless tell something other than the "truth" of the event. They show an ideal of reality that is precisely ritual. These images say both more and less at the same time, by reducing the difference between what the rite was (assembling a "having-been-there"[16]) and what it could have been in an ideal unfolding. It is to the individual and social memory of the one who looks at that these "perfect" images are addressed, as they propose the synoptic sight of an ideal—and the ideal of a synoptic sight—of a moment that tends irresistibly toward a history devoid of turbulence, in which all is clean, pure, and mastered.

Today we are still very close to this logic: video recordings and the great luxurious works commemorating the visits of the Pope, as well as royal marriages, and funerals, of which the British, with all the trials and tribulations of their Crown, are great consumers.

## THE SOCIAL FUNCTIONS OF THE RITUAL MEDIA

Five functions can be attributed to the ritual media. They are exercised by the institutions organizing the rite, as much as by its actors and its audience.

The first of these functions is *testimonial*. Essentially, the speech and images of the ritual media testify to something *which has occurred* by showing it, as though attesting to its authenticity. This memory can be approached through the double angle of recollection and commemoration, each one returning to different modalities of enunciation. In other words, the ritual media *testify*, or one could say they set in memory. The media also allow the formal expression of the emotion, joy, and sorrow of the people constituting the community of the spect-actors of the ceremonial event retransmitted.

In the same way, the ritual media *monumentalize* the event by constructing the official image of it that the collective memory will keep; above all, by restoring it through the magnificent and idealized prism that, by nature, creates and governs the ritual principle. Moreover, one may consider that the rite is a "political monument."

This function of monumentalization joins the preceding functions of memory. Further, in the case of the engravings representing royal entrances, this function takes on its full dimension by means of a very strong connection linking architecture to the book. It is indeed a rare, and, in fact, even a singular, case, in which it is the book that perpetuates an exceptionally *ephemeral* architecture that, etymologically, lasted "but a single day." This work was thus monumentalized, in the most literal sense of the word.

From time immemorial, stone and marble have been the materials of eternal memory, of petrified memory. This architectural petrification seemed to be proof of a primarily material perpetuity. Here, the opposite forced itself through: It was the book that kept and sustained. The epigraphic quotations in the book that captured the ephemeral character of provisional architectures were symbolic, because the perpetuation was editorial. As Jouhaud notes, "Thanks to its epigraphies, does the book not present itself as the last monument of the entrance? That which would contain everything and would alone be capable of giving a true end to the party?"[17]

Next, the ritual media tend to legitimize the events that they retransmit or retranscribe through the (obvious) function of *legitimation*.

To reach ritual mediatization is, de facto, for a personality or an institution, to be recognized as legitimate, *respectable*. Many institutions contribute in granting this legitimation, which becomes effective with the retransmission or media narration. It is as much the receiving authorities as the media protagonists who accept the interruption or modification of the usual programs so that a historical event may be broadcast, which in turn becomes historical, thanks to this retransmission. Here one can invoke the two televised funerals, which occurred a few hours apart, introducing Diana Spencer, Princess of Wales, and Mother Teresa into the pantheon of great women of the 20th century.

Whatever the questions or shadowy areas able to tarnish the life of "Lady Di," a funeral retransmitted in such a way is to some extent the history that recovers it and grants these women, a posteriori, the charisma of exceptional characters.

The ritual media *vectorize* ritual events in the same way. They may offer and occasionally succeed in producing a worldwide audience. That is their greatest success, their innovative character. For this reason, the papal blessings given *urbi et orbi* from St. Peter's constitute eloquent examples of the nature of the ritual media: Previously, only the pilgrims present in Rome were in attendance. Since the advent of television, however, hundreds of millions of people can take part in these blessings, incorporating themselves into the vast Catholic community, the great family of Christendom, and this is thanks to the gaze and the virtually shared emotion and prayer; that is to say, thanks to televisual technology. And the formula *urbi et orbi*, precisely, has found its full sense because television permits the world (*orbi*) to participate and at St. Peter's itself, the benediction is given in the city (*urbi*). Television has accomplished what was formerly just a metaphor, or mystical performance.

Finally, and above all, the ritual media proceed to a *dramatization* of the events that they retransmit. A joyful tonality habitually characterizes televisual speech. Functioning according to established codes, based on intimacy and genuine relaxation, the audiovisual media fulfill the function of social bonds through this bias. On the other hand, the ritual media establish a distance and space-time of programming that dramatize their retransmissions.

The rare media context (retransmission of big sporting events) during which the consumer can live an event in its total continuity, with unity of action in time and space, also belonged to the tragedy of antiquity. Only at this price—total immersion—will the spect-actors become aware of the historical dimension of that which they are in the middle of witnessing and grant it a form of credibility. This dramatization, which also expresses itself in the style of filming and commentary, establishes a particular context of reception, mainly the proof of the historicization of the event—because History with a capital H is serious by nature.

## A Singular Inversion, of Actuality With History

The case often made against the media charges them with making history banal. They would soften it to transform it into a "current affair," with a continual stream of flashes each day erasing the tide of images from the day before in a crazy and amnesic race forward. Television has been the first to undergo this trial. As a whole, the ritual media radically reverse these fears concerning the dilution of history and conceal the objections addressed to the information system. If the event retransmitted has a sufficient audience and legitimacy, the media engage the televiewers live with "history in the making."

These ritual media therefore manage to thwart this evolution of history, to radically reverse it, which is thanks to these five invaluable and complementary functions of *vectorization, legitimation, monumentalization, testimony*, and, especially, *dramatization*.

Social, political, and institutional changes arise due to the fact that the ritually received guest—sovereign, president, Pope—is able to make sense of and produce transformations in the symbolic order, finally acting only through ceremony: The guest presents "not a program, but a project"[18] that is primarily of the orders of desire

and dream. Above all, the guest introduces sense during a time of turbulence that is often caused by his arrival. The ritual guest is at the same time the poison and the antidote, the disorder and the order. He or she precipitates and catalyses a movement that is only paradoxical in appearance. This is what specifically maintains the guest's charisma. According to Dayan and Katz,

> The interpretation proposed by the actors is powerfully directive. Like the wizard of Lévi-Strauss, the ceremonial actor reformulates the situation in which he participates with the assistance of culturally accepted paradigms. This situation then acquires an intelligibility, but at the interior of a dynamic directed towards a precise outcome. It aims to "make do," and counts on a mythical development.[19]

Inscribed by political mythologies, the symbolic program proposed by the ritual guest fertilizes the social body and the communities concerned with its mobilizing power. It creates a bond then, by mobilizing springs that exceed it and are powerfully anthropological. That this arrival is mediated hardly changes things. The ritual mobs will be more numerous, only agreeing to take part, even remotely, in something magical, almost miraculous: a gift-contra-gift during which the actors facing off share a filter that reveals more than it veils, adding to the scene utopian desires of metamorphosis and fusion, introducing into the social body a share of this Utopia formatted by the rite, which founds an idealized social bracket and institutes a new *age d'or*.

The ritual community, regenerated by this historical and even mythical moment, will keep the diffuse, but sublimated, trace of it. "Having-been-there," "to have seen it," "to have lived it," and to be able to share these experiences, in which each first imprinted the body of the other, creates a shared history by all.

A reference must still be made to the *communitas* of Victor Turner, in which one grasps the extreme density of the audiences of these ritual media spectacles. Transgressing the established social strata, transcending the usual barriers and inertias, these retransmissions "produce their audience," which, although indefinite and transient before the usual programs, are "substantialized," or (one could say) become "flesh and blood," to become a true community, conscious of existing, and in which the members are living a historical moment together.

It is sometimes on the scale of a whole country that the ritual media raise the number of members of their diasporic community, which is evanescent and virtual, indeed, but oh, how powerful and dense! For they are masterfully welded and bound by an emotion, a memory, and a common gaze. On November 22, 1963, the day of the assassination of President John F. Kennedy in Dallas, the whole of America stopped in the middle of the afternoon. Tens of millions of people turned on their televisions or radios and began to cry together, sometimes so far from each other, but yet suddenly so close. Even the journalists cried, watching from the other side of the screen, which was in fact a mirror. A few days later, at the time of the funeral, this time openly and dramatically ritual, a large part of the planet communed together on the altar of emotion, tears, and history. Thus is the miracle and vertigiousness of the ritual media.

## NOTES

1. The expression *ritual media* will be used many times in these pages. To avoid it being used in such a manner that I could be accused of language abuse, I should first specify that a medium cannot have a ritual *nature*. By *ritual media* we understand ritual programs that emerge as a media type as a whole, thanks to some specificities of stylistic and morphological nature and considering their reception modalities.

2. The term *performative* comes from language science, and it is used by the American linguist J.-L. Austin, of whom we have already made reference. From "to perform"—to take action, to transform—the term signifies just words about acts that, by extension, can produce effects, and thus possess the force, in some contexts, to transform realities and reinforce the validity of another situation. For example, a *performative* path might go from the verdict to the court, from the diagnostic to the hospital, from the mystery of marriage to the church. J.-L. Austin discusses the bases of his theoretical point of view in the work *How to Do Things With Words* (originally a

William James lecture, 1955; 2nd ed., 1975, J. O. Urmson & M. Sbisà, Eds., Cambridge, MA: Harvard University Press).

3. D. Dayen and E. Katz, 1996, *La télévision cérémonielle*, Paris: PUF; 1992, *Media events: The live broadcasting of history*, Cambridge, MA: Harvard University Press. The latter book is based principally on the analysis of a body of mediated events with very strong political echoes, such as the first journey of Pope John Paul II to Poland.

4. We suggest the concept of "spect-actors" as a definition of the participants in community rituals. Indeed, a fundamental role is given to their vision of the ritual process, considering that while the ritual is occurring, nobody is just an actor or just a spectator. Its spectacular logic, the same as the construction that says the instrument reflects its own light, imposes that both "actors" and "spectators" watch at the same time they play their ceremonial roles. The face-to-face arrangement of the two groups in the "mirror" of the ritual shows that each group has its own different nature: The groups are totally asymmetrical but fundamentally complementary. This neologism of "spect-actor" has been used in other circumstances and by other authors, especially in reference to cinema theory.

5. Of course, rituals and mass media do not possess a conscience: At the back of some we will always find political, military, or religious institutions that refer to political and economic rituals in the mass media. At the same time, a convention has been created of retransmitting the big events: marriages, funerals, hosting of state officials, officials taking part in public functions. Dayan and Katz stop in their work at an important point: that of the discussions preceding the retransmitting of ritual celebrations and that of the premises of this "historicization."

6. Daniel Dayan, 1990, Présentation du Pape en voyageur: Télévision, expérience rituelle, dramaturgie politique [Presentation of the Pope during his journeys: Television, the ritual experience, and political dramaturgy], *Terrain, 15*("Paraître en Public"), p. 20.

7. Victor Turner, 1969, *Le phénomène rituel: Structure et contre-structure* [Ritual phenomena: Structure and counterstructure] (G. Guillet, Trans.), Paris: PUF.

8. Edited or recorded, the mediated ritual will actually be kept and contemplated. This is one of its functions: The memory that continues producing the history.

9. Daniel Dayan and Elihu Katz explain the fact that virtual a priori communities of ritual media tend to shape themselves as a body when people group together to contemplate these celebratory events. Televiewers gather and reconstitute in spontaneous communities, as these programs require a "collective view."

10. G. Balandier, 1988, *Le désordre: Eloge du mouvement* [Disorder: Elegy for the movement], Paris: Fayard.

11. C. Rivière, 1995, *Les rites profanes* [Profane rites], Paris: PUF.

12. Dayan and Katz, *La télévision cérémonielle, op. cit.*, p. 134.

13. Adopting—in a more prosaic manner—the significance of Dayan and Katz's reference to the fact that the mass media has a force that permits the transformation of history, the American information channel CNN explicitly exposes this as a principle: *to witness history in the making.*

14. According to the hypothesis of Dayan and Katz, ceremonial politics and big ceremonial policies would express a tendency toward fusion, demonstrated in situ but also in extension by collective participation in media retransmissions. These are thus used to create a continuity between the filmed groups and the televiewer groups. Such continuity provokes an oceanic feeling, a euphoric loss of the limits of the self, an imaginary integration into a congregation in a state of *comunitas* (Dayan & Katz, Présentation du Pape, *op. cit.*, p. 20).

15. The British royal family became specialists in these celebration reports, which proclaimed the life of the Crown. Very often happy, even if more recently dramatic, such reports fed on the fashion of the emotional community. They are always constructed in this manner, with an important amount of attention given to the manner in which the subjects of Her Gracious Majesty give life to the event transmitted live. In 2001, relative signs were transmitted through the media coverage of the royal celebrations of the British Crown from Buckingham Palace directly to the editorial staffs of the biggest newspapers and radio and TV channels. British journalists were amazed by what seemed to them unacceptable to their working freedom and their professional conscience.

16. This expression belongs to Roland Barthes, who, in *La chambre claire*, described the essence of photographic action: to observe precisely the "having-been-there" of what was observed. Roland Barthes, 1980, *La chambre claire: Note sur la photographie* [Camera lucida: Reflections on photography], Paris: Gallimard-Cahiers du cinéma.

17. C. Jouhaud, 1987, Imprimer l'événement [Publishing events], Roger Charier (Ed.), *Usages de l'imprimé aux XIVe-XVIIe siècles* [The culture of print in the 14th-17th centuries], Paris: Fayard, p. 414.

18. Dayan and Katz, *La télévision cérémonielle, op. cit.*

19. Daniel Dayan and Elihu Katz, 1995, Télévision d'intervention et spectacle politique: Agir par le rituel [Televisual intervention and political spectacle: Ritual action], *Hermès, 17-18*, p. 171.

# 8

# The Emergence of Religious Forms on Television

Günter Thomas

Fruitful research programs sometimes benefit from a risk-taking strategy. They derive their advantage from an imaginative and challenging yet methodologically controlled crossing of borders between traditional academic disciplines. When this happens, a concept or model familiar in one discipline can be used in a new way in another field. If we understand the theoretical apparatus of an academic discipline as analogous to, say, a pair of glasses that make certain things visible, these glasses are, in this case, being used to look at fairly unfamiliar material, material not normally analyzed by this specific set of spectacles. For researchers who want to keep their disciplines neatly separated and "clean," such an endeavor—to borrow a phrase from Mary Douglas—represents academic "pollution" (Douglas, 1966). Still, it seems to be irritation and pollution that keeps fruitful research going.

The following considerations will attempt to practice such disciplinary boundary crossing, insofar as they combine anthropological considerations on religion on the one side and media studies on the other side. The key question here is: When an anthropologically interested scholar of religion looks at television with spectacles (the theoretical apparatus) normally used for the investigation of religious phenomena, what then becomes visible in regard to these television programs of late-modern societies?

The following considerations are divided into three parts. At the outset, I would like to make a clarifying suggestion for the often vague and even confused discourse about the relations between religion and television. It will become clear that four levels of interaction between television and religion require four distinct levels of analysis. In the subsequent section, I will briefly name the motives and aims of the analysis of television that are presented here. What is the aim of this boundary crossing? In addition, I will address methodological considerations and clarify what I alluded to in the metaphor of the spectacles.

The third part of this chapter will deal with and present considerations of several relevant examples. Taking up two aspects of the aforementioned fourth level of analysis, I hope to throw a little light onto two religious aspects of late-modern television programs: the emergence of a ritualized liturgical order and the creation of a specific cosmology. These two religious forms have been selected only for the purposes of example and could, of course, be supplemented by additional

**Table 8.1**     Television and Religion: Four Levels of Interaction and Interpretation

|  | *Focus of Analysis* | *Examples* |
|---|---|---|
| Level 1 | *Self-presentations and presentations* by third parties of explicitly recognized religions, such as Christianity, Judaism, or Islam, or new religions | *Self-presentations:*<br>▣ Religious services<br>▣ The Epilogue<br>▣ "Religious television"<br><br>*Third-party presentations:*<br>▣ Nonfictional reports about the churches<br>▣ Fictional films on biblical themes<br>▣ Soap operas centered on the clergy |
| Level 2 | *"Religious" motifs, symbols, roles, stories, and themes* in fictional and nonfictional broadcasts that are taken from recognized religions or that can be traced back to them but for which there is no explicit reference to those religions | ▣ Mythical savior figures in films<br>▣ Paradise motifs in TV commercials<br>▣ Treatment of transience and death in TV series<br>▣ Sin and atonement; crime and punishment<br>▣ Persistence and forms of evil<br>▣ Confrontations between good and evil<br>▣ Sacrifice<br>▣ Pollution and purity or cleanliness<br>▣ Redemption or salvation and new beginnings (happy ending)<br>▣ Initiations and passages |
| Level 3 | *Adaptations and transformations of religious rituals* in TV broadcasts that adopt what were originally religious practices, beyond the reception of motifs, symbols, and themes, and that celebrate events | ▣ Wedding rituals<br>▣ Confessions and repentance rituals<br>▣ Collective "media events"<br>▣ Rituals of awe and wonder<br>▣ Condensed performances of a life, interpretations of the flow of a life (series)<br>▣ Performances of moral indignation and condemnation<br>▣ Ordering rituals (TV news) |
| Level 4 | *Religious cultural forms and functions* Structural aspects of processing, construction, and presentations of "reality" in and through television; individual and social functions of television relating to the "grammar" of religion | ▣ Organization of transcendences; "beyond the everyday"<br>▣ Social cosmology<br>▣ Social ritual and liturgical order<br>▣ Providing "ontological security"<br>▣ Mythical transformation of reality<br>▣ Creation of a feeling of a large or even worldwide community, a global ecumene<br>▣ Public celebrations of shared values |

forms. Yet both of these examples clearly call for an interaction between anthropology and television studies.

Table 8.1 offers an outline of the levels of interaction and interpretation as they pertain to television, with examples.

## TELEVISION AND RELIGION: FOUR LEVELS OF ANALYSIS

The relations between religion and the media have a long history, ranging back to the emergence of the first media of communication, which were used in rituals. If one applies a rather broad notion of "media," then media analysis has long been a part of anthropological studies. Every elaborated form of symbolism is in itself a medium of communication. Seen in this way, there is no society, no religion, and no ritual that does not use some media. However, the situation became more complex with the industrialization of print media and with the appearance of the audiovisual media, such as film, television, and the Internet. Against the background of this development, sociologists describe the media as one of the latest of society's functional subsystems (Luhmann, 1996). Due to the complexity of the relations between media and television, as well as the lack of a distinct academic home for the discourse, the debate on religion and media often resembles a post-Babel melee, with little conceptual clarity and mutual understanding (de Vries & Weber, 2001; Hoover & Lundby, 1997; Hoover & Schofield Clark, (2002); Thomas, 1998). To enhance conceptual clarity and promote understanding, a framework is required that can act as a guide for research questions and help distinguish various approaches to the large topic "religion and media." However, to create a suitable framework for our current goals, I will limit here the broad range of "media" to television alone. For this analysis of the relations between television and religion, a distinction will be made between four levels of inquiry.

*1. Self-Presentation and Third-Party Presentations.* The question of religion on television may refer to the *self-presentation of explicit traditional or publicly acknowledged religions,* such as Christianity, Islam, Buddhism, or Judaism. Broadcasts of religious services or *Wort zum Sonntag* (the most successful religious preaching format on German Saturday night television) or various types of so-called religious television in the United States would be included in this category of *self-presentation.* In these cases, the religious community itself uses television for self-descriptive purposes, which may supplement a particular religious ritual. A certain modification can be found in *third-party presentations,* in which nonreligious institutions provide descriptions of religious

communities, texts, or ritual practices. This subcategory includes informative (journalistic) and fictional (entertainment oriented) contributions; specifically, critical reports on the churches, films and features about public religious rituals, movies on Biblical themes and figures, soap operas centered on the clergy, and so on. Religious films broadcast on television belong to this group. Essential for this first level of interaction is the fact that television acts primarily as a medium of description, even though it may not be absolutely neutral.

*2. Motifs, Symbols, Roles, Stories, and Themes.* The picture changes significantly when we move to the second level. The search for interactions between religion and television can be directed at *motifs, symbols, roles, stories,* and *themes* in fictional and nonfictional broadcasts that are either taken from the historical religions or that can at least be traced back to them. Mythical "savior figures" pervade movies and televised detective series. Paradise motifs appear in TV commercials as part of the iconography of individual happiness. Ideas from religious wisdom literature, as well as treatments of foundational questions concerning the meaning of transience and death, among other concepts, can also be found (Heuermann, 1994; Jewett, 1993, 1998; Lawrence & Jewett, 2002, 2003; Schneider, 1993; Scott, 1994). The ongoing struggle between life-diminishing and life-enriching forces is played out every night on many channels. The movie *The Matrix* and its sequel is one of the more recent and striking example of "religious saturation" in audiovisual products. Every look into *TV Guide* finds programs dealing with the uncanny human potential for destruction and the quest for redemption. Without any doubt, these motifs, symbols, roles, stories, and themes are not intrinsically or even necessarily religious. Yet, in the not so distant past, they were clearly located in religious discourses. The religious heritage of humankind provides rich material for their interpretation.

*3. Performative and Ritual Event Television.* At the third level, scholarly attention moves away from individual motifs, symbols, and themes and shifts to the larger entities of TV broadcast units. Via certain types of TV broadcasts, events are created that go far beyond the reception of individual motifs. Instead, they aim at the consummation or subletting of originally religious practices and rituals. The instances of "performative event television" (Keppler, 1994, 1995) do not portray something but rather *perform* something with the broadcast. The aim here is construction, not merely portrayal. Performative event broadcasts do not just show, they really make something with people. In doing this, they copy and transform recognizable, extramedial religious forms: Some shows aim at performing wonders that appear to be close to miracles, wedding shows seem to substitute for real weddings, and many programs resemble public confessions or sacrifices (Reichertz, 2000a, 2000b; Schilson, 1997). In times of crisis, daily news becomes public ritual, maintaining and creating a sense of order. Some talk shows become celebrations of the moral order by observing moral boundaries "from both sides." As in the case of a media event (Dayan, 2000; Dayan & Katz, 1992), sometimes these programs shape and stage events that occur outside *and* within the medium, but in both cases only *through* the medium. Ritual forms that are deeply grounded in anthropology and are, to a certain extent, universal become structures for media formats. At this third level, television absorbs and modifies forms from the religious field, a process that becomes visible from a religiously informed anthropological perspective.

*4. Cultural Intervention.* The last level of interaction is concerned with aspects of the cultural invention of television programs. At this level, research questions are directed toward structural aspects and the form of television itself: the processing and presentation of reality in and through this medium. The goal is to describe similarities and analogies with religious forms, which are not tied to distinct broadcasts but embedded into the very form of the cultural institution. In this context, one could consider the broad complex of liturgy and ritual (Rothenbuhler, 1998, pp. 73-128) and the means of providing experiences of

"transcendence"; that is to say, occurrences of a varying range that extend beyond everyday experience. The mythical transformation and presentation of reality by television also belongs to this level of interaction (Bleicher, 1999, 2000; Silverstone, 1981, 1988, 1994). In addition, we should keep in mind that television is late-modern society's most influential institution for cosmologization; that is, for the provision of an encompassing view of reality. Here the subject of analysis is the media flow itself, the predominant presentation forms of television as a cultural invention, and their practice. At this fourth level, structural aspects are joined to considerations of the individual and social functions of television.

It is at this fourth level—that is, in dealing with the structural forms of processing and presentation and with the functions of television—that anthropological perspectives on television meet observations made in media studies. Depending on the results of this fourth level analysis, new light can then be cast upon the third and second levels; that is, upon the program types (level 3), as well as the motifs, symbols, and themes within the programs (level 2). We find this to be the case because two possible directions of interpreting the findings on these two levels suggest themselves: (a) exploitative reception and reprocessing of traditions and (b) syncretized arrangement of emerging media religiosity.

Religious motifs, symbols, and themes, as well as the types of programs mentioned, could be read as more or less exploitative receptions or as the reprocessing of traditional and explicitly religious traditions. They would then be receptions in favor of the attractiveness, acceptance, or marketability of the programs concerned. They would be used by filmmakers, authors, and artists to enhance the resonance of television products. Both the second and the third level of interaction would bear witness to the fact that not just the audience but also the producers are *bricoleurs* who weave together fragments of diverse cultural traditions into an emerging new product (Lévi-Strauss, 1968).

One could, however, take a slightly different reading of the findings on the second and third level: They may be examples, even indicators, of more or less syncretized arrangements of an emerging media religiosity with a cultural dynamism of its own. Even though this interpretation runs counter to the obvious and explicit self-description of producers and viewers, an anthropological observation would take this liberty and hold a view in opposition to the "commonsense" perspective. An anthropologically informed look at television in late-modern societies sees the emergence of religious forms in television.

Both interpretations are possible. Although they differ in regard to the larger sociocultural picture, they suggest the same kind of anthropological view of the media.

## CROSSING TRADITIONAL BOUNDARIES: METHOD AND PURPOSE

### Methodological Considerations Concerning the Identification of Religion

An anthropological view of television that is informed by religious studies as well as ritual studies cannot take common sense, even academic common sense, in the field of media studies as its starting point. The anthropological look at television seems to be counterintuitive. For this reason, the crossing of traditional boundaries requires methodological clarity and transparency. How can a complex of phenomena such as television, which displays religious aspects neither by the audience nor by its description of itself, come within the purview of the anthropological analysis of religion? At this stage, two closely interlinked paths appear navigable: the procedure of *metaphoric construction* and that of *polythetic classification*.

The procedure of metaphoric construction provokes a comparison that permits us to see one thing in the light of another (Debatin, 1995, chapter 2; Black, 1962); that is, it lets us see television in the light of religion and thus opens for us a new perspective. Religious insights become a creative,

heuristic set of instruments that lead to a new description of an all-too-familiar object: television. Quite often, this procedure is motivated by the perception of anomalous aspects in a familiar phenomenon. Familiar things are put into new contexts, many features are given a new weighting, and others are perceived for the first time. Without actually turning into an "identification as. . . ." procedure, metaphoric construction, in the selectivity of its comparison, operates on the basis of difference. "The insight into likeness is the perception of the conflict between the previous incompatibility and the new compatibility. 'Remoteness' is preserved within 'proximity.' To see *the like* is to see the same in spite of, and through, the different" (Ricoeur, 1978, p. 146; consider also Grimes, 2002).

Polythetic classification assumes that a cultural association of phenomena such as religion can be identified on the basis of the simultaneous appearance of several otherwise culturally ubiquitous elements without religions being reduced to an assumed common final reality (Needham, 1972, 1975; Platvoet & Molendijk, 1999; Poole, 1986; Saler, 1993; Smart, 1981, 1983, 1997; Thomas, 2001, pp. 329-364). Within the framework of this approach, the cultural forms that characterize religion create a heuristic grid or framework that has to be processed successively—an optical raster, so to speak—for considering television. Any concentration of the characteristics of religion indicates that religious aspects are really present. Within polythetic classification, "remoteness" is preserved within "identity."

Both metaphorical construction and polythetic classification may complement, or indeed supplement, the other.

### Aims and Purposes of Identifying Religious Forms in Television

What motives and purposes are pursued when anthropological questions are raised about the religious aspects of television (as understood by the third and fourth levels)? Here are three interconnected aspects that belong to the public responsibility of public discourses on religion:

1. The phenomenon of television takes such a central position in late-modern societies that any collaboration in analyzing its complex nature should be welcomed. There are several aspects that have been overlooked in classical media studies, as well as a good number of anomalies that call for anthropological considerations and for the activation of resources from other disciplines.

2. Anthropology, religious science, the sociology of religion, and theology share the task within academic discourse of enlightening the public about the transformations, shifts, and remolding of religion and religious forms. This specific enlightenment may of course be carried out in spite of itself; that is, at least in those cases in which religious aspects are discovered precisely where one is concerned with things that apparently have nothing to do with religion. In undertaking this task, public discourses about religion have to move beyond commonsense knowledge, as well as beyond the accepted common sense within the respective field.

3. Not only philosophy and sociology, but anthropology, and, finally, theology must undertake religious criticism. As with any self-critical reflection on the religious tradition, these disciplines are all too familiar with the possibilities of perverting religious forms and with the possibility that a culture may indeed be endangered by its religions. Any discourse about religion that is interested in helping design the life of a community in a life-promoting way will not be able to stop at a "neutral" observation of the media system. Not every form of religion is "life-promoting, dedicated to the truth and compatible with the dignity of the human individual" (Huber, 1998, p. 225)—and this insight also applies to the religious aspects of television.

At this stage, it should be self-evident that this is not a matter of an apologia for "religion in general"; neither is it a matter of demonstrating the inescapable religiosity of every individual, nor even of searching desperately for religion outside the churches (because it seems to be lacking within them). Rather, the question standing at the center of these considerations is whether the relationship between religion and media technology is "of a more systematic and intrinsic nature than theories of modernization and differentiation, disenchantment and secularization led us to expect" (de Vries, 2001, p. 14) and whether we can speak of a "religion of the media" (Derrida 2001, p. 69). Therefore, the basic assumption must be that beyond all instrumental relations, for religion, the medium is not secondary, and for media, the religious is not a mere epiphenomenon.

The following section will consider examples of two religious aspects of television: liturgy as a form of ritual and cosmology. Both have to be understood as religious forms, even though they present just two dimensions of religion and appear in many cultures without being necessarily religious. Both relate to an analysis on the fourth level, of the relationships between religion and television.

## EMERGING RELIGIOUS FORMS ON TELEVISION

### The Liturgical Order of the Program Flow

Complex liturgical orders are liturgies that must be conceived of as a concatenation of individual rituals (Rappaport, 1979, 1999). The notion of liturgical order combines (a) the idea of threads of distinct rituals forming an ordered ritual flow and (b) the notion of flow, which was introduced to television studies by R. Williams (1975, chapters 3 and 4). Television, with its many individual programs, offers itself as a program-shaped presentation continuum, which may be interpreted as an endless, eternal liturgy aimed in principle at infinity—indeed, as a liturgical order. The individual rituals of the programs are embedded in and linked by the liturgical stream and placed into a factual and temporal order. The individual streams of the liturgical order are structured into channel-specific program concepts, specific daily and weekly schemes, and certain channel structures. The liturgical flow unites programs across the entire field of genres: those which tend to treat extramedial occurrences as "whole events," so to speak; informative or documentary programs that relate to "outside" factors; and those elements that, like fictional films, only exist within the flow.

In the television liturgy, the limited amount of time normally available to the older religious rituals has been stretched to form a presentation that runs around the clock, infinitely, as a virtual eternity. The very flow of television has no scheduled ending. The perpetuity of the broadcast makes viewers forget the fleeting nature of what is offered. The moment the flow is broadcast, it vanishes without any memory that would keep this stream alive. Admittedly, the liturgy offers an "eternal present" in the form of an endlessly disappearing present. Yet despite this permanent decay, the liturgy is enormously stable and objective. It decays permanently without leaving a trace, and yet from the perspective of the viewer it is indestructible. As every viewer knows, even switching the TV off cannot interrupt the flow of programs. Without any participation of the viewers themselves, apart from the investment of attention, the viewing consciousness can attach itself to a continuum of perception and occurrence and resign itself to this continuum. This connection to another stable stream of consciousness, independent of viewers' thinking and feeling, differentiates television from the fragility of communication based on interaction. Viewers' inability to disturb or influence the stream resembles the fixed nature of the communication process in traditional religious rituals.

The individual rituals within the irreversible linear-flowing liturgical order are structured by rhythms, cycles, and repetitions. Through the hourly, daily, or weekly rhythms of periodicity, the linear time of the flow is interspersed with the cyclical time of familiar repetitions. On the one hand, the liturgical order depends on the extramedial temporal orders of work and leisure time. In its reporting, it also orients itself toward extramedial occurrences, but it increasingly decomposes and remolds even extramedial orders of time to fit themselves around TV time as a new chronometer.

The liturgy is a complex time form that has (a) an *inner* structure of individual offers, durations, specific cycles, and rhythms and (b) an *external* time form permitting an individually tailored structuring of everyday life determined by forms of reception: a "customized" liturgical order. Individual viewing habits allow endless variations of the liturgical stream without getting totally detached from the "master stream." Although the patterns of television reception are differentiated from each other, the building material of these individual or family patterns still stems from the same liturgical stream. This latter aspect makes it possible for one to adapt quite individually to a supraindividual order that has its origins in the "world beyond" everyday life, to simultaneously increase individuality and community (Whitehead, 1960, p. 86).

Corresponding to this relative exit from everyday life is an entry into so-called prefigured realms of experience. They lead to an experience of "restored behavior," to use a concept developed by the theater anthropologist Richard Schechner (1985, pp. 33-116). As inner ritual periods of time, these prefigured realms of experience simultaneously offer a modulation of time. Anyone can at any time join these "worlds beyond" everyday life, these self-representations of society and—via the "interface" of the TV screen—submerge themselves into these extraeveryday realities. In this way, the TV offers variations of small-scale transcendences that are "always at hand" and very much embedded in everyday life. A separate form of presence in this other reality is permitted by the TV-specific experience of oscillation between (a) the contingent "observation," so to speak, of the communication that is offered by the program (and the communication about it) and (b) the emotionally compact, perceptive involvement. The liturgical flow allows the viewer's consciousness to couple on, to participate in a relaxed fashion within this continuum of perception provided by the stream, to participate without actually being there, to let him- or herself fall without the risk of going astray. Television may be the greatest storyteller of all time, but the point about it is that it *performs* stories and thus permits entry into prefigured realms of experience beyond everyday life: an imagined "displacement" that simultaneously offers immediacy and safety, a daily "everyday escape from everyday-ness." In some specific broadcasts, which fall into the category of performative event television, TV offers "rites of transformation," while the whole flow of the liturgical order offers "rites of transportation" into other realities readily at hand (Schechner, 1985, pp. 117-150).

Television creates a form of "media present" in a "television space," which replaces the physical presence in interaction-supported ritual. The media religious experience follows the structure that, *in* the reality of human experience, opens up access to an "opposite world," *to* a different paradigmatic, actual reality, to a relative world beyond everyday life, and that opposite world in turn throws new light on the previous reality, allowing it to be seen from a different perspective. With a complexity that differs according to genre and program, this "other reality" invites the viewers to interpret the lives they have lived. The presence of televisions in public areas documents the efforts to prevent the interruption of communication, in this case an address to the individual via the medium, and contact between both worlds. The stream of the liturgical order reveals an odd reversal of traditional religious prayer.

Within the liturgical flow, various genres organize an evocation of anxiety and its control through their own form. With its reliability, its stable forms, well-known figures, and familiar shapes, the endless liturgy satisfies a need for continuity and intimacy—a need that it itself strengthens by its varied description of a chaotic world. Every surprise in an individual episode takes place in the context of the expectability of the liturgylike program and predictable, familiar program formulas. It is precisely through such a rigid form that the intensity of the affective or cognitive stimulation and the attraction of consciousness can be so enormously enhanced or reduced. Never mind what's happening outside in the world—the news is over in 20 minutes, and no feature film really has an "open" ending in the temporal respect. Whatever happens, reality can still be coped with.

The community the liturgical stream creates has a two-sided form. On the one hand, it is the "imagined community" (Anderson, 1983) of the TV viewers and at the same time—at least in fictional genres—it is the community of those whose experiences the viewers can, at a safe distance, willingly and affectively share, of those with whom one vicariously and imaginatively interacts. In this way, television individuates and communitizes, combining community (emotional proximity, "sharing" the fates of others) with the advantages of society (possibility of choice, privatization, distance).

## Cosmology: A Fragile Order for a Fragmented World

Modern societies and cultures are fragmented in several respects. Social subsystems follow their own rationality, lifestyles and cultural spheres become differentiated, lifeworlds lose their homogeneity, and normative contexts are relativized by recognized plurality. For more and more people, sectors of reality beyond direct everyday experience appear increasingly opaque. This development to a plural referentiality of reality is intensified through the extension of geographical and cultural perceptive horizons made possible by the media. Correspondingly, philosophy and the social sciences acknowledge the illusory nature of an epistemological "God's-eye view" and the end of traditional metaphysics as a means of sustaining the unity of reality.

In this much-lamented situation of new unclarity and opaqueness, the media system, and television in particular, produces a comprehensive self-description of modern society. This description has at least partially replaced traditional religious cosmologies in many respects.

Religious cosmologies serve, first, to integrate a plurality of world aspects into a single interpretive horizon via a unified and comprehensive description given by a "privileged observer." This interpretive horizon excludes, or at least reduces, the possibility of absolute meaninglessness and chaos. With this description, religious cosmologies offer, second, a symbolic medium for handling the development of a society. In this respect, they provide the configuration of "possibility spaces." Third, via this metacommunication regarding all other societal communication, cosmologies are aimed at the legitimation, formation, and coordination of other forms of social communication, of other realities. In its own individual way, television seems to be moving toward the function of a "sacred canopy" (Berger, 1967), as described by the sociology of religion—even although under the peculiar epistemological and ontological conditions of late-modern societies.

Liturgical orders themselves have a tendency to cosmologize.

> It is . . . in the nature of liturgical orders to unite, or reunite, the psychic, social, natural, and cosmic orders which language and the exigencies of life pull apart. . . . Liturgical orders bind together disparate entities and processes, and it is this binding together rather than what is bound together that is peculiar to them. (Rappaport, 1979, p. 206)

Liturgical orders generate their own representation of their social environment. The very fact that a flow is taking place communicates a basic observability and reliability of the world outside of direct environmental experience. To use the concept employed by Anthony Giddens (1991, pp. 35-69), it constantly renews "ontological security" (Silverstone, 1993). But approximation to the level of a cosmology can only be achieved, first, by the crystallization of unified aspects of order, which go beyond the largely additive processes of the liturgical stream, and, second, by the fact that this reality, with its ontology, leaves its mark on and colors other realities.

How then does television, in its description, order reality, when TV reality is constantly presenting itself as driven by catastrophes and scandals? What is the unity of the fragments in this liturgical stream, above and beyond the addition of the individual parts within the flow? On a very basic level, the liturgical stream unites an enormous number of tiny facets of multiple sociocultural realities. This view of the world is symbolized in most TV news by the use of some image of the globe. Even if one acknowledges this combination, however, it remains a rather clusterlike combination. To speak of a cosmology, it seems necessary to point out some unifying principles. What makes the TV cosmology so compelling and at the same time "invisible" are

two features: only what is (a) *interesting* (b) *at the moment* is included in the cosmology of television and can become part of the constantly decaying liturgical stream. Not substance, but time (actuality); not the unchanging, but that which creates resonance (the interesting) are the building blocks of this cosmology. Things that are uninteresting at the moment are, strictly speaking, not real inside this ontology. Everything that is interesting at the moment is subsequently processed by other genre-specific distinctions. This opens up a spectrum of genres. At one end of this spectrum, we tend to find the so-called nonfictional genres processing what is of topical interest by stressing—mainly in a highly selective way—individual interruptions of the social, political, or natural order in the processes of other extramedial realities. At the other end of the spectrum are the stronger fictional genres that, in the form of more or less completely fictitious possible worlds (e.g., feature films or serializations, respectively), thematicize the archaic-anthropological conflicts that are always topical. These conflicts generally cover love, death, betrayal, devotion, battle, destruction, and the endangering of the legal order. Here it is the relative restitution of the infringed orders that dominates in the mythically typified, small narrative world—fictional microcosms of television as story machine. Many intermediate forms will be found between the two ends of the spectrum. All of them are interspersed with commercials as an iconography of happiness and "the positive," such as adventure, newly fruitful relationships, and, fundamentally, wealth and attractive identities. If one considers the two ends of the spectrum, one sees that the liturgical stream unites what is happening today, here and now, with the ever-topical, mythically elemental. Thus a mixture of alarmism and confirmation—a dynamic standstill—is created. This neither accumulates behind us, providing a space that "imprints" a distinct and debatable cultural memory, nor creates before us a historically conscious space of social expectation and development, of direction and target orientation. An anthropologically oriented criticism of religion will have to start with these two distinctive temporal forms of television communication: the permanent "now" of topicality and the "history-less-ness" of the ever topical.

What makes this cosmology so evident? First, there is a strong drive toward personalization, something that marked archaic cosmologies. An audiovisual and "interesting" portrayal of even the most abstract relations (from a scientific perspective) has to be personalized to lead to a persuasive closeness of the everyday world. Along this line, there is a network of references binding this world to everyday life: actors who also actually exist off-screen; screens that claim to point to what they display; the "live reality" of news programs, in which television pretends to subject itself to the contingencies of real life. Then there is the evidence of the image, the obvious, which can generate a feeling of the evident and of the factual that is difficult to outbid. Even in times of computer enabled "morphing," many people still feel that "pictures don't lie." In contrast to mature philosophical or scientific cosmologies, television cosmology's presentational form is accessible to common sense. In its obviousness, it is able to render invisible its own massive efforts at abstraction.

## CONCLUDING REMARKS

At the beginning of this chapter, we started with the distinction between four levels of analysis, which served to set the anthropological approach presented here apart from others and relate it to alternative points of access to the religious functions of television. The investigation of emerging religious forms in the leading medium of television is part of a critical self-enlightenment of public discourse on religion and of a critical demonstration of religious forms in our cultural environment. Liturgy and cosmology are only two analytical perspectives that not only have to be worked out further but that also need to be complemented with considerations of normative communication, of mythical narration and typification, and of sacrifice—just to name a few. The development of possible sound criticism of these religious forms in television would also require better illumination of the types involved in forming

the community of the liturgical stream, the social ecology of attention, and the temporal structures of cosmology. Yet I hope that even this brief sketch of the fruitfulness of this perspective on the underlying question has made it clear that the program-shaped television of Western societies is not just some component of the cultural symbol household or of the economy of symbols. Television is not just a sign system people use to interpret their lives. It is not just a cultural system of symbols *per se*. Television in late modern societies is not just a text rewritten by every viewer. The remarkable fact rendered visible through an anthropological perspective geared to religious aspects is that within the stream of television, forms of communication emerge that bear a striking resemblance to well-known religious forms. With its liturgical stream describing a cosmos, television has recourse to distinctive, cultural communication forms of religion. To discover it will be a considerable challenge to discourses on religion and a source of light to media analysis that is at least worth considering.

## REFERENCES

Anderson, B. (1983). *Imagined communities: Reflections on the origin and spread of nationalism.* London: Verso.

Berger, P. L. (1967). *The sacred canopy: Elements of a sociological theory of religion.* Garden City, NJ: Doubleday.

Black, M. (1962). *Models and metaphors.* Ithaca, NY: Cornell University Press.

Bleicher, J. K. (1999). *Fernsehen als Mythos: Poetik eines narrativen Erkenntnissystems* [Television as myth: Poetics of a narrative knowledge system]. Opladen, Germany: Westdeutscher Verlag.

Bleicher, J. K. (2000). Das Narrationssystem Fernsehen und seine Vermittlungsstrukturen [The narration system called television and its structures of mediation]. In G. Thomas (Ed.), *Religiöse Funktionen des Fernsehens? Medien-, kultur- und religionswissenschaftliche Perspektiven* [Religious functions of television? Perspectives from media, cultural, and religious studies] (pp. 127-144). Opladen, Germany: Westdeutscher Verlag.

Dayan, D. (2000). Religiöse Aspekte der Fernsehrezeption: Große Medienereignisse im Spiegel des Rituals [Religious aspects of television reception: Large media events]. In G. Thomas (Ed.), *Religiöse Funktionen des Fernsehens? Medien-, kultur- und religionswissenschaftliche Perspektiven* [Religious functions of television? Perspectives from media, cultural, and religious studies] (pp. 191-204). Opladen, Germany: Westdeutscher Verlag.

Dayan, D., & Katz, E. (1992). *Media events: The live broadcasting of history.* Cambridge, MA: Harvard University Press.

Debatin, B. (1995). *Die Rationalität der Metapher: Eine sprachphilosophische und kommunikationstheoretische Untersuchung* [The rationality of metaphor: An analysis through language philosophy and communication theory]. Berlin: de Gruyter.

Derrida, J. (2001). "Above all, no journalists!" In H. de Vries & S. Weber (Eds.), *Religion and media* (pp. 56-93). Stanford, CA: Stanford University Press.

de Vries, H. (2001). In media res: Global religion, public spheres, and the task of contemporary religious studies. In H. de Vries & S. Weber (Eds.), *Religion and media* (pp. 3-42). Stanford, CA: Stanford University Press.

de Vries, H., & Weber, S. (Eds.). (2001). *Religion and media.* Stanford, CA: Stanford University Press.

Douglas, M. (1966). Purity and danger: An analysis of the concepts of pollution and taboo. London: Routledge.

Giddens, A. (1991). *Modernity and self-identity: Self and society in the late-modern age.* Stanford, CA: Stanford University Press.

Grimes, R. L. (2002). Ritual and the media. In S. M. Hoover & L. Schofield Clark (Eds.), *Practicing religion in the age of the media: Explorations in media, religion and culture* (pp. 219-234). New York: Columbia University Press.

Heuermann, H. (1994). *Medien und Mythen: Die Bedeutung regressiver Tendenzen in der westlichen Medienkultur* [Media and myths: The meaning of regressive tendencies in Western media culture]. München: Wilhelm Fink Verlag.

Hickethier, K. (1998). *Geschichte des deutschen Fernsehens* [The history of German television]. Stuttgart, Germany: Metzler.

Hoover, S. M., & Lundby, K. (1997). *Rethinking media, religion and culture.* Thousand Oaks, CA: Sage.

Hoover, S. M., & Schofield Clark, L. (2002). *Practicing religion in the age of the media: Explorations in media, religion and culture.* New York: Columbia University Press.

Huber, W. (1998). *Kirche in der Zeitenwende: Gesellschaftlicher Wandel und Erneuerung der Kirche* [The church at the turn of time: Social change and renewal of the church]. Gütersloh, Germany: Bertelsmann Stiftung.

Jewett, R. (1993). *Saint Paul at the movies: The apostle's dialogue with American culture.* Louisville, KY: Westminster/John Knox.

Jewett, R. (1998). *Saint Paul returns to the movies: Triumph over shame.* Grand Rapids, MI: William B. Erdmans.

Keppler, A. (1994). *Wirklicher als die Wirklichkeit? Das neue Realitätsprinzip der Fernsehunterhaltung* [More real than reality? The new reality principle of TV entertainment]. Frankfurt-am-Mainz, Germany: Fischer.

Keppler, A. (1995). Die Kommunikation des Dabeiseins: Formen des Sakralen in der Fernsehunterhaltung [Communication of togetherness: Forms of the sacral in TV entertainment]. *Rundfunk und Fernsehen, 43,* 301-311.

Lawrence, J. S., & Jewett, R. (2002). *The myth of the American superhero.* Grand Rapids, MI: William B. Erdmans.

Lawrence, J. S., & Jewett, R. (2003). *Captain America and the crusade against evil.* Grand Rapids, MI: William B. Erdmans.

Lévi-Strauss, C. (1968). Das wilde Denken [The savage mind]. Frankfurt-am-Mainz, Germany: Fischer.

Luhmann, N. (1996). *Die Realität der Massenmedien* [The reality of the mass media] (2nd ed.). Opladen, Germany: Westdeutscher Verlag.

Needham, R. (1972). *Belief, language, and experience.* Oxford, England: Basil Blackwell.

Needham, R. (1975). Polythetic classification: Convergence and consequences. *Man, 3*(10), 349-369.

Platvoet, J. G., & Molendijk, A. L. (Eds.). (1999). *The pragmatics of defining religion: Contexts, concepts and contest.* Leiden, Netherlands: E. J. Brill.

Poole, F.J.P. (1986). Metaphors and maps: Towards comparison in the anthropology of religion. *Journal of the American Academy of Religion, 53*(3), 411-457.

Rappaport, R. A. (1979). *Ecology, meaning, and religion.* Berkeley, CA: North Atlantic Books.

Rappaport, R. A. (1999). *Ritual and religion in the making of humanity.* New York: Cambridge University Press.

Reichertz, J. (2000a). *Die frohe Botschaft des Fernsehens: Kulturwissenschaftliche Untersuchung medialer Diesseitsreligion* [The good news of telelvision: A cultural analysis of a medial "this-world religion"]. Konstanz, Germany: Universitätsverlag.

Reichertz, J. (2000b). Trauung und Trost, Vergebung und Wunder: Kirchliche Dienstleistungen im Fernsehen [Marriage and consolation, forgiveness and wonder:

Religious "services" through television]. In G. Thomas (Ed.), *Religiöse Funktionen des Fernsehens? Medien-, kultur- und religionswissenschaftliche Perspektiven* [Religious functions of television? Perspectives from media, cultural, and religious studies] (pp. 205-221). Opladen, Germany: Westdeutscher Verlag.

Ricoeur, P. (1978). The metaphorical process as cognition, imagination, and feeling. In S. Sacks (Ed.), *On metaphor* (pp. 141-157). Chicago: University of Chicago Press.

Rothenbuhler, E. W. (1998). *Ritual communication: From everyday conversation to mediated ceremony.* Thousand Oaks, CA: Sage.

Saler, B. (1993). *Conceptualizing religion: Immanent anthropologists, transcendent natives, and unbounded categories.* Leiden, Netherlands: E. J. Brill.

Schechner, R. (1985). *Between theater and anthropology.* Philadelphia: University of Pennsylvania Press.

Schilson, A. (1997). *Medienreligion: Zur religiösen Signatur der Gegenwart* [Media religion: On the religious signature of our time]. Tübingen, Germany: Francke.

Schneider, K. J. (1993). *Horror and the holy: Wisdom-teachings of the monster tale.* Chicago: Open Court.

Scott, B. B. (1994). *Hollywood dreams and biblical stories.* Minneapolis, MN: Fortress Press.

Silverstone, R. (1981). *The message of television: Myth and narrative in contemporary culture.* London: Heinemann.

Silverstone, R. (1988). Television myth and culture. In J. W. Carey (Ed.), *Media, myths, and narratives* (pp. 20-47). Newbury Park, CA: Sage.

Silverstone, R. (1993). Television, ontological security and the transitional object. *Media, Culture and Society, 4,* 573-598.

Silverstone, R. (1994). *Television and everyday life.* London: Routledge.

Smart, N. (1981). The Philosophy of worldviews—that is, the philosophy of religion transformed. *Neue Zeitschrift für Systematische Theologie und Religionsphilosophie, 23,* 212-224.

Smart, N. (1983). *Worldviews: Crosscultural explorations of human beliefs.* New York: Scribner.

Smart, N. (1997). *Dimensions of the sacred.* London: Fontana.

Thomas, G. (1998). *Medien-Ritual-Religion: Zur religiösen Funktion des Fernsehens* [Media, ritual, religion: On the religious functions of television]. Frankfurt-am-Mainz, Germany: Suhrkamp.

Thomas, G. (2001). *Implizite Religion: Theoriegeschichtliche und theoretische Untersuchungen zum Problem ihrer Identifikation* [Implicit religion: Historical and theoretical analyses on the problem of its identification]. Würzburg, Germany: Ergon.

Vorderer, P. (Ed.). (1996). *Fernsehen als "Beziehungskiste": Parasoziale Beziehungen und Interaktionen mit TV-Personen* [Television: "More of a bind than a tie." Parasocial relationships and interactions with TV personalities]. Opladen, Germany: Westdeutscher Verlag.

Whitehead, A. N. (1960). *Religion in the making.* New York: Meridian.

Williams, R. (1975). *Television: Technology and cultural form.* New York: Schocken Books.

# 9

# THE CHURCH OF THE
# CULT OF THE INDIVIDUAL

ERIC W. ROTHENBUHLER

Why does celebrity work the way it does in the United States and other industrialized societies? Why are such large proportions of the communicative and cultural resources of such societies devoted to the making and unmaking, promotion, presentation, examination, and scandalization of celebrity personalities? Why do almost all people in such societies spend at least some of their time paying attention to the lives, activities, and performances of individuals unknown to them but who are presented by the media as celebrities? Why does the system operate in such a way that essentially one cannot be out of the presence of these star players on the public stage, as if they were essentially an element of the cultural environment? Is it because they *are* an essential element of that environment?

The proposal I explore in this chapter is that these mysteries can be answered if we understand the media as the *church of the cult of the individual*. The starting idea is that the cult of the individual, as Durkheim (e.g., 1898/1994) proposed, is the religion of modern society. Then I push the analysis deeper than Durkheim did, into the communicative infrastructure of modern society. If, as Goffman (e.g., 1959, 1967) showed, the person, the self, which is the sacred object of the cult of the individual, is a symbolic entity that can be known only through communicative processes, then the ceremonial practices of that cult (religion) must be in communicative processes.

Communication itself, then, is the location of the church of the cult of the individual. On the one hand are the rituals of interpersonal presentation and avoidance, greeting and parting, the

**Author's Note:** This chapter was presented as a paper at the International Communication Association Annual Convention, June 1-5, 2000, Acapulco, Mexico, to the Department of Communication, University of Ljubljana, May 15, 2001, and discussed at the Ritual Communication Workshop, University of Oslo, May 21, 2001. My thanks to the participants at each and the many other colleagues who have commented usefully on this study and related work over the years, including Steve Bailey, Gregor Bulc, Mihai Coman, Nick Couldry, Rob Drew, Walter Gruenzweig, Hanno Hardt, Birgitta Höijer, Morten Kansteiner, Knut Lundby, Breda Luthar, Arnt Maaso, Tom McCourt, Gunnar Saebo, Jonathan Sterne, Steve Wurtzler, and Espen Ytreberg.

performance of role and situation. More than just an instance of ritualistic structure in everyday life, these can be seen as the moments of communion in the cult of the individual. They are the high points of the ceremony, the moment of contact with the sacred object: the person. On the other hand is the profusion of discourses, texts, and artifacts about people and personalities, individuals and individuality, myths, moral dramas, passion plays, and rites of accession and denigration. The media provide the religious education of the cult of the individual. Along with church school, they provide the liturgy, sermons, hymns and hymnology, bible and commentary, evangelism, denominationalism, and ecumenism of the cult of the individual. That is why the celebrity system and its audience appear so large and its processes and products so pervasive—because it is so important.

## Durkheim on the Cult of the Individual

That the cult of the individual is a legitimate religious practice and a necessary characteristic of modern society is one of Durkheim's more intriguing ideas. Though never fully developed, the idea appears in widely scattered passages of books, articles, and posthumously published lecture notes from all parts of his career. Analyzed in the larger context of his sociology, as Pickering (1984, especially pp. 476-499) does, a vision of a new religion attuned to the needs of modernity can be inferred.

In this new, modern religion, the individual is sacred, and individualism is a sacred value system. The new religion would be based, at least in part, on "objective knowledge" of the world, proving useful in people's lives; it would emphasize justice. Beyond that, like all religions in Durkheim's (1912/1995) analysis, the new religion would express the unity of individual, society, and sacred principles and would engage in periodic gatherings and other ritual forms for the expression, promulgation, and reinforcement of its principles. In his clearest statement

on the issue, from an essay responding to the Dreyfus affair in 1898, Durkheim (1898/1994) said, "the religion of the individual is a social institution like all known religions. It is society which assigns us this ideal as the sole common end which is today capable of providing a focus for men's [and women's] wills" (p. 70).

My proposal is that the media system of consumer culture and celebrity has grown as a church of the cult of the individual. Goffman (e.g., 1959, 1967) has shown that interpersonal interactions are conducted according to ritual rules consistent with Durkheim's proposal that the person is a sacred object (this work is discussed later). The media function as an adjunct to this system, providing the religious education necessary to good performance of the cult.

Others have put forward seemingly similar proposals; for example, that television functions like religion for many people. These proposals, though, were formally functionalist and analogical, leaving questions of religious substance and practice unaddressed. By contrast, my proposal is literalist and analytical: that the media system really is a necessary working part of a real religion—although some of the evidence is based on functionalist analysis and some of the descriptive language is analogy.

### Moralities of Consumption

One of the mysteries of Durkheim's work is his lack of explicit reference to communication and media. He preferred discussion of such apparently more serious topics as morality and religion, economy, law, division of labor, psychology, suicide, and education. Yet the working mechanisms referenced in each of his explanations of social process and order, in all of his major works, is something we would today recognize as falling within the analytical category of the communicative (Rothenbuhler, 1993). This fundamental role of communication in his social theory was left mostly implicit—it was certainly never specifically named as the communication process on which society depends—and when he discussed symbols and signs, his language and analysis was stiff and anachronistic even in its own time. He showed no evidence of special interest in the developments of the mass press, telegraph, telephone, sound recording, cinema, or radio, and he could be disdainful of other sociologists who were paying attention, including both Tarde and the American pragmatists. This may have been a kind of blind spot in his work, an inhibition about drawing attention to its own historically situated foundations. Durkheim's enduring insight into the communicative foundations of social order and process may have been partly based on his luck in being alive at a time when communication systems and structures were changing with unprecedented rapidity. Along with the development of electrical systems that allowed communication to break free of physical movement, this rapid change allowed the fundamental importance of communication systems to be more readily observed. Yet Durkheim never said so. His self-understanding was that he was pursuing the science of morality and discovering evidence of otherwise invisible and theretofore unknown social currents and forces. Today, we would call them communication.

Williams (1982) argues for another set of affinities between historical setting and Durkheimian sociology—along with the work of Tarde and other turn of the century French social theorists. Her argument is that modern sociology and consumer culture were two currents of the same stream. Each in its own way expressed a vision of a world of mutable status, role, identity, and hierarchy. About this connection, too, Durkheim is mostly silent and occasionally disdainful or obfuscatory. Still, his proposals for the cult of the individual show striking continuities of logic with recent developments in the study of consumer culture, which, growing out of contemporary cultural studies, are purportedly entirely independent of any Durkheimian influence. Starting from the assumptions of neo-Marxist and post-Marxist cultural theory, this literature nevertheless converges with the present Durkheimian analysis on the seriousness and importance of the social identity processes conducted in the apparently optional worlds of consumption behavior and leisure activities. (See Nick Couldry's work, chapter 6 and 2003, for another example of this convergence.)

Assimilating Durkheimian sociology and consumer culture draws attention to the existence of moralities of consumption. Consumer behavior may often be mundane, but it is not unimportant. The choice of a soap product may be trivial, but it is not frivolous. Leisure may be play, but it is not without rule of reason. Consumption may not always or necessarily be so, but it can be a part of "the serious life." There are right and wrong, good and bad, beautiful and ugly ways to consume. These moralities of consumption exist because consumption is symbolic behavior that articulates self and social order.

This conclusion is also based on larger historical developments that have been examined from other important points of view. The history of play and leisure illustrates their origins in the serious life, showing how they became importantly distinct realms of optional behavior only with the rise of industrialization (Huizinga, 1955). Turner (1982) develops this theme in his important distinction between *liminoid* and *liminal*, liminoid being the more individuated, optional form, characteristic of ritual in modern, industrial societies. Following another line, Gadamer (1975) elucidates the essential role in the modern vision of culture of the idea of cultivating oneself. With the rise of modernity, culture was tied to education, its appreciation and production were seen as learned capacities, and it was valued for its meliorative effects on individuals. Thus, precisely as leisure and play became distinct social realms of optionality, culture was imbued with a vision by which the right choices in leisure could be self-improving. The necessary correlate of this proposition was that the wrong choices would be self-wasting, from which grew the study of deviance and disorder. To this day, commentary and study of mass communication and popular culture are wracked by differences in taste, value debates, and presumptions about the positive and negative character of effects. The cultural items produced and selected, the ideas and images expressed and enjoyed, as well as their social effects, are presumed to be the business of academics, public intellectuals, and politicians. It could not be that the public presumed to have a voice in other people's choices in such matters, unless on the background of a morality of consumption.

These connections demonstrate the serious, self-defining, and socially freighted importance of communicative and cultural choices in the domain of consumption behavior and leisure activities. These are communicative activities in which we can observe some of the invisible social forces to which Durkheim devoted his career. They are activities of the cult of the individual.

## The Production of Saints and Heroes

In providing the discourse environment for the cult of the individual, one of the media's most important activities is the production of saints and heroes, devils and ghosts, choirs, preachers, mullahs, gurus, and bishops. This is done through a complex mix of texts, artifacts, performances, discussions, and accounts. Moral dramas portray and news accounts report what happens to people who perform their individuality in good and bad ways. Myth and ritual do more than present heroes and villains; in this way, heroes and villains are created. All of the systems for recruitment, training, expulsion, status distinction, roles, hierarchy, and all of the other structures and processes of social organization must be present in the church of the cult of the individual. But as this church exists in communication and not in the organization of material bodies and resources, its structures and processes must exist in discourse, text, and artifact. Its structures must be semiotic and its processes hermeneutic.

## GOFFMAN ON THE CULT OF THE INDIVIDUAL

Goffman's work on interpersonal ritual is the only example we have of a sustained effort to follow up on Durkheim's idea of the cult of the individual (see, e.g., Goffman, 1959, 1967). His work was an ethology of the microdynamics of interpersonal interaction. Observation shows that interactions are structured in highly generalizable ways. The analysis explains these structures as having evolved to deal with the circumstance that the self has become a sacred object that, on the one hand, can only be known in interaction with others, although, at the same time, it is most likely to be damaged in interaction with others. The others in the interaction have the same dilemma. Interpersonal interactions, therefore, are structured as rituals of approach and avoidance in which selves are simultaneously presented and protected. Because both parties can benefit from success and either can be hurt by failure, the normal result is a cooperative ceremony. Surrounding this norm is an elaborate structure of rules for handling special cases and incompetent or uncooperative people (see Goffman, 1959, 1967; Rothenbuhler, 1998).

## GOFFMAN ON MEDIA REPRESENTATIONS

In *Gender Advertisements,* Goffman (1976) addressed media representations, advertising photography in particular. His important conclusion deserves to be generalized beyond the case materials he analyzed. That conclusion is that much of media content functions as a form of hyperritualization in which the normal rules of personal presentation are exaggerated, the normal stereotypes are more so, the distribution of types tends to extremes, and so on. In the media presentation of personal roles and performances—in advertising pictures, dramas, song lyrics, and talk—the range of realistic possibilities tends to be reduced to iconographic representations of selected, and thereby preferred, types. Second, because they are presented in the media, these types are given greater public presence and social authority. They become especially prominent examples of how to conduct oneself in the company of others. They become displays in the world that provide orientation (instruction) for how to display one's orientation to others in the world, representative examples of how to be a representative example (Rothenbuhler, 1998).

## CELEBRITY AND REPUTATION

The literatures of celebrity and reputation have developed in ways mostly separate from these Durkheimian sources. This is unfortunate, for celebrity and reputation have come to be understood as rather peculiar, semiautonomous dynamics. The celebrity system may be understood in its own terms—how celebrities rise and fall, for example—but not in its capacity as a system of symbolic expression for larger social currents. Reputational dynamics may be understood well enough to attempt manipulation of the system— as do public relations agents and campaign consultants—but they cannot be understood as parts of a larger system.

The literature on celebrity has settled on three standard stories (see, e.g., Braudy, 1986; Gamson, 1994; Marshall, 1997). One is a story of historical decline, from heroes of production to heroes of consumption (Lowenthal, 1944), from heroes famous for their accomplishments to celebrities whose fame is their accomplishment (Boorstin, 1961). A second story is of ideological displacement, in which celebrities are presented as if they were heroes. In these analyses, celebrities appear in one of four forms: glamorously different from us ordinary folks; just like us in most ways, but different nevertheless; as selected by luck; or as fated, magically endowed, or inexplicably special (see variously, Alberoni, 1972; Dyer, 1979; Marshall, 1997; Mills, 1959). A third story addresses the star system and the star-making machinery. In this account, celebrities are products of the rationalization of the industrial production of culture. Celebrity, by this account, is a decision-making tool that reduces the uncertainty of the management of media and culture industries.

All three of these stories about celebrity are suspicious of their subject matter. In the story of decline, fame once had a virtuous purpose in celebrating real accomplishments, but now it celebrates false accomplishments, reflecting and producing a debased culture. Similarly, the ideological perspective views celebrity as a device for distracting the attention of the masses from their real problems and their potentially real heroes.

Similarly again, the star-making–machinery analysis views celebrity as not what it appears to be but as a tool and product of business management and industrial production.

However, if Durkheim was right that the religion of the individual is the only value system that can unite a modern society and that therefore the practice of its cult is necessary to the social order, then the celebrity system, which produces the most famous individuals of all, must be a more important and more orderly phenomenon than any of these analyses present. It may be that the move from heroes of production to heroes of consumption is not a decline, but an evolution. In a simpler, smaller, and more collectivistic social order, perhaps people were selected and celebrated for their contributions to the order. In a larger, more complex order, working on more individualistic values, it would make sense to celebrate individuals as individuals. Far from an instance of ideological displacement, then, the celebrity system would be drawing the attention of the masses to instances and instructions for the operation of the values that work in the present order. Celebrity dynamics are more than just tools and products of the economy: They are fundamentally important expressions of the value system of the society.

Reputation has been analyzed in the contexts of social interactions and social control, as resource and commodity, in artistic and literary careers, and as celebrity (e.g., Becker, 1982; Goode, 1978; Lang & Lang, 1990; Rodden, 1989). One generalization across these contexts is that reputation as such tends to be most important in domains where the procedures, criteria, and indications of success are least tangible (Lang & Lang, 2002). Reputation as such is more important in art, for example, than in sports, and more important in politics than in business. It is probably more important in the less tangible areas of business— more important for managers than for stock traders, for example. The procedures, criteria, and indications of success in the performance of individuality are eminently, if not definitively, intangible. We should expect, then, that reputation would be a key currency in the cult of the individual.

## Two Modalities of Self

Combining Goffman's analysis of interaction ritual and selected ideas from the literatures on reputation and celebrity, we can construct a model of two modalities of the self: presentation and reputation. Normally, presentation and reputation are mixed, as in interactions between people who know or know of each other. Media presentations with known actors mix the two, as does news coverage that combines presentation and reportage. An interaction with a stranger would be all presentation. Media representations of anonymous, noncelebrity actors would be the analog. Situations of pure reputation would be rare, but urban myths and news reports of the form "so-and-so said such-and-such today" could be taken to qualify. Celebrity news and the features of gossip magazines would qualify. If the role of the media is to function as the religious literature, commentary, and church school of the cult of the individual, then it is not trivial that pure cases of the two modalities are more common in the media than in the interactions of everyday life. Mixed cases are realistic; pure cases are instructive.

## Modalities of Celebrity

The literature of celebrity is dominated by attention to Hollywood, film stars, and associated entertainments. This appears to follow public opinion, reflecting a general understanding of who the big stars are and where the big celebrity money is made. It would be helpful, though, to complement this with a comparative study of types of celebrity.

The film star is explicitly known as an actor; the television star is also known as an actor, but often in only one role. Musicians, artists, literary figures, news reporters, and politicians are also actors in the celebrity system, but they are not usually known as such, and their role and person are usually treated as the same. Film stars come to be appreciated for their performances in multiple roles, and they can also be known, appreciated, or denigrated for their performances as themselves on talk shows, at charity events, working for political causes, as spouses and family members, and so on. Some film stars are known as great actors who embody each different role they take. Others have a celebrity more apparently based on the idea that in one way or another they are playing themselves in the different roles they take. Any such distinction between person and role, however, is much more rare for musicians, artists, writers, reporters, or politicians. Their performances are less readily distinguished from their selves, and they work in cultural domains where honest expression is often seen to depend on a direct and uncalculated relationship between self and expressive work. They are, in the system, supposed to be themselves. (The case of writers is more complicated.)

Perhaps film stars make the best celebrities—or the most prominently popular ones—because their performance is the most useful analog of the tensions experienced by the everyday modern person in the many roles that this person must negotiate in the activities of everyday life. Film stars are displayed in and out of role, in different roles, front stage and back stage. They handle it with aplomb and attractive cool. When they do not, their deserved punishment and later apology is prominently displayed.

In contrast to film celebrities, who may be performing with grace under pressure in multiple roles, celebrity musicians, artists, and politicians are, perhaps, normally performing authenticity, genuineness, and fealty. A social system built on individualism could not work without emphasis on such reliability-producing values. Quite regularly, celebrities of these types are destroyed when the machinery of publicity is turned to a ritual of expulsion because they have attempted major changes of public thought and expression. Individuals whose convictions count for so little should not be trusted. Occasionally, though, celebrity musicians, artists, or politicians can change their style of thought or expression and survive as an appreciated celebrity. Such stars will normally be known as geniuses; again, this is a necessary form of individuality for a social system and thus successful cases are presented as such. Geniuses are needed, but it would be dangerous to the system should too many people think it an easy path to pursue. Therefore failed geniuses are presented as unreliable individualists, guilty of uncontrolled impulses, excesses of ego, unproductive idiosyncrasy—in a word, self-indulgence.

## HAGIOGRAPHY AND GHOST STORIES

A few disparate celebrities can be selected and analyzed for a strange phenomenon they have in common: Most of their celebrity is not only posthumous but peculiarly concerned with the relations of the living and the dead. George Orwell became, after his death, "Saint George," and the authority to tell his life story and claim his patronage was vigorously competed for (Rodden, 1989). If Orwell became a saint, Elvis Presley became a ghost. Indeed, the presence of his uninhabited image was already so pervasive in American culture that perhaps we were haunted already before he died. And now that he is dead, from imitators to memorials, from tributes to parodies, from relics to trinkets, Elvis is everywhere—awfully noisy, as Rodman (1996) says, for a dead man (Marcus, 1991). Frida Kahlo, the Mexican painter, has been the subject of a devoted posthumous celebrity known as "Frida-mania" that centers on identification between the fan and the imaged artist through the media of her paintings and myth (Lindauer, 1999). The blues musician Robert Johnson has not yet achieved one-name status, as have St. George, Elvis, and Frida, but his has become the most recognized name of any pre-World War II blues musician. Also, the dynamics of his posthumous reputation and the place of devils and ghosts in his story fix him in the same group (Rothenbuhler, in press).

The Elvis case raises an interesting question. If Elvis's image was haunting the culture before he died, and if his presence was at least as lively after, then was he in some ways already dead before

he died and still alive after? This could only be, of course, in his capacity as a saint or a ghost of the cult of the individual. Before he died, his role in that system was clearly defined. As his body began to fail to live up to that role, his spirit took leave and began its own career—not his Christian spirit, or his Buddhist one, but his spirit as a leader of the church of the individual. After the death of his body, his spirit-celebrity was that much more free to pursue its work.

Lindauer (1999) demonstrates something in the Frida Kahlo case that is also important in a more general way for artist-celebrities. Lindauer shows how, for her celebrity following, Kahlo's painting is understood as a natural, inevitable, direct expression of the artist. Kahlo the artist is also understood as a natural, inevitable, and direct expression of Kahlo the person, an uncalculated, expressive product of her biography. All of this is taken as iconographic representation of woman. The result is, as Lindauer puts it, "artist = paintings = woman." This equivalence allows the devoted Frida-following to know and appreciate any one term of the equation by knowing and appreciating the others and results, Lindauer claims, in consuming the follower through a fetishistic relation with the paintings. One appreciates and values oneself as a woman through empathy with Frida's biography and appreciation of Frida's paintings. One understands Frida's biography and paintings through one's own experience as a woman.

Elements of this analysis may not be generalizable from Frida-mania to the other cases of interest here. The system of equivalences is partly based on sexist ideas about the natural expressiveness of women painters, stories about the special role of feminine pain in Kahlo's life and art, and ideas about the centrality of such pain in the being of woman. The selection of some artists for celebration because they can be portrayed as embodying the idea that self = expression is surely a more general phenomenon. The Elvis case is strikingly parallel even as it seems bizarrely improbable. He is understood by his fans, against all odds, as just a nice country boy who loved to sing. His work is seen as an expression of who he is; who he is is understood through an appreciation of his work. Even his worst movies and music can then be seen as evidence of his honest being, simple origins, and limited ambitions. It is on this basis that Elvis is adored. Orwell's biography is told in radically different ways by the different schools contending to adopt him as forefather; it is a struggle for equivalence of biography and work. Robert Johnson's supposed biography—the one that was invented and embellished for decades before any real facts were discovered—is still the source of the most widely told tales about any blues musician. Why? Because it embodies the value of authenticity, the equivalence of life and work. The singer of lonely songs should be a lonely person. The writer of songs about ghosts and devils should live a haunted life.

There is more; this is no simple authenticity. The authenticity performed in the vision of artistic life in which person = work is authenticity at its highest level—it is self-sacrifice. The story of Robert Johnson is that his attempts to play guitar produced laughing ridicule from other musicians until he sold his soul to the devil. Suddenly he reappeared on the scene as a polished guitar player, in possession of techniques and chord voicings unknown to others. After that he had a few short years of playing before the devil came to collect his debt. Given poisoned whiskey by a jealous husband while playing at a juke joint, Johnson died a few days later—according to some versions of the myth, crawling on all fours and barking like a dog.

In the last 2 years of his life, before dying in 1938, Johnson recorded 29 songs. When rereleased on albums 30 years later, along with liner notes that sketched the myth, rock and roll musicians heard and read evidence of the sacrifice it took to become a blues musician. Reports of Johnson's ghost appeared soon afterwards.

Indeed, Johnson's songs became widely played by rock and roll musicians, starting in the 1960s and continuing to today. His name is often invoked in discussions of influences and inspirations. Prominent musicians have referred to Johnson's inspiring or fearful presence in their lives, not infrequently using religious, supernatural, or therapeutic language. Most recently, Eric Clapton and Peter Greene have devoted whole albums to his music, and John Fogerty pinned a comeback tour to an epiphany at the side of his grave. (Subsequent questions about whether Johnson is really buried there can perhaps explain the limited success of the comeback strategy.) (See Rothenbuhler, in press, for a fuller account of the strange career of Johnson's records and his posthumous reputation.)

## A MODERN RELIGION?

So, which of the stories about celebrity is true? What are the answers to the questions with which we started? On present evidence, we could not say. What is demonstrated here, though, is the possibility of a system of ideas by which certain mysteries of celebrity can be understood. This chapter is admittedly speculative, even playful, and the proposal that the media function as a church of the cult of the individual must remain a hypothesis.

The self-understanding of modernity is that it is a secular age; religious life, along with politics, industry, privacy, and more, has been differentiated from the whole and assigned its proper purview. No longer world making, religion in modernity is a specialized, institutional sphere. Indeed, the historical religions have been differentiated from politics and industry; they have been assigned their own institutional spheres, from which they largely act as conservative influences on other social processes.

Of course, Durkheim's great contribution was to identify the structures and processes underlying modern, secular life that operate by the logic of religion but without its name. Modernity has its religious element, even as it swears it does not. The flash of this insight has motivated much of the interest of media scholars in ritual and myth. This chapter demonstrates the possibility of building a more formal theory of religious structures and processes, ubiquitous in modern, secular life and peculiarly attuned to it, operating independently of traditional institutionalized religion.

Modern life is built on the cult of the individual. It is the religion that dare not speak its name; nevertheless, our communication practices; our cultural choices; our industries of information, entertainment, and consumption; our politics; our educational institutions; and, increasingly, our churches are built around the construction, display, critique, and improvement of selves. The self is the holy object of the society carried by the medium of the individual. It can only exist in communicative interaction, and therefore its churches must be communicative structures. Thus the media and their productions, distribution systems, and audiences grow ever larger. Manufacturing industries devote more and more to consumer design, becoming more and more communication industries also. The economies of industrial powers evolve toward service industries, with everything revolving around the individual consumer. Politics becomes (is) marketing. All of the institutional spheres differentiated in the evolution of modernity become more like communication industries. No one is in favor of it, and yet all participate. How else to explain it except as due to the inexorable, arational pull of religious faith. We must be our self and our self must be served. Attention to the self spreads, contagious and attractive as a religious ecstasy.

# REFERENCES

Alberoni, F. (1972). The powerless "elite": Theory and sociological research on the phenomenon of stars. In D. McQuail (Ed.), *Sociology of mass communications: Selected readings* (pp. 75-98). New York: Penguin.

Becker, H. (1982). *Art worlds.* Berkeley: University of California Press.

Boorstin, D. J. (1961). *The image: Or, what happened to the American dream.* New York: Atheneum.

Braudy, L. (1986). *The frenzy of renown: Fame and its history.* New York: Oxford University Press.

Couldry, N. (2003). *Media rituals: A critical approach.* London: Routledge.

Durkheim, É. (1994). Individualism and the intellectuals (S. Lukes & J. Lukes, Trans.). In W.S.F. Pickering (Ed.), *Durkheim on religion* (pp. 59-73). Atlanta, GA: Scholars Press. (Original work published 1898)

Durkheim, É. (1995). *The elementary forms of the religious life* (K. E. Fields, Trans.). New York: Free Press. (Original work published 1912)

Dyer, R. (1979). *Stars.* London: British Film Institute.

Gadamer, H. G. (1975). *Truth and method.* New York: Crossroad.

Gamson, J. (1994). *Claims to fame: Celebrity in contemporary America.* Berkeley: University of California Press.

Goffman, E. (1959). *The presentation of self in everyday life.* New York: Anchor Books.

Goffman, E. (1967). *Interaction ritual: Essays on face-to-face behavior.* New York: Anchor Books.

Goffman, E. (1976). *Gender advertisements.* Cambridge, MA: Harvard University Press.

Goode, W. J. (1978). *The celebration of heroes: Prestige as a social control system.* Berkeley: University of California Press.

Huizinga, J. (1955). *Homo ludens: A study of the play element in culture.* Boston: Beacon Press.

Lang, G. E., & Lang, K. (1990). *Etched in memory: The building and survival of artistic reputation.* Chapel Hill: University of North Carolina Press.

Lang, K., & Lang, G. E. (2002). Reputation. In *International Encyclopedia of the Social and Behavioral Sciences* (pp. 13210-13216). New York: Elsevier Science.

Lindauer, M. A. (1999). *Devouring Frida: The art history and popular celebrity of Frida Kahlo.* Hanover, NH: Wesleyan University Press.

Lowenthal, L. (1944). Biographies in popular magazines. In P. F. Lazarsfeld & F. N. Stanton (Eds.), *Radio research 1942-1943* (pp. 507-548). New York: Essential Books.

Marcus, G. (1991). *Dead Elvis: A chronicle of a cultural obsession.* New York: Doubleday.

Marshall, P. D. (1997). *Celebrity and power: Fame in contemporary culture.* Minneapolis: University of Minnesota Press.

Mills, C. W. (1959). *The power elite.* New York: Oxford University Press.

Pickering, W.S.F. (1984). *Durkheim's sociology of religion: Themes and theories.* London: Routledge & Kegan Paul.

Rodman, G. B. (1996). *Elvis after Elvis: The posthumous career of a living legend.* New York: Routledge.

Rodden, J. (1989). *The politics of literary reputation: The making and claiming of "St. George" Orwell.* New York: Oxford University Press.

Rothenbuhler, E. W. (1993, Summer). Argument for a Durkheimian theory of the communicative. *Journal of Communication, 43,* 158-163.

Rothenbuhler, E. W. (1998). *Ritual communication: From everyday conversation to mediated ceremony.* Thousand Oaks, CA: Sage.

Rothenbuhler, E. W. (2005). The strange career of Robert Johnson's records. In S. Jones & J. Jensen (Eds.), *Afterlife as afterimage: Understanding posthumous fame.* New York: Peter Lang.

Turner, V. (1982). *From ritual to theatre: The human seriousness of play.* New York: Performing Arts Journal Publications.

Williams, R. H. (1982). *Dream worlds: Mass consumption in late nineteenth-century France.* Berkeley: University of California Press.

# 10

# NEWS AS MYTH

## Daily News and Eternal Stories

JACK LULE

News stories do not arrive fully formed on the dusty computer screens of journalists, although journalists sometimes wish they would. Stories are shaped by many forces. The process begins early. Even as a story is assigned, editors and reporters make sure they have a mutual understanding of "the story."

Other forces then begin to act on the story. Colleagues may suggest their own interpretations. Expectations of the publisher or broadcast owner may be well known in the newsroom. Previous stories found in databases or clippings files have influence. Conventions and traditions, such as inverted pyramid leads and codes of objectivity, guide research and writing. Sources have their own view of the story. Questions asked by competing reporters are noted. Expectations of the audience and long-term circulation or ratings goals can be considered.

The single news story can often be forged from some or all of these forces. Stories, in this perspective, take shape before a word is written. For each event—an election, airline crash, murder, concert, football game, or fire—editors, reporters,

sources, and audiences try to understand: *What's the story?*

Editors and reporters do not have to conceive brand-new stories for each event. They do not have to tell stories never before written or read. Stories already exist. Journalists approach events with stories. They employ common understandings. They take from shared narratives. They draw upon traditional story forms. They come to the news story with fundamental and familiar stories. Sometimes the story changes as the journalist gathers more information. The story does not change into something completely new and never before seen, however. It changes into—another fundamental and familiar story.

Modern society calls the fundamental stories told by ancient cultures "myth." Modern society calls the fundamental stories told by the BBC or the *New York Times* "news." This chapter is about connections between news and myth. It suggests that myths take modern form in the news of today. I will first define myth and look back on scholarship that has studied news as myth. I will trace how archetypal myths take form in the news

---

**Author's Note:** This chapter is adapted from Jack Lule, *Daily News, Eternal Stories: The Mythological Role of Journalism* (New York: Guilford Press, 2001).

and argue that myths can be found every day within national reports, international correspondence, sports columns, human interest features, editorials, and obituaries. I will suggest that any discussion of journalism that does not account for storytelling and myth misses a vital part of the news.

In this view, journalists are part of a long storytelling tradition that includes fleet-footed messengers, minstrels, troubadours, carriers, couriers, criers, poets, chief priests, missionaries, rabbis, and medicine men. Journalists draw their tales from a deep but limited range of story forms and types that long ago proved their ability to hold audiences. The storytelling tradition is significant, probably crucial, to human lives and human societies. News is a vital part of that tradition.

We do not often think of news in this way. Our understanding of news is shaped by our times. We act as if news was invented for our modern era. We think of news as information for an information society. News, for us, is details and data about politics, products, crime, celebrities, technology, sports, and stocks. News gives us reports about candidates, companies, teams, movies, neighbors, and weather. News is much more, however: News is myth.

## MYTH DEFINED

The connections between news and myth at first may appear to be the product of overly imaginative professors who have spent a bit too much time in ivory towers. In popular use, *myth* can mean a false belief or untrue story. Myth also means an ancient tale of fabulous people and incredible places. News usually means a report of factual events and real people. To compare news and myth may seem like comparing black and white or true and false. Indeed, myth is often contrasted with reality, as in the possible title: "The Ivory Tower: Myth or Reality?"

For this discussion, *myth* will not be defined as a false belief or untrue story. Myth is not ancient and unreal. To compare news and myth does not suggest that news regularly passes down untrue stories of doubtful origins. It does not suggest that news is inherently false, biased, slanted, or spun. Myth is understood as a societal story that expresses prevailing ideals, ideologies, values, and beliefs. More broadly, myth is an essential social narrative, a rich and enduring aspect of human existence, which draws from archetypal figures and forms to offer exemplary models for social life (Eliade, 1958; Frye, 1951, 1957; Jung, 1959). This seemingly simple definition can have numerous social, cultural, and political implications. It sees the stories of myth as much more than interesting, entertaining, well-known tales. It places myth—and news—near the center of social life.

The definition emphasizes "archetypal figures and forms" and "exemplary models." I want to explain and explore further what these are. Archetypes are original frameworks. In terms of myth, they are patterns, images, motifs, and characters taken from and shaped by the shared experiences of human life, which have helped structure and shape stories across cultures and eras. Archetypes are fundamental figures and forces, such as heroes, floods, villains, plagues, patriarchs, pariahs, great mothers, and tricksters. Given life in narrative, they help create the primary archetypal stories that are at the heart of human storytelling.

Not all archetypal stories are myths. Archetypes influence much storytelling, from the imaginative play of children to daydreams to romance novels to Shakespearean plays. Myths are archetypal stories that play crucial social roles. That is, myth enters the picture when archetypal stories represent important social issues or ideals. For example, a tale of a hero can represent strength or bravery or compassion. A flood story can portray the wrath of an angry god or the humbling power of nature.

Used in this way, archetypal stories offer "exemplary models." They provide examples of good, evil, right, wrong, bravery, and cowardice. They are models of social life and models for social life. Myth draws upon archetypal figures and forms to offer exemplary models that represent shared values; confirm core beliefs; deny other beliefs;

and help people engage, appreciate, and understand the complex joys and sorrows of human life.

Archetypes often are associated with the theories of psychologist Carl Jung (1964, 1976). Although Jung provided many insights, his psychological framework, one element of which is the concept of the "collective unconscious," is not necessary for an appreciation of archetypes, models, and myth. In fact, a large number of theories and theoreticians have explored this terrain. I draw most frequently from the philosopher and historian of religion Mircea Eliade. A Romanian who lived for years in France and the United States, Eliade studied myth in hundreds of societies and had a breadth of experience that allowed him to see links among myths from many different cultures and eras, including our own. Eliade's political positions, which seem to range from far right to far left, have troubled some, but he is a towering figure in modern studies of myth.

In his studies, Eliade (1958) found that archetypes and exemplary models were key to myth. He stated:

> Religious life, and all the creations that spring from it, are dominated by what one may call "the tendency toward an archetype." However many and varied are the components that go to make up any religious creation (any divine form, rite, myth or cult) their expression tends constantly to revert to an archetype. (pp. 58-59)

Myth, Eliade argued, uses archetypes, such as heroes and floods, as models. He felt that myth is sacred, exemplary, and significant because it "supplies models for human behavior and, by that very fact, gives meaning and value to life" (Eliade, 1963, pp. 1-2). For Eliade, myth is often about origins and beginnings. Myth provides models based on these elemental creations. He said, "the foremost function of myth is to reveal the exemplary models for all human rites and all significant human activities—diet or marriage, work or education, art or wisdom" (p. 8).

Eliade (1958) found myth using archetypal models to guide all kinds of activities, "the act of procreation, 'the cheering of a despondent heart, the feeble aged and the decrepit,' inspiring the composing of songs, going to war." He said myth thus "provides a *model,* whenever there is a question of *doing something"* (pp. 410-411).

## Myth as Essential—Even Today

Seen in this way, myth is surely not ancient or old, fantastic or false. Myth is essential and always alive. The stories of myth are necessary to human lives and the societies they construct. Eliade (1963) argued that "certain aspects and functions of mythical thought are constituents of the human being" (pp. 183-184). He wrote:

> It seems unlikely that any society could completely dispense with myths, for, of what is essential in mythical behaviour—the exemplary pattern, the repetition, the break with profane duration and integration into primordial time—the first two at least are consubstantial with every human condition. (Eliade, 1960, pp. 31-32)

Joseph Campbell (1960) agreed: "No human society has yet been found," he said, "in which such mythological motifs have not been rehearsed in liturgies; interpreted by seers, poets, theologians, or philosophers; presented in art; magnified in song; and ecstatically experienced in life-empowering visions" (pp. 1-2). Jung too saw myth as essential. "Has mankind ever really got away from myths?" asked Jung (1976, p. 25). "One could almost say that if all the world's traditions were cut off at a single blow, the whole of mythology and the whole history of religion would start all over again with the next generation." Every society needs stories that confront the ultimate issues of the human condition. Every society needs myths.

Modern societies, though, have modern conceits. They especially like to pretend that they are more "advanced" than other societies. They believe myth is for ancient or primitive societies. They believe they have no need of heroes, villains, exemplary figures, portrayals of good and evil. They believe they have replaced myth with scientific knowledge, technological advances, and objective reports of the real world. They fool themselves.

Eliade, as I noted, studied myths in hundreds of societies. He raised his gaze to the modern world—and saw classic myths all around him. He said, "an adequate analysis of the diffuse mythologies of the modern world would run into volumes: for myths and mythological images are to be found everywhere, laicised, degraded or disguised; one only needs to be able to recognise them" (Eliade, 1960, p. 33).

He called these disguised mythologies "the survivals and camouflages of myth" (Eliade, 1963, p. 162). He and other writers revealed the "survivals and camouflages" of modern myth in many places, from cars to suburbia to modern art—but especially in the mass media (Campbell, 1949, 1972; Eliade, 1959). Comic books, plays, mystery stories, radio shows, romance novels, movies, television programs, and other forms of mass media continually reaffirm: Modern society too needs to hear the stories of myth.

## MYTH IN THE NEWS

With this background, we can take an arresting step: Like Eliade, we can recognize in some news stories the siren song of myth. News stories offer more than a retelling of common story forms. News stories offer sacred, societal narratives with shared values and beliefs, with lessons and themes, with exemplary models that instruct and inform. News stories are myths.

To be sure, there is no need to overstate the case for mythic stories in the news. Many news stories have no relation to myth. Many news stories are derived from rudimentary story forms and professional conventions of the trade, such as inverted pyramid leads or easy formulas for writing speeches, sports results, or fire stories: Official gives speech. Home team wins. Fire destroys building (Darnton, 1975; Eason, 1981; Schudson, 1982). Even Sigmund Freud warned against the danger of overanalyzing, of seeing symbolic content in every object. "Sometimes a cigar is just a cigar," Freud is supposed to have said. Well, sometimes, a fire story is just a fire story.

Sometimes, however, in describing some experience, in reporting some event, reporters and editors draw upon a fundamental story of earthly existence, a universal and shared story of humankind, and they use that story to instruct, inform, celebrate, or forewarn. Like myth tellers from every age, journalists can draw from the rich treasure trove of archetypal stories and make sense of the world.

Sometimes reporters do this consciously. They make explicit references to Icarus, infernos, Oedipus, or plagues. Sometimes they do this unconsciously. Their eyebrows raise when an observer points out ancient heroes, modern tricksters, and archetypal deluges on the front page. Consciously or unconsciously, however, journalists take their place among the centuries of storytellers who tell and retell the myths of humankind.

I want to extend this argument still further. I have come to believe, and hope to show, that, more than any mass medium, the daily news is the primary vehicle for myth in our time. News, of all things, has become the inheritor of humanity's essential stories. Other mass media possess the ability to tell myths. The news, however, when studied carefully, will show numerous, numinous links to myth.

## NEWS AND MYTH REPEAT STORIES

First, like myth, news offers the steady repetition of stories, the rhythmic recurrence of themes and events. Eliade noted that societies need to have their myths told again and again. Myths, he said, offer an "exemplar [sic] history which can be repeated (regularly or otherwise), and whose meaning and value lie in that very repetition" (Eliade, 1958, p. 430). In more difficult language, he wrote: "What is involved is not a commemoration of mythical events but a reiteration of them. The protagonists of the myth are made present, one becomes their contemporary" (Eliade, 1963, p. 19). Myth, he said, thus invokes

the prodigious, "sacred" time when something *new, strong,* and *significant* was manifested. To re-experience that time, to re-enact it as often as possible, to witness again the spectacle of the divine works, to meet with the Supernatural and relearn their creative lesson is the desire that runs like a pattern through all the ritual reiterations of myths. (Eliade, 1963, p. 19)

News too surely offers stories that are "new and strong and significant." Still, like myths, news stories are not really new. More than any mass medium, the news thrives on the ritual repetition of stories. The news tells us the same stories again and again. Like myth, news tells us not only what happened yesterday but what has always happened. Flood and fire, disaster and triumph, crime and punishment, storm and drought, death and birth, victory and loss—daily, the news has recounted and will recount these stories.

For readers, this connection between news and myth may help explain the almost formulaic recurrence of stories in the news, the strange sensation of listening to stories already heard, the odd ability to glance at a story and know precisely what it says. For journalists, myth may help explain the peculiar feeling of writing stories that already have been written, the dim awareness of telling stories that already have been told. "It's an old story," reporters will sometimes explain. It is.

## NEWS AND MYTH TELL "REAL" STORIES

News and myth also share an emphasis on "real" stories. News, of course, places special significance on "the real." Distinctions are drawn, and mostly observed, between fact and opinion, between nonfiction and fiction. Journalists are punished, sometimes fired, for making up facts, for straying from the real. Other mass media tell stories. Sometimes they tell real stories. Only news, however, places such a heavy emphasis on being *real*. Only news is first and foremost supposed to be a report of real events.

Myth, too, oddly enough, has privileged the real. Modern societies equate myth with unreal stories, but for centuries, societies have always been careful to distinguish between the real stories of myth and the false stories of fiction, fable, and legend. Myth, after all, explains origins, promotes order, and represents social beliefs and values. Myth needs to be seen as real and true. Eliade

(1963) said, "Myth tells only of that which *really* happened, which manifested itself completely." He added, "The myth is regarded as a sacred story, and hence a 'true history,' because it always deals with *realities*" (p. 6). The philosopher Ernst Cassirer (1946) also found that the images of myths "are not *known* as images. They are not regarded as symbols but as realities" (p. 57).

## NEWS AND MYTH ARE PUBLIC STORIES

News and myth also share a tradition of *public* storytelling. Stories are everywhere. Some stories are told to one individual by another. Children, couples, friends, and neighbors share stories with one another. Other stories entertain an audience. Plays, radio shows, movies, and television programs offer stories to engage and entertain audiences. News and myth, too, address individuals and audiences. However, as we will see, they also offer stories that inform, instruct, and enlighten *a public*. They address people not just as individuals, not just as audiences, but as members of a social, civic group.

As Mitchell Stephens (1988) made clear in *The History of News,* news stories were told to publics even before the advent of writing. Tribes gathered to hear news of battles and births from well-traveled messengers. Later, towns scheduled times and places for news criers. The Roman empire distributed copies of the *acta*—proceedings and transactions—and posted them in cities. News was understood as information of *public* interest. Myth, too, has addressed its audience as members of a public. As social charter or sacred story, as account of origins or geography of the underworld, myth speaks to a society *as* a society. It is a social narrative, a civic text. Myth and news are, after all, stories of public interest.

## NEWS AND MYTH USE FUNDAMENTAL STORIES TO INSTRUCT AND INFORM

News and myth thus will be shown to bear the closest social similarities. They offer and repeat stories. They draw stories from real life. They tell stories that confront issues of social, public life and they use these stories to instruct and inform. They are moral tales. They warn of disaster and disease, of degeneracy and decay. They tell tales of healing and comfort, of righteousness and reform. They offer dramas of order and disorder, of justice affirmed and justice denied. They present portrayals of heroes and villains, of models to emulate and outcasts to denigrate. News and myth speak to a public and offer stories that shape and maintain and exclude and deny important societal ideas and beliefs. Again, there is no need to overstate the case. Other mass media at times repeat age-old stories. They draw from the real, they address a public, they instruct and inform. Only news, however, regularly and daily, shows its allegiance to myth.

## How News Becomes Myth

How does it happen? How do story, myth and news merge? How do archetypal stories take dramatic shape in the news of today? To begin to answer, we must look more closely at the fundamental, archetypal stories. Storytelling, as we have noted, seems fundamental to human life. Every culture has left evidence of storytelling. Humans make sense of the world and their time in it through story. Even more intriguing, some stories appear fundamental to human life. Startlingly similar folk tales, legends, and myths can be found in different cultures and eras.

For example, the folklorist Stith Thompson (1955) worked for much of the 20th century on a multivolume index of folk literature. It began with a compilation of the world's myths. Thompson collected, collated, and cataloged thousands of myths from across centuries and cultures. When it came time to publish his work, Thompson did not organize the myths by country, culture, or time period. He organized the myths by *theme*. Similar work was compiled by James Frazer (1951). In other words, researchers looked across hundreds of years and cultures and found—the same stories.

How can that occur? Some anthropologists have been convinced that direct connections among these stories can be traced. They argue that neighboring societies borrowed ideas, customs, tools, recipes—and stories—from one another. They point out that great cultural centers of the ancient world were often great trading centers. Stories, they say, were traded too. Stories became part of an overall process of cultural diffusion (Day, 1984, pp. 1-32; Strenski, 1987).

Early psychiatrists and psychologists also observed fundamental stories. However, they advanced a different reason for the cross-cultural similarities. Freud and Jung, in particular, noted similarities between stories, folk tales, myths, and dreams. They asked: How could a 7-year-old girl, an unlikely candidate for diffusion, have dreams with plots and symbols taken from ancient stories? Jung was especially intrigued. He was, for awhile, Freud's foremost student and colleague. When he broke with Freud, one of his primary interests became the study of the "collective unconscious." Jung (1959, 1964, 1976) pointed out that humans were born with bodily organs that had long evolutionary histories. He believed that the human mind, too, had its own evolutionary history. This collective unconscious, Jung said, contains powerful, primordial patterns (archetypes) that lead to the creation of universal symbols, characters, motifs, stories, and myths.

Definitive answers about fundamental stories are not likely to be established by the anthropologists or psychologists. Perhaps the best answer combines the two. Some stories may be fundamental to humans, probably based on the shared experiences of being human. People are born into an almost infinite variety of circumstances, yet we all still share some experiences. We share birth, the entry into the world as small and helpless babies. We share infancy and have hazy, half-remembered images from childhood. We often have families or relationships with mother figures and father figures. We share feelings of fear, love, hate, anger, compassion, jealousy, and joy. We share bodily, natural sensations of hunger, thirst, and sexual desire. We need to sleep. We need to move. We produce and understand, tell and retell stories based on these experiences, and these stories sometimes have been, and will be, shared and spread.

These fundamental stories can be understood as archetypes. As we noted, the word can be used in its original, broader meaning, without reference to Jungian theory, to denote original figures or frameworks, powerful patterns, models to imitate and adapt. The fundamental stories of humankind are archetypal stories. They are patterns and models born from human experience to imitate and adapt. The flood that destroys and cleanses human society is an archetypal story adapted by hundreds of cultures. The trickster, that half-animal, half-human figure lurching through society, is an archetypal story. The hero is an archetypal story.

Once the fundamental stories are in place, they cast their influence on storytelling. Stories shape storytelling. As writers and societies attempt to understand and express their experience of the world, they consciously and unconsciously draw upon the special stories, the commonly shared, universally understood stock of archetypal stories. Writers find these stories within themselves and within their societies. A person may never have been told or taught the story of the flood, but the person has experiences: with the unpredictable forces of nature or with driving rain and wild winds or with sensations of being submerged in a bath, pool, lake, or ocean. The person can be led by those experiences to understand, and perhaps to tell, the story of the flood. Born from universally understood archetypal stories, the particular telling of these tales can have great emotional impact on listeners in every time—including today.

Every telling of the fundamental stories does not result in myth, however. Stories have their own status. Some stories are important just for individuals or small groups. If one of my children runs into the house crying, I will ask what happened. My child will put events into a story of the tragedy. That story is important to me and my child but probably not terribly important to society at large. Other stories, though, are meaningful and consequential for many people.

Just as storytelling seems fundamental to human life, storytelling seems fundamental to social life. Humans need stories, and their societies need stories. Through stories, a group of people define themselves. They tell stories of their origins. They tell stories of what they believe and do not believe. They tell stories of evildoers who threaten the group. They tell stories that ostracize some and celebrate others. They draw from the archetypal stories to pass on to their children and their children's children their ways of life, love, worship, and work. These societal stories attain sacred status. They become accepted and assumed. They narrate and illustrate shared beliefs, values, and ideals. They are myths.

Here we can achieve some understanding of how news becomes myth. We have seen that fundamental stories shape storytelling, that editors, reporters, sources, and readers consciously and unconsciously draw upon the universally understood stock of archetypal stories. When these fundamental stories become public, when these stories are told to a people, when these stories are narrated on a societal level to render exemplary models and represent shared social values and beliefs, news becomes myth. News stories can be understood as the modern recurrence of these stories. Society after society has attested to the enduring power of the archetypal stories. Our society is no different. News is the latest echo of stories uttered long ago. Journalists, as storytellers, cannot help but call upon the fundamental stories that long ago proved their worth to humankind.

## Which Myths Get Told, and Why

To sum up the matter perhaps too simply: Reporters, editors, sources, and readers draw from a large, though limited, range of fundamental stories to portray and understand events. Which stories ultimately get chosen? Which myths get told in the news, and why? The answer: News most often tells stories that support social order and sustain the current state of things.

This proposition is darker than I would like, but there is no way to read the news regularly and not see how news most often affirms the status quo, confirms the way things are and sustains the current social order. Many scholars take this further. They reduce culture and myth to ideology. For them, ideology is the starting point, the driving force that produces culture, society, myth, and news. For them, news and myth are told solely for the production of consent and the maintenance and support of ideology.

I try to resist such reduction, but the devil must get his due. Social order—no abstract, static entity—is acted out and affirmed each day as people participate in dramas great and small. News, as myth, participates decisively in social order. Myth not only offers order but insists on order. Myth not only confirms beliefs but constricts beliefs. Myth not only passes down traditions but sanctions traditions. In support of social order, news as myth daily defends the dominant social consensus.

As myth, news stories herald values of sacrifice and service through the myth of the Good Mother. News stories demean "other worlds," warn of their dark chaos and trumpet our own society's superiority. News stories celebrate modern versions of Heroes who embody social values. News stories degrade Scapegoats who transgress or protest too vigorously.

Modern society seems to abide dissent to social order. News, in particular, seems to have been established as a channel for dissent. After all, didn't U.S. news bring down a president during Watergate? Isn't the news constantly criticizing public officials? When studied carefully, however, news stories are shown to seldom challenge core values. They rarely question the very structure of society. They do not dispute the system of governance, apportionment of power, distribution of wealth, or other central features. News primarily tells stories that show society chugging along, through ups and downs, through changes in political parties, through wild swings in the stock market, and through natural disasters great and small. After years of watching dramatic spectacles and tumultuous accounts in the news, we lift our eyes and realize that things have pretty much stayed the same. Day after day, the news upholds the social order in which it holds, after all, a prominent position.

Yet news is messy and complicated, and each news story is a site of personal, social, and political struggle, from its conception by a reporter to its understanding by a reader. News stories and their influence are not predetermined. Thus, myth, thankfully, does not allow us to despair completely over the relationship between social order and news. As myth, news does not always manufacture consent, although it most often does. As myth, news cannot be reduced to ideology, although it often serves that role. Myth, although it throws all its weight to the protection and defense of social order, will survive the passage of any one order. The stories were told long before and will be told long after.

In fact, news can sometimes provide stories and exemplary models that can be used by groups to alter or shape social order. The work of independent U.S. journalist I. F. Stone, an icon to many on the political left, exemplified the ability of news to challenge social order. For decades, Stone produced a weekly newsletter that offered a radical perspective on the news. As the *New York Times* and other mainstream media faithfully echoed early official explanations for U.S. involvement in Vietnam, for example, Stone mined new information from government documents. He placed that information into stories—mythic stories—that not only opposed the dominant explanation but also offered an alternative perspective on the mendacity of government, the military, and U.S. global goals. Numerous European political movements have relied on their own news outlets for stories and myths.

Alternative news outlets on the political right and left ensure that news will not always serve social order. Challenging dominant social values and assumptions is difficult, but it can be done. Myth upheld long-ago regimes—but myth also helped overthrow them.

## The Poet, Historian, and Journalist

Myth reframes our understanding of news—and our understanding of news and public life. Put simply, journalists and audiences often conceive of public life too narrowly. Some see public life in terms of civic affairs. People are seen as citizens and voters, and journalism is cast in hallowed terms as a great informer and trustee for this public. Others see public life in more cynical terms as consumer affairs. People are understood as buyers, and journalism is cast as a great informer and trustee for a purchasing and investing public.

News as myth restores a broader view of public life. Myth suggests that news is intimately entwined with *all* the wide-ranging issues and concerns of human existence, not just civic duties or purchasing problems. The literary and social critic Kenneth Burke (1966) reminds us that stories are how people understand the world and their own lives. As myth, news confronts death as well as taxes, evil as well as crime, fate as well as elections, souls as well as sickness, salvation as well as sales. Myth argues that journalism must greatly expand its view of stories and public life.

News people ignore obvious evidence. Newspaper sales, magazine circulation, television news ratings, and Web site traffic all surge during dramatic and sensational events: schoolyard killings, royal weddings, hurricanes, assassinations, airline crashes, and inaugurations. What are people seeking? They are not going to use these stories to vote for a candidate or purchase a product. They want compelling dramas. They want satisfying or stimulating stories that speak to them of history and fate and the fragility of life. They want myth.

Myth offers people news they can use to comprehend the hand of history and fate, news they can use to understand hatred and fear, news they can use to consider the possibilities and shortfalls of their own lives. Myth means that the most complex phenomena of public life, from birth to death, will be captured in the dramatically compelling narratives of news.

We should keep foremost an appreciative sense of wonder for this perhaps jarring juxtaposition of daily news and eternal stories. It is humbling to consider that some stories have engaged and enthralled humans throughout existence, that people of the 21st century share stories of the human experience with people of the first century. We should appreciate that in our modern, high-tech, online world, we find stories and practices that date back to tribal times.

In *The Educated Imagination,* the literary critic Northrop Frye (1964), drawing upon Aristotle, tried to make clear the role of the poet in society. He contrasted the poet with the historian, saying:

> The historian makes specific and particular statements, such as: "The battle of Hastings was fought in 1066." Consequently he's judged by the truth or falsehood of what he says—either there was such a battle or there wasn't, and if there was he's got the date either right or wrong. But the poet, Aristotle says, never makes any real statements at all, certainly no particular or specific ones. The poet's job is not to tell you what happened, but what happens: not what did take place, but the kind of thing that always does take place. (p. 63)

The thought may be a bit inflated, but I think the journalist, through myth, can ultimately fulfill the social role of historian and poet. The journalist, at best, can get the date right and the meaning right. The journalist, at best, can tell you not only what happened but what always happens, what took place and what always does takes place. The journalist, at best, can offer us news and myth.

## REFERENCES

Burke, K. (1966). *Language as symbolic action.* Berkeley: University of California Press.

Campbell, J. (1949). *The hero with a thousand faces.* New York: Bollingen Foundation and Pantheon Books.

Campbell, J. (1960). The historical development of mythology. In H. Murray (Ed.), *Myth and mythmaking* (pp. 1-12). New York: George Braziller.

Campbell, J. (1972). *Myths to live by.* New York: Viking Press.

Cassirer, E. (1946). *The myth of the state.* New Haven, CT: Yale University Press.

Darnton, R. (1975, Spring). Writing news and telling stories. *Daedalus, 104,* 175-194.

Day, M. S. (1984). *The many meanings of myth.* Lanham, MD: University Press of America.

Eason, D. L. (1981, Fall). Telling stories and making sense. *Journal of Popular Culture, 15,* 125-129.

Eliade, M. (1958). *Patterns in comparative religion* (R. Sheed, Trans.). New York: Sheed & Ward.

Eliade, M. (1959). *The sacred and the profane* (W. R. Trask, Trans.). New York: Harcourt, Brace & World.

Eliade, M. (1960). *Myths, dreams and mysteries* (P. Mairet, Trans.). New York: Harper.

Eliade, M. (1963). *Myth and reality* (W. R. Trask, Trans.). New York: Harper & Row.

Frazer, J. (1951). *The golden bough.* New York: Macmillan.

Frye, N. (1951, Winter). The archetypes of literature. *Kenyon Review, 12,* 92-110.

Frye, N. (1957). *Anatomy of criticism.* Princeton, NJ: Princeton University Press.

Frye, N. (1964). *The educated imagination.* Bloomington, IN: Indiana University Press.

Jung, C. G. (1959). *Archetypes and the collective unconscious* (R. F. C. Hull, Trans.). New York: Pantheon Books.

Jung, C. G. (1964). *Man and his symbols.* New York: Dell.

Jung, C. G. (1976). *Symbols of transformation* (2nd ed., R. F. C. Hull, Trans.). Princeton, NJ: Princeton University Press.

Schudson, M. (1982, Fall). The politics of narrative form: The emergence of news conventions in print and television. *Daedalus, 111,* 97-112.

Stephens, M. (1988). *The history of news: From the drum to the satellite.* New York: Viking Press.

Strenski, I. (1987). *Four theories of myth in twentieth-century history.* Iowa City: University of Iowa Press.

Thompson, S. (1955). *Motif-index of folk-literature.* Bloomington: Indiana University Press.

# 11

# NEWS STORIES AND
# MYTH—THE IMPOSSIBLE REUNION?

MIHAI COMAN

The various studies focusing on the interface between media and myths lead to a natural question: Are *all* mass media products "symbolic instances" and therefore creations with mythic status? If not, what types of media, at what moments, for what reasons, by what means, and with what consequences become generators or bearers of mythic phenomena?

The opinions of researchers who have tackled the issue illustrate two significant approaches. One group (Barthes, 1957; Goethals, 1993; Koch, 1990; Lule, 2001; Martin-Barbero, 1997; Real, 1996; and others) proposes that mass media—as a system—have taken over the functions of the institutions that produced and circulated myths and mythologies in ancient societies. Outlining this position, Gripsrud (2000) states:

> The media are storytellers reiterating stories that, like ancient myths, serve as ways of thinking about existential and social matters individuals and groups have to deal with in their everyday life. Such function overrides distinctions between genres, such as those between factual and fictional genres, between news and other ostensibly informational genres on the one hand and those explicitly dedicated to entertainment on the other. (p. 295)

According to this perspective, which derives from the old *evolutionist* paradigm, mass media perpetuates in modernity the functions, contents, and social prestige of the myth; in other words, mythic constructs are an essential characteristic of culture, including modern culture and its mass media. These opinions suggest that the mass media system on the whole (the press institutions with their norms, the producers with their practices and values, the texts with their logic and the audience with its consumption techniques) takes over (is a living "relic") of the mythological system—with its production instances, creators, contents, and specific manner of performance and reception.

The other perspective (Bird & Dardenne, 1988; Breen & Corcoran, 1982; Coman, 2003; Hoover, 1988; Peri, 1997; Segre, 1997) states that the mythic dimension is present only in certain situations and characterizes only certain mass media products. According to Silverstone (1988), television crosses myth if the following conditions are observed:

(1) Television presents the content of myth, most significantly in its reporting of major collectively focusing events; (2) it presents a communication which in its various narrative and rhetorical aspects preserves forms of familiar and formulaic storytelling

that are the product and property of a significantly oral culture; (3) it creates by its technologies a distinct spatial and temporal environment marked by the screen and marking for all to see the tissue boundary between the profane and the sacred. (p. 29)

This perspective places the mythic features outside the field of journalistic discourse—they appear as *accidents* produced by either the surplus of mythological representations generated by major public events, the archaic framework of epic motifs updated by mass media–circulated narratives, or the specificity of the act of consumption, which is distinct from the other activities and creates boundaries analogous to those between the sacred and the profane.

These two main approaches place us in a dire situation: To set the myth at the heart of mass media means to claim that the journalists' discourse is symbolic in nature—which means that the press cannot contribute rationally and argumentatively to the public sphere; cannot create a public opinion based on logical, nonemotional thoughts and debates; and, last but not least, cannot represent the main actor of democracy. For an anthropologist, to place myth outside the mass media system and view it as an accident in the (normal) order of journalistic discourse means to accept the boundaries of "le grand partage" (Lenclud, 1992): the promotion of the sophisticated Western culture as profoundly and essentially different from "other" cultural forms (primitive, folkloric, popular, mass, etc.). This view, in turn, encourages the notion of a fundamental human difference between "us" (the civilized) and a group of "others" incapable of attaining superior levels of civilization.

Other cultural frames specific to the cultural traditions of the Western world increase this dilemma: (a) In the Platonic view of myth, myths are conceived of as untrue, empirically unprovable stories rooted in the irrational, though able to evoke certain "ideas" and to persuade through the power of emotions, in opposition to "logos." Emptied of both its symbolic prestige and heuristic power, "mythos" grew "to be defined through what it is not, in double opposition to the real, on the one

hand—the myth is fiction—and to the rational, on the other—the myth is absurd" (Vernant, 1974, p. 195). (b) There is also the conviction that, by carrying on reasoned debates and reporting certain and verified facts, mass media can accept the symbolic dimension only as an atypical deviation, an "exotic" error, appearing as a result of either unprofessional behavior or accidents (extraordinary circumstances, in which the information is produced and circulates abnormally, as through propaganda campaigns, manipulations, media skids). Thus the presence of myth in mass media can only be an intrusion, preventing the press from carrying out its specific mission, and it is an intrusion that ought to be suppressed. In this sense, Dahlgren's (1988) reaction, when he was facing atypical mechanisms of sense making in crime reportage, is clarifying: "This type of reading certainly has little to do with information about crime or about external social reality in any literal sense. It is not so much logos which is at work here, rather a small scale and trivial mythos" (p. 205).

## MYTH, MYTHOLOGY, MASS COMMUNICATION

The efforts to define *myth* encounter a triple obstacle: (a) The various definitions of *myth* put forth by various sciences create a fluid and often contradictory conceptual field; (b) the cultural segments evincing "constructs" labeled as myths are extremely heterogeneous: "exotic" cultures, "ancient" cultures, folkloric cultures, popular cultures, the field of cultural industries, "higher" forms of art and literature, and so on; (c) these cultural forms have been studied from a variety of theoretical and methodological perspectives, including those of history, linguistics, psychoanalysis, folklore, philosophy, sociology, anthropology, the comparative study of religions, literary theory, the history of arts, and so on, and these approaches have proposed definitions of the concept of myth and interpretations of mythic phenomena that have proved to be contradictory and even irreconcilable.

Most definitions of myth invoke a number of factors whose intersection ensures the specificity of this cultural form and, implicitly, the coherence of the concept they name and explain. Thus, J. Fontenrose (1971, p. 54) proposes the following specific features: Myth is a narrative, it is traditional, it is orally transmitted, it has a specific plot, it refers to the world of gods. W. Doty (1986, pp. 11-29) sets 10 defining features: integration in a myth network, cultural importance, the imaginary character, the narrative dimension, metaphorical and symbolic content, graphic imagery, the audience's emotional participation, reference to primordial events, the impression of a real world, establishment of social roles. C. Riviere (1997, pp. 53-55) identifies eight features: imaginary story, belonging to a symbolic world, polysemy, the atemporal character, the emotional dimension, orientation toward action, the rationality of the imaginary, and the initiatic character.

Other definitions work with a smaller number of features. Eliade (1968) says, "Myth narrates a sacred story; it relates to an event that took place in primordial time, in the fabled time of the beginnings. . . . Myth then is always an account of a creation: it relates how something was produced, began to be" (pp. 1133-1134). Raglan (1972) states: "We can then extend our definition and say that myth is not merely a narrative associated with a rite, but a narrative which, with or without its associated rite, is believed to confer life" (p. 124). Carrol (1996) believes that "first a myth is a story; second this story is concerned with the sacred, in E. Durkheim's sense of the word, that is person or things surrounded with reverence and respect in the society where the story is told; third, the events described in this sacred story are set initially in a previous age that is qualitatively different from the present age" (pp. 827-828).

If we apply so unified a schema, we notice that, within the mass-media system, *there are no myths:* In other words, one cannot isolate cultural forms capable of acting out all the attributes presupposed by a synthetic or cumulative definition of myth. The mass media does not offer us myths, obvious in themselves, but "texts," which include some elements that present (thematic) analogies with certain mythic manifestations or send to extratextual elements (social, psychological, or logical functions) identical to those of myth. Therefore it is hard to claim that we can identify "authentic" myths in the media; it would be more accurate to state that in certain mass communication products, anthropological research can reveal certain mythic sequences or disclose functions and logics similar to those of mythic thinking and creation. This means that the mythic elements are extracted and treated by the researcher based on certain analogies (of function, form, content, or deep cognitive structure) and less by invoking the sum of attributes specific to myth (the relationship to ritual, status of true and exemplary story, liminality, oral character, fantastic content, etc.). These elements are decontextualized, freed from the purposes they have in the modern media system, and projected upon a conceptual screen in which the mythic factions, meanings, and uses become obvious.

In spite of the lack of conceptual clarity surrounding the terms *myth* and *mythology*, the low interest of anthropologists in applying these notions when analyzing modern cultures; and the immense gaps in time, space, and cultural configuration that separate the world of myths from the modern world, many researchers have nevertheless attempted to explain certain news stories by relating them to the mythic universe. The analysis of studies and debates on the possible relationships between the news press and the mythic system shows that they used three interpretative paradigms: the *archetypal model* (mythic elements are the extensions, in journalistic accounts, of ancient epic and symbolic patterns, ever present in our cultural baggage), *the functionalist model* (news, just like myth, comes to answer eternal human needs), and *the cognitive model* (the news system and the mythic system represent mechanisms for thinking and signification, based on the same mental operations).

## The Myth as Hidden Text

Most studies dedicated to the mythic dimension of mass media products started from the feeling that the products themselves did not exhaust meaning, that certain elements "are signs of the eruption of another story through the text of an existing one; they are pieces of a shadow text that force their way into the nominal one, fugitive presences that testify to unresolved tensions between the event reported and the narrative that is doing so" (Manoff, 1986, p. 225). The aim of this kind of analysis is to find the hidden text, the (narrative, and possibly mythic) schema over which the various accounts of a particular event were built (independent of the journalists' immediate intentions).

The most elaborate embodiment of this approach is offered by Lule's (2001) research. He considers both news and myths to be the actualization of eternal stories, or archetypes, that have marked mankind's history and destiny since the most ancient times. "More than any mass media, the daily news is the primary vehicle for myth in our time. News of all things has become the inheritor of humanity's essential stories" (p. 19). As symbolic forms stemming from the same root, "news and myths thus will be shown to bear the closest similarities. They offer and repeat stories. They draw stories from real life. They tell stories that confront issues of social, public life. And they use these stories to instruct and inform. They are moral tales" (p. 21). Thus an analysis of the corpus of news stories reveals (and is reduced to) a limited number of mythic-narrative archetypes. Lule identifies seven mythic archetypes actualized by modern news: the victim, the scapegoat, the hero, the good mother, the trickster, the other world, and the flood. Obviously, they do not exhaust the archetypal vocabulary actualized by news—other research can reveal other eternal and original stories hidden in the reporting of contemporary events. The victim archetype is found in the media coverage of the Achile Lauro hijacking. In it, Lule noticed that the press gave a privileged position to Leo Klinghoffer: He is described in images suggesting a martyr's status, a hero sacrificing himself for others. The scapegoat appears in stories about the Black Panthers' leader Huey Newton: there, "the news was clearly offering an enactment of dramatically satisfying sanctions against one who would challenge the social consensus" (p. 79). The press's

reactions to football player Mark McGuire's athletic performance embodied the hero archetype; those about Mother Teresa, the good mother archetype; those about Mike Tyson's rape trial followed the trickster archetype; the news stories about political conflict in Haiti expressed the other world archetype; and Hurricane Mitch was represented as the flood archetype. This approach raises questions of both a general and a particular order: (a) What is the origin of these archetypes? The unity of the human being and the human psyche? The unity of narrative mechanisms for representing the world? The unity of civilizations? (b) Why do only a limited number of archetypes circulate, unchanged, throughout humanity's history? Is it due to mechanisms ensuring the faultless diffusion of cultural models in space and time? Is it due to a relationship between a limited number of set events and an equally limited repertoire of narrative models and standard characters? (c) Are these archetypes valid for all civilizations, or only for Indo-European and Western cultures (implicitly, the mass media)? If they are generally human, why are certain archetypes missing from certain mythologies? And, symmetrically, how did the mass media in other cultures present the events that have embodied the noted archetypes—in this eternal story code, or in another one? (d) What is the relationship between this list of archetypes and those generated by other researchers (Jung, Kereny, Durand, Eliade, Campbell)? In the area of Lule's analysis, I believe that in some cases they can be substituted—Mike Tyson and Huey Newton seem to be both scapegoat and trickster—and others sustain even less eloquently the identification with the proposed archetype—Haiti is pretty far from the archetype of the other world, and McGuire and his athletic performance are not necessarily the best embodiment of the hero archetype (civilizer or savior) of mythology. However, beyond these observations, which refer more to the interpretative paradigm chosen by the author, Lule's theoretical and analytical construction represent the most elaborate attempt to prove that there is a correlation between myth and news story within the frame of a coherent theory.

Other case studies assume an archetypal perspective as well. Thus, the drama of Korean

Airlines flight 007 (which went into Soviet airspace and was shot down by Soviet missiles) generated media coverage underscored by the myth of the "evil empire." The American press, as investigated by Corcoran (1986), saw in this event "a condensed symbol of the difference between the Russians and the rest of the world" (p. 302) and built (sometimes by ignoring certain information) a version of events that fell within the public's expectations of narratives and subterranean values, by which it defined communism within Cold War symbolic paradigms. Andersen (1992) saw the U.S. media discourse during the Oliver North hearings as a product of "a transcendent rhetoric of idealism and patriotism, while increasingly that idealism has to be understood through a free-floating body of fictional texts" (p. 187). In this sort of media discourse, there are (explicit or understood) symbolical references to emblematic figures of the "American Myth," such as Dirty Harry, Rambo, Jefferson Smith, and Luke Skywalker: "The North episode was a postmodern drama in which myth appeared more reasonable than the black world of covert policies, cynical motivation and the real lack of American values" (Andersen, 1992, p. 186).

In their frequently quoted study, Knight and Dean (1982) explain the way in which the *Globe & Mail* and the *Sun* presented the Special Air Service (SAS) Regiment operation of eliminating the terrorists in the Iranian embassy in London in 1980 by reactivating certain cultural themes: the legitimacy of repressing the enemy, the expertise of the defenders of the order, and the mysterious character of these troops. The media construction derives from a "dialectic of myth" combining two opposed versions: legitimate action and illegitimate violence. This interplay of symbolic systems promotes, especially in the discourse of *Globe* journalists, a shocking and very contradictory image of the SAS: "efficient, but chilling, successful but ferocious and lethal, representative of legitimate state, but dressed like criminals, heroes but always shooting to kill" (p. 156).

In all these studies, the archetype appears and is justified because of a premise (often assumed implicitly): The mass media system is, on the whole, a form of modern actualization of some *premodern cultural models.* Articulated by the opposition between high and popular culture, this argument is associated with the former values, such as rationality, a reflective character, seriousness, moral responsibility, and so on, and it places at the other pole the irrational dimension, spontaneity, entertainment (pleasure), absence of sophisticated ethical standards, and so on. Following this association, it is normal and easy to explain how the products of the popular press reactualize certain features (epic structure, types of characters, psychological functions, values or world representations, etc.) specific to some cultural forms of a folkloric nature such as legends, ballads, and myths.

## The Mythic Functions of Modern Communication

Most approaches focusing on the relationship between news media and the mythic universe are placed less at the level of microstructures (the relationship between the coverage of a certain event and certain archetypal constructs) and more at the level of global dimensions: They investigate the possibility of common frames of thought and behavior and are able to relate and explain the connection between myth and journalistic accounts. From this perspective, the association of mythic discourse with journalistic discourse appears as the expression of certain frames of thought and action (archaic, primitive, wild, prelogical) unchanged throughout the centuries and essential to the human condition. This time-honored approach to the study of myth leads to two types of explanation: a functionalist one (myth and news serve the same needs—for knowledge or emotion—that are basic to humanity) and a cognitive one (myth and news are products of the same processes—logical and narrative—common to human techniques of taking possession of and signifying the real world). In the first case, the linking element is provided by the unity of three factors: the human psyche, existential situations, and techniques for preserving social order; in the second, the relationship between myth and journalistic accounts is ensured by unitary mental structures (logical operations) and the coherence of human processes of signification.

The functionalist argumentation is most clearly expressed by Silverstone (1994):

> I have argued on a number of occasions that the ordinary of everyday life is sustained within our society and within others by forms of cultures which it has been most easy (but still intensely problematical) to call myth. Mythic structures and functions within contemporary communication can be identified and arguments about their significance sustained, as long as it is recognized that myths, like so much in culture, are Janus-headed. They provide in their narratives and in the formalities of their delivery within ritual or neo-ritualized occasions a framework for the creation and sustenance of ontological security. (p. 166)

This occurs because television is able "to mobilize the sacred," creating a liminal interval placed between everyday reality and extraordinary reality (be it fiction or unexpected events). Within this frame, the myths circulated by media communication have both a common dimension (they refer to everyday facts, situations, or people, they are consumed in familiar places and moments) and an extraordinary one (they can appear in ritualized contexts and can refer to fundamental moments of life). In the modern world, myths often materialize in news formats:

> News items are micro-narratives, textually closed, contextually open. . . . Their stories are those of heroic exploits and disaster; their concerns are with the cosmic and threatening; their function is the management of anxiety that they themselves in part create; they are ritually told at regular and predictable times of day; they make stars of their presenters, both liminal and liminary; they provide the stuff of everyday interaction; we are entirely dependent on them. (Silverstone, 1988, p. 39)

For this reason, news, just like myths, contributes to "the definition and maintenance of commonsense reality, constantly at work, translating and reassuring the boundary between the familiar secure world of the everyday and the unfamiliar insecure world beyond it" (Silverstone, 1988, p. 37).

Other scholars also propose such functionalist explanations, based on the common capacity of myths and news to serve permanent human needs. Thus, Breen and Corcoran (1982, pp. 128-130) argue that myths and news have the following common functions: (a) *instance of knowledge:* They are "a part of the perceptual system of culture through which unfamiliar situations . . . are interpreted and fitted into old symbolic forms"; (b) *exemplary model,* which offers behavior patterns accepted by society; and (c) *conflict mediator:* possible and real stress in everyday life is mediated, at a symbolic level, by story elements. In studying Yitzhak Rabin's postmortem image in the Israeli press coverage, Peri (1997) noticed that the creation of the myth of the committed politician contributed to the promotion of an unconflicting model of collective identity by remodeling social memory: "This was done by promoting the political ritual surrounding Rabin, building the myth of the man who becomes a symbol in his death. This the myth accomplished by addressing a critical point in the collective identity-construction of the collective memory" (p. 445; see also Berlioz, 1983; Campbell, 1995; Coman, 1996; Morin, 1969; Pouchelle, 1983; Segre, 1997).

The interpretation models built in this manner have the advantages and disadvantages of any functionalist explanation: They supply a relatively simple key to identifying the common features of journalistic narratives and mythic constructs. This key is so common that it suits many other cultural situations and phenomena. Thus it is obvious that people have common needs and that certain symbolic products serve these needs; because of this, it may be claimed that apparently different cultural forms are homologous—in other words, they have identical function, because they offer identical or similar solutions to satisfy the respective needs. The difficulty lies in the fact that, for instance, not only myths and news but also magic songs, ritual texts, novels, films, rumors, popular science works, and so on have the capacity to reduce unfamiliar areas, provide symbolic models for understanding the world, and guarantee "ontological security." Hence myths and news can indeed be similar cultural forms (because they have identical functions), but this comparison occurs within the very wide frame of symbolic human action, a frame within which almost all products can be said to serve the same respective functions. Under these circumstances, the functionalist explanation provides neither the specific differences, starting from which we could argue in favor of the existence of a specific homology between myth and news, nor the cultural and historical significance of this homology.

From an anthropological view, the functionalist interpretation of the relationship between myth and news reportage through the hegemonic function offers an easy, simply analogical explanation limited to certain specific situations, an explanation in which the term *myth* becomes a label for something that represents only a small (and debatable) part of mythic relationships. At the same time, though, through this operation of placing myth in the realm of ideology, the respective researchers were able to reduce the distance between mythic creation in nonmodern societies and the mass media universe, offering a common base and a reason for the plausibility of associating myth and journalistic products.

## A Space of Symbolic Bricolage

The cognitive paradigm appears, explicitly and coherently, in the landmark study by Bird and Dardenne (1988). They start from the premise that press-distributed information messages are not based on an argumentative system of a strict logical nature (as the parents of liberalism suggested) but rather on a vocabulary of symbolic representations: "we consider the news genre as a particular kind of symbolic system" (p. 68). This is due to certain profound cultural characteristics that push the referential dimension and the informative and interpretative functions into second place.

> Readers do not only consume news as a reflection of reality, but as a symbolic text that defines murder as more noteworthy than car thefts. News stories, like

myths, do not "tell it like it is" but rather "tell it like it means." Thus, news is a particular kind of mythological narrative with its own symbolic codes that are recognized by its audience. (Bird & Dardenne, 1988, p. 71)

To support such a clear-cut statement, Bird and Dardenne develop several series of arguments: They recall the recurrent epic themes appearing in popular narratives and journalistic accounts; they invoke the standardized patterns used by traditional creators of folkloric texts (the archetypal paradigm); they refer to the narrative's capacity (as a basis of myth and news) to offer security-enhancing versions of common experiences or to ensure social balance (the functionalist paradigm).

In this palette, the most important type of argument seems to be the cognitive one: News and myth are born from the same mental mechanism and through the same logical operation—that of defining reality with the help of cultural symbols. "The journalist-storyteller is indeed using culturally embedded story values, taking them from the culture and re-presenting them to the culture, and is thus akin to the folk storyteller who operates in a 'communal matrix' vis-à-vis the audience" (Bird & Dardenne, 1988, p. 80). When confronted with unusual events, journalists "have to fit new situations into old definitions; it is in their power to place people and events into the existing categories of hero, villain, good and bad and thus to invest their stories with the authority of mythological truth" (p. 80). In essence, like the "myth-makers" in non-Western civilizations, journalists are *bricoleurs* (the term is not used as such, but is implied by Bird and Dardenne) who ceaselessly build and rebuild the symbolic edifice of cultural representations, using narrative patterns, figures, values, and codes available in their cultural environment. For that reason, the most important factor is not the concrete referent to which news sends but the cultural code through which it builds a certain version of reality, which explains the crucial formula "News stories, like myths, do not 'tell it like it is' but rather 'tell it like it means.'"

The cognitive paradigm is also invoked by other attempts to justify the mythic status of journalistic accounts. Thus, for Newcomb and Hirsh (1985), journalists are "cultural bricoleurs seeking, creating new meaning in the combination of cultural elements with embedded significance; they respond to real events, changes in social structure and organization and to shifts in attitude and values" (p. 60). Barbara Philips (1976) appeals directly to Levi-Strauss's terminology. "As a concretizer, the journalist is kin to anthropologist Claude Levi-Strauss' primitive empiricist, the bricoleur; the journalist, like the bricoleur, tests reality by experiencing life, not by structuring the experience of life in a formal, systematic way" (p. 91). A similar perspective seems to also be assumed by Langer (1998) in explaining the perennial nature of human interest news:

> In the multiplication of the "other news" stories across bulletins everyday, day after day, a structure of sorts, which might be called mythic, does begin to emerge. The structure, which in its initial manifestation revolves around causality and its collapse might be re-posed in more general, abstracted terms—permanence and change. If the longevity and perennial journalistic production of the "other news" can be situated in relation to these terms, and if this process can be understood, not in ways of individual stories, but as part of an organized system whereby all stories are located in their relation with each other as specifiable types, a more fundamental structure, akin perhaps to myth, emerges, which articulates a continuously "spoken" discourse on patterns of permanence and change. (p. 143)

In the same paradigm falls my own study (Coman, 1993) of the coverage in the French press of the first week of what journalists called "the Romanian revolution." In the journalistic texts on the events in December 1989, I have identified numerous archetypal representations (Christmas, candles, fir trees, sacrificially dead young people, the children, the old king, etc.) and a number of binary pairs (young people and terrorists, sacrifice and crimes, revolutionary ideals and the pleasure of killing) that relate to symbolic pairs (hope and despair, future and past, life and death). These figures and codes structure the "referential" accounts of what was happening in Bucharest and signify events in revolutionary code (changing communist rule) and mythological code (the disappearance of the old, exhausted king and enthronement of the power of the young by the founding sacrifice of the heroes of the revolution).

This theoretical model is more coherent than the functionalist one, because it does not open the doors to an indefinite number of human necessities and social functions and an unending stream of analogies. However, in instituting the unity of acts of thinking and processes of building meanings, irrespective of era or geographical area, this conception must still show why it is exactly myth and news stories that form a homogeneous system of signifying the surrounding world. In other words, these interpretations did not lead to the elaboration of a paradigm that would explain why texts that refer to daily, palpable, certain realities use the same signifying mechanisms as texts that refer to fantastic deeds and beings, take place in another world and another time, and take an act of faith to be believed and socially valued. Inevitably, this model leads us to the multiple debates around such notions as "primitive thinking," "prelogical thinking," "wild thinking," and beyond this debate toward a theory of speech acts, of production of meaning, and of the human mind.

## CONCLUSIONS

Research attempting to interpret the functioning of the news and its signification by association with the mythic universe is between two poles. At one are the (very numerous) voices claiming that the cultural distance between the two categories is too great and that their association, being metaphoric and speculative, refers only to particular cases (deviations from the norms of the press) and cannot lead to scientifically valid generalizations. At the other pole are those who, with unbounded enthusiasm, consider that in mass media everything is myth and mythology. The various analyses discussed so far propose interpretations based on the ternary model, in which the relationship between mythic discourse and journalistic discourse is legitimized by reference to a third mediating element, a more general cultural category, which is able to explain the iconoclastic association between mass media texts and mythic constructs. These studies resort to the formal, functional, or cognitive unity of news stories and myth and have concluded, respectively, that narrative archetypes, common functions, or symbolic thinking can mediate the temporal and cultural distance between the two universes.

It is no less true that between myth (in the worlds and eras in which it was manifesting itself fully) and the press (the system, language, and modern society) there seems to be a great distance, historically, socially, and culturally. Both scientists and common opinion accept the idea of a modern continuity much more easily in ritual manifestations than in mythic phenomena: The existence of great ceremonies and public celebrations, as well as of numerous domestic rites and celebrations, sustains the feeling of a ritual continuity between ancient past and present and between exotic areas and those of modern civilizations. Myth, on the other hand, seems to be exclusively the product of "different" cultures; it functions as an indicator of "otherness" that, when it is identified in "our" world, stands witness to historical, social, or mentality enclaves, to uncommon situations (crises), and to the mistakes that we (still) make in the processes of applying rational, scientific mechanisms of explaining the universe. These common images of the place of myth in contemporary culture explain the insistence with which the researchers who have approached the mythic dimensions in mass media have sought *mediating cultural forms* capable of showing by which channels myth has sneaked from the ancient past into the present and of explaining the continuity of such symbolic constructs.

The investigations into the relationship between myth and news story, especially those published in the last few decades, are often persuasive and exciting. They remain, however, isolated attempts that, as opposed to the framework within which the relationship between mass media products and the ritual universe has been discussed (Dayan & Katz, 1992), have not generated a complete theory (such as that of "media events"), a homogeneous conceptual vocabulary, and a school of thinking or an intense and homogeneous current of research.

## REFERENCES

Andersen, R. (1992). Oliver North in the news. In P. Dahlgren & C. Sparks (Eds.), *Journalism and popular culture* (pp. 171-189). London: Sage.

Barthes, R. (1957). *Mythologiques*. Paris: Seuil.

Berlioz, J. (1983). Texte hagiographique, rock 'n roll et politique [Hagiographic text, rock 'n roll, and politics]. In J.-C. Schmitt (Ed.), *Les saints et les stars: Le texte hagiographique dans la culture populaire* [Saints and stars : Hagiographic text in popular culture]. Paris: Beauchesne Editeur.

Bird, E., & Dardenne, R. (1988). Myth, chronicle and story. In J. Carey (Ed.), *Media, myth and narratives* (pp. 67-85). London: Sage.

Breen, M., & Corcoran, F. (1982). Myth in the television discourse. *Communication Monographs, 49*(2), 127-137.

Campbell, C. (1995). *Race, myth and the news*. London: Sage.

Carrol, M. P. (1996). Myth. In D. Levinson & M. Ember (Eds.), *Encyclopedia of cultural anthropology* (pp. 827-831) New York: Henry Holt.

Coman, M. (1993). Naissance d'un contre-mythe (la Roumanie, décembre 1989, dans la presse française) [Birth of an anti-myth (the image of Roumania, December 1989, in the French press)]. *Réseaux, 59*, 107-118.

Coman, M. (1996). The metamorphosis of the intellectual myth: The case of Mircea Eliade. In J. M. Pomorskiego & Z. Bajki (Eds.), *Valeriana: Essays on human communication* (pp. 154-160). Krakow, Poland: Osradek Badan Pr.

Coman, M. (2003). *Pour une anthropologie des medias* [Toward an anthropology of the media]. Grenoble, France: Presses Universitaires de Grenoble.

Corcoran, F. (1986). KAL-007 and the evil empire: Mediated disaster and forms of rationalization. *Critical Studies in Mass Communication, 3*.

Dahlgren, P. (1988). Crime news: The fascination of the mundane. *European Journal of Communication, 3*(2), 125-136.

Dayan, D., & Katz, E. (1992). *Media events*. Cambridge, MA: Harvard University Press.

Doty, W. G. (1986). *Mythography: The study of myth and rituals*. Birmingham: University of Alabama Press.

Eliade, M. (1968). Myth. In *Encyclopaedia Britannica* (Vol. 15, pp. 1032-1140). London: International Copyright Union.

Fontenrose, J. (1971). *The ritual theory of myth.* Berkeley: University of California Press.

Goethals, G. (1993). Media mythologies. In A. Chris (Ed.), *Religion and the media.* Cardiff, Wales: University of Wales Press.

Gripsrud, J. (2000). Tabloidization, popular journalism and democracy. In C. Sparks & J. Tulloch (Eds.), *Tabloid tales: Global debates over media standards* (pp. 285-300). Boulder, CO: Rowman.

Hoover, S. (1988). Television, myth and ritual. In J. Carey (Ed.), *Media, myth and narratives* (pp. 161-178). London: Sage.

Koch, T. (1990). *The news as a myth: Fact and context in journalism.* New York: Greenwood Press.

Knight, G., & Dean, T. (1982). Myth and the structure of the news. *Journal of Communication, 33*(1), 144-160.

Langer, J. (1998). *Tabloid television: Popular journalism and the "other news."* London: Routledge.

Lule, J. (2001). *Daily news, eternal stories: The mythological role of journalism.* New York: Guilford Press.

Lenclud, G. (1992). Le grand partage ou la tentation anthropologique [The great division or the anthropological temptation]. In G. Althabe, D. Fabre, & G. Lenclud (Eds.), *Vers une anthropologie du présent* [Towards an anthropology of modern society] (pp. 9-37). Paris: Editions de la Maison des Sciences de l'Homme.

Manoff, R. K. (1986). Reading the news—by telling the story. In R. K. Manoff & M. Schudson (Eds.), *Reading the news* (pp. 197-229). New York: Pantheon Books.

Martin-Barbero, J. (1997). Mass media as site of resacralisation of contemporary cultures. In S. Hoover & K. Lundby (Eds.), *Rethinking media, religion and culture* (102-116). London: Sage.

Morin, E. (1969). *La rumeur d'Orleans* [The rumor of Orleans]. Paris: Seuil.

Newcomb, H., & Hirsh, P. (1985). Television as a cultural form. In *Mass Communication Review Yearbook.* Newbury Park, CA: Sage.

Peri, Y. (1997). The Rabin myth and the press: Reconstruction of the Israeli collective identity. *European Journal of Communication, 12*(4), 435-458.

Philips, B. (1976). Novelty without change. *Journal of Communication, 4,* 87-92.

Pouchelle, M. C. (1983). Sentiment réligieux et show business: Claude Francois objet de dévotion populaire [Religious sentiment and show business: Claude Francois, object of popular devotion]. In J.-C. Schmitt (Ed.), *Les saints et les stars: Le texte hagiographique dans la culture populaire* [Saints and stars: Hagiographic text in popular culture]. Paris: Beauchesne Editeur.

Raglan, L. (1972). Myth and ritual. In T. A. Sebeock (Ed.), *Myth: A symposium* (pp. 122-135). Bloomington: Indiana University Press.

Real, M. (1996). *Exploring media culture.* London: Sage.

Riviere, C. (1997). *Socio-anthropologie des réligions* [The socioanthropology of religions]. Paris: Armand Colin.

Segre, G. (1997). Les biographies d'Elvis Presley : Un récit mythique [The biographies of Elvis Presley: A mythological story]. In M. Segre (Ed.), *Mythes, rites, symboles* [Myths, rites, symbols]. Paris: L'Harmattan.

Silverstone, R. (1988). Television, myth and culture. In J. Carey (Ed.), *Media, myth and narratives* (pp. 20-47). London: Sage.

Silverstone, R. (1994). *Television and everyday life.* London: Routledge.

Vernant, J.-P. (1974). *Mythe et societé en Grece ancienne* [Myth and society in Ancient Greece]. Paris: Maspero.

# 12

# News as Stories

## Michael Schudson

A news story is news. It is also a story. Because it is a story, readers can expect it to have a beginning, a middle, and an end and to operate by some standard conventions of narrative prose. It is purportedly a true story; that is, a story about something that happened. Because it is a true story, it is responsible not only to literary convention but to a faithful rendering and even a verifiably faithful rendering of what really happened.

Journalists are often more aware of the claims they make to truth than the fact that they present their work in the form of a story. "I guess usually I don't consider myself a storyteller," said *Philadelphia Inquirer* investigative reporter William Marimow, "I consider myself a gatherer of facts."[1] Still, the reporter's job is to make meaning. A list of facts, even a chronologically ordered list, is not a story and is not a news story. From a list or chronicle, the writer must construct a tale, one whose understanding requires a reader or viewer to recognize not the sum of facts but their relationships. For this to happen, the news story must be recognizably a certain kind of news story—straight or feature, sports or politics, human interest news or breaking news. Implicitly or explicitly, the writer learns to tailor the facts of the matter to a form and format in which their relationships will come to make sense.

That is the abstract. The concept becomes concrete daily in the life of the working journalist. It takes shape around a number of basic workaday questions.

*1. Is This a Story?* Is there a story there in that set of facts or actual happenings? "All is calm but for a cat climbing a tree. The cat gets stuck in the tree. Firefighters are called. Neighborhood children gather to watch. Firefighters rescue the cat." This is a coherent narrative. It is also a story. It narrates a set of related events with a beginning, a middle, and an end. It defines a problem or obstacles, describes a set of activities directed toward resolving the problem, and finally resolves the problem and returns the world to normal.

But is this a news story? Perhaps it is, at least to enterprising sixth graders who are publishing a newsletter for the block they live on where the cat drama took place. For them, this might be front-page news, a big break from routine life on their street. The metropolitan paper or even the community weekly will, of course, not run the story. It is too familiar and too predictable. If ants published newspapers, it might be a headline every time you walked down the street and wiped out a few dozen of their leading citizens. However, stepping on ants is so much part of even a sixth-grader's daily life, and the ant victims are so far from sixth grade consciousness, that this kind of event will not make their school paper.

What if the cat belongs to the mayor? Better still, what if the cat belongs to the city councilman who just voted to reduce the fire department budget, complaining that the firefighters "spend too much time rescuing cats and not putting out fires"? Now, suddenly, reporters have a story, and a rather delicious one at that.

Why? Is it the pleasure of irony? In part. But if it had been an ordinary citizen who had just complained to neighbors that the fire department spends too much time rescuing cats, it would not be news. This citizen made a private statement, not a public one. Also, this citizen is not an elected official whose views are always potentially public acts, whose facial expressions will be scanned for their world import. The news story must be not only delicious but somehow impinge on or offer a kind of commentary on our public life. What counts as public life, of course, is not obvious. It changes from time to time and it varies from place to place. Part of the unsettling transformation of news in our own day is that large domains of life have newly moved from private to public.

*2. What's the Lead?* This is a more subtle part of the task of story construction. In this case, the reporter knows she or he has a story, but the heart of it has not quite been located. This should be a familiar enough anxiety to those who have written a term paper in which they had to choose their own topic rather than respond to a set topic provided by the instructor. The student must arrive at an interesting question, interesting enough to be a topic for a paper. Reporters face the same challenge in finding a lead. Is there an interesting topic in this general array of facts? What stands out as notable and newsworthy? At the Democratic National Convention in August 2000, candidate Al Gore gave a 40-minute acceptance speech and nearly every newspaper across the country identified the same headline and the same lead, quoting Gore's claim that "I stand here my own man." The lead provides a theme for the story as a whole. In narrating a complex event or one segment of an extended event, just as Gore's

speech was one notable but small segment in a year-long campaign for the presidency, the reporter must have an instinct for the heart of the matter. Sometimes it is obvious—which is to say, there is widespread consensus. Sometimes there is room for a variety of very different leads concerning the same set of events.

*3. Does It Have "Legs"?* A reporter constructs a story for a particular day's edition of the news. But is it a 1-day wonder, or is there an ongoing story—does it have legs? Our penny-pinching city councilman's cat is most likely a 1-day story, an amusing but incidental sidebar. It might suggest a follow-up on council members who take advantage of city services whose budgets they try to cut, but the story itself goes nowhere.

A story with legs, however, strikes journalists as a palpable force, one with a momentum of its own, one with a personality of its own, one that plays the journalist as much as the journalist plays the story.

A reporter directs these questions and others in the first instance to editors and fellow reporters and general patterns and norms of journalistic culture. Only indirectly do reporters consider the audience of news readers and viewers, but in the end, assumptions about what audiences want and what will please them are at stake. The response most journalists want to evoke in their audience is, at base, as media scholar Peter Parisi has written, "astonishment, not understanding." One reporter says that she wants stories that will make a man reading the front page at the breakfast table spit out his coffee and declare, "My God, Martha, did you see this?"[2] Media analysts have called these "what-a-story!" stories, while Bob Woodward at the *Washington Post* has advised the reporters he supervises to go after "Holy shit!" stories.[3] For all of the philosophizing one finds about news and democracy, the working journalist seeks, most of the time, a spitting-out-the-coffee response, not an engaging-in-public-debate response. The reporter hopes for readers who will be scandalized more than enlightened, who will marvel more than learn, who will feel irresistibly compelled to say to the next person they meet, "Did you hear about . . . ?"

Reporters cannot manufacture "Holy shit!" stories. They can seek them out. They can have a nose for news and follow their nose toward holyshit heaven. They can craft the story in a way to heighten or highlight this effect. Beyond this, they cannot go. They have to hope they will be lucky to stumble on just the right set of events or be the first on the scene when the Cessna crashes on the White House lawn.

Obviously, most stories do not produce the "what-a-story!" effect. Some do not even try. Investigative reporting seeks not spitting-out-the-coffee but a sputtering "There oughta be a law!" The investigative story seeks to evoke moral outrage. It carefully constructs, as Theodore Glasser and James Ettema have shown, an innocent victim and a guilty party, and it takes as its task not only a cognitive ordering of events for the audience but a moral ordering of responsibilities. The outcome will reinforce the common moral order—news stories do not challenge fundamental moral assumptions (although the events they narrate or the sources they quote may do just that). "Events on city streets and in county jails are not merely represented but rather made compellingly real because they are shown to belong to an order of moral existence that renders them meaningful."[4] These stories enable readers to "judge the moral significance of human projects . . . even while we pretend to be merely describing them."[5]

We tell stories for various reasons. People may tell stories to children at bedtime to ease them into sleep, or they may tell children stories on a long car ride to keep them awake until they get home. People may tell stories to impart lessons or to entertain. They may tell family stories to keep a tradition and identity alive; that is, they may tell stories as homage to the past. Or people may tell stories with an eye to the future, to inspire or to motivate. Journalists tell stories professionally, rather than as part of daily life, but they make use of all these possibilities, sometimes writing to soothe and sometimes to enliven, sometimes to honor and commemorate and sometimes to embolden and impassion. They tell stories competitively, seeking to do better than their rivals on the next newspaper or television station or their rivals at the next desk. They may seek the spitting-out-the-coffee story that astonishes or they may seek a community-building, ritually reaffirming story that covers a state funeral or a reconciliation of two political rivals in a way as to induce in the audience a sense of well-being and of belonging.[6]

Most understandings of the generation of news merge a "cultural" view, which centers on storytelling, with the various social organizational views of the manufacture of news I have already discussed. These two kinds of accounts are analytically distinct. Where organizational views take news to be a manufactured product created each day anew in interactional relations among firms, markets, and resources, a cultural view is more impressed with what news workers inherit than with what they create, and it emphasizes not social production so much as the symbolic determinants of news in the relation between "facts" and symbols. A cultural account of news helps explain generalized images and stereotypes in the news media—of predatory stockbrokers just as much as hard-drinking factory workers—that transcend structures of ownership or even patterns of work relations.

For instance, in their analysis of British mass media coverage of racial conflict, Paul Hartmann and Charles Husband note that "The British cultural tradition contains elements derogatory to foreigners, particularly blacks. The media operate within the culture and are obliged to use cultural symbols."[7] Frank Pearce, in examining media coverage of homosexuals in Britain, takes as a theoretical starting point the anthropological view that all societies like to keep their cultural concepts clean and neat and are troubled by "anomalies" that do not fit the preconceived categories of the culture. Homosexuality is an anomaly in societies that take as fundamental the opposition and relationship of male and female; thus homosexuals provide a culturally charged topic for storytelling that seeks to preserve or reinforce the conventional moral order of society—and its conceptual or symbolic foundation. News stories about homosexuals, Pearce says, may be moral tales, "a negative reference point . . . an occasion to reinforce conventional moral values by telling a moral tale. Through these means tensions in the social system can be dealt with and 'conventionalized.'"[8]

A cultural account of this sort can explain too much; after all, news coverage of homosexuality has changed enormously since Pearce wrote his article, a "universal cultural anxiety about anomalous categories" notwithstanding. Recent study of U.S. news coverage concludes that gays and lesbians appear much more in the news now than they did 50 years ago, that they are covered much more "routinely" as ordinary news subjects rather than as moral tales, and that although coverage is not free of antigay prejudice, it is generally fair.[9]

Similarly, broad cultural explanations of the prevalence and character of crime news as fulfilling deep societal needs for moral order must also be evaluated with some caution. It makes sense that broad and long-lasting phenomena—such as heavy news coverage of crime over two centuries across many societies—will have deep cultural roots, but it is also important to recognize fashions, trends, and changes in crime coverage. Joel Best's account of why some newly defined crimes receive only occasional or episodic press coverage and others, with better institutionalized support in a "victim industry," receive more systematic and ongoing treatment is a good example. What is at stake here is the interaction of general cultural and specific social-organizational dimensions of news.[10]

News is not one literary form but a set of literary forms. Some news forms are as predictable or as formulaic as the unfolding of a mystery novel, romance, or limerick. Others are more complex: Neither the practitioner nor the reader is entirely conscious of what the aesthetic constraints are. Even focusing only on political news, this varies from the breaking story, to the reflective news analysis, to the investigative series that takes 3 days to run, to the magazine essay, to the full-length book that is often a second look at material the writer first wrote as hard news. Even within a single story there is variation, from the headline and lead (which in the prestige press tend to defer to official sources) to the body of the story, in which alternative interpretations may appear. An account may even emerge deep in the story that undermines the official version reported near the top.

If elements of content fit conventional notions of ideology or the common sense of a hegemonic system, aspects of form operate at a more subtle level. By *form*, I refer to assumptions about narrative, storytelling, human interest, and the conventions of photographic and linguistic presentation in news production. For instance, there are systematic differences between the inverted-pyramid structure of print news and the "thematic" structure of television news. The inverted-pyramid form is the standard journalistic literary matrix, a form within which every reporter operates. According to this model, a news story begins with a lead that answers the basic questions who, what, when, where, and (sometimes) why in the first few sentences. In the most straitjacketed version of this model, all these questions are addressed in the first sentence. Following the lead, the story takes on the most important features of the reported event and moves from one topic to the next in decreasing order of importance. This form was a peculiar development of late 19th-century American journalism. It seemed to fit the technology of the telegraph—an inverted-pyramid story "telegraphs" the most important news first. It did much more than that, however. It fit not only a world of telegraphs but a world of an increasingly independent and cocky corps of journalists who were prepared to name on their own authority what aspect of the news they covered could be judged the most important. This feature of the narrative form, then, implicitly authorized the journalist as expert. In political reporting, it helped redefine politics itself as a subject appropriately discussed by experts rather than partisans. This is only to suggest that news is a form of literature and that among the resources journalists work with are the traditions of storytelling, picture making, and sentence construction they have inherited from their own artistic or expressive cultures or crafts.

Most research on the culture of news production takes it for granted that, at least within a given national tradition, there is one common news standard among journalists. This is one of the convenient simplifications of the sociology of journalism that merits critical attention and might, indeed, be a point at which a lot of current assumptions about how journalism works begin to unravel. Reporters who may adhere to norms of "objectivity" in reporting on a political campaign will not blink at filing a gushing report on a topic about which there is broad national consensus or writing derisively on a subject that lies beyond the bounds of popular consensus. It is as if journalists were unconsciously multilingual, code-switching from neutral interpreters to guardians of social consensus and back again without missing a beat. Elihu Katz and Daniel Dayan have noted how television journalists in Britain, the United States, Israel, and elsewhere who narrate live "media events" rather than ordinary daily news stories abandon a matter-of-fact style for "cosmic lyricism."[11]

Journalists, well aware of the formal and informal norms of professional practice, are less cognizant of the cultural traditions that specify when or how professional norms are called into play. Daniel Hallin[12] writes of three domains of reporting, each of which operates by different journalistic rules. In the zone of "legitimate controversy," recognition of a culturally sanctioned conflict (such as anything on which the two leading political parties differ) guarantees a professionalism dedicated to presenting both sides. In the zone of deviance, there is coverage of issues, topics, or groups beyond the reach of normal reportorial obligations of balance and fairness. These may be ridiculed, marginalized, or trivialized, because reporters instinctively realize they are beyond the pale—such as the women's movement in its earliest years.

The third zone is reporting on topics in which values are shared. It includes most feature writing, human interest reporting, much sports reporting, and occasional hard news reporting that can trust in a taken-for-granted human sympathy between reporter and reader. For instance, it is in theory conceivable that when expensive houses perched on the edge of canyons are destroyed by mudslides in California or when elegant vacation homes nestled in a flood plain are wiped out, a reporter would inquire of the devastated homeowners why they had been so stupid as to build there in the first place (or alternatively, they might ask the local zoning authority why it had allowed the building). A private citizen could not be interrogated with the kind of aggressive questioning public officials are routinely subjected to. By unspoken understanding, there are not two sides to human tragedies. No one teaches this at a journalism school, but everyone knows it. It is part of the culture of newsgathering, part of the etiquette of the profession.

Another crucial cultural distinction in journalism separates news into departments—local, national, and foreign or general news, business, sports, and features. These are very powerful and consequential ways of dividing the field covered by news reporting. Take the distinction between general news reporting, centering on politics, and business reporting. Executives of large corporations, who may often have more influence on the daily lives of citizens than government officials, are invariably less visible in general news. They may be highly visible on the business pages—but there the way they are covered is radically different from general news. On the front page, journalists write in anticipation of readers who ask, "What is happening in the world today that I should know about *as a citizen* of my community, nation, and world?" On the business page, journalists presume its readers ask, "What is happening in the world today that I should know about *as an investor* to protect or advance my financial interests?"[13] The reporter may be scrupulously professional in both cases, but, by the unspoken assumptions of the genre, the die is already cast as to what can or cannot become a story, what angle will or will not make sense.

That news operates by narrative conventions makes it sound too much like the conventions are under the control of the reporter. News writing, then, is just a matter of assembling the appropriate mix of elements—click on the icon for television, radio, or print; then select from Column A "breaking news," "news analysis," "investigative reporting," or "human interest";

from Column B the sphere of consensus, the sphere of legitimate controversy, or the sphere of deviance; and from Column C an expert, insider audience or a general, easily distracted audience. Of course, it does not work so mechanically. To see that news is a set of literary conventions is to recognize that news is culture and reproduces aspects of a larger culture that the reporter and editor may never have consciously articulated. News is produced by people who operate, often unwittingly, within a cultural system, a reservoir of stored cultural meanings. It is organized by conventions of sourcing—who is a legitimate source or speaker or conveyer of information to a journalist. It lives by unspoken preconceptions about the audience—less a matter of who the audience actually may be than a projection by journalists of their own social worlds. News as a form of culture incorporates assumptions about what matters, what makes sense, what time and place we live in, what range of considerations we should take seriously. A news story is supposed to answer the questions who, what, when, where, and why about its subject, but to understand news as culture requires asking of news writing what categories of person count as a *who*, what kinds of things pass for facts, or *whats*, what geography and sense of time is inscribed as *where* and *when*, and what counts as an explanation, or *why*. James Carey has argued brilliantly that news incorporates certain modes of explanation—and rejects, or makes subsidiary, others. For most news, the primary mode of explanation is "motives." Acts have agents, agents have intentions, intentions explain acts. In covering politics, the agent is ordinarily a politician or candidate; the motive is ordinarily political advantage or political power. If this mode of explanation seems insufficient to understand a given act or event, reporters may look also to "causes," broader social or institutional forces at work. The unspoken convention is that reporters may ascribe motives on their own authority, but if they have recourse to "causes" they must find "experts" to make the case.[14]

The *what* of news is equally a product of cultural presuppositions. Metropolitan newspapers are increasingly dependent on their suburban readers and will sometimes cater directly to their presumed needs and interests. However, as Phyllis Kaniss has observed in an important study of local news in Philadelphia, the central city remains the heart of local news coverage. Although a majority of readers do not live or work in the city or vote there, "news of the city government and city institutions . . . takes premier position over policy issues facing suburban communities." The development of suburban industrial parks is barely noticed, but downtown development or the renovation of the old train station win continuous coverage. "These projects are given a place of prominence in the local news media not because of their importance to the regional audience, but because of their symbolic capital."[15] The mass media carry a great deal of symbolic freight in urban and regional identity, more than they know, certainly more than they self-consciously engineer. They help to establish in the imagination of a people a psychologically potent entity—a "community"—that can be located nowhere on the ground. News, in this sense, is more the pawn of shared presuppositions than the purveyor of self-conscious messages.

All news stories are stories, but some are more storylike than others. That is, some of them remind us of the kinds of narratives we associate with the novel, the joke, the campfire story, the gossipy story, the moral cautionary tale, the various fictional or nonfictional but highly structured and purposive forms people typically associate with the word story. The classic, hard-news story that places all the critical information in the first sentence and does not compel many people to read to the end (because the end is never a conclusion or a moral but only the least important information of all the information that would fit in the allotted space) does not have this same character. The classic hard-news story operates more to convey information of utility efficiently than to build a shared world with readers emotionally. At one end of journalistic writing, then, is a model in which the reporter approaches the ideal of a piece of machinery conveying relevant information with accuracy; at the other end is a model of the reporter as a literary or photographic artist, connecting worlds more than conveying data. The former model is in some ways more closely connected with Habermasian visions of rational democracy, the latter model more closely linked to Andersonian visions of horizontal community. The telling of stories in the latter sense is part of the building of a community. This latter view of journalism sees news forms as part of a process of producing collective meanings rather than a process of transmitting information. It emphasizes the social, rather than the mechanical, feature of the news process.

The emphasis on stories, narrative, and story form also tends to lead thinking in a functional, rather than instrumental, direction. That is, it makes one think that understanding the news requires not so much that we know who transmits information to whom for what reason and with what effect but that the whole news process is part of a ritual process beyond the ken of any of its participants. Journalists do not have to read a handbook to know to shift from normal declarative reporting to affectively toned prose when they do human interest reporting or to the hushed tones and murmurs they adopt in covering a state funeral. They code-switch effortlessly. They may or may not catch themselves in this act—it does not matter. They are a part of a larger culture and they play their appointed role. It would not be a journalistic error to fail at this; it would be a kind of cultural sacrilege.

## NOTES

1. Cited in James S. Ettema and Theodore L. Glasser (1988, Summer), Narrative Form and Moral Force: The Realization of Innocence and Guilt Through Investigative Journalism, *Journal of Communication, 38*, p. 24.

2. Peter Parisi (1999), Astonishment and Understanding: On the Problem of Explanation in Journalism, *New Jersey Journal of Communication, 7*, p. 7.

3. Gaye Tuchman (1978), *Making News,* New York: Free Press, pp. 59-63, developed the first analysis of "what-a-story!" stories. Her work was taken up further by Dan Berkowitz (2000), Doing Double Duty: Paradigm Repair and the Princess Diana What-a-Story, *Journalism, 1,*

pp. 125-143, and (1992), Non-routine News and Newswork: Exploring a What-a-story, *Journal of Communication, 42,* pp. 82-94. Woodward's advice to his staff to locate "Holy shit!" stories became a vital point at issue in a libel suit brought against the *Washington Post* (ultimately unsuccessfully) by the chairman of Mobil Oil. See the discussion of this in Michael Schudson (1992), *Watergate in American Memory,* New York: Basic Books, pp. 121-123.

4. Ettema and Glasser, *op. cit.,* p. 23.

5. Hayden White (1981), The Narrativization of Real Events, in W.J.T. Mitchell (Ed.), *On Narrative,* Chicago: University of Chicago Press, p. 253.

6. The leading work on community-building television news is Daniel Dayan and Elihu Katz (1992), *Media Events: The Live Broadcasting of History,* Cambridge, MA: Harvard University Press. The most consistently interesting commentary on this feature of newspaper news (as well as television news) comes from the work of James Ettema and Theodore Glasser. See, for instance, Theodore L. Glasser and James S. Ettema (1994), The Language of News and the End of Morality, *Argumentation, 8,* pp. 337-344, and especially their book (1998), *Custodians of Conscience: Investigative Journalism and Public Virtue,* New York: Columbia University Press.

7. Paul Hartman and Charles Husband (1973), The Mass Media and Racial Conflict, in Stanley Cohen and Jock Young (Eds.), *The Manufacture of News: A Reader,* Beverly Hills, CA: Sage, p. 274.

8. Frank Pearce (1973), How to Be Immoral and Ill, Pathetic and Dangerous, All at the Same Time: Mass Media and the Homosexual, in Stanley Cohen and Jock Young (Eds.), *The Manufacture of News: A Reader,* Beverly Hills, CA: Sage, p. 293.

9. Edwin Alwood (1996), *Straight News: Gays, Lesbians, and the News Media,* New York: Columbia University Press, p. 315. See also Suzanna Danuta Walters (2001), *All the Rage,* Chicago: University of Chicago Press. Walters urges (p. 28) that gays and lesbians should never forget their oppression but "we must mark those rare and chaotic moments when all the verities come tumbling down"— and she sees the 1990s as a moment of just this sort.

10. Jack Katz (1981), What Makes Crime "News"? *Media, Culture and Society, 9,* pp. 47-75. This work offers a general "moral order" explanation. Joel Best (1999), *Random Violence: How We Talk About New Crimes and New Victims,* Berkeley: University of California Press offers a social-organizational explanation.

11. Katz and Dayan, *op. cit.,* p. 108.

12. Daniel Hallin (1986), *"The Uncensored War": The Media and Vietnam,* New York: Oxford University Press, p. 117.

13. Soviet journalists had one advantage over Western journalists in their day—they could cover business with the same access they had to government because business was government owned and managed. They had access to the shop floor that a reporter in the West could only gain with difficulty. See Dean Mills (1981), *The Soviet Journalist: A Cultural Analysis*, unpublished doctoral dissertation, University of Illinois, Urbana–Champaign.

14. James Carey (1986), Why: The Dark Continent of American Journalism, in Robert K. Manoff and Michael Schudson (Eds.), *Reading the News*, New York: Pantheon Books, pp. 146-196.

15. Phyllis Kaniss (1991), *Making Local News*, Chicago: University of Chicago Press, pp. 65-68.

# 13

# PERFORMING MEDIA

## Toward an Ethnography of Intertextuality

MARK ALLEN PETERSON

The scene is a baseball field in midwestern Pennsylvania. The first practice for the Teal Tigers Girls' Softball Team has just ended. The coach is playing a game with the girls to test their knowledge of baseball rules, asking them questions and tossing them candies when they answer correctly. The parents, mostly fathers, stand awkwardly in a circle watching. We are waiting to collect our daughters and take them home. We do not know one another yet.

The coach runs out of questions. She still has two girls who have not earned a candy and she does not want them to go home empty handed. She looks up at the parents, hopefully. "Can anybody think of another question?"

"Who's on first?" says one of the fathers. Several of us grin.

"What's on second?" asks another.

"I don't know," says the first man.

"Third base!" I offer. Two other men say it simultaneously with me. We are all grinning at each other now. The ice has been broken. We still do not know one another, yet some kind of connection has been made. The coach rolls her eyes. Our children gaze at us in perplexity.

In one sense, this is a typical linguistic performance by means of which a small group of strangers enter into an initial social relationship. What is interesting is the way in which it depends on intertextual knowledge of mass media, not only that of the initial speaker but of the other speakers in the interaction as well. By themselves, the words uttered made little referential sense. Their meaning depended on prior knowledge, on a capacity to recognize the utterances as mimetic representations. One of the men had offered a quotation from the vast symbolic repertoire available to Americans as a result of a century of media saturation. This quotation was answered by another and then by another. The four lines uttered have only minimal relations to one another. Coherence in performance depends on knowing how they are related in another text. The performance was improvised, yet drawn from a thoroughly familiar script.[1] Several of the fathers, ranging in age from their mid-30s to mid-40s, are

**Author's Note:** I would like to thank Mihai Coman, Dorle Drackle, Mark Pedelty, John Postill, and Eric Rothenbuhler for their comments on earlier drafts. This chapter extends ideas presented in my book *Anthropology and Mass Communication* (2003).

clearly familiar with the text; their children, just as clearly, are not.

Intertextuality—the decontextualization and recontextualization of symbols or discursive elements—is a central feature of all linguistic performance, spoken and written (Bakhtin, 1981; Kristeva, 1980). Media intertextuality, the interweaving of bits and pieces of dialogue, actions, or other symbols from mass media texts into everyday speech and action, is of particular interest to those studying the role mass communication plays in everyday life. Attention to intertextuality has much to teach us about how people attend to media texts and how media enter into the practices of everyday life.

Intertextuality has been widely examined by media scholars but almost always as a characteristic of texts rather than of social action. Assumptions are made about authors and readers, but these are reconstructed from features of texts rather than attention to social actors. For example, John Fiske's (1989) definition of intertextuality as "the use of recognizable textual references that allow viewers to read texts in relation to other texts" clearly places the primary agency for intertextuality on the producers of media texts. There is also a widespread recognition of artistic uses of intertextuality by *auteurs* like Woody Allen, for whom intertextual "pilfering is a fundamental part of the process of creation" (Stam, 1989, p. 198). Olson (1987) argues that the increasing self-conscious use of intertextuality by television writers, directors, and producers illustrates a coming of age of the genre (and presumes an equal sophistication among audiences). A medium such as television becomes "postliterate" when its codes of production and consumption have broken free of its mooring to the written word and are built on a foundation of prior television texts. But Andersen (1995) argues that the increasingly intertextual nature of television shows such as the American comedy *Seinfeld* is primarily aimed at extending consumer ideologies from the realm of advertising into entertainment media so that advertising and narrative become indistinguishable.

Such textual approaches, which link media texts to other media texts and involve the intentions of text producers, are not particularly useful in explaining performances such as the one described earlier, in which media texts are appropriated and harnessed by social actors to do the work of everyday life. In this chapter, I want to argue for an examination of media intertextuality as a characteristic of social action. My argument is based on the assumption that the roles of media in society are by no means limited to practices of consumption and interpretation. People are never *only* audiences constructing readings of texts, they also seize upon, remember, replicate, and transform elements from the media they consume. They quote dialogue, emulate styles, and whistle tunes they learned from television, radio, or the movies. Some of this intertextual borrowing may be random, idiosyncratic, and personal, but the bulk of such intertextual play is socially patterned. Knowledge of particular kinds of media texts and an ability to display this knowledge competently is a form of cultural capital valued in many social fields. Learning the appropriate media knowledge for particular situations can be an important aspect of socialization. People become performers of texts, and they also become producers of texts, weaving elements from the media they have consumed into new narratives and artifacts that can be displayed to construct particular forms of sociality. Much of this behavior becomes itself the subject of public discourse, as religious leaders, lawyers, educators, psychologists, and others speculate on the moral effects of such intertextual play. In this chapter, I will discuss media intertextuality as a social phenomenon, explore the possibility of ethnography as a methodology for studying it, and offer an initial typology of key domains of intertextual social action.

## INTERTEXTUALITY

As I am using it here, intertextuality is an active social process involving the extracting of a discourse or discursive element from one setting (decontextualization) and inserting it into another (recontextualization) (Bauman & Briggs,

1990; Briggs & Bauman, 1992; Silverstein & Urban, 1996). Intertextuality is an imaginative act through which consumers of texts draw links between texts as part of their everyday social practice. As a semiotic heuristic, intertextuality is intimately bound to such central linguistic concepts as genre, self-reference, plagiarism (and citation), parody, quotation, allusion, authorship, and irony.

As an interpretive practice, intertextuality is communicative insofar as links between the original setting and the recontextualized setting are recognized. Recognition of intertextuality by an audience does not require intent on the part of the producers of a text, although intent may be imputed to them. Likewise, recognition of intertextuality by some audiences does not imply recognition by all, nor does it imply that all audiences will make the same intertextual references. Intertextuality may be conscious or unconscious, deliberate or unintentional. These terms are not particularly useful, however, because they overstate the boundary between reflexive and unreflexive behavior. Bourdieu (1977) has drawn our attention to the extent to which actions can become unreflexive practices, and even deeply embedded habitual behaviors, without ever losing their strategic properties.

Intertextuality is a standard tool for social actors to use when faced with ambiguity. Gumperz (1995) argues that participants in communications that violate expectations always search for explanations; in this search, they "rely on previous communicative experiences and their ability to establish intertextuality by remembering specific ways of talking and the situations and activities indexically associated with their use" (p. 397). Intertextuality thus involves both personal and social constructions of meaning by active consumers who, in the process, shape and reshape mediascapes through their communicative behaviors.

Intertextuality is meaningful to its interpreters because it is a form of indexical signification. Intertexts, that is, signify not only by their content, but by the way they point to the other contexts in which the identical text occurs. This way

of understanding intertexuality is based on a Peircean semiotic, which recognizes a sign as something (*sign* or *signifier*) that stands for something (*object* or *signified*) to someone (*interpreter*) in some respect (*interpretant*). Here I want to emphasize the role of the interpretant as the "respect" through which signifier and signified are related. Peirce suggested three broad categories of signifying relationship: *iconic,* or signifying by resemblance; *indexical,* or signifying by connection; and *symbolic,* or signifying by some arbitrary cultural convention. All three signifying relationships are to some extent present in most cases of media intertextuality.

Indexicality, the link between the original text and its representation, is perhaps the most obvious semiotic aspect of intertextuality. The indexicality of an intertextual sign can be of many types. Peirce's own favorite examples tended to be relations of cause and effect, as when smoke indicates fire. But indexicality encompasses the whole range of metonymic relations, in which parts stand for wholes, categories stand for members, places stand for their inhabitants, and so forth.

Intertextual signs are never only indexical, of course; they are always also iconic. When we say that a text—a coherent unit of verbal, visual, or auditory signs—is taken from one context and recontextualized in another, we actually mean that it is replicated. "Who's on first" in the story at the beginning of this chapter was a quotation, a verbal replication by one man in a particular context of a prior utterance by another man in another context. It is the mimetic resemblance between a particular text and its other entextualizations that we recognize and that leads us to make indexical connections. The degree of exactitude of resemblance varies according to context. In the example, no effort was made by the speaker to reproduce Lou Costello's characteristic voice, nor did the speakers accurately reproduce the sequence of the original script. In some contexts, such as a performance by a professional comedian, the accuracy of mimetic reproduction might be very important.

As Eco (1976) and others have pointed out, indexical relations are always also symbolic, in that they are ultimately tied to arbitrary cultural codes through which it is possible to recognize connections. Smoke may indeed be *caused* by fire, but that fact must be learned before smoke *indicates* fire. Even gestural signs ultimately rest on social convention. As I write this, my 10-month-old son has not yet learned to understand the American gestural sign of the pointing finger. If I point to something, he looks at the finger and his gaze travels up my arm to my face—an indexical relationship but not the culturally appropriate one I am endeavoring to make him understand.

Peirce himself recognized that actually occurring signs in the world would be polysemic. His semiotic writing includes a complex typology of signs, including arbitrary iconic indexes and other combinations. Here, I am less interested in classifying intertexts than I am with three key questions raised by intertextuality:

1. *Indexicality:* What significance does the recontextualized text bring with it from its earlier contexts?

2. *Iconicity:* What changes does the intertext undergo as it is being recontextualized?

3. *Social convention:* How is intertextual play organized into practices that seek to accomplish specific ends in particular social fields?[2]

It is my contention that these questions can best be asked and answered through ethnographic description and analysis of everyday uses of media intertextuality.

## Ethnographic Strategies for Indexical Research

By *ethnography* I mean description based on intimate, long-term, reflexive encounters between social scientists and the peoples about whom they are writing. The classic model of ethnography is participant observation, which involves relatively long-term relationships between the ethnographer and his or her host community and in which researchers attempt to situate themselves within quotidian situations and events. Without an ethnographic research imaginary that forces us to

consider our interpretations of media texts in the light of encounters with other media consumers, we run the risk of replacing our own (multiple and fragmented) subjectivities for the intersubjectivities that offer us the best hope for understanding how mass media work in the contemporary world.

To the study of media, ethnography brings an attention to cultural difference, a commitment to close observation and recording, the provision of "thick" descriptive detail designed to reveal the contexts that give actions meanings to a community, reflexive engagement with the voices of the ethnographer's hosts, and attention to the contiguity of what is being described to broader aspects of social process. Media ethnography attempts to tease out layers of meaning through observation of and engagement with the everyday situations in which media are consumed, the practices by which media are interpreted, and the uses to which media are put.

In calling for an ethnographic approach to intertextuality, I am calling for attention to ways in which intertextuality is public and social. When I see a book on a friend's shelf written by Burnham and Woods and I laugh to myself because my imagination draws a link between these names and the charmed prophecy that protects Macbeth, this fragment of intertextual play does not strike me as worthy of ethnographic attention. But when my daughters use discourse from the children's program *Mighty Morphin Power Rangers* to position themselves among neighborhood boys and to regulate play with them, this strikes me as being of broader social significance. Such bits of everyday life speak to us of the subtle and yet significant intersections of media with gender roles, social performance, socialization processes, pleasure, and power.

There is a growing interest in intertextuality in the anthropology of media. Examples of recent anthropological work on media that focuses on intertexuality include Abu-Lughod (1993, 1995a, 1995b, 1997), Armbrust (1996, 1998), and Spitulnik (1996, 1999). For intertextuality to form the basis of a holistic approach to mass media, however, it must be more deeply theorized and shaped by anthropologists attempting to use it to explicate field situations. In this essay, I will borrow from the language of Gerard Genette's (1998) categories of "transtextuality" to offer five categories of intertextual social action:

1. *Intertextual performance:* The reproduction of media texts in social discourse

2. *Paratextual knowledge:* The knowledge about media texts one brings to media reception, intertextual performance, and other encounters with texts

3. *Architextual practice:* That aspect of interpreting media texts that creates meaning by recognizing intertextual connections, locating a text in a wider intertextual web, and assigning significance to the text within this web

4. *Metatextual discourse:* Discourse that comments on media texts and on people's textual practices

5. *Hypertextual production:* The creation of new texts out of elements appropriated from media texts

## DOMAINS OF INTERTEXTUAL ACTION

*1. Intertextual Performance.* Genette (1998) restricts the term *intertextuality* for the sort of performance highlighted in the introduction: "the presence of one text within another" (p. 2); that is, the quotation from or allusion to a media text in another text or, as in the case provided earlier, a social performance. Ethnographers of media-saturated societies have long recorded the ways in which intertextual references enter into everyday social performance. As early as 1937, Robert Lynd described how discursive elements were transferred from the movies and tried out in the everyday social worlds of movie viewers as part of the ongoing socialization of American youth.

The description and analysis of the circulation and performance of words, phrases, and discursive styles as they are appropriated from mass media and enter into social interaction is one of the most fruitful domains for the study of intertextual performance. As Spitulnik (1996) points out, such an approach has its origins in Bakhtin's

(1981) observation that certain forms of discourse have a "socially charged life" (p. 293) and Gumperz's (1971) recognition that "mass media and the prestige of their speakers tend to carry idioms far from their sources" (p. 223; cited in Spitulnik, 1996). The circulation of media idioms in the United States is obvious; phrases like "Who's on first?" "Play it again, Sam," "Beam me up, Scotty," "Make my day," "Toto, I don't think we're in Kansas anymore," and so forth appear frequently in a variety of speech acts and are immediately recognizable even by people who have never seen the movies or television shows from which they are borrowed (see Spitulnik, 1996). Similar phrases abound among audiences of every community in which media play significant roles. Still, because television, films, and other mass media are often transnational commodities, idioms from them can enter into social fields outside of those used in their communities of origin. For example, a 10-year-old Kashmiri boy of my acquaintance in New Delhi used to greet tourists with a barrage of phrases from Arnold Schwarzenegger films to evoke laughter, after which he would attempt to entice them into his uncle's rug shop.

*2. Paratextual Knowledge.* As shared intertexts circulate ever more widely, they become part of the general cultural knowledge within communities. Social actors cannot make use of media intertextuality as performers without a reasonable assurance that their audience will recognize the references. People who dwell in media-saturated societies are expected to know about an extensive series of media genres, storyworlds, and mediated figures beyond their face-to-face social experiences. They must know about relevant genres, currently popular texts, and a number of mediated figures, such as actors, athletes, authors, cartoon characters, fictional characters, musicians, politicians, religious leaders, and talk show hosts. Familiarity with such texts and figures and an ability to converse with others about their events and storylines or their diets, diseases, sexual escapades, divorces, and legal disputes is required for competent participation in many forms of conversational performance (see Caughey, 1984a, 1984b, 1995).[3] This body of knowledge about media texts I will call here a paratext.[4]

Genette (1998) uses *paratext* to refer to titles, bylines, epigraphs, citations, and other cues that make up the immediate surround of the text. At this level, paratext would seem to be parallel to what Gumperz has called, for social interaction, "contextualization cues" (Gumperz, 1990). Certainly paratextual cues—the need for a joke to break the ice, the fact that it was a softball game, and the coach's request for a question—served to stimulate the intertextual performance described in the introduction. But Genette also uses the term for the knowledge certain actors have of texts and which they bring to a reading of them. In defining media intertextuality in social performance, then, I will use paratextuality to refer to that unequally distributed yet socially patterned knowledge people have about media texts that influences both how they approach new texts (that is, their interpretive practice) and also how they talk about media with different interlocutors, in different settings, and toward different ends (that is, their metatextual discourse).

Paratextuality in this sense operates on at least two levels. On one level, it consists of knowledge of the storylines, history, themes, and running jokes associated with a television show, movie series, media figure, or other intertextual locus. In an ongoing television series, for example, regular viewers will accumulate knowledge of character relationships, as well as the narrative history of the storyworld of the show. But paratextual knowledge also includes detailed knowledge of the contexts that render such textual knowledge useful. This means not only being aware of specific media references but also being able to recognize which of these are appropriate to use in what situations.

*3. Architextual Practice.* The social fields in which people engage in intertextual play include those of media consumption. Genette (1998) uses the term *architextuality* to refer to the ways in which consumers recognize particular elements of texts as being shared by other texts they have seen and use this to construct particular "readings" of these texts. One of the fundamental aspects of architextuality is the capacity of media consumers to classify texts into genres. Such practices include, for example, the ability to recognize the differences between commercials and regular television programming, perhaps assisted by such paratextual cues as network announcements ("we now return to our program . . ."). It includes the ability to recognize certain fundamental structural patterns of commercials and to relate these to certain kinds of products. This kind of interpretation is both learned and socially patterned.

Interpretation is used here to describe a more active process than mere recognition of a set of regularized genres. Each new media text is not only generated by the preexisting notions of what such a text is but also possesses the possibility of changing some of those notions and so of generating a modified version. Television viewers learn genres not as a set of fixed, archetypal forms with which they mechanically recognize and decode types of advertisements but as part of a set of interpretive practices that includes recognition of discontinuity as well as continuity, transformation as well as reproduction.

Learning practices of media interpretation, including the ability to create and recognize intertextual connections on the basis of both formal properties and their transformations, is an ongoing process that includes the learning of interpretive schemes as well as the learning of interpretive practices. By *interpretive schemes* I mean "standardized elements of stocks of knowledge applied by actors in the production of interaction. Interpretive schemes form the core of mutual knowledge whereby the accountable universe of meaning is sustained through and in processes of interaction" (Giddens, 1979, p. 83). By *interpretive practices,* I mean the ability to define contexts in which media is encountered and to apply to them appropriate styles of perception, performance, cognition, and affect. Such skills are not consciously strategic so much as habitual (Bourdieu, 1977), built up out of years of socially organized media consumption activity. How much attention one pays to a particular genre or text, how one speaks and acts during media reception (at home versus at a movie theater), the ways in which one interprets the text, and the emotions one invests in or derives from the text are all part of interpretive practice. Interpretive practices are one of the links between media consumption and everyday life. They involve social performances and, like all social performances, they accomplish multiple ends.[5]

Genette's concept *architextuality* thus refers to the processes by which people imaginatively engage with media texts to construct their meaning. In particular, it refers to the ways people make indexical connections between the immediate text they are experiencing and other texts they have experienced in the past. Interpretation, in this sense, is always at least partly a form of play, of bricolage. Such play does not occur in a vacuum, of course. Interpretive practices take place in particular contexts. The physical setting, the social definition of the scene, the nature of the media technologies deployed, the relationships between those experiencing (or imagined as experiencing) the same text—these are just a few of the important considerations of the setting (Lembo, 2000; Peterson, 2003, pp. 127-138).

*4. Metatextual Discourse.* In addition to the context of situation, people's intertextual practices are conditioned by the cultural context. This cultural context of interpretation is not a static code but is itself a product of cultural performances. *Metatextuality* refers to texts about texts, to public commentaries and criticisms of texts and of real or imagined behaviors with texts. It refers to aesthetic assessments of media, sales pitches for media, discussions of favorite media texts and genres, discussions of the viewing habits of oneself and others, concerns about the effects of particular texts, genres, or media technologies on society, and so forth.

There are at least three key forms of metatextual discourses: those that are referential, those that seek to persuade, and those that use media to invoke moral worlds. Referential metatexts, including broadcast guides in newspapers, exposés, trivia games, discussions with the video store clerk about what is new on the shelves, and conversations with friends about new movies, seek to share referential information about texts. Such

metatextual discourses may lay claims to neutrality or objectivity but often invoke local aesthetics, create "buzz," or generate nostalgia. Even in their most neutral forms, such discourses tend to center around issues of genre, offering framings for media consumption.

These referential metadiscourses thus move imperceptibly into the realm of persuasive metadiscourses. Persuasive metatextuality overtly seeks to persuade people that the media text they are thinking of consuming will be worth the investment of time, energy, and money they must make to experience it. Such discourse includes all forms of media advertising, much of entertainment journalism (in which the actors, directors, technicians, and other artists interviewed speak only in the most glowing terms of current and soon to be released films), and decision-making negotiations among customers and sales clerks in video, music, or bookstores.

Yet a third category of metatextual discourse concerns moral public discourses about media. Public discourse about texts, clusters of texts, and genres is ubiquitous in many societies, and it is nearly always a value-laden discourse. "There are very few programmes that people will freely and plainly admit they like to watch; with the exception of perhaps the evening news, people seem to feel a need to explain, defend and justify their viewing habits." (Alasuutari, 1992, p. 561). Such metatextual discourses, although in the form of a commentary on media, have a semiotic life of their own, often serving as metaphorical ways of talking about moral issues that are not directly or obviously linked to the media. Richard Wilk (1995) points out that although we might expect public discourse about media to frame the ways in which people consume media, there is little evidence that talk about media has much to do with actual consumption. Rather, talk about media absorbs existing class, gender, ethnic, and other social distinctions and re-presents them as being about media texts, forms, or genres.

*5. Hypertextual Production.* By *hypertextuality*, Genette (1998) means appropriations, transformations, and alterations in media texts.[6] Such hypertextuality is common in intertextual performance—the fathers performing lines from the "Who's on First" routine do not perform the entire routine but an abbreviated version of it, intended to evoke rather than recreate the original text. Genette envisions such hypertextuality as involving original texts ("hypotexts") and transformed versions of them ("hypertexts"). This can create a complex web. Walt Disney's *Little Mermaid* (1989) is certainly a hypertext of author Hans Christian Anderson's hypotext, but the Disney version becomes in turn a hypotext for many other versions, both in the media and in oral retellings. Here I will use *hypertextual production* to refer to the production of new texts out of elements appropriated from prior texts, in which transformation of the texts is central to the meaning of the texts so created.

In many settings and communities, intertextual elements are not only performed in discourse but become objectified and commodified. Sometimes these are direct quotations from media. In 1981, after the attempted murder of the main character in the globally successful soap opera *Dallas,* one could find "Who Shot J.R.?" quoted on clothing, buttons, and other goods, not only across the United States but throughout Europe as well, both in English and in local languages. People use such secondary media as buttons, posters, t-shirts, and so forth for purposes of display, as ways of constructing particular identities. People are not only consumers of commodified entextualizations, however; they are themselves creators of media entextualizations. This form of hypertextuality is particularly characteristic of children's play and of film fan behavior (Bacon-Smith, 1992, 2000; Dickey, 1993, 2001; Jenkins, 1992), as well as of media industries, both large and small, that transform one another's texts to create new texts, forms, and genres.

It is important to emphasize that hypertextual acts cannot be understood outside the sets of social fields that help define and (metatextually) evaluate them. Children quickly learn that teachers reward literary forms of intertextuality but frown on intertextual play that embeds television and film texts into schoolwork. Likewise,

American adults learn very quickly that society urges those who engage in *Star Trek* fandom to "get a life," although it honors those who put the same amount of energy into opera or museum art. Fan transformations of media texts can even lead to legal battles with those who claim authorship or ownership of the original hypotexts (Mikulak, 1998). What to do about this—whether the social or personal rewards of hypertextual play outweigh the institutional sanctions—depends on a person's assessment of their social field.

## Conclusion

Studies of mass media have long been dominated by explicit or implicit notions of linear communication—notions of media texts moving from producers to consumers. Audience studies, although shifting attention from texts to the processes and situations of their interpretation, have nonetheless tended to reproduce this paradigm by putting the text and its interpretation at the center of meaning making. What I have tried to emphasize in this essay is that studies of reception (reading, hearing, viewing) and interpretation map only a small part of the terrain of social life in which media play a role. The ethnography of intertextuality offers a useful supplement to text- and reception-based approaches to media study and pays attention to the structural features of texts and to sites of reception, but it examines these in relation to the many other activities in which people make use of media.

The essence of the approach I am advocating is to treat intertextuality not as a property of texts but as a social strategy. As such, intertextuality is one among many strategies—reflexive and tactical as well as unreflexive and habitual—by which people use the mass media as part of their cultural capital, as part of the symbolic stuff they need to construct social identities and to accomplish the ordinary tasks of everyday life. To treat intertextuality as a strategy is to attempt to shift it from the realm of art or media effects to the poetics of everyday life. An anthropology of media that attempts to describe and explain the meanings of media in a society or community ought to be able to explain not only how cultural meanings are encoded in media texts but also the ordinary uses of media in social interaction. Such ethnographies of media intertextuality at once problematize standard reception studies and, at the same time, demonstrate profoundly the degree to which many people's lives are saturated by media and mediated social relations in the contemporary world.

## NOTES

1. "Who's on first?" is a comedy routine by the early 20th-century comedy team of Bud Abbott and Lou Costello in which Bud tries to talk about baseball players with the nicknames "Who" "What," and "I Don't Know," which Lou hears not as names but as queries. The routine was performed literally thousands of times on stage, radio, television, and film and has been part of the intertextual metatext for several generations of Americans.

2. The first two of these questions are discussed generally in Bauman and Briggs (1990) and Briggs and Bauman (1992). See also Spitulnik (1996).

3. Competent performance should not here imply positive regard. Disdain can be as legitimate a discursive position as enthusiasm. What is socially unacceptable is ignorance.

4. I have elsewhere, following Jenkins (1992), referred to this body of knowledge as a metatext (Peterson, 2003, p. 151). In this chapter, following Genette, I want to reserve *metatext* for a different kind of intertextual discourse.

5. On interpretive practice, see Beeman and Peterson (2001) and Peterson (2003).

6. The term *hypertextuality* is an awkward choice for this category of intertextuality, because *hypertext* has come to have a very specific meaning in electronic media. Preferable terms might be *entextuality* and *entextualization* (but see Silverstein & Urban, 1996).

## REFERENCES

Abu-Lughod, L. (1993). Finding a place for Islam: Egyptian television serials and the national interest. *Public Culture, 5*(3), 493-513.

Abu-Lughod, L. (1995a). Movie stars and Islamic moralism in Egypt. *Social Text, 42,* 53-67.

Abu-Lughod, L. (1995b). The objects of soap opera: Egyptian television and the cultural politics of modernity. In D. Miller (Ed.), *Worlds apart: Modernity through the prism of the local* (pp. 190-210). New York: Routledge.

Abu-Lughod, L. (1997). The interpretation of culture(s) after television. *Representations, 59,* 109-134.

Alasuutari, P. (1992). "I'm ashamed to admit it, but I have watched *Dallas*": The moral hierarchy of television programmes. *Media, Culture and Society, 14,* 561-582.

Andersen, R. (1995). *Consumer culture and TV programming.* Boulder, CO: Westview Press.

Armbrust, W. (1996). *Mass culture and modernization in Egypt.* Cambridge, England: Cambridge University Press.

Armbrust, W. (1998). Terrorism and kebab: A Capraesque view of modern Egypt. In S. Zuhur (Ed.), *Images of enchantment: Visual and performing arts of the Middle East* (pp. 283-299). Cairo, Egypt: American University in Cairo Press.

Bacon-Smith, C. (1992). *Enterprising women: Television fandom and the creation of popular myth.* Philadelphia: University of Pennsylvania Press.

Bacon-Smith, C. (2000). *Science fiction culture.* Philadelphia: University of Pennsylvania Press.

Bakhtin, M. (1981). Discourse in the novel. In M. Holquist & C. Emerson (Ed.), *The dialogic imagination: Four essays* (M. Holquist, Trans., pp. 259-422). Austin: University of Texas Press.

Bauman, R., & Briggs, C. (1990). Poetics and performance as critical perspectives on language and social life. *Annual Review of Anthropology, 19,* 59-88.

Beeman, W. O., & Peterson, M. A. (2001). Situations and interpretations: Explorations in interpretive practice. *Anthropological Quarterly 74*(4), 159-162.

Bourdieu, P. (1977). *Outline of a theory of practice* (R. Nice, Trans.). Cambridge, England: Cambridge University Press.

Briggs, C., & Bauman, R. (1992). Genre, intertextuality and social power. *Journal of Linguistic Anthropology, 2,* 131-172.

Caughey, J. L. (1984a). *Imaginary social worlds: A cultural approach.* Lincoln: University of Nebraska Press.

Caughey, J. L. (1984b). Social relations with media figures. In G. Gumpert & R. S. Cathcart (Eds.), *Inter/media: Interpersonal communication in a media world* (pp. 219-252). Oxford, England: Oxford University Press.

Caughey, J. L. (1995). Imaginary social relationships. In J. Harris & J. Rosen (Eds.), *Media journal: Reading and writing about popular culture.* New York: Allyn & Bacon.

Dickey, S. (1993). *Cinema and the urban poor in South India.* Cambridge, England: Cambridge University Press.

Dickey, S. (2001). Opposing faces: Film star, fan clubs and the construction of class identities in South India. In R. Dwyer & C. Pinney (Eds.), *Pleasure and the nation: The history, politics and consumption of popular culture in India* (pp. 212-246). New Delhi: Oxford University Press.

Eco, U. (1976). *A theory of semiotics.* Bloomington: University of Indiana Press.

Fiske, J. (1989). *Reading the popular.* Boston: Unwin Hyman.

Genette, G. (1998). *Palimpsests: Literature in the second degree* (C. Newman & C. Dubinsky, Trans.). Lincoln: University of Nebraska Press.

Giddens, A. (1979). *Central problems in social theory: Action, structure, and contradiction in social analysis.* Berkeley: University of California Press.

Gumperz, J. J. (1971). The speech community. In P. P. Giglioli (Ed.), *Language and social context* (pp. 219-231). New York: Viking.

Gumperz, J. J. (1990). Contextualization and understanding. In A. Duranti & C. Goodwin (Eds.), *Rethinking context* (pp. 229-252). New York: Cambridge University Press.

Gumperz, J. J. (1995). The linguistic and cultural relativity of conversational inference. In J. J. Gumperz & S. C. Levinson (Eds.), *Rethinking linguistic relativity* (pp. 374-406). Cambridge, England: Cambridge University Press.

Jenkins, H. (1992). *Textual poachers: Television fans and participatory culture.* New York: Routledge.

Kristeva, J. (1980). *Desire in language* (A. A. Jardine, Trans.). New York: Columbia University Press.

Lembo, R. (2000). *Thinking through television.* Cambridge, England: Cambridge University Press.

Lynd, R. (1937). *Middletown revisited.* New York: Harcourt, Brace.

Mikulak, B. (1998). Fans versus Time Warner: Who owns Looney Tunes? In K. S. Sandler (Ed.), *Reading the rabbit: Explorations in Warner Bros. animation* (pp. 193-208). New Brunswick, NJ: Rutgers University Press.

Olson, S. R. (1987). Meta-television: Popular postmodernism. *Critical Studies in Mass Communication, 4*(31), 284-300.

Pierce, C. S. (1977). *Semiotic and significs.* Bloomington: Indiana University Press.

Peterson, M. A. (2003). *Anthropology and mass communication: Myth and media in the new millennium.* Oxford, England: Berghahn.

Silverstein, M., & Urban, G. (Eds.). (1996). *Natural histories of discourse.* Chicago: University of Chicago Press.

Spitulnik, D. (1996). The social circulation of media discourse and the mediation of communities. *Journal of Linguistic Anthropology, 6*(2), 161-187.

Spitulnik, D. (1999). The language of the city: Town Bemba as urban hybridity. *Journal of Linguistic Anthropology, 8*(1), 30-59.

Stam, R. (1989). *Subversive pleasures: Bakhtin, cultural criticism and film.* Baltimore: Johns Hopkins University Press.

Wilk, R. (1995). "It's destroying a whole generation": Television and moral discourse in Belize. *Visual Anthropology, 5*, 229-244.

# 14

## AUDIENCE ETHNOGRAPHIES

### A Media Engagement Approach

ANTONIO C. LA PASTINA

In the last two decades, ethnography has acquired a central role theoretically and empirically in media studies. It also has acquired a rhetorical function. Rhetorically, ethnography has come to represent an opposition to positivistic paradigms toward data collection and analysis, as well as the relationship between research and the researched. Ethnography has represented a shift from empirical practices of data collection, pushing scholars to introduce nonobjective strategies to audience analysis and a greater level of self-reflexivity among researchers.

This turn, however, led to a problematic situation. The term *ethnography* has acquired great currency among media scholars, at the expense of a focused coherence on its meaning, a critique that has been advanced by other scholars. Murphy (1999) outlined the dilemma of ethnography use in reception studies. He argued that scholars of cultural studies have theorized about the importance of ethnography to an understanding of media and cultural practices at the same time that they have reached an almost paralyzing position in which the political and epistemological debates regarding the role of the researcher have limited rather than promoted the production of ethnographic media studies.

In this chapter, I argue that audience ethnography needs to be repositioned as a fieldwork-based, long-term practice of data collection and analysis. This practice allows researchers to attain a greater level of understanding of the community studied and maintain self-reflexivity and respect toward those they are attempting to understand within the everyday life of the community. Relying on my work in rural communities in Brazil over the last decade, I will discuss some of the ways in which ethnography, as a long-term, in-depth practice, can benefit our understanding of the reception dynamic as well as provide insights otherwise impossible to attain. I will propose a model for audience ethnography, which I term *media engagement*, to discuss how the process of ethnography functions to apprehend the complex dynamic that evolves between consumers and cultural products.

Murphy and Krady (2003), in their edited book, demonstrated how ethnography can provide a solid understanding of the engagement process between viewers and cultural products. Taking into consideration the complexities of location and the dynamics of gender, race, ethnicity, and class, the different chapters in that anthology showed how media (audience) ethnography could be performed as a long-term, in-depth project that allows for solid knowledge about media practices.

Ethnographers immerse themselves in a culture to retell the lives of a particular people, to narrate the rites and traditions of that people, and to understand and explain their cultural practices. In doing so, ethnographers contain, even if they do not intend to, the experiences lived, giving form and coherence to a multiplicity of experiences, to simultaneous events, sensations, feelings, and emotions. The ethnographer is trying to order the chaotic world in which theory and praxis are jumbled. According to Geertz (1973), this is accomplished through thick description:

> Ethnography is thick description. What the ethnographer is in fact faced with . . . is a multiplicity of complex conceptual structures, many of them superimposed upon or knotted into one another, which are at once strange, irregular and inexplicit, and which he must contrive somehow first to grasp and then to render. (p. 10)

For Geertz (1973), "understanding a people's culture exposes their normalness without reducing their particularity. . . . It renders them accessible: setting them in the frame of their own banalities, it dissolves their opacity" (p. 14). As ethnographers, Geertz explains, "we begin with our own interpretation of what our informants are up to, or think they are up to, and then systematize those" (p. 14). In this sense, what we observe and write is a retelling, from the researcher's perspective, of what happens in the locality. The intent of the ethnography must be to allow the systematization of these accounts, so the reader can understand the events described, knowing full well that these are the accounts of one observer who has framed and perceived the events within his or her limitations.

Rosaldo (1993), in discussing the work of Geertz and Turner and their role in developing methodologies for processual analysis in ethnography, argued that the danger of *thick* descriptions is that they may end in *thin* conclusions. His view is that the focus on social control placed on most of these authors' earlier works excludes "precisely the informal cultural practices whose study they elsewhere advocate and whose work their case studies so effectively illuminate" (p. 98). Rosaldo was not arguing against thick descriptions; he was developing an argument against the notion of culture as a form of orderly structure and controlling force: "One often equates culture with order (as against chaos) and social norms with regulation (as against anarchic violence)" (p. 99). For him, when culture was equated to a "control mechanism, such phenomena as passions, spontaneous fun, and improvised activities tend to drop out of sight" (p. 102). As ethnographers, we must be prepared to look at culture not as a system enclosed in itself but rather as a system in continuous motion.

Abu-Lughod (1993), in the introduction to *Bedouin Stories*, wrote that the concept of culture seemed to work as an essential tool for making "other." The author argued that in producing a discourse on culture that explains the "difference," "anthropology ends up also constructing, producing and maintaining difference" (p. 12).

> In his radical argument that "natives" are a figment of the anthropological imagination, [Appadurai] shows the complicity of the anthropological concept of culture in a continuing "incarceration" of non-Western peoples in time and place. He argues that by not looking to their histories, we have denied these people the same capacity for movement, travel and geographical interaction that Westerners take for granted. The fluidity of group boundaries, languages and practices, in other words, has been masked by the concept of culture. (Abu Lughod, 1993, p. 11).

The importance of the concept of culture in ethnographic work is that in gathering data or facts one inevitably will select some over others and, in doing so, will present a certain view of a group's "culture," creating a representation or a construction of a group's lived experience. As Scheper-Hughes (1992) argued, "all facts are selected and interpreted from the moment we decide to count one thing and ignore another, or attend this ritual but not another, so that anthropological understanding is necessarily partial and is always hermeneutic" (p. 23). This selectivity in which the ethnographer inevitably engages may result in generalizations that, according to Abu-Lughod (1993), lead to the creation of "coherent, self-contained" others, allowing for the "fixing of boundaries between the self and the other" (p. 7).

Still, these narratives that represent a particular segment of a group's life provide a deep understanding of the dynamics that form that group's practices and, for our purpose in this chapter, their particular engagement with media and popular culture. The diversity of methods and theoretical approaches delineated by Drotner (1994) clarifies the strength of the ethnographic method for the study of media practices. A method as open-ended as ethnography provides space for the researcher to incorporate information and build on it, as well as to recycle and reevaluate it the next day based on newly acquired information and renewed perceptions.

The advantage of using ethnography to engage in audience studies rests on its potential to provide both a domestic and a communal context of television and telenovela reception among the different groups in the community. It also facilitates an understanding of how the reception context can affect the interpretation of the message by viewers, individually and in groups (La Pastina, 2003b). Ethnographic research also allows the examination of the phenomena not only in its immediate social, political, and economic contexts but also in a larger historical framework, as well as its insertion in the broader regional, national, and global context.

Morley and Silverstone (1991) argued for the advantage of ethnographic methods in studying media audiences, explaining that they provide an "analysis of multiple structured contexts of action, aiming to produce a rich descriptive and interpretative account of lives and values of those subjected to the investigation" (p. 149-150). The importance of ethnography lies in the possibility of assessing the different elements involved in the reception process and how these elements interact within the context of the locality in which the observation is taking place, along with the culture and identity of the community members.

Television audiences are fluid; they present different characteristics in different situations and toward different programs. "Watching television should be seen as a complex and dynamic cultural process, fully integrated in the messiness of everyday life, and always specific in its meanings and impacts" (Ang, 1991, p. 161). According to Ang (1991), ethnographic research is the appropriate methodology for better understanding of viewing behavior in the specific concrete situation in which it takes place. She argues that ethnographic research can account for

> situational practices and experiences of those who must make do with television provision served them by institutions—an open-ended discourse that conceives quality as something relative rather than absolute, plural rather than singular, context specific rather than universal, a repertoire of aesthetic, moral and cultural values that arises in the social process of watching television rather than through criteria imposed upon [it] from above. (Ang, 1991, p. 167-168)

For Drotner (1994), media ethnography

> draws on a variety of classical anthropological and ethnological methods of investigation: participant observation, informal talks and in-depth or life course interviews, diaries kept by the informants as well as self-reports kept by the researcher. In addition, [the ethnographer] may apply textual analysis of, for example, selected television programmes, musical scores or magazine genres. (p. 97)

Drotner (1994) argues that these methods and theoretical approaches do not necessarily provide a more veridical picture; rather, it is the "discrepancies that are most significant and revealing" (p. 98).

The practice of audience ethnography remains a challenge. The need to focus on the complexities of the surrounding environment and on personal ideational values and attitudes makes this a process fraught with limitations. To observe and participate in the process of media consumption might limit a more general analysis of the societal process and the general trends that can be observed in a sociological study. Nevertheless, the understanding of individual and communal media consumption practices might help to apprehend the role of media texts.

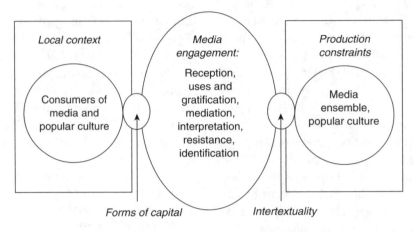

**Figure 14.1**    Media Engagement Model

The engagement between viewers or consumers and texts needs to be investigated as a process located in a context broader than the immediate site of the viewing interaction. I have identified four stages of this engagement process: reading, interpretation, appropriation, and change. The first phase takes place when the actual reading occurs, normally in the home, within a family context. This phase is best understood in terms of a factual explanation of the narrative structure and content. The second phase ensues when the text is interpreted, which happens not only at an individual level but also through social interactions that might impose norms, values, and beliefs shared by the community regarding the text. After interpretation, the third phase is appropriation, in which the issues brought up by the text and interpreted through mediating forces are used to explain one's own life or the social relations and cultural dynamics in which one is inserted. The processes of identification and catharsis are normally at work in this phase. Resistance also occurs in this phase. The final stage in this engagement model is behavior change, which in most cases is the hardest stage to document in this process of engagement. Ethnography has the potential to observe community and social changes that might be related to media presence, due to its ability to develop

longitudinal investigations. Although these four phases are an artificial attempt to impose an analytical frame on this unruly process, the stages are not discrete or present in all textual engagements (see Figure 14.1).

In the model shown in Figure 14.1, I propose that ethnography allows investigators to grapple with the complexity of the relationship between viewers or media consumers and media texts as an ensemble that connects all the available media sources.

I espouse the view that when viewers engage in this reception process, several things happen at the same time. The interaction between viewer and text is complex, multidimensional, and multilayered. No single term can explain this process. Viewers engage in several processes, often simultaneously: The text becomes part of a routine; it is used for gratification and leisure; its meaning is negotiated with family and community; some images, topics, and characters are rejected and others embraced; the text is inserted in a context that also mediates the process (Martín-Barbero, 1987/1993); and this process is continuously evolving, due to social interactions. Identification happens, interpretation happens, use for pure gratification happens, use for access to information happens, passive viewing happens, and highly active reading happens. Chatting about these texts might lead to interpretations and consequent acceptance or negation of values and attitudes presented in these narratives. Although they occasionally are nomads, subjects normally are predictable in their interpretive strategies.

The challenge in the study of audiences is that we are stepping into a field where no clear unified structure is in place. In this research, I am trying to go beyond the analysis of interpretations alone to discuss that transition at which text becomes reality, and sometimes reality seems to be the text. I am using *engagement* here to imply the totality of the media experience—from reading about the show, to watching it, to talking about it, to remembering it, and so on.

## TELENOVELAS IN RURAL BRAZIL: A CASE STUDY OF MEDIA ENGAGEMENT

To explain the advantage of the ethnographic process in understanding what I have termed *media engagement*, I will present an analysis of the confluence between a particular telenovela text and viewers' lives in a specific context. Telenovelas are layered structures of signification, with different sets of meanings associated with different aspects of the creative and production process. Telenovelas are melodramatic texts that favor traditional notions of class ascension and romance inherent to the genre. Nevertheless, in recent years, the Brazilian telenovela, especially as the genre has been developed by the Globo network, has become much more attuned to the national reality, discussing current affairs and the social and political structure of the nation (Hamburger, 1999; La Pastina, Rego, & Straubhaar, 2004). In doing so, telenovelas have become a space in which authors' agendas, and many times those promoted and supported by the network, become an important subplot in the narrative (La Pastina, 2004a; La Pastina, Patel, & Schiavo, 2004).

In *O Rei do Gado* (The Cattle King), the particular telenovela discussed here, adultery, premarital sex, and pregnancy raised important issues to viewers in Macambira, a small rural community that was struggling with more visible teen sexuality

and changing codes of moral behavior. It also underscored the questioning, by a large number of women, of traditional norms that limited women's sexuality but allowed men to retain their sexual freedom, even after marriage (La Pastina, 2004b). The subplot of land reform and political integrity included in the narrative clearly touched the local reality. In 1996, during the broadcast of *O Rei do Gado*, Macambira, the site of this fieldwork, was split by the rivalry between two political parties in the community. In this scenario of political rivalry, the notions of integrity, honesty, and land rights prompted viewers to discuss the images presented in the telenovela in relation to their own reality (La Pastina, 2004a). The commercial nature of telenovelas pervaded the narrative as well, with commercial insertions and tie-ins with material advertised during commercial breaks. Viewers, however, did not necessarily decode the commercial content of telenovelas evenly. Technological limitations reduced the access to commercial messages, and the remoteness of the community affected the engagement with the commercial messages, clearly establishing a hierarchy of viewer desires based on each individual's cultural, economic, and symbolic capital (La Pastina, 2001).

In Macambira, which is located in the interior of the Rio Grande do Norte state in northeastern Brazil, television was perceived as the ultimate form of entertainment. Years of savings were invested by some families in satellite dishes that allowed them to tune into 14 channels instead of the single one available to the majority of the population. Television was more than entertainment, however. For many viewers, it was the main, if not the only, source of information. Television and telenovelas provided access to a modern and urban reality in which male and female roles appeared to be different. Through television, viewers in Macambira knew what was going on in Brasilia, the nation's capital. They also knew the latest fashion trends in the industrialized South and the misery of communities a few hundred miles away. Television reminded these viewers about the gap between their lives and the lives of people in the urban centers of the South. Whether decadent and dangerous or "modern" and exciting, the lifestyles of other families were brought to those in Macambira through the telenovelas that featured conflicts, struggles, emotions, and romance.

Macambira was distant and isolated, not only physically and culturally, but symbolically and emotionally, from the urban and modern representation of the nation, the Brazil constituted in the political and social discourse of school textbooks and the news and entertainment media. This was reflected in physical distance, economic disparity, and large differences in values and daily life routines. These structural differences created a breach or perceived gap between viewers in Macambira and the modern, urban Brazil of the telenovelas (La Pastina, 2003a).

This gap created a fracture in the national identity, producing a regional and local sense of not belonging to the nation, generating diverse readings of the reality consumed through the media. For most in Macambira, television and radio remained the main sources of information about the outside world. Only very limited interpersonal contact with outsiders complemented that media knowledge. Migrants, particular temporary ones, represented a bridge to the outside world, providing personal stories on the opportunities and vicissitudes one had to confront to survive in the South. This lack of direct experience severely limited the cultural capital that rural Brazilians brought to understanding the telenovelas, such as in regard to many of the more unfamiliar consumer themes and product placement exposures, as well as instances of intertextuality between news and the telenovela plot.

In the year I spent in Macambira, I talked to men and women about their lives and the lives of the characters in one particular telenovela, *O Rei do Gado*. These viewers' views of their lives and those of the fictitious characters at many times resembled each other. At other times they were totally dissonant. Discussing the telenovela with males was almost always preceded by a disclaimer that this telenovela was an exception. Male viewers tended to deny enjoying watching telenovelas, except for those with realistic portrayals. The definition of realistic portrayals varied, however, from *O Rei do Gado* to *Irmãos*

*Coragem* (Brothers Courage) to *Escrava Isaura* (Isaura, the Slave), but mostly, males attributed realistic characteristics to those texts that dealt with rural lifestyles.

Men's and women's roles in Macambira were defined and influenced by the economic setup of the community. The embroidering industry, an informal economic system, was the main source of income. Most of the people engaged in embroidery were women, with a few men peripherally participating in this industry. Overall, men in the community had a limited number of job opportunities. They could try to get one of the few public jobs, mostly at the municipal level, with a very limited income, or they could work in agriculture and struggle with limited water resources, limited access to the land, and production costs that rose while selling prices declined. Through the years, a segment of the population migrated; temporary migration to São Paulo and Rio de Janeiro had become an important source of income for many males. This limited access to job opportunities had, according to some residents, led to an imbalance in which many men were powerless and women were empowered, a shift of power that led to conflict.

Erivaldo's family was from São Fernando, a small community 15 miles away from Macambira. Every time I met with his relatives, they would tell me how different Macambira was from São Fernando. One big difference was that in Macambira, women sat down at the bar and drank beer and cachaça without being intimidated. In São Fernando, they said, this did not happen. In Macambira, women went out to the few bars, drank at parties, and many times drank at home with friends. To many in Macambira, these behaviors were the result of women's ability to secure their own income. Dona Bezinha had no doubts: "Women have to work to be able to be independent. They need to secure their income so they don't have to ask their partners for money to do anything." What about the husbands that had to ask their wives for change to go have a beer with their friends? Although gender relations were colored by the local economic culture, undeniably there were clear leftovers from traditional patriarchal structures, in which men's rights and women's obligations were articulated. The reverse, women's rights and their partners' obligations, was the terrain of conflict. Males, in many cases, wanted to maintain their culturally granted rights, and women wanted to acquire what they perceived to be those rights of theirs that had been suppressed. It was within this struggle that telenovelas were embedded in Macambira. Males and females watched these shows, some more than others, depending on the particular show and the time of broadcast, but over time, telenovelas became part of many community members' lives. For some, telenovelas were just entertainment; to others they provided insights into another reality, into a world far away, into a world where men and women related differently, where women had more freedom, where parents and children talked about their problems, where affection was displayed.

What became clear through this ethnographic work was that viewers engaged with the different narrative plots within the telenovela, but the attention devoted to some elements was much greater than that paid to others. Gender was one of the most powerful elements in the process of interpretation and engagement with the telenovela text, far overshadowing cultural capital and other elements influencing the reading of the text.

Established gender norms and attitudes in Macambira structured in many ways the levels of engagement and the readings of viewers. Women's increasing economic empowerment created a fracture in the established traditional male-female domination patterns. This allowed women to question their role and men's role in the household and the community. The telenovela seemed to be one way through which women observed alternatives, which they then used to evaluate their own lives and the lives of the community in relation to those of the characters in the South. This finding supported earlier reception discoveries by Leal (1986) and Vink (1988).

Gender constructions also hindered the ability of males to engage with the text in a more complex manner, however. For many, there was a perception that their masculinity, many times

questioned by their inability to provide for their households, could be damaged even more by their association with a telenovela, a text still perceived as a women's program. This distancing that many males presented in relation to telenovelas was even more present when certain elements in the narrative were discussed. Males watching the telenovela preferred to talk about issues associated to land reform and rural lifestyle discourses. Consequently, many males presented a limited cultural capital regarding knowledge of the telenovela narrative structure and an inability to use situations in the telenovela to discuss their own reality, which many women did. Cultural capital in this context relates to the knowledge of certain elements in the telenovela, such as (a) narrative conventions and strategies employed by telenovela writers; (b) an awareness of previous roles played by a certain artist that can provide a framework for understanding his or her current role; (c) the career trajectory of writers and directors, which allowed viewers to notice stylistic threads from one telenovela that they worked on to their next; and (d) intertextual information regarding the telenovela relationships to other TV programs, other media texts, and real-life characters. The last two items are, in many ways, not only the result of telenovela watching but also of exposure to other media texts, the total available media ensemble, that provide contextual information about telenovelas.

Even if the text were perceived as feminine, males did use the rural lifestyle and the political narrative to think about their lives in relation to the urban, modern South. The images of farming and the technology associated with the big cattle-raising and milk-producing farms in the telenovela caught most males' attention, as did the discussion of politics and land reform. Males also were prone to comment on and rejoice over scenes of cattle herding and the lifestyle of the *peões* (herdsmen), including their singing and storytelling. This engagement with this element of the narrative seemed to indicate that perceived gender norms did in fact hinder the level of engagement with narrative layers, such as the more traditional melodramatic elements of love and betrayal. This, however, does not mean that males did not pay attention to those elements or were totally oblivious to them. It means they had a greater interest in talking about elements locally associated with the male sphere, such as politics and farm techniques, rather than in engaging with other elements in the narrative that were normally associated with the female sphere, such as raising children and romance.

Due to the rural nature of *O Rei do Gado*, it was easily perceived as a text pertaining to a male sphere. For women, telenovelas—and *O Rei do Gado* was no exception—were about romance. Women viewers in Macambira perceived the melodramatic roots of the genre and expected melodramatic genre conventions to be followed by the writers. The incorporation of a more contemporary social context in the telenovela's narrative seemed to be distancing these texts from their melodramatic roots, apparently making it harder for women to identify with the characters. Males, on the other hand, saw in this process of contemporanization a bridge with what they perceived to be a realistic narrative, which justified their viewing and enjoyment of the telenovela. However, the established norms and attitudes regarding gender roles in the community still limited the possibilities of males to acknowledge the melodramatic as enjoyable. Telenovelas, for those males, were valued according to their perceived informational and realistic content.

The political and commercial layers of signification in the narrative were not always available to all viewers in the same fashion. The newness or distance from Macambira's reality of these political and commercial themes and images clearly established a certain hierarchy of meanings available, based on cultural and social capital. Very few viewers successfully decoded the instances of political intertextuality, such as when the telenovela characters interacted in the plot with real-life politicians or when real-life politicians acknowledged in the news media the importance or relevance of the telenovela subplot on agrarian reform. Few also were able to decode many of the commercial product placement insertions. The available knowledge of the political debate in the nation and of a larger range of commercial

goods seemed to have limited the access to those sequences of many viewers with less cultural capital. The male identification with the rural plot line led many to see in the commercial insertions the kind of information they said they enjoyed in telenovelas. What was puzzling was that even viewers aware of Globo's merchandising strategy did not see an attempt to advertise in the placement of agricultural products (La Pastina, 2001). This may demonstrate that the pleasure derived from the rural imagery, even if it reinforced viewers' perception that they lived in the periphery of this modern world, reminded them of their own rural traditional values and identities.

The local political structure also hindered the readings of the political message within the telenovela. The electoral disputes in town and the tradition of local political fights and accusations of corruption and mismanagement served to create a local climate in which politicians were perceived as corrupt by definition. Residents questioned the honest politician in the telenovela, seeing him as one who did not understand how the system worked and therefore could not accomplish anything.

## MEDIA ENGAGEMENT AND AUDIENCE ETHNOGRAPHIES

This chapter has attempted to demonstrate how an ethnographic approach to media engagement between viewers and text(s) allows for a better comprehension of this complex process. Structural elements within the narrative, as well as within the viewing context, mediate the process of reception and appropriation of the narrative into viewers' lives. During the study, it became apparent that gender, both as social norms that are culturally based and as an element within the narrative, was key in the process of hindering and enabling viewers to engage with the text in their lives. Gender as a socially constructed category also was used to provide an element of comparison between male and female viewers, their expectations regarding the text, and their willingness to engage with certain narrative layers.

This ethnographic approach also contributed to providing a better understanding of the role of the local (versus the national or global) in the process of media engagement. It clearly established that the perception of the telenovela text as a representation of urban reality hindered the process of identification; at the same time, it created a bridge between the two realities, allowing viewers to engage with a discourse that they perceived to be modern. These representations of difference may lead, in some instances, to a desire to question one's life in relation to the lives of those on the screen. Men also questioned their limited power to farm and raise cattle, comparing their reality to the modern rural technology used in the telenovela farms. In that process, consumer items, lifestyles, and particular behaviors, as well as norms that challenge the local traditions, may become part of the local cultural capital that will be used to interpret situations in viewers' own lives.

In the long term, telenovelas, as well as other media text, have provided viewers in Macambira with an array of images and ideas about what the world beyond its borders looks like. In that process, it has allowed local teenagers to challenge the established local norms, led males to perceive their role in the community as one that could be changed and questioned, and given women an array of role models that strengthened their perceptions of their own rights. Ethnography allows researchers to investigate patterns of telenovela engagement that permit scholars to question how this process—from reception to appropriation of those messages into viewers' lives—may lead to an awareness about self and community and may ultimately promote social change.

## On Evaluating Good Ethnography

I would like to end this chapter by discussing some of the challenges to good ethnography. Evaluating ethnographic media research is tricky. In our discipline, ethnography has been a hodgepodge of possibilities. As I have argued in this chapter, media ethnography needs to return to a sense of commitment to traditional practices: a long-term, in-depth, site-specific, multimethod approach. A good ethnographic study must provide evidence that the data reported, the analysis, and the processes described are the result of a long and careful process of maturation of the information collected. This return to sound methodology does not preclude, nor should it, a greater level of self-reflexivity and an awareness of the ethical implications of conducting fieldwork.

Ethnography is time consuming and costly. It is hard for most researchers to devote an extended period of time away from other job obligations and family. It is also still quite difficult to secure funding to conduct extensive ethnographic research. The inability to generalize from ethnographic data should not be seen as a weakness but rather as part of a methodological process that allows scholars to attain a deeper understanding of particular processes. Nevertheless, generalizability might be reached in limited ways through replicability of ethnographic studies across several sites.

Ethnography requires a high level of commitment and a willingness to share your work and your life with a particular group that you care about. Many, such as Scheper-Hughes (1995), have argued that we should always engage in militant ethnography. I agree with her that once we are on the site, our presence affects the work we are conducting and the community in which we are working. I believe that good ethnographic work has to make that self-reflexive relationship clear and build on that knowledge of our own limitations and the role we have in the research process, but it must also acknowledge the central and vital role community members have in the final research product.

## References

Abu-Lughod, L. (1993). *Writing women's worlds: Bedouin stories.* Berkeley: University of California Press.

Ang, I. (1991). *Desperately seeking the audience.* New York: Routledge.

Drotner, K. (1994). Media ethnography. *Communications, 19*(1), 87-103.

Geertz, C. (1973). *Interpretation of cultures.* New York: Basic Books.

Leal, O. F. (1986). *A leitura social da novela das oito* [The social reading of the 8:00 telenovela]. Petrópolis, Brazil: Editora Vozes.

Hamburger, E. I. (1999). *Politics and intimacy in Brazilian telenovelas.* Unpublished doctoral dissertation, Department of Anthropology, University of Chicago.

La Pastina, A. (2001). Product placement in Brazilian prime-time television: The case of a telenovela reception. *Journal of Broadcasting and Electronic Media, 45,* 541-557.

La Pastina, A. (2003a, May 2-4). *Does national programming promote national identity? A case study of rural Brazil.* Paper presented at the Third Annual Media in Transition Conference, Massachusetts Institute of Technology, Cambridge.

La Pastina (2003b). "Now that you going home are you going to write about the natives you studied?" Telenovela reception, adultery and the dilemmas of ethnographic practice. In P. Murphy & M. Krady (Eds.), *Global media studies.* London: Routledge.

La Pastina, A. (2004a). Selling political integrity: Telenovelas, intertextuality and local elections in Brazil. *Journal of Broadcasting and Electronic Media, 48,* 302-325.

La Pastina, A. (2004b). Telenovela reception in rural Brazil: Gendered readings and sexual mores. *Critical Studies in Media Communication, 21*(2), 162-181.

La Pastina, A., Patel, D., & Schiavo, M. (2004). Brazilian telenovelas: The social merchandising approach. In M. Cody, M. Sabido, A. Singhal, & E. Rogers (Eds.), *Entertainment-education and social change: History,* *research, and practice* (pp. 261-279). Mahwah, NJ: Lawrence Erlbaum.

La Pastina, A., Rego, C., & Straubhaar, J. (2004). The centrality of telenovelas in Latin America's everyday life: Past tendencies, current knowledge, and future research. *Global Media Journal, 2*(5). Retrieved December 5, 2004, from http://lass.calumetpurdue .edu/cca/gmj/contents.htm

Martín-Barbero, J. (1993). *Communication, culture and hegemony: From the media to the mediations* (E. Fox & R. White, Trans.). Newbury Park, CA: Sage. (Original work published 1987)

Morley, D., & Silverstone, R. (1991). Communication and context: Ethnographic prospectives on the media audience. In K. Jensen & N. Jankowski (Eds.), *Handbook of qualitative methodologies for mass communication research.* London: Routledge.

Murphy, P. D. (1999). Media cultural studies' uncomfortable embrace of ethnography. *Journal of Communication Inquiry, 23*(3), 205-221.

Murphy, P., & Krady, M. (Eds.). (2003). *Global media studies.* London: Routledge.

Rosaldo, R. (1993). *Culture and truth: The remaking of social analysis.* Boston: Beacon Press.

Scheper-Hughes, N. (1992). *Death without weeping: The violence of everyday life in Brazil.* Berkeley: University of California Press.

Scheper-Hughes, N. (1995). The primacy of ethical: Proposition of a militant ethnography. *Current Anthropology, 36*(3), 409-420.

Vink, N. (1988). *The telenovela and emancipation: A study on television and social change in Brazil.* Amsterdam: Royal Tropical Institute.

# 15

# Picturing Practices

## Visual Anthropology and Media Ethnography

Graham Murdock and Sarah Pink

The industrial production and everyday consumption of visual imagery have long been major areas of interest in media studies, but it is only relatively recently that visual materials produced by researchers and participants have been integrated into the research process. In promoting this "visual turn," however, enthusiastic communications researchers have tended to ignore the rich tradition of relevant practice developed within anthropology (see, e.g., Gauntlett, 2004). This chapter addresses this gap by focusing on three key areas of work in visual anthropology:

1. The production of visual materials by the researcher as part of the research process

2. The analysis of visual material produced by participants both spontaneously (domestic photography, home Web pages, and cell phone pictures) and as part of the research process (asking participants to film and photograph some aspect of their environment or daily routines)

3. Using visual imagery, in combination with other materials, to represent the results of the research

We have singled these areas out for two reasons. First, they cover the three key "moments" in the research process: collection, analysis, and presentation. Second, they are particularly relevant to the project of developing research that seeks to understand both the multiple social uses of contemporary media and communications and the multilayered, imaginative and expressive environments generated by professional and vernacular practices.

Much of the work in visual anthropology that is most relevant to ethnographic work in media studies has been produced within the last two decades and has drawn on innovations in video technology and digital media to support more flexible and open-ended forms of research practice. At the same time, it has also been indelibly shaped by anthropological encounters with visual media that date back to the discipline's formation. These engagements have provided both exemplars to be drawn on and extended, as well as working assumptions and practices to be challenged and changed.

## Encounters: Anthropology, Media, Visuality

The emergence of modern anthropology coincides almost exactly with the development of the photographic and film technologies that dominated visual production and display until the advent of digital technologies in the last decade. In 1889, George Eastman introduced transparent roll film as an alternative to cumbersome glass plate technologies. Four years later, the Lumiere brothers' cinematographe show in Paris ushered in the age of cinema. Anthropologists were immediately drawn to these innovations, seeing the camera's mechanical eye as a guarantee that visual records would be "objective," uncontaminated by subjective bias. Franz Boas began using still photography in his fieldwork among the Kwakiutl Indians of the Northwest Coast in 1894, and when Alfred Haddon and his Cambridge team set off for the Torres Straits in 1898, he insisted on taking both photographic and film equipment. He was interested not only in making visual field notes but in integrating imagery into the presentation of the results. The film footage was never worked up into an ethnographic film, but photographs featured prominently in the six volumes that eventuated from the project.

As anthropology became more institutionalised within the academy, however, research increasingly centered on note taking and "writing up." In the process, "the active use of both the camera and the cinematographe was effectively banished from ethnographic practice" or relegated to a minor role (Grimshaw, 2001, p. 25). Bronislav Malinowski was instrumental in defining the core elements of the new fieldwork practice. He took a number of photos while working on his seminal ethnography of the Trobriand islanders between 1915 and 1918 but never integrated them into either his analysis or his presentation (see Young, 1998). Early ethnographic photographs also raise questions about the ideology underpinning fieldwork practice, Evans-Pritchard's (1940) classificatory photographs of near-naked Nuer having attracted particular attention (see Emmison & Smith, 2000; Hutnyk, 1990; Pink, 2003).

In contrast, in their research into character structure in Bali, Gregory Bateson and Margaret Mead set out to use visual records in genuinely innovative and open-ended ways. In 2 years of fieldwork between 1936 and 1938, they produced 25,000 still photographs and shot 20,000 feet of 16 mm motion picture film. They saw this material as central to analysing and presenting their work. Rather than regarding images as illustrations of a theory constructed elsewhere, "they considered the connections, explanations, and interpretations the photographs suggested as hypotheses to be explored further" (Hagaman, 2004, p. 4). This openness was followed through into publication, with a text that juxtaposed exposition against imagery and allowed readers to develop their own comparisons and sequences. The result, *Balinese Character: A Photographic Analysis* (Bateson & Mead, 1942), was genuinely path-breaking but included only 3% of the photos taken and excluded film footage. As we shall argue later, contemporary digital media have made their vision of dynamic and open texts "attainable in ways they did not foresee but probably would have appreciated" (Hagaman, 2004, p. 9).

Although innovative, Bateson and Mead's work remained firmly wedded to the idea that anthropologists specialised in the study of stable communities relatively untouched by capitalism and modern technologies. Not all ethnographers shared this romance with preindustrial life, however. In 1937, the British naturalist Tom Harrison and the poet and journalist Charles Madge teamed up to launch "Mass Observation," with the declared intention of producing an "anthropology of ourselves." Harrison had earlier embarked on an anthropological study in the New Hebrides, but it owed more to adventurism than to Malinowski, leading at one point to him leaving the island on the luxury yacht owned by the Hollywood film star Douglas Fairbanks. Harrison and Madge's first major British research site, Bolton, was far from glamorous, but in constructing a portrait of city life, they drew on a wider range of sources than most anthropologists of the time. They included photographs taken by the young cameraman, Humphrey Spender. Shooting in a wide range of settings, from christenings to pubs, he produced around 800 pictures in total, almost all them "candid" shots taken with a concealed camera, a technique the team felt would catch everyday action in its unvarnished actuality and avoid the compositional clichés of professional press photography. The original group also included the documentary film maker Humphrey Jennings. There was no attempt to integrate film into the Bolton project, but after leaving Mass Observation, Jennings did return to the city to make one of his best known shorts, *Spare Time* (1939), a record of recreational activities. Mass Observation's most important departure from established fieldwork practice, however, was their recruitment of volunteer observers and the incorporation of their accounts as an integral element in the published reports of the various studies. Their contributions were confined to notes and diaries, however. They were not asked to submit photographs.

Anthropologists, too, were beginning to bring ethnography home. After early work in Melanesia, arranged by Malinowski, the American ethnographer Hortense Powdermaker conducted fieldwork in Mississippi and went on to produce the first anthropological analysis of media production with a book on Hollywood (1950). This interest in industrialised image making was taken up again in the late 1960s when a new generation of sociologists and anthropologists turned their attention to the social organisation of television programme production (see, e.g., Elliot, 1972). Most ethnographic work of the time, however, followed Mass Observation in focusing on the ways mass-produced artefacts and images were deployed in consumption and leisure. This was a central thread in the work coming out of the newly emerging fields of Cultural and Media Studies. With some notable exceptions, such as Paul Willis's (1978) ethnographies of youth subcultures in a British Midlands city, however, most studies fell some way short of the prevailing anthropological definition of fieldwork as requiring sustained immersion in a single setting. Rather, they drew on personal observations, often made somewhat haphazardly, or employed qualitative methods, such as depth interviews and focus groups, that involved relatively fleeting encounters with participants, sometimes confined to one meeting. Nor, despite their fascination with popular media imagery and everyday

visual environments, did they incorporate either photography or film into their methods of research or presentation.

Anthropology's traditional focus on preindustrial societies was widely accompanied by an assumption that participants had no knowledge of modern media technologies. Robert Flaherty's seminal 1922 dramatised documentary of Eskimo life, *Nanook of the North,* for example, shows Nanook clowning with a phonograph record, feigning amazement. The truth was that, far from being naïve, "the Inuit were technologically sophisticated enough to maintain Flaherty's equipment" (Winston, 1995, p. 20). This assumption of ignorance became increasingly difficult to maintain in the postwar period, as former colonial territories achieved independence and employed television as a major tool of nation building. It became unsustainable as commercial satellite channels proliferated across established field fieldwork sites, such as India and Southeast Asia. This new visual environment has encouraged ethnographers working in those areas to take up many of the questions concerning consumption, identity, and media that have developed within media and cultural studies. As the subtitle of a recent anthology of this work makes clear, this is "new terrain" for many anthropologists (see Ginsburg, Abu-Lughod, & Larkin, 2002). Here again, however, the focus on popular imagery and visual experience has not been matched by a concerted effort to incorporate visual media into general anthropological practice. This effort has remained largely the preserve of ethnographic film making.

Much early activity in this area was devoted to recording ways of life on the point of extinction. As publicity for the long-running Granada television series *Disappearing World* put it, the aim was to produce portraits of peoples "whose way of life was under threat from the pace of change" (Off the Fence, 2004). This emphasis on explicating the unfamiliar and exotic often produced a didactic style of presentation typified by the trilogy of Granada films about the Mursi and Kwega of southern Ethiopia, which mobilised David Turton's anthropological expertise to provide authoritative off-screen commentary on the scenes and events filmed. As Jean Lydall, another anthropologist working in Southern Ethiopia, complained, his insistent lecturing made it "difficult to view the films from any other point of view than that offered by Turton" (Lydall, 1996, p. 2). In response, she constructed her own films around participants' own accounts, with unexpected results. As she later recounted, "I had discussed many things with them before. . . . I thought the women would explain things as I had come to understand them, but again and again, I was taken by surprise" as informants responded to being filmed by formulating their ideas in a much more comprehensive way (Lydall, 1996, p. 4). This potential thickening of description is an obvious attraction of incorporating film into the fieldwork process but does nothing to decentre the researcher's control over the way participants' accounts are edited and contextualised in the final presentation.

Following Sol Wirth and John Adair's (1972) path-breaking film work with the Navaho, this problem was increasingly addressed by encouraging participants to make their own productions. The introduction of easy-to-use video cameras a few years later made this an inexpensive, feasible and attractive option. Some initiatives, such as Eric Michaels's work with aboriginal communities in Australia (see Michaels, 1994) originated within the anthropological research community. Others, such as the BBC's *Video Nation* and *Video Diaries* series, were responses to grassroots demands for more access and representation within public broadcasting. In both contexts, professionals acted as facilitators rather than producers. They trained and advised participants on how to use the equipment but left the final editing decisions to them. As we shall see, contemporary visual anthropology now frequently draws on participant-generated materials in developing research and presentational strategies.

To sum up: What marks contemporary visual anthropology out as a distinctive approach is not simply its central project of building an "anthropology of visual systems or more broadly visual cultural forms" (Morphy & Banks, 1997, p. 5), but its commitment to using the full range of available visual technologies and resources at each stage of the research process—fieldwork, analysis, and representation. Drawing on artefacts manufactured within the cultural industries, participants' own productions, and researcher-made materials, visual anthropology aims to develop visually thick and open-ended accounts of everyday visual practices and visual environments. This ambition now goes well beyond film and photography to encompass art, drawing, video, new digital and visual media, and multimedia technologies, including hypermedia (Pink, 2001; Pink, Kürti, & Afonso, 2004).

Despite a rearguard action from mainstream ethnographers who continue to deny a place for film in anthropological practice (see Taylor, 1996), recent years have seen visual anthropology's tripartite commitment to visual methodology, visual analysis, and visual representation becoming more generally accepted as a valid and productive approach, both substantively and methodologically. At the same time, visual anthropology has had to respond to more general shifts in anthropological practice, particularly the rise of multisited ethnography. Although "community study" involving the researcher living and interacting with a stable group of people for a sustained time still exists as valid anthropological exercise, with some changes to its original form (see Amit, 2002), it is not currently the dominant practice in contemporary urban settings. There are good reasons for this, particularly in studies of media.

Much popular media activity is centred around the home, but as Miller (2001) points out, short of living with different families for extended periods of time, the long-term close relations formed by constant interaction in traditional fieldwork settings are simply not practicable in this context (see Pink, 2004b). Home-based research is inevitably multisited, as the researcher moves between different fieldwork encounters, with different sets of informants, behind closed doors. This stretched definition of ethnography moves anthropological practice closer to the qualitative methodological strategies developed within cultural and media studies and has prompted efforts to draw the disciplines together (see Crawford & Hafsteinsson, 1996). At the same time, media researchers interested in exploring how audiences actively reconstruct the meanings of media texts have started to go beyond the verbal accounts provided by depth interviews and focus group discussions and begun encouraging participants to make their own productions. David Gauntlett's (1997) study, in which children 7 to 11 years old were assisted in making videos about the environment as a way of gaining insights into how they processed media materials about environmental issues, is a case in point.

This convergence of interests and methods has been given additional momentum by visual anthropologists' increasing interest in developing academic and applied projects in the modern large-scale societies that have conventionally been the principle domain of researchers specialising in communications and cultural and media studies. This move has also prompted the development of sets of visual methods more adapted to these new field sites. These new visual methods both draw on and depart from methods used in earlier anthropological studies of media.

## PRODUCTIONS: PICTURING MEDIA PRACTICES

As we noted earlier, the idea that an ethnographer should photograph or film events and activities performed by the subjects of her or his research dates back to the formative years of professional anthropology. Visual sociologists, too, have long been active in photographing and filming the everyday lives they study. Since the initial development of these methods, however, both theory and practice have moved on considerably. The contemporary wisdom that guides the production of images as part of research (see, for example, Banks, 2001; Pink, 2001) insists that this process should be reflexive and collaborative and that the images themselves need to be understood in terms of the context in which they were produced rather than as unproblematic representations of a social reality. The examples that follow illustrate

how these guiding principles have been applied in a range of recent studies that have used photography, video, and Web-based media.

No matter what medium is employed, however, the primary justification remains the same. Visual technologies, whether still photos or moving images, allow for the recording and analysis of aspects of individual communication and social practice that cannot be transcribed onto the written or printed page without substantial reduction or loss. By capturing emotional expression, facial and body language, and spatial relations, they foreground dimensions of representation that have escaped from the prison house of language and are missing from accounts constructed solely on the basis of interview transcriptions. This is not to argue that pictures speak louder than words or that their meanings are self-evident and self-sufficient. Rather, the challenge is to work toward multimedia methods and forms of representation that combine still and moving images with participants' commentaries and researchers' analyses in ways that allow for interpretations to become more open ended. As Marilyn Strathern (2002) has noted, in doing ethnography, "you do not have to tie up all the loose ends; on the contrary, there may be data that will become a resource only from some vantage point in the future" (p. 309).

## Photography

As we have seen, there is a long-standing tradition of participant observation with a camera whereby the anthropologist takes photographs as she or he (or a collaborator) participates or observes within a particular cultural setting. In their Balinese fieldwork, for example, Gregory Bateson took photographs while Margaret Mead made field notes and their interpreter translated what was being said. Although this way of working requires the consent of participants, it does not usually entail their further collaboration. They become more involved when they are asked to comment on what the ethnographer has shot and when their responses and reservations are used as a starting point for rephotographing certain

**Figure 15.1**    Hand Phone Use for Photos

Source: Photo © 2004 John Postill. Used by permission.

scenes or settings. "Shared anthropology" can impose unexpected costs, however. The French ethnographic film maker Jean Roche was called back repeatedly to reshoot an annual lion hunt because his subjects "found the footage of their kills unsatisfactory" (Bickerton, 2004, p. 62). Participant input plays an even more central role in informant-directed photography (see Banks, 2001), during which informants prompt the researcher to photograph activities, objects, or persons that have particular significance for them. However, photography is, arguably perhaps, most productively and reflexively employed in research settings where informants are themselves also active photographers.

John Postill's (in press) current research on local new media and local governance in suburban Malaysia[1] is a case in point. His fieldwork is largely with middle class participants who have access to a range of advanced media and communications technologies. They create their own Web sites and are avid users of text messaging, e-mail, video cameras, and camera phones (see Figure 15.1).

Figure 15.1 depicts a frequent practice in Malaysia: Local people photograph a local event with their "hand phones" (the Malaysian English term for mobile phone). Their expertise produces an interesting reversal of the researcher's traditional,

and largely taken for granted, command over image-making technologies. In this situation, one effective methodological option is to become a participant observer who is also a cultural producer within that context. A series of digital photographs taken to support Postill's research during local public functions fed into the research process in several ways. First, they provided a detailed record of the way media were deployed in these settings, not only by professionals recording the events for newspapers and broadcasting stations but also by participants using camera phones and still and video cameras. Second, informants in the study who expressed an interest in the research photos were given copies on CD that they could load onto their personal computers. This helped cement the reciprocities on which full cooperation with the study depended. Third, the images were available to be incorporated into future presentations of the research, both in print and using hypermedia forms such as CD-ROMs and Web pages.

In contrast to the rapidly accumulating body of work on vernacular image making, anthropological studies of professional image production are rare, but the research conducted by Donna Schwartz and her team on press photographers covering the Super Bowl, the pivotal game in the

American football season and a major articulation of the core values of the national culture, illustrates their potential (see Schwartz, 1993). The study was based on the idea that knowing how news photographs are put together at a practical level was likely to produce fuller and better informed analyses of how these images are made to promote specific meanings on the page. Adopting a visual anthropological approach, the team members participated in the production process, gaining press passes and doing their fieldwork as participant observers with the press pack as they set about constructing a particular vision of the event. As well as learning the process that the press photographers engaged in, Schwartz and her colleagues produced their own set of "critical" images that responded to the "official" version. By providing visual demonstrations of the selective attention and omissions that characterised reporting of the event, the team added a significant new element to the standard critique of news bias.

## Video

Visual anthropologists have conventionally used video to produce a visual record of events and activities during fieldwork that can later be used as a resource for analysis or as a basis for the production of ethnographic documentaries. As the relatively stable communities addressed by traditional ethnographic techniques have been steadily eroded or dismantled, however, recent years have seen new uses of video develop as part of a more general effort to devise techniques of enquiry better suited to the study of everyday life in societies experiencing rapid social and cultural change and technological innovation. These methods are particularly appropriate for researching how people engage with established and emerging technologies and for exploring how they navigate their way through increasingly convergent technological arrays and visual environments.

Much of this work has been developed in the context of commercial marketing and audience research; most has focused on domestic space and shopping activity as the final links in the consumption chain. The problem of tracking increasingly

nomadic audiences as they integrate media activity into their everyday routines has been of particular interest. The work of Peter Collett and his colleagues is prototypical of one main current of work in this area.

A video tape recorder was installed in the main television cabinet in 20 British homes. Whenever it was switched on, the apparatus produced continuous video footage of all activity in the viewing area directly in front of the set, together with a record of the date, time, and channel and a small inset showing the programme as it appeared on the screen. The resulting 350 hours of videotape showed that the participants in the study only focused on the screen for two thirds of the time. "For the rest of the time, they attend to kids, groom themselves, read the newspaper, doze off— the list of distractions is endless," and even when they are watching, "they frequently engage in activities that have nothing to do with television watching" (Collett, 1987, p. 246). Although the study was funded by the body then regulating British commercial television, the Independent Broadcasting Authority, it was of particular interest to advertisers concerned with the dynamics of audience attention.

This basic technique has since been extended to monitoring home computer use. Although it requires the prior consent of participants, using "hidden" or unobtrusive cameras and monitoring software bears a close similarity to the ubiquitous visual surveillance systems installed to monitor activity in public sites and, increasingly, in domestic interiors as a means of checking on children and child minders. This raises ethical problems, particularly in relation to the subsequent storage and display of the footage shot. Methodologically, too, the limitations outweigh the advantages. On the one hand, it allows a large quantity of visual data to be collected over an extended period of time and provides a way of checking what people actually do against what they claim to do. On the other hand, because the camera or monitoring software is installed in a fixed position, it can only record what is happening in one location. It cannot track participants as they move between different sites of action. Even if multiple monitors were used, they would still only capture what is happening on the surface. Because there is no opportunity to probe participants' motivations or experiences by talking to them at the time, the resulting footage cannot be used in an exploratory way. It offers an extensive assemblage of "social facts" but rules out the development of interpretations that take full account of participants' own constructions of events.

The same stricture applies to recent work in product and marketing research, which has used hand-held digital video cameras to follow people as they move from one location to another. This has the added disadvantage of being very labour intensive. The less ambitious technique of the "video tour" offers one way of retaining the dynamism and mobility of tracking studies allowing the researcher to include a wider cross-section of case studies and providing spaces in which participants may offer their own accounts and interpretations. The method involves researchers and informants working together to show and explore an aspect of their everyday lives. In a series of projects designed to research people's relations to domestic space and household goods and routines, for example, informants were asked to show the researcher (and the video camera he or she was carrying) around their home, describing each room, the objects and artefacts it contained, the histories of how they had acquired them, and their feelings about them (Pink, 2004b). The idea of "home" as both a material space and a guiding narrative was used to prompt the particular features that respondents nominated for filming and to encourage open-ended commentary. Although this method has not so far been used extensively in communications research, it has the potential to make significant contributions to debates on current shifts in media use. First, in a situation in which new media technologies are increasingly promoted on the basis of style as well as utility, it offers a way of exploring how computers, mobile phones, video recorders, and digital television sets are incorporated into everyday settings as material artefacts and aesthetic objects. Second, the proliferation of communications devices in many homes, the expansion of mobile telephone use, and the migration of television viewing from the sitting room to the kitchen and the bedroom give added relevance to a method that tracks media installations and routines across the whole of domestic space. Third, conducting individual "video tours" with each member of the household offers a useful way of examining how media practices are structured by relations of power based in gender and generation.

As well as providing valuable material that can be analysed in its own right, collaboratively produced video recordings can also be reinserted into the research process by, for example, showing them to informants, eliciting their responses to both their own tapes and those produced by other participants, and using these as a basis for further explorations of their media maps and practices.

## DIGITAL MEDIA

As we saw earlier, Gregory Bateson and Margaret Mead's plans to open up multiple pathways to interpretation by presenting their visual material alongside their written exposition were radically curtailed by their reliance on print. The last decade, however, has seen the demarcation lines erected by analogue media technologies give way to the converging spaces produced by digital media. By translating all forms of human expression—speech, music, sound, writing, statistical data, and still and moving imagery—into the universal language of computing based on varying arrays of zeros and ones, digitalisation offers a range of new possibilities for the practice of visual anthropology. Three are particularly far reaching in their implications. First, for the first time, every kind of research material can be stored in a single archive, either on CD-ROM or on an Internet site. Second, these repositories can be searched and read in much more flexible ways, using key words and hyperlinks to create new juxtapositions, combinations, and sequences that may suggest new avenues for exploration. Third, the full interactivity offered by the Internet (particularly the most widely accessible portion of it known as the World Wide Web) enables archives to become dynamic and open to continuous addition, commentary, and critique.

As yet, digital media are not widely used as part of the visual anthropology research process, although a number of ethnographers are now exploring their potential.. The visual anthropologist Jay Ruby, for example, provides a log of visual and written fieldwork updates on a Web site that documents his fieldwork in the Oak Park community in the United States.[2] Other researchers are combining the multimedia and interactive possibilities of the Web to create sites that contain a combination of researcher-produced and informant-supplied research materials in a range of media. A good example is Stephen Lyon's Social Organisation, Economy and Development site.[3] Here, in an experiment in "open ethnography," Lyon includes stories, essays, and music supplied or produced locally by informants; his own field notes and updates; and users' comments. Such initiatives can be seen as harbingers of new forms of reflexive and collaborative work that assist the anthropologist in producing multimedia knowledge in which informants' voices are truly embedded.

## Incorporations: Using Vernacular Imagery

Incorporating informant-produced images into fieldwork accounts can never be undertaken innocently. On the contrary, it forces us to take the contexts within which they have been produced more fully into account.

### Found Images

The anthropology of personal or family photography is now well established as an area of study. Some of these images will have been posed and taken by professional photographers, although, as Christopher Pinney's (1997) work on local studios in India demonstrates, this may still allow considerable scope for individual customisation through the choice of particular props and backdrops. Others will be prints of images taken by participants themselves. Both may be found mounted on living room walls or mantelpieces, printed on mugs and refrigerator magnets, or pasted in the family albums analysed in Chalfen's path-breaking (1987) work. Following developments in visual technologies, recent work in this field has expanded to embrace a range of other forms of individual and household image making, from home videos and videotaped letters to personal and family Web pages and computer files of images downloaded from digital cameras and mobile phones (see Chalfen, 2002, p. 143). These stocks of imagery can be used as both a basis for interpretation and a prompt for further exploration. They provide a corpus of texts that illuminate respondents' ways of thinking and looking at themselves and others and their concepts of evidence. They also offer a jumping-off point for interviews exploring the social dynamics and aesthetic criteria that underpin their visual practices.

### Prompted Images

The exploration of everyday image making and the meanings it carries can also be useful when extended and tailored to the focus of particular projects by asking informants to produce photography, video, drawings, or computer imagery as part of the research process. Drawing on the model developed by the BBC *Video Diaries* programmes mentioned earlier, this might involve participants keeping a running video or photographic record of their media activities and encounters for a set period. This could combine the (audio) visual documentation of their everyday practices and the (possibly changing) context(s) of use with their reflective commentaries on their experiences recorded at the end of each day's shooting. Although video recording provides more information, it is not always practical in nondomestic settings. The alternative is to use digital cameras or camera phones. These provide a convenient and unobtrusive way of keeping visual records in public locations and can be easily combined with written logs or audio recordings. To understand how television is encountered and

**Figure 15.2**     Photograph of a Photograph

Source: Photo © 2004, John Postill. Used by permission.

experienced in public spaces, for example, one might ask an informant to photograph his or her immediate physical and social environment at the time they see a screen and to record their reactions on audio immediately afterwards. Camera phone and digital audio technologies are also well adapted to projects that ask media professionals to compile logs of their working day. Another alternative is to ask participants to develop a personal Internet Web log (or "blog") that combines a daily written diary with digital photographs uploaded from a digital camera or camera phone.

These developing digital media also have interesting applications in public contexts. John Postill's research in Malaysia demonstrates why, in a situation in which both researchers and participants have access to the same technologies, it is more important than ever to attend to the contexts and practices of image production and of representation as well as the content of the images produced.

Figure 15.2 shows the anthropologist in the field holding a photograph of himself and his informant, the local politician, Dato´-Lee Hwa Beng. It is a good example of the increasingly layered nature of photographic practice under conditions of equalised access. The photograph in the

anthropologist's hands was taken a few minutes earlier by Lee, with his digital camera, and then immediately printed out on his portable printer. The photo reproduced here, taken by an associate of the researcher, not only records the researcher and the informant sharing a spontaneously produced informant image but shows both of them constructing that moment as a photo opportunity.

## REPRESENTATIONS: COMMUNICATING RESEARCH

As noted earlier, ethnographic film and video production has long been the "conventional" medium for visual anthropological representation. It still offers a useful way of representing research on visual media, because it both replicates many of the key characteristics of the media under study and simulates the experience of viewing them. A still image of a photograph held on video replicates the experience of viewing the material photograph, for example. Two good examples of the possibilities for representing an ethnography of photographic practices and images on film and video are Tobias Wendl and Nancy du Plessis's

(1998) *Future Remembrance,* a film about studio photography and sculpture in Ghana, and David and Judith MacDougall's (1991) *Photo Wallahs,* about photography in an Indian hill town. By leaving a video camera running in a public space, the MacDougalls' experiment with ways of combining footage shot by the researchers with filmic representations of participants' practices in relation to that material and the technologies and social relations that produce it.

Photographic exhibitions, especially in museum anthropology, are another well-established method of visually representing aspects of other cultures. With the arrival of multimedia technologies, however, anthropologists are beginning to consider an array of new display possibilities using installation art and other established art and design practices to represent multisensory ethnographic experiences and realities. As the highly successful multimedia installations at the British Film Institute's (now closed) Museum of the Moving Image suggested, these approaches are of particular value in representing research on media and communications.

The growth of the Internet and the shift to high-density broadband connectivity have breathed new life into Andre Malraux's vision of "museums without walls." Since the 1990s, anthropologists have been very much a part of this general movement and have begun to develop new ways of representing visual research in the emerging hypermedia environment. As we noted earlier, the main digital media currently used by anthropologists are both multimedia and multilinear. The increasing availability of digital video and stills cameras and of user-friendly multimedia and Web-based software is expanding both these potentialities in exciting ways. Digitalizing research materials means that a CD-ROM or Web site can hold not only a researcher's report of a study but all the materials on which the study's interpretations and analysis are based. Theoretically, these might include not only interviews and field notes but all the photographs, sound recordings, film and video footage, computer games, and Web sites that were the focus of the research, together with the written, recorded, or filmed responses to this material produced by both the researcher and the participants. In practice, however, the public reuse of much of the media material produced by the cultural industries is hedged around by intellectual property laws, although these are constantly under negotiation, particularly in relation to educational as opposed to commercial uses of material. Nor are respondent-generated materials without problems, as displaying them in public may raise difficult issues of "ownership, anonymity and consent" (Parry & Mauthner, 2004, p. 149).

The emerging digital archives are also multilinear. The researcher's account no longer enjoys privileged status. It stands as one possible interpretation among others. By navigating their way through the corpus of research materials using multiple pathways, users are free to produce new comparisons and connections and generate alternative interpretations. Research archives housed on Web sites extend open endedness in two additional ways. First, by providing hyperlinks to other relevant Web sites, they can connect the presentation of particular projects to the wider corpus of theory and debate on the areas the research focuses on (see Pink, 2004a, for discussion of the question of making multimedia hypermedia projects "conversant" with existing debates in written anthropology). Second, they can use the Internet's interactive capacities to encourage participants and other researchers to add new material of their own or to question interpretations offered by the research team and by other contributors.

## MOBILISING CONVERGENCE: DIGITAL MEDIA, COLLABORATIVE INQUIRY

The digital image environment is still in the process of construction, with currently available technologies arguably at much the same stage of development as analogue photography and film were when Haddon embarked for the Torres Straits. It is already clear, however, that it poses far-reaching challenges to anyone interested in understanding how contemporary ways of looking, recording, and interacting are being reshaped by new technological possibilities. It is also clear that this is not simply a question of adding new topics to the list of research areas. The progressive convergence of expressive forms made possible by digitalisation coincides with an increasing convergence between media studies and visual anthropology, both in the questions being asked about contemporary visual cultures and the methodologies employed to tackle them. These intersecting movements offer unprecedented opportunities for creative development in both disciplines.

Realising these opportunities will require three basic conditions to be met. First, we need to dismantle the intellectual checkpoints that have traditionally separated visual anthropology from media studies and look for ways of developing collaborative, cumulative, and comparative research on the production and consumption of mediated visuality across the full range of possible fieldwork sites. Second, we need to focus on "globalisation" as an unfinished project in which old orders are being displaced and the contours of new ones are still emerging (see Burawoy et al., 2000, p. 348) and as a cultural arena in which visual imagery operates as both a homogenising force and a key resource for differentiation and contestation. Third and (we have argued) most important, we need to build on recent innovations in visual anthropology's techniques of inquiry and integrate the full range of contemporary visual media into our practices of investigation, analysis, and representation in pursuit of more reflexive, open-ended and collaborative styles of inquiry.

## NOTES

1. John Postill's research with the University of Bremen is funded by the Volkswagen Foundation. It is part of *Netcultures,* a comparative study of new media and local governance involving anthropologists from the Universities of Amsterdam, Bremen, and Manchester.

2. Ruby calls his site *Maintaining Diversity: An Ethnographic Study of Oak Park, Illinois—Progress Reports*, and much related information can be found there with the monthly log (http://astro.ocis.temple.edu/~ruby/opp/, last accessed 6 December 2004).

3. Retrievable from http://anthropology.ac.uk/Bhalot/ (last accessed 6 December 2004).

## REFERENCES

Amit, V. (2002). *Realising community.* London: Routledge.

Banks, M. (2001). *Visual methods in social research.* London: Sage.

Bateson, G., & Mead, M. (1942). *Balinese character: A photographic analysis.* New York: New York Academy of the Sciences.

Bickerton, E. (2004, May/June). The camera possessed: Jean Rouche, ethnographic cineaste: 1917-2004. *New Left Review, 27,* 49-63.

Burawoy, M., Blum, J. A., George, S., Gille, Z., Gowan, T., Haney, L., et al. (2000). *Global ethnography: Forces, connections, and imaginations in a postmodern world.* Berkeley: University of California Press.

Chalfen, R. (1987). *Snapshot versions of life.* Bowling Green, KY: Bowling Green State University.

Chalfen, R. (2002). Snapshots "r" us: The evidentiary problematic of home media. *Visual Studies, 17*(2), 141-149.

Collett, P. (1987, Fall). The viewers viewed. *ETC: A Review of General Semantics, 44*(3), 245-251.

Crawford, P., & Hafsteinsson, S. (Eds.). (1996). *The construction of the viewer.* Aarhus, Denmark: Intervention Press.

Elliott, P. (1972). *The making of a television series: A case study in the sociology of culture.* London: Constable.

Emmison, M., & Smith, P. (2000). *Researching the visual.* London: Sage.

Evans-Pritchard, E. E. (1940). *The Nuer: A description of the modes of livelihood and political institutions of a Nilotic people.* Oxford, England: Oxford University Press.

Gauntlett, D. (1997). *Video critical: Children, the environment and media power.* Luton, England: John Libbey Media.

Gauntlett, D. (2004, July 25-30). *Using creative visual research methods to understand the place of popular media in people's lives.* Paper presented at the Conference of the International Association of Media and Communication Research, Porto Alegre, Brazil.

Ginsburg, F. D., Abu-Lughod, L., & Larkin, B. (Eds.). (2002). *Media worlds: Anthropology on new terrain.* Berkeley: University of California Press.

Grimshaw, A. (2001). *The ethnographer's eye.* Cambridge, England: Cambridge University Press.

Hagaman, D. (2004). *Connecting cultures: Balinese character and the computer.* Retrieved December 6, 2004, from http://www.soc.ucsb.edu/faculty/hbecker/Bali.html

Hutnyk, J. (1990). Comparative anthropology and Evans-Pritchard's Nuer photography: Photographic essay. *Critique of Anthropology, 10*(1), 81-102.

Jennings, H. (Writer & Director). (1939). *Spare time.* London: GPO Film Unit.

Lydall, J. (1996, November). *Television and anthropology and the anthropology of television.* Paper presented at the Fifth International Festival of Ethnographic Film, University of Kent, Kent, England.

MacDougall, D. (Director), & MacDougall, J. (Director). (1991). *Photo wallahs: An encounter with photography in Mussorie, a North Indian hill station.* Berkeley, CA: Oxhard Film Productions.

Michaels, E. (1994). *Bad aboriginal art: Tradition, media, and technological horizons.* Minneapolis: University of Minnesota Press.

Miller, D. (2001). Behind closed doors. In D. Miller (Ed.), *Home possessions.* Oxford, England: Berg.

Morphy, H., & Banks, M. (1997). Introduction: Rethinking visual anthropology. M. Banks & H. Morphy (Eds.), *Rethinking visual anthropology.* London: Yale University Press.

Off the Fence. (2004). *Disappearing world revisited: Return to the remote tribes around the world.* Retrieved December 6, 2004, from http://www.offthefence.com/programs/shortseries/dwr/ dwr.html

Parry, O., & Mauthner, N. S. (2004). Whose data are they anyway? Practical, legal and ethical issues in archiving qualitative research data. *Sociology, 38*(1), 139-152.

Pink, S. (2001). *Doing visual ethnography.* London: Sage.

Pink, S. (2003). Interdisciplinary agendas in visual research: Re-situating visual anthropology. *Visual Studies, 18,* 2.

Pink, S. (2004a). Conversing anthropologically: Hypermedia as anthropological text. In S. Pink, L. Kürti, & A. I. Afonso (Eds.), *Working images.* London: Routledge.

Pink, S. (2004b). *Home truths.* Oxford, England: Berg.

Pink, S., Kürti, L., & Afonso, A. I. (Eds.). (2004). *Working images.* London: Routledge.

Pinney, C. (1997). *Camera indica: The social life of Indian photographs.* London: Reaktion Books.

Postill, J. (in press). *Media and nation building: How the Iban became Malaysian.* Oxford, England: Berghahn.

Powdermaker, H. (1950). *Hollywood, the dream factory: An anthropologist studies the movie makers.* Boston: Little, Brown.

Schwartz, D. (1993). Superbowl XVII: Reflections of the manufacture of appearance. *Visual Sociology, 8*(1), 23-33.

Strathern, M. (2002). Abstraction and decontextualisation: An anthropological comment. In S. Woolgar (Ed.), *Virtual society? Technology, cyberbole, reality* (pp. 302-313). Oxford, England: Oxford University Press.

Taylor, L. (1996, Spring). Iconophobia: How anthropology lost it at the movies. *Transition, 6*(11), 64-88.

Wendl, T. (Camera), & du Plessis, N. (Director). (1998). *Future remembrance.* Goettingen, Germany: IWF.

Willis, P. (1978). *Profane culture.* London: Routledge & Kegan Paul.

Winston, B. (1995). *Claiming the real: The documentary film revisited.* London: BFI.

Wirth, S., & Adair, J. (1972). *Through Navaho eyes: An exploration in film communication and anthropology.* Bloomington: Indiana University Press.

Young, M. W. (1998). *Malinowski's Kiriwina: Fieldwork photography, 1915-18.* Chicago: University of Chicago Press.

# Part III

## EVENTS, STORIES, ACTIVITIES

The ten case studies collected in Part III could be organized in a variety of ways. Of course they can each be read for the intrinsic interest of their case study materials: religion, artistic play, and group identity on the Web; construction of national identity through media and language in Québec and Israel; the rescue workers and 9-11; trauma, fear, and media practices. Each also represents a particular intersection of the concepts, methods, and issues that animate media anthropology. The chapters could be read to reflect the conceptual order of the chapters in Part II. Dayan's and Hoover and Park's chapters address religion. Shinar's, Danet's, Rothenbuhler's, Liebes and Blondheim's, and Zelizer's are each about ritual in their varying ways. Hammer's chapter, and also Rothenbuhler's and Liebes and Blondheim's, address myth. Berkowitz's and Bird's chapters are about stories and myth.

Most of the chapters in this section use ethnographic concepts or methods to one degree or another, although usually rather loosely. They are engaged in readings of the public scene, informed by the ethnographic idea, not loyal to the rite of an extended period of distant fieldwork traditionally required in the professional practice of anthropologists. Readers interested in visual culture and imagery can focus on the chapters by Dayan, Danet, Liebes and Blondheim, Rothenbuhler, and Zelizer. Those with a primary interest in discourse can look to Berkowitz, Bird, Hammer, Hoover and Park, and Shinar.

We decided to organize the chapters according to their focus on events, stories, and activities. This categorizes the chapters according to the type of their empirical object and allows the concepts and methods to vary across them, appearing as tools, if you will, applied this way or that according to the needs of the authors and their subjects.

Four chapters have a primary focus on events, and September 11 is central for three of them. Dayan's chapter, a study of Pope John Paul II's visit to Reunion Island in 1989, is a further development in the theorization of mediated, ceremonial events. Rothenbuhler's piece unpacks the layers of symbolism organized around Ground Zero and the central image of The Firemen in New York City after the events of 9-11. Liebes and Blondheim configure 9-11 in a chain of work that includes studies of media events and disaster marathons, with a comparative analysis of bin Laden's attack on the United States and Sadat's visit to Jerusalem. Zelizer offers a comparative analysis of the use of amateur photography as an aid to understanding and memory in the Allied Army's encounter with the Holocaust and New Yorkers' with 9-11.

Two chapters focus on stories. Berkowitz's chapter addresses the story aspect itself in regard to the "what-a-story" reaction of working journalists to big, unexpected news events. The story structure organizes the event: It provides an end, it provides meanings for the representation and understanding of the event, and it helps journalists to schedule their work. Bird's chapter analyzes a story that became strikingly successful with journalists and audiences alike, despite violating normal journalistic standards: There were no witnesses, and who did what, when, and where could not be verified. The story of an anonymous woman who was purposefully infecting men with AIDS fits a cluster of stories, beliefs, and fears about AIDS and about sexual relations more generally. It worked—it was credible—because it gave expression to otherwise vague, incoherent, and mostly unexpressed anxieties.

The three chapters that address the Internet can also be characterized as focusing on activities. In each case, emphasis is given to individuals, their activities, and a range of particular meanings. What do people do on the Internet in regard to ritualized play and aesthetic expression (in Danet's chapter), religion and the search for meaning (in Hoover and Park's chapter), myth and identity construction (in Hammer's chapter)? In each case, we see new communicative activities using a new medium yet still fitting enduring patterns of human culture. Aesthetic play, the search for meaning, and identity construction on the Internet are new expressions shaped by their particular circumstances and by the same cultural logics that have shaped analogous activities elsewhere.

Shinar's chapter, a comparative study of political struggles over language and identity in Québec and Israel, also examines activities. He uses a more molar level of analysis, though, and the work would perhaps be more accurately characterized as a study of processes. He proposes a model by which activities could be characterized as instances of one or another more typical process. This, of course, could bridge us back into the other ways of categorizing the chapters—for what is a ritual, myth, story, religion, or ethnography but a label for an activity characterized as an instance of a process? Thus we invite our readers to choose their chapters and their order of reading as it fits their own purposes.

# 16

## THE POPE AT REUNION

### Hagiography, Casting, and Imagination

DANIEL DAYAN

TRANSLATED BY PAUL GRANT

## EVENT AND MEANING

The concept of an event is ambiguous. It refers to several types of realities. Although these realities are distinct, they are all linked to the universe of meaning. All of them aspire to be rendered into speech; all beg access to narratives. Certain events are accidents, unpredictable or unpredicted happenings. Historians will eventually undertake to integrate such events into continuities. They will acquire meaning through a retrospective operation. Such events are presented by the English critic Paddy Scannell (2000) as "happenings," as "things that occur," things to which we try to ascribe meaning. When such events occur, the first requirement is that they be considered noteworthy. This involves a momentous decision, one that takes place long before any

historian considers allocating a more lasting meaning to them. This first *making sense of* is a matter of journalism. It often consists in finding someone responsible for "what happened." For want of being the consequence of an intention, the event may become the result of a negligence. Without becoming truly understandable, the event makes its entry into the universe of explicable things.

Other, often considerable, events take on a completely different temporality. Even though the latter events are also subject to reinterpretation by historians, their particularity is that of belonging to the universe of sense even before they happen. Their meaning is anticipated. It is proclaimed in advance. They are expressive events. Of course, the meaning proclaimed by such events will combine with the meaning they take on over the course of

**Author's Note:** This text was first presented at an international seminar, "Public Space in the Islands of the Indian Ocean: Madagascar, Reunion, Maurice," at the University of Reunion. For their comments and criticism, I would like to thank the participants at this seminar, especially Jacky Simonin, Philippe Breton, Sandrine Comment, Gilles Gauthier, Jean Mouchon, Mayila Paroomal, and Yves Winkin. My remarks on television and ritual benefited from exchanges with Gunnar Saebo and (much earlier) Christian Metz. My remarks on hybrid discourses were inspired by a conversation with Elihu Katz.

their unfolding, the one that will retrospectively remain their own. Still, it is remarkable that part of their signification comes under a prospective temporality instead of being retrospectively conferred upon them. Major ceremonial events pertain to this second category. They are *expressive events;* they are discursive acts, even though it is sometimes difficult to find out who actually speaks. In this way, the Pope's travels or "pilgrimages" can be seen as speeches—as speeches that are enacted and whose meanings are proclaimed long in advance. Does their expressivity eliminate the possibility of misunderstanding? No. The most emphatic statements can be misunderstood, and misunderstandings—especially collective misunderstandings—are often bearers of historical change. This is why, long after they are over, expressive events continue to require interpretation, calling for a reading that is not to be confused with their self-presentation, a comment that does not comply with the chronicle of their announced meaning. In other words, it is easy to spot expressive events but difficult to circumscribe their expressivity and unwise to focus exclusively on those voices explicitly delegated by the event. An expressive event speaks, but one does not always know who speaks through the event. Unexpected "happenings" emerge in the midst of the most carefully constructed ceremony. When an event speaks, we must sort out its many voices. This is what this chapter attempts, in connection with an already distant event.

The event is Pope John Paul II's visit to Reunion Island in 1989, during his tour of the Indian Ocean. The TV version of this visit belongs to the genre of "ceremonial television." Within this genre, it falls under a particularly prolific subgenre: that of the Pope's travels. This subgenre continues to be present on screens. As I start writing this text, the French channel LCI is broadcasting images of Pope John Paul II's trip to the Holy Land. After so many events of this kind, yet another new broadcast hardly seems necessary. Who needs the rambling commentary, the sight of ecclesiastics zooming across the screen with wind-blown cassocks and briefcases in hand? The event is losing all meaning amidst the confusion,

but the camera moves closer. The Pope is about to speak. He clings to his chair, lips sagging, head leaning on his chest. Amid the ravaged face, two dark cracks, and in the cracks, the pontiff's gaze: a will that turns television, the crowd of dignitaries, the trembling fingers, and the thick speech into one single dramaturgy. The nodding idol is transfigured. Something is happening.

## EVENT AND DISTANCE

Television is more than a witness of the event. It is one of its essential players. This is the television of expressive events, the television of occasions that Elihu Katz and I analyzed as "media events." It can content itself with offering broadcasts about rituals, but it may also be capable of miming ritual phenomena, thus offering not only images but equivalents of rituals (Dayan, 2000). Certain media events are not simply televised ceremonies, ceremonies whose images happen to be in mass circulation. Following a suggestion by Christian Metz (personal communication, 1987), one should speak instead of *televisual* ceremonies. Ritualization affects the very performance and reception of television, and TV ritualization easily coexists with the initial one. The crowd surrounding the pope in Saint Denis participates in a mass. The viewers throughout the world who watch "the Pope's voyage to Reunion" are invited to participate in another ritual that is no longer a mass and to invent responses that will ensure their participation. The ritual universe has developed a dimension that had previously been excluded: distance (distance between celebration and participation, distance between dispersed participants). One may, then, speak of rituals without physical contact, of "diasporic" rituals, of rituals to be reconstructed at home.

## EVENT AND VALIDATION

John Paul II. Prime Minister Rocard. The event is enacted, coorganized, and cosponsored by the heads of two communities, the representatives of two centers. Does this sponsorship affect the provided experience? Yes. Criteria for validation are quite different when happenings are involved (newsworthiness, reliability of information) and when symbolic events are involved. The latter, being enacted addresses, modes of discourse, gestures, are particularly fragile and vulnerable to criticism. Gestures can be momentous or they can remain mere gesticulations. Symbolic events can become history or fail to become more than pseudoevents. Where is the dividing line?

The answer might be offered by Clifford Geertz (1973), when, in his famous essay on Balinese cockfighting, he distinguishes between "deep play" and "shallow play"; when he explains why certain cockfights are considered crucial and attract large numbers of transfixed spectators and why other cockfights, equally violent, equally bloody, only attract scattered audiences. Why is it that some fights are considered "deep play" and others are considered "shallow"? The answer concerns not the nature of the fights themselves but the identity of the cock owners. A fight means much more and stakes are higher when prominent personalities are involved. The difference between shallow play and deep play is, in a way, a matter of validation. The same could be said of the difference between pseudoevents and effective symbolic events. The former are validated by no one other than the media that broadcast them. The latter must be validated in the name of major institutions. The running of an athlete is no longer the same when it is invested with the epic narrative and layers of meaning provided by the Olympics.

Of course, different sorts of symbolic events call for different sorts of validation. A protest demonstration is "deeper" when sponsored by significant segments of civil society (unions, parties, associations). A ceremonial event acquires "depth" when validated by representatives of the center (in the case of a national event) or, as here, by representatives of many centers. Are such centers stable, monolithic, unchanging? Not at all. One should see them as works in progress, caught in a perpetual process of transformation. As Barbara Myerhoff (1987) succinctly put it:

"Traditions are not transmitted the way you hand [a person] bags of potatoes." Receiving them is reinventing them. Center maintenance involves negotiating, bartering, making concessions. It often involves strategic reformulations, and such reformulations increasingly depend on the media. Does this mean that the notion of center is a myth? That "the center" does not exist? I do not believe so. Without a center, without an institutionalized core of values and beliefs, I do not see what the critiques of hegemony or the sociologies of reproduction could be about. Centers are constantly challenged, and they respond to challenge by reformulating themselves. They are eminently "constructed." Their "constructedness" does not contradict their "reality."

## EVENT AS ACTION: CENTERS, PERIPHERIES, PUBLIC SPHERES

Agenda setting is an easy way of identifying a public sphere. A public sphere is characterized by the nature of the ongoing debates and the identity of those who participate in the debates. However, the same event can be a part of several public spheres and it can be treated differently in each. This polymorphous dimension of major events was pointed out by Paolo Mancini and Daniel Hallin (1994) when they analyzed the different versions of the Gorbachev-Reagan meetings in the American, Russian, and Italian media. The diversity of accounts concerning the same event helped to underline the diversity of public spheres. The travels of Pope John Paul II are also at the intersection of several public spheres. How do they unfold in each?

### National, Colonial, or Regional Public Sphere?

In his commentary on Habermas, Philip Schlesinger (1996) stresses the existence of an implicit link between the public sphere and the nation-state. The nation-state seems a prerequisite to the existence of a public sphere, as it fixes the limits of the "common good" to be discussed in it. Of course, Habermas tries to undo an overly exclusive link between the concept of the public sphere and the framework of the nation-state. He does so by encouraging supranational debate, by insisting on the concept of a constitutional patriotism. In practice, however, supranational institutions seem to suffer from a "democratic deficit"; they are frequently accused, when making decisions, of sacrificing all debate to the pronouncements of experts. As for the identities linked to a "constitutional patriotism," they do not carry much weight in contrast to the resonance of the nation-state and its "deep identities" (Schlesinger, 1996).

What happens when we leave the national level for the regional?

Several authors are interested in the way transborder regions (such as Catalonia) generate regional public spheres. Does the example of Catalonia have any relevance when we talk about Reunion? Are we able to imagine institutions in which the three neighboring islands of the Indian Ocean (Madagascar, Maurice, Reunion) would discuss their common interests? One can certainly imagine such institutions, but a cursory glance at newspaper headlines in the three islands suffices to demonstrate the heterogeneity of agendas. Reunion is not very involved in a regional sphere. Still, as is often the case in situations still marked by a colonial past, it does not fully belong in the French national public sphere. Reunion voices are rarely heard in French debates. Reunion itself suffers from a deficit of visibility. When it enters the French public sphere, it is in the form of the "foreign news" (catastrophes, riots, earthquakes) described by Galtung and Ruge (1965). Will this change with the Pope's visit? Is this visit primarily concerned with the French public sphere?

## From Postcolonial Public Sphere to Catholic Public Sphere

Is the Pope going to kiss the ground at Reunion? Is he going to abstain, as he already had the opportunity to place his lips upon French ground? Will he act as if he were in France? Will he act as if he were somewhere else—and if so,

where? These are the questions on everybody's mind before the Pope's plane lands at Saint Denis.

The Pope's visit is accompanied by a radical status change. The Pope does not have the power to redefine the political status of Reunion. But the papal visit has the ability to lift Reunion—at least for a moment—from its marginal status within a postcolonial public sphere and place it for a few hours (for a few days) at the center of the world's attention. Submitted to this transformation, Reunion plays an eminently passive role. It constitutes the object of the Pope's solicitude. The world follows the gaze of the Pope as it moves around the planet and finally stops on this dot in the middle of the Indian Ocean. Reunion is drawn inside a new public sphere: that of Catholicism. Offering one of the many existing versions of globalization, one of its "imaginaries," this public sphere is placed under the sign of seduction, of intimidation. It proposes events whose splendor is meant to impress. A rigid cleavage organizes it in two domains. The first is inaccessible to the public: It is that of the *arcana imperii;* the Vatican, its councils, corridors, hierarchies, antechambers. The second is a stage for dramaturgies that are public, accessible to all, offered to the faithful and to potential converts. The Catholic public sphere perfectly illustrates the Habermasian concept of a public space of *representation*. It is a public sphere constructed by a center in view of exerting, maintaining, or reestablishing its control. In this regard, the Pope's visit is a "royal progress" of sorts. Like the progresses of Balinese monarchs in the countryside, the seduction exercised by the center is an offer of meaning: The center is defined by a capacity to represent, to illustrate a cosmic order (Geertz, 1980). The center is defined as a metaphor pointing to that order. It is an instrument of imagination. The Pope then proceeds to the periodic reactivation of his links with the periphery. The center of the Church's world moves towards its margins.

## Center, Periphery, Adventus

The Vatican's dramaturgy is also in line with a ceremony coming from late antiquity and instrumental in integrating the Roman empire. Later recovered by the Church as "translation," a ritual aimed at redistributing fragments of the relics of saints to the most remote communities of an expanding Catholicism, this ceremony is the ceremony of the *adventus or advent.* Every time a high-ranking Roman official visits one of the empire cities, the whole population is expected to meet and greet the dignitary. All the various groups of the population must be represented (the absence of any of them would be perceived as an offense). The moment of the meeting is celebrated by a panegyrist in charge of exalting the virtues of the visitor and of bringing out the meaning of the visit (Dayan, 1990; Kerns, 1982). One has only to replace the panegyrist with a journalist to recognize the familiar scenario of official visits. However, in the Pope's case, center and periphery are more than polite tropes. John Paul II is not simply the chief of a minuscule European state. He is the head of the Catholic Church, and he visits the faithful. He is indeed the center visiting the periphery. The throne of Saint Peter is transported to Reunion. What television broadcasts is an authentic *advent.*

## Local Event, Broadcast Event

TV *advents* are generally offered to three types of audience: (a) those who gather in dense crowds at the site of the event, (b) those who gather in their homes or public places to watch the event on television, and (c) those far-away spectators who choose to attend an event that does not directly involve their society or history. Watching the event on the site of its unfolding, audiences of the first type tend to be drawn into the performance: They become collective actors in the event. Following the broadcast from remote countries, audiences of the third type are "overlooking" an event that is not meant for them. Watching on TV an event that only a small part of a national population can directly attend, audiences of the second type are the target audiences of major ceremonial events. For a long time, media events have been conceived with such audiences in mind.

This is not the case here. The demographics and relatively small size of the island allow for a

return to traditional (theatrical) forms of ceremony. The Pope's visit is characterized by an immense amount of direct public participation. One fifth of the population is present during some phase of the event. There is practically no family without a member attending the Saint Denis ceremonies. Under such circumstances, the presence of television is no longer a prerequisite to the public nature of the event. The visit of Pope John Paul II would be a public event with or without any broadcast. To Reunion Islanders, television serves mainly as a complement, a confirmation, an instrument of memory.

However, the Pope's visit to Reunion is also addressed to audiences watching the event from remote countries. This is one of the particularities of papal communication. Of course, the pontiff's address originates from the center (Rome) and is directed to the periphery (Reunion)—but the Pope's performance is, in fact, addressed to other peripheries. The Pope seems to speak to a given society, but upon his arrival, that society becomes a dais on which he steps to address the rest of the Catholic world. The visited locale becomes a provisional center of Catholicity. To a certain extent, one could say that John Paul II was devoting his mandate to reconstructing the Catholic public sphere. Introducing television at the heart of ritual architecture, he redefines the center as a site that any periphery can occupy when its turn comes. John Paul II has invented a nomadic center. The Vatican is no longer in Rome. It has become portable.

## A Hybrid Architecture

The Pope's visit to Reunion thus appears as a hybrid event, an event coming under at least two public spheres: the postcolonial public sphere common to the French nation-state and its overseas "départements" and the Catholic public sphere, reconfigured to partake in the global flow of images. One could imagine this situation in terms of a confrontation, the Vatican competing with the French metropolis to impose a given vision of the periphery. It is in line with such a confrontation that the question "Should the ground of Reunion be kissed?" finds its relevance. The confrontation does not take place, however; it is carefully avoided. The event smoothly fits into several public spheres and is characterized by the congruence of the different frames imposed on it. Its discursive architecture juxtaposes several discourses, each of which has a specific author, a specific recipient, and a specific object. Thus the Pope's visit to Reunion involves at least five discourses.

1. The first discourse is held *by the center for the center*. It concerns the periphery: It is the discourse of the French press telling French readers what is happening in far-away Reunion.

2. The second discourse is held *by the center for the periphery*, and it regards the periphery. It is the discourse of the French prime minister, Michel Rocard, addressing the citizens of Reunion and conveying the greetings of the capital. It belongs in the local public sphere.

3. The third discourse is held *by the periphery for the periphery*, and it regards the periphery: It is the discourse of the Reunion Press on the exceptional presence of a Pope and a prime minister. It also belongs in the local public sphere.

4. The fourth discourse is held *by the periphery for the center*, and it concerns the periphery. It is the speech of the Reunion prelate, Monsignor Aubry, describing the situation of Reunion Catholics to the Pope. The center addressed here is no longer Paris but the Vatican. The prelate's speech is primarily situated within the Catholic public sphere.

5. The fifth discourse is held *by the center* (Rome) *for the periphery* (Reunion), and it is about that periphery. Because the referent and addressee of the discourse are in fact the same, this discourse is very likely to be imperative or performative. It is the Pope's speech. Of course, the pope's performance, although addressed to a particular community within the periphery, aims in fact at reaching all peripheries. This multiple address characterizes the new Catholic public sphere, once remodeled by the Pope. Public events are no longer capable of reaching their targeted audiences without being overheard, without reaching other, unintended, audiences. John Paul II turns this communicative problem into a major resource.

## Credoscapes

The action of Pope John Paul II inscribes itself in a world criss-crossed by various flows, a world the anthropologist Arjun Appadurai (1996) has attempted to describe in response to the diversity—ethnic, ideological, technological, economic, informational—of contemporary societies. To illustrate the basic heterogeneity of these societies, Appadurai appeals to a metaphor from landscape painting. The presence of different ethnicities turns most of the contemporary societies into "ethnoscapes," more or less contrasted, more or less diversified. Ideologies, in turn, are organized into "ideoscapes" that can be vast or narrow, open or closed. Technologies form predictable "technoscapes," combinations of complementary techniques or paradoxical juxtapositions of technical universes that one would believe incompatible. Thus the existence of the fisher-hunter-harvesters of the Amazon next to the Internet surfers of Sao Paulo is characteristic of the Brazilian technoscape. The globalization of economies requires contextualizing any given economy within a "financescape." Finally, the mass of images and information circulating from one end of the planet to the other is organized into diverse media landscapes. These "mediascapes" are characterized by the amount and nature of the diversity they offer; by their hospitality to, or rejection of, foreign images. Each mediascape represents a local window, a particular viewpoint on global flows.

There is, perhaps, an additional "scape." Religious beliefs also coexist in recognizable configurations. They form "credoscapes," which may remain stable for a long time and can then be shattered or remodeled by large migratory flows or the circulation of images. The inhabitants of certain credoscapes often try to insulate themselves from outside influences, particularly those coming from media. The media are indeed capable of introducing new forms of religiosity, of changing the composition of the credoscapes. Such is the case in Colombia and Bolivia, where anthropologists mapped the decline of Catholicism and the impressive progression of protestantism in its "electronic church" or "televangelist" variants

(Gutwirth, 1998). One can similarly document the impact of American-produced religious programs on Anglican communities in Zimbabwe. Although evangelism is mostly to be found on TV screens, its impact is far from negligible, and the existence of powerful charismatic movements tends to further strengthen the seduction exercised by "mediascape missionaries" (Lundby & Dayan, 1999). Such examples suggest one of the contexts in which the Pope's action should be understood. This action consists of regaining lost terrain, of proposing a new image of the Catholic Church, of severing the Church's remaining ties with a colonial past still present in many minds. It also consists of systematically using the resources of the mediascape. For centuries, Catholicism has been relying on the power of images, orchestrating this power with unparalleled virtuosity, producing munificent "patrons of the arts." John Paul II is no longer a patron of the arts, but he is a master of television. Through television, he recasts the Catholic "center" for the sake of the faithful and reminds others that the Church is open to them, that Catholicism can be an instrument of self-imagination, an existential option.

## EVENT AS RITUAL

The relationship between media and ritual raises many questions, some of which have been discussed within the analytic framework elaborated in *Media Events* (Dayan & Katz, 1992, 1996). Three seem particularly relevant here. The first concerns the consensual role to be played by media rituals or, in contrast, their propensity to exacerbate conflicts. The second is about the approach, compositional or functional, that one may have to these rituals. The third addresses the possibility of celebration from a distance: the existence of displaced rituals.

### Consensus and Conflict

Most of the events Elihu Katz and I studied in *Ceremonial Television* (Dayan & Katz, 1996) play an explicitly integrating role. Along with such events, James Carey (1998) proposes to take into account a whole series of other events equally mediated, equally ritualized, but generating dissensus. The bitter O. J. Simpson trial and the scandal concerning the nomination of African American Judge Douglas to the United States Supreme Court are in fact "dissensus rituals," ways of focusing the public's attention on the existence of social crises—of escalating such crises. However, if there is an opposition between the consensual role and the conflictual role that one might confer upon the rituals—especially the media rituals—this opposition proves to be relative (Roth, 1995; Saebo, 1997, 2003). As soon as we go into the details of their elaboration and performance, the most consensual rituals turn out to be ridden with tensions, agitated by conflicts (Lukes, 1975). To respond to Carey's argument, the simple fact of ritualizing a conflict, of formulating it on a symbolic register, diminishes its conflictual nature. Even the most savage of terrorist rituals includes a miniaturized dimension, a symbolic ambition that distinguishes it from a full-scale war.

The Pope's visit to Reunion enacts itself in a consensual register that does not stress tensions (between the Pope and the French government; between the Vatican hierarchy and the local episcopate; between the various cultural, religious, and ethnic groups that form the population of Reunion). These tensions appear rarely, if at all, in the open. The Reunion visit contrasts with those turbulent events in which Pope John Paul II plays hide and seek with the censors of Jaruzelski's Poland, or in which he is forced to hold mass against the background of Marxist frescoes in Nicaragua, raising his voice to cover a barrage of Sandinista slogans. One has the impression of a harmonious cooperation between the key players of the event (the Pope, French Prime Minister Michel Rocard, Monsignor Aubry). Nobody objects to the Pope's focus on the tragic realities of slavery. On the contrary, his call for awareness is perfectly heard by the French press. A smooth continuity is established between the ritual experience—what Victor Turner calls the "pedagogy of the shrine" (Turner & Turner, 1978)—and the agenda of the press.

## Functional and Compositional

The reference to ritual raises a second issue, which concerns definition. Media research may be interested in the ritual from a functional point of view or envision it from a formal or even "compositional" point of view (Roth, 1995; Saebo, 1997, 2003). From a functional point of view, one can propose that, in many historical situations, newspapers contain an immense amount of redundant information and do not therefore perform a truly informational role. Allowing the dissemination or strengthening of common values, the function of newspaper reading would then be to create or strengthen homogeneous communities of readers. One could therefore speak of the "ritual" functions of the press (Carey, 1975). As suggestive as such a formulation may be, its concept of ritual has little to do with the precise descriptions of temporal structures of Van Gennep (1909); with the detailed exploration by Victor Turner (1969/1990) of moments of separation and reintegration and of what happens in the interval between those two moments; with Wallace's (1966) and Myerhoff's (1982) description of the phases that may structure the ritual experience; and, finally, with Handelman's sketch (1990) of a general ceremonial grammar.

The difference between a functional vision and a compositional vision distinguishes rituals as social constructions with recognizable contours from all those other social objects that the analyst may decide to call rituals. In one case, only specific events are rituals. In the other case, all social relations are potentially so, and each interaction, no matter how casual, reaffirms the social contract. Functional visions of ritual tend to short circuit the necessity for a "double hermeneutics" (Roth, 1995; Saebo, 1997). They tend to ignore the notion that the designation of ritual should not involve the sole decision of an analyst whose knowledge should prevail over the lack of knowledge of the social players. If one defines ritual in functional terms only, no element of the social seems immune from possible inclusion. If one refuses to grant a prevalent position to the analyst, situations must be explicitly perceived as rituals by the participants.

The perception of participants is relevant not only when it comes to ascribing ritual status but also when it comes to defining ritual content. Functionalism is often taken as a synonym of consensualism. This leads to ignoring a whole tradition of ritual studies whereby no consensual ritual can be accepted as consensual simply because its actors say it is. In a conflictual society, any ritual only expresses conflict. If its participants say otherwise, one must denounce them: Their ritual is a fraud, a front, or a mask. In this sort of "conflict" functionalism, the interpretive tension called for by double hermeneutics gives way to the "hermeneutics of suspicion." Like all functionalisms, conflict functionalism is unfalsifiable. Still, if all rituals are conflictual in principle, what are we to do of those that are really conflictual? What are we to do of rituals of excommunication, purification, humiliation, assassination? Barthes (1978) once wrote that "language is fascist." If *all* language is fascist, what are we to do of "newsspeak"? What about the sociolinguistics of actual fascism?

## EVENT AS IMAGINATION

Forming what might be called a "paradigm of imagination," different trends in media studies emphasize the importance of the cognitive instruments that allow us to conceive the society in which we live, to build images of this society. Such images are crucial to political action, historical projects, and the very experience of belonging. Arjun Appadurai (1996) has emphasized the importance of contemporary mediascapes, the direct access they allow the general public to a globalization that is no longer automatically subjected to the mediation of elites. The immigration process is thus linked to a capacity to imagine the far away.

## Prefigurations and Figurations

The work of Benedict Anderson (1983) also addresses the problem of imagination. It shows that imagination—"generating an image of"—is capable of acting on reality, of bending or transforming it. For Anderson, the imagination process is first of all a "prefiguration" process. An imaginary community can prefigure an actual community; a national imaginary can lead to the birth of a nation. Starting with the administrative reality of the former colonial provinces, Anderson develops an argument inspired by Walter Benjamin. Mechanical reproduction plays an essential part in the process he describes, taking the form of the printing press or, more precisely, a "capitalism of print" capable of producing and disseminating newspapers and novels. Linguistically speaking, print capitalism leads to the disappearance of dialectal variations, the standardization of habits, and the appearance of a common language. In the literary field, the unification of dialects is prolonged by that of the represented spaces: Novel plots draw the contours of political entities that are still virtual; they construct regional geographies. Finally, the dissemination of newspapers, the simultaneous reference to events, each of which used to be specific to a given population, leads to the integration of distinct temporalities and to the emergence of a shared time. Using a standardized language, sharing a common temporality and a unified territory, the former administrative divisions of colonial empires can now imagine themselves as "communities," anticipating or prefiguring their conversion into national realities. The emergence of these communities responds to the encounter between a context (that of colonial administrative divisions), a medium (print capitalism), and processes of imagination(prefigurations of political realities).

Still, the role of imagination processes, as described by Anderson, consists not only in prefiguring new communities. Technologies of imagination also make it possible to figure already existing communities, to confirm their existence. National realities become imaginable through such instruments as the museum (a modern cult of the dead), the census (the counting of the living), and the map (the portrait of a territory). Every day, television complements these instruments by operating as (a) a kind of perpetual museum, (b) a constant census of the viewers'

communities, and (c) a constantly updated cartography of the public sphere.

## Casting

Indeed, one could study the way in which the media deploy constellations of social or political actors, the way in which the media are constantly involved in a process of "casting" (with the meaning this word has acquired in the language of film). Not unlike the credits that we see at the end of a movie, the media are continuously reciting lists of roles available in a society. They constantly present us with the actors charged with playing these roles. Imagining the social consists not only of highlighting themes or issues ("agenda setting") but of casting those who are concerned by, or involved in, these issues. In narrative terms, one could say that agenda setting provides verbs, description of actions. Casting, on the other hand, tells us about actors and the parts they fill. Behind every "issue" that an agenda incorporates, there is a social group. Because narrative discourse is omnipresent, casting is uninterrupted. We find it in the social casting of serials, political casting of news, cultural casting of set shows, demographic casting of reality shows. Castings may contradict each other, but they usually repeat each other, confirm each other, add up to each other in offering a demographic *commedia dell'arte:* a general picture of society, of the groups that compose it, and of the characteristics of these groups. The media allow us to imagine society through the enumeration of ongoing dramas and through that of their "dramatis personae" (Dayan, 2000).

## Reconfiguration

There is, however, an additional role that the media might play. This role does not consist in prefiguring a society on the verge of being born, or in figuring an already existing society, but in reconfiguring a given society, in transforming it, retouching—sometimes literally—its face.

Among the various scenarios ceremonial television permits, the most frequently used is the consensual celebration of a person, group, or institution. This celebratory scenario could be defined as a "coronation." Coronations are solemn affirmations of loyalty. Such is the case of the Pope's visit to Reunion—but to whom is this loyalty addressed? Who or what is being crowned? The event's dramaturgy seems to leave little place for doubt. The coronation is that of the Pope, triumphantly welcomed by the island's population. However, this dramaturgy is only that of the local event. The event as offered in the Catholic public sphere comes under another dramaturgy. It is about a *coronation* too, but this time it is Reunion that is offered as an example, presented as the illustration of universal norms, celebrated in its successful multiculturalism, hailed as a countermodel to Lebanon—also a multicultural country, but one traversed by hatred and discord. The event could be called "The Coronation of Reunion," in the style of 19th-century allegorical frescoes. Yet, as we have seen, it mobilizes a very contemporary strategy: encouraging faith wherever it is, not simply where it is theologically pure; promoting a Catholicism of diversity; accepting the validity of unorthodox manifestations of piety. Beyond celebrating Reunion, the thrust of the event consists in redefining Catholicism itself. Reunion offers the Pope an opportunity to recast the Church's image. The Pope performs an expositive; his gesture redefines the center. In the very gesture by which he recasts Catholicism, however, John Paul II also confers a face upon Reunion. This face summarizes the diversity of the island. The face is also substituted for this diversity. The face is not that of a slave; it is that of a white man. It is not the face of a martyr but that of an almost ordinary Catholic priest. By sanctifying Father Scubilion, John Paul II carefully constructs a certain version of Reunion. Scubilion's giant portrait, dominating the mass in Saint Denis, seems to be the reflection of Pope John Paul II's own face. Center and Periphery have been recast in the same gesture.

## Illocution

For a long time, it was believed that the effects of an event could only be posterior and exterior to the event. However, if such effects (effects that we could call "perlocutory") do exist, there are also other effects that, on the contrary, are immanent to the event and indistinguishable from its unfolding. These effects (which we might call "illocutory") are not the least considerable. The main effect of an event such as the Pope's visit is indeed confounded with the visit itself. It consists of the event taking place, realizing its ritual vocation, being attended to, becoming "deep play," benefiting from what Austin (1962) calls "felicity." Such a fate is far from being guaranteed. Many proposed events remain ritual propositions without any response. The public may reject these propositions or remain puzzled as to their exact meaning. How do you respond to a poorly handled script? To a dramaturgy obviously pulled in too many directions by the contradictory ambitions of the organizers? The success of an event such as the Pope's visit to Reunion is made possible by a consensus among the organizers, translated into a clear proposition. It allows a community to feel itself, see itself, measure itself, and to become aware of its own power. The success of an event—its illocutory effect—thus allows for a kind of charismatic census: It allows a group to self-imagine. But in whose terms? A casting has taken place. Should Reunion accept the part?

## References

Anderson, B. (1983). *Imagined communities: Reflections on the origins and spread of nationalism.* London: Verso.

Appadurai, A. (1996). *Modernity at large.* London: University of Minnesota Press.

Austin, J. L. (1962). *How to do things with words.* Oxford: Clarendon Press.

Barthes, R. (1978). *La leçon* [The lecture]. Paris: Seuil.

Carey, J. (1975). A cultural approach to communication. *Communication, 2*(2), 1-25.

Carey, J. (1998). Rituals of degradation. In T. Liebes & J. Curran (Eds.), *Media, ritual, identity* (pp. 42-71). London: Routledge.

Dayan, D. (1990, May). Présentation du pape en voyageur [The presentation of the Pope's journeys]. *Terrain, 15,* 15-29.

Dayan, D. (2000). La télévision: Miroir du rituel [Television: Mirror of ritual]. In P. Bréchon & J. P. Willaime (Eds.), *Medias et religion en miroir* [Media and religion face to face] (pp. 245-265). Paris: PUF.

Dayan, D., & Katz, E. (1992). *Media events: The live broadcasting of history.* Cambridge, MA: Harvard University Press.

Dayan, D., & Katz, E. (1996). *La télévision cérémonielle* [Ceremonial television]. Paris: PUF.

Galtung, H., & Ruge, M. (1965). The structure of foreign news. *International Journal of Peace Research, 1*, 64-90.

Geertz, C. (1973). *The interpretation of culture.* New York: Basic Books.

Geertz, C. (1980). Centers, kings and charisma. In J. B. David & T. Clark (Eds.), *Culture and its creators* (pp. 150-170). Chicago: University of Chicago Press.

Gutwirth, J. (1998). *L'église electronique: La saga des télévangelistes* [The electronic church: The saga of the televangelists]. Paris: Bayard.

Handelman, D. (1990). *Models and mirrors: Towards an anthropology of public events.* New York: Cambridge University Press.

Kerns, P. (1982). *Papal visit to the US.* Unpublished manuscript, Annenberg School for Communication, University of Southern California.

Lukes, S. (1975). Political ritual and social integration. *Sociology, 9*(2), 289-308.

Lundby, K., & Dayan, D. (1999). Mediascape missionaries: Television, religion and identity in a local African setting. *International Journal of Cultural Studies, 2*(3), 399-417.

Mancini, P., & Hallin, D. (1994). Rencontres au sommet: Vers une sphére publique internationale? [Summit meetings: Toward an international public sphere?]. *Hermes, 13-14*, 185-203.

Myerhoff, B. G. (1982). Rites of passage: Process and paradox. In V. Turner (Ed.), *Celebration* (pp. 109-135). Washington, DC: Smithsonian Institute.

Myerhoff, B. G. (1987, November). *On the engineering of holidays: A debate with Elihu Katz and Daniel Dayan* (Hillel lectures). Los Angeles: University of Southern California.

Roth, A. L. (1995). "Men wearing masks": Issues of description and analysis of ritual. *Sociological Theory, 13*(3), 301-327.

Saebo, G. (1997, July). *Media rituals and modern society.* Paper presented at the Congress of the International Communication Association, Glasgow.

Saebo, G. (2003). *Media, rituals, and the cultivation of collective representations* (doctoral dissertation). Oslo, Norway: University of Oslo Press.

Scannell, P. (2000). For anyone—as someone—structures. *Media, Culture and Society, 22*, 5-24.

Schlesinger, P. (1996). Europeanization and the media: National identity and the public sphere. In T. Slatta (Ed.), *Media and the transition of collective identities* (IMK Report Series No. 18). Oslo, Norway: University of Oslo Press.

Turner, V. W. (1990). *Le phénomène rituel: Structure et contre-structure* [The ritual process: Structure and anti-structure] (G. Guillet, Trans.). Paris: PUF. (Original work published 1969)

Turner, V., & Turner, E. (1978). *Image and pilgrimage in Christian culture: Anthropological perspectives.* Oxford, England: Blackwell.

Van Gennep, A. (1909). *Les rites de passage: Étude systématique des rites* [Rites of passage: Systematic study of the rites]. Paris: E. Nourry.

Wallace, A. (1966). *Religion: An anthropological view.* New York: Random House.

## ADDITIONAL SOURCES

Alexander, J. C. (1988). *Durkheimian sociology: Cultural studies.* New York: Cambridge University Press.

Brown, P. (1981). *The cult of the saints.* Chicago: University of Chicago Press.

Carey, J. (1989). *Communication as culture: Essays on media and society.* London: Routledge.

Dupront, A. (1973). *Pélerinages et lieux sacrés: Mélanges François Braudel* [Pilgrimages and sacred spaces: François Braudel's mixtures]. Toulouse, France: Privat.

Durham Peters, J., & Rothenbuhler, E. W. (1994). La réalité de la construction [The reality of construction]. *Hermès, 13-14*, 27-44.

Habermas, J. (1962). The structural transformation of the public sphere. Cambridge: MIT Press.

MacAloon, J. (Ed.). (1984). *Rite, festival, spectacle, game.* Chicago: University of Chicago Press.

Scannell, P. (1995). Media events: A review essay. *Media, Culture and Society, 17*, 151-160.

Scannell, P. (1996). *Radio, television and modern life.* Oxford, England: Blackwell.

Schudson, M. (1989). How culture works: Perspectives from media studies on the efficacy of symbols. *Theory and Society, 18*, 53-180.

Shils, E. (1975). *Center and periphery: Essays in macro sociology.* Chicago: University of Chicago Press.

# 17

# GROUND ZERO, THE FIREMEN, AND THE SYMBOLICS OF TOUCH ON 9-11 AND AFTER

ERIC W. ROTHENBUHLER

O n the morning of September 11, 2001, an act of war against civilians in a place at peace scrambled the categories of culture, cognition, and communication. This act killed 3000 people and injured scores more, eliminated two landmark buildings in a landmark city, and startled, stunned, scared, and confused the U.S. population and the communication system on which it depends for professional reassurance about how to think. The most skilled and prominent professional talkers, the smooth presences called the anchors of network news, were reduced to stammering and silence. This analysis focuses on New York City and the public response to the attack there, as the City came to be the center of public attention, housing the dominant symbols of all of the events of that day.

Hijacking the two planes and flying them into the World Trade Center towers was a sneak attack against noncombatants by unsoldiers of a non-nation. It converted tools of commerce and leisure into weapons of mass destruction. It converted workplace and tourist attraction into deathplace. It scattered debris and human remains over square miles of civil setting. It converted lives to bodies that could not be found because they no longer existed. It started a fire that could not be put out until the Twin Towers had become the Pit. It brought down the most prominent symbol of the most symbolically central city in the U.S. system of images and ideas. It was punctuated by ironies that added to the air of the fantastical: Concrete crumbled and burned while paper survived and flew away; the tallest buildings in sight

**Author's Note:** An earlier version of this essay was presented under a different title as the keynote address at the "Making Sense of September 11: News Media and Old Metaphors" conference, Ohio University, September 21, 2002, Athens, Ohio. My thanks to Jeffrey St. John, the conference organizers, and the thoughtful audience there. My thanks also to Carol Wilder for key suggestions and encouragement on the earliest drafts; Dan Cherubin for research assistance; and Jim Bass, Carol Blair, Mihai Coman, Jack Lule, Tom McCourt, Paul Ryan, Barry Salmon, Michael Schudson, Greg Shepherd, and anonymous reviewers for thoughtful comments on a later draft. Jane Martin's photographs, her aid in interpreting them, and her discussion of the ideas in this paper were essential to the project. My thanks also to the New School and its Department of Communication for supporting my research.

crushed themselves into piles while the subway stations and shops beneath them stood empty and whole; fine white ash coated everything so perfectly it created a ghostly visual aesthetic, attracting photographers for weeks; towering neighboring buildings such as the Marriott Hotel and Tower 7 were completely ruined, while tiny St. Paul's Chapel and its tiny, historic graveyard stood dusted but undamaged. As if all this was not enough, the attack was also a fantastical touching of coup. These enemies reached past the warriors, into the heart of domestic space, and touched America's citizens right on the forehead, before they could react.

The public response to the attack on the World Trade Center shows strong patterns of unspoken cultural work—rescue, relief, and memorial efforts were also symbolic repair work. The communicative element of the activities around 9-11 and the actual element of the communication— the things said in the doing and the things done in the saying—worked to unscramble, reconstruct, and reorder the damage done in the symbol system along with the damage done on the ground.

## NOTES ON CONCEPTS AND METHODS

This chapter serves as an example of media anthropology in its broad sense. It is an essay in interpretation, directed at a phenomenon of mediacentric contemporary life, drawing freely on concepts from across the anthropological literature and elsewhere. The analysis uses observations of events and activities in New York City and the media to help explain how Ground Zero and The Firemen came to be central symbols of the 9-11 events and their aftermath.

On the 11th, my colleagues and I witnessed the attack from our office at New School University, and after spending most of the day there, I participated in the exodus from lower Manhattan. Our university was closed for the first week, and some of the buildings were used for family and medical information centers. On the 13th, I returned to help answer phones and be available to displaced students. Taking advantage of the location below the barricades—the city was officially closed below 14th street on those first days—and following the lead of Jane Martin, a professional photographer with whom I collaborated, I set out to observe the scene on the streets where citizens were gathering to cheer the rescue and recovery workers. I kept a journal of observations and personal reactions and gradually built that into a more formal file of observation notes, annotated clippings, and interpretation ideas continuing through the anniversary period one year later. Martin began photographing public reaction to the events on the 11th, and through the first few months, she photographed and observed in most of the neighborhoods of lower Manhattan and at all the key centers of action. I used her reports to guide my own observations in public places, and her photographs served as a form of visual note taking.

The study focuses on the symbolic patterns that appear across media coverage, public talk, interpersonal talk, and the symbolic aspects of behavior in public places. All are treated as elements of the same tapestry, the methodological presumption being that they can be read as reflections, if not expressions, of communicative and cognitive structures. This is based on the classical hermeneutics of Dilthey (1976) and the synthesis of hermeneutics and structuralism of Ricoeur (1981). Such otherwise heterogeneous anthropologists as Geertz and Lévi-Strauss inspire the interpretation—see in particular Geertz (1988) on Lévi-Strauss as symbolist.

The concept of the sacred and the symbolic geography of proximity to the sacred are the central ideas of this work (see Douglas, 1978; Durkheim, 1912/1995; Eliade, 1959; van Gennep, 1908/1960; Turner, 1977). Douglas's analysis of dirt, hygiene, pollution, and taboo is especially important. The attack on the World Trade Center scrambled cognitive categories at a very fundamental level and reduced those buildings; nearly 3000 people; and the taken-for-granted idea of their lives as private citizens at peace, and thus potentially our lives as the same, to literal and symbolic dirt. This could not be left alone. Just as the rubble and the dirt needed to be sorted and the valuable parts recovered, the ground cleared, and the site rebuilt, symbolic distinctions and relations needed to be recovered, repaired, and rebuilt so they could settle once again into the taken-for-granted background of the routine flow of everyday life.

Symbolic repair work is carried forward by ritual: both formal ceremonies, which are given relatively little attention in the present analysis, and by the ritualistic elements of otherwise apparently practical social actions—the things implicitly said in the doing.

> When we honestly reflect on our busy scrubbings and cleanings in this light we know that we are not mainly trying to avoid disease. We are separating, placing boundaries, making visible statements about the home that we are intending to create out of the material house. (Douglas, 1978, p. 68)

Disorder and sacredness came powerfully and dangerously together in the death and destruction of the World Trade Center Towers. The disorder of concern was immensely more than matter out of place, although that alone was a massive enough problem. As elucidated in the analysis to follow, here was witnessed death as well as heroism out of place; war and all that it entails out of place; challenges to the most basic values; shocking disruptions of taken-for-granted knowledge and social schemas; and direct, personal contact with the sacred itself, all out of place. The dissolution of ordered organic function and the dissolving of consciousness were concretely represented in the obliteration of two buildings so tall they had become ubiquitous presences in the peripheral vision of all who walked in lower Manhattan—and many who only imagined it, as demonstrated by the presence of the twin towers on travel posters found around the world. The burning rubble pile and the void itself became for many a hierophany, a revelation of the numinous presence of the sacred (Eliade & Sullivan, 1987). Neither the physical nor the symbolic damage could be cleaned or repaired without a months-long effort, the first step of which had to be containment.

The analysis begins with attention to the symbolic geography centered on Ground Zero and then moves to consideration of The Firemen as a central symbol in the public response to 9-11. The cultural role of the firefighters, as elucidated later, is based on their crossing the borders and touching death at Ground Zero, in the sacred center of the symbolic geography of public response to 9-11 (see Marvin & Ingle, 1999, on border crossing and death touching). The symbol of The Firemen became a multifaceted paradox as they represented each and all of the prevalent forms of contact with the vital questions put into play at Ground Zero, a place where sudden and unexpected death was brought to some and not others, a place where the sudden death was followed by a months-long funeral pyre. The Firemen represented citizen-soldiers, rescuer-victims, inside-outsiders, manly men who cry, and more.

The Firemen as symbol is based in cultural logic and discourse practices; its centrality and importance is motivated by the work, sacrifice, risk, injury, death, and loss of individual firefighters who live in New York and whose families care how they are represented. The distinction between concrete individual men and women and The Firemen as social representation was confused in the debate over the Iwo Jima–like statue of three firemen raising a flag over the rubble. The statue portrayed them as heroic, fit, and handsome, one black, one Hispanic, and one white. The three guys who stole the flag and hung it protested that they, the actual men, were older, heavier, and white and should be shown as such ("Firefighters block a," 2002; "Three firefighters say," 2002). In our media-centered cultural system, photographs, videos, and news stories, each claiming their own version of verisimilitude, are dominant forms of cultural representation. Hence something like The Firemen as a symbol will often be portrayed in the recognizable form of an individual firefighter. The analysis, then, must walk a fine line with due respect to what lies on both sides, working to gain the benefits of cultural analysis without disrespect to the actual people whose lives are being represented as patterns of culture.

## GROUND ZERO AND THE IMPACT ZONE

The World Trade Center site began to be called Ground Zero on the day of the attack. The language comes from planning for atomic war, and there was initially some debate about its appropriateness in this use. Yet it was apt enough to become universal almost immediately. On the surface, it defines a site of complete destruction; ground zero is where everything is gone. Use of the term in the first days was even prescient, as it would not be understood until weeks later how human remains and even concrete and steel were pulverized in the crush and vaporized in the fire.

At a secondary, more implicit level, the term *ground zero* organizes a geography. In the case of atomic explosion, ground zero is the origin of the exploding force and spreading radiation. Everything can be measured by its distance from ground zero; in the case of planning for atomic war, survivorship probabilities can be calculated. The term, then, evokes a vision of spreading damage and danger, poison and contagion, away from ground zero.

Officially, "the immediate impact zone is defined as the area south of Chambers Street and west of Broadway, and the entirety of Battery Park City."[1] In the first days after the attack, the city was officially closed below 14th Street; that Friday it opened to Canal, although there were still many restrictions on movement north of there. As rescue operations at the World Trade Center site turned to recovery, official control of operations became stabilized, and cleanup progressed in the areas outside the immediate impact zone, the closed territory became smaller and more genuinely secure to nonofficial passage. Here we see a system of concentric territories with ground zero as the center of a pattern of disruption, surrounded by the immediate impact zone and the security controlled areas; then the larger impact zone, the Lower Manhattan Development Corporation's areas of concern, the territory of staging places for rescue and recovery, places where ash came down and people fled. This territory is organized by a series of decreasingly violent causes—explosion, fire, death, injury, debris, dust, emergency management, rescue, recovery, relocation, reconstruction—producing increasingly wider effects in decreasingly vital aspects of life, from life itself, through meaning and memory, relationships and organization, to transportation and commerce. At the center is the place of death, those who have been touched by it and those who touch it. At the barricades were those who came to pay tribute and bear witness—to be in proximity, as if to touch those who crossed the barrier. In the larger community was the place of the smell and the ash, the missing posters, candles, flowers, and public shrines. This territory extended out communicatively across the country. There was a flow of testimony, pictures, and description out and away from New York and a flow of volunteers, donations, gifts, and tourists back into New York.

Ground Zero, then, named a place that was more than the center of the impact zone, the site of maximum destruction, the origin of the explosive force. Ground Zero was the anchoring center of a meaningful organization of experience: in other words, a sacred place.

## THE ATTRACTION TO THE BARRICADES—THE ATTRACTION OF GROUND ZERO

The impact zone was set off by barricades, inside which only people with photo IDs and official business were allowed. In the first weeks, the area inside these barricades shrank until it defined specific sites of recovery and security work. From the second day through the next few weeks, these barricades were highly attractive sites. People wanted to be there. The most attractive barricades were the busiest ones, on the West Side Highway, for example, which rescue workers, ambulances, military vehicles, and others used for entrance and egress to the site and connection to St. Vincent's Hospital and other staging, command, and control sites. The barricade here was popular enough, and the social activity there exuberant enough, to attract its own name. It came to be called Point Thank You. (Note that the military-talk and citizen-talk styles are conflated, not accidentally, but with a bit of ironic flair, as if to point to the paradox.)

In the first couple of weeks, this barricade on the west side was a dramatic public play of singing, cheering, flag waving, piling up of supplies, cooking and eating, coming and going, and plain old social gathering. The barricades represented the border between the ordered world and the disordered one, and as the days and weeks progressed, they became more orderly places themselves. At first, volunteers, rescuers, crowds, and law enforcement nearly mingled. People brought materials to the barricades in shopping bags and carts; rescue workers moved in and out piled haphazardly into and onto private vehicles; the strictness of security enforcement varied. Later, the barricades were strictly regimented; proper IDs had been distributed, and access was carefully controlled. Supplies were properly stacked. Crowds were held back.

People were attracted to the barricades because they wanted to touch that border between ordered and disordered and to witness the crossing of the border. Crossing the border were a panoply of professionals, officials, and workers, and the occasional celebrity. They all got cheered. In one way, they were all rescue workers, working to rescue the order of civil society; crossing into the disordered territory and coming back again was a kind of repair work. As their work progressed, the location of the barricades could be moved, until the impact zone had, in this sense at least, shrunk right around Ground Zero itself, which, by that time, had become a tourist attraction. The *New York Times* estimated a million visitors by the end of 2001, before the viewing platforms had been built; *Newsweek* estimated (circa September 2002) that there would be 3.6 million by the end of 2002.

Ground Zero is, by this analysis, a legitimate tourist attraction. There is nothing different between this and visits to historic battlefields or national cemeteries. As the territory inside the barricades shrank toward Ground Zero, they became less celebratory places, less peopled by New Yorkers, less about recovering from the touch of the enemy, less about reordering the symbolic world of the city's residents. Simultaneously, the barricades became better places for silent witness, closer to the site of death, which slowly became less a smoldering, battlefield ruin, more controlled, and eventually a site of reconstruction. This is the place where those who were not touched came to pay tribute to those who were.

## THE FIREMEN

Why did the firefighters receive so much public attention after 9-11? They were rescuers, of course. Fifty thousand people worked in those buildings every day; an estimated 140,000 moved through them on a weekday. Early on, Mayor Giuliani estimated that 20,000 or more were safely evacuated that morning; later, more studied estimates were that up to 14,000 may have been in the buildings before the first plane hit and more than 10,000 were evacuated. On the ground, greeted by the press, many of those people said a word of thanks to the firefighters. This simple truth—the firefighters helped save people, and the people were grateful—is also a classic narrative seed lying at the core of countless children's stories, novels, movies, songs, speeches, and news reports. So of course, once loosed in the sphere of public discourse, it resonated. However, that is not the end of the story.

Many of the firefighters engaged in genuinely heroic acts of self-sacrifice; much larger numbers who did not die put themselves equally at risk for the benefit of others. No altruism is greater than self-sacrifice for the survival of others, and no social system can survive without commensurately elaborate rewards for it. Thus, in the normal course of things, when a firefighter dies in the line of duty, we expect a ritually heightened degree of public attention. Indeed, official fire department protocol and unofficial practice calls for an elaborate funeral ceremony, with large numbers of visiting firefighters, and it usually receives prominent local press coverage. When 343 firefighters die in one morning, we should expect something like 343 times as much attention.

There was another narrative element here as well. On the first day or two, someone was quoted as saying that the firefighters were running into the burning buildings and up the stairs while everyone else was running down and out. This verbal image became widely repeated and served as a fulcrum point for stories about survival and sacrifice. Fire department and city officials used it to talk about the heroism of the firefighters. Survivors used it in stories about their own escape. For some, perhaps, it increased the drama of their own escape, the closeness of their contact with death. Some appeared genuinely haunted by the unknown fate of the men they passed on the stairs. Some of the few firefighters who have told bits of their own story also used the image of passing people on the stairs, although they know what happened to their colleagues who went on higher than they did. At least one has told a powerful story of the capriciousness of duty, as his life was spared but his partner was killed because his partner told him to go down with a woman who was struggling.

## Citizen Soldiers

The quasimilitaristic ways of the fire department were also apt in the situation. They fit the public need to respond when civilians had received military-like injury. The fire department provided citizen soldiers, mediating figures at a time when the distinction had been damaged. Giving attention to a group that crossed that line professionally perhaps aided in the cultural repair work. The fire department uses ritual and symbol to define and control its border-crossing activities; issues of fire department rank, uniform, command, medals and commendations, funeral ceremony, and the widows and orphans fund (about which more later) were all of special importance in the months after 9-11. The fire department provided plenty of fodder for this type of attention.

The militaristic ceremonies of the fire department made their dead useful symbols in response to the violated sensibilities of the witnesses. (My analysis is based on observations of the public discourse, which was dominated by witnesses, not victims.) The key violation of the attack was that it brought military-like death to civilians engaged in their civil activities on an ordinary day. A firefighter killed by trauma in the line of duty

becomes a civilian given military honors. Firefighters do not carry guns in duty, but an honor guard fires guns at their funeral. They do not serve under the flag, but they are draped with one at death. The uniforms they work in look like work clothes; the ones they are buried in are military dress. They do not salute regularly in work life, but they are saluted prominently in death. In life they are attended by family, friends, and coworkers; in death they are attended by all firefighters everywhere.

I have drawn the lines starkly, as if the ritual converted fallen firefighters suddenly from guys with a job to members of a brotherhood of soldiers. In fact, the militaristic elements of fire department training and fire department life prepare this ground. Like new recruits of the armed forces and law enforcement, and novitiates of religious orders, fire department trainees are separated from their families and from other citizens, leveled, and remade as comrades to each other and as agents of the institution. This is a classic institutional structure for remaking subjectivities, analyzable as a total institution (Goffman, 1961) and as a rite of passage creating and protecting institutional communitas (Turner, 1977). Both the liminality vis-à-vis the rest of society and the communitas among the members is kept alive by the segregated life of the firehouse, which is analogous to the segregated life of a military barracks. Fire department training, lore, and life in fact prepare members to die for others. Just as Marvin and Ingle (1999) have shown of the armed forces, the liminal existence of firefighters protects the promise of duty: Their life is already given away. Firefighters have already promised *I will run in when others are running out.*

This militaristic, already-given-away life, though, was not emphasized in the public discourse after 9-11. Rather, the firefighters were "our guys," the comrades were a family, and the firehouse was a home. Newspaper stories emphasized the ordinariness of the firefighters. The prominent "Portraits of Grief" in the *New York Times,* excerpted in papers around the country, presented the firefighters right along with the rest of the citizens, pictured in family snapshots, their lives described in all the same ways, no one more prominent than the others. Firehouses in lower Manhattan became places where people sent flowers, sympathy cards, cakes, and pies. The public does not do this for military bases; they do this for friends and family who have lost a loved one. No doubt the families of fallen soldiers are treated like any other bereaved families, but the barracks are not portrayed as places of grief, receiving flowers, sympathy cards, and home-baked desserts. The public attention to the fire-fighters after 9-11 downplayed the already existing militaristic aspects of the fire depart-ment, as if to emphasize the contrast I was exag-gerating: the juxtaposition of the ordinary working class guy going about his work with his death in an "act of war" and his subsequent con-version to a person worthy of a military funeral. This made the fire department in general and the idea of the dead firefighters in particular a better fit to the symbolic troubles of the time. To join the long parade and paraphrase Lévi-Strauss: The firefighters were good to think with.

## Rescuer Victims

The firefighters were not only rescuers and not only citizen soldiers; they were also the most publicly visible victims and victims' families. The New York City Fire Department lost 343 people, disproportionately officers, leaders, and experi-enced men. Individual firehouses lost four, six, eight, even 12 people at a time. The number was not the only thing, however. The financial services company Cantor Fitzgerald lost 658 people and received quite a bit of notice, but neither before nor after 9-11 could this company be as symboli-cally central as the fire department ("Remains of a," 2002).

Before 9-11, firefighters and fire departments were objects of desirous attention. Little boys and girls wanted to be among them; grown-up boys and girls still liked them. After 9-11, the firefight-ers became, too, the best picture of a victim. Their yellow suits dominated; they looked like firefight-ers, no matter what any individual one of them may have looked like. In looking like few if any of us, they could stand in for any of us—all the

better to empathize with if we each have childhood memories of wanting to be among them.

Their status as both rescuers and victims, and the generally positive public perception accorded firefighters, made picturing them useful for busi-nesses and other institutions otherwise uncon-nected with 9-11, New York City, or its fire department. Major advertisers faced a dilemma after 9-11 and again during the anniversary period. Their normal business plans called for a large, visible presence in the media, yet the obvi-ously self-interested nature of advertising could appear too crass and produce negative public response. Full-page ads or 30-second commer-cials picturing and praising firefighters offered a solution. No one could be against the firefighters. The advertiser could appear to be doing some-thing charitable and associate itself with altru-ism. Simultaneously, it could keep its name before the public and continue to hold at least some of its usual advertising space. This, then, helped the firefighters become even more visible after 9-11.

The victimage of the firefighters was mobi-lized, too, by their radical innocence—not just by the fact that, like the rest of us, none of them had done anything to attract death that morning, and not just that, like members of law enforcement and the military, they died in the line of duty, but by the fact that their death was in the line of an innocent duty, a duty to aid the injured, not to bring injury. They died in a "war" the effects of which they were trying to prevent—as if it were medics and chaplains being killed in combat.

The fire department also provided the best-organized group of victim's families. With the sur-viving firefighters standing in for the families of the dead, the fire department was the only victims' organization that already existed before 9-11. It not only already existed, it was a depart-ment of city government, had a press officer, and was already a news beat.

## Inside Outsiders

The firefighters were rescuer-victims, citizen-soldiers, icons of victimage, and well-organized victims' families. They were also at the very center of official presence at Ground Zero, yet they represented outsiders, the unofficial, the victims, and the witnesses. The firefighters played the role of "inside outsiders," defending to the very last day the irrational, the symbolic, the sentimental, and the memorial against the bureaucracy of rebuilding. On November 2, about two months after the attack (although still more than a month until the fire would finally be put out), firemen and policemen got into a fistfight in the recovery area. This sort of thing does not happen very often.

Several hundred firefighters had gone to the site to protest a reduction in the number permitted on the grounds. They called for the resignations of the mayor and the fire commissioner. Giuliani said few bodies remained to be recovered; the protesting firefighters chanted "Bring our brothers home!" (Once again we see a militaristic value, but here mixed with an element of mysticism. Where have their brothers gone?) News stories on following days reported firefighters' claims that the World Trade Center was a burial site, hallowed ground, sacred, and that it must be defended. They promised that their people would be there until the last of their missing was found. All of this was explicitly personalized: A retired fire captain, Bill Butler, told the crowd, "My son Tommy, from Squad 1, is still in that building, and we haven't gotten to him yet." The crowd replied with the chant "Bring Tommy home!" ("Firefighters in angry," 2001).[2]

The Mayor's Office, under whose command the police were working, described the site as a hazardous workplace, where greater control was needed over the number of people and the movement of people and equipment on site. The contrast of instrumental rationality and universalism, on the one hand, and the logic of the sacred and personalism, on the other, could not have been more clear. Still, how did the firemen come to represent the position they held? How did a department of rules, ranks, orders, command, and control come to represent the opposition to instrumental rationality?

The Fire Department may be normatively structured by ranks, commands, and so on, but firehouse life is not so dominated; comradeliness and personalism dominate. On the morning of 9-11, volunteerism and personal, more than official, responsibility and risk were prevalent. Significant parts of the confusion at the scene were produced by fire crews arriving without orders and proceeding to work under no one's command. Fire stations were left abandoned because no one on duty would remain behind. Some number of the firefighters killed were actually off duty.

The personalistic element grew with the rescue operations and was finally sanctioned by an official policy that any fire department personnel who wanted to work rescue and recovery could. On the first days, almost any guy with work clothes and tools could get into the site; certainly any firefighter could. In that setting, the New York City firefighters were the kings. They were the ones with uniforms, experience, official local sanction, and some semblance of a command structure. The *New York Times* put it frankly: The firefighters owned the site—and although they were officially supposed to be there, their account of their presence was personalistic. Their brothers were under that rubble and they were going to get them out. Again, fire department policy sanctioned that: Any off-duty firefighters that asked to work recovery were granted permission. They were not ordered to Ground Zero; they were granted permission to go.

By early November, most of the action was done, and there were large numbers of firefighters standing by, waiting for the sighting of human remains. Why were they not willing to leave, or at least take turns? For the firefighters, Ground Zero was not a zero—there was not a nothing there. Even months later, in May, when the bodies and body parts had long been found and all that remained was dirt and ash and even that was flattened and scraped and driven over and hauled off, even then that was not undifferentiated ground. The bureaucracy could see the ground in terms of its probabilities of yielding recoverable body parts versus injury to workers and bystanders. In such terms, this ground could be compared to any other ground. "Where there is no differentiation there is no defilement" (Douglas, 1978, p. 160). For the firefighters, however, this ground was unlike any other, irreconcilable by any terms. This ground was radically differentiated from all others and capable of being differentiated within itself: This bit of it was more valuable than that; those were ruins, these were relics; that was dirt, this was ash.

And yet . . . Where were those bodies? What had become of those brothers? Was blood transformed to ash so completely? And how then could you tell this from that? Any shovelful might be the valuable shovelful.

After putting their volunteers on a schedule and limiting the numbers a bit, the Fire Department was allowed to continue with dozens of firefighters observing the full recovery operation, standing at the ready to drape a flag over a stretcher and form a recessional salute to every part sizable enough to stand for a body. On the last day, May 30, when the recovery period at the site was officially declared completed, the firefighters orchestrated the ceremony. The last flag-draped but otherwise empty stretcher was carried past lines of silent, saluting firefighters and police officers, in the same sort of recessional ceremony used so many times before. At the end, it appeared, then, that firefighters represented the victims, victims' families, rescue and recovery, and witnesses as well. (Although there was a second closing ceremony for the families on June 2, it was explicitly private and without official City presence. It received much less media coverage. There were also bits of ceremony and publicity in coming weeks as the unofficial but actual last firefighters left the scene, the nearby Fire Department identification center was closed, the landfill was closed, and so on.) From beginning to end, then, the firefighters represented a public; they represented all who received the blow or witnessed its destructive force, who felt it as a strike against their first-person collectivity, against "us." The firefighters represented the sentimental, irrational, unofficial interest of the symbolic citizens of the site, all those bound to it by their sense of trauma or witnessing from whatever their position in the events of the day and the flow of representations out of New York. The firefighters were, for that public, their human presence on the unempty ground at Ground Zero.

## Manly Men Who Cry

Like everything else in this story, there is another facet to the role of the inside-outsiders. The firemen were not just antiofficial insiders, they did not just represent sentimentality and irrationality against the bureaucracy; they were also pictured as manly men who cry. They were, on the one hand, hypermasculine men: large, strong, deep voiced, with rough faces, sweaty skin, and adorned in dirty, heavy, work clothes. There were, apparently, no women. These firemen were, on the other hand, repeatedly pictured with sad, distant stares, with heads hanging, with eyes glistening, or even openly crying. When interviewed, they were repeatedly represented either discussing their losses and their sadness or rather more inarticulately not knowing what to do. There was a great release of representations of men hugging, standing arm in arm, talking about their relationships and their feelings.

One scene from a documentary that aired around the time of the anniversary showed a firefighter in a blue t-shirt, looking everything like a regular working guy, sitting a bit slumped and tired at a table with open notebooks in front of him—not upright at a desk like someone who is accustomed to paperwork. He spoke to the interviewer, not to the camera like someone who is accustomed to media interviews. He rubbed his head and spread his arms, palms up, shoulders shrugged; "I don't know what I'm doing," he said. "I've never planned one funeral before, and now I have to plan eight." Such an ordinary guy with such an extraordinary responsibility—soldiering forth and yet voicing the frustrated cry we have all felt but tried not to speak: Why me? Why now? I can't carry this load.

## Why Fire*men*, Specifically?

New York City had unusually few female firefighters in 2001 (29, to be exact), their roles in fighting skyscraper fires were limited, and none of them died on 9-11. Averages of body size and muscle mass, as well as tradition and presumption, put more men than women in rescuer roles during times of physical danger. More men than women were then likely to be owed thanks, more likely to have risked self-sacrifice, and more likely to be lauded as heroes. The hero story itself is historically cast with a male lead. Given how few female firefighters there were in New York, even pictures of crowds of surviving firefighters would seldom show a female face.

Journalists who would have used circumspectly nonsexist language on September 10, lost "firefighter" from their vocabulary for months afterward, as if there were only fire*men* in the whole of New York City and only women and children among their families. This was part of a larger pattern of unleashing of prefeminist, and pre–new-economy, images of masculinity and of female sideline support and nourishment. Male volunteers worked in the pit; female volunteers cooked, massaged, bandaged, and talked with the lonely, tired men.

This trend reached a peak of sorts with dating stories spread through interpersonal networks and reported in the New York press. For example, Nino's, a downtown restaurant, remained open serving free food and providing a resting place for rescue workers after 9-11. It quickly became widely known for this and became a prestigious volunteer slot discussed on society pages. Nino's maintained a waiting list of people wanting to cook and serve food, and stretching into the fall and winter there were reports of people flying into New York from around the country for their volunteer day at Nino's. It was striking that essentially all of the Nino's volunteers were (it was reported) single young women dressed for dating. Many talked explicitly, the story goes, about their desires to date a fireman. An invitation to a private, guided tour of Ground Zero was most coveted. The veracity or generalizability of such stories is not the issue. The fact that they circulated enough to be reported in the legitimate press illustrates an important aspect of the symbolic role of the firemen in the months after 9-11 ("To serve and," 2001).

Along with the "men" of the fire department came the widows and children. The Fire Department's survivors' benefit was called the widows and orphans fund. The first time I read the term I thought I had been transported to a cowboy movie somewhere. Did people still talk that way? In the *New York Times?* They did after 9-11. Although it is true that no women of the Fire Department were killed on 9-11, it could have happened. Is the Fire Department and the press that covers it really so unprepared that they have no vocabulary for naming the survivors of a female worker? Can no one in the Fire Department name any beneficiaries other than women and children? No male partners? No fathers? And is everyone guaranteed children?

So dominating became the image of male victims and female and child survivors that President Bush in an interview broadcast by CBS on September 10, 2002, recounted a meeting with victims' families in which there was apparently no one but children remembering their dads and wives remembering their husbands. His memory was apparently clogged by the symbolic dominance of The Firemen, and their widows and children, in the intervening months.

The prototypical image of a rescue worker came quickly to look like the construction workers in Ford and Chevy truck commercials. Heavy, dirty clothes; sweaty skin; hardhats; square jaws; slim hips; and muscled shoulders. Whatever their look, these construction workers turned rescue and recovery workers were nearly as lauded as the firemen. What did they have in common? The construction workers did not die; they did not run into the burning building when others were running out. What they and the firemen had in common is that they touched death. The manly men whose image must have been so important in the months after September 11 to be granted license from the usual strictures against sexism were manual men, men who touch. What they touched was inappropriate death, the literal and symbolic remains of which needed to be put away. That hygienic behavior was also a ritual cleaning that was aided, apparently, by having its attendants portrayed as rather old-fashioned, masculine heroes.

The specific masculinity of these firefighters also worked as a kind of catalyst or accelerant on several of the other symbolic functions of The Firemen. The hypermasculinity of the representation of these sentimental, irrational, mourning, victims' families could not have been better for licensing the audience's own perfectly healthy needs for sentimental, irrational, mourning. On the one hand, the widows and orphans fund, on the other, the fireman-as-victim and family. Strength, resolve, and perseverance really do go well with sentimental surrender.

## Conclusion: Paradox and Representation

The firefighters in New York City were a social paradox in the period after September 11, a multi-faceted symbol that presented two contraries from any view. They were rescuer-victims, citizen-soldiers, inside-outsiders, sentimental-officials, masculine men who cry, and more; they became a multivalent symbol, The Firemen, that could be everything to all people. More perfect, this symbol was everything and its opposite too. Each thing the firefighters represented seemed to magnify the power of the next. In this sense they were not just an open text, usefully available to multiple interpretations; it was as if they were coded for that and more: a tool for thinking through socially necessary paradoxes. (We must remember that the firefighters we are discussing are not concrete individual men and women but social representations, a symbol, its logic, and its use, although that symbol may itself be represented by a concrete, individual man or woman.)

The Firemen as represented on TV, in newspapers and magazines, in talk and imagination, were a powerful symbol of paradox, and they were not just one paradox but many. The public was not looking at that symbol for its paradoxes, though. They were looking through that symbol and its paradoxes for the contact it provided with something else: the serious life, the vital center, ultimate questions. The firefighters represented this for us even as they crossed the lines and worked with their hands in that haunted dirt at the center of our impact zone.

In the public's response to this act of war against civilians in a place at peace, The Firemen symbol and the individual firefighters were border crossers and death touchers. They represented the public, the citizenry in intimate contact with the most vital questions of life: Who keeps it? When does death come? They performed and represented cultural repair work as the categories of citizen and soldier; peace and war; workplace, tourist attraction, and battlefield; air travel and weapon of mass destruction; duty, loyalty, rationality, and sentiment as all this and more was resorted after 9-11.

## Notes

1. This quotation was taken from a page on the official New York City Web site April 9, 2002. The page (http://www.nyc.gov/html/oem/html/other/frozen) no longer exists.

2. Other relevant details discussed in this section of the paper were reported in a series of *New York Times* stories, from this one on November 3 through November 17.

## References

Dilthey, W. (1976). *Selected writings* (H. P. Rickman, Ed.). Cambridge, England: Cambridge University Press.

Douglas, M. (1978). *Purity and danger: An analysis of concepts of pollution and taboo.* London: Routledge & Kegan Paul.

Durkheim, É. (1995). *The elementary forms of the religious life* (K. E. Fields, Trans.). New York: Free Press. (Original work published 1912)

Eliade, M. (1959). *The sacred and the profane: The nature of religion.* New York: Harcourt Brace Jovanovich.

Eliade, M., & Sullivan, L. E. (1987). Hierophany. In M. Eliade (Ed.-in-Chief), *Encyclopedia of religion* (Vol. 6, pp. 313-317). New York: Macmillan.

Firefighters block a plan for statue in Brooklyn. (2002, January 18). *New York Times*, p. B4.

Firefighters in angry scuffle with police at Trade Center. (2001, November 3). *New York Times*, p. A1.

Geertz, C. (1988). *Works and lives: The anthropologist as author.* Stanford, CA: Stanford University Press.

Goffman, E. (1961). *Asylums: Essays on the social situation of mental patients and other inmates.* Chicago: Aldine.

Marvin, C., & Ingle, D. W. (1999). *Blood sacrifice and the nation: Totem rituals and the American flag.* New York: Cambridge University Press.

Remains of a day. (2002, September 9). *Time.*

Ricoeur, P. (1981). *Hermeneutics and the human sciences* (J. B. Thompson, Ed. & Trans.). Cambridge, England: Cambridge University Press.

Three firefighters say flag came from yacht. (2002, April 2). *New York Times*, p. B3.

To serve and flirt near Ground Zero. (2001, December 9). *New York Times*, sec. 9, p. 1.

Turner, V. (1977). *The ritual process: Structure and antistructure.* Ithaca, NY: Cornell University Press.

van Gennep, A. (1960). The rites of passage (M. B. Vizedom & G. L. Caffee, Trans.). Chicago: University of Chicago Press. (Original work published 1908)

# 18

# MYTHS TO THE RESCUE

## How Live Television Intervenes in History

TAMAR LIEBES AND MENAHEM BLONDHEIM

Political commentators and cultural critics see September 11 as a catastrophic event after which "life would never be the same" (Didion, 2003). It is talked about as an "event that changed the course of history for the US." The death of more than 3000 people can arouse public empathy and unite the community around the victims and their families but cannot at first glance be thought to have changed history. This means that more than the horrific loss of life and physical damage caused by the Al Qaeda terrorists, it was the *symbolic* meaning invoked by the collapse of the Twin Towers and the mode of experiencing it that translated September 11 into a historical landmark.[1] The unexpected but deliberate shattering of a powerful icon adds a sense of humiliation and vulnerability to empathy, depriving the public of any illusion of fast or easy closure. Moreover, the sudden experience of tragedy and the practically simultaneous and universal exposure to it via mass media made the events of 9-11 a collective shock, generating the public notion of a shattering of the status quo and launching of a new departure. These symbolic and narrative elements place the icon of the falling Towers in a line with earlier events, experienced via media, which occupy a place of their

own in public memory. Such events can be catastrophes, natural or manmade; they can also be moments of great historical achievements of the human spirit.

For a number of decades, until the 1990s, the networks interrupted their routine schedules almost only for the latter type—preplanned ritual events, or events that represented major social, political, or technological breakthroughs for humanity (the moon landing, Egypt's president Sadat's visit to Jerusalem, and the collapse of the Berlin Wall), invoking a sense of collective gratification, even euphoria (Dayan & Katz, 1993). Since the 1990s, however, television schedules are also being interrupted for the broadcast of unplanned breaking news, typically major disasters (Liebes, 1998). Like traditional media events, these major disruptive events, paradoxically, also unite the collective, albeit through shared fear and shared mourning. Both types of events shower society with symbolic meanings, some of which cross societal boundaries to become universal symbols. As in the case of prearranged media events, the impact of catastrophes such as the explosion of the Challenger on takeoff and the Columbia on landing, the Kennedy and Rabin assassinations, the near disaster at Three Mile Island, and the real one in downtown New York on September 11, 2001, cannot be separated from the manner of their mediation and the ways in which they are experienced by the public at large.

In what follows, (a) we look at how television, normally the most pedestrian of media, transforms itself and its audiences by recognizing events as "historic" (in advance or while they are happening). (b) We observe two parallel but opposite events: The heroic visit of Egypt's President Sadat to Jerusalem (1977) and bin Laden's attack on the United States (2001), both pronounced as historic by their perpetrators, serving as commentators, and analyze their visual and verbal rhetoric. (c) We point to the practice of framing historic events through instant recognition of their transformative nature and by invoking distant historical or mythic archetypes. Whereas in both case studies the event is regarded as a watershed, in terms of causing a transformation of mental states (on the personal and collective levels), the competing versions of the ensuing public debate differ on whether the event drew public discourse "back into history" or "leached us" out of history.

## TRANSFORMING "MONITORING" VIEWERS INTO AN ACTIVE PUBLIC

When the bells are ringing and the princess gets married (or buried), or, *mutatis mutandis*, when disaster strikes and the towers collapse, everyday television comes to life like a Cinderella transformed. Exit bitsy, distracted, daily TV, rattling in the background, broadcasting to absent-minded, bored viewers, some watching but none noticing. Enter focused, amazed, and/or horrified TV, which grabs viewers from whatever they were doing and glues them to the little screen.

Notwithstanding newer, more technically sophisticated communication technologies, television still reigns supreme in its ubiquity, its accessibility, and the minimal effort it demands from viewers (Kubey & Csikszentmihalyi, 1990). This immense popularity gets no respect: Media scholars are prone to place television low

on their list in terms of the medium's capacity to actively involve viewers. Demoted to the marginal status of "wallpaper" (Liebes & Katz, 1993), television is perceived as useful for peripheral monitoring of the world outside, whereas novels and films–media that demand a greater investment in time, money, and cognitive or emotional energy—are thought to inspire "real" involvement (Booth, 1982; Chatman, 1981; Meyerowitz, 1985). We derive a sense of identity as individuals not from television but from books, says Meyrowitz. Unlike television (and film), says Booth, it is from books that we can follow ethical and philosophical debates of important social issues.

We glance at the little screen, says John Ellis (1994), to be reassured that the hurly-burly of daily life is rushing on, that there is no catastrophe pending. TV allows us to glimpse the uncertainty and craziness outside while "we" remain safely tucked in at home, our sanity intact. This description does not belittle the significance of the TV set in our lives. It does mean that television's importance lies not in enslaving viewers to actually watch it but in its capacity to *release* them from watching. It looks after us, as it were, acting as a buffer between our lives and what we are witness to (Lazarsfeld & Merton, 1948). This view may be a variant of the notion of television as the grown-up's "transitional object" (Silverstone, 1994). *As the World Turns* and Dan Rather signal stability in a world threatened by chaos. The few seconds it takes to glance at the set at any given time are sufficient to conclude that the world is churning on and that the Twin Towers are "still there," dominating the New York skyline.

But there are moments in which television disengages from its wallpaper marginality to reinstate itself at the center of living rooms and souls. It can rally the community or the nation, sometimes the world, around the current Olympics or, more often, the current disaster, sometimes reinventing the community (or the nation or the world). Casual viewers become intensely engaged and are joined by uncounted others who are alerted to the broadcast via other media, such as the cellular phone (Katz & Rice, 2003). With ratings exploding, the public is riveted to the screen, glance turns into gaze, and people seek company watching their TVs, as media and public face the unsolved issue that haunts their society. We refer to these kinds of events, unraveled by TV in real time, as "history making." Because they are history, the whole world watches, and, because the whole world is watching, they are crystallized into history.

As in the case of media events, in live disaster coverage, television transforms viewers into active and involved publics. In disasters, however, television takes on a much more active and critical role than in preplanned events. It becomes not only the stage on which the event is played out but the producer and mediator of the ongoing event. Live performance of such high-profile moments and the capacity to rally nationwide (sometimes worldwide) constituencies are integral to the experiencing of the event and, ultimately, to the way in which it is remembered. Only much later do we learn what "really" happened behind the drama on the screen. It was the collective sharing of the event in real time, however, through one single narrative, that made audiences feel part of a "historic event." Only the partnership between TV and its expanded audience can make such a truly public event possible; only the de facto partnership between TV and the event's perpetrators can put the show and its appropriate rhetoric on the road.

Like media events, the experience of disaster is of "one of those moments in which history splits, and we define the world as 'before' and 'after.'"[2] At these moments, in which the taken-for-granted collapses, television audiences are lifted above the daily drudgery. They envision new horizons for society, are traumatized by the uncanny, and look to television for news and also for much more. But whereas the success of media events is due to the union of establishment and broadcasters (Dayan & Katz, 1993), *disaster marathons*, brought about by an outside power (natural or human), surprise establishment and media alike, sometimes paralyzing the establishment, leaving media in charge

of lost and horrified viewers (Blondheim & Liebes, 2002, 2003).

On such momentous occasions, television gives expression to the experience its breaking news had launched. Broadcasters maneuver this fragile, liminal community of distraught viewers gathered round the set, horrified by human brutality or intensely identifying with human suffering. In such moments, media professionals need to resort to some instant, familiar script that befits the occasion, one that evokes the greatness or the gruesomeness of the experience at the same time that it shares the elation or despair of the viewers. In such cases, the script must be instantly recognizable.

## THE SCRIPTING OF RITUAL EVENTS AND CATASTROPHES

In the case of preplanned ceremonial events, professionals have a script to follow. This script emerges from the voluntary contract they had made with the powers that be, and although they may resent it, broadcasters play their reverent roles. In disasters, the script disappears altogether. Reporters, anchors, and editors, caught by surprise on air, have to create a tentative script then and there, constantly reassessing and adapting the narrative as they go along. It is a dual process of unraveling the script of the antagonist and of producing their own script against the grain. Media events compromise professional norms by uncritically aligning broadcasters with the establishment. In disaster, professionalism is compromised by a move in the direction of the audience.

The media are as bewildered as the viewers in these events—unscheduled eruptions rob them of the advance knowledge that characterizes news editing. In this way, media professionals become part of the public at large. As high-profile figures standing in, as it were, for the equally surprised powers that be, media professionals are at higher risk as potential targets (recall those news professionals who became targets for anthrax). By abandoning professional distance and allowing themselves to disclose personal emotions—expressing surprise and horror, identifying with the suffering victims—reporters and anchors tend to abandon the stance of disinterested objectivity.

The switch from routine coverage to catastrophe coverage happens with the realization that the event that is transpiring should be "grasped as history . . . not only as chronology and narrative" (Carey, 2002). Thus, on September 11, the daily style of coverage, signifying a sense of professional control and continuity (in turning from one item to another, equally important or unimportant), broke down. That happened at the moment the second plane hit the towers, cruelly ending the putative framing of "major accident" and acknowledging a phenomenon that could not be dealt with by routine conventions. From the moment in which ABC's correspondent exclaimed: "Oh, my God, that looks like another plane," the show switched from "chronology" to "history." This was evidenced in the exclusivity of the event (filling the whole screen, erasing of other news, let alone advertisements), in the emotional performance of reporters (allowing themselves to lose their cool—"it is terrifying, awful," "Good Lord, it just. . . ."), in the collapse of taken-for-granted reality they conveyed. Ultimately, the sense of history in the making was seen in anchors' and commentators' quest for major landmarks on the cultural horizon that might give meaning to the perplexing event without sacrificing its uniqueness.

Before placing the responsibility for the "mythic" framing on media professionals only, it should be remembered that what characterizes both ritual events and catastrophes, in contrast to the genre of news, is the endowment of the perpetrators with enormous power to put their own mark on the way in which the event is interpreted. A closer look into the cases of Anwar Sadat's landing live in Jerusalem and bin Laden's emissaries exploding live in New York illustrates the creative use made by the protagonists—one on stage, one backstage—of the long hours allocated to them in the public eye. Riveting the audience, these two men were out to conquer; they were the source of inspiration for the action

(Sadat directly, bin Laden indirectly), involving mythic allusions and ancient visions.

## MOBILIZING TELEVISION AND INVOKING MYTHIC ICONS: THE OPPOSITE VISIONS OF SADAT AND BIN LADEN

A look at the mobilization of television in the cases of September 11, 2001, and Anwar Sadat's visit to Jerusalem in 1977 (following the Yom Kippur war)—treated here as structurally similar, but diametrically opposite, case studies—will serve to demonstrate the political implications of media acceptance of the perpetrators' definition of the situation, thereby relinquishing professional responsibility. We proceed by showing how the two perpetrators situated themselves within a "larger than life" paradigm (in the sense of the planned effect of their acts), moving on to observe the rhetoric inherent in their staged performance and verbal strategies and those of the reporters on the spot, as well as by subsequent commentators. Our focus is on the way in which the two protagonists set up the event, their own performance, and their planning of the event's media coverage throughout; notably, on their method of ensuring a transformative experience. Both cases, we suggest, illustrate the effectiveness of a strike on prevailing consciousness, the strategy of a performative "leaping out" of the immediate historical processes and invoking the distant past and ancient archetypes.

In juxtaposing the events of Jerusalem and New York, the first step is to acknowledge their dissimilarity. The two protagonists, Sadat and bin Laden, were oriented toward diametrically opposite courses. bin Laden was bent on general anarchy and destruction, in which no negotiation was possible and in which the final unilateral goal could be only achieved in some mythic future. Sadat was engaged in a project of negotiating with the enemy, for which, he reckoned, a dramatic "psychological" breakthrough was needed. However, there were striking similarities in the double play each had to perform vis-à-vis two kinds of audiences.

The respective acts of the two protagonists were played on the home court of "the enemy," each performer knowing full well that although the whole world was watching, only two constituencies really mattered: the opponent, and the home-team fans. Sadat's act vis-à-vis his opponent was the trickier of the two: He had to transform public opinion in a country in which he was seen as the arch-enemy. At the same time, he had to prevent potential opposition in his own country from destroying his effort. He knew he had a chance to convince the Israeli public, used to heated debates and changing policies, but having to contain potentially dangerous opposition within Egypt made achieving the first goal all the more complex. bin Laden's task vis-à-vis the enemy was straightforward enough: It was to succeed in delivering a blow spectacular enough to change the status quo and change hearts and minds in both Occident and Orient.

Unlike Sadat, who had to walk the tightrope of convincing Israelis without alienating Egyptians, bin Laden could deliver an unequivocal message. As a leader of a movement striving for an Islamic revolution in different countries, with no official standing anywhere, he had nothing to lose. Moreover, far from proposing a revolutionary outlook, he drew on conservative religious sentiments. Infiltrating the politics and social organization in Moslem countries, however, could be achieved only by a supremely effective mobilization of media. By demonstrating his power to strike the "infidels," taking a free ride on their screen, as it were, bin Laden stood to capture symbolic influence, the only potential resource for mobilizing support for a revolution by hundreds of millions of Moslems deprived of any hope for a better life.

## Mobilizing Media: Sadat, bin Laden, and the Adversary's Television

Both perpetrators counted on television to promote their project and to maximize its impact. Both made sure they delivered the goods—a performance not to be missed. In the context of a preplanned performance, broadcast live, Dayan and

Katz see the show as proceeding in a five-phase process. The build toward the climax begins with a *latency* stage, in which the tension leading to the climactic event is only dormant. The latent issue emerges on the public agenda with a prospect of its resolution in a phase of *signaling*. The proposed resolution explodes on public consciousness via a dramatic symbolic event *modeling* the new departure. The act both proclaims it and rushes it forcefully to the center of a new public agenda. A phase of verbal explication, or *framing*, of the overall meaning of the dramatic event that models the proposed new departure is closely linked to the event; it may even be an integral part of it. Finally, the event itself reverberates throughout the societies involved and is digested by them with the collective evaluation of their meanings and effects.

The latent background for Sadat's act was the stalemate between Egypt and Israel, both exhausted in the aftermath of the Yom Kippur war. The rise of the right wing to power in Israel's 1977 elections led to a process of secret signaling, then covert negotiations, and even tentative agreements between the two sides. In the course of negotiations, it became clear that a major, dramatic event was necessary to change minds on both sides; in other words, signaling would have to be extended to the greater public. To extend signaling to that public, Sadat announced his daring initiative to visit Jerusalem in November 1977, on American TV. Telling his friend Walter Cronkite, and the rest of us, that he would go to the end of the world, even to Jerusalem, to put an end to war, he produced a no less public invitation from Prime Minister Menachem Begin. The visit was planned as a friendly act, intended to offer Israel diplomatic recognition in return for territorial concessions. For the Israeli public and even Israeli media, miraculously unaware of the foreplay, the gesture was just as inconceivable as bin Laden's terrorist attack.[3]

Revealing acute media acumen, Sadat made live coverage of Israeli television, throughout, a condition of his visit. His strategy of talking to the Israelis as if "over the heads" of their government (and then over the heads of Israelis to his own people), addressing the enemy in the second person—as "you," rather than "they"—was the essence of the move. It provided evidence not only of the power of face-to-face encounters but also of the potential power of television to create a transformation in the reality of conflict.

Television's live broadcast throughout was the key element in enabling Sadat to model his visit to Jerusalem as a romantic conquest of the hearts of Israelis. Talking to Israelis in real time; his creative use of ancient historical texts to "prove" a common origin and a common history for the two peoples; and the omitting of elements of competition, conflict, and contradiction were the necessary framing. Sadat presented his own persona as a hero who, by virtue of having taken huge risks for the attainment of peace, had the moral right to demand an even bigger sacrifice from his hosts. His decision to take the trip, he told whomever would listen, was made against the advice of his closest advisers. Invoking the American icon of the lone cowboy who rides unarmed into the enemy camp, the shrewd Sadat was well aware that the danger lay less with Israelis[4] than within the extremists in his own camp. And, it worked. Sadat's charm; his charismatic personality; and, paradoxically, his not giving up on the tough territorial conditions he demanded in return for his offer of symbolic goods (that is, for recognition) convinced Israelis that he was sincere.[5]

As in the case of Sadat, the effect of bin Laden's attack depended to a great extent on its being broadcast live. In contrast to Sadat's visit, which was preceded by a bilateral process of *signaling* before the grand crescendo of *modeling* and *framing*, in bin Laden's case the preliminary steps were essentially unilateral. The gulf between the Western and Islamic worlds and the increasing contact between them through processes of globalization constituted the latent tension leading to the September 11 drama. bin Laden's side was much more aware of this problem than the other side. The phase of signaling before bringing the tension to a head was once again mainly unilateral. The failed 1993 attack on the Twin Towers; the 1997 attacks on

American embassies; and, in 2000, the attack on the *U.S. Cole* were clear signals of a pending—desperate and hopeless—"war" on America. The signals seem to have been directed only to, and regrettably decoded only by, extremists in the Arab world. After all, disaster, unlike ceremonial event, is unexpected by the victim. Hence the complete shock of the 9-11 attacks to Americans and Westerners.

Modeling the new departure he wanted to bring about, bin Laden once again would act unilaterally. He could count on the cooperation of an inadvertent accomplice in the other camp—media in general and television in particular. In Sadat's case, the dramatic event could be presented as if it had been decided on spontaneously; in actuality, it depended on the voluntary cooperation of the media (and the Israeli government). bin Laden's project, although hinged on complete surprise, could rely on media's practice of the routinizing of the unexpected, provided the event was ruthless, tragic, and traumatic enough to justify TV's cooperation. Even then, however, the symbolic impact needed the right images. Although the professional camera was almost sure to miss the attack on the first tower, there was potential for the camera to be there for the attack on the second (17 minutes later), documenting and showing it in real time.[6] Whether by stroke of luck or by the precise carrying out of meticulous planning and timing, this potential materialized.

By these contrasting means, both Sadat and bin Laden managed to undermine the status quo. They both needed more than that, however: Their ultimate success would depend on sustaining the aftershock of their dramatic move, launching, in effect, a new reality. Indeed, the two managed to bring about the kind of media cooperation that far exceeded the high-profile event, the kind that would live for a few days in the ordinary "Breaking News" genre (Wolfsfeld, 2004). Sadat, through inspiring words and brilliant diplomatic maneuvers, managed to make his Jerusalem visit the opening act of—in fact a model for—a high-profile diplomatic process, which would reign for months over headlines, ultimately leading to the implementation of the script he had imprinted on the minds of Israelis through the transformative event he staged.

If Sadat's tools in sustaining a new consciousness were words and high-visibility gestures, bin Laden took the opposite tack: His weapons for controlling the agenda were near silence and the provocative shadow of invisibility. By lurking enigmatically behind the scene, he managed an event that would provide him exclusivity for days and would dictate the political agenda for months, maybe for years to come. By leaving open the questions of who and why, as well as of where next and when next, he prevented closure and raised suspense. His outlandish shadow cast a mysterious nonpresence as large and as captivating as Sadat's charismatic and charming persona.

## MODELING: SYMBOLIC UNDERPINNINGS OF THE EVENTS

The performances of Sadat and bin Laden were directed at their respective antagonists—the Israeli and American publics. Both Sadat's itinerary of gestures and bin Laden's itinerary of destruction started with the sight of a vessel coming out of heaven. For Israelis, seeing the Egypt Airways jetliner descend from heaven to earth, then move to join a staircase with the El Al insignia (causing Bob Simons, then of CBS, to exclaim "will miracles never cease?") was a dream come true (Dayan & Katz, 1993). In diametrical opposition to this fairy tale from heaven, Americans witnessed, with the horrified shock of a nightmare, jetliners from the sky above descending, then gliding smoothly into the WTC. The destruction itself seemed immaculate, with no villain and a horrifyingly few injured individuals and distorted human remains in sight. Both New York's landmarks and their inhabitants vanished as though by the stroke of a ghostly wand.

Sadat mobilized a variety of rhetorical resources for his mission: He enlisted the various symbolic elements of the ancient and new scenery around Jerusalem, in a careful mix that balanced Muslim and Jewish-Israeli signifiers. Thus, during his 3-day visit, he paid tribute to the sacred symbols of Jews and Muslims—praying in the al Aqsa Mosque, visiting Yad vaShem, the Jewish memorial for the holocaust, and placing a wreath in the national military graveyard. He also appealed to primordial universal feelings and family ties. Shaking the hands of his enemies from the Yom Kippur war who had gathered in line to receive him at Ben Gurion airport, he received a present from Golda Meir (prime minister at the time of that war), "from a grandmother to a new grandfather," and responded by admitting, with a smile, that he used to call her "the old lady." Sadat thus attempted to convey the fundamental humanity common to him and to his hosts, graciously trying to establish rapport.

In parallel to the euphoria caused by the miracle of seeing Sadat in Jerusalem, bin Laden created a larger than life national trauma that owed as much to choreography and casting as to the actual damage done. His choice of targets that symbolized the American spirit was inseparable from the method chosen for demolishing them: human beings in the role of a Trojan horse. This was an unthinkable twist by the standard of the American ethos symbolized by the Twin Towers. Just as awe striking, however, were the killer angels' tools in trade, which were chillingly familiar: They were the workaday vehicles of the routine system of modern transport, which could be relied on for getting to the right place at the right time, derailed and subverted by weapons purchasable in any dollar store. The creative genius here was in attaching the enemy's most mundane systems to generate the closest thing to a miraculous execution and produce the appropriate pictures for the greatest horror show ever played on TV or generated by Hollywood's creative minds.

In effect, the weapon was in itself a demonstration of the message of the event. Undiscoverable, it lay in the religious psyche and motivations of the suicide pilots, far beyond the comprehension of the host culture and unfathomable by the institutional infrastructures on which the attackers piggybacked. Thus the mechanics of the attack were a model of the ultimate incompatibility between the two antagonists, symbolizing the impossibility of any communication between bin

Laden and his followers and secular, open, Western civilization.

The targets of choice could easily be identified as icons of American, and global, television, and, presumably, for the genre of Disaster Marathon, with the power of exploding twice: first, in conveying the initial, shocked, gut reaction ("My god, I don't believe I am saying this. . . ." to quote Yaron Wilenski of *Galatz* Radio on September 11); later, in the more reflexive readings that decoded and interpreted the primordial and mythic meanings conveyed by the vanished icons and by the missing perpetrators. At least as important as presenting to the United States and the West a model of a war to come was bin Laden's message to his own people. By successfully and devastatingly striking at Western icons, he could signal to his own side that the mission of toppling the West was not impossible.

Sadat, in his media performance, presented himself as the hero, fully responsible for his own epic initiative. bin Laden, at various times, chose the more humble and ambiguous role of apostle of, and sometimes mere commentator on, a godly process. Unlike any other commentator, strictly limited to a particular event and to a point in time (with words that tomorrow might sound old and irrelevant), the videotapes that surfaced periodically with what might or might not be bin Laden's voice conveyed general ideological thinking and were therefore equally relevant or irrelevant at any time, serving as a diversion more than a fundamental aspect of his project. In that sense, they mystified more than clarified.

## SEPTEMBER 11: "BACK INTO HISTORY" OR "LEACHED US OF HISTORY"?

When the dust settled, the post-facto evaluation of September 11 had a number of foundations to build on, emerging from media representation and discourse. The first was the experience of witnessing the event on TV itself and realizing, with the improvised, emotional, and engaged text of its broadcasters as background, its monumental dimensions. Another was the (belated) voice of the presumed perpetrator making use of the world's unsatisfied curiosity over the question of "Who did it?" to market the ideological and eschatological dimensions of the catastrophe. A most significant foundation for evaluation, however, was the mythic framing of the event as proposed by publicists, pundits, and intellectuals.

Historians (at least the less romantic and more locally oriented) debated the most appropriate analogies in national experience, with Pearl Harbor often serving as point of departure, but the likes of the American Revolution and the War of 1812, even Antietam, were invoked and remembered in the effort to frame the outrage. Allusions to the Crusades and Armageddon brought religious history into play, and cultural commentators invoked structural similarities between the collapse of the Twin Towers and past cosmic disasters. The suicide bomber tactics caused one critical cultural analyst to draw on the metaphor of the biblical Samson, who brought down the pillars of a Philistine temple on himself and on his enemies. It appears that this commentator was being overgenerous, neglecting the important elements of the proxies sent by bin Laden from his relatively secure hiding place. Other observers, by invoking the Tower of Babel, highlighted the threesome of religious, communicative, and world-order transformation in what supposedly signaled a new beginning of history.[7] The myth of the ancient Tower of globalism, fraught with relevant symbolic meaning involving seemingly invincible powers and pointing to the hand of God, could be made part of a "useful history" for a shocked society, disoriented in its notions of time and space. Such icons were seized on as signifying fundamental human traits (hubris, self-destruction, self-sacrifice) or social and cultural values (eschatology, materialism, globalism). But all this exegesis had something in common: It was an attempt to locate the mammoth event in—or out—of a familiar spatial and historical landscape. This effort to make the connection between bin Laden's attack and events with similar narrative and symbolic elements may be seen as a way of writing it into history.

In contrast to viewing and interpreting daily events within the historical process of which they are a part, the surprise attack of 9-11, the context of which is still somewhat obscure, achieves its larger than life meaning from media commentators and scholars, who extract the patently mammoth happening out of context, aligning it, by what Walter Benjamin calls "tiger leaps," with distant, heavily symbolic events, seen as analogous. Such a process of framing associates the contemporary events that represent the victory of the human spirit, or its destructive potential, with historical events, or mythic texts, that belong to different times and places, by virtue of their expressing identical or similar human failures or the greatness of human spirit, on an individual or collective level.

The tiger leaps between eras and places grant freedom to invoke paradigmatically similar heroes or villains, sometimes divine (good and evil) forces with which audiences are familiar from their history books or from the mythic, ancient texts of their culture. This may be used as a rhetorical strategy for pushing the meaning of the immediate event to an unequivocal extreme. In the case of 9-11, media discourse of "mythification"—"Doomsday America," "The worst terrorist outrage in history; is this the end of the world?" (*Daily Star,* September 12, 2001, p. 48)— can serve the government by justifying military retaliation of mythic proportions.

The terms used by journalists, commentators, and media scholars in the aftermath of the September 11 attack reverberate with Walter Benjamin's (1970) idea of seeing both personal and collective history as a kind of "awakening"; that is, the raising of a "not yet conscious knowledge [of] what has been" into awareness. This model assumes that understanding of the way history works is activated in sudden flashes and leaps, to paraphrase Benjamin, as awakenings into deeper and deeper states or more profound levels of awareness—a sort of "dialectic awakening" that has no specific ending. Looked at in this light, the harsh wakening of 9-11, from a sense of security to chaos and threat, is such a "dialectic moment," suspended between the dream world of the past and the transformative energy locked in the present.

Benjamin's insight, according to which history is seen as a sudden revelation, invoked by "a moment of danger," could not be better illustrated than through the way in which veterans of the September 11 experience a new understanding of history. Cultural theorists, notably James Carey, see this as "an awakening" from "a holiday from history" in the 1990s, characterized by a vision of a united world ("one market, one culture, one politics": Carey, 2002), into the reality of an uncertain world. The process of awakening had its own stages: Recalling the mental transformation she had undergone following September 11, political writer Joan Didion (2003) described herself as operating, in the first week after the attack, in a "protective coma, sleepwalking" through her preplanned schedule. The actual moment of awakening occurred while she was reading aloud on the stage, hitting on a sentence she had written decades earlier. It was a description of New York "as no mere city" but rather as "the mysterious nexus of all love and money and power, the shining and perishable dream itself." Now, she found, she could not say the word "perishable." This, for her, was the beginning of a new phase. Thus, the process of Didion's "awakening" was neither immediate nor automatic. Her first reaction to the trauma was a numb repression. Only the invoking of an innocent, naïve, pretraumatic word from her past rushed the painful realization into consciousness.

In parallel to the new painful awareness caused by catastrophe, the euphoria of Israelis caused by Sadat's dreamlike visit produced sufficient optimistic energy for carrying out the evacuation of Israeli settlements in the Sinai peninsula (and, similarly to 9-11, the series of suicide bus bombings in 1997 were moments of "awakening," invoking flashes of structurally similar past moments in the minds of Israelis, causing another rewrite of history, for some making the Oslo process seem a misunderstanding of history).

Regardless of the contradictory interpretations regarding the meaning of the new phase, in the wake of September 11 (as in the case of Israel following the Sadat visit), commentators share the following: (a) They believe that Americans, as individuals and as a collective, have undergone a transformative experience that has radically altered their understanding of history. (b) The boundaries between describing personal intimate experience (their own feelings, the reaction of their children; Rosen, 2002), the trauma undergone by the community, and the way in which media professionals gave expression to the tragedy are blurred, and commentary shifts freely among the three. (c) The model, and terms of reference, for interpreting the experience are historical, cultural, and psychological (or rather, psychoanalytic). (d) Taking off from the perpetrators' ambitious symbolism, historical allusions sometimes move into the realm of the prehistoric or mythic, or into the realm of popular fictional figures and narratives, or customs and stories of oral tribal societies. (e) Psychoanalytic processes are made use of for looking into the collective psyche, extrapolating from Freudian mechanisms (such as repression, displacement, condensation) as they operate within the individual psyches to their expression in the culture (which moves between denial, repression, and realization of history).

Here, however, agreement ends. For certain cultural critics, the attack—"historic" by virtue of its causing a shift in the perception of history—has provided a healthy shock for journalism, and may be the beginning of releasing it from "slavish dependence on the laws of the market" (Carey, 2002). Other critics credit the entertainment industry (rather than the press!) with issuing public "warnings" before 9-11, in the form of a premonition of an inevitable sudden drop from an idyllic materialist fantasy onto a harsh "desert of the real." Big best sellers (in Hollywood—*The Truman Show, The Matrix*) were loaded with flashes of intuitive (semiconscious?) insights into the undercurrents threatening to break through the falseness of the virtual American utopia (Zizek, 2002).

Other commentators severely criticize the way in which the multiple attacks were handled by television's journalists (and in public discourse in general), both during and following the events, seeing journalism and terrorists as confined to their parts as players in the greatest show on earth and its aftermath. Joan Didion (2003) is particularly scathing, seeing the post–September 11 processing of the "single irreducible image" as a systematic effort bent on obscuring and "leaching" the image

out of history, and thus draining it of meaning, finally rendering it less readable than it seemed on the morning it happened.

In conclusion, we suggest that (a) both historical rituals and manmade catastrophes are the moments in which television steps out of its role of ensuring casual viewers that reality outside is under control and acquires the role of *conferencier,* mediator, and movable stage, rallying viewers, alternately euphoric or overwhelmed by anxiety or grief, to what is declared as a transformative event. (b) In both preplanned ceremonial events and surprise attacks, the event's initial framing is supplied by the perpetrators and accepted (in advance or after the fact, as the case may be) by television. (c) The elevation of such events beyond the workaday is achieved by television's interrupting its routine schedule, moving to live broadcasting that places its (festive or anxious) viewers in a liminal mood. Whether television collaborates with the perpetrators ahead of time or is kidnapped for the cause, the perpetrators' framing of these occasions is achieved via the performative aspects of the event, accompanied and legitimated by the invocation of primordial images and emotions (known to everyone from their own lives and families) and by the allusion to shared symbols and mythic memories as imprinted in the culture's texts, such as ancient religious works, commentaries, or fairy tales, that allude to mythic events and symbols. (d) Both in the case of preplanned ceremonial events, when TV collaborates with the powers that be, and in the case of terrorists' hijacking of the screen, when TV itself takes charge, these allusions work to integrate society around the values it shares.

## NOTES

1. The discussion of the September 11 attacks in the following text focuses on the New York theater, the more salient of the four attacks.

2. *New York Times*, September 12, 2001.

3. This, in spite of an earlier terrorist attempt on the World Trade Center and other warnings. The momentous meaning of Sadat's visit can be realized when considering contemporary diplomacy: Consider President Clinton's failed attempt to get Syria's Assad to negotiate with any

Israeli prime minister, or the fact that Egypt's Mubarak never came to Israel.

4. For the Israeli right-wing religious movement—the most extreme political faction—withdrawal from the Sinai was far less problematic than withdrawal from the West Bank, as it is not considered a part of the country to which Israelis have a historical right.

5. Daniel Dayan has argued that looking at the visit from an anthropological perspective, it can be seen in terms of what anthropologist Marcel Mauss has called "potlach" (Liebes-Plesner, 1984). It is the ceremonial visit of one African tribal chief to a nearby tribe, to which he proposes to give a present that demands mutuality of the recipients. The hosting tribe is expected to reciprocate by giving an even bigger and more expensive present than the one it has received. Otherwise, the insult is unbearable and cannot be ignored. As Egypt's demands to Israel were to give up material (territorial) gains, and the security that a buffer zone supplies, in exchange for symbolic goods (that is, the promise of legitimacy), Sadat's creation of his own persona as the hero and his framing of the visit as carrying tremendous risks for the hero were essential tactics. The setting up of the visit as a ceremony of "potlach" may have clinched the immediate transformation of public opinion.

6. Thus Israel has learned from the foreign coverage of suicide bombers who strike arbitrarily that because everything is cleaned up by the time the cameras get to the scene, coverage is limited to fleeting seconds.

7. Significant examples of rhetorical and substantive applications of the biblical story in the discourse of the Twin Tower disaster include, among many others, http://www.guardian.co.uk/saturday_review/story/0,3605, 623670,00.html;http://www.ucc.org/911/100501a.htm; http://allafrica.com/stories/200109240131.html; and Paul Frosh's "The Apocalypse Will Be Televised: A Response to Nick Couldry," at http://www.opendemocracy.org.uk/servlet/net.opendemocracy.cms.cda.utils. PDFDownload?id=13.

# References

Benjamin, W. (1970). Theses on the philosophy of history. In H. Arendt (Ed.), *Illuminations.* London: J. Cape.

Blondheim, M., & Liebes, T. (2002). Live television's disaster marathon of September 11 and its subversive potential. *Prometheus, 20*(3), 271-276.

Blondheim, M., & Liebes, T. (2003). From disaster marathon to media event: Live televison's performance on September 11, 2001, and September 11, 2002. In A. M. Noll (Ed.), *Crisis communication: Lessons from September 11.* Lanham, MD: Rowman & Littlefield.

Booth, W. (1982). The company we keep: Self-making in imaginative art old and new. *Daedelus, 111*(4), 33-59.

Carey, J. W. (2002). Globalization isn't new; anti-globalization isn't either: September 11 and the history of nations. *Prometheus, 20*(3), 289-294.

Chatman, S. (1981). What novels can do that films can't (and vice versa). In W.J.T. Mitchell (Ed.), *On narrative.* Chicago: University of Chicago Press.

Dayan, D., & Katz, E. (1993). *Media events: The live broadcasting of history.* Cambridge: Harvard University Press.

Didion, J. (2003, January 16). Fixed opinions, or the hinge of history. *New York Review of Books,* pp. 54-59.

Ellis, J. (1994). *Visible fictions.* London: Routledge.

Katz, J. E., & Rice, R. E. (2003). The telephone as a medium of faith, hope, terror, and redemption: America, September 11. In A. Michael Noll (Ed.), *Crisis communications: Lessons from September 11* (pp. 83-97). Lanham, MD: Rowman & Littlefield.

Kubey, R. W., & Csikszentymihalyi, M. (1990). *Television and the quality of life: How viewing shapes everyday experience.* Hillsdale, NJ: Lawrence Erlbaum.

Lazarsfeld, P. F., & Merton, R. K. (1948). Mass communication, popular taste, and organized social action. In L. Bryson (Ed.), *The communication of ideas.* New York: Harper.

Liebes, T. (1998). Television's disaster marathons: A danger to democratic processes? In T. Liebes & J. Curran (Eds.), *Media, ritual and identity* (pp. 71-86). New York: Routledge.

Liebes, T., & Katz, E. (1993). *The export of meaning: Cross cultural readings of* Dallas. Cambridge, England: Polity Press.

Liebes-Plesner, T. (1984). Shades of meaning in President Sadat's Knesset speech, *Semiotica, 48*(3-4), 229-265.

Meyerowitz, J. (1985). *No sense of place.* New York: Oxford University Press.

Rosen, J. (2002). September 11 in the mind of American journalism. In B. Zelizer & S. Allen (Eds.), *Journalism after September 11.* New York: Routledge.

Silverstone, R. (1994). *Television in everyday life.* London: Routledge.

Wolfsfeld, G. (2004). *Media and the path to peace.* Cambridge, England: Cambridge University Press.

Zizek, S. (2002). *Welcome to the desert of the real: Five essays on September 11 and related dates.* Tel Aviv, Israel: Resling.

# 19

# FINDING AIDS TO THE PAST

## Bearing Personal Witness to Traumatic Public Events

BARBIE ZELIZER

W e find the past compelling because of what it tells us about the present. It is no wonder, then, that nearly everyone with a voice claims territory in it—wide-ranging collectives such as nation-states; large-scale interested groups bonded by ethnicity, class, and race; professional communities driven by expertise, such as that of historians, filmmakers, and journalists. Each strives to colonize connections to the past as a way of lending credence, cohesion, or even a simple perspective to life in the present.

However, the past's compelling aspects—in particular, its lived and experienced dimensions—do not begin when we position ourselves as members of groups. Rather, they draw us already as individuals, amateur presences who connect through a personal need to interact with the past. This need makes us act in atypical ways, particularly when we face public events of a traumatic nature. Situated as bystanders to history in the making, individuals in such cases often respond in ways that are out of the ordinary. They hoard and store newspapers from events of days long past. They compile personal videotape archives of television news broadcasts from events as wide ranging as the Kennedy assassination, the Gulf War, and the death of Princess Diana. Also, as in the recent case of thousands of New Yorkers and others who painfully plodded to the site of the World Trade Center attacks, they allow time to stand still as they search for a way to respond to the trauma that unfolded there.

What is it, then, that propels actions that are so out of the ordinary yet patterned in their typicality across space and time? In this chapter, I attempt to clarify what it means to forge a personal connection with a traumatic public past and ponder whether there is a space for connecting as an individual to the past that, in turn, shapes the past's ensuing collective appropriations. The project is unevenly structured, considering two very different kinds of traumatic pasts—one long gone, another that we are still experiencing: It uses the responses by individual liberators to the liberation of the concentration camps in World War II as a template for considering the responses now being shaped to the September 11 World Trade Center attacks by residents, firefighters, police, and

**Author's Note:** This chapter is a revised version of Zelizer, B., Finding aids to the past: bearing personal witness to traumatic public events, in *Media, Culture, and Society, 24*(5), September 2002, 697-714. Reprinted with permission of Sage Publications, Inc.

emergency medical personnel. In each case, the personal need to respond to traumatic public events generates individual acts of bearing witness that unify the collective, forged primarily through one mode of documentation—photography. Photography, and the ritual practices it involves, helps individuals establish moral accountability in a way that helps them move on; in so doing, they reinstate the collective after traumatic events temporarily shatter its boundaries.

## BEARING WITNESS
## TO A TRAUMATIC PAST

Although *trauma* initially denoted a term for physical wounds causing pain and suffering, it now reflects a range of cognitive-emotional states caused by suffering and existential pain. Scholarship on public trauma first came to light during the late 19th century, when spreading industrialization and the use of technology produced industrial accidents to which the public was unaccustomed (Young, 1996). Technology increased both the occurrence of traumatic acts and access to them.

Responses to traumatic events unfold in patterned ways. Public trauma occurs when actions—wars, major disasters, and other large-scale cataclysmic events—rattle default notions of what it means morally to remain members of a collective. Individual response is key here, for individuals face fundamental questions about the collective's capacity to accommodate both the personal and group needs arising from the trauma at hand. It is no surprise, then, that when faced with public trauma, people work toward recovery by drawing on personal aspects of their identity, which remain at the core of recovery's three stages—establishing safety, engaging in remembrance and mourning, and reconnecting with ordinary life (Herman, 1992, p. 155; also Caruth, 1996; Crane, 1997; Owen & Ehrenhaus, n.d.). The connection between the individual and collective remains interdependent throughout this recovery process: Although the sense of self is rebuilt necessarily in connection with others, with recovery taking place "in the context of relationships," groups are rarely the first resource to consider in the aftermath of a traumatic

event (Herman, 1992, pp. 133, 218). Instead, the individual remains the linchpin through which the upheaval and dislocation caused by trauma begin to be replaced by shared social meanings and a renewed sense of collective purpose.

Personal response thereby marks the process of recovering from trauma. Individuals experiencing trauma tend to respond first in individuated states connected to personal roles—as parents, children, or spouses—even when asked to activate professional roles in connection with the trauma at hand.[1] A space is created within which individuals work through the encounter with trauma first as individuals and only afterward as members of a broader collective. In the cases under discussion here, photographs fill that space, facilitating the work in which individuals establish moral accountability, move on from the trauma, and in so doing help return the collective to its pretraumatic, unified state.

It has long been argued that bearing witness offers one way of working through the difficulties that arise from traumatic experience, by bringing individuals together on their way to collective recovery. Defined as an act of witnessing that enables people to take responsibility for what they see (Zelizer, 1998, p. 10; also see Irwin-Zarecka, 1994), *bearing witness* moves individuals from the personal act of "seeing" to the adoption of a public stance by which they become part of a collective working through trauma together. In Shoshana Felman's (1992) words, bearing witness is "not merely to narrate, but to commit oneself and . . . the narrative to others: to take responsibility for history or for the truth of the occurrence. . . . [It is] an appeal to community" (p. 204). The act of bearing witness helps individuals cement their association with the collective as a post hoc response to the trauma of public events that, however temporarily, shatter the collective. By assuming responsibility for the events that occurred and reinstating a shared post hoc order, bearing witness thus becomes a mark of the collective's willingness to move toward recovery.

It is fair to assume, however, that despite the impulse to come together with others, individuals remain central actors in the movement from trauma to recovery. Even as time moves on and bearing witness moves into mediated forms, the personal need to respond to trauma does not disappear. Rather, it shapes and is shaped by the collective appropriations at its side. What, then, is the personal dimension of bearing witness—and what role does photography play in its shaping?

## PHOTOGRAPHY AND BEARING WITNESS

For many, seeing (at some level) constitutes believing. In that regard, photos offer a vehicle by which individuals can see and continue to see until the shock and trauma associated with disbelieving can be worked through. This suggests that the movement from trauma to a posttraumatic space may be facilitated at least in part by photography, not only in its strategic relay—the making of photographs—but in its usage over time, as well.

The capacity to forge a personal connection with a traumatic public past depends first on the materiality of photographs, whereby photographic images stand in for the larger event, issue, or setting they are called to represent. Photographs fix memory in an accessible and easily understandable fashion, externalizing events in a way that allows us to recognize them as real, concrete proof of the events being depicted. Photography thereby aids the recall of things and events past so effectively that photos often become the primary markers of memory itself. We need only think of the broad familiarity of the image of Lee Harvey Oswald being shot by Jack Ruby to recognize how far a photograph can go when standing in for a depicted event.

Still, invoking photographs to shape a collective past has its limitations. Photos at best offer arbitrary, composite, conventionalized, and simplified glimpses of the past. They are "conventionalized, because the image has to be meaningful for an entire group; simplified, because in order to be generally meaningful and capable of transmission, the complexity of the image must be reduced as far as possible" (Fentress & Wickham, 1992, pp. 47-48). They are also schematic, lacking the detail of the images of personal memory. Collectively held images thus act as signposts within definitive limitations, directing rememberers to preferred meaning by the fastest, if not the most all-encompassing,

route. When taken together, these aspects of the image create a mnemonic frame in which people can remember with others.

The collective's ability to remember through images also depends on a recognized means of storage. For unless cultures have the "means to freeze the memory of the past, the natural tendency of social memory is to suppress what is not meaningful or intuitively satisfying . . . and substitute what seems more appropriate or more in keeping with their particular conception of the world" (Fentress & Wickham, 1992, pp. 58-59). The capacity in modern cultures to freeze, replay, and store visual memories for large numbers of people—facilitated by museums, art galleries, television archives, and other visual data banks—has enhanced our ability to make the past work for present aims. Both display and storage have personal dimensions, however, and indeed, perhaps for no one has the photograph proved as valuable as it has for the individual.

Literature on amateur photography stresses the importance of making and using images for individual purposes. Amateur photographers take photos for fun, as records, and to satisfy personal obligations. Amateur photographs help people order their memories and demonstrate cultural membership (Chalfen, 1987). They offer therapeutic value in events associated with death and grieving (Ruby, 1995), and, even in families with traumatized pasts, they unify (Hirsch, 1997). Photography thus helps individuals mobilize with others in a way that is necessary for collective working through of events experienced in common.

On such impulses are predicated the personal dimension to the response of bearing witness. The private person is involved in the two activities crucial to photography—making and using images. Bearing witness succeeds when images are made and used by individuals in patterned, often ritualized personal behavior that in turn helps cement the collective.

## Ground Performance:
## Bearing Witness to the Holocaust

The role of individuals in bearing witness was aptly illustrated following the liberation of the Nazi concentration camps in 1945. The circumstances surrounding the camps' liberation created a fertile environment for recognizing photography. The liberation of the camps was the first major traumatic event to occur after the consolidation of photography in daily news. It took place when miniature cameras were on the rise, and many soldiers went into battle with cameras in their pockets. When the camps on the western front were liberated in the spring of 1945, there was a mandate to "see" what was going on in the camps, to help people believe the circulating stories of Nazi atrocity. General Dwight Eisenhower ordered photographers within 100 miles to change course and tour the camps to take pictures of what they found inside. He arranged trips for journalists, editors, and parliamentarians, to see the camps. On the home front, newspapers and journals were urged to print the images, with people encouraged to attend sidewalk exhibits of poster-size atrocity photographs. This made the act of bearing witness into a mission to which most Americans subscribed for both individual and collective reasons, and photography helped them do it.

Liberators were not the only agent responsible for bearing witness; certainly, much has been made of the role of the media themselves in creating public awareness about the camps and Nazi atrocity (Zelizer, 1998). However, one of the untold pieces of the visual documentation of the liberation of the camps was that of amateur photography. The liberators who "opened" the concentration camps to the free world became the involuntary holders of what remains one of the most atrocious and unbelievable memories in recent history. These barbarities were rendered, through photography, into captured experience for a population that then found itself in need of working through the trauma caused by what it saw. Facing scenes that were unexpected, horrific, and beyond belief, the liberators needed to personally engage in the act of bearing witness to work through to recovery. The availability of cameras made the act of taking pictures an obvious way to respond personally to trauma.

Thus, as the liberators entered the camps, they took snapshot after snapshot of what they saw, to the extent that making and using photos would become a standard of action for responses to later traumatic public events. A veritable cottage industry emerged from the need to bear witness. This amateur photographic record produced numerous memory pamphlets, military booklets (such as *Yank*), organs of specific divisions, or pamphlets (such as the Rainbow Division's *The Badge*), and military unit histories (such as *Timberwolf Tracks,* the history of the 104th Infantry Division). Each included images taken by soldiers with private cameras during the camps' liberation. Furthermore, individual liberators compiled personal albums of the shots they took of the camps.

The amateur mission in snapping shots of the camps was largely personal, motivated by a desire to record the scenes for posterity. "What I took was there," offered one former soldier. "It was fact" (Kushlis, 1979). Photos were often taken by company commanders, who positioned members of their units so that they could be seen against the display of Nazi atrocity, and these were later made into duplicates for unit members. At times, soldiers alternated, taking photographs with each other's cameras alongside the bodies (Mercer, 1980).

This reflected a desire to record the scenes for history. As one soldier later put it, "We weren't taking pictures of each other. We were taking pictures of conditions" (Baker, 1980). One liberator, when asked to share photos he had taken of the camps, described them in a matter-of-fact fashion:

> Oh yeah. This right here is Omar Bradley. This is Walton Walker. These are some of the dead bodies, as you can see here. And this is General Patton right here. . . . I took these photos myself. These photos are so well done that there is no grain in the picture because I took them with aerial photography film. (Mercer, 1980)

On the back of the photo, he had scribbled "I took these pictures. Send them home to mother after you have seen them. Look in *Time* magazine of 14 May 1945 and you will see General Eisenhower talking to the man under the arrow." After sharing another photograph, he pointed out to his interviewer that "this is General Eisenhower, as you can see. I walked right up to him and took the picture" (Mercer, 1980).

Amateur photographs of the liberation took on a patterned photographic aesthetic that echoed the aesthetic set in place by professional photographers (see Zelizer, 1998, pp. 86-140). The aim here was clear: to construct a visual template that could help individuals take responsibility for what they saw. This was the template necessary for bearing witness.

The record produced by the amateur photographers was uneven. On the one hand, certain liberator shots were blurred and unclear. One American GI recalled that the photos he took were "dim, for I was not a photographer" (Young, n.d.). Yet other photographs resembled the shots of professional photographers, reproducing familiar scenes of boxcars of dead bodies outside Dachau, pits of bodies in Belsen, and stacks of bodies in Buchenwald that differed only by the addition of a soldier in one corner of the photo. Sometimes the amateur photos were printed in the press, although generally at a considerable delay from the time they were taken. Soldiers returning to the home front years later sent their personal photos of the camps to local newspapers for publication. One such photo, printed as part of a letter to the editor 33 years after the camps were liberated, was published in response to a book review on Dachau that then appeared in the paper (Raper, n.d.).

As with the professional photos (Zelizer, 1998), the amateur images of bearing witness produced four kinds of depictions. To begin with, they extensively and repeatedly depicted the trauma at hand. The patterned depiction of stacks of bodies, piles of human bones, and human carnage that was displayed in the popular press was repeated here. Numerous shots depicted similar views of human carnage, suggesting that soldiers lined up by turn to take snapshots of the atrocities at their side.

The act of bearing witness produced three other kinds of depictions, each of which also appeared in the popular press: depictions of people bearing witness by looking at the cause of the trauma; people looking at the cause of the trauma without evidence of the trauma; and people taking photographs of the trauma and of other people bearing witness. In the depictions of people bearing witness, the horrified faces, shocked eyes, and often gaping mouths become testaments to the core difficulties involved in the act itself. Former liberators took shots of corpses spilling from the train cars at Dachau, with GIs standing in the photos' midspace and staring at the bodies or standing around bodies in Ohrdruf. Such photos have a resonance that persists over time. For instance, in 1979, a New York Rockland County paper ran—in its sports section—a personal photo of a former liberator, a Manhattan College track coach, as he looked over the ovens in Dachau in 1945 (Varner, 1979).

Amateur photos also depicted people looking at the trauma without evidence of the trauma itself. This kind of depiction—by which the act of bearing witness was visually separated from the trauma people were experiencing and was thereby given a prolonged space within the representation—was crucial in the capacity to work through trauma. Pictures of this sort were prevalent in the popular press of 1945, when numerous photos appeared with the atrocities positioned beyond the camera frame. Here too, liberators took and kept photos of themselves looking at the atrocities that appeared nowhere in the frame. Numerous liberators kept images of themselves looking over boxcars at Dachau or stacks of bodies at Buchenwald. This kind of photo had a specific function that was relevant to the larger aims of working through the trauma; it forced viewers to fill in the blanks by connecting what they were seeing with what they did not see but knew was beyond the frame.

Finally, personally bearing witness produced depictions that showed persons looking at or taking photos of the atrocities. These depictions played a key role in working through the trauma of Nazi atrocity. For instance, one liberator was pictured in 1984 looking at personal photos he had taken of Dachau before turning them over for museum display. The accompanying story told of how he had searched for the photos for 3 years until he found where he had carefully hidden them in his attic (Markowitz, 1984).

Following the war, the photos took on a patterned importance that highlighted their ritual use for the individuals who had taken them. Many liberators hoarded their photos in places set off from the space of everyday life—in attics, basements, locked closets. One told of how he had kept his photographs in an old file cabinet in the basement and retrieved them only when interviewed about his experiences. Another kept the images "helter skelter" in a cigar box and arranged them once called upon to do so. Still other liberators participated in the voluntary destruction of their photos, tearing up the images and maintaining that they were too graphic and painful. As one liberator later recalled:

> I have destroyed many of [the photographs], and particularly those that were taken up very close to the bodies and the expressions on the faces, because of small children from time to time seeing them in my collection of pictures (Baker, 1980).

Yet others hauled their images out for periodic public viewing, at liberators' conferences or reunions of military units.

Over time, the extensive images of the trauma had a long-standing impact on the liberators' capacity to remember what had happened. Retelling the story of the liberation of the camps took on two focal points: (a) in conjunction with the photograph and (b) in conjunction with the collective. In other words, liberators remembered the camps in a way that both relied on photographs and played to shared memories of the collective. When called on to recount what they had seen decades earlier, many liberators opted to tell their story of liberation through the photographic lens, offering testimony that paid tribute to specific photographs as a way of remembering the events they had experienced. For instance, in one archival attempt to secure testimony from liberators during the 1970s and 1980s, none of the liberators interviewed were asked to bring photographs to their sessions with their interviewers, yet many did so. Moreover, close to 85% of the liberators structured their recollections around the photographs that they had brought with them,

sharing photographs that had been taken by other people in their military unit. In a sense, then, they substituted their own individual, personalized memory for a shared, collective memory as it had been documented for the group by one of its members. As one of the liberators told it, "We have a few pictures that some of my men took at the time and gave me copies of them at the end of the war" (Baker, 1980). Thus, despite the interviewer's expectations that each liberator would provide his or her own experience of the liberation, many liberators instead offered the collective interpretations, as facilitated by the group photos.

Many testimonies were structured as stories of the photographs that the liberators had taken. At times, the images authenticated events that were difficult to recount in words. As one liberator who had served with the combat engineers entering Dachau said, "You're in combat, you're mentally geared to kill, and things of this sort, but you see things like that . . . in fact, I've got some pictures somewhere. I didn't have a chance to look them up before you came. . . . They're similar to what you've seen in all the magazines and everything, where these bodies are just stacked up there like cordwood" (Allen, 1978).

In other cases, photographs were invoked as stabilizers against challenges to the authenticity of what had happened. When asked about the fact that some people were saying that the Holocaust never occurred, one former Dachau liberator offered the following observation: "Well, I can testify to the fact that it happened. There are photographs of it. It happened" (Allison, 1979). The irony here was that even when he had personal memory to contradict the Holocaust deniers, the former GI preferred to invoke the photograph as a preferred tool of memory. In that the photograph externalized memory, it somehow seemed preferable to the personalized, internal memories of individuals.

All of this suggests that for individuals undergoing personal trauma following the camps' liberation, personal acts of bearing witness offered a way to move toward recovery. Bearing witness involved the display and use of personal images in a way that made such images important both individually and to the collective. In other words, photographs helped make recovery possible.

## Repeat Performance: Bearing Witness to the World Trade Center Attacks

The intersection between photography and bearing witness, set in place so aptly after the liberation of the Nazi concentration camps, has been repeated in numerous events in the years that have lapsed since the unfolding of that traumatic event. It is no surprise, then, that, following the September 11 attacks on the World Trade Center, photography played a central role in helping both individuals and groups work through the trauma.

The parallel here was twofold: On the one hand, the popular press turned over enormous amounts of space to photographic images in a way that paralleled the display of images appearing after the liberation of the camps in 1945 (Zelizer, 2002). On the other hand, the actions of individuals—amateur presences who themselves experienced personal trauma as residents, firefighters, emergency medical personnel—paralleled the responses displayed by liberators of the camps. Individuals took scores of pictures of what they saw. They shared them with friends, compiled personal albums, scribbled personal notations, borrowed negatives, and at times displayed them in public settings for others to see as well. These practices, which comprise the familiar template for bearing witness, helped individuals work through the trauma associated with the event. As one person who took more than 20 amateur photographs of Ground Zero said, "I feel guilty in some way taking a picture of this, but I don't know what else to do. . . . I think I need to record it visually so maybe I can understand it" ("Many come to," 2001).

The amateur photographic record of the disaster took on public proportions almost immediately. Impromptu grieving spaces of the missing were structured around the display of personal home photos and other amateur images, often blown up to poster size. Countless individuals trekked to the explosion site to pay homage, taking snapshots of what they found there. In the words of one volunteer rescue worker, interviewed on *Oprah* after he

quit his job in Kentucky and traveled to New York City to help in the recovery, "I took pictures. That way I wouldn't have any doubt about what I had seen" (Branham, 2001). Individuals lauded the capacity of personal photographs to make the events real in a way that the media could not.

Photographic booklets and memorial pamphlets connected with firefighters' unions and police station units began to appear within weeks of the disaster, celebrating through a "moving photographic tribute . . . every engine, ladder, and battalion that lost its brother on that fateful, terrible day" (McCourt, 2001, outside front cover; also, Barron, 2001). Amateur photos were featured as part of the more professional visual record being set into place. One tribute to persons who died in the line of duty used a cover image and two internal photos taken by a police department photographer (not identified as such in the text) who took pictures of NYPD personnel clearing out the rubble from the World Trade Center (Von Essen, 2001). Even a commemorative volume produced by Magnum Photographers included images by individuals not employed by Magnum. A six-shot series of images, called by the *New York Times* "a Zapruder film for our time" (Boxer, 2001), was included with the following explanation:

> Cameraman Evan Fairbanks had been working in downtown Manhattan on the morning of the attack and ran out with his video camera when he heard the commotion. As he was filming the towers, the second airplane appeared and crashed into 2 World Trade Center. Fairbanks called us that evening, and when we saw his extraordinary footage we concurred that it was a good fit with our documentary tradition. So Magnum agreed to distribute his videotape and the still images from that shoot, including those reproduced on these pages. (Magnum Photographers, 2001, p. 5)

From mid-November, Fairbanks' video film was also shown on an endless loop at the New York Historical Society as part of its September 11 exhibit. The images of two additional amateur photographers—one a darkroom printer and the other a Magnum intern—were also included in the collection. Said one of the amateurs: "I wasn't really experiencing what was happening. I really feel I was hiding behind my camera. It was my camera that was bearing witness" (Magnum Photographers, 2001, p. 64).

Here, too, individuals involved in the act of bearing witness structured their images around the photographic aesthetic set in place with Nazi atrocity. The four types of shots that proliferated following the liberation of the concentration camps reappeared in the later event— extensive depictions of the site of trauma, depictions of people viewing the site of trauma, depictions of people viewing the site of trauma without evidence of the trauma, and depictions of people taking and viewing photographs of the site of trauma. Together, they provided the visual template associated with bearing witness.

To begin with, depictions of the explosion site were manifold, with images taken from every possible perspective. Varying minimally but in patterned ways—distance, angle, temporal positioning, and focus—nearly every photo centered on the site as it transformed from burning towers to smoking rubble. Although different from the photos of Nazi atrocity due to the absence of bodies, the photos in every other respect—scope, number, prominence, and focus—were remarkably similar.

Depictions of people bearing witness to the World Trade Center immediately appeared in public. Amateur and personal photos quickly made their way into the popular press and were positioned in impromptu galleries around the country. For instance, the *Washington Post,* with some delay, published a jarring amateur photo of a woman's body outlined against her porch, watching the towers smoke in the distance (White, 2001). The photo, taken by an amateur photographer of his girlfriend, was his way of "taking a picture of what was happening in a way that it would mean more in the future" (E. Nederlander, personal communication, January 29, 2002).

Individuals also took photos of people looking at the atrocities without evidence of the atrocities. For instance, one photographer, not on assignment, walked outside his apartment and snapped shots

of people looking upward at some undepicted horror. The photograph, he said, was a reflection of what he saw as he walked the streets (P. Witty, personal communication, January 23, 2002). Similar depictions showed people looking (presumably) either at the site itself or at its mediated representations, such as the television screen. These shots showed no evidence of the disaster site itself, forcing spectators to fill in what they knew rested beyond the camera's frame. The cause of the trauma, again, was undepicted but was necessary to understand what was being shown.

Finally, bearing witness produced depictions that showed people engaged in the basic act of taking photos or looking at photos of the attacks. Published pictures showed hordes of people at Ground Zero, snapping images of the site and of each other, often in throngs of people. One such image showed police officers taking pictures of each other, angled against the altered New York skyline. The caption told readers that they had come from Homestead, FL, to serve as volunteers for the city (Ung & Hill, 2001). In unpublished pictures, too, individuals snapped hundreds of images of people bearing witness to the photos.

One photographer said she took scores of shots of the act of bearing witness (J. Martin, personal communication, November 2, 2001).

The making of photos did not, however, deplete the value of the image in working through trauma. Rather, such photos provided a setting that established photography's presence as an integral part of the act of bearing witness over time. Photography's positioning as a coping mechanism for trauma allowed for numerous ritualized activities that compounded and elaborated on its presence. Those activities, in turn, helped individuals over time reconnect with the collective.

Again, these activities paralleled those displayed by the liberators after World War II. People saved, stored, and shared photos. As with the liberation of the camps, exhibits of the photos sprouted up in almost every corner of the country. Such exhibits displayed a wide range of images, including both life-size portraits and photographs of firefighters, combined displays of photographs and artwork, and historic collections of images of events similar to the World Trade Center attacks.

One such exhibit in Soho, which took over two Prince Street storerooms under the title "HereIsNewYork: A Democracy of Photographs," became one of the most active sites for bearing witness to the tragedy. Beginning in early October, 2001, the exhibit sold digital copies of photos for $25 apiece (to be donated to charity) and collected more than 4000 images, submitted by more than 500 photographers.

The exhibit instantly became an event (Smith, 2001; also Sozanski, 2001). Packed to capacity, individuals crowded the space and the sidewalks outside, taking pictures of people looking at the photos strung on wires across the wall and under the ceiling. Significantly, in the *New York Times'* words, the exhibit was

> a major archive in the making, one that reflects history in a new, egalitarian way, containing images by professionals and amateurs alike . . . the show represents the photography world's attempt to experience one of many signal facts about the tragedy: that it was witnessed and photographed by more people than any event of a similar magnitude. (Smith, 2001, p. E1)

Displaying photos by amateurs and professionals side by side, the exhibit depicted primarily images of the event's aftermath, with the organizers taking one photo from all who submitted. Photography's importance to the mission of repairing the broken community was explicitly articulated. In the words of one of the organizers, "the gathering of work—not only of famous photographers but of policemen, firemen and amateurs alike—is a cathartic expression and helps to unify us all" (C. Traub, personal communication, November 13, 2001). The *Times* proclaimed that the amateur and professional photographers were no different from the "big soup kitchens set up by Tribeca restaurateurs to feed the rescue workers," another instance of "New Yorkers trying to contribute to the physical or emotional mending of the city by pursuing their usual lines of work, only differently" (Smith, 2001, p. E1).

Taken by "ordinary people, students . . . witnesses helplessly watching. And some . . . by those caught up in the havoc—people running for their lives, relief and rescue workers, a subway motorman" (Smith, 2001, p. E1), the photos were displayed in the exhibit without captions or labels. Identified only by number, in a way that reinforced the collective over the identity of its constitutive members, the images, said one critic, were "chilling in their duality, [offering] a measure of the enormity of the event in single, personal units. They also testify to the taking of a photograph as a common human response, a way to deal with a reality almost beyond comprehension" (White, 2001, p. C4). In that light, many of the photographs were delivered with stories about how they had been taken. According to the exhibit's organizers, "People want us to see these pictures. They know we probably won't hang any more pictures of the towers on fire, but they want us to see their pictures of the towers on fire so that we know they were there" (White, 2001, p. C4). In another's words, "the photographs are the memorial to September 11" (C. Traub, personal communication, November 13, 2001). It was hardly surprising that the exhibit met resistance when it attempted to close. Months after its original closing date, it not only remained open but spawned additional displays of parts of its collection both across the United States and around the world, with 500 images set to go to Berlin in late January for an exhibit sponsored by the Ministry of the Interior, and 1500 images being lent to Chicago for a public exhibit (A. Wentz, personal communication, January 23, 2002). The act of bearing witness, created from primarily amateur individual acts of taking and displaying photos, generated a symbolic space in which to bear witness. In so doing, individuals were able to work through the trauma induced by the event, gradually coming together as a collective once again.

## CONCLUSION: FINDING AIDS TO THE PAST

Although it is impossible to predict what role the photos of the World Trade Center attacks will play over time, the personal response to the liberation of the concentration camps is undeniably being repeated here. Photographs provide the setting for bearing witness that is necessary for both individual and collective recovery. The act of seeing and taking responsibility for the horrors depicted in the images helps the collective move on, with its boundaries gradually becoming reinstated.

Significantly, though, this is a first in contemporary memory: Such a nearly complete photographic template for bearing witness, originally set in place after World War II, has been repeated in none of the major atrocities that occurred in the years since. Rather, the events of September 11 offer the first set of circumstances since 1945 that imitates almost completely the earlier photographic aesthetic. Although the September 11 depictions do not offer the images of human carnage that we saw in 1945, in every other respect the contemporary act of bearing witness is virtually identical to that witnessed half a century ago.

Why is photography so important here? Bearing witness requires a space for visualizing trauma in a fashion that can move individuals— and, by extension, collectives—toward and through recovery. Photographs are an instrumental part of making that happen. They offer a way to travel from the highly individuated experience of trauma to a posttraumatic space where the collective can again emerge. Numerous ritualized practices associated with the image—displaying photos, talking about photos, visiting exhibits of photos—help individuals cement associations with others as a post hoc response to trauma. Thus, by taking personal snapshots at the time of a traumatic event's unfolding, people move toward recovery, and they use the images in ritualized ways that, in turn, help reinstate the boundaries of the collective.

This suggests that photographs are a crucial vehicle for bearing witness, moving individuals to the posttraumatic reinstallment of the collective. In this respect, photography acts like the finding aids of archives. Much as finding aids force archival researchers to separate long enough from the larger research project so they can, for the moment, develop its discrete details, photographs force the creation of a personal space for as long as that space is necessary before it is reintegrated as a part of the larger collective. Photographs ease the work of reintegration after trauma. In that sense, they are not only finding aids to the past but to the future, as well.

## NOTE

1. Examples here abound: When Oprah Winfrey interviewed journalists who had covered the World Trade Center attacks, she asked for professional stories and instead received personal tales of retrieving children from school, checking on spouses, and securing the homefront (*Oprah Winfrey Show,* October 3, 2001). ABC's Peter Jennings choked up on air on September 11, 2001, while talking about calling his children. Walter Cronkite told of how he needed to check on his personal effects, when he was interviewed by Larry King (*Larry King Live,* October 5, 2001). Also see the article "Ground Zero" (2001).

## REFERENCES

Allen, H. F. (1978, December 10). Interview, Holocaust Project [Transcript]. Emory University, Atlanta, GA.

Allison, B. (1979, July 29). Interview, Holocaust Project [Transcript]. Emory University, Atlanta, GA.

Baker, J. H., Jr. (1980, February 27). Interview, Holocaust Project [Transcript]. Emory University, Atlanta, GA.

Barron, J. (2001, December 2). Book of photos serves as a glossy homage to lost firefighters. *New York Times,* p. B7.

Boxer, S. (2001, November 22). Documenting the world in an act of transformation. *New York Times,* p. E1.

Caruth, C. (1996). *Unclaimed experience: Trauma, narrative and history.* Baltimore, MD: Johns Hopkins Press.

Chalfen, R. (1987). *Snapshot: Versions of life.* Bowling Green, OH: Bowling Green State University Popular Press.

Crane, S. A. (1997). Writing the individual back into collective memory. *American Historical Review, 105*(5), 1372-1385.

Felman, S. (1992). The return of the voice: Claude Lanzmann's *Shoah.* In S. Felman & D. Laub (Eds.), *Testimony: Crises of witnessing in literature, psychoanalysis and history.* New York: Routledge.

Fentress, J., & Wickham, C. (1992). *Social memory.* London: Basil Blackwell.

Ground zero. (2001, October 5). *TV Guide,* pp. 12-16.

Herman, J. (1992). *Trauma and recovery.* New York: Basic Books.

Hirsch, M. (1997). *Family frames: Photography, narrative and post-memory.* Cambridge, MA: Harvard University Press.

Irwin-Zarecka, I. (1994). *Frames of remembrance: The dynamics of collective memory.* New Brunswick, NJ: Transaction.

Kushlis, J. B. (1979, March 30). Interview, Holocaust Project [Transcript]. Emory University, Atlanta, GA.

Magnum Photographers. (2001). *New York, September 11.* New York: Powerhouse Books.

Many come to bear witness to the devastation at Ground Zero. (2001, September 18). *New York Times,* p. B6.

Markowitz, B. (1984, August 9). Saharovici receives Holocaust pictures. *Hebrew Watchman* [Dachau file, Holocaust Project, Emory University, Atlanta, GA].

McCourt, F. (2001). *Brotherhood.* New York: American Express Publishing.

Mercer, F. (1980 June 8). Interview, Holocaust Project [Transcript]. Emory University, Atlanta, GA.

Owen, A. S., & Ehrenhaus, P. (2000, August 3-6). *Towards a visual rhetoric of witnessing: Reflections on the representation of traumatic memory.* Paper presented at the Visual Rhetorics, 2000 Conference, University of Iowa, Iowa City. Retrieved December 23, 2004, from http://www.uiowa.edu/~obermann/symposia/visualrhetoric/abstracts/Owen-Ehrenhaus_abst.html

Raper, C. (n.d.). Letter to the editor. *Greensboro Daily News* [Dachau file, Holocaust Project, Emory University].

Ruby, J. (1995). *Secure the shadow: Death and photography in America.* Boston: MIT Press.

Smith, R. (2001, October 9). Snapshots of September 11: A gathering of witnesses. *New York Times,* p. E1.

Sozanski, E. J. (2001, October 21). After tragedy, an outpouring of art. *Philadelphia Inquirer,* p. H13.

Ung, E., & Hill, M. (2001, September 30). Businesses try to hang on as N.Y.C. recovers. *Philadelphia Inquirer,* p. A23.

Varner, B. (1979, October 7). Holocaust and horror part of this coach's life. *Sunday Journal-News,* p. 3D.

Von Essen, T. (Ed.). (2001). *In the line of duty: A tribute to New York's finest and bravest.* New York: HarperCollins.

White, B. (2001, October 22). New York's apocalypse in photos. *Washington Post,* p. C4.

Young, A. (1996). Suffering and the origins of traumatic memory. *Daedalus, 125*(1), 245-260.

Young, R. J. (n.d.). Letter to John B. Coulston. In *Jews in the American Army liberation of Ohrdruf* (Doc. No. B/60, K/15/82). Yad Vashem Pictorial Archive, Jerusalem.

Zelizer, B. (1998). *Remembering to forget: Holocaust memory through the camera's eye.* Chicago: University of Chicago Press.

Zelizer, B. (2002). Photography, journalism, and trauma. In B. Zelizer & S. Allan (Eds.), *Journalism after September 11* (pp. 48-68). London: Routledge.

# 20

# Telling What-a-Story News Through Myth and Ritual

## The Middle East as Wild West

Dan Berkowitz

Airliners crash, celebrities die, war erupts. Each time, a frenzied newsroom commotion ensues. Journalists have begun pursuit of yet another big story—a highlight of their professional careers—a "what-a-story."

What-a-story newswork involves a large-scale effort within a media organization to cover a highly unexpected event of major consequences. The full staff is usually called in to help. The regular news of the day is discarded, and the majority of coverage centers around the unexpected event. The newsroom staff is stretched to its limits to get the job done, as journalists work together excitedly to catch the story, put the pieces together, and present it to their audiences.

A journalist's race for news represents more than just another big story to report on, however. What-a-stories serve as cultural triggers that activate journalism's professional ideology and its corresponding news values. They also represent a point on the cultural terrain for the reproduction of political ideology, culture work that journalists accomplish through the retelling of a society's enduring myths.

This chapter builds on ideas that have come earlier in the book—myth, narrative, ritual—to show how what-a-story newswork draws from myth to get the job done, using as an example news about a terrorist bombing in Tel Aviv.

## Conceptual Framework

The discussion here requires the reader to make a departure from thinking about news through the lens of professional ideology and to consider instead how journalists adopt and execute an "emergency routine" to *simulate the ideals* of professional ideology and its practice. By designating something as a what-a-story, journalists are

**Author's Note:** Thanks to Hillel Nossek, College of Management, Israel, and Dina Gavrilos, Arizona State University, for their ideas in earlier phases of my study of myth and newswork. I also thank James Rossen, University of Iowa, for his thoughtful discussion of the emergency routine training and practice in medical settings.

provided with cues about the nature of an occurrence that guides them toward organizational (and, perhaps, journalistic) success. In turn, myth facilitates journalists' efforts to report on what-a-story news by defining a story form a priori that will be culturally resonant to a society.

For the notion of myth, I draw on Lule's (2001) work, which discusses a long-standing "societal story"—a social narrative that expresses central values, beliefs, and ideologies. Myth appears over and over in news discourse, taking basic story plots and actors and adapting them to specific occurrences and the people who are involved. Especially important in this use of myth is the notion of ideology, because myth carries embedded messages about the dominant social order.

For the notion of ritual, I draw on the work of Ehrlich (1996), which has a particularly good fit to this discussion through his integration of ritual with the sociology of news literature. He explains how *ritual* contrasts with the more mechanical *routine* by the way in which actions of journalistic ritual carry meaning about the high-level ideals of the professional journalistic culture. To enact a journalistic ritual is to perform a culturally sacred activity. Although these rituals must be well known, they are rarely practiced. When they *are* practiced, they surface in specific ways that shape the nature of news content.

The term *what-a-story* is applied to news of a highly unexpected occurrence that has large consequences for society. A what-a-story holds venerated standing within journalistic culture: It is something that journalists are eager to cover when it is found. More important than the occurrence itself, what-a-story news affects newsroom work routines, changing the day's content through its all-consuming nature.

Despite the highly unexpected nature of the what-a-story, everybody knows what needs to be done when one occurs, much as hospital workers know a routine for dealing with a patient's cardiac arrest. One important contrast, however, comes from the ways journalists and physicians learn how to perform their emergency routines. In medicine, medical coursework teaches a predetermined procedure for dealing with cardiac

arrest. Physicians learn what steps to take and how their role fits in with that of other medical personnel. They drill together to learn the routine, and they engage in regular practice. When a patient suffers cardiac arrest, all medical personnel launch into their emergency routine, each person performing an agreed-on role.

Journalists, however, do not work quite the same way as physicians in learning and executing their emergency routine for the what-a-story. Most important is that the professional ideology of journalism does not allow acknowledgment of a "predetermined" approach to covering news. Instead, professional ideology begins with a "good journalist" who knows how to dig up information and cover the story "correctly" through professional expertise. Although some media organizations may have a plan for covering a local earthquake or hurricane, they do not have a corresponding plan for every big disaster—every what-a-story—that might arise, nor do they even want to. Most simply, professional ideology requires that journalists treat occurrences "objectively," determining how the net should be cast for a specific story only after carefully filtering facts through their expertise, learned "by osmosis" from living the journalistic culture (Breed, 1955). It is an expertise more or less uniformly possessed by "good journalists." Thus what-a-story newswork draws part of its intrigue from journalists who are not "supposed to" approach an occurrence in a formulaic manner, yet somehow, they predictably capture the essence of an occurrence and then package it as news in a predictably successful way.

The first hint that what-a-story news is linked to myth and ritual comes from the term itself, which contains the label "story," suggesting that a well-known mythical dimension is contained within. Some scholars have come close to identifying this link explicitly but, usually, through a different set of terms. In capturing the news of a plane crash, newsworkers typify occurrences from their "mental catalog" of stories learned on the job (Berkowitz, 1992; Kitsch, 2002). Although she did not use the term *what-a-story* specifically, Zelizer (1993) invoked a similar idea when she described how journalists draw on their historical sense of the field's big stories—a durational mode of interpretation—to determine the story elements that should be involved.

At a basic level, then, these characterizations of what-a-story connect simply to story, but if one looks a bit deeper, they cannot be seen as content neutral. That is, if what-a-story news pertains to big stories—those stories with large social meaning and significance—then what lurks within is the same cultural stuffing from which myth is made. It is important to add that very few stories gain the anointment of what-a-story, and as Schudson (2003) explains, "Some do not even try" (p. 180).

When an occurrence is able to gain the what-a-story designation, though, myth becomes a handy and efficient means for accomplishing newswork. That is, myth is both culturally and ideologically resonant, springing forth from that duality and working regularly to reinforce it. When news draws on myth and incorporates it correctly, the news content that results is automatically resonant for both journalists and their audiences. Further adding to this resonance is the ritualized nature of what-a-story newswork. For journalists, what-a-story newswork represents high ritual in the professional culture. It is not to be tampered with, and it must be respected in both its central actors and its basic story line.

When an occurrence has been deemed by journalists to have the correct characteristics to be considered a what-a-story, the newsroom undergoes a transformation so that it can take on two tasks. One task is to initiate the ritual work activities of the what-a-story. The other is to connect the basic nature of the occurrence—although probably not explicitly and outwardly—to a specific mythical setting.

To initiate ritual newswork, journalists engage in their ritual exclamations of "What a story!" "Holy shit!" and similar phrases, lifting their arms and bobbing their heads (Tuchman, 1978). With general agreement that a what-a-story has taken place, newsroom managers pick up their telephones and begin to call in reinforcements. All staffers, even those on their day off, will be called in to help out. With the staff in place, newsroom managers begin a command post approach,

holding meetings to consult on coverage strategies and plan deployment of personnel.

With the ritual begun, its application to journalistic work needs to be determined, and this is accomplished by casting the occurrence into a mythological perspective. This casting serves two purposes: to select the appropriate mythological story line and to select the types of actors who should be involved (Berkowitz, 2000). Drawing on these elements is an efficient newswork strategy, because it sets forth a shared storyline, one that carries the archetypal actors to be included in the story. These general elements can then be transformed to fit specific instances, focusing the information reconnaissance effort and simplifying the task at hand. Not only does the mythical framework provide shape for a what-a-story, it comes equipped with an ending to both the story and the work process. For mythical narratives, these endings often reaffirm core ideological beliefs of a society, and for news, they do the same.

Overall, myth and what-a-story news provide a lovely journalistic fit, all at once determining how news of an occurrence should be told and facilitating the working plan needed to get the job done.

## Applying the Framework to a Terrorist Event

To demonstrate how what-a-story newswork is told through myth, I draw on the instance of a 1996 terrorist bombing in downtown Tel Aviv's Dizengoff shopping center. In this situation, a Palestinian man wearing a bomb belt attempted to enter Israel's largest shopping mall. He was turned away but went to a nearby intersection outside and detonated his bomb. Fourteen people died and 130 were wounded. This alone did not cast the occurrence as a what-a-story, because other kinds of bombings had preceded it. Even though this terrorist act came in a new form (most previous terrorist acts had either involved bus bombings or hijackings of buses, ships, or planes), the newness of this event on its own would not qualify it as a what-a-story.

What made this occurrence a what-a-story was a bizarre element of irony—many of the victims of the bomb blast were children, and further, these children were dressed in costumes for the Jewish festival of Purim. It was a highly unexpected occurrence, one not easy for American journalists to explain to their audiences back home. Yet it had to be covered, and it had to be covered that very day. It was vivid and surreal, the kind of occurrence from which myths are built.

One additional element needs to be highlighted regarding the transformation of the Dizengoff story to myth: The occurrence was ideological and carried a clear moral judgment. Here, the judgment was that terrorism against adult civilians is one thing, but terrorism against children, costumed children in joyous celebration, violates a society's moral standards. The bombing thus cast the terrorist as a savage, somebody not bound by even the most basic beliefs of American society. In sum, this terrorist bombing set up a working parallel with the recurring myth of the Wild West.

## Contemporary Ideological Implications of the Wild West Myth

The basic theme of the Wild West myth involves the brave, hardy townspeople's quest to further their growing, advancing civilization, vigilant in their resolve to challenge the elements of the frontier wilderness (Cawelti, 1984; Melching, 1979; Parks, 1982; Slotkin, 1992). All the while, townspeople face *external* challenges from marauding savages who attack the people and the town itself. Townspeople also face more *internal* challenges from villains, both through greed (e.g., an unscrupulous banker) and through more violent means (e.g., outlaws who gun down townspeople and rob their businesses).

Clearly, the Wild West myth is steeped in the ideology of American society. The story casts society as insiders and outsiders, the good and the bad, the civilized and the Other. The *townspeople,* for example, symbolize the hard-working middle class establishment, people who believe in success through collective and individual "gumption." Their lives are hard and their rewards are simple, as they carry forth the values of the ruling society "Back East" through sacrifice and perseverance. The *hero* reflects the rugged individualism of American leaders, people who make personal sacrifices for the good of society. Heroes carry the message that society's values (its dominant ideology) demands a mission from its citizens. The *savages*—the American Indians—represent a clear oppositional force to both the values and lifestyles of those pioneering the western frontier. Somewhat less common in this scheme is the *noble savage,* an actor who chooses to live apart from the dominant ideology yet does not challenge it, a hapless victim symbolizing the weakness of the old ways.

The hero becomes the clearest counterpoint to the savage. As he engages in self-sacrifice to mediate between civilization and savagery, he may be seen as the savior of the townspeople. One aspect that sets the hero apart from the savage is the way in which each inflicts violence. For the hero, the kill is "clean," accomplished through sophisticated weapons and done only reluctantly, when no other option exists. The savage brings a clear contrast, with a messier, cruder kill accomplished with knives, clubs, and arrows. The kill of the savage is less calculated, less discriminating—it violates the underpinnings of the advancing civilization.

As a counter to the ideological role of the savages, the *cavalry* represents the power to maintain dominant ideology. The cavalry is composed of men who are self-sacrificing for the sake of progressive society. Finally, holding only a minor part in this ideological drama, the *citizens of Back East* and their *elected leaders* step into the unfolding drama to reaffirm that they are clearly in charge and that all who struggle on the frontier are their charges, their representatives in the spreading society. The elected leaders, in particular, carry the message that what has been done by the society and its representatives is fair, just, and the correct path to have taken for the sake of humankind.

## Translating the Middle East Into the Wild West

The story of the Dizengoff terrorist bombing follows the Wild West storyline quite clearly, beginning with the surprise of the bombing, the Israeli government's foray into the West Bank, and, finally, a large-scale gathering of American and Middle East leaders, symbolic of the many treaties signed between the American leaders and the American Indians of the original American frontier. Although an examination of news content cannot view ritual newswork directly, the Dizengoff story nonetheless shows how what-a-story news draws on common myths of dominant ideology to provide a quick response to a surprise occurrence—a response that both appears ideologically correct and allows for quick agreement about the parameters of how it will be covered.

It is important here to mention the historical context of the relationship between America and Israel as long-standing allies in furthering the ideology of American democracy. For many American newspaper readers, the connections are clear enough, so that adapting the story of the Wild West to the Middle East should not require a large mental stretch. The young nation-state of Israel symbolizes the new western frontier, and the Israeli people become its pioneers and settlers. After several years of suicide attacks, hijackings, and other "savage" efforts by the Palestinians to undermine dominant ideology, Israeli cities such as Jerusalem and Tel Aviv come to represent key "frontier towns" in perpetual danger from attacks by the savages. Building from the basic template, the Palestinian "savages" live in the wilderness, on a kind of reservation—the West Bank and Gaza—like American Indians in the original Wild West. In a similar way, the Israeli army takes on the role of the American cavalry, forging forth into the wilderness in response to the savages' attack. In the role of hero comes U.S. President Bill Clinton (and other U.S. officials), who provides military support to the Israelis (pioneers). As a mediator, Clinton calls for a peace summit, bringing the "chiefs" of the Middle East together, including the "chief" of the savages, Palestinian president Yassar Arafat, and the leader of the "pioneers," Israeli prime minister Shimon Peres.

To accomplish a textual analysis, this chapter draws on news articles, opinion pieces, and letters appearing in the *New York Times* and *USA Today*,

organizations that Lule deems America's cultural scribes. In all, 51 items were examined from the *Times* and 37 from *USA Today*, beginning with the first mention of the Dizengoff Center attack and continuing until the story faded out. These two newspapers were examined in conjunction to gain a broader picture of myth telling, rather than for purposes of comparing their approaches to the story.

## Telling the Dizengoff Center What-a-Story Through Myth

In what-a-story news, language becomes more vivid as the journalist takes on the role—more consciously—of a storyteller. An excerpt from a *USA Today* item (Price & Stewart, 1996) shows the storyteller at work, setting the scene and conjuring up the mythical image of an ongoing cultural battle:

> Outside a bank in Israel's largest shopping mall, a Palestinian terrorist sets off a bomb wrapped around his body. At least 14 are killed, hundreds are wounded and the delicate balance between warring peoples teeters yet again. (p. A1)

Moving forward with the storytelling, another *USA Today* item made the point that this Wild West violence was counter to the expected plot, with *violence of the wilderness* taking place in a city symbolizing the *success of progressive society,* an Americalike place. The writer explained that Tel Aviv was supposed to be different:

> "To bomb the center of life in Tel Aviv is to strike squarely at the new Israel," says Israeli-born drama teacher Ilan Vitemberg. "Jerusalem is old Israel. It's a political city, a city of many wars and many walls, symbolic of people who must defend themselves." (Grossman, 1996, p. A4)

With this assertion, what-a-story coverage moved ahead, both setting up the "gee whiz" factor of the occurrence and signaling that mythical narrative was being employed. The narrative quickly continued to pit the *wild* Wild West (Jerusalem) with the Wild West that had been successfully tamed and developed (Tel Aviv). Rabbi Marc Lee Raphael of the College of William & Mary explained that "bombing Tel Aviv is like escalating terror to Los Angeles, New York or Chicago" (Grossman, 1996) and, as a *Times* article quoted criminologist Chaim Kleg, "Listen, if this happened in Times Square, people would also go hog-wild" (Schmemann, 1996). Descriptions of a modern society and its amenities firmed up this depiction of the tamed frontier, a place with all the expected cultural niceties, "It's lined with banks, shops, cafes and nightclubs. Nearby are the symphony, theaters and art galleries" (Grossman, 1996).

In this narrative mode of what-a-story news, imagery became quite vivid, clearly more so than these media organizations would ordinarily present. This vividness was a way to facilitate reporting the story when details were scarce, the audience was minimally knowledgeable about the overall situation, and immediate coverage was a necessity. A *Times* editorial drew on this imagery-rich language to get the job done, using terms such as "cycle of bloodshed," "savage attacks," "spasm of terror," in a "convulsed Israel," caused by "a small group of fanatics" (Schmemann, 1996). The story told of "victims sailing through the air," some of whom were children, just as one *USA Today* story explained through an eyewitness account: "'I helped a guy whose eye was coming out,' he [a witness] said. 'Then I saw a little kid with part of his leg blown off and smoke coming out from him'" (Rubin, 1996a, p. A3).

Adding to this image of a savage attack on the frontier, another *USA Today* story quoted Bethlehem's Palestinian children, who were chanting a tribute to a recently assassinated bomb maker, "Our beloved man, bomb, bomb Tel Aviv" (Rubin, 1996b, p. A1). This kind of image further spread the gap between the civilized society of the pioneers and the crudeness of the savages, showing that even when young, they were bloodthirsty throughout. The same held true for Palestinian institutions of higher education, which the cavalry—Israeli troops—raided as "breeding grounds" for terrorism, a term more commonly applied to animals or vermin (Rubin, 1996c, p. A5). That perspective, on its own, evokes Lule's

depiction of the *trickster,* a character constantly undoing himself and his culture through his penchant for violence. Thus the irony here is that colleges are designed to be uplifting, to lead their students toward a more "civilized" society, yet for the Palestinians in their mythical role of savages, the academic setting is a place that furthers the opposite outcome.

Another dimension of the savage in the Wild West is that of sneakiness. In the original story, savages arrive under cloak of darkness, employing ruthless tactics to destroy the pioneer's towns, shooting flaming arrows into homes and businesses, scalping innocent victims in a bloodthirsty frenzy. A contemporary version of this sneakiness appears in the Dizengoff story: "There was no telling how many young zealots were already in Israel, and those who had set off bombs in the last nine days had evidently dressed as Israelis, either donning military uniforms or affecting the style of Israeli youths" (Schmemann, 1996, p. A1).

## HARDY PIONEERS AS VICTIMS: COPING ON THE FRONTIER

In stark contrast to the brutality of the savages, the settlers of this modern Wild West frontier (the Israelis) were portrayed as brave, resilient citizens, martyrs for their efforts to advance civilization. A *USA Today* item, for example, described a scene in which "some men unfurled a huge Israeli flag" over the Dizengoff shopping center as the downtown crowd applauded, sang the national anthem, and wept (Rubin, 1996d, p. A5). Later in the story, an Israeli journalist emphasized the pioneers' heroic sacrifice: "We tried. God knows we tried. We tried to make peace. We were ready to pay a high price. . . . This is it." Linking the bombing in the "frontier town" with the dominant society "Back East," the story mentioned the recent opening of a Burger King in the shopping center, a move done because of the corporation's belief in future peace in the region.

In the Wild West myth, we often hear about the rugged people on the frontier enduring hardships—especially the brave "widow woman" who kept the ranch going after her husband was killed by savages. In the modern Wild West, this role was taken on by Leah Rabin, widow of the slain prime minister (Puente, 1996). In *USA Today*, Rabin commented on the ongoing peace efforts and her concern for keeping frontier life strong and safe. "We just have to continue on that road," she urged, telling a *Times* reporter in a clearly ideological statement, "The good will eventually prevail over the evil" (Hanley, 1996, p. A9).

This theme depicting the fortitude of hardy pioneers appeared once again in a *Times* item titled "Day's Routine Now a Test of Courage" (Greenberg, 1996). There, the writer described anxious bus riders sitting in nervous silence, of Tel Aviv shoppers "burdened with heightened concern that disaster might confront them at the next street corner" (p. A12). Ordinary individuals—a telephone technician and a carpenter—spoke of their resolve: "We have to keep riding the buses as usual. It's our country" (p. A12).

## To the Rescue: The Cavalry Arrives

In the story of the Wild West, when savages attack the townspeople, the cavalry rides into town to save the day and restore the dominant order. In this modern version, the same holds true, as the Israeli army begins moving into the Palestinian wilderness to drive back these symbolic savages. A *New York Times* story dramatically explained:

> After midnight, the army reported that it had sealed off cities, towns, and villages across the West Bank and was bringing reinforcements into the region. The move in effect restricted people to their immediate communities and augured tough Israeli actions in Palestinian regions that only recently were celebrating the lifting of Israeli occupation. (Schmemann, 1996, p. A1)

Thus, news coverage conveyed this as an attack-chase storyline of the Wild West, a clash between cavalry and savages in the savages' own lands. Troops went out to "seal off safe houses where terrorists are trained, armed and dispatched to kill, and die" (Rosenthal, 1996, p. A23). Other soldiers "fanned out," sealing off homes

while members of the radical Islamic organization Hamas were "rounded up." Much like the Wild West imagery of the cavalry that scoured the hills outside pioneer towns, capturing or killing bloodthirsty savages, Israeli troops conducted "an intensive search for a 24-year-old Islamic radical trained in Sudan and Syria . . . suspected of masterminding the suicide bombings" (Schmemann, 1996, p. A1). Other troops took on a more general task, with a "round up" of 300 Islamic militants.

## Ideological Counterpoint: The Suffering of the Noble Savages

In the Wild West story, the noble savage fulfills a different victim role, clinging to a fading, traditional lifestyle. This story element shows how the new society's values are meant to dominate within the "progress" of humanity, again affirming the merits of this new social order. The noble savages are willing to live peacefully among conquerors, even though their new lifestyle is far less fulfilling and enduring.

One *New York Times* story, for example, shows noble savages as simple people suffering because of a few bad apples among them. Readers learn that Mahmoud Abu Ein, the owner of a cooking pot factory preparing his wares for the Israelis' Passover holiday, was not able to enter Tel Aviv for raw materials. Despite a relatively simple product—much like the savages' beads, furs, and blankets—Ein spoke of failed dreams for a successful life: "'You know, once I thought I might be a king not of just pots and pans, but of all housewares in the Middle East,' he said. 'My dream I suppose is still alive somewhere, but I am just standing still'" (MacFarquhar, 1996, p. A14).

Following suit, a *USA Today* story explained that "the result has been devastating for local business and morale. Palestinian areas have become near–ghost towns" (Rubin, 1996). This becomes a clear reference to the failed towns of the frontier, although applied to an unusual context. Nonetheless, this notion makes sense when fitted to the lives of the noble savages, who maintain ideological attributes of both the savages and the settlers.

Palestinian academics, too, fit into the role of the noble savage, as they began to condemn the violent acts of other Palestinians for the first time: "Never in our history has there been a demonstration against another Palestinian group," commented a Palestinian journalist (Rubin, 1996d, p. A5).

Yassar Arafat, in the role of the savages' chief, fills an ambiguous role, at once both conciliatory and untrustworthy. His visual image—a checkered keffiyah on his head—appears much like a chief's feathered bonnet in the old Wild West, further affirming this ideological ambiguity. Oddly, few of the other "savages" appear in the same mode of dress. As an Israeli telephone technician explained, "We depended on Arafat, and now we are paying the price" (Greenberg, 1996, p. A12). A *Times* editorial furthered this portrayal of uncertain trust, explaining that Arafat was the head of just one Palestinian faction, one tribal chief among many, with some chiefs bringing more peaceful motives than others. Likewise, a *USA Today* opinion piece called Arafat a "66-year-old terrorist-turned-peacemaker" who "Just a decade ago . . . might have joined Hamas in celebrating the carnage" ("Arafat, Peres, Bear," 1996, p. A10).

In sum, the role of the noble savage provides an ideological paradox to the Wild West story, a story character who does not fit cleanly with either the ideological insiders or the ideological outsiders. Ultimately, this ambiguity continues to reinforce the position of dominant ideology through its depiction of social weakness.

## THE MEDIATING HERO: PRESIDENT CLINTON AND THE SUMMIT OF THE CHIEFS

The Wild West story, like many myths, would not be complete without a hero figure. In this case, U.S. President Bill Clinton filled that role. The hero is often a savior of civilization, struggling against the odds—and occasionally making personal sacrifices—to accomplish a monumental task. Clinton's role was to help rescue the frontier government by coming to the aid of the frontier leader, in this case Israeli Prime Minister Shimon Peres. Firming up the ties between dominant society "Back East" and the new frontier, Clinton affirmed, "the United States has always stood with the people of Israel through good times and bad, and we stand with them today" (Purdum, 1996a, p. A12). An item in *USA Today* carried that affirmation forward and also separated the new frontier society from that of the savages with Clinton's statement: "We stand with you today to bring this horror to an end and bring those responsible to justice" (Katz, 1996, p. A1). Thus explicit links between dominant society and its offspring on the frontier were affirmed for the media audiences.

To accomplish the job of restoring the new social order on the frontier, several leaders stepped forward to speak and reinforce the hero's mission so that there really was an "aggregate" hero role. For example, former Secretary of State Warren Christopher admonished Arafat to control his people before continued support from the dominant society would be forthcoming (Katz, 1996). The heroes of dominant society made it clear that the territorial government—Israeli leadership—had little to do with restoring peace in the region. This was instead a task for the heroes, who would accomplish the task through modern weaponry and advanced defense tactics. A *New York Times* story reported that Clinton sent "sophisticated bomb-detection equipment" along with the "technical experts to help operate them," something beyond the means of the humble, suffering pioneers (Purdum, 1996a, p. A12). This is much like the gun-toting hero who uses skill and precision to kill, in clear contrast to the savages' bloodthirsty approach, and on a grander scale.

Accordingly, we read in the *Times* about "clutches of soldiers with automatic weapons" on patrol, part of a special antiterror task force "signaling that intelligence operations, and not brute military force, will take precedence in the campaign against Hamas" (Schmemann, 1996, p. A1). Sharply contrasting was a *USA Today* description of how "a terrorist sets off a bomb wrapped around his body" (Price & Stewart, 1996, p. A1).

In some forms of the Wild West story, dominant society demonstrates its evident superiority to the crude life of the savages through a meeting on the frontier. Chiefs arrive in full regalia, feathers, fringes, and beads gleaming in the midday sun. They ride in bareback atop their tamed wild horses, moving slowly and cautiously toward their impending treaty and change of lifestyle as "the Other." The cavalry also comes in on horseback, but on dark, domestically bred horses decked with polished saddles, their shiny black boots in smooth stirrups. Each group stands behind its respective leader as agreements are signed and the future affirmed.

In this new Wild West story, the heroes also mediate a peace treaty, as hero Clinton calls an antiterrorism summit with 31 Middle East leaders and Europe. The correspondence between Arab leaders and savage chiefs is striking, as an openly acknowledged symbolic saga begins (Purdum, 1996b). "What you will have is the peacemakers, shoulder to shoulder, demonstrating condemnation of the terror and support for peace," asserted one U.S. official as the figurative assembly began in Sharm el Sheik, Egypt (p. A1).

## CONCLUSION

This chapter began with the idea that when highly unexpected occurrences take place—occurrences that journalists see as worthy of the what-a-story designation—an emergency routine is quickly implemented to facilitate coverage within the everyday newswork schedule. Journalists further face the challenges of producing this fast-track news in a way that requires little explanation to the audience and little depth of understanding from the journalist. Cultural myths become the means of accomplishment for these tasks, a way of producing news that is culturally resonant and ideologically harmonious.

The case example offered here demonstrates the plausibility of this conceptual vantage point by showing how a particularly enduring and broad-sweeping myth—the taming of the Wild West—was used to accomplish what-a-story reporting in two key ways. First, the myth was politically resonant with the American media

audience (Slotkin, 1992). This mythical narrative was easy to follow and readily recognizable. Second, the narrative's high degree of character and plot complexities provided the opportunity for journalists to quickly package a lot of ideas into a single grand scheme. As journalistic ritual, this what-a-story news effectively united the minds of journalists and allowed a common sense of purpose to quickly emerge.

Although the Wild West story is broad in scope, simpler mythical stories also have utility for facilitating what-a-story newswork, such the Trickster, the Good Mother, and the Other World. Each contains the elements of predictability and ideological resonance that make for streamlined storytelling.

Finally, a key aspect of this chapter's context is that the what-a-story had clear cultural connections yet was geographically distant. It contained mysteries of another world of which the audience was not particularly familiar, and it was ripe for storytelling. Occurrences taking place within the United States—plane crashes, school shootings, political upheaval—all bring their own complexities, but their geographical proximity brings quicker cultural understanding. When news takes place within the United States, the story told is literally "our story" in a political, cultural, and ideological sense. What-a-story news taking place outside American borders, ironically, also becomes our story. Whether explaining the demise of Princess Diana as a fairytale princess or telling the story of a distant war, what-a-story news builds on American cultural myths to turn the news of others, ultimately, into the stories of ourselves.

## REFERENCES

Arafat, Peres, bear heavy burden in quest for peace. (1996, March 6). *USA Today,* p. A10.

Berkowitz, D. (1992). Non-routine news and newswork: Exploring a what-a-story. *Journal of Communication, 42,* 82-94.

Berkowitz, D. (2000). Doing double duty: Paradigm repair and the Princess Diana what-a-story. *Journalism: Theory, Practice & Criticism, 1,* 125-143.

Breed, W. (1955). Social control in the newsroom: A functional analysis. *Social Forces, 33,* 326-355.

Cawelti, J. (1984). *The six-gun mystique.* Bowling Green, OH: Bowling Green State University.

Ehrlich, M. (1996). Using "ritual" to study journalism. *Journal of Communication Inquiry, 20,* 3-17.

Greenberg, J. (1996, March 6). Bombing in Israel: The mood. Day's routine now a test of courage. *New York Times,* p. A12.

Grossman, C. (1996, March 5). Heart of "new Israel" pierced. *USA Today,* p. A4.

Hanley, R. (1996, March 5). Bombing in Israel: The widow. Leah Rabin tells Israelis to be strong. *New York Times,* p. A9.

Katz, L. (1996, March 6). U.S. backs "strong action" by Israel. *USA Today,* p. A1.

Kitsch, C. (2002). "A death in the American family": Myth, memory, and national values in the media mourning of John F. Kennedy. *Journalism & Mass Communication Quarterly, 79,* 294-309.

Lule, J. (2001). *Daily news, eternal stories: The mythological role of journalism.* New York: Guilford.

MacFarquhar, N. (1996, March 7). Israeli crackdown renews anxieties of Palestinians. *New York Times,* p. A14.

Melching, E. (1979). Patricia Hearst: Myth America 1974, 1975, 1976. *Western Journal of Speech Communication, 43,* 168-179.

Parks, R. (1982). *The western hero in film and television: Mass media anthology.* Ann Arbor, MI: UMI Research.

Price, R., & Stewart, S. (1996, March 5). Bombs deeply wounded real target: Peace. *USA Today,* p. A1.

Puente, M. (1996, March 5). Bombing causes outrage, sadness in USA Jews, Arabs condemn terrorism. *USA Today,* p. A4.

Purdum, T. (1996a, March 6). Bombing in Israel: The White House. U.S. is sending technology to help intercept bombers. *New York Times,* p. A12.

Purdum, T. (1996b, March 6). Clinton to meet foreign leaders on the Mideast. *New York Times,* p. A1.

Rosenthal, A. (1996, March 5). On my mind: Now it's Israel's job. *New York Times,* p. A23.

Rubin, J. (1996a, March 5). Grieving Israelis' anger, anguish spill over: Hundreds gather outside bombed shopping center. *USA Today,* p. A3.

Rubin, J. (1996b, March 5). Israel: Hamas can't hide. Fourth suicide bombing kills 13. *USA Today,* p. A1.

Rubin, J. (1996c, March 7). Israel detains 100 activists. *USA Today,* p. A5.

Rubin, J. (1996d, March 7). Palestinians openly criticize Hamas attacks. *USA Today,* p. A5.

Schememann, S. (1996, March 5). Bombing in Israel: The overview. 4th terror blast in Israel kills 14 at mall in Tel-Aviv. Nine-day toll grows to 61. *New York Times,* p. A1.

Schudson, M. (2003). *The sociology of news.* New York: W. W. Norton.

Slotkin, R. (1992). *Gunfighter nation: The myth of the frontier in twentieth-century America.* New York: Atheneum.

Tuchman, G. (1978). *Making news: A study in the construction of reality.* New York: Macmillan.

Zelizer, B. (1993). Journalists as interpretive communities. *Critical Studies in Mass Communication, 10,* 219-237.

# 21

## CJ's Revenge

### A Case Study of News as Cultural Narrative

S. Elizabeth Bird

On October 10, 1991, ABC's news magazine *Prime Time* ran a story titled "Angel of Death." It began with a montage of shots in bars and other night spots, showing people dancing and drinking against a background of flashing neon signs advertising topless shows and other dubious pleasures. Over the throbbing dance beat, Diane Sawyer intoned:

> She is called the Black Widow. She says she has AIDS, and she's bent on revenge. She says she's going to clubs and bars and sleeping with lots of men so that she won't be the only one to die. No one knows who she is, but she's the most talked about and most feared person in Dallas.

Reporter John Quinones then retold a story that had been causing a sensation in Dallas since early September, reaching the national press by the end of the month (Clemmons, 1991). It began when *Ebony* magazine published a letter in its "Advisor" column signed "CJ, Dallas, Texas." The entire text of the brief letter was as follows:

I have AIDS. No one knows it. I go to clubs more now so I can meet new men. I feel that I am a beautiful person and I couldn't believe I got it. I sleep with four different men a week, some times more. I've slept with 48 men so far, some of them married. I feel if I have to die a horrible death I won't go alone. I know I'm not right in what I'm doing. Can you tell me what's wrong with me? Why don't I feel guilty? (CJ, 1991, p. 90)

*Prime Time* reporters were told by the *Ebony* managing editor that the letter was not verified but was printed "as a warning to readers." The "Advisor" compared the letter writer to a serial killer and advised him or her to seek treatment and "stop your vengeful actions," adding that "the purpose of publishing your chilling letter is to warn those who are still in the habit of picking up strangers . . . that there are people like you on the loose who won't hesitate to do them in." The letter led to a flood of calls to a local African American radio talk show host, Willis Johnson, who told *Prime Time* that he had received "the exact same letter" from a woman in 1989. Later, a woman had

**Author's Note:** This chapter is a heavily edited version of chapter 6 in the author's *The Audience in Everyday Life: Living in a Media World*, used by permission of Routledge/Taylor and Francis Books, Inc. I wish to thank Dave Overton, News Director of KXAS-TV, Channel 5, Dallas–Fort Worth, who provided tapes of 12 stories on the CJ case aired between August 30 and October 21, 1991.

introduced herself to him in a Dallas nightclub, claiming to be CJ. He was completely convinced that her claims were real. Johnson issued a plea for CJ to call him, which she apparently did on August 31, 1991. He set up an interview with her on September 4. Extracts from the interview were played on *Prime Time* over footage of a reel-to-reel tape slowly rolling, spliced with more darkly lit shots of bars. The recorded voice of "CJ" is interspersed with comments from Johnson.

| | |
|---|---|
| Willis Johnson: | Do you feel guilty at all about.... |
| CJ: | Doing what I'm doing? |
| Johnson: | Yeah. |
| CJ: | No, I don't. I wanted a marriage, I wanted children, but I can't do that now. I blame it on men. Period. Not just one man—he gave it to me, but I'm doing it to all the men because it was a man that gave it to me. |
| Johnson: | [Voiceover] On the other end of the phone was a devastating woman. She was cold, calculating, and this methodical about what she was doing. |
| Johnson: | But CJ, realize how many lives you are affecting here. Men who have families and children and.... |
| CJ: | Well, that's not my concern. That's their concern. |
| Johnson: | Do you feel anything at all? |
| CJ: | No, I don't. |
| Johnson: | Nothing? |
| CJ: | Nope. Revenge. |

Later in the same show, *Prime Time* interviewed Assistant District Attorney George West, who had made it a personal crusade to arrest CJ. Police in Dallas had refused to get involved because no one had filed a complaint, but after media and public pressure, they too mounted a search for CJ on October 9. Then on October 22, the Dallas police announced ("Dallas Police Discount," 1991) that they had located the writer of the letter, a 15-year-old girl who did not have AIDS but who was grieving for a friend who had died of it. The 29-year-old woman on the tape turned out to be the most prolific of about half a dozen women who had called local media. She did not have AIDS, and her motives were unclear.

As I watched the saga unfold, I was convinced that no actual CJ would ever be found or arrested. The reason? I saw the story as, undoubtedly, an urban legend run wild—a product of oral folk tradition that, because of its cultural salience, had become transformed into "news." This chapter is about how that happened, and how an essentially anthropological analysis of this case study may shed light on our understanding of news as a form of cultural narrative.

## AIDS IN LEGEND

The folklore literature is full of AIDS jokes, legends, and other popular responses. AIDS was first diagnosed in 1981; as early as 1982, a story was circulating in San Francisco about a gay AIDS sufferer who would have sex indiscriminately and then show his lesions to his sex partner with glee, saying "I've got gay cancer. I'm going to die, and so are you" (Smith, 1990, p. 116). By 1986, as AIDS invaded the straight community, the commonest form of the legend involved an infected woman. *USA Today* printed this report in October 1986:

> Novelist Jackie Collins . . . shared what she said was a true story on Joan Rivers' show. A married Hollywood husband picked up a beautiful woman at a bar. They enjoyed a night of passion at a good hotel; in the morning he rolled over to find a sweet thank you note. Class, he thought, real class. Then he walked into the bathroom and found, scrawled on the mirror in lipstick: "Welcome to the wonderful world of AIDS." (*USA Today*, October 22, 1986, quoted in Goodwin 1989, p. 85)

Fine (1987) collected many similar versions, and Smith (1990) documents the story in several European countries. Newspapers and magazines were reporting it, sometimes as a legend, sometimes as an interesting, if unverified story, and word of mouth was doing the rest. Smith also points to the numerous antecedents to the AIDS story, in the form of similar lore about herpes, gonorrhea, and syphilis. The oldest example he cites is a tale told by Daniel Defoe in his 1722 *Journal of the Plague Year,* about the 1665 plague, in which "a poor, unhappy gentlewoman" was confronted by a plague sufferer. "He caught hold of her, and kissed her; and which was worst of all, when he had done, told her he had the plague, and why should she not have it as well as he?" (Smith, 1990, p. 131). Similarly, Vietnam veterans told tales of prostitutes who deliberately infected GIs with "Black Rose," a supposedly incurable form of venereal disease (Gulzow & Mitchell, 1980). This name is echoed in some versions of the AIDS story, in which the victim receives black roses from the person spreading the disease.

The updated AIDS version continued to circulate widely throughout the 1990s, when the Internet bulletin board FOLKLORE was reporting variants from almost all U.S. states. By 2002, it had become one of the most thoroughly documented legends on the popular urban legends Web site snopes.com (Mikkelson, 2000). In recent years it has faded somewhat, as AIDS has become culturally assimilated and supplanted by new horrors, such as terrorism, although new variants continue to surface. We may assume that stories like these were also in circulation in Dallas, and the original letter writer was inspired by them. It may also be that the letter itself was an item of folklore, of the kind that circulates through photocopied versions of jokes, parody memos, and letters—and now the Internet.

## From Legend to News

Why, then, did the newspapers and other media, such as *Prime Time,* cover the Dallas story so extensively and, in the case of broadcast media, so

uncritically? We tend to think of news and folklore as the opposite of each other: News is factual and verifiable; legends are false and unverifiable. More recently, cultural researchers have sought to show that the line between news and legend is not so clear (e.g., Bird, 1992; Bird & Dardenne, 1988; Lule, 2001). News, like folklore and myth, is a cultural construction, a narrative that tells a story about things of importance or interest. Journalists like to think that news somehow mirrors reality, that it objectively describes events; news is "out there" to be discovered. However, news does not exist until it is written, until it becomes a story, and what is deemed newsworthy owes as much to our cultural conceptions of what makes a "good story" as it does to ideas of importance or significance. Student journalists are encouraged by their textbooks to "find the story" in an event, using the same kind of criteria—conflict, drama, novelty—as any good oral storyteller.

As Bennett (1983) points out, the drive toward story tends to formularize news: "Any communication network based on stories will become biased toward particular themes" (p. 88) Thus reporters learn to find familiar stories in disparate events—the "passenger who missed the plane that went down" or narratives of government waste or inefficiency. As Berkowitz (1997) shows, reporters are able to handle apparently unique, "what-a-story" events through the use of conventional narrative techniques that call on familiar themes. Perhaps this was shown most dramatically in the news media's response to the terrorist attacks of September 11, 2001, when all media, from tabloids to TV to "serious" newspapers, offered similar stories of heroes, survivors, and villains (Bird, 2002).

Most important in this context, news both reflects and reinforces particular cultural anxieties and concerns. It goes in waves; many scholars have demonstrated, for example, that waves of reporting about teenage suicide or child abuse do not necessarily reflect actual changes in the rates of these problems. In the United States, the summer of 2001 was dubbed "the summer of the shark" because of several highly publicized shark attacks. In reality, there were no more attacks than usual, and sharks suddenly disappeared from the media after September 11. News reflects waves of interest and, in turn, feeds the anxieties that first produced the interest (e.g., Best, 1990, 1991b). These scares develop in part because of the very nature of news reporting. Notions of objectivity require that information be verified, but verification frequently involves simply confirming that someone indeed said something. The quote itself becomes a "fact" when reported in the media. Thus, folklore about poisoned candy or about children mutilated in mall bathrooms or abducted by Satanic cults is shared and passed on by everybody, including people who function as news sources (Victor, 1993). Sources provide stories, and legend becomes news.

Goss (1990) documents this process in assessing the case of the "Halifax slasher" in 1930s Britain. Over several months, a man armed with a razor was reported to be attacking people at random in Halifax, Yorkshire. The case received wide media coverage, and people were quoted as having been attacked or at least as having known someone who had been. Eventually it was dismissed as a hoax. As Goss comments: "uncatchable 'super-criminals' always pose questions about how the 'system' is performing and the ways in which it has left us anxious and vulnerable" (p. 103). CJ became a sort of "super-criminal," as "ordinary people" were quoted as saying she must be found and prosecuted as a mass murderer. She certainly left people, particularly men who frequented singles bars, anxious and vulnerable. KXAS-TV, a local station in Dallas–Fort Worth that covered the story extensively, frequently featured interviews with bar patrons who described how they had changed their ways and become more cautious. Other stories on the same station had experts analyzing CJ: "She doesn't have a positive self-esteem" (September 9, 1991). CJ's existence became a given, essentially because enough objective "facts" were being generated about her.

The feeling of cultural vulnerability was what the CJ scare was all about; to see it as simply a hoax on the media shows a one-dimensional view of news communication. In the 1990s, AIDS was widely perceived as a new plague; like syphilis during the Renaissance, it was seen as "disease that [is] not only repulsive and retributive but collectively invasive" (Sontag, 1989, p. 46). Legends typically grow from anxiety and fear—maniacs on the loose, corporations that poison us, tanning booths that fry our insides. Media quite frequently see legends as exactly what they are and disregard them; a *Dallas Morning News* reporter did make the connection between CJ and the AIDS legends, offering the hoax theory as one possible explanation (Precker, 1991).

Media are part of our culture too, however, and reflect its concerns. Fringe tabloid newspapers, unconstrained by questions of objectivity and fact, know that and consciously feed from it. As a tabloid writer told me: "When looking for ideas for stories, it's good to look at fears, and . . . at real desires. That's why a lot of people win lotteries in the stories, and why people get buried alive all the time" (J. Hogshire, personal communication, March 13, 1992). Mainstream media are more cautious and responsible, but they are still part of the cultural complex that saw AIDS as one of the greatest threats ever. The vague, locally variable legends about the AIDS carrier were convincing enough to make many papers, because they struck a resonant chord. The story "felt" true.

The media also gave a specific name, face, and voice to the anonymous threat. In sociological terms, "labeling" functions as a way of defining a threat. Thus the media, by providing specific nicknames, bring the identity of mass murderers into focus—the Boston Strangler, the Halifax Slasher, the Beltway Sniper. The women purporting to be CJ provided that label and even provided a voice, personifying the anonymous peril of AIDS and giving the media real quotes, real "facts" that turned a legend into news. In effect, news stories that seem most credible to reporters and audiences alike develop legitimacy through the construction of a body of "objective evidence" derived through a conventionalized process of newsgathering. The CJ story provided a wealth of such evidence, which unfolded as the story grew. First we had the direct quotes, taken from the letter and audiotapes. A Dallas reporter recalls the impact of the audiotape: "That's what sold this thing, that it was such a convincing tape. . . . It was this good, sexy sound bite that made all the difference" (M. Precker, personal communication, April 27, 1993). Then the "person in the street" (or bar) was encouraged to comment angrily, fearfully, and colorfully, against a backdrop of visually striking stock footage of "the bar scene." As the story progressed, an artist's drawing was commissioned by KXAS-TV, using Willis Johnson's recollections of the "CJ" he had once met in a club, and this image was used everywhere, usually with total acceptance of CJ's reality: "A woman . . . is using the disease to kill. The woman is CJ, and this is what she looks like" (KXAS-TV, September 4, 1991). To frame the story conventionally, the audience heard the opinions of police, district attorneys, psychologists, and other "experts." All the pieces were in place to transform the vague, dispersed legends and rumors into the concrete, labeled reality of news.

## THE CULTURAL SALIENCE OF CJ

This process would not have been so complete if the story had not already been culturally resonant; the AIDS-CJ story is a relevant narrative for many audiences in several ways. For one thing, AIDS has been generally perceived as the most lethal plague in generations; it is a genuine threat. Many AIDS sufferers have spoken about their anger and bitterness at becoming a victim and their consequent wish to lash out; the scenario is plausible. As Quam (1990) mentions, "in the case of AIDS, the culturally-defined line between sickness and crime is blurred" (p. 34). The AIDS sufferer is a victim-turned-villain in the popular mind, reminiscent of the lepers and maimed, crippled evil-doers of popular culture. Best (1991a) discusses the major role of "villains," such as mass murderers, in folklore and popular culture, including news, talk shows, and other informational media. All these media emphasize that these evil figures are lurking, ready to strike anyone at any time The tale, then, strikes a chord that is as resonant in oral traditions of story as it is in media definitions of story, because both have the same cultural roots.

More specifically, in the CJ stories, the AIDS villain is almost always a woman. This is inconsistent with the way AIDS is actually spread through heterosexual contact; although women are relatively likely to be infected by men, men have only a small chance of catching AIDS from a woman. Still, the woman perpetrator is perfectly consistent with wider cultural attitudes. In legend, the man she infects is usually married or is at least seeking illicit sex (in earlier variants, the woman is often a prostitute). She is, then, the embodiment of the just reward. Grover (1988) points out that non–drug-using prostitutes have lower HIV infection rates than other women, probably because they are more aware of the risks involved in their job. She argues that "prostitutes are taken as embodiments of infectiousness less for their actual risks and rates of infection than for their symbolic and historical status" (p. 26). Although CJ is not characterized as a prostitute, she is seen as a predator, an abnormally promiscuous woman. In fact, KXAS-TV ran a story that underlined the perception of CJ as even worse than a prostitute, interviewing a self-identified "hooker" named Maggie Patterson (October 10,1991). Patterson's opinion: "Well, I think she's low-down. . . . She's making it bad, you know, on other women that's out there selling their bodies. . . . I use plenty of rubbers and things, but she ought to turn herself in." The message is clear: Prostitutes are open about what they are doing, and men know what they are getting into, but women like CJ purport to be "ordinary" women yet harbor and spread death among the unsuspecting.

Thus both the legend and the CJ story spread like wildfire among the singles bars and pick-up joints of Dallas, as a cautionary tale for *men*, rather than for women. CJ, like the woman in the legends, was a horrific siren for the AIDS age. She was characterized as unusually beautiful, seductive, and difficult to resist. We use the sexually aggressive, always-ready woman as a pervasive dream figure, yet we fear the damage she might cause. CJ is a sexually available dream figure whose polluted body turns the encounter into a nightmare—she is worse than clearly disfigured villains, because her pollution is invisible.

During the earlier days of AIDS, gays and bisexuals were assigned the role of "Contaminated Other." As awareness of heterosexual infection grew, prostitutes were given that role, as they had been in other plagues, and the earlier AIDS legends feature prostitutes as carriers. Later, the labeling extended to any sexually active woman, as reflected in the legends, including the particular legend variant that became the CJ story. As Treichler (1988) notes, in the early 1980s, women were generally regarded as particularly well-protected against AIDS, but gradually this changed, until women were perhaps the most suspect of all: "Like the virus, wearing an innocent disguise, are we not double agents, in league with the enemy ?" (p. 221). Once again, we see a precursor to that notion of woman as "double agent" in the iconography of syphilis. Gilman (1988) describes a gradual shift from the notion of a male "victim" to that of a female "source of corruption," pointing to such images as a title-page illustration for a 19th-century text on syphilis that shows a syphilitic woman hiding her ugliness behind a mask as she attempts to seduce a male victim.

Thus a woman "carrier" is more likely to strike fear into the general populace. As long as AIDS could be dismissed as a "gay disease," the "moral panic" (Cohen, 1980) about AIDS was relatively muted, and gay victims of the disease could be stigmatized as guilty and deserving of their fate, in contrast to "innocent" victims. The early 1980s legends of the gay man who deliberately infected others had little salience outside the gay community. Likewise, as long as the media characterized AIDS as confined to gays, widespread perception of a universal threat was absent. Only when children, straight men, and women became victims was the stage set for general "moral panic." The Dallas TV coverage of the CJ scare illustrated that panic clearly. An early story discussed reaction to the CJ letter, which was posted in the bathrooms of many Dallas clubs. "Experts say folks need to know that AIDS is no longer, or never was, a white gay man's disease. . . . The disease has spread to the heterosexual society, and no one is safe" (KXAS-TV, August 30, 1991). The story ends with the reporter speaking over the familiar dark dance-bar scene: "It's Friday night, it's the Dallas club scene. Tonight folks are having fun. But tonight, folks are thinking about a deadly disease that could end their lives."

A woman, and particularly a beautiful, hard-to-resist woman, is especially evil, deceitfully carrying the virus out of the closet (where it belongs) and into the world of "normal" men. Significantly, the original letter to *Ebony* never identified CJ as a woman, only as "a person." If CJ had been perceived as a man, infecting other gay men, the furor would never have developed. Quickly, she became known as a woman, in keeping with the time period's folk legends. As Sontag (1989) points out, although "at risk" (and therefore already stigmatized) groups are terrifying in the role of carrier, in many ways, the "innocent" are more frightening. The moral panic surrounding CJ was so great because she was seen to *masquerade* as innocent; the perception was that she used this mask to cross the boundaries and infect the truly innocent.

Furthermore, CJ was not just a beautiful woman; she was a beautiful African American woman, whose image was a perfect example of "colonized" notions of black beauty (Worth, 1990) in that she was light skinned, straight haired, and slender. This apparently made her especially threatening. Television news coverage of the story did not make an issue of race verbally, but visually it tended to reinforce stereotypes of African American sexuality. Stories repeatedly used the same footage of African Americans dancing in dimly lit nightclubs, apparently disregarding the beautiful threat lurking among them. The stereotypical beauty of CJ allowed her image to be "mainstreamed" beyond the African American community, as she fit so perfectly the age-old image of the promiscuous, exotic, "dusky" woman who lured white men into sin (di Leonardo, 2000). When the CJ story began, accounts suggested that she was targeting African American men in particular, but this aspect quickly disappeared, so that by the time *Prime Time* covered the story, the familiar club scenes included dancers of all races.

Meanwhile, for women the tale may function as a revenge fantasy. Fine (1987) suggests that women may find the story attractive because it pays men back for abuse or rape. Indeed, that seems to have been the motivation of the main caller who claimed to be CJ. She expressed her anger and hatred of all men and her desire to wipe them all out. If she was looking to scare men, she was clearly successful.

Within days after the *Prime Time* piece aired, the mother of the girl who had written the *Ebony* letter went to the police. Following this, Dallas Deputy Police Chief Ray Hawkins told the *New York Times:* "Our attitude is that there is no CJ as purported to be. However, there are lots of CJs out there, either knowingly or unintentionally spreading HIV" ("Dallas Police Discount," 1991, A14).In Texas, such an action is a felony punishable by up to 10 years in prison. At the time, Dallas had a high incidence of AIDS, ranking 12th nationally, with 3200 cases diagnosed by September 1, 1991. During the height of the CJ scare, AIDS awareness grew dramatically, with activists handing out CJ t-shirts, leaflets, and condoms. The AIDS hotline received 1200 calls in 3 days, more than in the previous month. The hotline added a new tape to its computer menu, called "CJ," which callers could access for counseling and advice (Krepcho, Smerick, Freeman, & Alfaro, 1993). According to the local health department director, "I look at what happened with CJ as a fire drill, something that has made people aware of danger and risk" ("Dallas Police Discount," 1991, A14).

For 200 years, the media have been subject to hoaxes, as Fedler (1989) amply demonstrates. These may be the result of deliberate misinformation campaigns, but they are always most successful when they seem plausible, because they speak to something current in the culture. The CJ incident was not a deliberate hoax, yet like true hoaxes, it depended for its vitality on the cultural climate being right, which legitimized the sources of the story. Because the story reached so deeply into cultural myths and stereotypes, it took on a life of its own. Essentially, it was the coming together of anonymous rumors, tales, and legends, initiated by one individual but fed by oral tradition and media alike. George Bernard Shaw once

commented that it took the media blitz surrounding the Jack the Ripper murders to draw attention to the terrible conditions faced by the poor women of Whitechapel who became prostitutes and potential murder victims (Goss, 1990). The 15-year-old girl who wrote the letter said she did it not to deceive but to increase awareness of the deadly threat of AIDS. With the help of folklore and the media, she apparently did just that.

## Conclusion

Traditional accounts of news tended to see it as a product of sociological or historical forces. More recently, the notion of news as storytelling has become increasingly conventional, as part of an interdisciplinary reevaluation of storytelling. Much of this reevaluation has focused on the structural aspects of narrative—for example, how journalists construct stories in particular, stereotyped ways. This has opened up the study of journalistic practice immeasurably. However, the ways in which news narratives interrelate with the stories and concerns of the wider culture at specific moments in time is currently a neglected area, which should be explored. For instance, Lule (2001) argues for an understanding of news as myth and makes a good case for journalists' role as "scribes," analogous to ancient storytellers and bards.

However, Lule's application of "myth" is limited because of its dependence on Eliade's (e.g., 1949/1958) and Campbell's (e.g., 1949) emphasis on archetypal or universal themes, with a nod to Malinowski's (1954) more functional, anthropological interpretation. The weakness of this "universalist" approach is that it pays scant attention to the differences in time and place that produce particular cultural moments and narratives, rooted in particular histories. Furthermore, it ignores the participatory role of the culture in which the myth is embedded. For Lule, as for many others who have analyzed news as mythical narrative, the focus is on the journalist, who is given the burden of defining the myth. Thus "the language of news is what matters" (Lule, 2001, p. 5). Strangely, Lule argues that "rather than plumb the depths of the human mind, myth stays on the surface of the printed page" (p. 146). This statement seems to fly in the face of a truly anthropological understanding of myth more as process than as text, as well as a joint product of storyteller and audience. Although Lule suggests that the news audience—the cultural context in which the news exists—is almost irrelevant to the role of news as myth or narrative, I would suggest that it is crucial.

Journalism is driven by a need to explain, and AIDS is something that is, in many respects, inexplicable. The legends frequently leave it unexplained, but journalism seeks answers, often through stories that personalize the vague, anonymous forces "out there." Carey (1986) writes, "Explanation in American journalism is a kind of long distance mind reading in which the journalist elucidates the motives, intentions, purposes, and hidden agendas which guide individuals in their actions" (p. 180). Individuals and names make news stories, as CJ shows us. The *Ebony* letter writer gave the anonymous threat a name, the talk show caller gave her a voice, and the local news gave her a face, all of which other media enthusiastically disseminated. More recently, we saw the same process in action with the international circulation of a story that expressed not fear, but desperate hope. In the aftermath of the World Trade Center bombing, a story went around the world about a man on the 83rd floor of the 110-story south tower who survived the building's collapse by "riding the rubble" to the ground. Beginning as a vague rumor among rescue workers, it solidified, as reporters first identified the man as a firefighter, later naming him as Sgt. John McLoughlin, a New York Port Authority police officer and father of four. *Newsweek* confirmed the story, and only later did it gradually emerge in the media that McLaughlin did not exist and that it would have been impossible for such a thing to happen. But in the meantime, "in addition to giving the public and the rescue workers hope, it gave the world's media a target for one of the most astonishing survival stories ever" (Alderson, 2001).

Thus we can see news not as something entirely distinct (though clearly having its own distinctive generic properties) but rather as one strand in the web of culture. News is a complex genre; its mythological or storytelling function is only one dimension, along with the more conventional function of setting an agenda and chronicling major events. As Carey (1986) writes, "In fact, journalism can present a coherent narrative only if it is rooted in a social and political ideology, an ideology that gives a consistent focus or narrative line to events" (p. 161). Sociology, history, narrative theory have all helped to increase our understanding of the process of news. In my analysis of the CJ story, I have tried to draw more on the holistic, cultural focus of anthropology, reaching out from the story itself toward a set of connections between it and notions simmering in the culture at large. News as a genre is indeed distinct, but unless we start to see those connections, we will find it harder to understand why particular stories have salience at particular moments. "Big stories" and "moral panics" are not created by journalists alone; rather, journalists may be the brokers for the stories a culture is already telling.

## References

Alderson, A. (2001, September 23). Letter from New York: World Trade Centre myth that kept hope alive. *news. telegraph*. Retrieved December 18, 2004, from http://urbanlegends.about.com/gi/dynamic/offsite.htm?site=http://news.telegraph.co.uk/news/main.jhtml%3Fxml=/news/2001/09/23/wald23.xml

Bennett, W. L. (1983). *News: The politics of illusion*. New York: Longman.

Berkowitz, D. (1997). Non-routine news and newswork: Exploring a what-a-story In D. Berkowitz (Ed.), *Social meanings of news: A text reader* (pp. 363-375). Thousand Oaks, CA: Sage.

Best, J. (1990). *Threatened children: Rhetoric and concern about child-victims*. Chicago: University of Chicago Press.

Best, J. (1991a). Bad guys and random violence: Folklore and media constructions of contemporary deviants. *Contemporary Legend, 1*, 107-121.

Best, J. (1991b). "Road-warriors" on "hair-trigger highways": Cultural resources and the media's construction of the 1987 freeway shootings problem. *Sociological Inquiry, 61*, 327-345.

Bird, S. E. (1992). *For enquiring minds: A cultural study of supermarket tabloids.* Knoxville: University of Tennessee Press.

Bird, S. E. (2002). Taking it personally: Supermarket tabloids after September 11. In B. Zelizer & S. Allen (Eds), *Journalism after September 11* (pp. 141-159). London: Routledge.

Bird, S. E., & Dardenne, R. W. (1988). Myth, chronicle, and story: Exploring the narrative qualities of news. In J. W. Carey (Ed.), *Media, myths and narratives: Television and the press* (pp. 67-87). Newbury Park, CA: Sage.

Campbell, J. (1949). *The hero with a thousand faces.* New York: Pantheon.

Carey, J. W. (1986). The dark continent of American journalism. In R. K. Manoff & M. Schudson (Eds.), *Reading the news* (pp. 146-196). New York: Pantheon.

CJ. (1991, September). [Letter to the "Advisor" column]. *Ebony, 46,* 90.

Clemmons, C. (1991, September 3). A fearful fallout from AIDS Letter to magazine. *Times-Herald,* pp. C1, C5.

Cohen, S. (1980). *Folk devils and moral panics: The creation of the mods and rockers.* New York: St. Martin's Press.

Dallas police discount AIDS revenge tale. (1991, October 23). *New York Times,* p. A14.

di Leonardo, M. (2000). *Exotics at home: Anthropologies, others, American modernity.* Chicago: University of Chicago Press.

Eliade, M. (1958). *Patterns in comparative religion* (R. Sheed, Trans.). New York: Sheed & Ward. (Original work published 1949)

Fedler, F. (1989). *Media hoaxes.* Ames: Iowa State University Press.

Fine, G. A. (1987). Welcome to the world of AIDS: Fantasies of female revenge. *Western Folklore, 46,* 192-197.

Gilman, S. L. (1988). AIDS and syphilis: The iconography of disease. In D. Crimp (Ed.), *AIDS: Cultural analysis, cultural activism* (pp. 90-102). Cambridge: MIT Press.

Goodwin, J. P. (1989). *More man than you'll ever be: Gay folklore and acculturation in middle America.* Bloomington: Indiana University Press.

Goss, M. (1990). The Halifax Slasher and other "urban maniac" tales. In G. Bennett & P. Smith (Eds.), *A nest of vipers: Perspectives on contemporary legend V* (pp. 89-112). Sheffield, UK: Sheffield Academic Press.

Grover, J. Z. (1988). AIDS: Keywords. In D. Crimp (Ed.), *AIDS: Cultural analysis, cultural activism* (pp. 17-30). Cambridge: MIT Press.

Gulzow, M., & Mitchell, C. (1980). "Vagina dentata" and "incurable venereal disease" legends from the Vietnam War. *Western Folklore, 39,* 306-317.

Krepcho, M., Smerick, M., Freeman, A., & Alfaro, A. (1993). Harnessing the energy of the mass media: HIV awareness in Dallas. *American Journal of Public Health, 83,* 283-285.

Lule, J. (2001). *Daily news, eternal stories: The mythological role of journalism.* New York: Guilford.

Malinowski, B. (1954). *Magic, science and religion, and other essays.* Garden City, NY: Doubleday.

Mikkelson, B. (2000). *AIDS Mary..* Retrieved December 18, 2004, from http://www.snopes.com/horrors/madmen/aidsmary.htm

Precker, M. (1991, October 12). CJ's story draws national attention. *Morning News,* pp. 1C, 3C.

Quam, M. D. (1990). The sick role, stigma, and pollution. In D. A. Feldman (Ed.), *Culture and AIDS* (pp. 29-44). New York: Praeger.

Smith, P. (1990). "AIDS: Don't die of ignorance": Exploring the cultural complex. In G. Bennett & P. Smith (Eds.), *A nest of vipers: Perspectives on contemporary legend V* (pp. 113-143). Sheffield, UK: Sheffield Academic Press.

Sontag, S. (1989). *AIDS and its metaphors.* New York: Farrar, Strauss & Giroux.

Treichler, P. A. (1988). AIDS, gender, and biomedical discourse. In E. Fee & D. M. Fox (Eds.), *AIDS: The burden of history* (pp. 190-266). Berkeley: University of California Press.

Victor, J. S. (1993). *Satanic panic: The creation of a contemporary legend.* Chicago: Open Court Press.

Worth, D. (1990). Minority women and AIDS: Culture, race, and gender. In D. A. Feldman (Ed.), *Culture and AIDS* (pp. 111-136). New York: Praeger.

# 22

## RITUALIZED PLAY, ART, AND COMMUNICATION ON INTERNET RELAY CHAT

BRENDA DANET

I n a novel form of image-based communication on Internet relay chat (IRC), participants interact in real time, not via typed words but via the display of brilliantly colored images created from typographic symbols on the computer keyboard. About a dozen channels (chat rooms) on various IRC networks have featured this phenomenon, but it has particularly flourished on #mirc_rainbow[1] (henceforth *rainbow*) on the Undernet.[2] This chapter will show that the classic anthropological concepts of play, myth, and ritual help illuminate this novel phenomenon.

*Rainbow* activity draws on the basic constitutive and regulative rules of face-to-face interaction ritual (Goffman, 1967), as well as on the traditional exchange of paper greeting cards (Herrnstein-Smith, 1978; Jaffe, 1999). As in greeting cards, the imagery and verbal texts in *rainbow* art are largely prefabricated.[3] In this ethnographic study, I draw on 6 years of participant observation and on a database of approximately 6000 images, mostly captured while they were displayed online. Others come from image sets available via the channel's Web site.[4] I also incorporate material from semistructured interviews and e-mail exchanges with 36 "ops"—operators, individuals who help run the channel and create most of the art that is shared by all. Interviews were collected by e-mail during summer and fall 2002.

Participants treasure their pseudonymity; they use "nicks" (nicknames), which resemble Citizens' Band radio "handles" (Bechar-Israeli, 1995; Kalçik, 1985), graffiti writers' "tags" (Cooper & Chalfant, 1984), and stage or screen names of actors and other performers. With the players' agreement, actual online nicks are used here, as well as the actual name and URL of the channel.

Images are appreciated for themselves but are primarily a medium of communication, which tends to be playful and artful to call attention

**Author's Note:** An earlier version of this paper was presented at the Third Annual Conference of the Association of Internet Researchers, Maastricht, the Netherlands, October 13-16, 2002. For introductory information on Internet Relay Chat (IRC), see http://www.irc.org/.

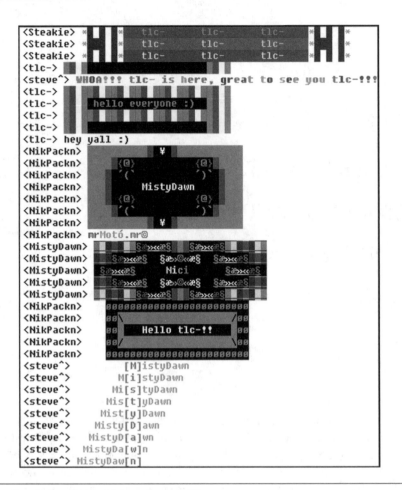

**Figure 22.1**    Greetings on #mirc_rainbow, August 2002

to itself. Richard Lanham (1993, p. 4) noted the "bi-stability" of the surface of digital text, compared to the transparency of texts in print culture. I attend both to the form and content of *rainbow* images *and* to their communicative functions in context.

## INTRODUCTION

In Figure 22.1, a sequence of live interaction captured in August 2002, five players have deployed six images and one line of ready-made text to greet or honor others. The nick of each player appears at the left, just as if the person typed ordinary text. First, <Steakie>,[5] a male signage installer from Pennsylvania, greets <tlc->, a male Mississippi carpenter in his 30s who has just arrived, with an image containing nine repetitions of his nick

(nicknames are presented in angle brackets, just as they appear online.) All images in Figure 22.1 had been prepared beforehand, by various *rainbow* artists, and are used as shown in the figure as tokens for interaction. I estimate that some 150 artists have created the art shared by all.

After the initial interchange shown in Figure 22.1, <steve^>, a 50-year-old English oil tanker driver, interjects a prescripted minitext, adding the recipient's nick: "WHOA!!! tlc- is here, great to see you tlc-!!!"

<tlc-> now displays an image with the message, "Hello everyone :)," adding, "hey yall :)."[6] Then <NikPackn>[7] greets <MistyDawn>, a secretary in her 30s from Missouri, <tlc->'s real-world wife and fellow op. <NikPackn> is a 50-ish female nursing administrator from Virginia. <MistyDawn> reciprocates with yet another

image. Next, <NikPackn> acknowledges <tlc->. Finally, using a script that transforms repeated nicks into visually attractive images, <steve^> greets <MistyDawn>.

## The Players and Their Leaders

Dissatisfied with the atmosphere on a channel called #mirc_colors, in May 1997 a group of players defected to found *rainbow*. Despite some ups and downs, this channel has flourished. Most players are Americans; concentrated in smaller cities and towns in the South, West, and Southwest; generally of high school education; employed in lower middle and working class occupations. There is a smattering of players from other countries. About 60% are women, although men play central roles as senior ops and programmers.[8]

Several leaders have higher educational attainments. The first was <texxy>, a male with a B.A. in public relations who led the group from 1997 to 2001. At the time, he was the customer service manager in a Texas office supplies store. The second leader was <patches>, a woman with a B.A. in music, and as her nick hints, an experienced quilter. When she withdrew from IRC in April 2002, <sher^>, the group's most popular, most prolific artist, an Illinois housewife and high school graduate married to a coal miner, took over.

## The *Rainbow* Motif

The name of the channel is rich in associations for the players. For centuries, the rainbow has been a prominent symbol of hope, optimism, and spiritual aspiration in Judeo-Christian tradition (Boyer, 1959; Gage, 1993; Lee & Fraser, 2001). These meanings also appear in William Wordsworth's (1802) famous poem:

My heart leaps up when I behold

A rainbow in the sky

For Philip Fisher (1998), the rainbow is "the central instance of the aesthetics of wonder" (p. 33). We wonder at, and are momentarily transported by, the unexpected. Rare and ephemeral, the rainbow offers us the pleasures of color and of regularity of geometric shape—a perfect half circle. Thus the channel name points to the players' longing for experiences that transport them out of humdrum routine and troublesome life situations.

In interviews I asked, "What do you think of when you think about the name of the channel? Why is 'rainbow' a good name for the channel?"<Litty>, an Indiana housewife in her 40s and a former alcoholic and drug addict, wrote, "Rainbows always brings [*sic*] a smile to your face." <kassy>, a disabled, African American former factory worker from Kentucky, replied, "Rainbows are good things make you smile. . . ." <MotoTsume>, a Canadian male computer technical support person, commented, "A Rainbow to me is a nice sign that storms are over (so it is a calm place to be and also a little magical)."

Today, the rainbow is a symbol of acceptance of diversity, for the gay and lesbian community and the African American Rainbow/PUSH Coalition.[9] This connotation is pertinent here too. For <MistyDawn>, the name "fits for the people . . . there are so many different people . . . from so many different places . . . with so many different personalities." For <patches>, another association was to *The Wizard of Oz* (Baum, 1956; Rushdie, 2002), and especially to the song, "Over the Rainbow." Below a motif on the *rainbow* Web site in the late 1990s were the words, "Click on above image to step into a world where dreams do come true," an almost exact quotation from this song.

## ASCII Art and IRC Art

IRC art is an elaboration of ASCII (pronounced *AS-kee*) art, an earlier form of text-based computer art. In the 1960s and 1970s, programmers, hackers, and computer professionals, who were mainly male, created it. By the 1990s, people of all walks of life, women and men, young and old, were doing so.[10] The acronym ASCII stands for American Standard Code for Information Interchange, the code that established the basic set of seven-bit typographic characters used in "plain text" across all operating systems; for example, in e-mail.[11]

ASCII art images are usually displayed in white on black or black on white[12] and are usually

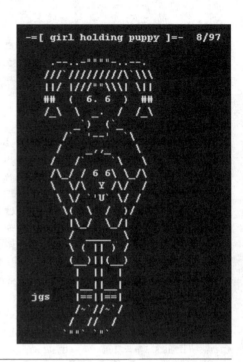

**Figure 22.2**    Solid Style and Line Style in ASCII Art

Credits: Skull and bones, artist unknown; girl with puppy, Joan Stark.

created in "solid style," in which clusters of repeated symbols create filled shapes, or "line style," in which typographic characters are used to "draw" the outlines of objects (Figure 22.2). Some art combines the two styles.

Early ASCII art often dealt with stereotypically male themes: space travel, sports, war and aggression. With increased participation in the 1990s of women, such as Joan Stark, the Ohio housewife who created the girl with puppy in Figure 22.2, imagery turned softer, more stereotypically feminine.

Surprisingly little verbal communication takes place on *rainbow*. Interaction is similar whether strangers or old-timers are greeted. IRC art emerged after 1995, when the Window-based IRC software enabled use of 16 different colors and exotic typographic symbols (extended ASCII characters[13]) to decorate text, as in

Wé£çômé to #Mìrç_Ráînbōw RickS

or, more often, to create visual patterns, as in Figure 22.3. Images are created as in knitting and ordinary wordprocessing: left to right, top to bottom.

This phenomenon juxtaposes computer skills with naïve aesthetic expression and partially resembles traditional crafts and folk art—weaving, embroidery, and quilting (Danet, 2003). Images are either abstract (Figure 22.3) or figurative (Figure 22.4). Abstract images usually contain elaborate play with typography or, less commonly, consist of blocks of solid color. Figurative images are mostly "drawn" with typographic symbols.

## Functions of *Rainbow* Activity for the Players

*Rainbow* activity fills many functions for the players. A paramount motivation for many is their love of the art and its colors. Asked, "What place does *rainbow* have in your life?" <Sea-mist>, a California office manager in her 40s, replied, "I go there to have fun, relax and enjoy the . . . colors and art work." <Serina>, another Californian in her 30s, who cleans houses, wrote, "I like the

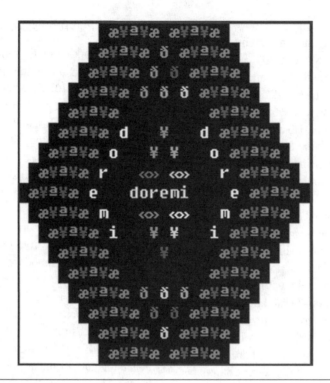

**Figure 22.3** Abstract Design

Credit: <blu->.

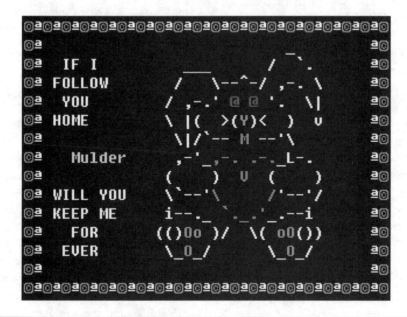

**Figure 22.4** A Figurative Image

Credit: Adapted by <glint> from a work by "flump," Haley Jane Wakenshaw ("hjw"), http://www.kersbergen.com/flump/.

colors and the playfulness that we all have." <Tammy>, a Florida sales representative in her 30s, said, "The colors are pretty awesome and what first attracted me to the channel."

Many participants are bored, unhappy, or lonely and looking for diversion. A Maryland writer in her 40s nicknamed <Desiree> told me, "Most are lonely people expressing their feelings through art." <Steakie> wrote that "being there is relaxing . . . and it helps pass away the boredom of a single life." For <Kassy>, the disabled Kentuckian, "*rainbow* is a special warm place when I can log on when I am having a bad day and just get a hug or a poke." <dholli>, a single Pennsylvania man in his 50s who underwent bypass heart surgery in 2002, said, "When your [*sic*] down u [you] can go to the ppl [people] and talk about it." <glint>, a New Zealand housewife in her 30s, wrote that *rainbow* "enriched my life so much its [*sic*] given me an out on days when I just want to crawl back into bed." There are a half dozen recovering drug addicts and alcoholics; others on *rainbow* have serious health problems or handicaps or have family members with such problems. For them, *rainbow* functions as a support group.

Some players cultivate friendships behind the scenes, via private e-mail and chat and on a second channel, #mirc_*rainbow*2, where they get technical help, rehearse displays, and chat verbally. Fourteen of the 36 interviewed used the word "family" spontaneously: <Citybear>, a 30-ish Texas housewife, keeps coming back because "it's like a family you never had before." <elp>, a formerly homeless male cook at a hospital in Texas, confessed, "I dont [*sic*] have friends in real life and I created a family in *rainbow*." Other functions of channel activity include a sense of mastery and increased computer literacy, the enjoyment of meeting people from all over the world, and satisfactions derived from helping others.

## PLAY AND RITUAL IN *RAINBOW* ART AND COMMUNICATION

*Rainbow* communication is a form of ritualized play—propelled by, and giving expression to, the group's central myths, thereby creating a sense of *communitas* (Turner, 1969, 1974).

## Play and Playfulness on *Rainbow*

In a reworking of Johannes Huizinga's (1955) classic formulation of the nature of play, Roger Caillois (1961, p. 10) characterized play as free, separate, uncertain, unproductive, governed by rules, and make believe. Most of these features characterize *rainbow* activity too, although playful activity online is not located in a separate physical space. Following J. Nina Lieberman (1977, p. 6), I distinguish three types of online playfulness: spontaneity, manifest joy, and a sense of humor. In differing degrees, all are present on *rainbow*. <crmsoda>, a female Web designer from California, uses the art "to emphasize my moods, chats and playfulness." There is spontaneity in the unpredictability of who participates and which images are displayed and by whom. For <Steakie>, *rainbow* is special "because the 'family' there all enjoys seeing someone 'LightUP' with joy after they have been helped or taught how to make their own files and play them." <Litty> said that "*rainbows* [*sic*] has the best of al [*sic*] worlds in it. Fun love. Joy. And most of all GOOD ppl." Humorous images are sometimes displayed, though sentimental ones predominate. <redmoon>, a divorced female psychiatric nurse from Texas with Cherokee roots, wrote, "I have had many a laugh at most of the antics that go on there."

### Why So Playful?

Three factors promote playfulness on *rainbow*. First is interactivity, the dynamic quality of the medium, its flexibility and speed, and the ability to interact with others in real time (McMillan & Downes, 2000; Rafaeli & Sudweeks, 1997). Second is the influence of hacker culture. Hackers cherish virtuoso play with symbols, words, typography, and spelling, often deliberately transgressing customary usage to challenge readability (Danet, 2001a, pp. 26-27, 2001b; Raymond, 1996). *Rainbow* artists share with them a love of play with writing and of extending what programs can do, although not their transgressive spirit. The masking of identity also fosters playfulness, because it reduces accountability for action (Danet, 1998; Turkle, 1995).

## Play, Ritual, and Liminality on *Rainbow*

Although primarily a form of play, *rainbow* activities also contain elements of secular ritual (Moore & Myerhoff, 1977; Rappaport, 1979, 1999; Tambiah, 1985). For present purposes, I adopt Stanley Tambiah's (1985) definition of ritual as presented in his famous essay, "A Performative Approach to Ritual":

> A culturally constructed system of symbolic communication . . . constituted of patterned and ordered sequences of words and acts, often expressed in multiple media, whose content and arrangement are characterized in varying degree by formality (conventionality), stereotypy (rigidity), condensation (fusion), and redundancy (repetition). (p. 128)

Drawing on Bateson (1955, 1972) and Rappaport (1971), Handelman (1976) suggests that the metamessage of the ritual frame is "This is ritual . . . *all messages included within this frame are true*" (p. 188). In contrast, the metamessage of play is "This is play . . . *all messages within this frame are false*" (p. 189, italics added). Ritual says "Let us believe"; play says "Let's pretend; let's act as if we believe." We will see that *rainbow* myths and canonical beliefs are of both types.

Both play and ritual are liminal phenomena. In liminal periods or events such as carnivals, hierarchical status differences and ordinary normative constraints are temporarily suspended; all experience sentiments of *communitas*, heightened awareness of belonging to a group (Turner, 1974, p. 44). Many spaces on the Internet, including *rainbow*, are liminal, or aspire to liminality despite their year-round nature. There is tension on *rainbow* between efforts to maintain the liminal frame and the organizational needs of the group.

## COMPONENTS OF RITUAL IN *RAINBOW* COMMUNICATION

### Canonical Beliefs

As is true in real-world ritual (Rappaport, 1999; Rothenbuhler, 1999, p. 92), *rainbow* activity expresses and entails more than meets the eye, more than most players can articulate. The logo on the channel Web site from 1998 to 2001, a pair of outstretched arms encircling nine small faces, also included the words "We love everyone here on #mirc_*rainbow*!!! Come join us and enjoy the rainbow of colors :)" This logo indicates that the group aspires to offer instant friendship and unconditional social acceptance to all and, at the same time, an enjoyable aesthetic experience.

Figure 22.5 is a formally stated list of beliefs underlying *rainbow* activities. The central belief is, "The real world is an insecure, unsafe, unloving place full of troubles. *Rainbow* is a secure, safe, loving place, a trouble-free haven where all are accepted, honored, appreciated, and loved, fully, instantly, and unconditionally." This formalization elaborates the proclamation, "we love everyone here on #mirc_*rainbow*."

Second and third, all are welcome and all are equal. The fourth belief expands the notion of unconditional love. Overt expression of love is available instantly to all. People may remain pseudonymous, although some may eventually reveal personal information as they come to trust others. These beliefs are based on a premise, unstated by *rainbow* members, that it is *possible* to love everyone fully, instantly, and unconditionally. I have also included a belief stating that virtual love and friendship are as valid as real-world forms of love and friendship. Another is that childhood is a happier, safer, more secure time of life than adulthood, a belief that helps explain the preference for childlike figurative imagery, as is apparent in figurative illustrations for this chapter. Last is the belief that all artists are equally talented and deserving of recognition.

## Formality: Formulaic Predictability, Repetitiveness

The degree of formality—of formulaic predictability—in all social situations varies along a continuum from least to most formal. In the restricted range of *rainbow* communicative acts, what changes are the identities of the greeters and those greeted and the images mobilized. Repetitiveness, a well-known feature of ritual, is

1. The real world is an insecure, unsafe, unloving place full of troubles. *Rainbow* is a secure, safe, loving place, a trouble-free haven.

2. People of all ages, from children and teenagers to the elderly, are equally welcome on *rainbow* regardless of gender, skin color, social class, ethnic background, or geographic location.

3. All who participate on *rainbow* are equal.

4. All participants are loved fully, instantly, and unconditionally, even if they do not reveal information about themselves and their real-world lives, and regardless of what information they choose to reveal or is unintentionally revealed.

5. It is possible to love everyone fully, instantly, and unconditionally.

6. Virtual love and friendship are as valid and as valuable as real-world forms of love and friendship.

7. Childhood is a more satisfying, happier, safer, and more secure time of life than adulthood.

8. All artists are equally talented and equally deserving of recognition.

**Figure 22.5**    *Rainbow* Canonical Beliefs

abundantly present. In addition to repetition of typographic symbols within images and incessant acts of greeting and honoring, there is repetition over time with minor variations in figurative images—scores of teddy bears, Valentines, cute animals, children, and so on. Another prominent form of repetition is bilateral symmetry (Danet, 2004), in which the two halves of an image mirror each other, as in Figure 22.3. Repetitiveness in image form resembles verbal *parallelism*, "the foregrounding of certain aspects of text or discourse by the introduction of *extra regularities* not called for by the basic rules of language" (Leech, 1969, p. 64; italics added). Parallelism is a pervasive device and idiom in formal speaking, chanting, and singing, and in greetings, farewells, petitions, and courtship overtures. Especially throughout the world's oral traditions, it is a "speech form or language stratum reserved for special situations, for the preservation of past wisdom, for the utterance of sacred words, *for determining ritual relations,* for healing, for communication with spirits" (Fox, 1975, pp. 127-128, cited in Tambiah, 1985, p. 140; italics added).

In work on the language of legal documents, I noted the prominence of one form of parallelism—word pairs, or binomial expressions (Malkiel, 1959), such as *aid and abet, cease and desist.* These pairs are usually partially redundant and contain striking formal regularities, such as assonance and alliteration and "thickening" of the language to enhance its performative power (Danet, 1984).

These reflections illuminate why earlier ASCII art was entirely figurative, whereas in IRC art we see the dramatic turn to patterning—systematic repetition of elements. ASCII art is created and viewed in solo conditions, whereas IRC art is a fundamentally social phenomenon. *Repetition within images and repetitiveness across images are related to the social and psychological functions of the display of images in context,* facilitated by and expressed through ritualization.

## Invariance

Often an exchange with a newcomer looks the same as one between old friends, although if players are friends, they may add a few words of personalized text. Occasionally, a visual exchange *is* fully personalized. Once, when <Nicky> greeted <iaaron> with a humorous image of a face sticking its tongue out, he responded with an image originally designed by <Nicky>. By playing it, <iaaron> honored her personally. Also, players

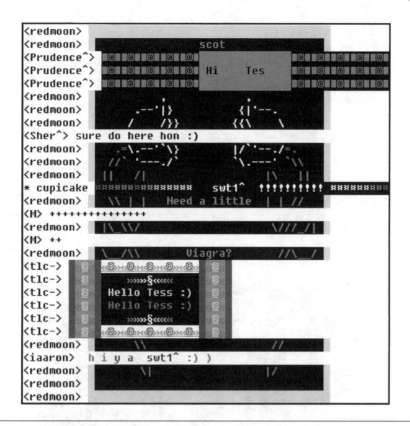

**Figure 22.6**    *A "Picture Collision"*

sometimes greet others with custom-designed nick files, displaying individual nicks in a highly decorative fashion. However, only a minority of images displayed are personalized in these ways.

Concern for face-saving is rare. One situation in which issues of face might arise, but rarely do, is "picture collisions," the messy overlap of images unintentionally displayed simultaneously (Figure 22.6). In this visual equivalent of people talking at once, <redmoon>'s image is interrupted by smaller ones and some typed text. Sometimes when collisions happen, one person apologizes, but usually in a humorous or playful manner. Mostly, people just laugh.

## Repertoire of Communicative Acts

A typology of the seven most common communicative acts on *rainbow* is presented in Figure 22.7.

In opening greetings, the words "hi" or "hello" may have been embedded in the original design

by the artist. Sometimes the word "hug" or "hugs" appears instead (Figure 22.8), indicating that images (including those without the word "hug") are intended and experienced as virtual hugs, gestures of affection.

By far the most common category is *honorings*, acts of acknowledging a given player, initially or *any time later*. In addition to those honorings containing only a nick, there are sentimental expressions of love and friendship (Figure 22.9) and offers of virtual goods and services, such as a cup of coffee. Humorous images may contain clever wordplay.

Other categories in Figure 22.7 are requests for love, attention, or friendship ( Figure 22.10); invitations, generally of a mock nature and often expressed metaphorically (Figure 22.11); and compliments, such as "You're beary sweet," in the spirit of paper greeting cards.

Requests for love, friendship, or attention may be embarrassingly explicit ("Please give me loving," Figure 22.10) or indirect. Invitations

> 1. Opening greetings
>
> 2. Acknowledgments
>
> 3. Any-time honorings
>
> 4. Requests for love, attention, friendship
>
> 5. Invitations
>
> 6. Good-byes or partings
>
> 7. Thank yous

**Figure 22.7**  A Typology of Visual and Verbal Communicative Acts on *Rainbow*

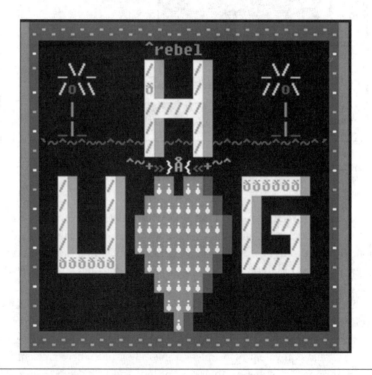

**Figure 22.8**  A Virtual Hug: An Image Containing the Word *Hug*

Credit: <angltooch>.

(Figure 22.11, "Wontcha come swing with me?") are closely related to requests; technically nonexecutable, they are another way of asking for attention. These five types of communicative acts constitute the bulk of all communicative activity on *rainbow*.

Two additional aspects of interaction also undermine seriousness of intent. In "*multiples,*" from 2 to 20 or more nicks can be inserted, instead of just one (Figure 22.12 ). In some, the nicks displayed are *randomly assigned* by the script embedded in the file. Thus, recipients are not really "being honored" by anyone. The players find this perfectly acceptable.

Second, I discovered that for a short period in 2002, a bot (mini-program or script) nicknamed

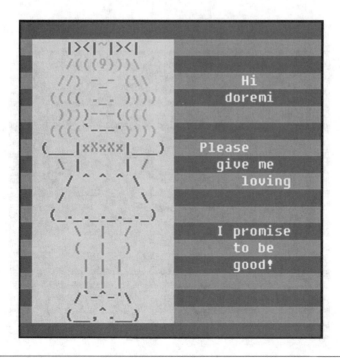

**Figure 22.9**     A Sentimental "Honoring" by <puriel>

Credit: Original by Normand Veilleux.

**Figure 22.10**     A Request for Love

Credit: <bamacutie>.

**Figure 22.11**    An "Invitation"

Credit: <gigi8>; teddy bear originally by Haley Jane Wakenshaw ("flump").

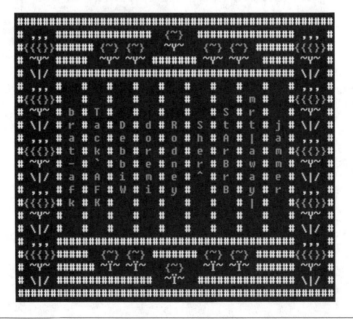

**Figure 22.12**    A "Multiple"

Credit: <sher^>.

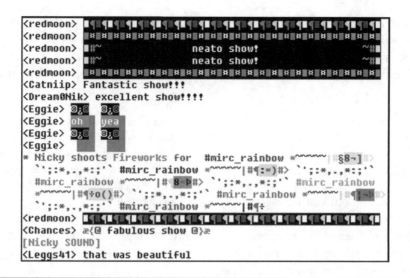

**Figure 22.13**    Audience Enthusiasm After Rainbow's First Anniversary Show

<eveline> seemingly greeted others. I was taken in: I thought that <eveline> was a person! I asked <sher^> whether others were taken in too. She claimed that although this did occasionally happen, the "victim" generally just laughed, rather than being upset. Eventually I noticed that the automated display was often grossly inappropriate. Sometimes the bot greeted itself. It displayed a Christmas greeting in April. The players were not bothered by these anomalies, partly because they enjoyed them as "art," and could instantly download the images. However, they also tolerated the anomalies because communication was partially ritualized.

## Performance

Performance is central to both play and ritual. In traditional oral genres of communication, the audience is invited to attend to the quality of the individual's performance. In Richard Bauman's (1992) well-known formulation,

the act of communication is put on display, objectified, lifted out to a degree from its contextual surroundings, and opened up to scrutiny by an audience. Performance thus calls forth special attention to and heightened awareness of the act of communication and gives license to the audience to regard it and the performer with special intensity. Performance makes

one communicatively accountable; it assigns to an audience the responsibility of evaluating the relative skill and effectiveness of the performer's accomplishment. (p. 44)

In contrast, in ritual, the quality of the individual performance does not matter; what matters is *doing it right.* Thus, in a marriage ceremony, it does not matter if one speaks loudly or softly; saying the correct words in the presence of authorized others is what counts (Austin, 1970). There are performers in both drama and ritual, but in drama there is also an audience. In ritual, on the other hand, all present are part of a *congregation* (Rappaport, 1999, p. 39).

*Rainbow* activities include not only regular communication but also occasional scheduled "shows," during which the group changes from "congregation" to "audience" and, technically, only the moderator may speak or display images. After the show, audience members "clap," type "bravo," and compliment the artists (Figure 22.13). Such audience behavior does not occur in regular channel interaction.

Whereas *rainbow* shows have clear beginnings and endings, spontaneous, continuous *rainbow* communication does not. Participants come and go any time they want. Another critical aspect of ritual is also missing: the absence of spiritual or social transformation. Participants do not emerge transformed from sequences of interaction. Consequently, ordinary *rainbow* activity is best viewed as ritualized play rather than full-fledged ritual.

## Discussion

### Canonical Beliefs: Mock or Serious?

*Rainbow* activity is both a form of lighthearted play with typography and visual imagery *and* a poignant pursuit of friendship and *communitas.* The channel offers a relatively risk-free environment where people who have low trust of others, are emotionally damaged, have unmet social and psychological needs, or have difficulties creating real-world social ties can reach out to others behind the scenes while creating and playing *rainbow* art and having fun.

Are the canonical beliefs I have discussed mock or serious? There is no pretense in the belief that all are welcome. However, the other beliefs involve a degree of pretense, notably the belief that *rainbow* is a secure, safe haven where all are loved. The guiding metamessage is, "*Let us pretend that this is so,*" or "Let us act *as if* this were so."

Interviews and correspondence with the players indicate that some of these needs *are* met, at least for a time—if they are lucky, even for years. However, one should not romanticize the phenomenon. Online social relationships may be more tenuous and volatile than those in real life. Asked in July 2002 what place *rainbow* has in her life, <redmoon> had written,

> I was [initially] in *rainbow* in a very insecure time of my life. Being loved is fun. Being adored is even better. I felt secure. I still feel a sense of security there. *Rainbow* saw me through a very lonely time in my life.

At the time, her husband was being unfaithful, and she was miserable; she was later divorced. The sense of well-being on *rainbow* did not last. Outraged by her demotion in spring 2003 to a lower ops status because of reduced participation,

she withdrew abruptly from all *rainbow* activity. In May 2003, she wrote me:

> For a channel who [*sic*] doesn't pay much attention to op levels, this really chapped my a**. If they continue to base ops on strickly [*sic*] performance, and who can color [create art] and who shows up, that channel will have the personality of a dead cat. Don't get me wrong, I loved *rainbow*. Had more fun in there than a body had a right too [*sic*]. But showing up when I could, and I felt being kicked in the pants for it. Well, that didn't suit me at all.[14]

### Presence, Appeal to the Senses and the Future of Online Ritual

Two additional aspects of ritual, not yet discussed, are also absent from *rainbow* activities: physical copresence of participants and direct, unmediated, rich appeal to the nonvisual senses. Attention to these aspects can help us assess the prospects for full-fledged online ritual in the future.

Unmediated oral ritual appeals to the senses in many ways. Besides verbal formulas, there are often stylized gestures, ceremonial objects, dress and body adornment, special food and drink, and decoration of the setting (Danet, 1997; Moore & Myerhoff, 1977). With regard to online religion, Lorne Dawson (2000, 2001) has debated whether authentic religious experience is compatible with the heightened reflexivity of life in cyberspace.

Writing about presence in relation to theater, Roger Copeland (1990, p. 32) noted that technological components may intensify living presence, producing sensory overload and even heightening the sense of presentness. Participants in many online modes, including *rainbow* displays, do experience a sense of copresence, even in the limited state of today's technologies. A critical element is *immersion:* "When [participants] feel immersive presence they are involved . . . absorbed . . . engaged, engrossed" (Lombard & Ditton, 1997). A practitioner of text-based online theatrical performance wrote, "Players in online theater consistently report a unique sense of total immersion and exaltation" (LaFarge, 1995, p. 421). Even in bare-bones textual form, many kinds of real-time interaction are experienced as emotionally gripping—occasionally, even traumatic (Dibbell, 1996).

Live, televised media events comprise powerful forms of mediated ritual, performing important integrative functions for the millions who watch them (Dayan & Katz, 1992). Viewing televangelism broadcasts enables audience members to experience *communitas*, to deepen religious experience, and to pursue help in dealing with crisis and loss (Alexander, 1994; Hoover, 1988). Varieties of interactive online ritual are likely to be at least as powerful, if not more so.

Acting individually online, people are already engaged in many ritual activities. Millions have sent or received digital greetings celebrating birthdays, holidays, and graduations (Danet, 2001a, chapter 4) or have signed virtual condolence books and lit virtual candles following the deaths of Diana, Princess of Wales; Mother Teresa; Yitshak Rabin; and Ronald Reagan and after collective disasters, such as the events of September 11, 2001. Virtual prayer is encouraged on the Web. Catholics can e-mail a request for intercession by St. Francis. Jews can e-mail a prayer to the Western Wall in Jerusalem, which is printed and inserted between the stones by someone there. A Buddhist site invites people to download digital prayer wheels for their computer. As for fully interactive, online religious ritual, most studies have been about "religion online"—utilization of the Internet by institutionalized religions, such as the Catholic Church (Brasher, 2001; Hadden & Cowan, 2000)—rather than "online religion" (Fernback, 2002; Helland, 2000; O'Leary, 1996; Schroeder, Heather, & Lee, 1998; Telesco & Knight, 2001).

The mixing of playful and ritual elements seen in this chapter is not new. Rappaport (1999) notes, for instance, that "Clowns have important roles to play in the rituals of the Tewa . . . and other American Indians, in Sri Lanka . . . and elsewhere" (p. 33; see also Handelman, 1981). As for the Internet, there is already evidence for the mixing of serious and playful, even hilariously parodic elements in virtual weddings on IRC and MOOs (Jacobson, 1996). The first simulated wedding in a three-dimensional virtual world took place in

May 1996 on "AlphaWorld," a graphical chat interface. After the ceremony, the groom drove from Texas to Seattle to join his virtual bride (Damer, 1997). Experiments by noninstitutional groups, such as Technopagans, also mix ludic and serious components (O'Leary, 1996; Schroeder et al., 1998).

Although these experiments may seem silly or inauthentic, we must have an open mind as to what is to come. Ultimately, all ritual is "made up" and requires a leap of faith for participants to believe in its efficacy. Even real-world ritual often involves simulation. Taking communion in Catholic ritual is a way of partaking of the body and blood of Jesus. By eating matzoth at the Passover Seder, Jews relive the Exodus from ancient Egypt. When fully immersive technologies of virtual reality become available, flooding the senses, obliterating awareness of the medium and one's physical surroundings and maximizing the sense of copresence (Grau, 2003; Murray, 1997), we are likely to see a flowering of online ritual, perhaps including elements of playfulness as well.

## NOTES

1. The number or pound sign (#) is the symbol marking every IRC channel. "mIRC" is the name of the Windows-based version of the IRC software.

2. There have been channels of the same name on other networks. This group is the best known.

3. To view this phenomenon online, download and install mIRC for Windows from http://www.mirc.co.uk/. Once the program is activated, log onto an Undernet server and type /join #mirc_rainbow in the main window.

4. See the downloads page at http://www.mirc-rainbow.net/.

5. Information on the social background of individual players is from online interviews.

6. The collection of punctuation marks shown as :-) is a "smiley," an emoticon—a sideways smile, viewed by tilting one's head toward one's left shoulder.

7. <Nici> and <NikPackn> are the same person: The temporary nick "Nikpackn" signals that <Nici> is packing for a trip, not paying full attention.

8. Because there has been quite high turnover in the group, it is difficult to establish a reliable social profile. This one, from Danet (2001a, pp. 248-252), was based on

minibiographies of players on the channel Web site. Unfortunately, the current version of the Web site, http://www.mirc-rainbow.net, no longer contains such minibiographies. Interviews with ops in summer and fall 2002 suggest that the profile has not changed significantly.

9. See http://www-2.cs.cmu.edu/afs/cs.cmu.edu/ user/scotts/bulgarians/rainbow-flag.html and http://www. rainbowpush.org/about/index.html.

10. For a history of ASCII art, see Danet (2001a, chapter 5).

11. ASCII code is "A text standard that consists of 128 characters (0-127) covering alphabetical, numerical, punctuation, and a few text control characters" (Computer Knowledge, 2004). There are 95 characters available for writing.

12. In earlier (DOS) times, they were displayed in phosphorescent amber or green pixels on a black screen.

13. These are eight-bit characters rather than the seven of plain text.

14. <redmoon> later rejoined the channel, despite her reduced ops status.

# REFERENCES

Alexander, B. C. (1994). *Televangelism reconsidered: Ritual in the search for human community.* Atlanta, GA: Scholars Press.

Austin, J. L. (1970). *How to do things with words.* Oxford, England: Oxford University Press.

Bateson, G. (1955). The message "This is play." In B. Schaffner (Ed.), *Conferences on group processes.* New York: Columbia University Press.

Bateson, G. (1972). *Steps to an ecology of mind.* New York: Ballantine.

Baum, F. L. (1956). *The wizard of Oz.* Chicago: Reilly and Lee.

Bauman, R. (1992). Performance. In R. Bauman (Ed.), *Folklore, cultural performances, and popular entertainments: A communications-centered handbook* (pp. 41-49). New York: Oxford University Press.

Bechar-Israeli, H. (1995). From <bonehead> to <clonehead>: Nicknames, play and identity on Internet relay chat. *Journal of Computer-Mediated Communication, 1*(2). Retrieved January 17, 2005, from http://jcmc/indiana.edu/vol1/issue2/

Boyer, C. B. (1959). *The rainbow: From myth to mathematics.* New York: Thomas Yoseloff.

Brasher, B. (2001). *Give me that online religion.* San Francisco: Jossey-Bass.

Caillois, R. (1961). *Man, play and games.* Glencoe, IL: Free Press.

Computer Knowledge. (2004). *ASCII—American standard code for information exchange.* Retrieved December 21, 2004, from http://www.cknow.com/ckinfo/index.php?ToDo=view&questId=57&catId=3

Cooper, M., & Chalfant, H. (1984). *Subway art.* New York: Henry Holt.

Copeland, R. (1990). The presence of mediation. *TDR: The Drama Review, 34,* 28-44.

Damer, B. (1997). *Avatars! Exploring and building virtual worlds.* San Francisco: Peachpit Press.

Danet, B. (1984). The magic flute: A prosodic analysis of binomial expressions in legal Hebrew. *Text, 4,* 143-172.

Danet, B. (1997). Speech, writing and performativity: An evolutionary view of the history of constitutive ritual. In B. L. Gunnarsson, P. Linell, & B. Nordberg (Eds.), *The construction of professional discourse* (pp. 13-41). London: Longman.

Danet, B. (1998). Text as mask: Gender, play and performance on the Internet. In S. G. Jones (Ed.), *Cybersociety 2.0: Revisiting computer-mediated communication and community* (pp. 129-158). Thousand Oaks, CA: Sage.

Danet, B. (2001a). *Cyberpl@y: Communicating online.* Oxford: Berg Publishers.

Danet, B. (2001b). *Cyberpl@y: Communicating online* [Home page]. Retrieved January 20, 2005, from http://pluto.mscc.huji.ac.il/~msdanet/cyberpl@y/index.html

Danet, B. (2003). Pixel patchwork: "Quilting in time" online. *Textile: The Journal of Cloth & Culture, 1*(2), 118-143.

Danet, B. (2004). "If you have a lot of clutter it messes up the popup": The pursuit of good gestalts in an online folk art. *Textile: The Journal of Cloth & Culture, 2*(3, Special issue), 226-254.

Dawson, L. L. (2000). Researching religion in cyberspace: Issues and strategies. In J. K. Hadden & D. E. Cowan (Eds.), *Religion on the Internet* (pp. 25-54). New York: JAI Press.

Dawson, L. L. (2001). Doing religion in cyberspace: The promise and the perils. *The Council of Societies for the Study of Religion Bulletin, 30*(1), 3-9.

Dayan, D., & Katz, E. (1992). *Media events: The live broadcasting of history.* Cambridge, MA: Harvard University Press.

Dibbell, J. (1996). A rape in cyberspace, or how an evil clown, a Haitian trickster spirit, two wizards, and a cast of dozens turned a database into a society. In

P. Ludlow (Ed.), *High noon on the electronic frontier* (pp. 375-396). Cambridge: MIT Press.

Fernback, J. (2002). Internet ritual: A case study of the construction of computer-mediated neopagan religious meaning. In S. M. Hoover & L. S. Clark (Eds.), *Practicing religion in the age of the media: Explorations in media, religion and culture* (pp. 254-275). New York: Columbia University Press.

Fisher, P. (1998). *Wonder, the rainbow, and the aesthetics of rare experiences.* Cambridge, MA: Harvard University Press.

Fox, J. J. (1975). On binary categories and primary symbols. In R. Willis (Ed.), *The interpretation of symbolism* (pp. 99-132). New York: Wiley.

Gage, J. (1993). *Color and culture: Practice and meaning from antiquity to abstraction.* London: Thames & Hudson.

Goffman, E. (1967). *Interaction ritual: Essays on face-to-face behavior.* Garden City, NY: Anchor.

Grau, O. (2003). *Virtual art: From illusion to immersion.* Cambridge: MIT Press.

Hadden, J. K., & Cowan, D. E. (Eds.). (2000). *Religion on the Internet: Research prospects and promises.* New York: JAI Press.

Handelman, D. (1976). Play and ritual: Complementary frames of meta-communication. In A. J. Chapman & H. Foot (Eds.), *It's a funny thing, humour* (pp. 185-192). London: Pergamon.

Handelman, D. (1981). The ritual clown: Attributes and affinities. *Anthropos, 76,* 321-370.

Helland, C. (2000). Online-religion/religion-online and virtual communitas. In J. K. Hadden & D. E. Cowan (Eds.), *Religion on the Internet: Research prospects and promises* (pp. 205-223). New York: JAI Press.

Herrnstein-Smith, B. (1978). *On the margins of discourse: The relation of literature to language.* Chicago: University of Chicago Press.

Hoover, S. M. (1988). *Mass media religion: The social sources of the electronic church.* Newbury Park, CA: Sage.

Hoover, S. M., & Park, J. K. (2005). Religion and meaning in the digital age: Field research on Internet and Web religion. In E. W. Rothenbuhler & M. Coman (Eds.), *Media anthropology* (pp. 247-259). Thousand Oaks, CA: Sage.

Huizinga, J. (1955). *Homo ludens: A study of the play element in culture.* Boston: Beacon.

Jacobson, D. (1996). Contexts and cues in cyberspace: The pragmatics of naming in text-based virtual realities. *Journal of Anthropological Research, 52,* 461-479.

Jaffe, A. (1999). Packaged sentiments: The social meanings of greeting cards. *Journal of Material Culture, 4,* 115-141.

Kalçik, S. (1985). Women's handles and the performance of identity in the CB community. In R. Jordan & S. Kalçik (Eds.), *Women's folklore, women's culture* (pp. 99-108). Philadelphia: University of Pennsylvania Press.

LaFarge, A. (1995). A world exhilarating and wrong: Theatrical improvisation on the Internet. *Leonardo, 28,* 415-422.

Lanham, R. A. (1993). *The electronic word: Democracy, technology, and the arts.* Chicago: University of Chicago Press.

Lee, R. L., Jr., & Fraser, A. B. (2001). *The rainbow bridge: Rainbows in art, myth, and science.* University Park, PA, & Bellingham, WA: Pennsylvania State University Press & SPIE Press.

Leech, G. (1969). *A linguistic guide to English poetry.* London: Longman.

Lieberman, J. N. (1977). *Playfulness: Its relation to imagination and creativity.* New York: Academic Press.

Lombard, M., & Ditton, T. (1997). At the heart of it all: The concept of telepresence. *Journal of Computer-Mediated Communication, 3.* Retrieved January 17, 2005, from http://jcmc/indiana.edu/vol3/issue2/lombard.html

Malkiel, Y. (1959). Studies in irreversible binomials. *Lingua, 8,* 113-160.

McMillan, S. J., & Downes, E. J. (2000). Defining interactivity: A qualitative identification of key dimensions. *New Media & Society, 2,* 157-179.

Moore, S. F., & Myerhoff, B. G. (Eds.). (1977). *Secular ritual.* Assen, Netherlands: Van Gorcum.

Murray, J. H. (1997). *Hamlet on the holodeck: The future of narrative in cyberspace.* New York: Free Press.

O'Leary, S. (1996). Cyberspace as sacred space: Communicating religion on computer networks. *Journal of the American Academy of Religion, 64,* 781-808.

Rafaeli, S., & Sudweeks, F. (1997). Networked interactivity. *Journal of Computer-Mediated Communication, 4*(Special issue). Retrieved January 17, 2005, from http://jcmc/indiana.edu/vol2/issue4/

Rappaport, R. A. (1971). Ritual, sanctity and cybernetics. *American Anthropologist, 73,* 59-76.

Rappaport, R. A. (1979). *Ecology, meaning, and religion.* Berkeley, CA: North Atlantic.

Rappaport, R. A. (1999). *Ritual and religion in the making of humanity.* Cambridge, England: Cambridge University Press.

Raymond, E. S. (1996). *The new hackers' dictionary*. Cambridge: MIT Press.

Rothenbuhler, E. W. (1999). *Ritual communication: From everyday conversation to mediated ceremony*. Thousand Oaks, CA: Sage.

Rushdie, S.(2002). *Step across this line: Collected non-fiction 1992-2002*. New York: Random House.

Schroeder, R., Heather, N., & Lee, R. M. (1998). The sacred and the virtual: Religion in multi-user virtual reality. *Journal of Computer-Mediated Communication, 4*. Retrieved January 17, 2005, from http://jcmc/indiana.edu/vol4/issue2/schroeder.html

Tambiah, S. (1985). *Culture, thought and social action*. Cambridge, MA: Harvard University Press.

Telesco, P., & Knight, S. (2001). *The Wiccan Web: Surfing the magic on the Internet*. New York: Citadel.

Turkle, S. (1995). *Life on the screen: Identity in the age of the Internet*. New York: Simon & Schuster.

Turner, V. (1969). *The ritual process: Structure and anti-structure*. Chicago: Aldine.

Turner, V. (1974). *Dramas, fields, and metaphors: Symbolic action in human society*. Ithaca, NY: Cornell University Press.

Wordsworth, W. (1802). *My heart leaps up when I behold*. Retrieved December 21, 2004, from http://www.4literature.net/William_Wordsworth/My_Heart_Leaps_Up_When_I_Behold/

# 23

## The Anthropology of Religious Meaning Making in the Digital Age

Stewart M. Hoover and Jin Kyu Park

Among the many speculations that have circulated about the nature and implications of the digital era has been a robust discourse about *religion* in the digital or online age. What seems to reside beneath this discourse is a deceptively simple question: How is the emergence of digital and online communication changing religion? It goes almost without saying that to answer this question it is necessary to understand both *online* and *religion* better than most scholarship in either area has previously seemed to. It is our purpose here to explore this question through reference both to emerging scholarship on the Internet-Web-online-digital world and to ongoing fieldwork on religion and meaning making in the media age.

A scholarship on media and religion is emerging around the notion that the natures of both *religion* and *the media* are undergoing change and are, in fact, converging in important ways (Hoover, 2001). Religion in the industrialized West is becoming increasingly an individual

matter. Based in late-modern trends identified by Giddens (1991), modern consciousness now finds itself in a more or less constant quest to construct an ideal "self," with much social and cultural practice oriented toward that project. Religion—including practices that share a family resemblance to religion but that may no longer be thought of as "purely" religious—can be seen as a dimension of that project of the self. In fact, an important strain of contemporary scholarship on religion identifies a self-oriented, autonomous spiritual seeking as one of the primary modes of contemporary religion and quasireligion (Roof, 1999). At the same time, the media sphere seems to be offering more and more material of a religious, quasireligious, or implicitly religious nature. There is, further, reason to suspect that the online world is one that is particularly prone to be a site of certain kinds of religious and quasireligious seeking and formation (Brasher, 2001).

As an emerging social and cultural reality, the Internet-Web-digital has been approached by

**Authors' Note:** Earlier versions of this chapter were presented at the Association of Internet Researchers 3.0, Maastricht, Netherlands, October 2002, and appeared as "Religion and Meaning in the Digital Age" in Horsfield, Hess, and Medrano (2004).

scholars through a range of approaches. Descriptive and anecdotal work is important. So are case histories, case studies, observations, interpretations, and (as the Pew Internet in American Life project has demonstrated) even large-sample representative studies. This will always be the case. The thinking and work we present here are intended to represent only one of many possible approaches to these questions. Reflexively speaking, our project is intended to (a) bring a more sustained focus to questions of religion and those ideas, symbols, and practices that bear a family resemblance to religion and (b) explore what can be learned from a specific kind of fieldwork: ongoing qualitative interview studies in media households.

As we noted, religion has been a fairly common theme in scholarly and lay discourse about the digital age. A number of books and studies have been produced. Much remains to be done, however. What we will do here is briefly review some of the initial work we have conducted on this in our research projects, focusing on two areas: (a) the emerging textual landscape of religion on the Web and (b) the results of initial interviews relative to these questions in our sample households.[1]

## Religion Online Versus Online Religion

Christopher Helland (2000) has introduced an elegant way of looking at this turf: the distinction between "religion online" and "online religion." Simply put, *religion online* is the self-conscious use of the online context by religion organizations or movements for purposes of publicity, education, outreach, proselytization, and so on. *Online religion,* by contrast, is the far more interesting issue of the online context becoming or being used as a locus of religious, spiritual (or other similar) practice. In a way, *religion online* is the easier side to study. Its sources, intentions, and resources are easier to see and account for. *Online religion,* by contrast, is more difficult and elusive.

Both of these "sides," of course, evolve from a set of concerns that should be entirely familiar to

us. Throughout modern history, each succeeding evolution or revolution in communication, from the printing press to television, has evoked hand wringing about its potential impact on religion. In the case of television, the controversy really took hold in the 1970s and 1980s with the emergence of televangelism. Some of the concerns are the same. For example, with both televangelism and the potential for online religion, some religionists are surely concerned about how this new medium might be *harming* "traditional" religion.

As was found with televangelism (see, for example, Hoover, 1988), it is likely that such concerns are too simplistic and too facile. The situation is surely more complex. It is likely, though, that one of the major implications of televangelism also applies to the Internet-Web-online context. In both cases, one important "effect" will have been in the area of social legitimation. Just as televangelism served to legitimize certain aspects of religion, in all probability, so will the Internet. This remains to be seen.

Returning to Helland's taxonomy, how do we go about understanding the intriguing area of online religion? Much of the most interesting work, such as that of Brasher (2001), Zaleski (1997), and Lawrence (2002), has worked at description and explanation. The basic outlines are that in the online world, a vibrant religious, spiritual, and transcendent set of discourses and practices has emerged. This is significant on its own terms. Although the balance of what we present here might be read as raising questions about the size and significance of the developments described by Brasher, Zaleski, and others, that is not our point. To the extent that online religion has developed in the ways they detail, there are potentially very important consequences for religion and culture as we have known them.

Our purpose is to look in a different direction. As media audience researchers, we are interested in what we can learn by standing with the audience, "looking back" with them, as it were, toward the mediated cultural world they inhabit and understanding the symbols and practices that emerge as meaningful—even religiously or spiritually meaningful—to them in that context. This theoretical and methodological approach has been described in detail elsewhere (Hoover, 2002, in press; Hoover & Russo, 2002). It is rooted in interactionist social theory and posits that the media sphere constitutes a "symbolic inventory," out of which audiences select symbols, values, associations, discourses, and ideas they use to infuse their lives with meaningful identities.

Looked at in this way, both religion online and online religion potentially provide resources for meaning making, although with radically different associations, saliencies, and potentials.

## CONTEMPORARY RELIGION THEORY AND RESEARCH

An important part of the project of understanding these things is a review of the valuable emergent scholarship in the area of religion. Unfortunately, a good deal of the work that has gone before has tended not to take advantage of this resource. An important comprehensive review of this work by Stephen Warner (1992) calls it "new paradigm" religion research. As opposed to traditional ways of looking at religion, in which history, symbol, and doctrine were seen as determinants of belief and action, Warner argues that we now must begin to look at religion as *achieved* rather than only as *ascribed*. The focus of this work is thus on the meaningful actions of communities and individuals in achieving meaning and insight rather than on investigating the ways in which adherents do or do not "get" the orthodoxies of various religious *traditions*.

This dovetails, of course, with the most persuasive directions of contemporary cultural studies as they have been applied to the media. Qualitative methodologies and interpretive sensibilities dominate in this new religion research, along with narrative studies and a focus on popular practice.

A basic assumption of this new religion research that has emerged is the powerful idea, itself derived from the work of social theorists such as Giddens, that the contemporary religious project is—like the contemporary social project—a project of the construction of the *self* and *identity*. In the context of religion research, this has evolved into a range of studies and approaches stressing the autonomous actions of individuals in making these kinds of sense. Most prominent among these ideas—as we noted earlier—has been the idea of religious or spiritual *seeking*. Most extensively understood through the work of Wade Clark Roof (1999), seeking underlies religious practice across a range of traditions and contexts. At its most basic, it replaces other structures of motivation and action with a process whereby the individual is self-consciously and reflexively engaged in a process of cultural, identity, and meaning construction. The terms of reference revolve around the individual and his or her needs and motivations.

## ONLINE RELIGION

This religious seeking pervades most traditions and contexts today, from the more traditional movements to and including movements that are on the religious and spiritual fringes. The most obvious examples of seeking come from the package of sensibilities and practices generally referred to as "new age" spirituality. New age defies a normative definition but generally includes those groups and practices that combine seeking with active processes of cultural and symbolic appropriation, creating hybrid traditions that combine Christianity with Eastern and Native American traditions, for example. New age is also interconnected with secular therapeutic resources, such as the variety of 12-step and other self-help programs. Most significantly for our purposes here, new age has always been mediated and commodified, its resources having been made available most commonly through books, tapes, seminars, and other paraphernalia.

Although new age is in some ways the proto-example of seeking, it is in fact the sensibility of seeking itself that is most important here. As an emergent religious practice, seeking expresses itself across a wide range of traditions and sensibilities.

More important for our arguments here, though, is the relationship of seeking to the online context. As a religious or spiritual practice, seeking fits well with the emergent online context. The market-place of symbols and contexts in the Web is open to the seeker. There is no priesthood, no dominant tradition or doctrine. There are no barriers to entry or participation. Further, the Web is a place of tremendous creativity, variety, and volubility. It is typified by playfulness, invention, and novelty.

In fact, many of the Web sites (representative of religion online) assume that seeking is taking place. They provide resources, handles, information, links, and so on designed to attract the seeker and bring her or him in. More interesting, though, is the relationship between seeking and online religion. The elasticity and subjectivity of the "selves" that presumably "seek" online enable them to integrate their quests into the kinds of settings and locations present in the Web (see, e.g., Brasher, 2001, for a more complete discussion). A further issue is rooted in the inherent subjectivity of these practices. As autonomous seekers move into the online environment, their practices need not bear any necessary relationship to established or ascribed categories of religious, spiritual, or meaning practice. Put another way, there is no necessary contingency between the constructions and intentions of the creators of Internet sites and the meanings or practices they invoke or relate to in online seekers.

## The Focus of This Study

The balance of this chapter will chart, in a rudimentary way, a theoretical and methodological route through the terrain of online-Web-digital religion and spirituality. The basic argument is as follows. The most interesting and challenging aspect of these matters is the online religion side of Helland's typology. It is interesting because it would be the most portentous in terms of its implications for what we used to think of as "religion." It is challenging because it is the most difficult to study. It is possible, as previous studies have demonstrated, to locate an online community of interest and carry out interviews, observations, and other sorts of research interventions. The kind of online audience activity that is most relevant should be that which is rooted in the mode of religious practice called seeking, and the Internet-Web-digital context should be particularly amenable to this mode. The nature of practice, as well as the outlines of the online religion that is achieved, should be of certain kinds—more individualistic, more subjective, less "traditional," more open to construction and reconstruction, less "fixed," more "fluid," yet grounded (Roof, 1999) in certain kinds of histories and meanings and symbols.

In contrast to such a theoretical argument, it is far more difficult to study these matters in a way that addresses questions dealing with (a) the varieties and levels of meanings, motivations, and practices that underlie or lead to online spiritual or religious activity; (b) the relationship between interest, motivation, the mode of seeking, and actual online involvement or behavior; (c) the capacities (structural, textual, and otherwise) of online sites to serve practices of seeking; (d) the issue of what Clark (2002) calls "implicit" religion online, in which religious and spiritual meanings and associations may be achieved regardless of the textual or structural intentions of site designers; (e) insights into the prevalence of online religion in various cultural, demographic, and social categories.

These latter questions, which get more at the "horizontal" and less at the "vertical" levels of online religious activity, are best addressed in ways other than textual case studies. They require a kind of sampling of Internet options, audiences, and practices to make possible the capture of significant information about what might be going on. The discussion of field research that follows approaches this type of method. We engage households in in-depth discussions of their narratives of self, family, and community, with special attention to the place of their media use in these constructions. Households have been included in our study by means of what Lindlof (1995) calls "maximum variability sampling," a technique in which interview sites are chosen for their variability along a range of demographic categories. Thus our conversations look for both particularities and commonalities in their expressions and seek to probe the capacities of various media practices to support various kinds of social and cultural action.

## Examples From Field Data

There follows a series of excerpts from our field data. These give a flavor of the kind of material we have to work with. Each is accompanied by a brief interpretive note. In each case, we identify which of our colleagues conducted the interview.

*Chris Chandler*[2] is a 35-year-old single father. He was interviewed by Anna Maria Russo, one of our colleagues.

Interviewer: So would you describe yourself in terms of religion or spirituality?

Chris: [Confused; laughs] You know I have my core Christian Catholic belief but then there is also I love Zen, I love the beliefs of the American Indians, Tao. It all fascinates me but ultimately all comes down to God and I try to.

I: The Catholic God?

C: Yeah, for the most part. And I try to pray, I try to count my blessings. I try to say "Thanks, God" every day, I try to [give] thanks for giving me Alicia [his daughter], thanks you know for keeping me healthy you know it's not like I get down and kneel. Usually when I get in the car, you know because I spend all day driving for work and so usually when I get in the car.

I: So do you ever seek out anything related to religion or spirituality on TV or on the Internet or in other media, movies?

C: Definitely Internet.

I: Yeah, where, what about it?

C: Um, I can't really give sites' names but definitely when I am in those moods where I just search you know and I think to myself well OK I am going. . . . I will have a search like. . . . I always had a thing for the American Indians, you know so. But I can't say definitely that is all religion but you know . . . but I can't say about TV at all. Do you mean as far as like religious?

I: Or spirituality, spiritual things or themes.

C: Let's say if it's on I see something but I can't say that I search for it. Maybe we are just different in semantics. . . . I don't watch *Touched by an Angel.*

I: Can you find meaningful things related to your spiritual beliefs in movies or TV shows or anywhere else that relates to your values. . . ?

C: I would say probably more music for me in that way. I would say definitely more music. When I am searching for some kind of spirituality I would say definitely more in music.

### Interpretation

For Chris Chandler, who works as a field credit representative, the Internet is the most useful medium for providing cultural resources for the construction of his own spirituality. He employs the Internet in the process through which he incorporates his interests in the spiritual qualities of various spiritual traditions, such as Zen, American Indian, and Tao, into his "core Christian Catholic beliefs." His use of the media for religious purposes seems to be very important in the course of positioning his religious identity. Another interesting point is that although Chris clearly recognizes his use of the Internet for religious purposes, he tries to refuse to relate his television viewing to his spirituality, because he does not want to be identified with the kind of people who search for religious meanings by watching such TV shows as *Touched by an Angel*. In that sense, the Internet provides him with both an acceptable and an efficient way of seeking resources for his own spirituality. It fits with his seeker sensibility (in his view) in that it is not as determinative as television.[3]

*David Mueller* is a 30-year-old father of three. He, his wife, and his children were interviewed by our colleague Dr. Joseph Champ.

| | |
|---|---|
| Interviewer: | Getting back to beliefs. Do you ever seek out inspirational, transcendent, religious information in media at all? Or do you mostly get that when you go to church? |
| David: | The church has an extensive amount of Web sites. And you can go there and you can get spiritual thoughts, there's resources as far as scriptural resources, like, you know, a lot of talk preparation type of materials, teaching materials, like to teach young children, to teach other people. It's really, if you want to learn anything about the church, their Web site is. . . . I mean, you can do anything from family history, genealogy, you can find your ancestors, as far as a religious point of view, they've utilized the available media to get that out. It's more for a distribution kind of thing. |

## Interpretation

The Muellers are a distinctive case among our respondent families because of their relatively higher income, as well as their elaborate knowledge of computers. Computer use is so ingrained in this family that even Reese, a 4-year-old boy, sometimes e-mails his friends. For this committed Mormon family, the Internet is a medium in which they can easily find much information and many resources to reinforce their commitment to Mormon religious beliefs. David also believes that the Internet offers a great potential for the church (not as a local church, but as the whole organization of the Church of Latter-Day Saints) to "distribute" the religion and that this potential is being realized. In other words, to this family, the virtual space of the Internet is very much concentrated in, or confined to, their religion. An apt comparison is to Chris Chandler. In comparison, the Mormon Mueller family is decidedly nonseeking. As to the question of the utility of the Internet, David Mueller is clearly unable to think outside of an "informational" mode; he clearly thinks of the Web as a resource for Mormons such as himself.

*Katy Cabera* is a 32-year-old single mother of two. She was interviewed by Christof Demont-Heinrich.

| | |
|---|---|
| Katy: | . . . I was pretty much clueless. Um . . . I wasn't involved in any kind of youth group or anything. We just went [to church]. Usually if my mom felt bad about something we went because we were Catholic. We could feel bad and then we could be, you know, we could repent on Sunday and everything would be OK. Act bad and then go back on Sunday and everything would be OK. And I had a really big problem with that because as a young kid I didn't think that that's |

exactly how it's supposed to be. . . . You try to be just as good as you possibly can all the time. You don't try to buy your way into heaven or you don't try to justify evil or immoral acts, or whatever it is people do during the week before church on Sunday. Um, and I see a lot of that on certain shows, that it's OK to be one way but then you can be a good Christian on Sunday. So, I have big problem with that.

Interviewer: Which shows?

K: Ah, usually movies. If you watch gangster movies, the mob movies, they go out and kill people and then they go to church on Sunday. What are they? They're Catholic!

I: Ah huh. . . .

K: And I don't like seeing that. I have a big problem with it. A huge problem with that. And, um, it can also be joked about late night, you know. On *Saturday Night Live* I've seen a couple of skits like that and, so, um, that's one of the reasons why I left the Catholic Church and stopped going to church. And when I started dating this one man 4 years ago, ah, he's the one who introduced me to the Lutheran faith. And there's a very close connection with Catholicism. I don't know if you knew that Martin Luther was a Catholic priest married to a nun. So, I, you know, started researching it and found that it, ah, was something that I fit into very well. So, I really like it.

I: So you talked a little bit about movies that weren't too favorable in terms of some aspects of Catholicism. Have you seen any of that in terms of the Lutheran faith do you think?

K: I don't know. Really with the Catholic thing, I've seen several like that. I remember one show in particular—oh yeah, I must have been maybe 12 or 13—and the show was called *The Wanderers*. It was a movie set in the 1950s about gangs. And, you know, rival gangs, you're in my neighborhood, you're on my turf and we're going to beat you up now. I mean, it was an interesting movie, but I remember this one gang went to the church to pray for forgiveness before going out and killing.

I: And the movie was called *The Wanderers*?

K: *The Wanderers*. Yeah. That was the first glimpse that I had of it and I can't pinpoint every single movie that I've seen but I know there are Catholic churches, you know there's the cross, the priest, the kneeling, and the praying, blah, blah, blah. And I just have big problem with that, just having to see that. [laughing]

I: Do you ever seek out anything related to religion on TV or on the Internet or on radio?

K: No, uh uh. I don't do any of that. I think the reason I don't really touch on going to any religious sites or anything is because I've got my mind set

I:      on what I believe and that's what I believe.

I:      So what about Lutheran sites, does your church have a Web site?

K:      Our church does have a Web site. But I'm there [at the church]. I don't need to go to the Web.

I:      So even surfing to sites that align with your beliefs is not of interest?

K:      I've never tried it. But I probably will now. I've got my sports and news. As soon as you leave I'm going to put the news on. I do that way too much at work too.

### Interpretation

The case of Katy Cabera suggests at least three dimensions of relationship between media and religion. First, as she noted in several references to TV programs and movies in her account of her journey from Catholicism to Lutheranism, popular culture provides crucial resources in people's religious identity process. Second, the Internet seems to have less potential for religious use for someone for whom religious identity is strongly established. Katy maintains that her reason for not using the Internet for religious purposes is that she already has set religious beliefs. Third, online religious community building is closely related to involvement in the offline religious community and subjective feelings about the involvement. She has no desire to go to the Web site of her church, just because she is already "there." This is clearly an instrumentalist view of the Internet. It is also clear that she sees the Internet's primary significance to be influence over religious choice—thus a "*not* for me" view.

*Wyonna Fallon* is a 39-year-old single mother of two. She was interviewed along with her daughter Jill, 14 years old, by Christof Demont-Heinrich.

Jill:      And there's—[to Wyonna] what's that site that you have that you can look at Bible verses?

Wyonna:      Heartlight.org.

J:      Yeah.

W:      And every day you get—

Interviewer:      Heartlight.org?

W:      Yeah. You get different things every day. Like that screen saver is different every day.

J:      You have a different wallpaper every day.

I:      Oh, really, what is that one? [pointing to the computer]

J:      Blessed is the nation whose God is the Lord. Psalm 3:12. They're usually Bible verses. They used to be important quotes. But now we got Bible verses. And then there's always a little picture that goes along with it.

I:      And that's what heartlight.org focuses on?

W:      It's actually done by the Church of Christ in Texas somewhere. And it has daily verses, or like articles and Bible. . . . [Here W. and J. are talking across one another, as they often do.]

J:      Stories and what not. . . .

W:      Study things that you can look at different verses or something like that. Put in a word and it'll show all the verses with that in it and stuff like that.

I:      How did you find out about it?

W:      Ahh . . . somebody told me about it, I believe.

## Interpretation

This is an example of a use of the Internet for religious purposes in which it "primes" religion in daily life. This family has no TV in their living room. Three years ago, Wyonna decided to get rid of cable because her daughters were spending too much time watching TV. The only TV set, used for video watching, is kept in the daughters' room. Instead, a computer takes the place of a TV, with a religious screen saver on the screen. From the site where she got the screen saver, Wyonna also gets wallpaper containing Bible verses and religious pictures delivered automatically through e-mail. The technology of the Internet is thus seen to provide more efficient ways for people to integrate religiosity into their everyday lives.

*Donna Baylor* is a 38-year-old mother of four. She was interviewed along with her husband by Christof Demont-Heinrich.

| | |
|---|---|
| Interviewer: | OK, we're going to switch gears and then come back to computers at the end. There's a section here on media and beliefs. We talked about this a little in the family interview, but not in depth. Do you ever seek out inspiration or information or encouragement in the media? And, if so, where and when have you done this? Can you think of any specific examples? I think you talked about going. . . . you have a whole set of bookmarks. You have a religion folder. |
| Donna: | Yeah. I do. |
| I: | So you're doing some seeking out online. |
| D: | Yeah. |
| I: | What kinds of stuff are you doing more specifically? |
| D: | Well, first, I have a daily e-mail that comes that's just a scripture: *The Daily Manna.* But I like it because it's just a scripture. It's not a commentary on it. It's just what's in the Bible. I like that. I like to read that every day. And then in my folder, I've got—well, my Crossings book club is in there. They're a religious book club. I think it's called Power and Glory. It's like Columbia House. It's a division of Columbia House, their Christian side of it. So that's in there. |
| I: | And that's music? |
| D: | Ah huh. And then I've got a thing in there. I don't know if it works anymore, but Hobby Lobby is a Christian organization and they used to every Christmas put in a full-page ad that had nothing to do with their stores, just the Christmas message. They also had it online. So I had saved some of those. Because they're really cool. |
| I: | Are you going online often to search for things and bookmark them? Or is this something—you have a folder that's already been created and you don't add to it very often? You keep going back to the same places? |
| D: | Well, it depends. If I find something new, I'll stick it in there. I've cleaned it out a couple of times because some of the things that I had found previously were gone, were not good anymore. I'd review it and go through it every now and then |

and put in new things and take out the old. You know, what's relevant and what's not. I have some Web sites in there on different religions that I've looked at—if I've gotten into a discussion with someone over. Well, I guess my big thing would be Mormonism. Since I have in-laws and relatives that are Mormon and Bill used to be Mormon. I try and research that a lot so that I have a lot information to work with that way.

I: So you don't have anything bookmarked on Islam or Buddhism. . . .

D: I haven't found any. I look around for ones that I like and that I can understand, are clear enough for me to get.

### Interpretation

Like Wyonna Fallon, Donna uses the Internet to get daily scripture. An interesting point she makes is that the reason she likes the daily e-mail system is that it sends passages of the Bible and not commentaries on it. She emphasizes her own ability to make meanings out of the scripture by refusing to take religious authorities' intervention in the process. This suggests that she is a bit of a contradiction. She also uses the Internet to seek information about various religious traditions. This is not so much an act of "religious and spiritual seeking," as in Chris Chandler's case; Donna shows many characteristics of a kind of dogmatism. She uses information about other religions, especially the Latter-Day Saints, to deal with her Mormon in-laws. It should be noted that, for her, the Internet offers a convenient way to gain access to the various religious traditions. At the same time, though, her attitudes regarding religious authorities and their Biblical commentaries suggest she is suspicious of received religious authority and

thus has some seeking in her religiosity—an interesting combination.

*Paula Wilcox* is a 41-year-old single mother, who lives with her daughter and her own mother. She was interviewed by Christof Demont-Heinrich.

Interviewer: So we were talking about seeking information, inspiration, and encouragement online or in the media.

Paula: Well, I like books. There's plenty of good books out there. On the Internet, people send me inspirational things all the time. I don't go looking for them, but people send them to me. Um, there's good shows out there too.

### Interpretation

Paula sees that religion is one of the important topics transmitted through the Internet. This is a very tacit or matter-of-fact understanding of the role of the Internet. This is understandable because, although this mother of a 10-year-old girl articulates that the computer is very important to her daughter's future and her success, she admits that it is not central in her own life or her friends' lives. However, it is interesting to find that, even for her, religion is a salient topic that is easily found in her limited access to virtual space.

## Discussion

There is much of interest here. At the same time, though, concrete evidence of online religion is hard to come by. Informants typically have difficulty in connecting their media and Internet use to questions of religion. Even Chris Chandler (the first case shown here), who so definitively states that he uses the Internet for religious purposes, has little to say about specifics. He clearly exhibits the characteristics of new-age seeking but gives us little insight into how his practices of seeking are satisfied or addressed through his use of the Internet.

Others, such as Katy Cabera, eschew any notion that the Internet might have a place in her religious or spiritual activities. She is a seeker in terms of the means by which she came to her current religious position, but now that she has settled there, she sees no need to go online. Katy shares something in common with many of the informants here: a sense that the primary purpose of the Internet or Web is a kind of informational function more closely associated with Helland's religion online category.

There is some evidence here, then, that the category of seeking does seem to go with an online religion morphology of Internet use. If this is true, we can see how it might be so and how contrasting categories of use might also function. For informants whose religion and spirituality is more or less "fixed," a contrasting source of symbolic or meaning resources naturally is seen as less important. For informants for whom seeking has become dominant, sources such as the Internet or Web seem somehow logical contexts for working out religious and spiritual identity. In neither case could it be said that the digital context is somehow determinative of practice; rather, it must somehow fit into existing lines of motivation and behavior.

These data are not, of course, representative in demographic terms. The samples were drawn for the sake of contrast rather than generalizability. Whatever we might say about findings, we must recognize them as exploratory if our primary purpose is prediction. However, they provide opportunities to generalize about what seems to be logical and possible, given what we know about emerging religious sensibilities and about the capacities, practices, and motivations of online activities.

On another level of analysis, there are some clear interactions between online practices and at least three domains of identity and meaning. The first is the domain of the informant's own religious, quasireligious, or spiritual needs and motivations. This is a dimension that seems to vary among these informants, with Chris Chandler most closely approximating the ideal type of the new-age seeker motivated primarily by internal logics of the self. Others, however, including Donna Baylor, although less exemplary of that morphology, nonetheless seem motivated by something internal in the way of need and motivation to seek resources on the Internet.

The second domain of interaction is between the Internet and other media. This is not a theme in all of these interviews, but it is particularly significant with Chris Chandler. The Internet is clearly seen as a different kind of place. For Chris, it is the preferred space for the kind of exploration in which he wishes to engage. For others, there is no particular motivation to seek out the Internet; other media are more of a tacit part of their practice.

The third domain is the interaction between the Internet and many informants' traditional religious commitments and beliefs. This is most obvious in the case of the Mormon family but is significant in all the cases. For some of the informants, received traditions and practices are treated as "givens" against which other sources and resources, such as media and the Internet, are measured. For others, traditional tastes and desires are normative, but resources are found in the online world. Donna Baylor provides an interesting case here. Although she appears pretty traditional in her Christian beliefs, she seems at the same time to suspect received authority and is attracted to the Internet as a place where she can get pure, unadulterated (uninterpreted) resources.

We have gained some insights here into the central questions we raised at the outset. First, there are a variety of ways that these various domains interact in the meanings and motivations related to online activity. These are, however, complex and subtle issues and questions, worthy of further reflection and study. Second, the mode of seeking, as we identified it in an ideal form in connection with new age sensibility, does seem to find some commonality with the online context. This is conditional, however, as demonstrated with our purest case, Chris Chandler. Third, the online environment, at least for these informants, seems to support these various activities primarily through its provision of information. Few of them appear to be involved in online religion–type activities. Again, some nuance is called for here. The kinds of resources Wyonna Fallon and Donna Baylor are using do bind them, in a way, to an online context that is, in a way, distinct from some of the others. Fourth, we do not have much evidence here of Clark's category of "implicit" religion. At the same time, though, a different set of questions might be implied if that were our primary purpose. Finally, we are not able to say much overall about online religion other than to suggest that its presence must interact well with the other domains we have identified and that there are ways in which it may be seen to be, for some informants, actually connected with fairly traditional sensibilities.

Our method here differs markedly from that of previous studies that have looked at online religion. We did not select these households because of their religious, quasireligious, or seeking status. What we have, then, are interviews that begin with a different premise and get to the question of the Internet as part of an overall discussion of religious practice. In that way, the conversation is about conventional religious practice more than it is about Internet religion. We might well have found more of specific relevance to Internet religion online if we had begun with those questions first and foremost.

## SOME FURTHER EXPLORATIONS

Further work is, of course, warranted here. If, as we have said, seekers are central to our understanding of the potentials of online religion, then a more sustained focus on such seekers is a next step. The sampling techniques we use are not adequate to this task, or seem not to be, so far. This suggests, anecdotally only, that seeking may be a relatively infrequent aspect of this landscape, or that the ways we have of asking about it are in need of refinement.

A number of approaches present themselves. We might look at the use of Web sites that are geared toward seekers. This would be consistent with some previous work. We might select seeking-oriented religious groups or movements in the

offline world and, through them, interrogate the relevance of the online world to their practice. We must also, obviously, continue to explore both our sampling methods and our instrumentation for ways that we might refine and improve our understanding of both our theory and method and our informants.

## NOTES

1. The field material and analysis presented here comes from an ongoing, multiyear, qualitative study of meaning making in the media age, under the direction of the first author and Dr. Lynn Schofield Clark. The research team includes the second author and the interviewers responsible for the specific interviews excerpted here: Dr. Joseph Champ, Dr. Anna Maria Russo, and Christof Demont-Heinrich. The authors wish to acknowledge and thank these colleagues for their efforts, advice, and input into this article. More information about the overall project, including notes on methods, is available at http://www.colorado.edu/Journalism/mcm/mrc/mrc.htm.

2. In keeping with our protocols, we have changed the names of all informants. All live in the Front Range area of Colorado, within a 100-mile radius of our base at the University of Colorado at Boulder. Under our protocols, none of our informants come from the city of Boulder itself.

3. Chris's articulation of a "received cultural script" involving the differences between television and the Internet is suggestive of a much larger and more interesting set of issues. For a complete discussion, see Hoover, Clark, and Alters (2004).

## REFERENCES

Brasher, B. E. (2001). *Give me that online religion*. San Francisco: Jossey-Bass.

Clark, L. S. (2002, April). Young peoples' Internet practices and spirituality: Preliminary findings from the Teens and the New Media@Home Project. Paper presented at the First Meeting of the Pew Internet & American Life Advisory Board, Chicago.

Giddens, A. (1991). *Modernity and self-identity: Self and society in the late modern age*. Stanford, CA: Stanford University Press.

Helland, C. (2000). Online-religion/religion-online and virtual communitas. In J. K. Hadden & D. E. Cowan

(Eds.), *Religion on the Internet: Research prospects and promises* (pp. 205-223). New York: Elsevier Science Press.

Hoover, S. M. (1988). *Mass media religion: The social sources of the electronic church.* London: Sage.

Hoover, S. M. (2001). Religion, media, and the cultural center of gravity. In D. Stout & J. Buddenbaum (Eds.), *Religion and popular culture: Studies on the interactions of worldviews* (pp. 49-60). Ames: Iowa State University Press.

Hoover, S. M. (2002, July). Religion, media and identity: Theory and method in audience research on religion and media. Paper presented at the Annual Meeting of the International Communication Association, Seoul, Korea.

Hoover, S. M. (in press). *Religion in the media age.* London: Routledge.

Hoover, S., Clark, L., & Alters, D. (2004). *Media, home and family.* New York: Routledge.

Hoover, S. M., & Russo, A. M. (2002, July). Understanding modes of engagement in research on media and meaning-making. Paper presented at the Conference of the International Association for Mass Communication Research, Barcelona, Spain.

Horsfield, P., Hess, M., & Medrano, A. (Eds.). (2004). *Belief in media.* London: Ashgate.

Lawrence, B. B. (2002). Allah on-line: The practice of global Islam in the information age. In S. M. Hoover & L. S. Clark (Eds.), *Practicing religion in the age of the media: Explorations in media, religion, and culture* (pp. 237-253). New York: Columbia University Press.

Lindlof, T. R. (1995). *Qualitative communication research methods.* Thousand Oaks, CA: Sage.

Roof, W. C. (1999). *Spiritual marketplace: Baby boomers and the re-making of American religion.* Princeton, NJ: Princeton University Press.

Warner, R. S. (1992). Work in progress toward a new paradigm for the study of religion in the United States. *American Journal of Sociology, 98*(5), 1044-1093.

Zaleski, J. (1997). *The soul of cyberspace: How new technology is changing our spiritual lives.* New York: Harper Collins.

# 24

# WEAVING TRICKSTER

## Myth and Tribal Encounters on the World Wide Web

ANITA HAMMER

Cyberspace is a "space" that, according to deconstructive theorists (Haraway, 1991, 1997; Stone, 1992, 1996), is changing not only the way people communicate on an everyday level but changing human identity itself. "Digital culture" has been posited by postmodern theorists as exemplifying and underlining the postmodern notion of fragmented and decentred human selves. This is part of an overall postmodern worldview of technology and technological reproduction as catalysts for a new turn of the human mind from the centred to the noncentred, from representation to simulacra, from boundaries of body to transgressed boundaries via technology. This postmodern view of technology is dominant in the field. Is it, however, the best way of viewing human use of information and communication technologies?

By applying a combination of anthropological theory, performance theory, and an overall perspective of cultural history, I argue in this chapter that

▣ The notion of a human decentered self expressed by, and due to, computer technology lacks historical and comparative context.

▣ This can be shown by viewing various states of human consciousness experienced by use of computer technology not as "new" and decentered but rather as technologically reframed activities that actually predate their computer manifestations: namely, imagination, play, theatre, masquerade, and ritual.

▣ Images of physical space represented as specific place and self-presentation by metaphors of the flesh are at the core of the "nonspatial" realm of cyberspace.

▣ Cyberspace activities are in between the social and the ritual or aesthetic and may be categorised as "reflective."

▣ These activities take place between individuals in a collective realm, by means of computer representation.

▣ From this, I argue that the human need for ritual and play, which is set apart or framed off from everyday life, has merely found another way of expressing itself through computer technology.

The conclusion I draw from these arguments is that human interaction within computer frames may serve as a "liminal" space, in contrast to everyday rational living but not a new version of it.

## BACKGROUND

From 1998 to 2001, I engaged in fieldwork in the nonplaceal and nonidentified space of "cyborgs" (Haraway, 1991, pp. 149-181). These years of research into digital cultural (defined here as human encounters taking place by means of computer technology) have brought me into contact with various forms of expression and self-presentation. More specifically, the object of my study has been the frames and modes of communication between individuals in computer interaction that takes place simultaneously in time, particularly in those environments known as MOOs (multiuser domains, object oriented). These are environments in which people create or represent themselves in various ways by means of textual interaction (Haynes & Holmevik, 1998). This textual interaction is done by means of the human imagination's capacity to "build" rooms and character descriptions by means of a computer program. Thus they are based on representation of place and human identity within the frame of a computer interface operating in "real time."

Since the appearance of the first public MOO, LambdaMOO, created by Pavel Curtis in 1990 (Curtis, 1998), the so-called social MOOs have been the object of much research and discussion. These computer programs are used to share imagery and transform human experience through a communication process in which the boundaries between created, imaginary, personal life and transpersonal interaction are not clear. It may be argued that this very uncertainty over the mode of operational reality provided by the opacity of the computer interface is the real attraction and source of popularity for these kinds of chatrooms.

Sherry Turkle (1997) proposed that the presentation of the human self as experienced by and through digital representation in social MOOs is an indication that the human identity can no longer be considered as originating from the "center" of a "self"; it must be seen as originating from a multiplicity of selves, or a "multiple self."

Traditional ideas about identity have been tied to a notion of authenticity that such virtual experiences actively subvert. When each player can create many characters and participate in many games, the self is not only de-centred but multiplied without limit. (Turkle, 1997, p. 185)

Turkle's suggestion is derived from postmodern theory, as well as from a belief that digital media have a profound impact on cultural identity. Contrary to this, I have argued that "multiple identity" is a concept that can only be considered original where there is ignorance of the history of theatre and ritual.

Viewed from an angle of theatricality, the plots that organise the actions on the stages emerging from Internet-based digital interaction constitute themselves through a masquerade of the soul. There is a denial of the very important aspect of masquerade that, in my view, is often the very attraction of these forms of digital interaction. Even in the cases in which room and character descriptions are clearly imaginative in their quality—when they are based on historical or mythological frameworks of contents, for example—the fictional frame is not clear. In contrast, when the frame is defined as "realistic" according to some aspect of everyday life outside the digital, the images of life are so clustered with the imaginary that a division between fictional and social life cannot be upheld.

This play between self and identity that takes place may relate to some deeper human need that can perhaps no longer be met by Western traditional art; that is, the need to participate, create, and play on a collective level. The key words *imagination, play, ritual, theatre,* and *myth* help explain how these aspects manifest in Internet communication and relate to an overall cultural context.

## "Material Imagination"

The French philosopher Gaston Bachelard's (1884-1962) concept of material imagination may be illuminating for understanding the representational code of textual MOOs. First, it describes how the human imagination, through images of matter and of the sensual world, constitutes the communication in any space defined as "nonspatial."

Second, the term "material imagination" (Bachelard, 1983, pp. 1-18) explains how not only theatrical aesthetic practices but also practices not necessarily ascribed to the aesthetic frame can be viewed as "images of matter" (Bachelard, 1983, p. 1).

In the textual MOO, the experience of the presence of the characters, behind which the players, or the programmed robot lines, exist, occurs in the room in the MOO. A *room* in the MOO is a spectacle of imaginary place based on textual representation.

Atmosphere and emotion stemming from the subject's experience of the physical world are recreated by a combination of memory and imagination in a MOO. Therefore, analogy to physical space is a fundamental element of the creation of MOO places.

> Besides the images of form, so often evoked by psychologists of the imagination, there are—, as I will show—images of matter, images that stem directly from matter. . . . When forms, mere perishable forms and vain images—perpetual change of surfaces—are put aside, the images of matter are dreamt substantially and intimately. They have weight, they constitute a heart. (Bachelard, 1983, p. 1)

Being entirely based on the memory of physical space, the entire totality of "places" existing in textual MOOs may be viewed as constituted by human imagination of matter.

In his work *The Poetics of Space*, Bachelard (1994) suggested that images of houses and rooms are at the centre of human imagination, the function of inhabiting being a "primary virtue" (Bachelard, 1994): "For our house is our corner of the world. As has often been said, it is our first universe, a real cosmos in every sense of the word" (p. 4). He further suggests that "a really inhabited space bears the essence of the notion of home" (Bachelard, 1994, p. 5).

The descriptions of place in MOO are decisive in determining the kind of behaviour that may be expected from the human participants in each room. The room descriptions are related or semi-related to the characters' description of self. Each communicational frame has clear spatial indicators defining the "roles" of the participants. Descriptions of place are determined by, and constitute, the "world," or fictional universe, large or small, in which the participant is expected to move, "physically" and psychologically. It also seems to be the case that the more accurate and precise the room description, including hearing, smelling, seeing, and tactile sensation, the more there is for the character to relate to, and the more "clues" she or he is given for character creation and appropriate behaviour.

It may be possible, by relating the representational code of MOO to Bachelardian thinking, to identify MOOing as not primarily a social but a reflective practice, much closer to traditional aesthetic practices than to the traditionally social.

Language is used to set in motion this common field of experience through a combination of recognition, creative association, and imagination framed by precise descriptions. The participants of a MOO create and recreate not only subjective images but cocreated images that may function as a shared field of poetic exploration and experience. Julian Dibbell, a writer whose extensive experience as an online participant qualifies him as a unique authority, also defines MOOing as an activity of the imagination (Dibbell, 1998).

The imagination of another body, both as body of self and of the other, is, according to Dibbell, taking place without regard to any "actual reality" in front of the keyboard. Dibbell himself calls this "play." Provided the players are actively choosing their parts and following them through in a manner of "willing suspension of disbelief," the activity described here may also be perceived as strongly involving aspects of play in the theatrical sense. Dibbell describes the phenomenon as a "self abandonment to the principle of play" (Dibbell, 1998, p. 144).

It is a play constituted by very specific images of the physical body and physical space, producing a fictional contract strongly involving analogy to sensuous perception. This contract can even support sexual interaction as recreations of sensuous memories into images. It is the corecreation of these memories that stimulates imagination, which again activates further sensational memories in the body. In regard to the capacity of the human mind for memory, Bachelard (1994) states: "All memory has to be re-imagined. For we have in our memories micro-films that can only be read if they are lighted by the bright light of imagination." He adds, "Dreams, thoughts and memories weave a single fabric" (p. 175). In Bachelard's concentration on material images, there is also a centring around the specific. Memory is viewed not as a flow, but as a centring upon specific images. It is crucial for Bachelard (1994) "to consider imagination as a major power in the human nature," and this major power, he states, balances "the function of reality" and "the function of unreality" in the human psyche (p. xxxiv). A weakness in the function of unreality is, to Bachelard, as dysfunctional as a weakness in the reality function.

Moving into a MOO and experiencing the abundance of images presented and used there as both spatial and psychological navigators, I experienced objects, rooms, and characters as sprung from an intention of using material imagination as means of creating activities lingering between aesthetic and social frames of communication. The "cosmic wormholes, the magical books, the mirrors, paintings and plastic-snow filled crystal balls" (Dibbell, 1998, p. 50) all lend their existence to the sensual world in that they are, in some form or other, analogous. MOO practices may be perceived as reflective practices in the sense that their creation is dependent upon material imagination based on practices of previous reference in the sensual world.

## Between the Social and the Reflective

Victor Turner (1988) refers to Gregory Bateson's (1972) "play frame" (pp. 177-193) as "a frame which encompasses a special combination of primary and secondary processes, and is likely to precipitate paradox" (Turner, 1988, p. 107). Obviously, the notion of "virtual space" and the digital realm, perceived as nonspatial or paraspatial, is already at play within a cultural dream of the impossible and is viewed from that context as a paradox by its very existence. When looking, then, at examples of various sensual perceptions

derived from sensual reality and dreamed up as material imaginations in the digital realm, one may see all places and objects of a MOO as playing with notions of reality. The paradox that arises is that the more precise are the descriptions of sensual perceptions that come through, the closer the virtual world comes to the imagination of "real experience" and the further it moves away from nonreality.

A MOO is playfully furnished, and its furniture may be perceived as reflections upon social life and culture. The MOO's furniture reflects various modes of reality outside the digital realm. The computer interface is, in itself, clearly "framed off" from noncomputer activities in any given space. Whether naming it a "mirror," a "window" (Turkle, 1997) or a "portal" to the world, the framing is definite, and it is through this frame that reflective activity can take place. Most computer software imitates the precomputer world through icons and textual analogies, but the imaginative language of MOO goes much further. MOO furnishings are reflections of the imagination. Turner (1982, pp. 13-14) traces the term *performance* from the old English *parfournir*, meaning "to complete" or "to carry out thoroughly." Within the computer framing of digital experiences, the reflection of the sensual world becomes furnished, or completed, through the joint imaginations of the MOO participants. In this sense, the furniture of a MOO is "performed"; in the sense that here, by means of digital technology, these reimagined variations of experiences of the senses are shared by the participants.

## Ritual Places?

Richard Schechner (1994) notes that when comparing human activity to the ethological studies of "ritualistic" animal behaviour, no difference is "more decisive then the fact that only humans permanently transform the space by 'writing' on it or attaching a lore to it" (p. 155). Going back to the first known ceremonial centers, the Palaeolithic cave paintings, it may be seen that cultural places are distinguished from the houses in which people live their daily lives. Schechner holds that "The transformation of space into place means to construct a theatre; this transformation is accomplished by 'writing on the space'" (p. 156).

Eliade (1994) holds that the construction of holy places, places that are outside the practicalities of everyday life, whose only function is cultural performance, marks the human need for creating a "centre of the earth" to which humans may orient themselves within a chaotic heterogeneity. He argues that in modern society, the patterns developed by human history relating to the transcendent reality inherent in the construction of ritual places continue to inform human behaviour and reshape themselves into contexts whose contents deny their religious aspects (pp. 120-127). If, as a working tool for understanding the attraction of immersement in textual virtual worlds, one uses a functional notion of religion, the ritualistic qualities of these activities may come to the fore. MOO activity may be serving as a ritual function for an overall worship of cyber experience. If viewed this way, MOOing could be described as quasireligious behaviour, and as such, it is not particularly different than any other contemporary quasireligious behaviours. I suspect, however, that even the keenest MOOer would be the last to accept such interpretation.

Margaret Wertheim (1999), in her work *The Pearly Gates of Cyberspace*, points out that

> The fact that we are in the process of creating a new immaterial space of being is of profound psychosocial significance . . . any conception of "other" spaces being "beyond" physical space has been made extremely problematic by the modern scientific vision of reality. (p. 231)

The very notion of creating a "cyber" world or "virtual reality," regardless of its contents, is, by itself, a longing for transcendence.

The attraction of a Moo, realised by place and objects materially imagined, is spectacle. This is the result of communication dependent on sensual descriptions of objects and place. On this ground, the cyberplace of the MOO represents the expression of a need to reritualise place and object.

It may be argued, then, that the concept of the MOO is the material imagination of a previously actualised ritual or theatrical place. In this case, the performance of place is here found on a metalevel. Perhaps various parts of the MOO represent various ways of reestablishing a principle of immanence. Because these digital practices emerge from a play frame that includes the very appearance of the medium as such, however, there will be a constant play between the belief of immanence in the appearances and its negation. This is due to the nonmateriality of the digital representational code of text as material imagination.

The reality-status of objects and place as immanently manifesting the belief system of a community during a communal ritual, however, is turned upside down in the case of "communal" MOOing. The play concept from which digital representation in the MOO departs is already undermining its own ontological status by negating itself (Bateson, 1972, pp. 179-180). Still, what happens in the MOO is that the set frames are played with.

It is possible to apply Gregory Bateson's (1972) theoretical framework of "reality status" of place and objects to a MOO and reach the following conclusions:

- ▣ By "pretending" that the textual digital place is synonymous (Bateson, 1972, p. 180) with physical space and simultaneously negating this statement (as is done by the term *virtual reality*), the distinction between the appearance of the phenomenon and its denotation is negated.
- ▣ If it is true that in the MOO the relation between appearance and denotation is negated and negated again, the result is a double minus of mathematics that may lead to a metaplus or, more specifically, an activity that has defined itself as identical with its own denotation (Bateson, 1972, p. 180).
- ▣ If these two statements are true, the MOO might be considered a case of postmodern retribalisation or ritualization, as it represents an attempt to be "mistaken for real" (Bateson, 1972, p. 182).

The fascination with meeting "wired" representations of various persona within the place created on the computer screen is the fascination with places created beyond place and with the "overcoming" of physical space and limitations.

Encounters on the Internet bear the quality of a landscape of dreams and longing and hope, as if these encounters could redeem everyday life and reality. Both theatre and ritual have traditionally been spatially framed off from other places and distinguished from everyday life practices. Places framed off by computer interfaces are merely invitations to another kind of worship.

The images of place are reborn images of matter, which by their very "second nature" bear a message of redemption through the mythological dream expressed in a technological belief.

## Actions of Ritual and Their Mythologies

The thought of a deeply rooted and actively functioning connection between media use and religious belief is by no means new. It has been explored by thinkers from the social sciences, such as Emil Durkheim (1965); from social anthropology, such as Victor Turner (1969, 1976, 1982, 1988); and from media studies, such as Eric Rothenbuhler (1998), just to name a few.

In my approach to the analysis of the MOO in a broader cultural context, however, it is the term *religion* that particularly matters, as much as the terms *myth* (or *mythology*) and *ritual*. In my work I have suggested that MOOing, by function of *place* analogy, may contain ritual aspects and, by *character* and *play,* constitutes certain specific *frames*. I have reviewed these in relation to both a *functional* and a *substantive* view of *ritual* and *myth*.

If all culture is seen as embedded in myth, historically as well as synchronically, this also includes digital culture.[1] A mythological image, however, is always imbedded in a storytelling structure. In ancient mythologies, an image never stands alone; it must be understood by the structure of the story within which it is told.

The term *myth* in this context denotes images produced by, and functioning within, a certain culture. These images, by the unity of their contents and structure, carry and reveal the deeper aspects of nonconscious or subconscious cultural belief.

It is possible that the postmodern deconstruction of the human self is actually an expression of the ritual structure underlying simultaneous interactive digital communication. MOOing may be the ritual counterpart of the myth of deconstruction.

One may then view the computer screen interface as a secluded place in which place and time change their meaning in reference to everyday life. The imaginary worlds of a MOO are a shared imaginary space, characterised by Margaret Wertheim (1999) as a "collective mental arena," a place in which the participants "might share with other minds" (p. 231). Typical of ritual frames is a very firm framing, which is, as seen from the outside, characterised by its simplicity. The firmness and simplicity of the outer frame allows for a flexibility of movement in time and between actors and spectators that could not happen if the framing were not familiar to and accepted by everyone involved.

Trance and ecstasy are a common, and often a necessary, part of ritual practice (Eliade, 1978, 1994; Schechner, 1994; Turner, 1969). The experience that one may have after hours of MOOing at the computer—of blending into the MOO environment as a character, losing track of time, being surprised by the course of action that one's character has taken when blending with others in the intense present encounter at the computer—is a similar phenomenon. It is the descriptions of such experiences that have led some researchers to proclaim the notion of "identity change" or "multiplicity of self" by means of computer technology. Rather, I have suggested that "social" MOO framing has a lot more in common with ritual. The firm frame, which is the computer interface itself, and its textuality allow for a lot of comings and goings, mingling and interchange in space and time, precisely as does a firm ritual frame in any ethnological theatre. My argument here is that what is considered "new" in the representation of character as aspects of a self divided via digital media may, in fact, not be new at all. It may be that electronic media, by providing a "secluded place" for character representation exchanges, are reenacting and expressing one of the most basic characteristics of humankind: experimentation with play and ritual. Digital representation merely adds another chapter to the story of *homo ludens*.

MOOing may be viewed as a ritual whose purpose is to reinforce a belief system in which human interaction and shared participation outside everyday life may provide purpose and direction. If this should be the case, simultaneously interactive digital communication functions as a series of punctual actions related to the overall belief system so widespread amongst digital consumers: resurrection by means of technology. These observations are based solely on the functioning of MOOing as structure, not as substance. The myth of deconstruction of self and identity via technology belongs to the Western culture outside the MOO, in which the MOO is embedded. Therefore the MOO itself reflects the myth rather than revealing the mythic content explicitly.

MOO places share the quality of ritual places in that their representation of physical objects, bodies, and room descriptions are distinctively separated from everyday life. Like rituals, they are interlinked with the everyday life of their participants and have a huge impact on participants' extraritual existence (Dibbell, 1998; Stone, 1992). MOOs can be viewed as transpersonal and collective places where repressed or "unlived" actions can find their outlet "elsewhere."

Dibbell (1998), gazing down from "the scarlet balloon" he entered to overview and "map" LambdaMOO, came to the realisation that

> At that moment, the view from the balloon looked to me like anything but a metaphor for a culture suffering through the final, delirious stages of advanced modernity. I looked, instead at nothing as much as a metaphor for the cure . . . what I saw now for the first time . . . was the remarkable cultural object all that collective creativity had produced. (p. 63)

Victor Turner (1982) explains that traditional ritual is related to "beliefs in invisible beings or powers" (p. 79). Digital communication departs from a belief system of nonbelief, in religious terms. The belief in the "reality" of the events taking place in MOO and their "identity-transforming" effects is rooted in the belief in technology as a redeemer. There is, perhaps, as Dibbell (1998) suggests, an attempt at "curing" the loneliness and

identity crisis of postmodernity through technology. Margaret Wertheim (1999) regards this possibility as the most positive aspect of cyberspace: "We may see cyberspace as a kind of electronic res cogitans, a new space for the playing out of some of those immaterial aspects of humanity that have been denied a home in the purely physicalist world picture" (p. 230). The Western intellect, refusing to believe in religions or "spiritual" powers, has produced the new communication technology. However, due to refusal in MOO to distinguish between character and player, a belief in the magic of forces that transcend presence reoccurs. The refusal to distinguish between the social and the aesthetic realm, between digital representation and physical body, reveal a belief system that is, in the end, contradictory to the rational ground from which it departs.

Victor Turner (1982) describes the liminal phase as a stage leading from one state of mind, position, or consciousness to another. In tribal ritual action, this stage is "frequently marked by the physical separation of the ritual subjects from the rest of society"(p. 26). Applying this to the MOO situation, the individual is not physically but mentally separated from everyday life. She or he is separated into character. If the experience of this is not being identified as creation of character and identification with it but as "multiplication of identity" (Turkle, 1997, p. 185), the result will surely be one of experience of dissolution of identity and of being in an intermediate state of "abysmal depth" (Turner, 1982, p. 82), of chaotic disorder in one's orientation to reality. The problem, however, is that there is no shaman or priest present in the MOO to guide the novice into a restructuring of reality, as the function of the "Archwizard" of a MOO is basically to overlook the technical side. "Novices" are left to their own judgement and may spend months or years coming to terms with the relation between digital representation and everyday life.

Dr. Kimberly Young (1998) runs a centre of Internet addiction in the United States. Her clients' descriptions of their Internet experience and their relationship to the computer strongly reveals what, for the theatre historian, could be taken for a description of Dionysian ritual. In my view, the "addiction" depends on the previously described fusion of distance and intimacy. This mixture, when understood as an extension of identity, with no distinction between player and character, has in fact been promoted by the hype of digital technology as an agent for change.

The social drama of which MOOing is a ritual counterpart leads one into a state of liminality where one can, through ritual social drama, question: What is human identity? Sherry Turkle (1984, 1997) has done a very good job of identifying this as the issue at stake. In relating this issue to theatre, however, I do reach some different conclusions.

The room, the place aspect of the MOO, may, as an archetype, be viewed as an image of the human psyche, and the characters appearing there as a search for salvation from the individual loneliness that underlies so many social and psychological problems of the Western culture of today.

The imagery by which digital technology presents and creates itself is so heavily loaded with ancient mythological imagery that it is very reasonable to ask whether this phenomenon is a conscious "restaging" of ancient mythology or whether it represents a less conscious but no less effective longing and dreaming backwards, leading to a state of postmodern tribalism. I view this phenomenon as a spontaneous manifestation of collective imagery that is more or less consciously projected. The reference to "another" world is very strongly expressed by the notion of "cyberspace" itself. The term *avatar*, a term commonly used for the representation of character in textual and iconic imagery within computer interaction, is derived from the Hindu concept of, in Sanskrit, *avatara*. Avatara means "descent," and the word is used to describe the incarnation of a god in a human body.

Multiple human selves and cyborgs seem to have free passes to become the new avatars of humanity. This is, I argue, due to a refusal of postmodern theory to view the cultural phenomenon of Internet interaction from a broader historical perspective—without which cultural theory is in danger of becoming the trickster tricking itself.

Liminal activities should be recognised for what they are: some of the borders of everyday life, but not identical with it. Playing with the concept of play has led Richard Schechner (1993) to characterise activities that cross the boundaries between social and aesthetic practice as "dark play" (p. 36), which lead to a form of "postmodern tribalism." It may be that such postmodern tribalism is weaving its way through threads of encounters in cyberspace.

## NOTE

1. For a host of discussions on digital culture, see the Digital Arts and Culture 98 International Conference Web site at http://cmc.uib.no/dac98.

## REFERENCES

Bachelard, G. (1983). *Water and dreams: Essays on the imagination of matter.* Dallas, TX: Dallas Institute of Humanities and culture.

Bachelard, G. (1994). *The poetics of space.* Boston: Beacon Press.

Bateson, G. (1972). *Steps to an ecology of mind.* New York: Ballantine Books.

Curtis, P. (1998). Not just a game. In C. Haynes & J. R. Holmevik (Eds.), *High wired.* Ann Arbor: University of Michigan Press.

Dibbell, J. (1998). *My tiny life in cyberspace: Crime and passion in a virtual world.* New York: Henry Holt.

Durkheim, Emil. (1965). *The elementary forms of religious life.* Glencoe, IL: Free Press.

Eliade, M. (1978). *History of religious ideas.* Chicago: University of Chicago Press.

Eliade, M. (1994). *Det Hellige og det Profane* [The sacred and the profane]. Oslo, Norway: Gyldendal.

Haraway, D. (1991). *Simians, cyborgs, and women: The reinvention of nature.* London: Free Associations Books.

Haraway, D. (1997). *Modest_witness@second_millennium.femaleman_meets_oncomouse: Feminism and technoscience.* London: Routledge.

Haynes, C., & Holmevik, J. R. (1998). *High wired.* Ann Arbor: University of Michigan Press.

Rothenbuhler, E. (1998). *Ritual communication.* Thousand Oaks, CA: Sage.

Schechner, R. (1993). *The future of ritual.* New York: Routledge.

Schechner, R. (1994). *Performance theory.* New York: Routledge.

Stone, A. R. (1992). *Will the real body please stand up.* In M. Benedict (Ed.), *Cyberspace: First steps.* Boston: MIT Press.

Stone, A. R. (1996). *The war of desire and technology at the close of the mechanical age.* Boston: MIT Press.

Turkle, S. (1984). *The second self: Computers and the human spirit.* New York: Simon & Schuster.

Turkle, S. (1997). *Life on the screen: Identity in the age of the Internet.* London: Orion Books.

Turner, V. (1969). *The ritual process: Structure and anti-structure.* New York: Cornell University Press.

Turner, V. (1976). Social dramas and ritual metaphors. In R. Schechner & M. Schuman (Eds.), *Rituals, play and performance.* New York: Seabury Press.

Turner, V. (1982). *From ritual to theatre.* New York: PAJ.

Turner, V. (1988). *The anthropology of performance.* New York: PAJ.

Wertheim, M. (1999). *The pearly gates of cyberspace.* London: Virago Press.

Young, K. S. (1998). *Caught in the net.* New York: John Wiley.

## Additional Sources

Aarseth, E. (1997). *Cybertex: Perspectives on ergodic literature.* Baltimore, MD: Johns Hopkins University Press.

Eliade, M. (1963). *Myth and reality.* New York: Harper & Row.

Giegerich, W. *Das Begragnis der Seele in die Technische Zivilisation.* Retrieved January 4, 2005, from http://www.cgjungpage.org/content/view/376/28/ (A condensed version of this text can be found at http://www.cgjungpage.org/content/view/375/28/ under the title *Reflections on Wolfgang Giegerich's "The Burial of the Soul in Technological Civilization."*)

Hammer, A. (1999). *Inanna in hieros gamos: A processual representation* (KUBE series, No. 3). Trondheim: Norwegian University of Science and Technology.

Hammer, A. (1998, November 26-28). *Role and theatricality in virtual worlds: Extending the theatrical, and investigating thresholds of mythic identity.* Paper presented at the Digital Arts and Culture 98 International Conference, Bergen, Norway. Retrieved December 23, 2004, from http://cmc.uib.no/dac98/papers/hammer.html

Hammer, A. (2001, February 12-13). *Understanding digital communication by tools of theatre.* Paper presented at the Computers at the Crossroads International Conference, Trondheim, Norway.

Hammer, A. (2002). *Weaving plots: Frames of theatre and ritual in simultaneous interactive digital communication* (Doctoral dissertation, KUBE series No. 2). Trondheim: Norwegian University of Science and Technology.

Rheingold, H. (1993). *The virtual community: Homesteading on the electronic frontier.* New York: Addison-Wesley.

Rothenbuhler, E. (1993, Summer). Argument for a Durkheimian theory of the communicative. *Journal of Communication, 43*(3), 158-163.

Segal, R. A. (1998). *Myth and ritual theory.* Oxford, UK: Blackwell.

# 25

## The Mass Media and the Transformation of Collective Identity

### Québec and Israel

Dov Shinar

The cases of Québec and Israel illustrate the shift of identities that typifies cultural transformation, social restructuration, and transitions between order and disorder. In Québec, the nationalist *"projet de société"* has worked to articulate a new *Québécois* collectivity. Among Diaspora Jews, the Zionist movement, combined with the *Shoah* (Holocaust), produced in 1948 a sovereign state, Israel. Both cases involve a rearticulation of collective identity through the development of particular relations between history and memory (Allor, Juteau, & Shepherd, 1994; Horowitz & Lissak, 1989; Smith, 2003). Québécois linguistic, political, and national feelings of uniqueness have been challenging federalist Canada. Political Zionism has been accompanied by linguistic revival, together with religious, cultural, political, and ethnic strife. Following previous works on the role of language in the formation and transformation of collective

identities (Shinar, 1996; Shinar, Olsthoorn, & Yalden, 1990), this chapter explores the roles of the mass media, particularly broadcasting, in such processes in Québec and Israel.

## The Model

The present analysis of mass media roles in forging of Québécois and Israeli identity is based on a conceptual framework, which maintains that

- All social groups, be they natural units of sociocultural process (Turner, 1977) or imagined communities (Anderson, 1991), go through successive phases in which regularization and adjustment couple with inconsistency, ambiguity, discontinuity, contradiction, and conflict.
- Rituals help to make sense of this interplay of order and disorder. As mechanisms of temporal change, built by a well-defined linkage of symbols,

they create mental models that enable a group to feel that it controls reality through the cyclical meaning given to social and cultural ruptures. Departing from one state and leading to another, rituals symbolize and occur in liminal time, which allows imagined communities to be "neither here nor there betwixt and between the positions assigned by law, custom, convention or ceremonial" (Turner, 1964, p. 5) or by the media. This "legitimized freedom from cultural constraints" (Turner, 1968, p. 581) supplies symbolic links between the past and the future of a society.

▣ Depending on the cultural resilience of societies, postliminal phases range from regeneration to oblivion, from "reaggregation" (re-membering) to dis-memberment.

Three anthropological variables help to operationalize these concepts:

*Root paradigms* are cultural models of an allusive, metaphorical kind, cognitively delimited, emotionally loaded, and ethically impelled, which give form to action in publicly critical circumstances (Turner, 1977). Root paradigms have been invented, revived, and imported in monarchic and Islamic Iran, by Israelis and Palestinians, and by separatist movements (Barber, 1995; Hobsbawm & Ranger, 1983; Shinar, 2003; Tehranian, 1979).

*Formulative efforts* are the concerted use of organizational principles and entities to give practical meaning to abstract ideas (Myerhoff, 1980). They supply root paradigms with organization and structure, such as those provided by governmental machineries; political, religious, and educational movements; trade unions; professional organizations; and bureaucratic structures.

*Transformative agents* are action catalysts, such as collective memory and awareness (Ignatieff, 1993; Myerhoff, 1980), media or language, that take formulative efforts on behalf of root paradigms to the masses to mobilize popular support for ideas and symbols. They include, first, specialized formal and informal media and traditional, modern, established and improvised, mediated and interpersonal, local, regional, and global channels; second, the performance of communication roles by social institutions, such as religion, family, the arts, and educational and political systems; and third, seduction, bribery, coercion, and terrorism.

Thus *re-membering* is the use of formulative efforts on behalf of root paradigms and their legitimization and support by the action of transformative agents. Examples include (a) Ataturk's revolution in Turkey, in which governmental formulative efforts used transformative agents (i.e., compulsory Romanization) to promote re-membering around root paradigms of national consciousness, modernity, secularism, and Europeanism vis-à-vis a weakened Islamic root-paradigm and (b) the almost full mobilization of the United States media on behalf of root paradigms (patriotism, freedom, antiterrorism, democracy) defined and promoted by the American administration and armed forces (i.e., formulative efforts) during the war in Iraq.

*Dis-membering* is the use of transformative agents in the dilution and replacement of root paradigms, or internal fragmentation. Examples include the dissolution of the USSR and Yugoslavia and the plight of the Shi'ite minorities in Lebanon (Ajami, 1986), and in Saddam Hussein's Iraq.

## The Dynamics of Re-membering and Dis-membering

Dis-membering processes have been documented in writings on the collapse of empires or the "deglobalization" of religions and ideologies. The study of re-membering has focused on the invention of traditions, the forming of collective consciousness, and the promotion of ideologies (Hobsbawm & Ranger, 1983; Ignatieff, 1993; Smith, 2003). Nationalism was the major root paradigm in the efforts to form federal Switzerland, based on "elevated sentiments, for God, Freedom and Country, union and fraternization" (Hobsbawm & Ranger, 1983, p. 6). Transformative agents included traditional practices—songs, contests, marksmanship—and modern media, modified, ritualized, and institutionalized for new purposes.

Three major features characterize the dynamics of re-membering and dis-membering:

*Competition.* The stability and prevalence of any re-membering triad (root paradigm–formulative efforts–transformative agents) are in constant competition with other re-membering or dis-membering triads. In Israel, a confrontation of "civil" and tribal identities has evolved since the 1967 war (Kimmerling, 1995). The civil root paradigm envisages a modern "State of Israel," an open society focused on concepts of citizenship, rights and duties, and voluntary participation. The tribal-religious root paradigm regards Jewish Law as the source of authority and has as its goal the running of a Jewish religious state in Biblical "*Eretz Israel*" (the Land of Israel). Israeli democracy has failed to create mechanisms for resolving this dilemma, and in the early 21st century, the clash between the two root paradigms is still unresolved.

*Preliminal, liminal, and postliminal stages:* When a re-membering triad declines in popularity, credibility, or action, it enters a liminal stage of competition with other triads. In the resulting open-ended postliminal stage, it might recuperate and remain dominant or be replaced by another triad. In the former Yugoslavia, Tito succeeded in the late 1940s in gearing formulative efforts (party, unions) to a re-membering process around three root paradigms: local "brotherhood and unity," regional anti-Stalinist socialism, and the Non-Aligned Movement. All three collapsed in the 1990s. Tribal affinity proved stronger than "brotherhood and unity," the socialist root paradigm collapsed altogether, and it is not possible to "be non-aligned between something and nothing. . . . There was no rationale any longer to keep the construct going" (Galtung, 1993, p. 6).

*System, end, and time:* Root paradigms become consensual or dominant when supported by effective organization and action. The process is open ended and can be time consuming. In Switzerland, a decision of the federal government in 1891 marked the establishment of the Confederacy of Schwyz, Obwalden, and Nidwalden in 1291 as the official founding of a national state (Hughes, 1975). Thus, six centuries passed until federal nationalism achieved predominance. This long period was needed to overcome the resistance of other root paradigms (i.e., linguistic diversity; political conservatism; backward economic, political, and cultural structures; and religious cleavages) and to give adequate formulative efforts and transformative agents, such as the increasing legitimacy of "nation" as a universal norm and the development of communication technologies, time to mature (Anderson, 1991).

## Root Paradigms in Québec and Israel: Survival and Growth

Over the centuries, the threat of dis-membering has introduced survival as a permanent root paradigm in the lives and collective consciousness of francophones in Québec and Jews in the Diaspora. For two centuries, between 1760 and the 1960s, French Canadians in Québec conceived "*la survivance*" (survival) in a defensive antiassimilationist stance of maintaining French-Catholic purity and avoiding contamination by the English. In the 1960s, this was replaced with a "*maitres chez nous*" (masters in our own house) metaphor and narrative, promoted by the Montréal francophone middle class, which aimed at bringing Québec into the modern world but maintaining its unique cultural identity. This "Quiet Revolution" was followed in the 1970s by efforts to maintain francophone supremacy through political action that combined peaceful negotiation with some violence.

As in Québec, Jewish survival in the Diaspora featured religion-based isolationist feelings, which were quite successful in preventing assimilation. In the middle of the 19th century, inevitable external contacts enhanced secularization and changed this trend. These characteristics have not disappeared with the establishment of an independent state. In Israel, survival has been a major re-membering agent against real dangers and against perils fabricated and nurtured by nationalist, irridentist, and messianic groups.

In both cases, survival was joined by another root paradigm, socioeconomic and political growth. In Québec, two centuries of a "lost paradise" narrative and of survival-oriented re-membering efforts began in the 18th century, after the double blow of the British conquest ( "*la Conquête*") and the desertion by France of its colonists. This was followed by further humiliations, such as the defeat of a rebellion in 1837-1838; imposed conscription in the two world wars; the invocation of the War Measures Act by the federal government in 1970 to deal with political terrorism; and the "Night of the Long Knives" in 1981, when the federal government and nine provinces agreed to patriate the constitution without Québec's consent (Francis, 1997). Since the 1960s, a contest of two visions is typical of francophone Québec's identity building: a Liberal *"ratrappage"*—"catching up" with English Canada—and an ideology of separatism. In this period, the re-membering arena has been defined by a double-edged struggle against anglophone dominance and against the traditional isolationist *survivance*. The apparent resolution of the conflict between traditionalism and modernization induced by Québec's Liberal government commitment to industrialization and urbanization was not entirely successful. The collapse of traditional culture made it increasingly difficult to maintain a distinctive identity.

The *Parti Québécois* (PQ) had tried to deal with this conflict since its establishment in 1968, through a successful unification of all *indépendiste* movements that brought the PQ to power in 1976. The political leadership that replaced the former elites was decisively defeated in the referenda of 1980 and 1995, however, and in the general election of May 2003. The resulting frustration introduced a neoliberal economic stance criticized by separatists as a strategy that has failed to replace the more flattering imagery of francophone ideological re-membering.

A growth root paradigm has joined the survival motif in Israel, too. Statehood, one of the most successful Jewish collective achievements in modern times, resulted from ideological root paradigms expressed in demands to normalize the socioeconomic structure of the Jewish people (increasing the rate of productive workers), settlement policies, technological innovation, and the hegemony of the labor movement. Statehood, however, triggered an interplay of re- and dismembering forces that eroded the earlier root paradigms and replaced them with a constant left-right, secular-religious, humanist-chauvinist, pendulumlike balance of power. The cultural patterns engineered by the prestate elite were not sufficiently strong when faced with hopes anchored in religion. A return to tradition in the last decades has legitimized the promotion of renewed root paradigms: religion, on one hand, and

consumption values, on the other, have been replacing most of the previous ideological commitment.

## FORMULATIVE EFFORTS

Several types of formulative efforts are typical of both cases:

*Political formulative efforts* in Québec include the *Parti Québécois*, famous for its takeover of the Québec government in 1976, and the currently active *Bloc Québécois*. They were preceded in the 1960s by movements such as the *Rassamblement pour l'indépendance nationale*, Québec's first mass-based separatist political party, which became a leading force, and in the 1970s by the *Front de libération du Québec* and the *Movement Québec français*. The former were francophone "urban guerrillas" and the latter a francophone pressure group that organized petition campaigns, demonstrations, marches, and "popular assemblies" intended to keep the language issue in the public eye. In Israel, such efforts included the activity of broadly based organizations, as well as political parties, movements, and lobbies.

*Armed formulative efforts* in Québec have included the "*Patriote*" movement, which led an unsuccessful uprising against the British in 1837-1838, and groups such as the *Rassamblement pour l'indépendance nationale*, inspired by U.S. civil rights movements, and the *Front de libération du Québec*, which planted bombs and conducted kidnapping operations in the 1960s and 1970s. Israeli armed formulative efforts included, in the prestate phase, underground movements that tried to overpower Arab movements and expel the British from Palestine. With the establishment of the State of Israel, the Israel Defense Forces took over these and other formulative efforts (immigrant socialization, education, and social services).

*Economic formulative efforts* were launched in Québec mostly during the Quiet Revolution of the 1960s. The nationalization of Hydro-Québec is an example of how economic enterprises supplied root paradigms with organization and structure. Hydro-Québec was formed in 1944, after the provincial government purchased the Montréal Light, Heat and Power Company. However, until 1962, some 80% of Québec's energy was controlled by anglophones. Waging the 1962 election as a referendum on the Hydro-Québec purchase of all remaining private electric companies, the then Natural Resources Minister René Lévesque (who led the PQ to a spectacular electoral victory in 1976 and became Québec's Premier) maneuvered the Liberal Party into nationalizing Hydro-Québec. This was intended to end francophone economic subordination to English interests and consolidate the separatist root paradigm.

The election of the PQ in 1976 established additional enterprises as viable economic formulative efforts. Levine's (1990) list of Montréal projects illustrates the process: infrastructural highway and bridge projects, a new international airport, schools, hospitals, the *Palais de Justice,* the francophone Radio-Canada building, the *Place des Arts* (home of the Montréal Symphony), the *Palais des Congres* convention center, the underground mass transportation system, Expo 67, and the 1976 Olympic games.

Although differing in timing and orientation, some similarities exist between Québécois and Israeli economic formulative efforts. The *Histadrut* is an example of such economic re-membering efforts active in Israel's prestate period and in the formative years of the state. As in Québec, Israelis have been charged with ideological tasks. The *Histadrut* was established in Palestine by the Socialist wing of the Zionist movement in 1920. It acted as a classic trade union federation, as well as a formulative effort on behalf of a re-membering socialist root paradigm, first, in initiating and maintaining the largest concentration of construction and industrial firms up to the 1980s, as well as the largest bank in Israel, and second, in providing services—public housing, health, work, welfare, education, and culture—particularly in the prestate period. Its nature as a major formulative effort can be illustrated with the phrase "the state in the making," with which it was baptized due to its role in institutionalizing the ideology. The *Histadrut's* leadership in Israeli economy and politics lasted until the 1980s, when it suffered a rapid decline, along with the entire socialist movement.

*Civic and cultural formulative efforts* included in both cases ethnic, cultural, religious, and professional associations. In Québec, a Ministry of Cultural Affairs was established in 1961 to preserve French language and culture and to act as a Québécois counterpart to the federal Canada Council. The *Parti Québécois* emerged as a nationalist alternative to the federalist Liberal Party.

Along with French-speaking unions, the party conducted cultural and legislative campaigns, which largely account for its triumph in the 1976 election. In Israel, *Histadrut* components, such as the teachers, civil servants, and academics unions and the cultural units of the World Zionist Organization and of the Jewish Agency, were effective in the performance of civic and cultural missions.

## TRANSFORMATIVE AGENTS: THE MEDIA

The media, particularly broadcasting, have played important roles in reflecting and molding Québécois and Israeli identities (Shinar, 2000; Thomas, 1992). In Québec, the weakening of traditional root paradigms and the shifts of *rattrapage* and separatist ideologies have paved the way for the advent of media and language as major transformative agents since the 1960s. In Israel, the promotion of modernization and secularization by political Zionism produced root paradigms based on the "cultural engineering" of symbols, rituals, and language. In later years, this orientation lost power and influence, giving way to new root paradigms that featured materialism and individualism, on one hand, and sectarian, religious, and messianic motifs, on the other. Media and language have been integrated in the promotion of all root paradigms. The slogan "Hebrew Is My Homeland" illustrates the nature of language as one of the most resilient transformative agents in the Zionist revolution. The frequent dilemmas expressed by media professionals concerning how to present genuine Israeli contents reflect the importance of this aspect.

The analysis of the media as transformative agents features normative, institutional, and symbolic dimensions.

## THE NORMATIVE DIMENSION

The normative dimension refers to dilemmas and strategic choices. The view that the media should perform integrative, cultural, and symbolic identity-building tasks has been common to the Québécois and Israeli normative approach to the media. Conflicts over the status and character of the media reflect such normative dilemmas, options, and decisions.

*The Media as Ideological Transformative Agents.* In Québec, the traditional vision of francophone identity emphasized distinctiveness; nationhood; and control of culture, language, and communications. This position was expressed in the demands of Québec's leaders to legitimize the predominance of the French language and culture in media policies. These demands have been consistently denied by Canada's federal government, which maintained that broadcasting should act on behalf of a federal Canada rather than of a Québécois identity. As early as 1929, a provincial law act was enacted that was intended to establish Québec's jurisdiction over broadcasting. Following several appeals, the act was rejected in 1931 by the Canadian Supreme Court and in 1932 by a London Privy Council's judgment. Results were similar when such confrontations resurfaced in later years. The war over the control of cable TV in 1977 was perhaps Québec's last attempt to retain full jurisdiction. It ended in defeat, following a Supreme Court decision. However, Québec's demands did not fade away. The federal government's position was tested in 1934, when anglophones in Québec, Ontario, and Western Canada rejected the presence of French on the air. Separation into two parallel radio services was completed in 1941. Likewise, in 1952, when television was introduced in Québec, francophone protest against bilingual programming was successful when an English-language station went on the air in 1954. Thus, normative strife created two media systems differentiated by language, culture, and consumption patterns (Fletcher, 1998). The result was double edged: On one hand, since the 1950s, efforts have been made in Québec to preserve francophone media, language, and culture in the scant maneuvering space left by federal policies. The creation and production of materials in French by writers, directors, actors, journalists, and others was warmly welcomed by the francophone audience, enabling Québec to recognize itself as the core of a new national identity (Thomas, 1992): "For the first time in their history, French Canadians in Québec were watching . . . a picture of themselves transmitted from one end of the province to the other" (Balthazar, 1997, p. 47).

Normative aspects of identity in the Israeli media have been less complicated. The early "melting pot" hegemonic social philosophy in Israel assigned to the media (as it did to other mobilization and socialization agents) integrative, cultural, and symbolic identity-building tasks. This resulted in the establishment of a single public broadcasting system, designed to perform nation-building services and to supply the needs of the audience. This structure prevailed until the 1980s, first under direct governmental control and then, beginning in the mid-1960s, under a BBC-like public broadcasting structure.

*The Media as Industrial Transformative Agents.* Crises in public broadcasting, favorable political conditions, and the impact of globalization from the 1980s onward introduced an industrial orientation into broadcasting in Québec and Israel (Savageau, 1998; Shinar, 2000). The general criticism of public broadcasting on the grounds of poor management, inefficiency, and bureaucratization applies to Québec and Israel alike. Also, Israel has been criticized for political interference and corruption, along with the inability of a single system to cater to the needs of the entire population. However, instead of improving the public broadcasting system, both societies encouraged the private sector, first through subcontracting and independent production and later through full industrialization.[1] Moreover, defeats in several referenda (1980, 1992, 1995) lowered Québec's separatist expectations, inducing a loss of interest in the re-membering functions of the media. In Israel, the downfall of the left in 1977 encouraged the multiplication of channels, encouraging the emergence of industrial interests in the media. Globalization enhanced this trend, mostly through transforming economic arguments into ideological tools. The myths of the public sector's inefficiency and of the "intrinsic" superiority of the private sector joined forces with the argument on the need to reduce the national debt in creating a normative basis for the industrialization of broadcasting.

Globalization also helped to legitimize media concentration through the argument that only big, national corporations can face international conglomerates. The opposition to any state intervention has been a final contribution of globalization to the industrial orientation of broadcasting in both Québec and Israel (Fletcher, 1998; Savageau, 1998; Shinar, 2000; Thomas, 1992).

*A Normative Shift.* Media industrialization indicates the emergence of an Ottawa-Québec consensus on media policy in the province. Since 1980, federal Canada and Québec alike reduced their budgetary responsibility for broadcasting and privatized television production and introduced commercial cable television. Québec's similar approach reduced its previous interest in the national and social tasks of the media. This produced the first agreement regarding communications between Québec and Ottawa. Industrial in spirit, the agreement aimed at technical innovation and support for the production, development, and marketing of communications goods and services. The agreement was not changed in later years, even as the political debate intensified.

In Israel, the introduction in the 1990s of privately owned cable television, two additional broadcast television channels, and a regional commercial radio system expresses the official policies of eliminating the monopoly of the public Israel Broadcasting Authority. An "open skies" governmental policy has encouraged the licensing of private broadcast channels, special-purpose cable stations, and satellite-based media, marking a clear trend of industrialization. The legislation on cable television is a significant expression of this trend. While legal texts on open broadcasting specify the national, cultural, and social roles of the media, cable television has been regulated by a technical amendment to the telecommunications law of 1982. There is no law in Israel that addresses the contents of cable television.

Two implications are typical of this normative shift. First, industrial media economics in Québec and Israel have favored foreign imports of (mostly U.S.-produced) television programs. Some studies indicate that the success of French broadcasting in attracting significant audience levels in Québec for indigenous television has not made French television impermeable to the dangers of the economic rationale (Desaulniers, 1985; Raboy, 1990). In Israel, television imports have increased, but so has local production. The second implication is that notwithstanding the criticism of its low cultural standards and of the focus on private interests rather than on re-membering (Raboy, 1996; Shinar, 2000), industrialization has paradoxically addressed deeper issues. This has been expressed in Québec by decisions that acknowledged for the first time the parallel bilingual development of Canadian broadcasting and recognized the special nature of French-language TV, parliamentary hearings on distinct needs of different markets, and a more equitable distribution of resources (Raboy, 1996). In Israel, legislation on commercial broadcasting reinforced demands that owners and operators pay adequate attention to local production.

The discussion illustrates the view that normative importance does not necessarily depend on formal acceptance. Like nations that have integrated defeats in war into the tales of heroism that make part of their collective identity, so the demand of control over the media has become part of the Québécois collective identity. Moreover, even when the normative dimension does not yield all the desired results, its re-membering function remains alive: It inspires and steers all dimensions of transformative agents and equips them with directions for action.

## The Institutional Dimension

The institutional dimension is where structural strategies are applied. In Québec, the failure of provincial legislation of media policies led to replacing this normative strategy with institutional action, with a "software approach" that focused on Québec-oriented and French-language programming.

Institutional action included the establishment of agencies and programs to promote francophone re-membering, such as a ministry of communications, fiscal measures intended to favor French media production, communications departments in Québec universities, and assistance to community media.

The "software approach" can be illustrated with production and audience studies, which show that, for example, since the 1970s, more than 50% of Canadian news in francophone CBC-TV dealt with Québec, compared with less than 20% in the English news. In later years, the tendency to focus news coverage on Québec-related issues was also found in French-language private TVA (Desaulniers & Sohet, 1980; Siegel, 1977). In the 1980s, French drama occupied 10% of broadcast time and 20% of viewing time in Québécois productions, compared with 2% of broadcast time and 2% of viewing time in English-Canadian drama (Task Force on Broadcasting Policy, 1986).

The advent of industrial broadcasting and the introduction of new services in Québec resulted in the fragmentation of francophone audiences. Since the late 1980s, Radio Canada and its affiliates dropped from 42% to 29%, and private TVA declined from 52% to 42% (Task Force on the Economic Status of Canadian Television, 1991).

In Israel, institutional action followed normative decisions. Israeli media have dedicated more airtime and more choice (along with an increase in imported programming) to local production and to catering to more defined segments of the audience. The shift has been expressed by higher rates of broadcast and cable-cast contents; music; and performers related to ethnic, social and cultural groups.

This has helped to overcome the basic problem of public broadcasting in Israel; namely, the impossible mission of supplying all communication needs of all groups in the population through one single agent, the Israel Broadcasting Authority.

## THE SYMBOLIC DIMENSION

The symbolic dimension refers mostly to the rhetorical and behavioral assignment of meaning through the creation and manipulation of symbols.

Symbols create a "constitutive rhetoric"; that is, language- and media-powered constructs and symbols are used to create, change, and legitimize root paradigms (Charland, 1987).[2] In both Québec and Israel, the media have performed symbolic functions through the use of narrative, semiotic, and ritual mechanisms.

## Narrative Mechanisms

One such mechanism features "formative documents," such as the ones issued for the various Québec referenda, Israel's declaration of independence, and historical programs in the media that refer to such narratives. They portray the historical background, ordeals, bravery, struggle, sovereignty, and the tools for its achievement, following the view that "it is within the formal structure of a narrative story that it is possible to conceive a set of individuals as if they were one" (Charland, 1987, p. 140). Thus, although no one alive today actually lived the French defeat in the battle for Québec in 1759, it became a media-based myth that has accompanied most Québécois during their entire lives. In the Israeli re-membering discourse, motifs such as the *Shoah*, "heritage," and historical awareness have made up part of mythological educational and media television series, such as *Amud Haesh* (Pillar of Fire), which narrates the history of the Zionist movement up to the holocaust, and *Tkuma* (Revival), the narrative of the revival and the establishment of Israel.

## Semiotic and Ritual Mechanisms

Semiotic mechanisms in Québec and Israel feature the typical "replacement strategy," whereby terms are introduced and disseminated through the media, and "media naming," which occurs mostly through the naming and framing of media organizations as identity symbols. Fictional in every logical and practical sense, these value-loaded types of connotative discourse and their dissemination through the media symbolize identity and belongingness.

Replacing the former *French-Canadian* in 1967, the term *Québécois* is considered to have created a new type of political identity in Québec. It is the same with the replacement of the word *province* with the word *state* by a Québec minister of cultural affairs (Levine, 1990). The British victory over Québec in 1759 provides such a media semiotic mechanism: The term *humiliation* appears frequently in the French press to convey a long-lasting sentiment, and it serves Québec's media as a useful term with which to interpret contemporary events (Fletcher, 1998).

Examples of "media naming" are *Radio Québec, Radio Canada,* Israel's public radio *Kol Israel* (The Voice of Israel), and *Channel 7,* a right-wing settlers' pirate radio station that uses the symbolic meaning of the number seven in Jewish tradition.

The ritual dimension involves repetitive, performative, and representational linguistic and media mechanisms that enhance the mobilization and regularization of behavior on behalf of root paradigms and formulative efforts. These are behavioral extensions of rhetoric, ranging from slogans to rites of intensification.

Québec's slogan of 1979, "*Vivre en Français au Québec*" (to live in French in Québec), matches Ben Yehuda's call of almost 100 years earlier, "Let us live a Hebrew life" (Basil, 1985). These are examples of ritual expression officially adopted by media linguistic policies. The replacement in 1977 of "*La Belle Provence*" (the beautiful province) on car license plates by "*Je me souviens*" (I remember), Québec's motto since 1873, illustrates the use of representational behaviors as mobilizing cues ("Debats de l'Assemblée," 1977). So does the loud collective, repetitive, and performative reading by Jews during the annual Passover seders. The broadcasting of the Exodus story also extends historical narrative into behavioral representation.

Repetitive and performative representations also include media audience and professional rituals. News consumption on radio and television has been one of the most observed secular ceremonies in Israel. The 5- to 10-minute–long hourly newscasts on radio in "normal" times (when there was no official war or major security events) in Israel's early days were supplemented in the

1960s with four additional daily hour-long news magazines, followed later by "news flashes" every half hour. Since the 1980s, this has been the broadcasting pattern of the public *Kol Israel* and of the army-operated *Galei Zahal* (IDF-Waves). On television, nationwide open-broadcast channels 1, 2, and 10 transmit at least three regular daily newscasts of 30 to 60 minutes each, supplemented by longer daily and weekend magazines. Breaking news and reruns often interrupt regular programming, which is preempted in emergencies. This ritual can be explained by immediate instrumental needs. Against a sense and a psychohistorical background of physical threat, the constant surveillance of the environment becomes a basic need. The growth of this practice into a national ritual can be considered part of Israel's existential anxiety syndrome, which produced the survival root paradigm.

In Québec, professional media rituals include the prominence given by the major French media in Québec to provincial politics and to Canadian issues in the context of Québécois interests, much as foreign correspondents would report on a neighboring country (Siegel, 1996); for example, the coverage of federal elections, in which francophone news focuses on constitutional and language issues and English news emphasizes economic issues. This ritual is also typical of Israel, with "Israeli angles" consistently taking precedence over other materials.

## THEORETICAL AND PRACTICAL IMPLICATIONS

The conceptual model explored here demonstrates both the relativity and the finite nature of re-membering and dis-membering: There is probably no full or predictable re-membering after the total collapse of nations and cultures. The model also encourages systemic analyses of how ideological constructs, power structures, and media evolve and change and of each component in the system, their interaction, and the growth or collapse of one component under the influence of others. As each component—root paradigms, formulative efforts, and transformative agents—can function as a "trigger" or "release" of re- or dis-membering processes, this is a circular and nonlinear dynamic. Thus the model allows for studying open-ended change.

The typology and internal composition of root paradigms (survival and growth), formulative efforts (political, armed, economic, civic, and cultural) and transformative agents (normative, institutional, symbolic) is applicable to both Québec and Israel, regardless of differences in nature, structure, and circumstances. The study of other cases might supply similar, additional variables.

The model allows for the contextualization of variables in terms of specific space, time, society, and culture and thus for avoiding pressures toward analytical standardization and reductionism.

One should be aware, however, of a conceptual difficulty in the analysis of transformative agents. Language, the arts, religious and educational networks, the media, and other such agents can be functional in assisting social organization and change, if these agents are effectively fused with root paradigms and formulative efforts. However, the dependence of transformative agents on other re-membering components makes them less powerful than their popular image display. Transformative agents never enjoy the autonomy of root paradigms and formulative efforts. If a transformative agent is not supported by compatible values and organization, the outcome of change will probably be dysfunctional. This was the case for Mohammed Saeed al-Sahhaf, the last minister of information in Saddam Hussein's government. He kept serving as spokesperson of the Iraqi regime even after it collapsed, Baghdad was being captured, and adequate root paradigms and formulative efforts stopped supporting his function of transformative agent. The obvious result was a grotesque performance.

The activity of transformative agents, particularly that of the media, has accompanied the emergence and popularity of dominant root paradigms in Québec and Israel alike. As long as survival was the leading root paradigm, ideological, nationalist, community-oriented transformative agents prevailed. Industrialization defused the ideological emphasis of the media in both Québec and Israel; paradoxically, it encouraged cultural expression. Still, transformative agents can never enjoy full autonomy.

Finally, the model allows for dealing with various scenarios of identity formation and transformation, which appear sometimes on their own and sometimes simultaneously. They include

*The "Avis Syndrome"* ("We know what we want and we try harder"): Promoters of root paradigms search for organization, power, and action agencies during liminal phases to reach re-membering dominance in postliminal phases. In the Avis Syndrome, root paradigms (ideological, religious, ethnic, etc.) are the crucial component of the triad; they seek effective formulative efforts. Examples include contemporary left-wing political parties and movements (such as in Israel, Italy, or France) who have kept their root paradigms but, due to political ineffectiveness, are not backed by good organizational frameworks and are short of good media coverage. Another example is the search for adequate changes in Québec and Israeli public broadcasting, conducted by promoters of this root paradigm who wish to improve rather than to abandon this broadcasting model.

*The "Pirandello Syndrome"* ("six characters in search of an author"): In certain liminal situations, supporters of formulative efforts, sometimes helped by action agencies, seek the legitimacy supplied by root paradigms to reach re-membering dominance or consensus in postliminal phases. In this case, formulative efforts are the crucial component; they are focused on seeking the legitimization of root paradigms. Postrevolutionary situations are good illustrations of this syndrome, as shown by prerevolutionary organizational structures in Eastern Europe (such as the civil service) that remained operative after the collapse of the communist root paradigm and have helped to define a new one, sometimes using the media.

*The "Che Guevara Syndrome"* (exporting transformative agents): Action agencies (transformative agents) in liminal phases look for the legitimacy supplied by root paradigms and the strength provided by formulative efforts to achieve re-membering power and consensus in postliminal stages. Examples include media-based political personalities, governments, and movements that are kept alive by effective transformative agents (Saddam Hussein's Iraq, for example); election consultants in Western democracies who offer their skills to sometimes contrasting and contradicting root paradigms; and "perpetual revolutionaries," terrorist groups, and subversive organizations around the world that influence national governments and international coalitions of whatever shade to support them on behalf of ideologies or beliefs.

## NOTES

1. At least in Israel, subcontracting and independent production enhanced the emergence of "hidden unemployment" in public broadcasting; the workload of permanent production staff was thus reduced, but they were still kept on the payroll. This added a financial burden to the increasing frustration and inflicted a heavy blow on the morale and professional prestige of public broadcasters.

2. For the purposes of this chapter, the use of media was added to Charland's conceptualization of "constitutive rhetoric." Like language, the media are conceived of here as (transformative) agents that create, change, and legitimize root paradigms through the manipulation of textual, rhetorical, and pictorial constructs and symbols.

## REFERENCES

Ajami, F. (1986). The vanished Imam: Musa al Sadr and the Shia of Lebanon. Ithaca, NY: Cornell University Press.

Allor, M., Juteau, D., & Shepherd, J. (1994). Contingencies of culture: The space of culture in Canada and Québec. *Culture and Policy, 6*(1), 29-44.

Anderson, B. (1991). *Imagined communities* (Rev. ed.). London: Verso.

Balthazar, L. (1997). Quebec and the ideal of federalism. In M. Fournier, M. Rosenberg, & D. White (Eds.), *Quebec society: Critical issues* (pp. 45-60). Scarborough, ON: Prentice Hall Canada.

Barber, B. R. (1995). *Jihad vs. McWorld*. New York: Times Books.

Basil, L. (1985). *La législation linguistique et l'évolution du Français au Québec* [Language legislation and the evolution of French in Québec]. Montréal: Office de la Langue Française.

Charland, M. (1987). Constitutive rhetoric: The case of the *Peuple Québecois*. *Quarterly Journal of Speech, 73*(2), 133-150.

*Debats de l'Assemblée Nationale du Québec*. (1977, August 17). pp. 3016-3017. Québec: Assemblée Nationale du Québec.

Desaulniers, J.-P. (1985). Television et nationalisme [Television and nationalism]. *Communication Information, 7*(3), 25-38.

Desaulniers, J.-P., & Sohet, P. (1980). L'univers du téléjournal québécois [The world of Québécois newsmagazines]. *Communication Information, 3*(2), pp. 199-210.

Fletcher, F. F. (1998). Media and political identity: Canada and Québec in the era of globalization. *Canadian Journal of Communication, 23*(3). Retrieved December 31, 2004, from http://www.cjc-online.ca/viewarticle.php?id=472&layout=html

Francis, D. (1997). *National dreams: Myth, memory, and Canadian history*. Vancouver, BC: Arsenal Pulp Press.

Galtung, J. (1993). The role of communication in rethinking European identity. *Media Development, 4*, 3-7.

Hobsbawm, E., & Ranger, T. (1983). *The invention of tradition*. Cambridge, England: Cambridge University Press.

Horowitz, D., & Lissak, M. (1989). *Trouble in Utopia: The overburdened polity of Israel*. Albany: SUNY Press.

Hughes, C. (1975). *Switzerland*. New York: Praeger.

Ignatieff, M. (1993). *Blood and belonging*. Toronto: Penguin.

Kimmerling, B. (1995, November 8). Habrith haBilti kdosha [The unholy covenant]. *Haaretz*, p. b-1.

Levine, M. V. (1990). *The reconquest of Montréal: Language policy and social change in a bilingual city*. Philadelphia. PA: Temple University Press.

Myerhoff, B. (1980). Re-membered lives. *Parabola, 5*(1), 69-72.

Raboy, M. (1990). *Missed opportunities*. Montréal: McGill-Queen's University Press.

Raboy, M. (1996). Linguistic duality in broadcasting policy: A microcosm of Canada's constitutional politics. In H. Holmes & D. Taras (Eds.), *Seeing ourselves: Media power and policy in Canada* (pp. 154-172). Toronto: Harcourt Brace.

Savageau, F. (1998). Millennium blues: The 1997 Southam Lecture. *Canadian Journal of Communication, 23*(2). Retrieved December 26, 2004, from http://www.cjc-online.ca/viewarticle.php?id=452&layout=html

Shinar, D. (1996). Re-membering and dis-membering Europe: A cultural strategy for studying the role of communication in the transformation of collective identities. In A. Sreberny-Mohammadi & S. Braman (Eds.), *Globalization, communication, and transnational civil society* (pp. 89-103). Cresskill, NJ: Hampton Press.

Shinar, D. (2000). And all the people see the voices: Homogeneity and sectoriality in the media. In J. Kop (Ed.), *Pluralism in Israel: From "melting pot" to "salad* bowl" (Interim report, pp. 185-198). Jerusalem: Institute for the Research of Social Policy in Israel.

Shinar, D. (2003). Peace process in cultural conflict: The role of the media. Conflict and *Communication Online, 2*(1). Retrieved December 26, 2004, from http://www.cco.regener-online.de/2003_1/pdf_2003_1/shinar.pdf

Shinar, D., Olsthoorn, J., & Yalden, C. (1990). *Dis-membering and re-membering: An improved conceptual framework for the analysis of communications in sociocultural change.* Montréal: Concordia University.

Siegel, A. (1977). *A content analysis. The CBC: Similarities and differences in French and English news.* Ottawa: CRTC.

Siegel, A. (1996). *Politics and the media in Canada.* Toronto: McGraw-Hill Ryerson.

Smith, A. D. (2003). *Haooma baHistoria* [The nation in history]. Jerusalem: Historical Society of Israel.

Task Force on Broadcasting Policy. (1986). *Report.* Ottawa: Minister of Supply and Services.

Task Force on the Economic Status of Canadian Television. (1991). *Report.* Ottawa: Minister of Supply and Services.

Tehranian, M. (1979). Iran: Communication, alienation, revolution. *Intermedia, 7*(2), 6-12.

Thomas, E. (1992). Canadian broadcasting and multiculturalism: Attempts to accommodate ethnic minorities. *Canadian Journal of Communication, 17*(3). Retrieved December 26, 2004, from http://www.cjc-online .ca/viewarticle.php?id=99&layout=html

Turner, V. W. (1964). Betwixt and between: The liminal period in Rites de passage. In J. Helm (Ed.), *Symposium on new approaches to the study of religion: Proceedings of the 1964 Annual Meeting of the American Ethnological Society* (pp. 4-20). New York: American Ethnological Society.

Turner, V. W. (1968). Myth. In *International encyclopaedia of the social sciences* (Vol. 10, pp. 576-582). New York: Macmillan/Free Press.

Turner, V. W. (1977). Process, system and symbol: A new anthropological synthesis. *Daedalus, 1*, 61-80.

# Part IV

## THEORY INTO PRACTICE

What is the point of media anthropology? What is it good for? To study the world, of course, and to improve it, maybe, as well. A world that is better understood is already a better world, for it contains more knowledge, a larger range of useful perspectives, richer questions, deeper understandings. This is the faith of academics, and we share it. Media anthropology, though, beyond improving our understandings of the media, holds promise for improving the media practices of our world.

Susan Allen (1994) provided a history and topography for one version of a field of media anthropology that would, in principle, include the training of journalists in anthropological theories and methods (see also Bird, 1987). Discussed in more detail elsewhere in this volume, this version of media anthropology grew out of the interest of anthropologists in participating in the media and reaching the public—in having a positive effect on media reporting of anthropologically sensitive issues, including international affairs, minorities, culture, and arts. Allen pushes the idea farther in useful ways and summarizes it with the apt slogan "informing global citizens." In her model, there is a research branch of media anthropology under which anthropologists adapt their theories and methods to the study of media processes, structures, functions, content, and audiences. This area has received much development, as witnessed by the chapters in this volume and the voluminous literature they reference. Applied media anthropology has also continued in the business of providing anthropological expertise to media producers (see Allen and Bruns, chapters 26 and 27). A paradox of applied media anthropology is that its most successful practitioners will always want to do more; it is likely that dissatisfaction is endemic to the practice.

While interest in the media was slowly growing among anthropologists in the 1970s and 1980s, communication scholars were making increasing use of concepts and methods with roots in anthropology, under the heading of cultural approaches to media studies. A broadly anthropological approach to media studies is now well established, if outside the institutional discipline of anthropology proper. These ideas are even present in the training of journalism students at the many journalism schools that are associated with mass communication research programs and that require courses in theory and research. The next step would be to make these ideas more prevalent in reporting, writing, and editing courses.

Communication, media studies, and journalism straddle the social sciences, fine arts, humanities, and professional training. It is a peculiar location in the structure of modern intellectual life, where clean divisions of labor are preferred. Sociology and social work, for example, have become two different fields. Methods in sociology are designed for observation and explanation; methods in social work are designed for intervention. No such clean distinctions are enjoyed in communication and media studies. In those fields, future practitioners and future academic observers, future artists and future industry managers are mixed together in the same classes that are also taught by a mix of professional observers and practitioners. Movement between academy and industry is not unusual and is sometimes encouraged.

When both scholars and students are participants in the thing studied, then, most obviously, there is no independent position for an autonomous observer in the study of human communicative life, no clear division of labor between practitioners and scholars. If we can accommodate theories designed for practice as well as for explanation, then there can be opportunity as well as awkwardness in this combination of science, art, and professional training. We could found a new communicative practice, grounded in a more adequate understanding of the anthropological complexities of our world.

We have a responsibility to equip students with knowledge of the full range of possibilities of communicative practice present in the historical, anthropological, and industrial record and to cultivate in them the tools of imagination, that they may be ready to try to do it differently, to try to do it better. There could be no better opportunity to have a laudable effect on media practices, no matter how small the chance.

Ideals and values are necessary to this vision of teaching and research, for the betterment of practice. There could be no other way to discuss "the better." Of course, values must be made explicit; they must be subject to debate; they must be chosen and intentionally applied. What follows in this section, then, is a series of arguments about the possibilities for improving the world by improving media practices via the judicious use of anthropological knowledge, perspective, methods, and questions.

For Susan Allen (1994 and chapter 26), the media are an instrumentality. Current media operations tend to produce disjointed knowledge, duality, and lack of understanding. If the media could be used to distribute anthropological perspectives, however, and if anthropological knowledge could be brought to bear on news and political events, this could improve the chances for a better understanding of conflict resolution and for equality and democratic participation.

Merry Bruns, in chapter 27, addresses a more specific question: What are the processes and impediments for the distribution of scientific knowledge via the press? It turns out that they are mostly cultural. She is working as an anthropologist of professional practices, as if to explain the anthropological difficulties of answering the call for an applied media anthropology.

Elizabeth Bird and Gerd Kopper, each in their own way, devote their chapters to potential uses of anthropological concepts, methods, and perspectives for improving the practices of journalism. Bird focuses on the similarities and differences between journalistic and ethnographic investigative and writing styles, pointing to opportunities to enrich journalism with judicious use of ethnographic questions, perspectives, and, occasionally, methods. Kopper addresses journalism education as itself a kind of cultural problem: What are the unwritten rules, the codes of knowledge, the institutional structures? He also asks, How can journalism education be improved by our anthropological reflection, by our culturally informed awareness of our role in this culture-producing institution?

Dahlgren, in his chapter, addresses these same issues at a higher level of analysis. His concern is with civic cultures as resources for healthy public spheres. Here we have a problem of political science and social theory—namely, democracy—that has come to be widely understood as being crucially dependent on communication and media processes; for example, in the theory of the public sphere or in Putnam's conception of social capital. Dahlgren shows how both communication processes and democratic outcomes are dependent on a range of phenomena best understood as cultural, hence anthropological in the larger sense.

Across these chapters, we see a concern for social improvement, for healthier, more participatory, more democratic societies characterized by more knowledge and deeper, more nuanced, mutual understandings. These kinds of societies and understandings can be promoted through a more responsible, tolerant, and wise journalism. Media anthropology can offer journalism and journalism professionals a toolkit of concepts, methods, ideas, and questions, and, perhaps most important, a vision for the possibility of improving media practices. Toward such an end, if media anthropology could even only imagine contributing, it would be a thought worth thinking.

## References

Allen, S. (1994). What is media anthropology? A personal view and a suggested structure. In S. Allen (Ed.), *Media anthropology: Informing global citizens* (pp. 15-32). Westport, CT: Bergin-Garvey.

Bird, E. (1987). Anthropological methods relevant for journalists. *Journalism Educator, 41*(4), 5-13, 33.

# 26

## ACTIVIST MEDIA ANTHROPOLOGY

### Antidote to Extremist Worldviews

SUSAN L. ALLEN

At this writing, I am 35 years older than I was when, as an anthropology student, I so innocently wondered why anthropologists and journalists did not provide combined training for those of us wanting to work in public education. The impulse to share anthropology's enlightening and grounding insights—about holism and whole-system perspectives, about connectedness and the interdependence of the earth and its creatures, about the twin survival requirements of diversity and commonality—seemed so sensible to me. In fact, I have pursued this bridging work throughout my professional life.

In *Media Anthropology: Informing Global Citizens* (1994), I speculated that perhaps those of us who were learning to see anthropology's holistic principles applied to "whole" cultures at that chaotic time were in a position to notice that they also applied to any system, from subparticles of atoms to relationships to the universe itself.

When I thought seriously about the ways in which anthropological perspectives would improve journalism and at how the information channels and methodologies created by journalists could allow the essence of anthropology to reach a critical mass of global citizens, I was, in

the vernacular of the day, blown away that no one was training people in both skills sets.

It seemed clear to me, for example, that it was wrongheaded to define *balance* in a journalism story as the inclusion of opposing points of view. Emphasizing polarities rather than taking into account the richer complexity of our reality leads to the dualistic thinking that results in absolutist and extreme positions.

That either-or, point-counterpoint framework is what I think we, as individuals and societies, need to grow beyond. Our goal as journalists and educators should be to broaden perspectives, not validate polarization! This insight about holism certainly is not new, but it did come out of the blue, in a manner of speaking. It arrived, for me, in December 1968, with the pictures of the earth seen from space for the first time.

What has happened since those early insights? We all know the answer. Despite all of our miraculous tools, with which we now can conceive of a "global village" and inform the entire global citizenry, we are constantly limited to a view of events and issues (peace-war, good-evil) that is simplistic, not complex; extreme, not contextual; short sighted, not far reaching. We are shown a black-and-white world instead of the more realistic continuum of possibilities between extremes or the spectrum of influences and connections in which seemingly single extremes exist.

With respect to public information, surely the Fox News Network represents the zenith of a swing toward extremist, corporate journalism. The question is open, however, whether we citizens—and we media anthropologists—will sit by while journalism's fundamental role in American democracy crumbles or whether we will insist on and create something better.

As my little activist mother would say, it is "high time" for some responsible group of professionals to begin systematically bringing perspective-building information and insights to global citizens, and, as fortune sometimes has it, that is exactly what media anthropologists can do.

In retrospect, one sobering reality and one encouraging insight have most influenced my thinking about media anthropology in the years since I edited *Media Anthropology: Informing Global Citizens*.

## THE SOBERING REALITY

Guardians of the status quo have reasserted (what they perceive as) their historic privilege since we began talking about media anthropology in the late 1960s. Those who held the social-economic-political reins of power liked that control just fine, thank you very much, and they did not sit idly by when citizens began to gain perspectives that would cause them to further question traditional assumptions. In retrospect, we naive folk who were working to share ideas that could move the world toward greater power sharing did not have a chance—at least, not if quick victory was our only goal.

Although (actually, because) the changes we had in mind would lead to more justice, not more inequity; to stronger democracies and less chance of tyranny; and to a safer and more sustainable world, the "tragedy of the commons" effect continued to influence "the few" who have an upper hand to want to keep the power over "the many"—at any cost to the many.

We simply did not foresee the strength of resistance to inclusive social justice from power holders in threatened, tradition-bound societies who, by this time in our history, had institutionalized their power into our social structures, including the communications media (which we saw as the primary vehicle for progress).

We thought individual human beings were ready for a "league of nations" and to function as a global citizenry. As it has turned out, we were and still are tightly controlled by something akin to a band of 14-year-old boys who prefer violence, entitlement, and short-term gain to peace, justice, and long-term sustainability.

With respect to media anthropology specifically, those who opposed the teaching of critical thinking skills; "wiring more people into the system," as futurist Alvin Toffler (1972, p. 124) said; and disseminating diverse views through media channels calmly went about their Business, with a capital B. They asserted their privilege by strengthening control over the media through writing policy, spending wildly, and severely limiting media access. In addition, some media-savvy, politically astute power holders began tutoring a cohesive and willingly regimented block of the population (mostly religious fundamentalists) in how to use (and buy) new media technologies to organize opposition to economic, political, and religious change. That group has succeeded practically unchecked.

Lots of people noticed this social right turn, which began with renewed permission after the 1980 U.S. presidential election, although in 1994, those of us working on the first media anthropology book continued to expect more "promise" than "threat" (Cherry, 1971, quoted in Allen, 1980) from the new communications technologies. We still thought that if we learned to use the new technologies, combined them with our world-shrinking "anthropological" insights, and used these tools for public education and real democracy building (including our U.S. "democracy"), we could help global cultures evolve toward a more sane, equitable, and sustainable future.

President Kennedy had said, "Our greatest challenge is to make the world safe for differences," and that is what we had intended to do.

Generations of progressive people, working in fields as diverse as physics, economics, environmentalism, religion, and journalism, had taken steps in that direction. Anthropology contributed by building a whole-world database of information that illustrated clearly the biological, as well as cultural, need for diversity, as well as revealing our common ground. We thought that if decision making and problem solving could occur from within the framework of this holistic cognitive frame of reference, people would make more fair, inclusive, and sustainable decisions. People would agree to work toward dynamic balance in the greater system because to such "global citizens" it would be obvious that to sustain life as we know it on our interconnected, interdependent little planet, we must either achieve win-win solutions—or eventually we would all lose.

American journalism had created channels for mass communication and a philosophy that called for an informed, educated populace. At the time we wrote, just a dozen years ago, there still were thousands of independent American newspapers, radio stations, and many points of view among traditional media outlets.

The idea of anthropology, journalism, and public education joining forces to create ways and means to bring grounding insights to everyone seemed like a logical next step toward global social justice and a more peaceful future. Those interested in the history and philosophy behind my version of media anthropology might look at my 1994 book and 1980 dissertation.

In retrospect, where did our plans fall short? For one thing, human lifespans are shockingly short compared with social evolution, a fact we did not fully appreciate. The communications and transportation revolutions, in fact, have brought us closer together and made apparent the necessity to our survival of mutual interchange and more creative problem solving.

It could be that we media anthropologists and our allies just have not finished our work.

## The Encouraging Insight: Reframing Media Anthropology as Part of a Larger Social Change Movement

In the years after 1994, I discovered that my distress about corporate takeovers, capitalist greed,

fundamentalist religious uprisings, and the resulting crawl of progress toward anything akin to "wholeness" in the world had jolted me into the very same polarized thinking I had been so hopeful that media anthropology would help transcend!

I used to talk about media anthropology providing "a tree to climb" to get a perspective on the entire forest. It took some years for me to see that we could reframe and revitalize media anthropology by grafting our healthy branch onto a bigger tree. We do not need to resign ourselves to the black-or-white mode of thinking that does not seek the whole color wheel of alternatives.

Today, my view is that media anthropologists can be part of a larger movement of people who are working for organic balance in the world. Some call it the global social justice movement. I call it the nonviolence movement. By whatever name, we can work together to share perspectives that will help citizens grasp the survival requirement of organic balance in relationships and systems, and that, in my mind, is the underlying mission of media anthropology. Now, however, I think we need to develop smarter strategies and multiple ways of sharing our information and insights, including using smaller, more personal, and less controllable media, as well as using "people power."

We can practice "media anthropology" through "The Media," as we said in 1994, and also by recognizing and collaborating with groups of citizens (large movements and small groups, as Margaret Mead said) who have changed their minds about how they want to interact in relationship with one another and the earth.

## In the Meantime—Linking Media Anthropology and Nonviolence

I took a position as director of a university women's center following publication of the 1994 book. It seemed like an odd job for someone who, by training and temperament, is a media anthropologist. In fact, my interest in the patterns of culture and some knowledge of social change turned out to be helpful in my new job, because I seem to have looked at problems of violence on campus with different eyes than those people who typically are in charge of responding to it. Ultimately, the real-world problems at the Women's Center helped me see the links between media anthropology and larger social change movements.

Here are two examples of how anthropology and my new work are connected.

While doing fieldwork on international news flow in the South Pacific in the 1970s, I became fascinated by what Johan Galtung (1971) referred to as the "structure of imperialism." I could plainly see how the vertical, linear power structures of former colonial governments continued to overpower attempts at horizontal, "weblike" regional communication organization. For example, if a hurricane hit an island in French Polynesia, news of the event traveled up the communication chain to Tahiti, then to Paris, then to the United States before it was transmitted back down to American Samoa, which is geographically next door.

I also could see the confusion and growing anger from "rising expectations" in poorer regions when new satellite transmissions brought television advertisements for goods and opportunities in rich countries that, of course, were not accessible to the poorer areas.

In other words, I stored away some experience with issues of personal and institutionalized power (and imbalances of power) that applied to social change, including those addressed by small organizations such as women's centers. I had not thought about imperialism in the context of personal relationships, but I knew in the recesses of my mind that the global nonviolence movement idea of "If you want peace, work for justice" translated locally to, "If we really want a safe campus, we need to work for equality and better balances of power."

Those lessons from media anthropology fieldwork applied to the issue of violence at all levels because oppression is oppression; abuse of power causes injustice and dysfunction in any system; and power is never given up or shared easily, no matter the arena.

After recognizing that dynamic, the challenges in my new job became: How could we create a grassroots movement for change that could underlie the hierarchy (and, actually, the patriarchy)? How could we develop a gender-neutral, nonthreatening language that would create allies instead of opponents? How could we work around resistant but powerful people when necessary? How could we use public education and private communication as tools for organizing our efforts?

These insights led me to help create a campaign for nonviolence in our small community "system." Those interested in hearing more about how we accomplished this may want to read my article "Activist Anthropology in a Women's Center" (Allen, 2001).

My point is that being assigned the task of attending to problems of violence on a college campus helped me see that the aims of media anthropology applied in daily life, not just globally or philosophically. Muddling around in the culture of violence led me to see that *relationship* (within a partnership, a group, the globe) describes "connected systems"; that dynamic, organic balance in these systems is sine qua non to a relationship that lasts; and that the underlying goals of a women's center and media anthropology are essentially the same: to help people break out of thought prisons caused by "reductionist" thinking—specifically, to share holistic perspectives.

In 1994, I advocated using journalism to share these kinds of perspectives. Now I think we can make use of many more tactics, tools, and strategies for tackling the job of global public education and rebalancing power.

## Underlying Issues

When I began working on the front lines at the Women's Center, facing problems caused by abuses of power against less-powerful people (women, gays and lesbians, ethnic minorities), I began once again to bump against people's inability to view the world beyond "this-or-that" extremes. I also began to grasp the very real threat of system failure that lurks beneath any situation of imbalance, because I could see first hand the inevitability of violence in situations where there is too little justice or when violence is met only by counterviolence.

In this case, I consistently ran into the unwillingness of the powers that be to address violence in contexts more encompassing than the isolated, individualistic "solutions" offered by the legal-health-economic-education systems. I noticed also that others in the population inevitably go along with the ineffectual handling of conflict because adequate information to assess the situation is not available to them.

I began to wonder why people failed to examine these issues within the honest complexity of organic systems, where intervening variables can be examined both now and through time. Why wouldn't they budge beyond a simplistic view of conflict that isolates single events and ignores systems, as well as isolating individuals and ignoring community?

I thought that if we examined violence in its holistic context, where strings in the knotted ball of interconnected precursors to violence could come into view, we might then convince people that it is in their own best interest to assume some responsibility for violence as a systemic public health problem rather than deny it or push it out of sight by labeling it an individual aberration. In addition, we might show one another that widespread, anticipatory participation in problem solving before the crisis stage might actually be effective.

Guess what! I again came up against the same resistance to change that occurs any time someone is asked to share power. Even modestly powerful people in "small ponds" (and their inattentive followers) would rather keep conflict out of the public agenda than make changes in themselves or in the power structures that, in the near term, appear to keep them safe and financially sound.

Needless to say, the barriers we face trying to change local systems governing violence in our community parallel the problems we media anthropologists faced when trying to bring real change to the U.S. media monolith—the same problems faced when anyone attempts to alter the seeming safety of the status quo.

## MAKING CONNECTIONS

Eventually, issues from the Women's Center—and my insistence on the need to "get ahead" of the violence instead of only "cleaning up after" it—led me to think about conflict as it actually exists: within one whole, systemwide spectrum of possibilities that encompasses both violence and nonviolence.

As synchronicity sometimes has it, the year 2000 was approaching, and I read that the United Nations was to declare the first 10 years of the millennium a "Decade for a Culture of Peace and Nonviolence." I started reading nonviolence literature, and that was when I realized that my violence work in the Women's Center, the ideas behind media anthropology, and also the goals of the nonviolence movement connected and shared an overarching mission: to share contextual, "anthropological" perspectives and to teach about holism so we could equip ourselves to assume more responsibility for ourselves and our world.

There are many excellent nonviolence movement writers beyond Mahatma Gandhi and Martin Luther King, Jr.: Gene Sharp, Howard Zinn, Coleman McCarthy, and Jonathan Schell are among them. I would like to quote from just one of the relevant nonviolence sources:

> What has drawn me most strongly to nonviolence is its capacity for encompassing a complexity necessarily denied by violent strategies. By complexity I mean the sort faced by feminists who rage against the system of male supremacy but, at the same time, love their fathers, sons, husbands, brothers, and male friends.
>
> I mean the complexity which requires us to name an underpaid working man who beats his wife both as someone who is oppressed and as an oppressor. Violent tactics and strategies rely on polarization and dualistic thinking and require us to divide ourselves into the good and bad, assume neat rigid little categories easily answered from the barrel of a gun.
>
> Nonviolence allows for the complexity inherent in our struggles and requires a reasonable acceptance of diversity and an appreciation for our common ground. (McAllister, 1988)

As I began designing a campaign for nonviolence on my campus, as a way to place a campuswide, participatory, violence-prevention network beneath the radar of anyone opposed to changes in the status quo, and as I was gathering materials and ideas for a nonviolence studies course, I became for the first time a serious student of the history and methodologies of the "nonviolence movement."

When I did that, suddenly a whole world of ways to think about system imbalance brought about by dualistic thinking opened before me.

I clearly saw that all systems, all relationships, change. Life *moves*. Whether the movement is toward the positive or toward the negative depends on many factors, of course. Always, however, dynamic balance has to be maintained if the system is to survive. Using violence (meaning any abuse of power) as a means to control change sacrifices sustainability. Abuse of power (tilting the balance to the extreme) can "work" for awhile, sometimes a long while if you do not care if the relationship lasts—an abusive husband can overpower his wife, a country or culture can dominate or oppress another, humans can pollute the earth. Eventually, though, the dysfunction will cause system failure. Nonviolence methodology, on the other hand, recognizes the vast array of possibilities between "either" and "or" and works for organic balance— fair relationships, win-win solutions to conflict— precisely so the system can be maintained.

## THE CHALLENGE OF TURNING ABSTRACT IDEAS INTO CONCRETE ACTIONS

Readers familiar with my 1994 media anthropology text may recall that I illustrated what media anthropology would look like when applied to journalism. I showed how journalism "reduced" the events of our lives (the stories of those lives) in a way that causes them to appear disconnected from the influences surrounding and connected to them. I tried to show how media anthropology would add a w, for *w*hole system, to the traditional 5-w questioning framework used by journalists, the who, what, when, where, and why of news stories (Allen, 1987).

In the same era, I drew illustrations of balance in systems, for classes such as Women's Mental Health and Comparative Spiritualities. I wanted to talk about internalized dysfunction caused by polarizing concepts such as right brain versus left brain, spirit versus matter, even male versus female (emphasis on the *versus*), and I needed to show a dynamic kind of balance to do it.

It is hard to share abstract ideas—such as nonviolence, for example—because they compete with concrete, sexy ideas such as violence. Who wants to think about whole systems and prevention when daily drama is available?

I decided to use the ancient yin-yang symbol for many reasons but mostly because it contains wholeness and movement instead of the dualistic, mechanistic, "teeter-totter" model of balance more widely understood in our culture. Dynamic, asymmetrical balance is vital to all living systems; and it seemed reasonable to borrow this pattern that exists in the nature of everything from the DNA double helix to the simulation of star formation. With this symbol I could make more concrete the requirement of organic balance for system sustainability without using inflammatory or moralistic language.

To supplement the yin-yang, I used the mathematical Möbius strip to illustrate seamless wholeness; I used an old-fashioned, 1960s-style mobile to illustrate interconnectedness and interdependence; I used the gyroscope (a yin-yang symbol laid flat and given an axis) to show how imbalanced systems are guaranteed to fail. (I am adding illustrations for continuum and spectrum now, but the ones listed here have worked well.)

More recently, after meeting blank stares when I tried to talk about violence and nonviolence within the context of whole systems, I pulled out the old illustrations and updated them for a chapter in the book *Community and the World: Participating in Social Change*. The chapter, "Organic Balance as a Conceptual Framework for Social Change Movements" (Allen, 2003), can, I think, give us a new rationale for media anthropology and new options for applying holistic perspectives.

Through media anthropology, we can offer a cognitive framework, a filter, a frame of reference that can transcend dualities and reveal the folly of extremist thinking. If we join forces with the nonviolence movement, we can help to rebalance systems from a more personal approach.

## PARTICIPATING IN SOCIAL CHANGE

If we want people to sense connectedness, to participate in community, to care about the world, and to assume some response-ability, then someone needs to help empower citizens (inclusively, by the millions) with the ability to respond. That means making accessible the information and insights people need to participate.

If problems are set before us (if *life* is before us) only in the extremes (succeed or fail, right or wrong, peace or war), we are made to respond extremely, or we feel powerless to respond at all. We conclude that "someone" must know more than us; someone must be in charge. It must be the president or God or at least someone like Gandhi—but certainly not me!

If, on the other hand, we help people envision a holistic, cognitive blueprint and present problems and questions in their natural contexts and along a continuum of possibilities, people can begin to see ways in which they can participate and intervene in dysfunctional systems before the crisis point. People will learn how to "be the change they wish to see in the world," as Gandhi said.

An anthropologist friend from my younger life worked in the peace movement, and she used to talk about starting an "Anthropologists for Social Justice" group. I thought it redundant at the time. However, like her, at some point I started to wish anthropologists would be more socially active— even if we risked losing some credibility among colleagues who disapproved of public education or frowned on participation in the anthropologist's own culture.

If we anthropologists really believe our work is important and our ideas are sound—who are we saving them for?

One of my favorite ideas from the nonviolence movement is this:

Question:  Why are we violent but not illiterate?

Answer:  Because we are *taught* to read. (McCarthy, 2002)

The point is, none of us have been taught how to practice nonviolence in our daily lives. In fact, the few people who think at all about the "nonviolence movement" associate it only with famous circumstances and not with something in which ordinary people can participate every day. This includes anthropologists who have the particular mission of bringing nonviolence concepts and anthropological perspectives to the global citizenry.

I use my anthropology daily, in participatory, as well as media, activities, and I strive to "be the change I wish to be in the world." I insist to activist students that we focus on balance and perspective building rather than on polarizing, but I believe in the need for global-social rebalancing, and I think anthropologists can play a key role in keeping this movement smarter and less extreme.

## Examples of Nonviolence and Activist Media Anthropology

Nonviolence is another concept, like media anthropology, that seems bewildering to people who insist on absolutism and concreteness in their world. *Nonviolence* is especially difficult in the English language, where it seems to be negative or inactive rather than something one "does." However, nonviolence is neither passive nor abstract. I've come to think about nonviolence in a very practical way. Nonviolence can be seen as learning to see our lives, along with their inevitable problems and conflicts, within the context of whole systems—and, then, taking action to bring dysfunctional systems, large and small, into better balance by imagining, creating, developing the ways and means to attend to imbalances (we hope) before a crisis occurs, and afterwards, too, through conflict resolution, mediation, and other nonviolent methods. In fact, I think human cultures only now have reached a point in personal and technological development at which a critical mass of citizens may be able to obtain and integrate the complexity necessary to apply nonviolent practices in relationships of all kinds. It is now time to begin teaching these practices in earnest.

Conflict occurs in specific contexts, with a finite number of possible outcomes. Unlike violent responses to conflict, in which ending relationship is considered acceptable, *nonviolence* means devising and moving toward outcomes that have the best chance of sustaining the long-term health of the system. After all, we are going to end up living in the world with the things we label negative, including our opponents, whether we like it or not.

After studying the nonviolence movement in this light, the concrete, real-world problem of addressing violence on a college campus came to look like a microcosm for the whole issue of rebalancing power (and other energies) in our culture and world. Eventually, trying to address local injustices, such as rape or discrimination or economic injustice, led me back to the philosophical and global problems and solutions I associated with media anthropology's raison d'être.

The following is the working definition of violence-nonviolence I use for my Introduction to Nonviolence Studies class and elsewhere (it came originally from the syllabus for the 2004 class):

> We examine violence and nonviolence within a holistic, interlocking web of problems and outcomes, not as "black or white" polarities. Violence is individual and institutional, personal and political. It might be silence, bullying, harassment, physical assault, suicide, oppression, exploitation, war. . . . Violence is injustice that results in dysfunctional, imbalanced relationships—among people, groups, nations; [between] people and [the] environment, even within one body or mind. Nonviolence in this context means moving toward dynamic balance—justice, health, peace—by devising creative interventions into the dysfunctional systems—ideally, before a crisis occurs, but with conflict resolution, direct action, and other creative, nonviolent methods, afterwards. Nonviolent action generates win-win outcomes for inevitable conflict and change; it moves toward better balance in relationships with the goals of wholeness, fairness, and sustainability.

Is sharing that point of view "media anthropology"?

I think it probably is.

A series of public service announcements that the university's football coach has agreed to read on behalf of the local campaign for nonviolence provides, I think, another example of "socially active media anthropology" and "active nonviolence." The first announcement, for example, introduces the use of organic (win-win), instead of mechanistic (win-lose), methods of addressing problems and conflicts in the real world. It does that by talking about the difference between games and life.

| Coach: | I'm Bill Snyder, football coach at Kansas State University. |
| Student Athlete: | I'm Marquis Clark, high jumper, KSU Track and Field. |
| Student Athlete: | I'm Kendra Wecker, K-State women's basketball. |
| Snyder: | [Over shots of coach on the sidelines, Kendra shooting a basket, Marquis jumping] In sports—we either win or we lose. |
| Wecker: | But leave it on the court! |
| Clark: | Leave it at the track! |
| Snyder: | Leave it on the field! |
| Wecker: | Learn the difference between games and life. |
| Snyder: | Practice nonviolence in daily life. |
| Clark: | Look for win-win solutions to problems and conflicts. |
| Wecker: | In relationships and in community. |
| All: | If we don't *all* win, we all lose. |

Is this public service announcement a form of "media anthropology"? I think it is.

## TEACHING THE TEACHERS

Most of us global citizens have internalized the same dualistic, cognitive worldview that has brought our world so perilously close to system failure. After all, it has been our sanctioned reality for generations. Following that, however, and this is important, most of the world's citizens—including most individuals in progressive social change movements—still need to become aware of the holistic perspectives that media anthropology can help provide. Unless most who are working for change incorporate a holistic organizing framework that helps us transcend the "given" mechanistic worldview that leads to extremism and polarization, we, ironically, risk falling into the same dysfunctional cycle of attack and counterattack used by the fundamentalists who oppose any changes in the balance of power whatsoever.

Most progressives, including the intellectuals, environmentalists, anthropologists, and democrats among them, have done a lousy job of articulating the meaning and consequences of interconnectedness, having instead resorted to their own brand of reductionism and polemics. If this is because they have not yet embraced an organic conceptual model for analyzing their mission, they need to do it soon.

Media anthropologists have a big job to do, and we cannot limit ourselves to "either" using the established media "or" keeping our holistic perspectives to ourselves. We need to use alternative ways and means of getting our messages out. We can practice media anthropology by circumventing the controlled media and finding allies within them. We can make use of newer, smaller, and more independent electronic technologies.

We have to stick our objective little necks out there and say we believe in critical thinking and in holistic or anthropological perspective. If we are willing to do that, we can get involved personally with movements of people struggling in diverse ways to reveal connections and create sustainable community. We can use our perspective-building form of activism to show people why such pronouncements as "you are either with us or against us" is suitable in sports but is not appropriate language for the leader of a just nation. We can learn to focus the gaze of the media, large and small, in ways that help the "whole world watch" and thus end the secrecy that feeds tyranny, oppression, exploitation, selective denial, and other personal and institutional abuses of power.

We can help provide an intellectually sound, contextual cognitive framework that can help people make sense of a world that otherwise appears random and disconnected. We can help show that, surrounding any issue formerly framed as black or white, there is an entire color wheel of possibilities.

## MEDIA ANTHROPOLOGY AND THE NONVIOLENCE MOVEMENT?

I see a growing, global nonviolence movement as one (still loosely defined) organizational network of which media anthropologists could become a part. Certainly, an anthropological presence could provide cultural expertise and substance (not to mention perspective)—if anthropologists choose to participate.

I think the languages of anthropology and nonviolence can provide at least two powerful assets to those seeking a more just and peaceful world: a gender-neutral, nonthreatening, relatively baggage-free vocabulary based on critical thinking skills and holistic perspectives, and a whole world of alternative possibilities for direct participation by like-minded people working in diverse situations.

By going beyond the original conception of "media anthropology," and by adding active nonviolence to our repertoire, we can tap into what the 1960s knew as "people power." By doing this, we can use more personal and less controllable media, such as the Internet, cell phones, and other personal communications technologies to connect and organize people. (The Web-based organization MoveOn.org and Governor Howard Dean's 2004 presidential primary organization are early examples of these methodologies.) Also, we can apply a whole gamut of nonviolent methods to "speak truth to power" when power would limit our freedom.

I do realize these suggestions seem improbable, but becoming a student of nonviolence has taught me not to dismiss as hopelessly naive the efficacy of individuals-together who make up their minds to create change for the better and who refuse to cooperate with injustice. People building better balance in the world by practicing nonviolence can, in fact, become a "force more powerful" than money, tyranny, and tanks, and media anthropology can participate by helping connect and inform the necessary critical mass of global citizens who are working for a more just, peaceful, and sustainable future.

## REFERENCES

Allen, S. L. (1980). *Media anthropology: Concept and Pacific Islands case study*. Unpublished doctoral dissertation, University of Kansas, Lawrence.

Allen, S. L. (1987, Summer). "Adding a w": How journalists can practice media anthropology. *Journalism Education, 42*(2), 21-23.

Allen, S. L. (Ed.). (1994). *Media anthropology: Informing global citizens*. Westport, CT: Bergin & Garvey/ Greenwood.

Allen, S. L. (2001, December). Activist anthropology in a women's center. *Voices, 5*(1), 11-15. Retrieved December 27, 2004, from http://sscl.berkeley.edu/%7Eafaweb/Voices.pdf

Allen, S. L. (2003). Organic balance as a conceptual framework for social change movements. In T. D. Dickinson (Ed.), *Community and the world: Participating in social change*. Hauppauge, NY: Nova Science.

Galtung, J. (1971). *Members of two worlds: A development study of three villages in western Sicily*. New York: Columbia University Press.

McAllister, P. (1988). *You can't kill the spirit: Stories of women and nonviolent action*. Santa Cruz, CA: New Society.

Toffler, A. (1972). The strategy of social futurism. In A. Toffler (Ed.), *The futurists*. New York: Random House.

Beeman, W. O. (1995, September). Media anthropology: Informing global citizens (Book review). *American Anthropologist, 97*(3).

Center for the Advancement of Nonviolence. (2004). [Home page]. Retrieved December 27, 2004, from http://www.nonviolenceworks.org

Fellowship for Reconciliation. (2000). *Celebrating the decade for a culture of peace and nonviolence 2001-2010: A resource manual*. Nyack, NY: FOR.

Kansas State University. (2004). *Campaign for nonviolence: Kansas State University*. Retrieved December 27, 2004, from http://www.ksu.edu/nonviolence/

Kansas State University Women's Center. (2004). [Home page]. Retrieved December 27, 2004, from http://www.ksu.edu/womenscenter/

San Antonio peaceCENTER. (2004). [Home page]. Retrieved December 27, 2004, from http://www.salsa.net/peace/index.html

Sharp, G. (1973). *The politics of nonviolent action* (Parts 1-3). Boston: Porter Sargent.

Solnit, R. (2004). *Hope in the dark*. New York: Nation Books.

United Nations Association in Canada. (2002). *The United Nations and the culture of peace*. Retrieved December 27, 2004, from http://unac.org/peacecp/decade/

Zinn, H. (2002). *The power of nonviolence*. Boston: Beacon Press.

## ADDITIONAL SOURCES

Allen, S. L. (1975, Spring). Predicting reader interest in anthropology column. *Journalism Quarterly, 52*, 124-128.

Allen, S. L. (1984, November). Media anthropology: Building a public perspective. *American Anthropological Association Newsletter, 25*, 6.

# 27

# SPEAKING WITH THE SOURCES

## Science Writers and Anthropologists

MERRY BRUNS

The relationship between anthropologists and journalists forms part of the larger academic field of science communications: the study of how scientific information passes from primary sources to the public. Many of the concerns voiced by anthropologists about coverage of their work are shared by scientists in other fields.

News or feature stories are written to attract and interest the general reader, who often has little interest in science. Media goals and methods dictate the style in which journalists write, how they handle scientific complexity, and the focus they give to the story. These methods and goals often vary dramatically from the way in which anthropologists and other scientists present their material in professional publications. When the two styles conflict, anthropologists or scientists can feel frustrated, annoyed, or confused when others cover their work.

Anthropology sometimes receives a great deal of media coverage, in which case the problems may lie more with the type of coverage rather than the quantity. Anthropologists cannot always control which parts of their work will draw the most attention or be considered most newsworthy. For example, a conference whose theme held wide interest for anthropology as a field received no media attention at all, but a single speaker—whose paper tied in with a current news story—received a great deal of media coverage. It may not be what the conference sponsors were hoping would be covered, but it is what interested the reporters.

To work successfully with media, anthropologists should understand something about the way journalists work (which, in essence, is understanding another culture). As Carol Weiss and Eleanor Singer note in their 1988 book *Reporting of Social Science in the National Media*:

> The kind of social science that appears in the media depends on the interaction of two professional fields, journalism and social science. The interaction takes place on the home court of the journalist, and it is journalistic rules that prevail. Still, it seems reasonable to expect that actions that social scientists take or fail to take can affect the nature of the outcome. (p. 4)

Scientists from various fields, as well as anthropologists, may have similar complaints about their experiences working with media and the ways in which their research is sometimes depicted. They worry that reporters do not understand their science well enough to write about it. They fear they will be quoted out of context or that they will be portrayed as "instant experts" on a subject not in their field, which damages their credibility with peers. They are concerned that reporters will misrepresent their work in the story, leave out critical data, round off significant statistics, or oversimplify their comments. They often feel that news stories ignore the processes by which information has been acquired, leaving only the bare bones of their research.

All of these concerns stem from the unavoidable fact that a news story and an anthropology paper differ in almost every way. Understanding these differences and what drives media coverage of science can help reporters and scientists achieve a more satisfying compromise on the finished product.

## SCIENCE WRITERS AND MEDIA COVERAGE

The anthropologist who wants to communicate with the public through media channels should try to find a professional science writer to work with. Science writing has a history of serving the sciences well. Journalists become science writers because they have an insatiable desire to find out the *why* of science and because they love the process of research. They are in the field because they want to share their excitement with the public. Charles Petit of *U.S. News & World Report* explained, "We're writing for that teenager who's excited about science and want to encourage him to pursue his science interests" (Workshop Panel, 2000).

Many science writers started out in research themselves, only to find that they preferred writing about the science itself. Coming from surprisingly varied backgrounds, they cover medicine, technology, space, the environment, and social science—and most have science degrees. Their interests are wide, and their curiosity and willingness to delve into the complexity of science makes them among the most responsible of journalists.

Historically, poor reporting of science has often resulted when editors have offered stories to journalists lacking scientific training.

They don't have enough background to ask intelligent questions, or write intelligent stories . . . no broadcast exec would expect to send out a general assignment reporter and ask him to cover sports, play by play . . . yet any reporter that's available gets sent to cover a science story. (Dunwoody, Friedman, & Rogers, 1986, p. 33)

Although science writers operate under the same constraints as general reporters, they are better able to fit the science story into the type of media they work in because they are knowledgeable about the subject and know how to treat it responsibly. To a science writer, accuracy is as important as telling a good story.

## SCIENCE AND THE NEWS

Journalists are required to report science the same way they report politics or business news. Journalists pick up science and anthropology stories from press conferences, science journals, press releases from science associations, papers presented at science meetings, and through other sources.

News coverage requires, first and foremost, that the story be current. News is what is new. A science news story is sometimes whatever is the latest or the newest scientific information, and the choice of what to run is sometimes made by editors.

Problems in science coverage often arise when inexperienced general reporters get a "scoop" on a local science or medical story that they perceive to be of major significance. Because of their lack of background . . . they are more likely to portray a story as "newer" or "bigger" than it actually is. (Dunwoody et al., 1986, p. 89)

Science writers often have to make the case to an editor—who sometimes knows little or nothing about the subject—that the story is worth covering. Former anthropologist and science writer Cindy Lollar states, "Magazine editors care about your data, but only insofar as they are enabled to comprehend them through an energetic narrative told in a lively voice" (Allen, 1994, p. 42).

News may be defined as something specific that has never occurred before, is measurable or quantitative, and is, often, visual. However, one of the difficulties in covering anthropology is that the discipline is often nonquantitative. Anthropology seems to some writers to be "nonstatistical," lacking the rigor that hard sciences such as physics or astronomy provide. Science writers often see anthropology as a "soft science," which is particularly hard to convert into news that will satisfy editorial demands for stories with more definitive information.

Reporting on anthropology skillfully requires more than just reporting facts, however. "It demands the ability to raise and pursue pertinent interpretive questions, and the perseverance to seek out opposing arguments, and the integrity to report with equal vigor contradictory information that might emerge later" (Weigel & Pappas, 1981, p. 480).

To provoke a reader's interest, science stories must be important enough either to stand alone, or they must be able to "piggyback" on current news. This is especially true for newspapers, TV, and radio coverage—less so for feature stories or longer magazine articles.

## The Human Angle

Editors and journalists generally look for the "human interest" in their stories by focusing on the parts that speak personally to the reader. "According to most news personnel, the best stories are those that have drama and human interest" (Dunwoody et al., 1986, p. 26). A science story is often framed around the effect it will have on the reader and is written to start out with that focus. "Whatever a news outlet produces needs to be keyed to the interests of its particular audience. To reach the greatest number of newspaper readers or television viewers, science news must be simplified and translated into lay terms" (p. 19).

Unless the story is running in a large market, stories about science often have to interest a local readership as well, especially in smaller towns, where most science stories arrive through national wire services. Editors will often ask a science writer to justify the "local interest" in stories before they are even assigned.

## Targeting the Reader

Most news articles begin with a strong lead paragraph that is designed to attract and interest the reader and give the gist of the story. A careful science writer will strive to maintain accuracy as well as create compelling opening sentences. As the most important information is often contained in later paragraphs, it is up to the writer to maintain readers' interest in the story long enough to get them there. Skilled writers can do this by working source quotes and important information into the first part of their article.

Feature stories for magazines or newspapers have longer lead times and allow the writer to present subjects in greater depth. Although feature stories must also be focused around the reader's interests, they are not as constrained by a hard news "peg" as news stories. They are better vehicles for complex stories, as there is more room for background and a better understanding of the processes involved in the science.

Journalists writing news stories about anthropology and other sciences turn academic writing on its head by using an "inverted pyramid style." This standard journalistic technique gives the conclusion of the story first, followed by additional information in descending order of importance. Feature stories do not always adhere to this rule but are still focused more strongly on the conclusion of the story. Although this style can irritate academic and scientific writers—whose style is more linear—journalists have a different goal. Their writing must grab the reader's attention right away by letting them know what the story is about, then lead them through the process of getting there.

## Deadline-Driven Writing

Journalists usually operate under extremely tight deadlines. Stories must often be written in a few hours, particularly for newspapers, radio, and TV. During this time, the journalist may have to identify, search for, and call scientists to interview, make sure the facts are correct, come up with a reader-friendly take on the material, and write the article. This deadline-driven culture constantly forces the journalist to make decisions about the amount of detail he or she can put in the story. Sometimes meeting a deadline boils down to getting a quote or finding data quickly enough to get the story in on time.

Writing stories on deadline can also affect how sources are used or identified. Space limitations mean that anything considered not essential to understanding the storyline gets cut out. Sometimes only one, highly generalized aspect of a source's work might be mentioned ("a specialist on the Middle East") instead of a more complete citation ("an anthropologist examining Bedouin tribal nomads in the Middle East"). Under ideal circumstances, more than one source should be quoted in a story to provide balance or an additional viewpoint. But the "just find me an expert!" stress of writing on deadline can mean that sometimes only one, well-used source gets quoted in the story.

Science writers dislike the deadline-driven news mentality, perhaps more than other reporters. "Science reporters need more time to read and study. Reporters traditionally base their stories on interview notes. But science writing of any depth requires more understanding, which requires time. I feel my stories are often skimpy because they were rushed to meet deadlines" (Storad, 1984).

## MAKING THE COMPLEX CLEAR

A news outlet must gear its products to the interests of its audience. "To reach the greatest number of newspaper readers or television viewers, science news must be simplified and translated into lay terms" (Dunwoody et al., 1986, p. 19). Writing for the general reader differs from academic writing, which is meant to be read only by peers. The science writer uses a straightforward and concise style, because he must make sure that a general audience will be able to understand every word.

An anthropologist and former TV news anchor, Jim Lett, humorously claims that "journalists must satisfy much broader audiences, and the result . . . is that most of journalism is readable, and much of anthropology is not" (Lett, 1987, p. 356).

Newspaper and magazine readers' interest can decrease with the additional degree of technical complexity in a story. To overcome this, journalists write for the general reader in a direct, uncomplicated style, using analogies to explain complex subjects or focusing on the results, rather than the process, of the science. Although it may be easier to sell the "implications" of a science story than the facts, both must be skillfully woven together (Rowan, 1990, p. 27).

Effective journalists use the active voice to make the story more direct and compelling. They may write about the personalities of the scientists in addition to their research to make the story more accessible and interesting to a general reader. Unlike the rigorously depersonalized style of academic papers, science stories are often highly personalized to create empathy and curiosity in the audience.

## SCIENCE WRITERS AND ANTHROPOLOGISTS

I carried out a survey of science writers (Bruns, 1995), asking their perceptions of anthropology and anthropologists as news resources. Most respondents were print journalists, most had advanced science degrees, and all were members of the National Association of Science Writers, a professional organization. The survey data revealed both expected and unexpected information.

In general, those who had prior experience with anthropology or had anthropology degrees themselves tended to have more positive viewpoints about using it as a news subject. Those who were unfamiliar with the field were more cautious and, in some cases, negative about its value.

On one hand, some writers valued anthropologists for giving a sense of perspective to news stories.

Several appreciated their "unique viewpoint" and the way they took "the long view" of current news and added "good depth to stories"—all being good reasons to interview anthropologists. Anthropologists were valued as well for their "expertise across cultures" and their focus on "the human condition." Because science writers are often looking for the reader focus in news stories, anthropologists could provide "the human angle" to science. "Readers like reading about people," one reporter wrote; another stressed that anthropologists reminded him of the "importance of culture in our lives."

Overall, there was agreement that anthropologists were "knowledgeable experts to interview" who provided a sense of context and depth to stories. In addition, anthropologists could offer reporters a unique or counterintuitive view of a subject, giving an unexpected twist to an otherwise conventional article.

## PROBLEM AREAS

Some writers I interviewed appreciated the broad range of subject matter covered by anthropology. They felt that anthropologists offered news stories a good selection of "interesting topics, and study areas." At the same time, many writers had a more limited view of what anthropologists study and said they would not think to interview an anthropologist about "sports, military, politics, or foreign affairs"—areas about which anthropologists could provide a great deal of information.

Many journalists also had trouble differentiating between archeology, biological anthropology, cultural anthropology, and linguistics and had no idea which field to go to for an expert source. Some who had problems using anthropologists as sources apologetically cited their own "lack of knowledge of the field," which they felt made it difficult to know what *kind* of anthropologist to look for. Stating they "don't know which one to call," most writers were unaware that the American Anthropological Association, the Society for American Archeology, and other organizations might be good places to start looking for an anthropologist to interview.

Some stated that anthropology itself "wasn't newsworthy" and that anthropology as a subject was "not relevant to readers." One survey respondent stated that finding anthropology stories to cover was difficult, as there were "no journals available," and there were "no abstracts forthcoming from institutions."

Technical terminology was often seen as a real issue. Journalists often have trouble with specialists who use jargon when talking about their subject, because they have to translate it into language that their readers can understand. Many wished that anthropologists could "speak in lay terms," thus making their job easier. Some survey informants complained that there was "too much qualifying" when anthropologists talked about their research and that anthropologists were unable to make definitive statements about their work. Skilled science writers understand the reason behind this and realize that they will have to wade through a great deal of verbiage to write a tight story for the reader.

## PLAYING BY THE OTHER SIDE'S RULES

This overview of the relationship between science writers and anthropologists can be a starting point for anyone interested in communicating anthropology to a general audience. By being alert to the problem areas, the anthropologist can understand that science writers operate under a completely different set of rules for an entirely different readership. Learning to play the media's game by their own rules gives a great advantage to anthropologists and helps to ensure that their work is covered in an acceptable and responsible manner.

## RESOURCES FOR
## WORKING WITH MEDIA

Blum, D., & Knudson, M. (1997). *A field guide for science writers.* New York: Oxford University Press.

National Association of Science Writers. (n.d.). *Communicating science news: A guide for public information officers, scientists and physicians.*

Retrieved December 28, 2004, from http://www
.nasw.org/csn/ (Best practices for scientists on
working with the media.)

National Association of Science Writers. (2004).
[Home page]. Retrieved December 28, 2004, from
http://www.nasw.org (Resources and information
for science writers and public information officers.)

## REFERENCES

Allen, S. L. (1994). *Media anthropology: Informing global
citizens.* Westport, CT: Bergin & Garvey.

Bruns, M. (1995). [Survey of science writers: Evaluation of
their perception of anthropology as a news resource].
Unpublished raw data. Center for Anthropology
and Science Communication, Washington, DC, and
Center for Applied Anthropology, University of
South Florida, Tampa.

Dunwoody, S., Friedman, S. M., & Rogers, C. L. (1986).
*Scientists and journalists: Reporting science as news.*
New York: Free Press.

Lett, J. (1987). Commentary: An anthropological view
of television journalism. *Human Organization, 35,*
356-359.

Rowan, K. E. (1990, Summer). Strategies for explaining
complex science news. *Journalism Educator,* 25-31.

Storad, C. (1984, June). The state of the art: Science writers evaluate their field. *Quill, 29.*

Weigel, R. H., & Pappas, J. J. (1981). Social science and the
press: A case study and its implications. *American
Psychologist, 36,* 480-487.

Weiss, C. H., & Singer, E. (1988). *Reporting of social science
in the national media.* New York: Russell Sage
Foundation.

Workshop Panel. (2000). *Meet the press: Science writers
talk with anthropologists.* Workshop presented at the
Meeting of the American Anthropological Association
Meeting, San Francisco.

# 28

# THE JOURNALIST AS ETHNOGRAPHER?

*How Anthropology Can Enrich Journalistic Practice*

S. ELIZABETH BIRD

As this book amply shows, *media anthropology* can mean many things, from the anthropological analysis of media texts, producers, and audiences to applied efforts to present anthropological concepts effectively in the news media (Allen, 1994; Bruns, 2000).

In this brief chapter, I explore another, related question: What is the relationship between doing anthropology and doing journalism? Can journalists benefit from considering anthropological methods and approaches as they report and write the news? It has long been argued that social science and journalism are markedly different enterprises, based on different knowledge claims. These arguments often draw from Robert Park's (1967) distinction between abstract "knowledge about," through which the social scientist fits facts into theoretical frameworks aimed at predictability, and intuitive "'acquaintance with," through which the journalist accumulates facts that then, somehow, speak for themselves.

Phillips (1977) commented some years ago "that the journalist's way of knowledge . . . personally, professionally, and organizationally—is structured in one direction and the social scientist's

is structured in another is an important factor underlying their frequently mutual incomprehension and distrust" (p. 75). However, she also mentions the then-brewing movement in social science toward interpretive approaches, which she describes as beginning to "blur the traditional social science distinctions between knower and known, research and subject, theory and practice" (p. 75). She concludes that this approach "may later come to bridge the seemingly unresolvable distance between social scientific and journalistic notions of objectivity" (p. 75).

Indeed, as we look at the relationship between social scientific and journalistic approaches a quarter century later, we see significant "blurring" between the two, although it is clear that journalistic accounts are still "suspect in academic circles" (Shankman, 2001, p. 49). In cultural anthropology, descriptive and interpretive approaches have always been at the core, epitomized in the ethnographic method, and there has long been debate within the discipline about whether ethnography is a science, an art, or perhaps a bit of both. These days, there is a growing recognition among anthropologists that ethnographic methods,

**Author's Note:** This chapter is an extensive revision and updating of Bird (1987).

developed to holistically study isolated societies, must be adapted to the realities of a globally interconnected world, with ethnographers developing many new techniques (which often resemble journalistic methods) and applying them in familiar societies (see, e.g., Abu-Lughod, 2000; Marcus, 1998). Wolcott (1999) argues that, although ethnography is not in itself a clearly defined "method," a "central and unifying" principle of all ethnographic work is "a commitment to cultural interpretation" (p. 76).

It would seem that the same commitment is behind the last few decades' surge of interest in forms of journalism that go beyond traditional event-oriented reporting. For instance, the "cultural journalism" movement, inspired by such grassroots initiatives as the Foxfire project, "focuses on . . . everyday experiences and traditions in a community, as described by its residents, more than on the extraordinary . . . described by reporters as news" (Olmstead, 1986, p. 6). The academic home of the movement is the Salt Center for Field Studies, affiliated with the University of Maine, where students from many disciplines, including journalism, anthropology, sociology, and history, gain experience and training in what amount to ethnographic and documentary techniques aimed at capturing everyday experience. There is also "new journalism," which, as Shroder (1994) writes, rather more flamboyantly "penetrated the logic and customs of an exotic group and comprehended the world in the group's own terms" (p. 63), an enterprise that sounds much like ethnography. Such exercises in cultural reporting are often best suited to magazines, but many newspapers have also showcased extended, richly detailed feature stories with no traditional "news angle." Indeed, some believe this is one way to counter increased competition from broadcast news, as these kinds of stories can be done so much more effectively in print.

Thus there are certain genres of journalism that have already consciously developed an ethnographic stance, with an interpretive, rather than factual, goal. In this chapter, however, my aim is to discuss the relevance of the anthropological approach to journalism in a more general

sense—how some acquaintance with (or even knowledge about) ethnographic approaches might help general reporters. Drawing on my own background as both journalist and anthropologist, as well as my experience in teaching journalistic writing and anthropological methods classes, I suggest ways in which an appreciation of anthropological ways of knowing might help young journalists become more effective and perceptive in their future careers.

## ANTHROPOLOGICAL PERSPECTIVES AND JOURNALISTS

An anthropological perspective necessitates a particular relationship between researcher and "subject." Interviewing is obviously as important in anthropology as in journalism, but the stance of the ethnographer tends to be different from either social science or traditional news interviews, hinging on the difference between viewing the interviewee as source and research subject and as informant.

To a journalist, the "source" is exactly that—a source of information that is, in a way, separate from the personality of the individual. Similarly, sociologists traditionally treated the subject as a repository of information that could be tapped, the information becoming objectifiable and quantifiable. Although journalism textbooks now regularly discuss "social science" approaches to sources and data, stressing the importance of valid surveys, quantifiable information, and so on, they rarely explore the more time-consuming and humanistic approach to sources that characterizes ethnography.

Unlike the traditional sociologist, the anthropologist is less wary of the dangers of "subjectivity" and, in fact, aims and expects to relate to the informant as an individual. Anthropologists rarely interview an informant only once; a first interview is usually a preparatory, "getting-to-know-you" session, in which the interviewer will be less concerned with extracting facts and more concerned with reaching an understanding of the person and her or his particular concerns.

Furthermore, interviews may follow (or be embedded in) varying periods of observation and familiarization with the social scene. The questions to be asked in subsequent interviews should emerge as much from the impressions gathered from that first interview as from preconceived scientific hypotheses. Later interviews will probe more deeply but should all be in the context of mutual cooperation rather than one-way information flow, and these interviews will be enriched by the other interviews and informal observation that are necessary components of the anthropologist's method. For many anthropologists, the ideal interview is akin to a conversation (Camitta, 1990), and whatever the specific context (face-to-face, telephone, virtual, and so on), the goal is to see the world from the informant's point of view (Bird, 2003).

How is this relevant to a busy journalist working on deadline or to a harried journalism student trying to turn out a story assignment? The magazine writer or "cultural journalist" may have the luxury to spend the same amount of time on fieldwork that an anthropologist might, but what about general assignment journalists or beat reporters? I believe such journalists can practice seeing things ethnographically, even within the confines of the daily news regime. For instance, they might attempt to develop empathy with sources—communicating with them rather than interrogating them. To a journalist, the source is too often seen as a "representative," a unit that speaks for other like units, rather than as an individual. At the same time, although anthropologists encourage interaction with informants as individuals, their holistic approach encourages a perception of connections between individuals; this perception would be valuable in making journalists see the relationships between their sources and the wider cultural context.

Too often, journalists see each interview as an entity that bears little relationship either to previous interviews with the same person or to other interviews and observations related to the particular story. The tendency to use the telephone from the isolation of the newsroom may have something to do with that. The broader, more cultural approach fostered by anthropology encourages the appreciation of patterns and connections and should help to break down the compartmental approach of journalism, which treats every story, every source as unique and new.

The anthropological approach could be especially useful for beat reporters, who must develop a sense of continuity and connectedness in meaning. It is obviously important for a beat reporter to continue working with sources over time and to develop a sense of broader patterns—stories that lead to other stories and so on. Beat reporters could learn from anthropologists the relevance of keeping a complete "field diary" of their interaction with sources and happenings on the beat (see Emerson, Fretz, & Shaw, 1995). Once again, we see the difference between reporting discrete events or interviews aimed at particular stories and keeping a record of the whole "web of significance"—the beat, or the field, that allows the journalist-anthropologist to draw informed, broader conclusions about what is really happening. For instance, Shroder (1994) describes covering student government politics as a journalism-anthropology student, using his anthropological training to see beyond the story on election-brokering he was assigned.

> Instead of focusing on the scandal . . . we were interested in how the participants in the system perceived their roles, how they maintained their public morality or realigned it, and how the in-groups viewed the rest of the campus community. . . . [The result was] a different kind of story from what would have been written by a traditional journalist . . . [making it clear that] the election brokering continued to exist because it fulfilled an important function in a community. (p. 63)

The journalist habitually sets out on an interview with a particular story in mind, armed with some previous knowledge of the beat, and perhaps the evidence of stories written before and retrieved from the morgue. Still, each story is approached as separate, "irrelevant" notes may be discarded or never made in the first place, and only "timely" questions are asked. One wonders how much richer and multifaceted beat coverage might be if it could draw on notes made over time, observations jotted down that, although not relevant at the time, could suddenly throw light on later developments.

Certainly there are real time constraints, and the journalist may not have the leisure to produce the volume of notes that an anthropologist can, but it is not so much time as a difference in perception that prevents the average journalist from seeing the value of such an approach. Even in introductory newswriting classes, I have found it rewarding to work on this holistic approach to students' chosen beats or interest areas, and some students have been able to produce series of stories that demonstrate a growing awareness of connections and context. Similarly, the development of an appreciation of the complex cultural context of an interview may help journalists—general assignment or beat—in framing their questions and recording answers more effectively. Too often, journalists and their editors "know" what the story will be before they even start work—they may even have leads running around in their heads. It becomes an easy task to prove that this story is indeed the right one by asking the right sources the right questions and managing to ignore other issues that may come up in the course of the interview or the event. It is not deliberate bias or distortion, but it is an inevitable byproduct of the particularistic, event-oriented perception of the journalist.

Furthermore, as more and more research shows, what "the story" is depends a great deal on the conventions of information gathering, as well as on the conventions of narrative (Bird & Dardenne, 1988). As reporters, we think we have the story when we have spoken to a selection of acknowledged authorities and possibly one or two token symbols of the people. The ethnographer also uses authority figures, and indeed some have been criticized for lazily relying on very few key informants. Ideally, however, the anthropologist never assumes the story is complete; more people must be interviewed as the understanding from previous interviews accumulates, one line of questioning leads to another, and we return to a previous informant who then tells us more. The anthropologist's field is everyday life, and any member of the culture is a valuable source of understanding. The journalist's field is too often the network of officialdom, whether the White House or the local school board. A reporter with anthropological training should never again find it possible to perceive that network and its never-varying and limiting range of potential questions as sufficient. The anthropological perspective demands constant reframing of questions, revision of ideas, and cultivation of new sources; the ethnographic process is dialectical rather than linear, as fieldworkers study their data, discerning patterns and principles that then have to be followed up with further interviews and observation (Agar, 1996). This curiosity and unwillingness to settle for easy questions, easy answers, easily obtained, would be something that any journalism student might well learn to develop—even under the kind of time constraints that anthropologists have the luxury of escaping.

## WRITING THE STORY

Journalists could learn not only to rethink their approaches to gathering information but also to writing and analyzing it. Although anthropology shares with journalism an orientation that is more "acquaintance with" than other social sciences, it also involves a more rigorous element of "knowledge about" than journalism displays. Facts do not speak for themselves, yet journalists abdicate responsibility by displaying them as if they do. When journalists have to draw facts together, they frequently rely on known narrative conventions to make sense of the information rather than on theories or patterns that seem to emerge from the accumulation of data, as anthropologists would. This difference stems not only from time constraints but from an explicit difference in purpose: The journalist ostensibly seeks to inform and be "fair," and the anthropologist seeks to interpret. As Lett (1994) observes, "anthropologists and journalists have distinctly different notions about the nature of 'objectivity.' For . . . anthropologists, objectivity means being fair to the truth; for . . . journalists, objectivity means being fair to everyone involved" (pp. 102-103). Lett, an anthropologist and TV journalist, describes his discomfort at being ordered to "ignore the truth of the matter in hand in the interests of being 'fair' to the people involved . . . e.g. to report that evolution is 'just a theory' as a means of being fair to creationists" (p. 102). The richness and complexity offered by anthropological perspective can be a valuable corrective to the simplistic journalistic notion of "balance"—that the story is complete when one has spoken to a designated spokesperson from "each side" of an issue. However, it also demands that the researcher explicitly draw conclusions, and this, of course, is where journalists are often most uncomfortable.

## Problematic Issues

Once a journalist or student has been exposed to the complexity of information that anthropological fieldwork methods obtain, it should not be so easy to write news stories that are as one dimensional and conventional as so many now are. An anthropologically trained journalist would virtually by definition have to be an interpretive journalist. That in itself poses a problem for traditional journalism, because interpretation and analysis are supposed to be anathema to unbiased news reporting (unless clearly labeled as such). Culturally oriented journalism is controversial not only among journalists themselves but also to audiences; some readers or viewers react favorably to rich journalism that does not fit the "objective" mold, but many others do not. Probably as many readers or viewers believe in the commonsense paradigm of news as "just the facts," no matter how frayed that paradigm has become among scholars. A recent and typical case in point was the reaction to an ambitious series of stories in the *St. Petersburg Times*, one of the few newspapers whose freedom from corporate chain ownership occasionally allows reporters to indulge in extended cultural reporting. The series, *13,* was a six-part exploration, totaling more than 40,000 words, that chronicled the lives of seventh graders in Tampa and was based on several weeks of essentially ethnographic fieldwork with the teenagers (French, Fields, & Nguyen, 2003). It had no "news value" in the conventional sense, it certainly was not "objective," but it effectively conveyed the sense of the world through 13-year-old eyes. Many readers responded with enthusiastic letters to the editor. The series "made me feel the unfortunate reality of the transformation of child to adult"; it was "well written, truthful"; it "opened a door onto a world few ever see or remember, and you have given it due justice, explanation, sympathy and beauty." It was "outstanding . . . the writing team captured the essence of the age of innocence with a humorous and sympathetic 'adult' understanding" (Letters to the Editor, 2003, p. 13A). Others were less enthusiastic, disliking the subjectivity, the detail, and the lack of "real news" appeal: "My family . . . is astounded, disgusted and outraged . . . blatantly attempting to tear down their morals and defy, harass and ridicule parents"; it was "major overkill that could have been covered in one or two articles"; and it was a "silly series" (Letters to the Editor, 2003, p. 13A).

The lesson is that when journalists become more like anthropologists, they also shed the protective cloak offered by news values and objectivity and open themselves to the same criticisms anthropologists have long faced: subjectivity, overidentification with informants, personal bias, and so on. These criticisms have formed the basis for the periodic "scandals" in anthropology about accuracy, such as the dispute over whether Margaret Mead or Derek Freeman was "right" about Samoan culture (Shankman, 2001) and whether Napoleon Chagnon's accounts of the Yanomami were inaccurate, demeaning, and damaging to them (Tierney, 2000).

Ethnography by its very nature requires greater empathy and involvement with sources than is usual for journalism, and this may seem threatening, unsettling, or just plain hard work. At a practical level, the relationship of source to journalist is usually fairly clearly understood: The source offers information, perhaps in return for publicity. Journalists do develop relationships with their sources, maybe even socializing with them, but one of the acknowledged and very legitimate problems in journalism is the danger of becoming identified with sources and their interests. Indeed, an awareness of this problem may result in editors transferring reporters to a new beat just when they have become familiar with their current one.

The potential for involvement in anthropology is probably even greater, given the encouragement to develop relationships that are more long standing, more intense, and based on more probing, personal questions. Anthropologists are always wary of the dangers of "going native" and becoming an advocate for the culture of "their" people; nevertheless, they continue to do it. In fact, there is a constant and probably unresolvable tension in anthropology between the need to become assimilated and the need to remain the "professional stranger" (Agar, 1996). The tension is neatly illustrated by the comparison between the disparaging term, *going native* and the much-quoted instruction from Clifford Geertz (1983) to see culture "from the native's point of view," a goal he later modified (Geertz, 1988). Anthropologists worry about this issue, fearing it will interfere with their professional credibility. Journalists, however, may have even more to worry about, because they have the added burden of the public's "right to know." Often the public would be better informed if the reporter had used the broader, more contextual approaches of anthropology, but there will surely be times when the journalist must be adversary, not ally. The intimacy of the anthropological approach could blind reporters to the necessity of offering unflattering exposes rather than empathetic stories.

At the same time, the empathetic approach may in the end be more effective than the confrontational approach in reaching a deeper understanding, and professional journalists may be guilty of fostering the idea that only adversarial, *60 Minutes*–style reporting is really effective in discovering the "truth." I have certainly been struck by the pervasiveness of this attitude among journalism students, eager as they are to rush out into the "real world" and expose evil. Many seem reluctant to accept the possibility that a deeper understanding could result from building relationships with sources rather than setting

out to expose them. In discussing this point in class, I have used my own experience, including one instance in which I had the opportunity to interview a local Ku Klux Klan leader in the mid-1980s. I found the use of a wide-ranging, nonconfrontational approach to be extremely effective in encouraging the source to expand his ideas and even to seek me out for further interviews when he recalled other topics he wished to develop. The final picture that emerged was more complete and informative than would have been painted using an adversarial approach. It was certainly more useful than a quick round-up of phone calls to local official sources asking standard questions about Klan activity.

The problem of overidentification with sources is shared by journalists and anthropologists. Nevertheless, although it is not an easily resolved problem, its existence is not enough of a reason for journalists to reject the deeper understanding that anthropological approaches may offer—when the occasion is appropriate. Anthropologists who criticize journalists' lack of empathy must, however, also be aware that journalists at times have a responsibility to the public that anthropologists can justifiably avoid.

Related to this issue is another question that has more direct ethical implications. The code of ethics of the American Anthropological Association states unequivocally that anthropologists' primary responsibilities are to their informants. At all times, their privacy must be safeguarded and respected; specifically ruled out are such techniques as surreptitious recording, misrepresentation, and so on. In recognition of the cooperative role of informants in the creation of an ethnography, many anthropologists are now recommending that informants should be encouraged to read and critique the accounts made of their cultures.

It would be unusual to find a journalist who could share these ethical standards. Although all would surely endorse the need to respect privacy and sources' rights, would many support the idea that responsibility to a source overrides all other considerations, such as the requirements of a good story or the need to expose an injustice? My own limited study of ethical standards related to surreptitious recordings (Bird, 1985) was similar to other studies in that it suggested that newspaper editors, who would certainly hold to ethical codes in theory, would break them if a particular story merited it—although none would do so lightly.

One of the great advantages for anthropologists in collecting information is that they are not constrained by the fear of informants that intimate secrets will be published or broadcast. Anthropologists routinely (though less so recently) have given informants anonymity; the general patterns that emerge from their fieldwork are more relevant than the specific identification of one individual. Their copious fieldnotes provide the backup that may be necessary to convince colleagues.

If journalists start to use the more in-depth techniques of anthropologists, they are likely to face more difficult ethical dilemmas. The information they gather may be more intimate and personal, less like the official pronouncements they are used to. There may be more requests for anonymity or even for the right to preapprove stories, which journalists rightly avoid at all costs. The actual gathering of the information is, in any case, likely to be harder when informants know they are talking to journalists, not anthropologists.

However, this may not be such a bad thing. Once journalists become aware of their sources as people, perhaps they will become more critical of the kinds of easy answers that claim the story comes first and that ethics are negotiable. When studying the ways in which ethical dilemmas are faced by ethnographers, journalism students may begin to ask, for instance, if there are other ways information may be obtained before deceptive means must be resorted to. At a more general level, the added perspective seems to help journalists learn to become more self-conscious of what they see as normal, routine ways of interacting with their sources.

## CONCLUSION

Notwithstanding the efforts of new journalism or cultural journalism, the rituals and strategies of journalism have become entrenched as so much "common sense." In this essay, I have offered some thoughts on the contribution that an understanding of anthropological perspectives might bring to the working or student journalist. This contribution might best be summed up as ways in which to nudge journalists out of the comfortable, commonsense routine in which so many conduct their work and challenge them to expand their newsgathering techniques—perhaps even their definitions of what news can be.

The best place to begin this endeavor is in the classroom, where would-be journalists will have more time than ever again to ponder the complexities of how knowledge is gained and how stories are told. At a time when the audience for news is more distracted then ever and newspapers are losing readers (Bird, 2000), we should be aiming to produce graduates who are able to question some of the taken-for-granted certainties of journalistic practice. Journalists are not anthropologists, nor should they be (Grindal & Rhodes, 1987). The two professions have different missions, and they work in different environments and under different constraints. Still, their goals are enough alike that some appreciation of the insights of anthropologists, and perhaps some training in ethnographic methods, could be one fruitful way of expanding the horizons and the richness of journalistic practice.

## REFERENCES

Abu-Lughod, L. (2000). Locating ethnography. *Ethnography, 1*(2), 261-267.

Agar, M. A. (1996). *The professional stranger: An informal introduction to ethnography* (2nd ed.). San Diego. CA: Academic Press.

Allen, S. L. (1994). *Media anthropology: Informing global citizens.* Westport, CT: Bergin & Garvey.

Bird, S. E. (1985). Newspaper editors' attitudes reflect doubts on surreptitious recording. *Journalism Quarterly, 62,* 284-288.

Bird, S. E. (1987). Anthropological methods relevant for journalists. *Journalism Educator 41*(4), 5-13, 33.

Bird, S. E. (2000). Facing the distracted audience: Journalism and cultural context. *Journalism: Theory, Practice and Criticism, 1,* 29-33.

Bird, S. E. (2003). *The audience in everyday life: Living in a media world.* New York: Routledge.

Bird, S. E., & Dardenne, R. W. (1988). Myth, chronicle and story: Exploring the narrative qualities of news. In J. W. Carey (Ed.), *Media, myths and narratives* (pp. 67-86). Newbury Park, CA: Sage.

Bruns, M. (2000). *Media anthropology: A brief background.* Retrieved December 28, 2004, from http://www.sciencesitescom.com/CASC/medan.html

Camitta, M. (1990). Gender and method in folklore fieldwork. *Southern Folklore, 47*(1), 21-31.

Emerson, R. M., Fretz, R. I., & Shaw, L. L. (1995). *Writing ethnographic field notes.* Chicago: University of Chicago Press.

French, T., Fields, M., & Nguyen, D.-P. (2003, May 18-20, 23-25). Series: 13. *St. Petersburg Times.* Retrieved December 28, 2004, from http://pqasb.pqarchiver .com/sptimes/337915541.html?MAC=07d034116b 4cf3c7f93ba0fbcf4f1fa8&did=337915541&FMT=FT &FMTS=FT&date=May+18%2C+2003&author= THOMAS+FRENCH&printformat=&desc=4+UR+ EYES+ONLY+Series%3A+13.

Geertz, C.(1983). *Local knowledge: Further essays in interpretive anthropology.* New York: Basic Books.

Geertz, C. (1988). *Works and lives: The anthropologist as author.* Stanford, CA: Stanford University Press.

Grindal, B., & Rhodes, R. (1987). Journalism and anthropology share several similarities. *Journalism Educator, 41*(4), 4, 11-13, 33.

Lett, J. (1994). The anthropologist as television journalist. In S. L. Allen (Ed.), *Media anthropology: Informing global citizens* (pp. 91-103). Westport, CT: Bergin & Garvey.

Letters to the editor. (2003, May 31). *St. Petersburg Times,* p. 13A.

Marcus, G. (1998). *Ethnography through thick and thin.* Princeton, NJ: Princeton University Press.

Olmstead, K. J. (1986). Twenty years of cultural journalism. *Journal of Experiential Education, 9*(3), 4-8.

Park, R. E. (1967). *News as a form of knowledge: On social control and collective behavior.* Chicago: Chicago University Press.

Phillips, E. B. (1977). Approaches to objectivity: Journalistic versus social science perspectives. In P. M. Hirsch, P. W. Miller, & F. G. Kline (Eds.), *Strategies for communication research.* Beverly Hills, CA: Sage.

Shankman, P. (2001). Requiem for a controversy: Whatever happened to Margaret Mead? *Skeptic, 9*(1), 48-53.

Shroder, T. (1994). The anthropologist as newspaper journalist. In S. L. Allen (Ed.), *Media anthropology: Informing global citizens* (pp. 61-65). Westport, CT: Bergin & Garvey.

Tierney, P. (2000). *Darkness in El Dorado: How scientists and journalists devastated the Amazon.* New York: W. W. Norton.

Wolcott, H. F. (1999). *Ethnography as a way of seeing.* Walnut Creek, CA: Altamira Press.

# 29

# JOURNALISM EDUCATION AND PRACTICE

GERD G. KOPPER

## INTRODUCTION TO THE DEBATE

Taking journalism education as an issue in the context of media anthropology is by no means meant to overemphasise the practical meaning and the true importance of this type of instruction. Journalism education, despite its existence for about 100 years in some Western societies, is still a field requiring growth in quality and in theoretical foundation. It is with the knowledge of some essential deficits in this field that I confront the practice of journalism education with the kind of reflection that can be gained through media anthropology. In this chapter, I demonstrate that some shortcomings concerning the horizon of theoretical insight supporting journalism education might be overcome through perspectives derived from approaches consolidated within media anthropology.

Journalism education is a very special sort of construct, with its goal of educating people to enter into a job of rather imprecise requirements that has become one of particular visibility among some pivotal professional segments in modern societies. It is a job segment, though, that is especially indicative of the process of modernisation that started in the early 19th century through industrialisation in many Western countries. One

has to remember that the beginning of the 19th century saw the beginning of the institutionalization of teaching as a profession. Here began a distinct professional category, when instruction within families, the churches, at feudal courts, and among the various artisan fields did not suffice. During the latter part of that century, engineering began to develop as an independent professional segment. Teacher training and engineering schools and colleges became a matter of course in all modern societies during the era of industrialisation. The journalist, in his modern incarnation as a salaryman (and, somewhat later, -woman), belongs to this type of avant-garde population at the beginning of modern society as we know it.

Journalism education, though, as a special institutionalised training, started very late, comparatively, in most modern societies. The earliest institutionalised journalism education at the college level was in the United States at the beginning of the 20th century. France had one specialised institute of higher education in this field shortly before World War I. University programs of journalism education in Germany, though, started only in the mid-1970s. Similar programs have not yet been launched, so far, in countries such as Japan. This broader look at the development of journalism education shows, on the one hand, that journalism is a general indicator of modernisation in societies. It shows, on the other hand, that journalism education is an indicator of different types of cultures of journalism, in terms of deep-seated national job traditions and specific developmental histories of the mass media industry.

Many disciplines have probed into journalism since its advent, and most have assumed that because of its dependence on modern techniques of communication, production, and distribution and because of its inherently international and global outlook, this field of activity follows, basically, equal rules and standards worldwide. This assumption, of course, is exemplified by the daily work of international news agencies and by the obvious similarities and look-alike appearance of newspapers, magazines, and TV programmes around the globe. A closer look, though, shows that journalism is uniquely based on national cultures. The lines between the dimensions I have noted of international commonalty and cultural specificity are extremely difficult to differentiate. One will find enormous latitude in journalistic practice, indicating that, on the one hand, journalism, obviously, is practiced along common and international standards and, on the other hand, is only to be understood within its national context. I think that essential elements necessary in understanding journalism practice have, so far, been left out. It is because of this missing analytical perspective that even empirical research continues into those theoretical contradictions I have noted.

My hypotheses will, in this respect, go beyond hitherto existing empirical evidence of common grounds in international journalism. Until recently, the ultimate common ground of journalism appeared to be found in the evident homogeneity of certain work routines and in the adherence to certain accepted rules of news management. The discovery of crossnational trends in news reporting (Galtung & Ruge, 1965), for example, seemed to corroborate the view that "journalism" could be defined by common and mostly general elements of daily practice worldwide. At least there was evidence for this in the Western world. In contrast to this view, I show here that the common grounds of "journalism" in Western society are to be found underneath

such functional practices. Such grounds might be found in the results of a special education that determines the very nature of viewing things, of behaving in certain situations, of describing certain events. It is an education that is better described as a professional *transformation* that establishes a whole, closely knit system of vision and of codes. This process, however, is not to be misunderstood as equal to *journalism education*. It is by analysing journalism education and journalism itself more closely that differences may become clearer.

## JOURNALISM AND JOURNALISM EDUCATION, REVISITED

The practice of journalism can be divided into components that follow a set of explicit (transmitted) and implicit (untransmitted) rules. It is the untransmitted and, apparently, untransmittable character of this work that is the object of my analysis. The transmittable part of the rules, and their foundation, have become common knowledge within those disciplines that are foremost in observing and analysing this field of practice (see, among many others, Berkowitz, 1992; Breed, 1955; Campbell, 1995; Dayan & Katz, 1992; Lule, 2001; Schudson, 2003; Tuchman, 1977, 1978; Tunstall, 1971; Zelizer, 1993). To become an accepted member of this working environment and to be considered a "good journalist," however, the adherence to such a standard conglomerate of rules and its horizon of functionality is not enough. There are particular ways and modes of engaging in the job and of handling the daily tasks that cannot entirely be defined by "social algorithms." It is this element of "something more" to the job that needs to be better understood to grasp journalism as a special and apparently essential type of work in modern societies (Carey, 1998; Coman, 2003; Garnham, 2000; Handelman, 1990; Neveu, 2001; Peterson, 2003; Shroder, 1994).

Following these auspices, it is necessary to consider the process of evolving from novice to "old hand" in the trade of journalism. This consideration is especially significant if we are to understand a journalist's assessment of "quality" as represented by something that surpasses the rules and routine schemes that reign in the daily practice of journalism and have a central bearing on journalism education.

If one had to reinvent journalism education, one would, of course, follow the models set by the training of teachers and engineers: One would look for obvious sets of insight that would ease the passage into practice. In this way, one would look for rules explicit in terms of the organisation of journalism as such. In the end, one would have training modules that dealt with different modes of production, standards of efficiency, and, due to the nature of the work of journalists, questions of style and focus in regard to texts, perspectives on specific types of scenarios, and technical matters, such as the editing of a film or video sequence, the selection of photographs, and so on. All this could be collected and put into a book: *Introduction to Journalism.* According to varying perspectives and theoretical and practical emphases, there would be a full spectrum of such books, as well as books organised according to different national cultures of journalism. There exists even now a worldwide bibliography of such volumes.

Journalists, as a group of people doing the kind of work that they do, living in most cases a good life according to their type of work, and being an accepted part of societies of the Western type of lifestyle and culture, are a rather new phenomenon in the working environment and in our societies; their existence in this format being less than 200 years old, sometimes just a little longer than 100 years. There are societies in the world today in which modern development still lags so far behind (compared to the European or North American context) that journalism and "the journalist" in the modern form are still not common.

The understanding of rules that govern the existence and role of journalism in our society has to rely on an understanding of the element of change and expectation that goes with the development and historical shaping of this particular and rather new group of special workers within the context of the modernisation of Western societies. These rules and patterns differ considerably among nations, societies, and cultures, as well as within the Western and most modernised world. This is why, in recent studies, the term *journalism cultures* has been on the rise, signifying, first of all, the impressive degree of incoherence in even the most practical levels of style, storytelling, values attached to the significance of events, hierarchy of news values in general, and so on—in, for example, British, French, and German journalism (see Christophe, 2001; Kopper & Mancini, 2003).

It is quite clear, historically, that there is a deep-seated cluster in the modernisation process within each nation, in which journalism constitutes one singular but highly connected element of reference and reflection among a great number of other activities that, in total, combine to form that specific cluster of general expression, expectation, and reflection called *national culture.* The differences among "journalism cultures" that show up during the technical production processes of different media are considered an outcome of historical and social roots, different as they are among national cultures. There is, nevertheless, an overall understanding and a descriptive framework of reference that describe the operating aspects of journalism and disregard such journalism cultures and their particularities. The descriptions of what a journalist does and has to do are abstractions of functional differentiation attached to particular media, channels, and technical requirements. The differences between these two sets of systematic description and understanding of journalism—on the one hand, technical and operating requirements and on the other hand, particular cultural elements—lead toward clearer insight into the role of journalism education and illuminate one of its central deficits.

Journalism education starts in the context of modernisation at a particular stage of development: The fluent elements of versatility in coherent decision making concerning content and style that rely on the knowledge of literature, of rhetoric, and of the making of politics, to name just a few fields, prove to be insufficient when technical functions and continuous advances in technology turn the world of traditional media into that of complex and competing organisations requiring specialists' knowledge on all levels and in all wakes of constantly new trades that spin off during this process—the sports section, the business section, the entertainment section, and so on (Delporte, 1999; Fernenczi, 1993). If specialists were the solution to these sorts of problems, journalism education would not be an urgent requirement. The use of a plain-spoken economist in the editorial office and the integration of some sports aficionados would, at times, be sufficient. Specialisation, however, in the process of modernisation, generally requires a counterbalancing element—that is, a growing expertise in contexts—as an ingredient of modernisation. Journalism education is, foremost, a counterbalance concerning the requirement of context in this sense (if it is not simply technical training or the use of specialists as journalists).

Three pillars might constitute journalism education in the future; hitherto, only two elements have been deemed obligatory. The requirements, as we know them, are (a) introduction into the essentials of a national journalism culture and (b) grasping the complex technical nature of the operative work of journalism. The new one that I am proposing here is (c) understanding the coded and nontransmitted fundamentals underlying the two traditional pillars of culture and technology (i.e., elements a and b) in the field of journalism.

The argument must progress by shortcuts that indicate some major areas and questions. It will not be possible, at this stage, to elaborate the full debate, as necessary as it may be. I shall be interpolating my understanding as I have outlined it, in terms of looking for some of the missing links in journalism education. Those links may be seen in very basic and usually untransmitted constellations of communication codes that define the active field of journalism and that serve as fundamentals underneath the specific spectra of national journalism cultures. I shall expose seven of those linked codes: codes that one might derive from existing empirical knowledge and research.

## SEVEN UNTRANSMITTED CODES AS FUNDAMENTALS OF MODERN JOURNALISM

Modern journalism is patterned by seven coded fundamentals that constitute discursive perspectives

that, ordinarily, do not openly enter into the debate of practice. At this point they are not reflected in journalism education and thus have not found their proper place of reflection. Therefore it should be possible to lay out a kind of evolutionary background of the development of technical communication and its impact on codes. Central formative patterns of modern journalism seem to have their common grounds within this sphere. Such patterns and their foremost coding may be seen in the following phenomena.

## The Rigour of Seeing Things the "Right Way"

Empirical research shows that under most practical conditions, people entering into a daily situation of either banal or outstanding nature will recollect "what happened" in a most individual and diverse manner. The insiders who know most about this, and suffer from it, are those practising law. Apart from the most obvious facts of a case, everything mostly fluctuates in terms of reference, recollection, and simple observations. Because we know about our larger world in modern society basically through the services of media that present to us a world of predigested "facts" and fundamentally reduced contradiction, we usually are not aware of the immense scale of incongruity that is the basic nature of raw reality as constituted within the multitude of awarenesses existing in a population and reaching through organised masses exposed to their own reality (see Goffmann, 1974).

The primary element of coherence among stories being told resides in the most trivial essentials such as whether actors are male or female, group sizes, and general emotions (aggression or nonaggression, etc.). Essential parts of cultural training in modern human societies are aimed at acquiring standards of common understanding that define situations in terms of patterns for common discourse as well as in terms of common emotions (Wouters, 1999, pp. 137-141). The more patterns that exist and the more patterns that have a long-standing and intensely invoked entrainment, the more homogeneity there will be in recollection and mutual information transfer and the more repetitive communicative acts there will be. Entire functional systems in modern societies serve to maintain homogeneity of mutual classification and pattern understanding in given situations.

The shock to all novices in the job of journalism in modern times is the feeling of pressure to answer strong formative requirements; that is, to grasp the set standards of how to report a given situation *in its context*. All journalists of good standing report a given scene in essentially similar manners. Following the notion of contingency that in essence rules such situations and with regard to the full spectrum of human reaction possible in understanding and interpreting such situations, a result like that produced through journalism in its daily practice is, in fact, extreme. It is based on the success of education and training to fulfil this job with exactly those results in mind. It is, furthermore, the outcome of strong requirements of form, of constant pressure, and of collegial reassurances through entire cycles of work. Journalism education at present plays a large role in this process in many modern countries. However, this role is only a part within a larger context of many systematic factors. Parts of the function of journalism education are to validate the rigour of journalistic scheme procurement (e.g., in terms of the standardisation of work results); to gauge, constantly, the given construct of reality; and, generally, to introduce newcomers into methodologies of self-assessment and ensuing adaptation to given requirements. Even the credit that is given for selected individualistic stances and for journalistic insight constitutes part of the total formative rigour: These are indicators of a consensual spectrum within which the formative schemes are allowed to develop.

Contrary to the traditional role imagery and self-esteem one finds in the general literature on journalism and in most of its self-descriptions, one of the fundamental functions of journalism education and its practices resides in reinforcing standard social schemes of discourse and communication. This helps society in accepting a system of common daily reference concerning the enormous and complex array of situations and questions that arise every day. Most of the information and reporting transferred through journalists and media, though, absorbs material in a very rational manner. Instead of covering all, which would be impossible, coverage is coded: My life as a user of journalistic products is normal and on the right track if I read the code that tells me the catastrophe is a continent away, that there is no imminent threat to my personal life and economy, and that there is an option to be entertained. Formative social power that coincides with one of the major underlying discourse schemes of journalism thus helps to sustain a reliable notion of "things being normal" within a given society.

This mechanism works best if journalists accept this extremely artificial adherence to predefined schemes as the "natural way" of understanding the world in human terms. Journalism education and its mainstream curricula will reinforce this understanding of the "natural character" of scheme-based conceptualising so formative in the job world of journalism. Structural changes have become visible through new kinds of Internet-based journalism, its formats and services, and these might, in the future, become more critical in regard to the "naturalness" of the most widespread schemes in journalism practice.

## The Scheme of Knowing How to Tell Something in an Accepted Manner

Next to accepting a situation in a typified manner and reproducing it through an accepted scheme in standard journalism ranks the competence and ability to phrase texts according to accepted standards. A dozen different writers reporting a schemed situation will produce texts of extremely similar character: Sentences will run to a particular length, they will follow a particular rhythm, they will consist of similar verbs and nouns. The structure of the text will follow similar rules. However, there will be no general acceptance that all of these texts really look alike.

Variance within an accepted bandwidth of style and construction is considered of high value in the industry. Standardisation thus rules the industrial process on the one hand; variance, on the other hand, constitutes the impression of personal commitment, individual presence, and directness. These are characteristics that the public favours and tends to accept as a major element of the deliverables of mass media. Identification with individual journalists among readers, listeners, and viewers requires variance. This variance, however, is legitimised through structured adherence; that is, the boundaries set by standardisation of text production.

It is very clear that this process, furthermore, defines particular paths of describing the world and depicting situations and personalities. It is a logical outcome that an enormous spectrum of alternatives and variations, including perspectives and views much more complex than the standard, will thus be entirely excluded. This is not to declare the complete loss of such views: They simply have no legitimate position in journalism. There are ever so many fights to exclude them from journalism. Of course, there are grey zones that span from journalism to literature, or from journalism to documentary filmmaking, or from journalism to audio art. From the point of view of journalism, however, the working field constitutes itself by common practical insight into the borders that divide journalism from everything else (Schlesinger, 1990).

The particular social service referred to as journalism is based on a rigid constitution of rituals at the very heart of the exercise of the job; that is, how to see things and how to describe things (Carey, 1988; Ehrlich, 1996; Koch, 1990). Journalism education is, in its overwhelming effort, an exercise of introduction into the core rituals of the job. Questions remain, of course, as to whether this emphasis will determine the future of journalism education in the long run. Journalism education has entered the world of universities, and it is increasingly forced to open up to transdisciplinary enquiry. It is on this path that some metaquestions, as outlined in this chapter, enter traditional journalism education.

## The Acceptance of Being a Servant to a General Process

Due to the noted mysteries of the role and job of journalists, beginners in this practice, especially during their training period, tend to aspire toward a "career," usually connected to some vision of influence. However, it is the subtext of practical initiation into the "real" practice of this job to not only convince novices that they are just a simple and small part in a much larger machine but to press this notion inextricably into the core vision of the working ego. This is the most basic of all understandings that goes with being an accepted member of the working group. It is for this reason that this essential is never talked about. Based on this deep-rooted acceptance, there exists an elementary structure of coherence among practicing journalists of all sorts. The boundaries between "our group" and "them" (nonjournalists) follow these lines. Journalists who, within some media and formats, have gained a special status, performing singularly and as prominent brand names of shows, no longer belong to the "real group"; they are a "different sort," because they no longer interact with peers along those subtle lines of the complex process of division of labour that effectively surpasses the context of one particular medium or payroll environment. This division of labour includes the entire daily process of journalism. Everybody feeds on somebody else, and everybody knows it, accepts it, and is part of it.

Journalism education forms only part of these hidden convictions and traits, because its instruction will never form the "real" practice of journalism. Sometimes this type of education will turn out to be detrimental to the necessary ease of accepting the emotional basics of the job. Any kind of disciplined and planned education tends to focus on and emphasize the individual and his or her accomplishments. The same holds true for journalism education. If it creates a strong belief in individuals' potentials, journalism education also tends to outmanoeuver dispositions toward coherence that form the very fundamentals of the profession at large.

## Knowledge Regarding
## the Scale of an Event

Between journalism education and the beginning of their practice, there will not be a single day for novice journalists in which—without any overt say so—the most central of all messages will be clear: that there is a hierarchy of events and situations that happen in the world and that a journalist has to work according to this scale. To accept this scale of events and to understand it enough, within a short span of time, that it is ready at all times for the journalist to use in making decisions on the spot, makes the framework similar to the trained heart of a long-distance runner.

The exciting aspect of this performance, however, rests in the fact that there seems to exist some collective abstraction working behind the value hierarchy that delivers the scaling of events. Some efforts have been made to decipher the "inner mechanism" energising this abstract process (see Berkowitz, 1992; Rothenbuhler, 1998).

Thus, without relevant insight into the very nature of these processes of scaling, journalism education is operating like the science of medicine before the advent of the natural sciences. Elementary research that builds a link to this particular type of professional education is still, in large part, missing.

## The Certainty to
## Withstand Involvement

One of the basic patterns of human development has been the active dimension of support. The development of families, of groups, of cohorts, of larger and even abstract entities of modernity relies on strong dimensions of mutual support, whatever inherent aspects may be involved—procreation, dependency, aggression, and so on. In regard to this broad developmental trait, some of the socially accepted and required exceptions prove to be especially instructive; specifically, role patterns that are excluded from direct support. One of those peculiar role patterns of modern times is that of the journalist. It is generally, and without exception, accepted that

there are human beings who do not intervene positively in situations in which people are at the brink of death, in catastrophic situations, in situations of mental breakdown, and so on. It is accepted that journalists take pictures, that they ask questions, that they take down notes, soberly, patiently, while human beings are jumping out of flaming apartment buildings.

To be able to neglect any movement toward support in any given and assigned situation requires a trustful reliance on the valour of the role of the assigned work and on a good, functioning mentality that can distance itself from the situation without inner aggravation. A new kind of empirical research into journalism would require a closer look at the human components of the "real situation," at the complexity of social culture as the particular context of the "distanced view and mentality" of journalism, and at the very workings and performance of the industry that trades in such assignments.

Journalism education reflects only glimpses of the complexity involved, mostly under the heading of "ethics." It is clear that even within this sectored view, again, one finds more of an inner circle kind of debate concerning the do's and don'ts of the produced results of journalism. The intricate human exception that constitutes journalism is not being generally debated. It has become an object of increasing public interest, however, whether such performance is sustainable. Evidence of this is the increasing number of documentaries, TV features, and analytical reports concerning the work of war reporters worldwide.

## The Reduction of the
## Weakness of Hindsight

Much of the progress that led to modernity was built on inventions, innovations, services, and ideas that have one element in common: their measurable reliability. There are many dimensions to reliability, such as punctuality, freedom from risk, and so on. I do not expound on those details here. The amazing fact rests in a closer look at journalism as one of the key developments of modernisation: Its major overt characteristic is a connotation of reliability (embedding it in modernity), whereas its pragmatic covert nature is that of gross unreliability. It has even developed into a statutory legacy that not one mass medium in our age will guarantee the truth and reliability of its information in the strictest sense. The media will guarantee that their customary practice is their best work—work according to the rules. However, it is work built on tons of errors, misunderstandings, and outright betrayal. Because of this foundation, journalists could not be able to carry on through an entire working life if they were to strictly follow the accepted rules of reliability that reign over modern times. Stories written turn out to have been built on false assumptions; reports that never reach any approved status are circulated; there is news that ruins the lives of innocent people; and so on. To go on despite this quagmire, journalists are trained to forget the bad trail; they live on the positive results of their work, and colleagues remember them for their best scoops (which are rare). The worst thing that could happen to a journalist would be to be confronted with a meticulous record of all the things he or she has produced. The banalities en gros and the immense spectrum of error and stupidity will not be the unbearable insight to a few exceptions but to the majority of the journalist's (gross and impalpable) experience. The older journalists grow in their trade, the more they know about this invisible burden, and the sooner they learn never to think about it.

It is because of this side of the nature of their job that journalists tend to build up heroes among themselves within each national journalism culture. Journalism education is in danger of building a kind of subliminal church to this particular kind of heroism. A better and richer future for journalism education would require developing new research and teaching to cope with the very problem underlying the job of the journalist and its inner and individual dysfunctionalism.

## The Assurance of Individual Functional Uniqueness

Without a constant assurance of the individual functional uniqueness of each journalist, the entire and complex system of journalism would not be able to perform at all. Within a background that contains so many inherent and mostly hidden traits of the trade (in terms of the patterns of communication involved), the enormity of this particular "educational requirement" as a part of journalism must certainly be considered explicitly dramatic and bizarre. Apparently, this requirement is positioned in opposition to a number of the built-in schemes just outlined. Contradiction, as shown in this aspect, underlies the very nature of this job and its performance in modern societies. Without the constant belief in the singular value and functional uniqueness of the individual journalist, some essential requirements of the practice would not be demonstrable, such as inquisitiveness, perseverance, precision, clarity, and so on. These are qualities that cannot be pressed upon a group or an individual. Such qualities must be built upon characteristics already within the individual.

## Conclusion

A closer look at the underlying traits of journalism in the context of modernisation of Western societies shows quite clearly that the role of journalist reflects some key contradictions and dilemmas in the journalistic process in general and in general anthropological terms: Interpretation of the world as it is was removed from the hands of a select few of high esteem in literature and the arts at the beginning of the liberal and bourgeois period and made a process of manufacturing and, later, of a full-scale industry built on an intricate system of division of labour and technical know-how. The birth of a new spectrum of jobs summarized as "journalist" packed into that designation values and rules and elements of self-esteem dating back to the beginning of the mass press and comprised the ideas that these white collar workers have a special status vis-à-vis the public, moral issues, and basic human values. Because of the amount of contradiction involved in maintaining this job in a practical and industrialized manner, some essential supportive cultural communicative fundamentals exist that remain invisible and are never talked about. These fundamentals are codes that are never disputed or reflected on, so that an understanding of things and processes as "of natural order" may be maintained and thus also an undisputed surface to social life as well. Journalism education has, so far, been a coherent agent within this process of assigning social value to the system of journalism as it now is. Using the insight gained through media anthropology, journalism education will have to enter into a new kind of reflection of its role and instruments. Journalism, in this respect, has not entered the kind of richness of theoretical reflection that constituted the beginning of sociology as a new discipline at the end of the 19th century, when its task was, among others, described as "la conaissance de la conaissance."

# REFERENCES

Berkowitz, D. (1992). Non-routine news and newswork: Exploring a what-a-story. *Journal of Communication, 42*(4), 82-94.

Breed, W. (1955). Social control in the newsroom: A functional analysis. *Social Forces, 33*(3), 326-355.

Campbell, C. (1995). *Race, myth and the news.* London: Sage.

Carey, J. W. (Ed.). (1988). *Media, myths and narratives.* Newbury Park, CA: Sage.

Carey, J. (1998). *Communication as culture: Essays on media and society.* Boston: Unwin Hyman Press.

Christophe, C. (2001). *La crise des sociétés impériales: Allemagne, France, Grande Bretagne 1900-1940* [The crisis of imperialist societies: Germany, France, Great Britain 1900-1940]. Paris: Seuil.

Coman, M. (2003). *Pour une anthropologie des médias* [Toward an anthropology of the media]. Grenoble, France: Presses Universitaires de Grenoble.

Dayan, D., & Katz, E. (1992). *Media events: The live broadcasting of history.* Cambridge, MA: Harvard University Press.

Delporte, C. (1999). *Les journalistes en France 1880-1950: Naissance et construction d'une profession* [Journalists in France 1880-1950: The birth and construction of a profession]. Paris: Seuil.

Ehrlich, M. C. (1996). Using "ritual" to study journalism. *Journal of Communication Inquiry, 20*(3), 3-17.

Fernenczi, T. (1993). *L'invention du journalisme en France: Naissance de la presse moderne à la fin du XIX siècle* [The invention of journalism in France: The birth of the modern press at the end of the 19th century]. Paris: Plon.

Galtung, H., & Ruge, M. (1965). The structure of foreign news. *International Journal of Peace Research, 1,* 64-90.

Garnham, N. (2000). *Emancipation, the media and modernity: Arguments about the media and social theory.* Oxford, England: Oxford University Press.

Goffmann, E. E. (1974). *Frame analysis: An essay on the organization of experience.* Cambridge, MA: Harvard University Press.

Handelman, D. (1990). *Models and mirrors: Towards an anthropology of public events.* New York: Cambridge University Press.

Koch, T. (1990). *The news as a myth: Fact and context in journalism.* New York: Greenwood Press.

Kopper, G. G., & Mancini, P. (Eds.). (2003). *Kulturen des Journalismus und politische Systeme: Probleme internationaler Vergleichbarkeit des Journalismus in Europa—verbunden mit Fallstudien zu Großbritannien, Frankreich, Italien und Deutschland* [Cultures of journalism and political systems: Problems of international comparison. Case studies in Great Britain, France, Italy, and Germany]. Berlin: Vistas.

Lule, J. (2001). *Daily news, eternal stories: The mythological role of journalism.* New York: Guilford Press.

Neveu, E. (2001). *Sociologie du journalisme* [The sociology of journalism]. Paris: La Découverte.

Peterson, M. A. (2003). *Anthropology and mass communication: Myth and media in the new millenium.* Oxford, England: Berghahn.

Rothenbuhler, E. (1998). *Ritual communication: From everyday conversation to mediated ceremony.* Thousand Oaks, CA: Sage.

Schlesinger, P. (1990). Rethinking the sociology of journalism: Some strategies and the limits of media-centrism. In M. Ferguson (Ed.), *Public communication: The new imperatives* (pp. 61-83). London: Sage.

Schudson, M. (2003). *The sociology of news.* New York: W. W. Norton.

Shroder, T. (1994). The anthropologist as newspaper journalist. In S. L. Allen (Ed.), *Media and anthropology: Informing global citizens* (pp. 61-65). Westport, CT: Bergin & Garvey.

Tuchman, G. (1977). The exception proves the rule: The study of routine news practices. In P. M. Hirsch, P. V. Miller, & G. Kline (Eds.), *Strategies for communication research* (pp. 43-62). Beverly Hills, CA: Sage.

Tuchman, G. (1978). *Making news: A study of the construction of reality.* New York: Macmillan.

Tunstall, J. (1971). *Journalists at work.* London: Constable.

Wouters, C. (1999). *Informalisierung* [Informalising]. Wiesbaden, Germany: Westdeutscher Verlag.

Zelizer, B. (1993). Journalists as interpretive communities. *Critical Studies in Mass Communication, 10*(2), 219-237.

# 30

## THE PUBLIC SPHERE

### Linking the Media and Civic Cultures

PETER DAHLGREN

The history of modernity is inexorably related to the emergence of the media; ours is a "mediatized" society, where ever more modes of social contact take place through mediated communication. One of the consequences of mediatization is what Thompson (1995) terms an increased "publicness" or "visibility" in society, an enhanced transparency in regard to politics, the power structure, and "society" more generally. Certainly among that which has been rendered more visible is the public itself: We are offered ongoing symbolic constructions that portray who we are and how we think. Factual, fictional, and mythic renderings in the media have contributed to a collective sense of who we are—a sense of multiple, overlapping, and at times conflictual collective identities. Taking a historical perspective, Chaney (1993) tells us that "new relations of dramatization for collective experience have been forged" (p. 113). In the late modern world, this holds true even in transnational contexts, as the institutions of the media and their representations go global.

One could pursue this theme in cultural terms, from an anthropological angle, as some authors do (e.g., Hannerz, 1996), looking at how the media help people weave networks of meaning across societies and across the globe. However, the notion of mediated publicness and modernity invokes another analytic tradition: that of the public sphere, which is tied to concerns about democracy. With anthropological traditions in the media highlighting cultural themes, on the one hand, and the public sphere tradition focusing on politics and democracy, on the other, it is in a sense my aim to try to bring these hands a bit closer together, to demonstrate the importance and utility of a cultural perspective in understanding democratic participation.

Increasingly, discussions on issues of democracy and the media are framed within the concept of the public sphere. In schematic and idealized terms, a functioning public sphere is understood as a constellation of institutionalized, communicative spaces that permits the circulation of information and ideas. These spaces, in which the mass media figure prominently, serve to foster the development and expression of political views among citizens as well as facilitating communicative links between citizens and the power holders of society. The key text here is, of course, by Jürgen Habermas (1989). Habermas's point of departure is a critical one; he underscores the many ways in which the publicness of the new media had, by the early decades of the 19th century, come to distort rational communication and contribute to ideological misrepresentation and political powerlessness among the public.

There are problems and ambiguities in his book, as many critics have pointed out (see, for example, Calhoun, 1992), yet from an analytic and normative standpoint, the concept itself remains compelling.

There is in Habermas a strong leaning toward the rational; communication is theorized in a rigorous manner that emphasizes formalized deliberation. Among the common criticisms leveled against his approach is that he seemingly reduces democracy's communication in a manner that excludes affective, rhetorical, symbolic, mythic, bodily, humorous, and other dimensions (see Dahlgren, 1995). This may generate a solid platform for criticism of the media, but, as I will suggest later, it may also too readily lead us to reject all forms of journalism and other media content that do not follow Habermas's strict rational lines. It is my view that this would lock us into an all too narrow view of what a viable mediated public culture for democracy might look like.

Further, and more central to my discussion, Habermas and others underscore the importance of civic interaction, of citizens who are together on public issues. Indeed, politics, the realm of the political, is constructed and interpreted precisely in such everyday encounters. This perspective on citizen interaction emphasizes the discursive, participatory side of democracy (see, for example, Barber, 1984; Benhabib, 1996). There is little in Habermas, however—more in fact, in Dewey—concerning the theme of how people become engaged citizens, how they learn to participate. What is lacking, in short, is a cultural perspective on citizenship as a mode of agency. For this purpose, I introduce the notion of civic cultures.

*Civic cultures* refers to those dimensions of everyday life that have bearing on how democracy actually functions. Civic cultures can thus be understood as sets of preconditions for populating the public sphere. Such cultures are important

in facilitating engagement in the broad domain of what we might term the *politically relevant*, in creating a climate that is conducive to citizen participation in the shaping of society's political life, and in fostering fluid communicative borders between politics and nonpolitics. Civic cultures can include a large array of parameters, including knowledge, value systems, and forms of daily practices, but in this chapter I focus in particular on the notion of citizenship as a form of identity. With the notion of civic cultures—a sort of "cultural turn"—the public sphere is rendered more available for anthropological investigation, as something more than the site for the spread of information and for rational deliberation. Highlighting the perspective of civic culture invites investigation into how a variety of modes of everyday interaction among citizens—not just formalized "deliberation"—might bear relevance for democracy.

I will begin by briefly summarizing the notion of the public sphere, suggesting three analytic dimensions. From there I move on to talk briefly about the media and their development. With this background, I then turn to some critical perspectives on first the public sphere, then on democracy more generally. I try to bring together these strands by emphasizing the importance of civic cultures and highlighting citizenship as a form of identity, to offer a nonmediacentric perspective on the public sphere, a perspective that emphasizes agency within the cultural frameworks of everyday life.

## THREE DIMENSIONS

As a starting point, I find it helpful to conceptualize the public sphere as consisting of three constitutive dimensions. Evaluation of how well the public sphere of a particular society functions (I am for the moment discounting the global perspective) must take all three dimensions into account. Moreover, these three dimensions constitute a network of interdependence that both constrains and enables the functioning of the public sphere. I refer to the dimensions as the *structural*, the *representational*, and the *interactional*.

The structural dimension has to do with the formal institutional features of the public sphere. Most obviously, this includes media organizations, the policies and issues of their financing, and the legal frameworks defining the freedoms of and constraints on communication (e.g., libel and privacy issues). The legal framework also includes questions of ownership, control, procedures for licensing, rules governing access, and so on. Beyond the organization of the media themselves, however, the structural dimension also analytically encompasses society's political institutions, which serve as a sort of "political ecology" for the media and set boundaries for the nature of the information and forms of expression that may circulate. At this level, the public sphere's entwinement with society's overall political situation comes into view. A society in which democratic tendencies are weak is not going to give rise to healthy institutional structures in the public sphere. In turn, the representational dimension will be inadequate.

The representational dimension refers to the output of the media; that is, their forms and contents. In this dimension, one can raise all the traditional questions and criteria about media output—for example, fairness, accuracy, pluralism of views, sensationalism, infotainment, and diversity of cultural expression. There is also a growing complexity in the representational dimension. We find ourselves in a historical situation in which more and more of our social relations are dependent on various forms of media, and a great deal of our time in everyday life is filled by the use of both mass media and interactive media. Moreover, an ever-growing portion of social life and institutional activity are accommodating themselves to the general requirements of media (e.g., politics, sports, commerce, and religion have all evolved in various ways to adapt to the logic of the media). Today, the media have become the language of our public culture, and the grammar of this language affects the way we experience and think about the world and about ourselves. Also, although the media are central to the public sphere, they generate a semiotic milieu that far exceeds the boundaries of the public sphere.

Ours is a society thoroughly saturated by the media, yet only a very small portion of this saturation is explicitly concerned with current political questions. However, in the larger, overarching media milieu, we find symbolic and even mythic dimensions that both promote and hinder a democratic public sphere without necessarily being expressly political. For example, recurring and even banal representations in dramatic TV series or even sitcoms that show women engaged in arguing for their rights or pursuing careers contribute to a cultural taken-for-granted that such are proper roles for women—a democratic plus. On a negative note—and continuing with the gender theme—we can observe that all too often, and perhaps increasingly over the past decade or so, women are represented as victims or sex objects in much media output. Such images over time enter into the realm of the collective social imaginary—even if they are not shared by absolutely everybody.

The dimension of interaction needs emphasis, as this element tends often to be neglected, given the mediacentrism that colors most discussions of the public sphere. Interaction consists of two aspects. First, it has to do with citizens' encounters with the media—the communicative processes of making sense of, interpreting, the output. It is an old truism in communication theory that "the receiver" does not necessarily derive the same meanings, or make the same uses, of "messages" as the "sender" intended. This perspective became particularly prominent in the qualitative audience research of the 1980s, and although the degree of audience interpretive freedom is at times contested among researchers, the active component of meaning construction within the media-audience interface is firmly established. The second aspect of interaction is that between citizens themselves. This perspective was prominent in the older sociology of the media (I am thinking here especially of the "two-step flow" tradition), but it often gets ignored in discussions about the public sphere.

Here it is useful to recall Habermas, as well as other writers, such as Dewey (1954), who argue that "a public" should be conceptualized as something other than just a media audience. A public, according to Habermas and Dewey, exists as discursive interactional processes; atomized individuals, consuming media in their homes, do not comprise a public. There are, of course, strong interests in society that have a stake in defining *the public* in terms of aggregate statistics of individual behavior and opinion, and such approaches certainly do have their uses from the standpoint of marketing, the official political system, and not least from media institutions themselves. However, from the standpoint of democracy, it is imperative not to lose sight of the classic idea that democracy resides, ultimately, with citizens who engage in talk with each other.

To point to the interaction among citizens is to take a step into the sociocultural contexts of everyday life. Interaction has its sites and spaces, its discursive practices, its contextual aspects. I am not arguing that to have a firm understanding of the public sphere we must explore every possible nook and cranny of the social world. Rather, I suggest that we keep in view the process and conditions within everyday life that shape and color how people make use of the media, how they respond to it. Not least in this regard, media use in everyday life has a strong ritual quality to it, something that anthropologists increasingly underscore. The public sphere does not begin and end when media content reaches an audience; this is but one step in a larger communication chain that includes how the media output is received, made sense of, and used by citizens in their interaction with each other. We must keep in mind that "audiences" consist, at bottom, of citizens, and democracy has to do with citizens interacting with each other, shaped by—and giving shape to—a civic culture. We should also underscore that the boundary between public and private spheres is hardly an ontological given. It is constructed and reconstructed in the course of historical evolution, within everyday encounters as well as in media representations.

## EMERGENCE OF A CRITICAL PERSPECTIVE

In Habermas's (1989) view, a public sphere began to emerge within the bourgeois classes of Western Europe in the late 18th and early 19th centuries.

The institutional basis for this public sphere consisted of an array of milieu and media, such as clubs, salons, coffeehouses, newspapers, books, and pamphlets, all of which in various (though incomplete) ways manifested Enlightenment ideals of the human pursuit of knowledge and freedom. For Habermas, the key here was not only the institutional basis but the manner in which communication took place in this burgeoning public sphere. However imperfectly, he saw that interaction in this social space embodied the ideals of reason; that is, the Enlightenment goals of rational thinking, argument, and discussion.

As he continues with his historical narrative, Habermas sees the public sphere growing and deepening in the first few decades of the 19th century with the spread of mass literacy and the press. Gradually, the decay sets in. Journalism increasingly loses its claim to reason; public discourse degenerates into public relations. As the logic of commercialism increasingly shapes the operations of the media, the domain of rationality diminishes. Moving into the 20th century, Habermas observes with pessimism the trivialization of politics, not least in the electronic media; the industrialization of public opinion; the transformation of publics from discursive to consuming collectivities; and an array of other ills that many other critics have also often noted.

Habermas more recently has seemed to take a less militantly pessimistic view of the contemporary mediated public sphere and is now prone to acknowledge its sprawling character (Calhoun, 1992, chapter 17, pp. 421-461; Habermas, 1996, chapter 8, pp. 329-387). Media researchers of the critical school have long been making use of the public sphere as an analytic horizon with which to highlight the problematic character of the media and their relationship to democracy under late capitalism. Today, however, mere repetition of this generalized bird's-eye perspective has given way to more specific, concrete analyses. Also, many mainstream, liberal critics today come to conclusions about the public sphere that at base are very similar to the analyses inspired by Habermas.

At bottom, the public sphere rests upon the idea of universality, the norm that it must be accessible to all citizens of society. This puts key structural aspects of the media into the limelight. If the media are a dominant feature of the public sphere, they must be technically, economically, culturally, and linguistically within reach of society's members; any a priori exclusions of any segment of the population collide with democracy's claim to universalism. Seen from this angle, the vision of a public sphere raises questions about media policy and economics, ownership and control, the role of market forces and regulation, issues of the privatization of information, corporate power, and so forth. The practical tasks of shaping media policy are often conceptually complicated and politically difficult, given the array of competing interests at stake. Promoting the idea of the public sphere becomes all the more of a challenge in an era when market forces have such a strong influence on policy formation.

Institutionally, the modern media are in the midst of a pervasive global restructuring, yielding fewer but larger global conglomerates, which in turn further accentuates the processes of commodification (a perspective that is well argued in Herman & McChesney, 1997). In terms of communicative practices, most analyses of journalistic practices in the press and on television—as manifested in routine political and social coverage, as well as in election campaigns—come to rather dismal conclusions (see, for instance, Blumler & Gurevitch, 1995; Downie & Kaiser, 2002; Gans, 2002). I would posit that popularization can and has been, in many cases, a positive development, bringing more people into the public sphere. We can even see a mythic dimension, in which the "voice of the people" is invoked in talk shows, encouraging a sense of belonging and participation. Indeed, democratic politics must inevitably walk at least in part with popular culture, to resonate with people generally; clinging exclusively to high-brow forms of journalism will not promote engagement—and, of course, it will not work in today's market. At the same time, by most accounts today, popularization is degenerating into trivialization and sensationalism, with the ideals of journalism increasingly subordinated to the imperatives of the market. The

public sphere, as a space, can never be totally separate from the space of the market; the challenge is to combine the two in a creative manner. Today the problem is that market and the public sphere in the media present very different profiles: the one robust, expansive, ideologically ascendant; the other frail, diminutive, and on the defensive.

If the public sphere, on the one hand, is implicated with the market, on the other hand, this space has become increasingly interwoven with private space, to the point that the distinctions between public and private space are not always as self-evident as they seem to have been in the past (Thompson, 1995, offers a useful discussion of this theme). For example, the public space of the media is, to a great extent, intertwined with the private space of the home: Media reception is still mostly a domestic activity. Further, the discourses of the public sphere often deal with private matters, such as the personal lives of politicians and celebrities or general topics having to do with "lifestyle" questions or moral issues about how we live (e.g., abortion). This blurring of public and private spheres is, in fact, a key feature of late modern culture (see Fornäs, 1995).

## DEMOCRATIC DEFICITS

Thus, in the modern world, we can note two domains of "otherness" within the space of the public sphere: One is the market; the other is the realm of the personal, the private. Further, these two domains become more and more functionally intertwined with the development of consumer lifestyle culture. This has consequences for the public sphere, as market-driven lifestyles and personal identities—in the media and in everyday life—compete for attention and engagement with the political. Places in which we are "invited" to see ourselves as citizens are rare compared to those spaces in which we are admonished to think like consumers. These two core identities, however, do not necessarily comprise clear-cut alternatives. They are intertwined, they collude as well as collide, as we struggle to make sense of ourselves and our world; for example, we see increasingly how consumer issues can become politicized; that is, of concern to people in their roles as citizens.

The public sphere is predicated on interaction between citizens, not just on the media, and this interaction is, of course, shaped by social hierarchies, economics, work circumstances, welfare, and education. Such factors tend often to be disregarded—in, for example, discussions about declining participation in the formal political system (see Bennett, 2003a, 2003b)—and "apathy" and other ills are often treated as expression of citizens' seemingly enigmatic subjectivity, decontextualized from material circumstances. The importance of these factors leads us directly into classic arguments such as those of T. H. Marshall (1950) regarding the necessity of securing the *social* conditions of citizenship if democracy is to function. Needless to say, the weight that should be accorded to such assumptions and the social policy measures that should follow from them are politically contested in Western democracies, especially in recent years as welfare state traditions are eroding in the face of neoliberal initiatives.

Much of the received wisdom about what democracy is or how it should function seems not to correspond in an encouraging manner with the realities of the late modern epoch. The condition of democracy in Western societies varies, but some general trends are apparent. The arena of official politics does not command the degree of support and participation that it has in the past. Voter turnouts are declining, even in countries such as Sweden, which had considerable stability in its electoral patterns during the earlier postwar decades. Party loyalty is declining, especially among the young. The formal political system of most Western nations appears stagnant, reactive rather than proactive, eclipsed by developments in the realms of large-scale capitalism and technological innovations. A destructive climate of cynicism is emerging in many places. This cannot be understood as merely a response to the media, although this is no doubt part of it. Rather, this atmosphere of "antipolitics" must be seen as the consequence of the political system's inability to meet social expectations. Economic insecurity, unemployment, low wages, declining social services, and growing class cleavages are all part of the picture. If the causes are complex, it is nonetheless clear that what we are faced with is a serious erosion of civic engagement.

Carl Boggs (1997) calls this "the great retreat," a withdrawal from the arena of common concerns and politics and a retreat into "enclave consciousness," away from larger collective identities and community sensibilities. To illustrate, he refers to a 1995 survey of 240,000 U.S. college freshmen, which finds that fewer than one third say they keep up with current events, and only 16% say they ever discuss politics. Boggs adds, however, in an acerbic afterthought, that given the banality (in the 1990s) of contemporary formal politics, it is hard to imagine the students responding differently. The extensive disenchantment with formal politics that the survey suggests is a theme addressed by many today (Putnam, 2000, is most often cited in this regard). We have a crisis of civic culture and citizenship, which can be linked to a more pervasive cultural malaise (e.g., Bellah, Sullivan, Madsen, Swindler, & Tipton, 1986). Many people in Western societies seem to have at best very rudimentary identities as citizens, as members and potential participants of political society. They do not feel themselves to be a part of a larger democratic project.

## Civic Culture and Citizenship

The condition of the public sphere and democracy more generally give cause for serious concern. At the same time, there is evidence that can evoke other trains of thought. For example, from her fieldwork, Nina Eliasoph (1997) finds that in the microcosms of everyday life, people reveal that what may appear on the surface as apathy toward politics and contemporary issues is really a disguise for something else. In discursive situations, she finds that the seemingly apathetic are actually working very hard to *avoid* the political, to refrain from contextualizing their life circumstances in terms of public issues. Thus political disengagement may not necessarily be the "easy way out" but rather something that, whatever the motivation, in many instances requires a concerted effort. Seemingly, the potential for political engagement stubbornly remains.

It is precisely this kind of ambivalence that holds the door open for constructive thinking about a democratic future. The growing withdrawal from official politics must be interpreted as a response to the present arrangements of power and the current ways in which the political system operates. The ostensible political apathy, disenchantment, and disaffiliation from the established political system may not necessarily signal a disinterest in politics per se. That is, if we look beyond formal electoral politics, we can see various signs that suggest that many people have not abandoned engagement with the political but have, rather, refocused their political attention outside the parliamentarian systems (Fenton & Downey, 2003). They may also be in the process of redefining just what constitutes the political (Mouffe, 1993). Observers see a strong shift toward what is called "lifestyle politics" (Bennett, 1998), which is characterized by personalized rather than collective engagement and an emphasis on single issues rather than on overarching platforms or ideologies. The various manifestations of so-called new social movements can also be seen in this light (see, for example, Eschele, 2001; van de Donk, Loader, Nixon, & Rucht, 2004).

What will emerge from these developments is still unclear, but what is apparent today is that there are interesting things going on precisely within everyday life. It is here that we find the footprints and signposts of civic culture (or civic cultures; even here we would do better with the plural form!). I conceptualize civic culture as a circuit of dimensions that are mutually reciprocal and that may promote or hinder democratic virtues, however understood (for a fuller discussion, see Dahlgren, 2003). The key dimensions are knowledge and competence, democratic values, trust, and affinity, as well as practices and, not least, identities. Knowledge can take many forms, especially in an age of new media technologies; we should not be locked into traditional notions of learning. Democratic values foster openness toward and affinity with other citizens, and this, in turn, can promote a degree of trust. Practices include not just voting but a whole range of forms, most fundamentally discussion, talking with other citizens (Dahlgren, 2002). Finally, the category of identities highlights the importance of the subjective side of citizenship: People must be able to experience themselves as members of political communities and feel that their participation in society and politics is meaningful.

The idea of civic culture takes as its starting point the notion of citizens as social agents, and it asks what the *cultural* factors are behind such agency (or its absence). Civic cultures point to both the conditions and the manifestations of such participation; they are anchored in the mindsets and symbolic milieu of everyday life. Civic culture is normative in that it asserts the necessity for these dimensions to be anchored at the level of citizens' lived experiences, personal resources, and subjective dispositions if a viable democracy is to exist. It is also empirical: The various dimensions offer points of entry for research investigation. Civic culture is potentially both strong and vulnerable: It helps to promote the functioning of democracy and can serve to empower or disempower citizens, yet like all domains of culture, it can easily be affected by political and economic power.

The framework of civic culture thus seeks to address questions about why people engage in the public sphere or do not and to provide empirical starting points for analysis. The civic culture frame is interested in the processes of becoming—it explores how people develop into citizens, how they come to see themselves as members and potential participants in societal development. Civic culture is an analytic construct that seeks to identify the possibilities of people acting in the role of citizens; the political and politics are seen as not simply given but as constructed via word and deed. Citizenship has traditionally been defined in terms of sets of rights and obligations accorded the individual in her or his relationship to the state. Citizenship can also be seen in terms of social agency, as particular sets of activities and practices—and congruent virtues—relevant to particular kinds of situations.

One of the definitive characteristics of late modern society is the pluralization of our "selves."

Without getting tangled up in any postmodern theorizing, we can simply take note that in our daily lives we operate in a multitude of different "worlds" or realities; we carry within us different sets of knowledge, assumptions, rules, and roles for different circumstances. Some of these elements reside closer to the core of our identity; others are more toward the periphery. Still, all of us are, to varying degrees, composite people. The idea of composite identities also pertains to citizenship. Recent theoretical work on identity and subjectivity has emphasized that in our polydimensional construction of our selves, citizenship must be an integral aspect of our identity (Clarke, 1996; Mouffe, 1993).

The civic culture concept does not presuppose homogeneity among its citizens; it in fact assumes that there are many ways in which citizenship and democracy can be enacted. It does, however, suggest the need for minimal shared commitments to the vision and procedures of democracy, which in turn entails a capacity to see beyond the immediate interests of one's own group and its interests. Needless to say, this is a challenging balance to maintain. However, different social and cultural groups can express civic culture in different ways, theoretically enhancing democracy's possibilities.

The development of democracy is dependent upon a productive interplay between the civic culture of everyday life and the formal political system. In a sense, the public sphere functions as a link between the two. A democratic political system needs the continual input of democratic norms and processes from the civic culture. Such values can be found embedded in the vast terrain of domestic life, sociability, associations, organizations, social movements, and other forms of collective involvement outside of the formal political system. The civic culture of everyday life in turn needs, from the formal political system, robust institutional support and clear legal guarantees if it is to thrive.

The various currents at play today within civic culture means we should probably not anticipate a unitary, singular civic culture. Moreover, the shift in emphasis from media structures and media representations to citizen interaction does not suggest that we should automatically replace the troublesome picture of democracy and the public sphere I sketched earlier with something more cheery. Rather, focusing on interaction and on civic culture turns our attention to agency, to people doing things together within cultural contexts. Interaction among citizens is, of course, conditioned by media and factors of power and economics yet remains undetermined: The potential of the new, the contested, the altered remains viable. This is, of course, no news, but in the context of the media and the public sphere, it is a perspective that has often fallen by the wayside, replaced by the somewhat bleak view that emerges from an excessively mediacentric way of looking at the public sphere.

## Citizens and the Media

Drawing together these reflections provides us with a fresh perspective on the media, the public sphere, and democracy. Although the overall drift of democracy is troubling, and media developments seem to exacerbate rather than alleviate the troubles, evidence suggests that people have not given up on political engagement and visions. Instead, they are disappointed by the ways in which the present political system operates. Beneath the surface of apparent apathy, we find a good deal of engagement in a variety of forms, which signals newer definitions and initiatives in the realm of politics. In this context, it is important to highlight the interactive dimension of the public sphere—people talking to each other about current affairs—and understand how the conditions and character of this interaction relates to the broader terrain of civic culture. It is here that we can readily conceptualize social agency and the importance of citizenship as a form of identity.

The media play an important, and often negative, role in this regard, yet we must bear in mind that people do not merely reproduce the thoughts and perspectives of the media—they respond and react to them as well. The media are used as resources by citizens, but the media can also function as catalysts, at times promoting unanticipated consequences. In the new, emerging media environment, where interactivity of many kinds is made possible by the Internet and other technological developments, deterministic perspectives on what citizens will do and what kinds of politics will emerge become extremely hazardous. The democratic impact of the Internet is promising and dramatic, even if the long-term consequences are far from clear (see Anderson & Cornfield, 2003; Cammaerts & van Audenhove, 2003; Jenkins & Thornburn, 2003). Claims for a "cyber public sphere" must be modified by sociological realism. Whatever the outcome, however, it is abundantly clear that a major shift in communication capacity, media logic, journalistic practices, and cultural patterns is now underway. More people have more access to more information and more other people than ever before. Moreover, the Internet is further extending the reach, as well as transforming the logic, of the traditional mass media, as they go online and develop interactive capacities. This alters their structural and representational dimensions in various ways. More people will have more opportunities to consider what their identities as citizens might involve. Civic culture and the public sphere will not be unaffected. Instead of simply choosing pessimism or optimism in the face of these developments, we would be wise to follow them closely and analytically.

## REFERENCES

Anderson, D. M., & Cornfield, M. (Eds.). (2003). *The civic web: Online politics and democratic values*. Lanham, MD: Rowman & Littlefield.

Barber, B. (1984). *Strong democracy: Participatory politics for a new age*. Berkeley: University of California Press.

Bellah, R. N., Sullivan, W. M., Madsen, R., Swindler, A., & Tipton, S. M. (1986). *Habits of the heart*. New York: Perennial Library.

Benhabib, S. (Ed.). (1996). *Democracy and difference: Contesting the boundaries of the political*. Princeton, NJ: Princeton University Press.

Bennett, L. W. (1998, December). The uncivic culture: Communication, identity, and the rise of lifestyle politics. *Political Science and Politics, 31*(4), 741-761.

Bennett, W. L. (2003a). Lifestyle politics and citizen-consumers: Identity, communication and political action in late modern society. In J. Corner & D. Pels (Eds.), *Media and political style: Essays on representation and civic culture* (pp. 137-150). London: Sage.

Bennett, W. L. (2003b). New media power: The Internet and global activism. In N. Couldry & J. Currans (Eds.), *Contesting media power* (pp. 17-37). Lanham, MD: Rowman & Littlefield.

Blumler, J., & Gurevitch, M. (1995). *The crisis of public communication*. London: Routledge.

Boggs, C. (1997). The great retreat: Decline of the public sphere in late twentieth-century America. *Theory and Society, 26*, 741-780.

Calhoun, C. (Ed.). (1992). *Habermas and the public sphere*. Boston: MIT Press.

Cammaerts, B., & van Audenhove, L. (2003). *Transnational social movements, the network society and unbounded notions of citizenship*. Amsterdam, Netherlands: ASCoR, University of Amsterdam.

Chaney, D. (1993). *Fictions of collective life: Public drama in late modern society*. London: Routledge.

Clarke, P. B. (1996). *Deep citizenship*. London: Pluto Press.

Dahlgren, P. (1995). *Television and the public sphere*. London: Sage.

Dahlgren, P. (2002). In search of the talkative public: Media, deliberative democracy and civic culture. *Javnost/The Public, 9*(3), 5-26.

Dahlgren, P. (2003). Reconfiguring civic culture in the new media milieu. In J. Corner & D. Pels (Eds.), *Media and political style: Essays on representation and civic culture* (pp. 151-170). London: Sage.

Dewey, J. (1954). *The public and its problems*. Chicago: Swallow Press.

Downie, L., Jr., & Kaiser, R. G. (2002). *The news about the news*. New York: Random House.

Eliasoph, N. (1997). "Close to home": The work of avoiding politics. *Theory and Society, 26*(5), 605-647.

Eschele, C. (2001). *Global democracy, social movements, and feminism*. Boulder, CO: Westview Press.

Fenton, N., & Downey, J. (2003). Counter public spheres and global modernity. *Javnost/The Public, 10*(1), 15-32.

Fornäs, J. (1995). *Cultural theory and late modernity*. London: Sage.

Gans, H. (2002). *Democracy and the news*. New York: Oxford University Press.

Habermas, J. (1989). *Structural transformation of the public sphere.* Cambridge, England: Polity Press. (Original work published 1984)

Hannerz, U. (1996) *Transnational Connections.* London: Routledge.

Herman, E., & McChesney, R. (1997). *The global media.* London: Cassell.

Jenkins, H., & Thornburn, D. (Eds.). (2003). *Democracy and new media.* Cambridge: MIT Press.

Marshall, T. H. (1950). *Citizenship and social class.* Cambridge, England: Cambridge University Press.

Mouffe, C. (1993). *The return of the political.* London: Verso.

Putnam, R. (2000). *Bowling alone: The collapse and revival of American community.* New York: Simon & Schuster.

Thompson, J. B. (1995). *The media and modernity.* Cambridge, England: Polity Press.

van de Donk, W., Loader, B. D., Nixon, P., & Rucht, D. (Eds.). (2004). *Cyberprotest: New media, citizens and social movements.* London: Routledge.

# INDEX

# ABOUT THE EDITORS

**Mihai Coman** was born in Fagaras, Romania, in 1953, graduated from the College of Letters within the University of Bucharest in 1976, and attained his Ph.D. in Letters in 1985. He has been a teacher in a Romanian high school (1976-1982), journalist (1982-1989), and publisher (1989-1990). He was the first Dean of the School of Journalism and Mass Communication Studies at the University of Bucharest and the first coordinator of doctoral studies in communications. Dr. Coman is considered to be the founder of journalism and communication education in Romania. Until 1989, he specialized in cultural anthropology studies of Romanian folklore. He has published four volumes of mythology studies (*The Sources of Myth*, 1980; *The Sister of Sun*, 1983; *Mythos and Epos*, 1985; *The Point and the Spiral*, 1992) and a vast synthesis on animal mythology (*The Romanian Mythological Bestiary*, 1986, 1988, with a second edition published in 1996). Other of his mythology studies have appeared in scientific journals, including *L'Ethnologie Francaise, Etudes Indo-Europeennes,* and *Kurier.* After 1989, he published the reference volume *Introduction to Mass Communication,* and he coordinated the two volumes of the *Journalism Handbook,* which sold more than 20,000 copies. In the 1990s, he began to elaborate the theoretical and analytical framework of mass media anthropology through studies published in scientific journals, such as the francophone *Reseaux, MediaPouvoirs,* and *Communication,* or in collections, such as *La Transition en Roumanie: Communication et Qualité de la Vie* (edited by

Roger Tessier, 1995); *Valeriana: Essays on Human Communication in Honour of Valery Pissarek* (edited by J. M. Pomorskiego & Z. Bajki, 1996); *2001 Bogues: Globalisme et Pluralisme* (Vol. 1: *TIC et Societé,* edited by Bernard Miege & Gaetan Tremblay, 2003); and *INA: Television, Memoire et Identité Nationale* (2003). In 2003, as a synthesis of these investigations, he published *Pour une Anthropologie des Medias.*

He has also published numerous scientific studies in journals and books dedicated to the transformations in the mass media in post-communist countries, including "Romänischer Journalismus in einer Übergangspériode," in *Medienlandschaft im Umbruch,* 1994; "The Third Elite," *Media '95,* 1996; "Les Journalistes Roumains et Leur Idéologie Professionelle," in *Télé-révolutions Culturelles: Chine, Europe Centrale, Russie,* 1998; "Developments in Journalism Theory about Media 'Transition' in Central and Eastern Europe" (1990-1999), in *Journalism Studies,* 2000; and *Media in Romania (a Sourcebook),* 2004.

Dr. Coman was Visiting Professor at Institut fur Journalistik, Dortmund University, Germany (2000-2001); at the Department of Communication of the University Stendhal, Grenoble, France (1998-1999); at the Department of Communication of the University Paris XIII, France (1996); at the Department of Communication, University of Quebec at Montreal (1993); and a Fulbright researcher at the Department of Communication, California State University, Chico (1999). He is a member of several international organizations

(American Association of Anthropology, Association of Educators in Journalism and Mass Communication, International Association of Mass Communication Research, International Communication Association) and is on the editorial boards of communication journals such as *Reseaux, Communication,* and *Journalism Studies.* Dr. Coman may be reached at mcoman@fjsc.ro.

**Eric W. Rothenbuhler** is Professor of Communication at Texas A&M University. He was previously Director of Graduate Media Studies at New School University (2001-2004) and on the faculty of Communication Studies at the University of Iowa (1985-2001). At the University of Iowa, he was an affiliated faculty member with American Studies and faculty advisor to the student radio station, KRUI, 89.7 FM, where he had a weekly radio show on the history of rhythm and blues. He earned his doctorate at the Annenberg School for Communication at the University of Southern California in 1985 and his B.A. and M.A. from Ohio State University. He has been a visiting faculty member at the University of Kansas (twice), Scholar in Residence at the Center for Advanced Study in Telecommunication at Ohio State University, and has participated in doctoral workshops and teaching seminars at the Universities of Dortmund, Ljubljana, and Oslo.

Dr. Rothenbuhler's research and teaching address communication systems ranging from ritual through community to media industries. His dissertation research on the living room celebration of the 1984 Olympic Games provided the first statistically representative evidence for television audience behavior and attitudes consistent with the theory of media events. This work was published in *Journal of Communication, Critical Studies in Mass Communication,* and other outlets. His work on decision-making processes and industrial market structures in the radio and music businesses, in a series of articles beginning in 1982 in *Journal of Communication; Communication Research; Media, Culture, and Society;* and several books, is also widely cited. This work continues with research on American radio in the 1950s, in collaboration with Tom McCourt, and has so far produced an article in *The Radio Journal* and a forthcoming book manuscript. Dr. Rothenbuhler's essay "Symbolic Disorder and Repair After Witnessing 9/11" is being translated and published in France, as was an earlier essay with John Peters, "The Reality of Construction." Part of his work on the posthumous career and reputation of the American blues musician Robert Johnson is forthcoming in a book chapter called "The Strange Career of Robert Johnson's Records."

Dr. Rothenbuhler is the author of *Ritual Communication: From Everyday Conversation to Mediated Ceremony* (1988), which has been translated into Polish (2004). With Greg Shepherd, he coedited *Communication and Community* (2001). He was Review and Criticism Editor for the *Journal of Communication* (1997-1999) and has authored or coauthored more than 50 articles, chapters, essays, and reviews on media, ritual, community, media industries, popular music, and communication theory.

# ABOUT THE AUTHORS

**Susan L. Allen** holds a doctorate in Media Anthropology (Special Studies, University of Kansas, 1980) and an M.S. in Journalism and Mass Communications. She was Research Intern at the East West Center in Honolulu in 1977 and 1978 and has done fieldwork in the Pacific Islands and Japan. She edited the first media anthropology text, *Media Anthropology: Informing Global Citizens* in 1994. She worked in Washington, DC, for Kansas Senator Nancy Kassebaum and produced a small ethnic newspaper before joining the Kansas State University Women's Center in 1993, where she serves as Director.

**Dan Berkowitz** earned his Ph.D. at Indiana University in 1988. Currently he is Associate Professor at the University of Iowa. His research interests focus on the sociology of news, including media and terrorism, the relationship between media and community, local television news, and the role of myth in news. He teaches public relations, media and terrorism, the sociology of news, and computer-assisted reporting and has been a visiting professor at Tel-Aviv University and the University of the West Indies. He is Editor of the book *Social Meanings of News: A Text-Reader* (1997) and has published articles in *Journal of Broadcasting & Electronic Media; Journal of Communication; Journal of Public Relations Research; Journalism: Theory, Practice and Criticism; Journalism and Mass Communication Quarterly; Ecquid Novi; Public Relations Review;* and *International Journal of Public Opinion Research.*

**S. Elizabeth Bird,** Ph.D. (University of Strathclyde), is Professor of Anthropology at the University of South Florida. She is the author of *The Audience in Everyday Life: Living in a Media World* (2003), winner of the 2004 Best Book Award from the International Communication Association; *For Enquiring Minds: A Cultural Study of Supermarket Tabloids* (1992); and Editor of *Dressing in Feathers: The Construction of the Indian in American Popular Culture* (1996), and she has published widely in the fields of media studies, folklore, and cultural studies.

**Menahem Blondheim** teaches Communications and American Studies at the Hebrew University of Jerusalem and serves as Director of the university's Smart Family Institute of Communications. His research and publications focus on communications in American and in Jewish history and culture, as well as on communication technologies, old and new. He may be reached at mblond@huji.ac.il.

**Merry Bruns** is Director of the Center for Anthropology and Science Communications in Washington, DC, and has been involved in anthropology communications since the early 1990s. She is a member of the National Association of Science Writers and has written and done research on communication problems between anthropologists and science media. She gives annual American Anthropological Association workshops and academic sessions on communicating anthropology to the public, hosts roundtables between anthropologists and local science media, does volunteer work with the American Anthropological Association's Press Department, and works as a Content Strategist for science Web sites through her company, ScienceSites Communications (http://www.sciencesitescom.com).

**Nick Couldry** is Senior Lecturer in Media and Communications at the London School of Economics and Political Science. He earned his undergraduate degree in Classical Literature and Philosophy at Oxford University, with subsequent masters and doctoral degrees in Communications at Goldsmiths College, University of London. His research interests cover media power, cultural studies, ritual, and public engagement in mediated politics. He is the author of *The Place of Media Power: Pilgrims and Witnesses of the Media Age* (2000), *Inside Culture* (2000), and *Media Rituals: A Critical Approach* (2003), and coeditor of *Contesting Media Power* (with James Curran, 2003) and *MediaSpace* (with Anna McCarthy, 2004).

**Peter Dahlgren** is Professor of Media and Communication at Lund University, Sweden. He received his doctorate at City University of New York in 1977 and has taught at Fordham University, Queens College, and Stockholm University. He has also been Visiting Scholar at the Université de Paris II, Rhodes University in South Africa, the University of Stirling, and l'Université de Québec à Montréal. At present he runs an exchange program with l'École des Hautes Études en Sciences Sociales in Paris. His research focuses on democracy, the evolution of the media, and contemporary socio-cultural processes. Most recently, he has begun looking at how young citizens make use of new communication technologies for democratic engagement and identity work. He has published numerous articles and authored or edited several books in English and Swedish. His most recent book is *Media and Civic Engagement* (in press).

**Brenda Danet,** Ph.D. Sociology, University of Chicago, 1970, is Professor Emerita in Sociology and Communication, Hebrew University of Jerusalem, and Research Affiliate in Anthropology, Yale University. Her interests have included bureaucracy and the public, language and law, oral tradition and literacy, aesthetics in everyday life, and communication and culture on the Internet. She has published *Pulling Strings: Biculturalism in Israeli Bureaucracy* (1989); *Cyberpl@y: Communicating Online* (2001); *Bureaucracy and the Public: A Reader in Official-Client Relations* (with coeditor Elihu Katz, 1973); and *Art as a Means of Communication in Pre-literate Societies* (with coeditors Dan Eban and Erik Cohen, 1990). With Susan C. Herring, she guest-edited "The Multilingual Internet: Language, Culture and Communication in Instant Messaging, Email and Chat," a special issue of the *Journal of Computer-mediated Communication* (2003). Her chapter on ritual, "Speech, Writing, and Performativity: An Evolutionary View of the History of Constitutive Ritual," was published in *The Construction of Professional Discourse* (Britt-Louise Gunnarsson et al., Eds., 1997). Other articles of hers on IRC art have appeared in *Textile: The Journal of Cloth & Culture* (2003, 2004). She may be reached at brenda.danet@yale. edu, and her Web site is at http://pluto.mscc.huji.ac.il/~msdanet/.

**Daniel Dayan** is Directeur de Recherches at Centre National de la Recherche Scientifique and Professor of Media Sociology at Geneva University and the Ecole des Hautes Etudes en Sciences Sociales in Paris. After being Roland Barthes's research assistant, Dayan lectured at numerous universities, including the Annenberg School for Communications, Hebrew University, Stanford University, Institut d'Etudes Politiques, the Sorbonne, and Oslo University. He has been a Fellow of the Rockefeller Center, Bellagio (2000) and is currently a Fellow of the Media Program, European Science Foundation. His work analyses the experience of the public in regard to the sociology of performances and the management of collective attention.

**Faye Ginsburg** is David B. Kriser Professor of Anthropology and Director of the Center for Media, Culture and History at New York University, where she also codirects the Center for Religion and Media. Her teaching and research interests are directed toward cultural activists and social movements, with particular attention to the politics of reproduction in the United States and the development of indigenous media in Australia, for which she has received Guggenheim and MacArthur fellowships. Her books include *Contested Lives: The Abortion Debate in an American Community* (1989, 1999), which won four awards; *Uncertain Terms: Negotiating Gender in American Culture* (edited with Anna Tsing, 1992); *Conceiving the New World Order: The Global Politics of Reproduction* (edited with Rayna Rapp, 1995); and *Media Worlds: Anthropology on New Terrain* (2002). She received her Ph.D. in Anthropology from the City University of New York Graduate Center in 1986.

**Anita Hammer** has been working with theater and performance in Norway and New Zealand. She has a special interest in work with ritual theory and ritual theater, as well as in anthropological approaches to theater and ritual study. She has worked with analyses of cultural development in Sumerian ritual, as well as applied ritual approaches to contemporary studies of performance. She has lectured nationally and internationally on ritual approaches to performance. Her doctoral dissertation, *Weaving Plots: Frames of Theatre and Ritual in Simultaneous Interactive Digital Communication,* was defended at the Norwegian University of Science and Technology in 2001. Currently she is Associate Professor in Theater Studies in the Department of Music and Theater, University of Oslo, Norway.

**Mark Hobart** is Director of the Media and Film Studies Programme at the School of Oriental and African Studies, University of London, where he completed his doctorate after graduating from Cambridge in Social Anthropology. His teaching has ranged from regional ethnography, film, and semiotics to anthropological and general theory in the human sciences and, more recently, Southeast Asian cinema, media, and cultural studies theory and its broader philosophical implications. His work is based on more than 8 years of field research in Indonesia, and he has a long-standing interest in philosophical issues in the human sciences. His recent book, *After*

*Culture,* is available online free at http://www.criticalia.org. He has been active in developing media and cultural studies in Indonesia, including one of the largest extant archives of television materials (see http://www.bajra.org), for which he was recently awarded the Dharma Kusuma for his contribution to Indonesian cultural scholarship.

**Stewart M. Hoover** is Professor of Media Studies, Religious Studies, and American Studies at the University of Colorado at Boulder. He has served two terms as Interim Dean of the School of Journalism and Mass Communication at the university. His primary research has focused on the relationship between media and religion in both North American and European contexts. His current research interests include the public projection of religious symbolism, the religious practices of the Baby Boom and post-Boom generations in the media age, and religion journalism. His books include the forthcoming *Religion in the Media Age* (2006) and *Religion in the News: Faith and Journalism in American Public Discourse* (1998); *Practicing Religion in the Age of the Media* (coedited with Lynn Schofield Clark, 2002); *Media, Home, and Family* (coauthored with Lynn Schofield Clark and Diane Alters, 2004), and *Rethinking Media, Religion, and Culture* (coedited with Knut Lundby, 1997).

**Gerd G. Kopper** studied Industrial Sociology, Communication Sciences, and Law at the Free University of Berlin. He is a Fulbright Scholar with an M.A. in Journalism from Indiana University, Bloomington (1965) and a Ph.D. from the Free University (1967). He has worked as a journalist, journalism trainer, and editor and served as Permanent Consultant of the OECD, Paris, in 1968 and 1969. He was Head of research and development at Bertelsmann Publishing from 1971 to 1972 and Guest Research Fellow at the University of Tokyo, Todai. While in Japan, he also worked for NHK-Broadcasting and as a foreign correspondent. A research and development consultant for German government institutions at Bonn since 1974, since 1978 he has also been Full Professor at the Institute for Journalism, University of Dortmund, as well as Chair for Policy, Economics, and Law of Mass Media. In 1992 and 1993, he was President of the European Journalism Training Association; since 1991, he has been Director of the Centre for Advanced Study: Erich-Brost-Institute for Journalism in Europe. He has published in the fields of journalism and media structures and policies and is Coeditor of *Journalism Studies*, a quarterly periodical.

**Antonio C. La Pastina** is Assistant Professor in the Department of Communications, Texas A&M University, College Station. He holds a Ph.D. from the Radio-TV-Film Department of the University of Texas at Austin. His research interests are in media ethnography; the representation of otherness in mainstream media and its role on diasporic cultures, and the implications of the digital divide to peripheral communities. He has conducted research in the Lower Rio Grande Valley and central Texas, the northeast of Brazil, and Central Italy. He teaches courses in intercultural communication, ethnography, globalization, media, gender and race, and U.S. and Latin American popular culture. His work has appeared in *Critical Studies in Media Communication*, *Journal of Broadcast and Electronic Media*, *International Journal of Cultural Studies*, *Communication Research*, and *Intercom*, as well as in several edited books. Before moving to the United States in the late 1980s, he worked as a journalist in São Paulo, Brazil, his native country.

**Pascal Lardellier** is Professor of Information and Communication Sciences at Bourgogne University (Dijon, France). He is the author of two works: *Les Miroirs du Paon: Rites et Rhétorique Politiques dans la France de l'Ancien Régime* [Mirrors of the Peacock: Political Ritual and Rhetoric in the France of the *Ancien Régime*] (2002) and *Théorie du Lien Rituel: Anthropologie et Communication* [A Theory of Bonding Ritual: Anthropology and Communication] (2002). His chapter in this book reexamines and develops some of the suggestions contained in these earlier works.

**Tamar Liebes** is Professor and Chair of the Department of Communication at the Hebrew University of Jerusalem. She has written about media audiences, television genres, television's coverage of war and terror, and mass media and national and cultural identity. Among her books are *American Dreams, Hebrew Subtitles: Globalization from the Receiving End* (2003); *Reporting the Arab Israeli Conflict: How Hegemony Works* (1997); and, with Elihu Katz, *The Export of Meaning: Cross Cultural Readings of Dallas* (1992). She is Editor, with James Curran, of *Media, Ritual, Identity* (1998), and with Elihu Katz and John Peters, of *Canonic Texts in Media Research* (2003).

**Jack Lule** is the Joseph B. McFadden Distinguished Professor of Journalism at Lehigh University. His research interests include cultural and critical studies of news, online journalism, media, sports and society, and teaching with technology. He is the author of *Daily News, Eternal Stories: The Mythological Role of Journalism* (2001). Called "a landmark book in the sociology of news," the book argues that ancient myths can be found daily in the pages of the news. The book won the 2002 Lewis Mumford Award for Outstanding Scholarship from the Media Ecology Association. Dr. Lule is the author of more than 35 other scholarly articles and book chapters; he is also a frequent contributor to newspapers and periodicals. A former reporter for the *Philadelphia Inquirer,* he received his Ph.D. in Mass Communication from the University of Georgia in 1987. He has been teaching at Lehigh since 1990.

**Graham Murdock** is Reader in the Sociology of Culture at Loughborough University and a past Visiting Professor at the University of California, San Diego, and the Universities of Bergen, Stockholm, Brussels, and Mexico City. He has published widely on aspects of contemporary culture and communication and has been translated into 15 languages. He has long-standing interests in visual media and in the everyday organization of communication. He is currently codirecting a major research project on the ways households deploy domestic digital technologies.

**Francisco Osorio** is an anthropologist at the University of Chile. His M.A. (1996) and Ph.D. (2002), also from the University of Chile, are in

Epistemology of the Social Sciences. He has been Chief Editor of a Latin American e-journal of epistemology, *Cinta de Moebio* (http://www.moebio.uchile.cl) since 1997. He is a Fulbright Scholar who studied with Elihu Katz between 1999 and 2000 at the Annenberg School for Communication at the University of Pennsylvania, focusing on the relationship between anthropology and mass media. He may be reached at fosorio@uchile.cl.

**Jin Kyu Park** is a doctoral candidate and research assistant for the New Media @ Home Project at the School of Journalism and Mass Communication, University of Colorado at Boulder. He is a Korean national with a B.A. in Mass Communications from Yonsei University, Korea, as well as a master's in Journalism from the University of Texas, Austin. His research has focused on religion as a component for audiences' cultural text reading, religious and ethnic identity construction and media use, the popularity of Japanese animation (anime) in Western culture and its religious and spiritual implications, and the Internet as a medium for religious expression and meaning making. He is working on his dissertation on relationships between media, religion, and culture in contemporary Korea.

**Mark Allen Peterson** is Assistant Professor of Anthropology and International Studies at Miami University of Ohio. His work centers around semiotic and ethnographic analysis of the diverse ways in which media have become a part of everyday experience and practice. Educated at the University of California, Los Angeles, and Brown University, he has done fieldwork in north India, Egypt, and the United States. He is the author of *Anthropology and Mass Communication: Myth and Media in the New Millennium* (2003).

**Sarah Pink** is Senior Lecturer in the Department of Social Sciences at Loughborough University. She has a B.A. (1988) and Ph.D. (1996) in Social Anthropology from the University of Kent and an M.A. in Visual Anthropology (1990) from the University of Manchester. She was Lecturer in Sociology and Social and Cultural Studies

(1995-1999) and Reader in Anthropology (1999-2000) at the University of Derby. Her research has been in Spain, Guinea Bissau, and England, focusing mainly on visual and material culture, the senses, gender and performance in public contexts and in the home, and the use of visual images and technologies as part of research and representation. Her books include *Women and Bullfighting* (1997), *Doing Visual Ethnography* (2001), *Working Images* (2004), and *Home Truths* (2004).

**Michael Schudson** is Professor of Communication and Adjunct Professor of Sociology at the University of California, San Diego, where he has taught since 1980. He is the author of six books and editor of two concerning the history and sociology of the American news media, advertising, popular culture, cultural memory, and the history of civic and political participation in the United States. He has been a Guggenheim fellow, a resident fellow at the Center for Advanced Study in the Behavioral Sciences, Palo Alto, CA, and a MacArthur Foundation "genius" fellow. His latest work, *The Sociology of News* (2003), distills much of what he has written about the press over the past 20 years. His chapter here is adapted from it.

**Dov Shinar** holds a Ph.D. in Communications from the Hebrew University in Jerusalem. He is, at present, Professor and Dean of the School of Communication, College of Management in Tel Aviv, and Professor of Communication at Ben Gurion University of the Negev, as well as Professor Emeritus at Concordia University, Montréal. Shinar's teaching and research interests include the cultural significance of the media, media and collective identity, war and peace in the media, peace journalism, and the social impact of new media. His most recent publications are *Internet: Communication, Society and Culture (A Book of Readings)* (2001, in Hebrew); "Constructing Collective Identities and Democratic Media in a Globalizing World: Israel as a Test Case" (in *Democratizing Global Media: One World Many Struggles*, edited by R. A. Hackett and Y. Zhao, forthcoming in 2005); two entries in the *Encyclopedia of the Modern Middle East and*

*North Africa,* "Printed Press in Israel" and "Broadcast Media in Israel" (2004); and two articles in the journal *Conflict and Communication Online,* "Peace Process in Cultural Conflict: The Role of the Media" (2003) and "Media Peace Discourse: Constraints, Concepts and Building Blocks" (2004).

**Günter Thomas** is Professor of Protestant Theology at Ruhr-Universität Bochum in Germany. He holds a Th.M. in Theology from Princeton University, a Ph.D. in Theology from Heidelberg University, and a Ph.D. in Sociology from Tübingen University. His research interests include systematic theology in the 20th century, North American theology, media studies, ritual studies, and theory of religion. He has published a number of papers and several books, including *Medien-Ritual-Religion: Zur religiösen Funktion des Fernsehens* [Media, Ritual, Religion: The Religious Function of Television] (1998); *Implizite Religion: Theoriegeschichtliche und theoretische Untersuchungen zum Problem ihrer Identifikation* [Implicit Religion: Historical and Theoretical Studies of the Problem of Its Identification] (2001); and, as editor, *Religiöse Funktionen des Fernsehens? Medien-, kultur- und religionswissenschaftliche Perspectiven* [Religious Functions of Television? Perspectives from Media, Cultural, and Religious Studies] (1999).

**Barbie Zelizer** is the Raymond Williams Professor of Communication at the University of Pennsylvania's Annenberg School for Communication. A former journalist, Zelizer's books include *Taking Journalism Seriously: News and the Academy* (2004); *Reporting War: Journalism in Wartime* (with Stuart Allan, 2004); *Journalism After September 11* (with Stuart Allan, 2002); and *Remembering to Forget: Holocaust Memory Through the Camera's Eye,* which won three awards (1998). Zelizer has received a Fellowship from the Shorenstein Center for the Press, Politics, and Public Policy at Harvard University, a John H. Simon Guggenheim Memorial Fellowship, and a Media Studies Center Research Fellowship for her work on journalism as cultural practice, collective memory, and images in crisis.